Instructional Strategies for Secondary School Physical Education

Sixth Edition

Instructional Strategies for Secondary School Physical Education

Marilyn M. Buck
Ball State University

Jacalyn L. Lund
Georgia State University

Joyce M. Harrison
Brigham Young University

Connie Blakemore Cook
Brigham Young University

Boston Burr Ridge, IL Dubuque, IA Madison, WI New York San Francisco St. Louis
Bangkok Bogotá Caracas Kuala Lumpur Lisbon London Madrid Mexico City
Milan Montreal New Delhi Santiago Seoul Singapore Sydney Taipei Toronto

INSTRUCTIONAL STRATEGIES FOR SECONDARY SCHOOL PHYSICAL EDUCATION
SIXTH EDITION

Published by McGraw-Hill, an imprint of The McGraw-Hill Companies, Inc., 1221 Avenue of the Americas, New York, NY 10020.

Some ancillaries, including electronic and print components, may not be available to customers outside the United States.

 This book is printed on recycled, acid-free paper containing 10% postconsumer waste.

3 4 5 6 7 8 9 0 QPD/QPD 0 9 8 7

ISBN 978-0-07-284413-9
MHID 0-07-284413-2

Editor-in-chief: *Emily Barrose*
Sponsoring editor: *Christopher Johnson*
Developmental editor: *Melissa Mashburn*
Senior marketing manager: *Pamela S. Cooper*
Production supervisor: *Randy Hurst*
Production service: *Valerie Heffernan, Carlisle Publishing Services*
Interior design: *Violeta Diaz*
Cover design: *Marianna Kinigakis and Violeta Diaz*
Cover photo: *Scott Barrow/Imagestate*
Compositor: *Carlisle Publishing Services*
Typeface: *10/12 Times Roman*
Printer: *Quebecor Printing Book Group/Dubuque, IA*

Library of Congress Cataloging-in-Publication Data

Instructional strategies for secondary school physical education / Marilyn M. Buck . . . [et al.].—5th ed.
p. cm.
Rev. ed. of: Instructional strategies for secondary school physical education / Joyce M. Harrison . . . [et al.]. 4th ed.
Includes bibliographical references and index.
ISBN 0-07-284413-2
1. Physical education and training—Study and teaching (Secondary)—United States. I. Buck, Marilyn M.
GV365.I37 2007
796.071'273—dc22

2005054186

To all the instructors, students, and colleagues
who have inspired and challenged me
in my work.
—Marilyn M. Buck

To Bill Gaylor, for all his support.
—Jacalyn L. Lund

Brief Contents

CONTENTS

PREFACE

Now in its sixth edition, *Instructional Strategies for Secondary School Physical Education* provides a comprehensive overview of core material that balances theory coverage with detailed, class-tested teaching strategies. In addition to tying research in education and physical education to curriculum design and instruction, the text also provides a large number of practical applications and examples. The text is written at an undergraduate level, but it can also be used as a resource for graduate students.

Instructional Strategies for Secondary School Physical Education is intended to help prospective teachers acquire the skills necessary to design and implement effective instructional programs in secondary school physical education, including middle schools and junior and senior high schools. Successful programs require both effective instruction and a balanced curriculum—the aspects of physical education programs discussed in detail in this book.

APPROACH AND ORGANIZATION

The new edition of *Instructional Strategies for Secondary School Physical Education* reflects the most current research in education and physical education. Every chapter has been thoroughly updated and extensive coverage of standards-based education has been integrated throughout the text.

This new edition of *Instructional Strategies* continues the emphasis on learning domains that has been a key feature of previous text editions. The text examines the three learning domains—cognitive, psychomotor, and affective—in detail as it provides students with a basis for the design and implementation of instructional strategies. The National Association for Sport and Physical Education emphasizes the importance of teaching students the conceptual background of physical education as well as teaching physical fitness and skills. In order to achieve this goal, prospective teachers must understand the cognitive and affective domains along with strategies for teaching psychomotor skills. The development of positive student feelings toward physical education is the key toward students' continued participation in physical activities in and out of school. Traits such as fair play and teamwork, which fall within the confines of the affective domain, are essential to the continued enjoyment of physical activities; it is important for physical educators to know how to teach their students about these concepts.

The sixth edition retains a unit approach to organization. Unit I—A Framework for Physical Education—reviews material that may have been included in a foundation or motor learning class. The purpose of including this information is to provide students with everything they need for effective program development and teaching in one text. This allows students to transfer the knowledge they have gained in other classes to their teaching efforts. This unit includes an updated chapter discussing liability issues in physical education.

Unit II—Planning the Instructional Program—begins with curriculum planning and then moves to unit and lesson planning. The curriculum chapters relate specifically to the entry-level teacher and can be taught most effectively by forming curriculum committees of three to five students and actually designing a curriculum. The final chapters in this section discuss specific aspects of unit and lesson planning, including writing objectives, choosing instructional styles and strategies and different program activities, and assessing student performance. This unit contains numerous practical examples that give students a real-world understanding of teaching challenges.

Unit III—Organizing and Managing Instruction—discusses classroom management first with the idea that many (if not most) discipline problems can be avoided by the use of proper teaching strategies and classroom management techniques. Proper motivation can also decrease discipline problems.

The final process in instruction and program design is evaluation. Unit IV—Evaluating Instruction and Programs—discusses the process of evaluating instruction and then the evaluation of instructional programs and provides students with guidance on how to make the necessary revisions.

PEDAGOGY AND ONLINE ANCILLARY MATERIALS

Readers of *Instructional Strategies* can easily review and apply the text material to real-world situations using Study Stimulators placed at the beginning of each chapter and Review Questions placed at the end of main sections. The Study Stimulators introduce the main ideas of each chapter in a question format and can be used to guide subsequent study sessions. The Review Questions allow students to review new chapter material and apply that material to their own experiences.

An array of online ancillary materials is available to instructors who adopt the sixth edition. Materials include an Instructor's Manual with Test Items and PowerPoint presentations. In addition to multiple-choice and true/false test questions, the Instructor's Manual includes chapter overviews, learning objectives, key terms, suggested readings, learning activities, sample unit and lesson plans, transparency masters, and reference lists. These materials may be accessed at www.mhhe.com/buck6e. Please contact your McGraw-Hill sales representative for login information.

ACKNOWLEDGMENTS

Throughout the writing of the sixth edition of this textbook, many colleagues and friends for whom we are grateful have provided encouragement and support. We appreciate the thoughtful comments provided by our reviewers and those authors and publishers who generously consented to have their work reproduced or quoted. The reviewers whose excellent comments and suggestions are evident throughout the pages of this new edition are:

Thomas Johnson *Albion College*
David Meyer *Concordia University*
Katherine J. Riggen *Southeast Missouri State University*
Sandy E. Weeks *Texas A&M University—Commerce*
David Wittenburg *University of New Mexico*

We especially want to acknowledge Joyce Harrison and Connie Cook for their work on the first five editions, which are the foundation upon which the sixth edition has been written. Jacalyn Lund also thanks Jessica Weller and Rachel Gurvitch.

Instructional Strategies for Secondary School Physical Education

U N I T

A Framework for Physical Education

CHAPTER

1

The Roles of Education and Physical Education

Study Stimulators

1. Is education synonymous with schooling?
2. What similarities and differences exist among the various listings of educational goals?
3. Do educational goals influence changes in the purposes of education?
4. Do you agree with the purposes of education stated in the text?
5. Is there presently a crisis in education?
6. What global changes and trends might impact education? How might education be different in the future?
7. What are the goals or outcomes of physical education?
8. How do the goals of physical education fit with the national goals of education?
9. What are the values of physical education?
10. What is the current status of physical education in the United States?
11. Describe the physical education program of the future.

What Is Education?

Have you ever stopped to ponder the question, "What is education?" As a high school or college graduate, do you feel "educated"? Do you think you will ever be truly educated? *Webster's New Collegiate Dictionary* defines *educate* as "to provide schooling for" and *education* as the "process of imparting knowledge or skill."[1] Goodlad explains education from a more personal perspective, stating it is the deliberate *cultivation* of desirable traits and sensitivities.[2] He includes socialization as part of education with an encompassing of culture. Gardner discusses the concept of multiple intelligence substantiating eight aptitudes, or intelligences for which we must impart knowledge (see Chapter 4).[3] Goleman and others believe that emotional intelligence ought to be a part of the educational mix for our children, linking sentiment, character, and moral instincts. He stresses that the present generation of children is more troubled emotionally than the last: more lonely and depressed, more angry and unruly, more nervous and prone to worry, more impulsive and aggressive.[4] We know that 22 percent of all children born in America are born in poverty, and the suicide rate of children has increased 300 percent in the last thirty years. Further, by age sixteen, the average child will have seen 200,000 acts of violence on TV. In 1997, one-third of all male students reported carrying a weapon; in just over ten years, more children have been killed by gunshots than all the U.S. soldiers killed in Vietnam; and America has the highest murder rate in the world—seven times that of Canada and forty times that of Japan.[5]

Review Question: How would you define education?

Do you think that education always results from, or even develops most efficiently through, formal schooling? Komoski points out that students spend only 19 percent of their potential learning time in school.[6] Someone once said, "Don't let your schooling interfere with your education." Consider the classroom in which the students were interested in an exhibit of frogs, only to be told, "Come and sit down. We're going to have science now!" Consider, too, the following students, one listening to the driver education teacher talk about how to change a tire when the previous weekend she had rotated all the tires on the family car, or one jogging two laps of the track during physical education class when the night before he had run five miles preparing for an upcoming race.

Aristotle said, "All men by nature desire to know." Coming to "know" might take place in the formal classroom, but just as likely it will transpire in another setting. Historically, education occurred in the home, on the farm, or in the artisan's shop. Even today, much learning occurs on the job, in the home, or by way of the media. *Education is a process of learning, not a place.*

Today's advanced technological society requires continuous learning for effective living and working. Before the turn of the twentieth century, Spencer declared that the function of education is to prepare for complete living.[7] The living process, as characterized by society, is ever changing. The educational process and its purposes must adapt to changes in society in order to prepare citizens to function in an effective way. Teachers play a key role in shaping society as they prepare citizens for complete living. To say that teachers and the education profession have a profound impact on society would be an understatement.

Krajewski and Pettier illustrated how education must adapt its purposes to changes in society with the following story:

> This is a story of civilization of some thousands of years ago. The people lived in the warm lands, covered by streams fed by glaciers far to the north. They supported themselves by spearing fish and by trapping tigers.
>
> The glaciers moved south. The lands became cold. The tigers left and sediment from the glaciers choked the rivers. Still, the people remained.
>
> Before the advent of the cold weather the people had prospered and in their prosperity they felt that they should embellish their society and they set up a school system. In that school system, quite logically, they taught the spearing of fish and the trapping of tigers. Then the cold came and the fish left and the tigers left. The people of this area now survived by snaring eel and hunting bear. And they prospered again. They went back to examine their school system. They asked the headmaster what he taught. And he said, "I teach spearing fish and trapping tigers." And they said, "Well, do you not teach snaring eels and hunting bears?" He said, "Well, of course, if you want a technological education; but for a well-rounded education I prefer the classics."[8]

Physical education is one part of a total educational program and should not be de-emphasized.

Review Question: What are examples of "spearing fish and trapping tigers" in education today?

The Purposes of Education

The educational process reflects what the people in a given society think, feel, believe, and do. Teachers in any setting are given the charge of training, disciplining, developing, and instructing. Teachers working in the formal school atmosphere must take this charge and enhance the purposes of education. In general, the purposes of education in any society include one or more of the following:

1. To preserve and maintain the desirable aspects of the society or culture by transmitting them to the young.
2. To teach the skills and competencies needed to function effectively as an adult member of society, both socially and vocationally.
3. To help the individual act in a responsible manner, both currently and in the future, and function within society so both the individual and the group attain their fullest potential.
4. To teach the individual to think critically, to constructively evaluate societal issues, and to influence the social order by contributing to ordered, purposeful change.

The purposes of education remain constant even though society, in which the educational structure operates, is an institution of change. As change occurs, the educational process adapts to meet the needs of society. Historically, American society has been a world role model, and its purposes of education have been unique in that they are intended to reach out to all Americans.

The Current Status of Education

Throughout the history of American education in the twentieth century, groups were organized with the charge to determine principles or goals for education. Table 1.1

TABLE 1.1 A Perspective of the National Goals of Education

Cardinal Principles [1918]	Educational Policies Commission [1938–44]	Imperatives of Education [1964]	National Goals [1973]
	AIMS Self-realization Human relationship Economic efficiency Civic responsibility		
	TEN IMPERATIVE NEEDS OF YOUTH		
Health (physical fitness)	Good health and physical fitness	Deal constructively with psychological tensions	Adjustment to change (mental health)
Command of fundamental processes	Think rationally, express thoughts clearly, read and listen with understanding		Communication skills
Vocation	Develop salable skills	Prepare for world of work	Computation skills
Civic education	Understand the rights and duties of a citizen. Develop respect for others, live and work cooperatively with others	Keep democracy working Work with other peoples of the world for human betterment	Critical thinking Occupational competence
Worthy home membership	Understand the significance of the family		Responsibility for citizenship
Worthy use of leisure	Use leisure time well	Make the best use of leisure time	*Respect for law and authority
Ethical character	Develop ethical values and principles	Strengthen the moral fabric of society	*Appreciation of others
	Know how to purchase and use goods and services intelligently	Make intelligent use of natural resources	*Clarification of values
	Develop capacities and appreciate beauty in literature, art, music, and nature	Discover and nurture creative talent	Clear perception of nature and environment
	Understand the influences of science on human life	Make urban life rewarding and satisfying	Economic understanding
			*Appreciation of the achievements of individuals
			*Knowledge of self

shows a dramatic shift from very open-ended, general guidelines in the early 1900s to specific benchmarks targeted at improving schools at the turn of the century. Goals 2000 specified all students should have access to physical education and health education to ensure well-being and fitness.

In January 2002 President George W. Bush signed the No Child Left Behind (NCLB) Act of 2001. Table 1.2 lists the goals for NCLB. The current expectations for schools are to close the achievement gap, to hold schools accountable for student learning, and to have qualified teachers in every classroom. NCLB resulted from a belief that all children can learn and deserve a quality education. Figures 1-1 and 1-2 show the racial balance of public school students and their teachers. Differences in achievement in reading, math, and science among groups of children in elementary and secondary school are a major concern. Figure 1-2 illustrates the achievement gap in twelfth-grade math and science scores.

NCLB requires schools to make adequate yearly progress (AYP). The standards are established by each state. Schools that do not meet AYP standards are listed as needing improvement. Ninety-five percent of the students must participate in the testing. At some point, parents of children in a school that is not meeting AYP can choose to

TABLE 1.1 Continued

Seven New Cardinal Principles [1978]	Four Essential Goals for High Schools [1983]	National Education Goals [1990] By the year 2000:	Call to Action: Pres. Clinton Education in 21st Century
			Incorporate rigorous national tests in fourth-grade reading and eighth-grade math
Personal competence and development	Develop critical thinking		Provide a talented and dedicated teacher in every classroom
Skilled decision making	Prepare students for further education	*Preschool programs:* nutrition and health care, parental training	Ensure every student reads independently and well by the end of third-grade
	Increase students' career options	*Student testing:* national tests in grades 4, 8, 12	Expand Head Start and encourage early parental involvement
Civic interest and participation	Build a spirit of community service	*Student performance:* students test first internationally in math and science	Expand educational choice and accountability
Global human concern		*High school graduation rates:* rise to 90 percent	Provide safe, disciplined, drug-free schools
Family cohesiveness			Modernize school buildings
Moral responsibility and ethical action			Make thirteenth and fourteenth years of education as universal as high school.
Respect for the environment		*Literacy:* every adult skilled and literate	Offer adult education through simple skill grants
		Schools: all safe and drug-free	Connect every classroom and library to the Internet, encouraging students in technology literacy

*Process goals

TABLE 1.2 No Child Left Behind Act of 2001

- Improving the academic achievement of the economically disadvantaged
- Preparing, training, and recruiting highly qualified teachers and principals
- Language instruction for limited English proficient and immigrant students
- Giving parents choices and creating innovative education programs
- Making the education system accountable
- Making the system responsive to local needs
- Helping all children learn to read
- Helping children with disabilities

send their children to other schools. The schools are also required to have highly qualified teachers. At the moment teachers in English and mathematics are the only ones required to meet the following standards: (1) a bachelor's degree, (2) full state certification or licensure, and (3) demonstrated competency in each subject they teach. Soon, other subjects are expected to be included as well.

The 2004 Phi Delta Kappa/Gallup poll asked questions about NCLB as well as the usual questions about the quality of education and issues regarding school performance. Forty-one percent of the public gave their local school an A or B rating, whereas 61 percent of parents rated their school as A or B, up from 55 percent in 2003. Twenty-six percent of the public give the nation's schools an A or B rating while

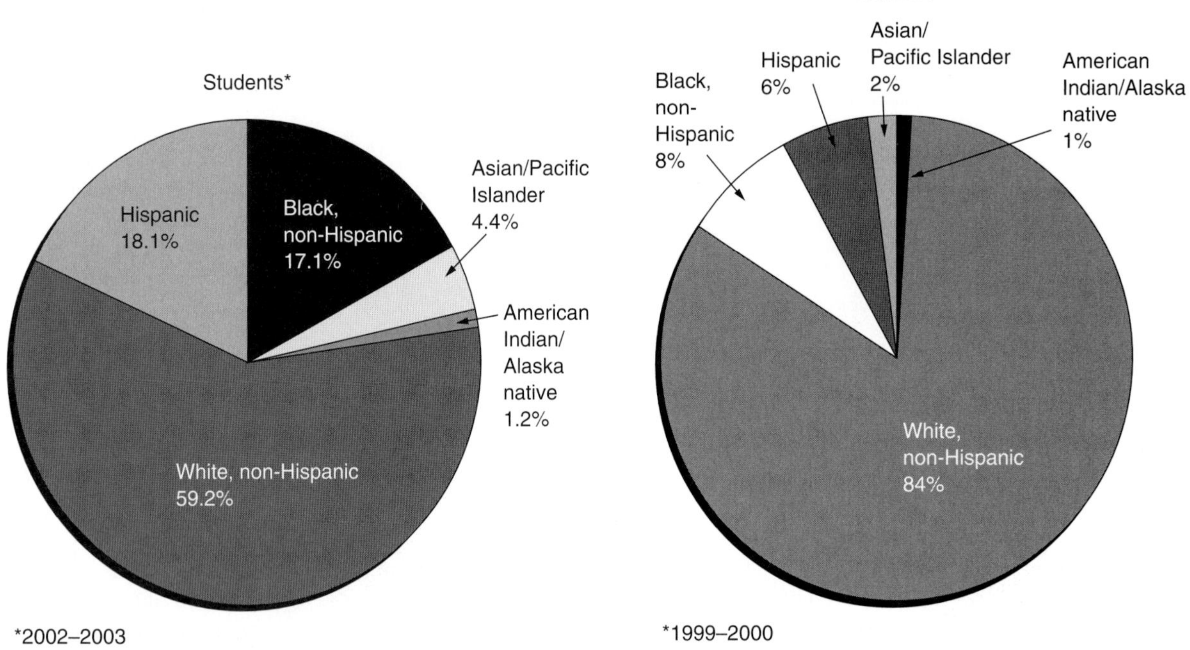

Figure 1-1

Public elementary and secondary students and teachers, by race.

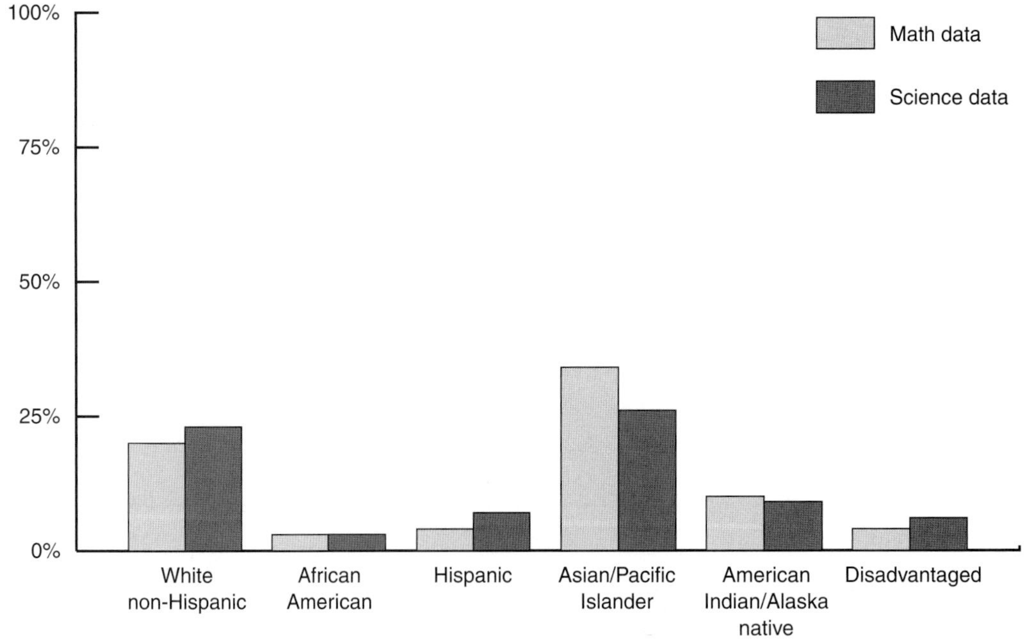

Figure 1-2

The achievement gap: twelfth grade math and science, 2000.

only 22 percent of parents believe the nation's schools deserve an A or B rating. "The closer people are to the public schools, the better they like them."[9]

Narrowing the achievement gap is a major goal of NCLB, and this view is shared by 88 percent of the public. Among these same individuals, however, 74 percent believe that the achievement gap is related to factors outside the school. Those factors are listed in Figure 1-3. When asked what was the most important factor in closing the achievement gap, 90 percent chose "to encourage more parental involvement." Forty-five percent of respondents believe that parents are the most important factor in student performance, 30 percent consider teachers most important, and 22 percent consider the students themselves most important.

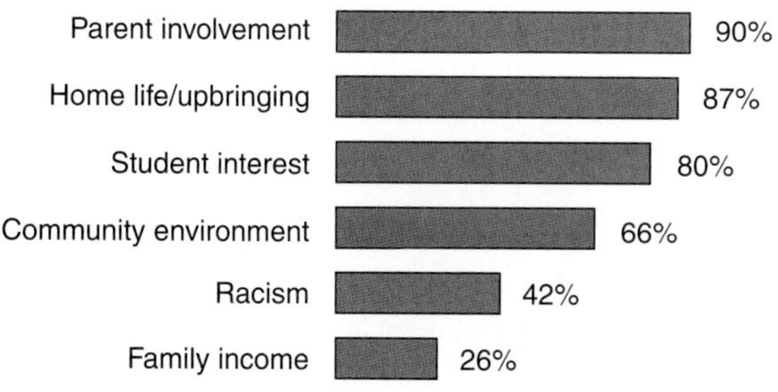

Figure 1-3

Factors judged very important in contributing to the achievement gap (2003).

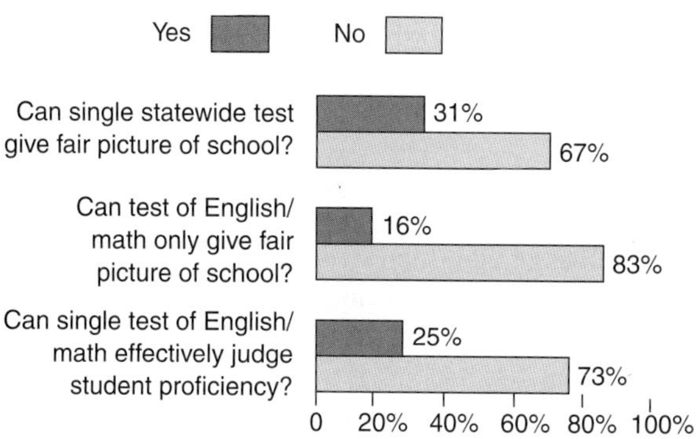

Figure 1-4

NCLB use of a single test.

Another central feature of the No Child Left Behind Act is holding schools accountable for student learning. The 2004 Phi Delta Kappa/Gallup poll asked the public to indicate their beliefs about using standardized tests in English and mathematics to determine the quality of a school. Figure 1-4 indicates the public's dislike of using single tests for this purpose.[10]

NCLB is the most recent attempt to reform education. The major thrust to begin educational reform occurred between 1983 and 1985 when more than a dozen reports critical of current education practices were printed. One of the first was *A Nation at Risk* issued in 1983 by the National Commission on Excellence in Education.[11] From it came the spine-tingling declaration that "the educational foundations of our society are presently being eroded by a rising tide of mediocrity that threatens our very future as a nation and a people."[12] Recommendations to correct school shortcomings stemmed from this and other reports. The more important recommendations included the following:

1. The schools must stress science and math and move away from the "frills."
2. The teaching profession must be strengthened by concentrating on the quality, pay, and autonomy of teachers and bolstering teacher-education programs.
3. The school curriculum should be more related to the job market and to perceived needs of industry (including computer literacy).
4. Foreign-language instruction ought to start in the elementary schools and should generally receive a high priority.
5. Students should spend more time in school, and their time should be used more effectively for instructional purposes.[13]

The 1990s began with a heightened public concern for education, including backing for a standardized national curriculum, upgraded educational outcomes, and support to increase taxes.[14] The first presidential State of the Union address of the decade highlighted societal ills affecting the educational process. Bringing about decreases in illiteracy, school dropout rates, and drug abuse became national priorities.

On the other hand, the Sandia Report, which was commissioned by the U.S. Department of Energy, contradicts the results of the previous reports. This report, never allowed to be published, although it is supported by the research of others, stated that the schools are doing as well now as they ever have.[15] This is especially amazing "given the severe decline in other social institutions."

A middle-of-the-road posture has been taken by some who believe the crisis has been manufactured by government, business, and the press to divert attention away from the real problems in education. Some issues of student achievement, funding, production of scholars, teacher training, decreasing of moral values, unhappy citizens, and private schools have resulted in myths that must be viewed from all angles to achieve a proper perspective.[16]

Bracey acknowledged that the schools have problems that need to be resolved. The schools most in need of help are the rural schools in low-income areas.[17]

Students need to come to school desiring to learn and possessing a readiness to do so, and schools will have to provide a conducive atmosphere. Students who come to school *prepared to learn* do well.[18] Lawson stated, "Schools cannot achieve their assigned goals if children and youth do not come to school ready and able to learn. . . . Only rarely do ['at-risk' children] come to school healthy, ready, and able to learn. All too frequently, they are hungry, need rest, and are seeking adult guidance and support. Today's schools cannot be expected to work for these young persons."[19] Herein lies the challenge for education in the future.

Review Questions: What do you believe are the issues facing the schools today?

What solutions would you propose for those issues that are problematic?

What is the purpose of NCLB and how is it attempting to meet the goals of improving education for all students?

Using state department of education sources, determine the status of your local schools in meeting AYP and other requirements of NCLB.

The Future of Education

The purposes of education in the future will be the same as the four purposes of education listed earlier in the chapter. How those purposes are achieved will dramatically change to meet the needs of a changing society. Jensen points out the changes that are happening in America, such as availability of information because of technological transformation, social ills (disintegration of families, drug problems, high school dropout rates, unskilled labor force, gangs), medical advances, ethical issues (loss of faith in government), environmental issues, and a transforming educational system.[20] A graduate today would be a part of the following broad international picture: in a village of 1,000 people, 564 would be Asians, 210 Europeans, 86 Africans, 80 South Americans, and 60 North Americans. Of those, 510 would be female and 490 would be male. Eight hundred would live in substandard housing, 700 would be unable to read, 500 would suffer from malnutrition, 700 would be nonwhite, and 300 would be white. Only 10 would have a college education, with 50 percent of the wealth being in the hands of 60 people (most of these being U.S. citizens). In this village, 300 would be Christian, 180 Muslim, 130 Hindu, and the rest atheists, with no knowledge of any religion.[21] The United States is a diverse nation with increasingly heterogeneous demographics, and these demographics should be considered by educators today.

Schools are changing, in everything from how classes are scheduled to who makes decisions. How many of the following thirteen issues facing public education today would you put on your list?

High Technology and Moving into the Information Age

In the first decade of the twenty-first century, a third of the world's population will be linked by computers that will be even more compact. Nearly two billion people can click a button to connect with other educators and integrate information and programs.[22] The Internet has virtually brought bookstores, libraries, and video cables into the school setting, and schools need to do all they can to capitalize on technology. Distance learning is another viable option. Colleges and universities are now able to pipe courses into high schools, even across oceans. However, students are often more technology literate than their teachers. Teachers need to be able to take advantage of this vast arena of technology. Most teachers have computers on their desks making materials accessible to help with such everyday tasks as attendance. Heart monitors and other technology are becoming commonplace in physical education programs. Each physical education teacher must be technology literate, and ask "How can this information age and new technology improve my program?" Technology and physical education are discussed in more detail later in the chapter.

Brain Research

The information age includes an emphasis on emerging brain research. "We are learning about the brain at an unprecedented rate," says Jensen.[23] Technology has paved the way with brain scanners like Magnetic Resonance Imaging (MRI) and Positron Emission Tomography (PET). We can better understand and see inside the brain. Jensen notes, "We are on the verge of a revolution: the application of important new brain research to teaching and learning. This revolution will change school start times, discipline policies, assessment methods, teaching strategies, budget priorities, classroom environments, use of technology, and even the way we think of the arts and physical education."[24] Teachers today will be much more effective if they keep up on the latest brain research information, realizing that information over three years old is most likely out-of-date. Entire textbooks have been written on this subject. Included here are several findings especially pertinent to teachers of the new century.

Emotions Activate the Brain

While our emotional system is acting independently, it is also acting cooperatively with the cortex of the brain. Teachers need to be especially cognizant of fear, threat, and stress. Research has shown that under threats, anxiety, negative stress, and induced learner helplessness, the brain operates differently. There is an altered blood flow and electrical activity pattern in the brain, minimizing its potential. It is less capable of planning, judging problem solving, and other higher-order skills. Actions by the teacher or peers that lead to embarrassment or humiliation are damaging to the learning process. Threatening comments, score-keeping discipline strategies, sarcasm, unannounced pop quizzes, unforgiving deadlines, and cultural or language barriers are other forms of threat and stress.[25] To increase productivity and learning in the schools, both teachers and students would do well to practice anger-management techniques and preventive programs.[26]

Motivation Calls for Stimulation and Novelty

Students may be temporarily unmotivated due to associations from the past, which, when triggered, provoke a negative or apathetic state. For example, a teacher's voice, tone, or gestures may remind a student of a previous, disliked teacher. In addition, students not taught in accordance with their learning style may react with a lack of motivation. To determine how each individual student best learns, teachers may want to retrieve learning-style information from such sources as Rita and Kenneth Dunn's

Profile, Ned Herrimann's Brain Dominance model, the Gregorc/Butler model, Meyers-Briggs,[27] or Kolb's Cycle of Learning.[28] Finally, a clear picture of well-defined goals and a perception that "I can succeed" aids motivation.[29]

Recent research caused teachers to rethink external rewards. Such things as candy, trophies, and certificates appeal to each student in a different way. They may actually cause a decrease in motivation for some students. Teachers should strive to reach the internal hypothalamic reward system of the brain. Pleasure-producing behaviors such as affection, entertainment, caring, or achievement will do this.[30]

"Choice remains critical to maintaining motivation," says Jensen.[31] When participants are given control over the content and process of their learning, motivation goes up. They need to make choices about personally relevant aspects of a learning activity. When given choices, burnout is reduced, discipline problems decrease, and achievement motivation increases.

Enrichment

Jensen emphasizes that challenge + feedback = brain enrichment.[32] Too much or too little challenge will cause students to give up or get bored. Mental challenge can come about with new material; adding degree of difficulty; varying time, materials, expectations, or support; novelty; and change in room decor or strategies. Chen and Darst have shown that students' low motivation in learning physical skills is attributable to the lack of interesting learning tasks. They suggest teachers should use tasks that facilitate exploration in learning and emphasize enjoyment rather than excessive challenge. They also suggest that novelty in an activity can be easily interpreted by students as challenge. Also keep in mind, "without our magnificent system of feedback, we would be unable to learn."[33] Feedback must be specific, not general. It is ordinarily most useful when immediate, although a stressed or threatened learner may prefer to have it delayed. Group interaction provides effective feedback. Most teachers should be using much more appropriate feedback, perhaps twenty times more.

Brain Rhythms

Researchers have found that the best time for short-term memory activities, rote learning, problem solving, test review, math, and science is between 9 A.M. and 12 noon. On the other hand, the best time for movement-oriented tasks, computer work, singing, and art are after noon. The best time for doing sports, music, theater, and manual dexterity tasks are between 2 P.M. and 5 P.M.[34] This means we should be starting school later, especially for teenagers (no earlier than 8:30 A.M. and preferably 9:00 A.M.). Recent research suggests that teen biorhythms are different from those of the average adult. Teenagers need more sleep than children and adults. They need to begin that sleep later at night and need to sleep later in the morning. Sluggishness during the first two periods of the day may be due to sleep deprivation. Edina High School in Edina, Minnesota, starts school at 8:30 A.M. and this experiment is proving to be a "phenomenal" success.[35]

Gender Differences

There has been considerable discussion about brain differences between boys and girls that may affect their learning. Research tells us that women are better learners the two weeks after their menstrual period is over.[36] We know that females do better at mathematical calculation, while males do better at mathematical reasoning. However, researchers are now finding that boys are not outperforming girls on national tests, and that the gender gap all but disappears with time and experience.[37] Researchers have documented differences in growth patterns, brain-structure differences, hearing, vision, touch, activity patterns, smell, and taste. Females usually learn to speak sooner and begin puberty changes sooner. Males have better distance vision and depth perception than females. Females excel at peripheral vision. Females have a more diffused and sensitive sense of touch as well as a stronger sense of smell. These differences are good to be aware of, but may not significantly affect the learning environment. The culture often perpetuates differences that have nothing to do with genes, such as that girls aren't good at math or science. Often girls' academic confidence and grades start to slump just at the time their bodies develop, their periods begin, and their self-confidence grows shaky.[38] Effective teachers strive to maximize the potential of each student, no matter what the gender.

Rehearsal Time

Teachers must capitalize on the brain's ability to rehearse. Repeating information is helpful when done with the brain in mind. Those items most recently taught are remembered better. However, when items are also presented at a slower rate, subjects remember not only the last items on the list, but the first ones as well. When presenting refinement cues, they should be given one at a time and repeated often. A fewer number of cues has a greater possibility of being remembered because students remember the first and the last, tending to forget the middle. The most important information should go at the beginning and the end, taking into account *recency and primacy* effects. These effects play on the short-term memory, and it is suggested that constant repetition moves simple information to long-term memory. More complex and meaningful information will need to be related to concepts and ideas already in memory.[39]

Mind and Body

"In times of diminishing financial resources, educators must make hard choices. Do dance, theater, and physical education belong in the budget? Are they frills or fundamentals?" Brain research reveals strong links between physical education, the arts, and learning. Further, the cerebellum, the small portion of the brain close to the brain stem, is commonly linked to movement. It takes up just one-tenth of brain volume, but contains over half of all its neurons. Researchers have shown it to be a virtual switchboard of cognitive activity, and people with cerebellar damage have impaired cognitive function. As pathways from the cerebellum are traced to the brain, it has been found that the same part of the brain that processes movement is the same part that's processing learning. Movement is very important in learning because it stimulates not only the cerebellum but the inner ear. Sensory data are regulated in the inner ear and help one maintain balance, turn thinking into action, and coordinate movement. Playground games that stimulate the brain and inner ear motion, like swinging, rolling, and jumping, are valuable. There is no single "movement center" in our brain, as movement and learning have constant interplay. Early movement is critical to the ability of a child to experience pleasure as well as readiness to read. Researchers now know that exercise not only shapes muscles, heart, lungs, and bones, but also strengthens the basal ganglia, cerebellum, and corpus callosum. It also fuels the brain with oxygen and feeds it neurotropins, thus enhancing growth and greater connections between neurons. It has been found that autistic children have smaller cerebellums and fewer cerebellar neurons.

Research studies now suggest strong links between the cerebellum and memory, spatial perception, language, attention, emotion, nonverbal cues, and decision making, suggesting the value of physical education, movement, and games in boosting cognition. In Seattle, Washington, third-grade students boosted reading scores by 13 percent when involved in dance activities. Researchers believe that working out, even twenty minutes three times a week, better prepares the brain to respond to challenges rapidly. Pollatschek and Hagen found children engaged in daily physical education showed superior motor fitness, academic performance, and attitude toward school as compared to those who did not engage. At Scripps College, those who exercised seventy-five minutes a week demonstrated quicker reactions, thought better, and remembered more. In Canada, school children who spent an extra hour each day in physical education far outperformed, at exam time, those who didn't exercise.[40] Silverman found that students will boost academic learning when engaged in games and so-called play activities.[41]

Jensen expands the mind-body vision, stating "give a school daily dance, music, drama, and visual art instruction in which there is considerable movement, and you might get a miracle."[42] He suggests drama, theater, role plays, stretching (to get more oxygen), and cross-laterals (arm and leg crossover activities such as jumping, touching opposite elbows or heels) to force both brain hemispheres to talk to each other better.[43] Miles supports the importance of music to the brain.[44] She says listening to music increases coherence between different areas of the brain. For example, music accesses both the left and right hemispheres of the brain and listening unites these hemispheres. The corpus callosum is what unites these hemispheres. Studies of adults who received early musical training show that their corpus callosums are larger than average, indicating increased interhemispheric traffic. Fast, rhythmic, loud music leads to arousal of the autonomic nervous system including heart rate, pulse, breathing, blood pressure, muscle tension, and galvanic skin response.

Given this body-mind brain research, it makes sense to enhance programs of physical education and the arts. Why is it that these are often the programs that are reduced when schools are faced with a budget crunch?

Violence

Niehoff presents research substantiating that violence can be controlled by focusing on the development of the brain.[45] The brain should be protected from alcohol and substance abuse both in the womb and afterward, especially in the formative years. A safe, caring social environment is also necessary to halt aggression. As pointed out earlier, emotional well-being is very influential to the functioning of the brain.

Teaching to Outcomes Formulated by National, State, and District Organizations

The establishment of *outcomes* or *educational standards* defines what a student should know and be able to do. This represents a new way of thinking, a paradigm shift, about American students. Such an emerging framework suggest two kinds of educational standards: (1) content standards: what students should know and be able to do; and (2) performance standards: how good is good enough. This new emphasis provides a basis for assessment based on individual achievement. Physical education has jumped on this moving train with its own standards framework. The National Standards for Physical Education, formulated by National Association for Sport and Physical Education, were first published in 1995.[46] All curriculum K–12 should be based on these standards and most states have used them as a framework for their own standards. The standards were revised in 2004.[47]

Changing Health Habits

Much more is known about health and fitness today. As a result, Americans are changing their health habits and physical educators should be a critical agent for change. The surgeon general has zeroed in on two health behaviors, publishing reports on nutrition and health (1988) and physical activity and health (1996). These reports have made Americans aware of fat grams, cholesterol, and physical activity as a means to a better quality of life. Both reports have the potential to change the professional agenda of physical educators. Although it is known what creates good health, many Americans do not adhere to recommended guidelines. Many of these health issues involve behavior and lifestyle choices. Bishop and Aldana report that even though people have knowledge about good health, for many their behaviors don't reflect this, and few people are willing to change.[48] For example, reports of poor physical fitness have been in the forefront since the 1960s. Recently, the surgeon general reported that more than 60 percent of U.S. adults do not engage in the recommended amount of activity, and approximately 25 percent of U.S. adults are not active at all.[49] The report emphasizes that nearly half of American youth aged twelve to twenty-one years are not vigorously active on a regular basis, and about 14 percent of young people, especially females, report no recent physical activity. Further, in the United States more than 600,000 children already have some form of heart disease, while 13 percent of fifth- through eighth-grade students had extremely high (200 mg/dl or higher) cholesterol levels. The public has also noted increased concerns over the level of obesity in the country, especially in the student population. Futurists predict that along with the current health issues, there will be new health issues, due in part to the new technologies.[50]

The schools will need to be involved in programs of education and change concerning health and fitness issues. Physical education and health classes should be the center of such efforts.

Safer, Drug-Free Schools

Reports about school violence continue to appear in the media while at the same time statistics compiled by the federal Centers for Disease Control and Prevention and the National Center for Education Statistics show that school is still the safest place in America for a child. Children are far safer in school than at home, on the street, or at the mall. The probability that harm could happen at school is greater because large numbers of young people are gathered there.[51] When the 2004 Phi Delta Kappa/Gallup poll asked what the biggest problems were in the schools, only 6 percent of respondents cited fighting, violence, and gangs.[52] Many organizations are calling for stricter gun laws, such as the Children's Gun Violence Prevention Act of 1999, to avoid such tragedies as those at Pearl, Mississippi; West Paducah, Kentucky; Jonesboro, Arkansas; Edinboro, Pennsylvania; Springfield, Oregon; Lakewood, Colorado; and Conyers, Georgia. We must also listen more carefully to children and pay more attention to troubled children and youth.

Drug statistics are alarming. Self-reports by students who have graduated from high school indicate that 29 percent are regular smokers, 44 percent have tried marijuana, 90 percent have tried alcohol, and 33 percent have been recent heavy drinkers. Mohnsen reports statistics indicating one-fourth of all fourteen- to seventeen-year-olds have alcohol-abuse problems.[53] The most popular drug-abuse prevention program in the schools, D.A.R.E., has shown disappointing results. "Few if any, are invulnerable," report Evans and Bosworth.[54]

The National Education Association (NEA) and American Federation of Teachers (AFT) offer resources to help educators make schools safe. They have joined together to produce materials to train educators in safe school practices and classroom management skills. These materials can be viewed at the websites of these organizations and some materials can be downloaded for quick and easy utilization. Schools are urged to investigate a "no-taunting pledge" taken by students.

Those who teach in the public schools today must be prepared to deal with students who live with drugs and violence and are addicted or violent. The turn of the century will see more laws dealing with these issues.

School Choice

Policymakers are attempting to introduce increasingly greater choice and competition into American public school selection. This allows participation in programs without regard for the neighborhood in which students live, giving parents greater voice in the education of their children. Metcalf and Tait report more than 95 percent of adults in the United States believe parents should have more choice regarding the education of their children. The two most common choices are *charter schools* and *voucher* programs. Other choices include magnet schools, alternative schools, tax credits for private school tuition, intradistrict and interdistrict choice plans, and alternative programs within a single school.[55]

Charter Schools

Charter schools are governed by contract, deregulated, autonomous, and independent of the rules and regulations that govern traditional public schools, yet are funded by tax dollars. This puts them in a position to compete with public schools.[56] Charters are built on the premise "that schools can help youngsters. All kinds of youngsters."[57] Charter schools are indeed serving a diverse population. Researchers found that in 1996–97, half of charter school students were minority group members, compared with one-third in conventional public schools. Forty percent were poor, compared with 37 percent in conventional public schools, 13 percent had limited English proficiency, and 13 percent had disabilities. Nearly half reported that their performance prior to attending a charter school was "failing," "poor," or "average."[58] The basic strategies for charter schools include (1) teachers, parents, or community creating new schools or converting existing schools; (2) state authorization of an official sponsor such as a local school board or other public body; (3) contract specifying accountability for improved student achievement; (4) waiver of virtually all rules and regulations governing public schools so each school is a discrete legal entity; (5) full per-pupil allocation of funds to move with the student to the charter school; (6) teachers supported in trying new strategies by having their status protected; (7) no academic or athletic admissions standards, no tuition or fees, and no religious instruction; and (8) charter revoked if school fails to deliver on its contracted promises.[59] The movement expanded from one school in 1992 to about eleven hundred schools in thirty-three states and the District of Columbia in the 1998–99 school year.[60]

Vouchers

These certificates (vouchers) are for a set amount of money from the state to pay tuition at the student's choice of public, private, or parochial schools. This is a hotly debated alternative and advocates on both sides of the issue become passionate. The Phi Delta Kappa/Gallup poll reveals that the public fluctuates in its support of vouchers used to send a child to a private school. In 2004, 42 percent were in favor and 54 percent opposed the use of public funds for attending private schools.[61] The public is more receptive to tax credits than vouchers. Virtually all such proposals have been defeated by the voters. Menendez reports that this issue has been placed on the ballot twenty-two times since 1996, and the voters have rejected it twenty-one times, resulting in those programs existing at the turn of the century only serving a small percentage of eligible students.[62] The Florida voucher program bypassed the public voters and was signed into law in 1999 but may never take effect due to issues of constitutionality.[63]

Voucher programs differ from most other *programs of choice* in at least three different ways. First, parents can use the voucher to select from among both public and private schools. Second, they include schools with religious affiliations. Third, programs often operate on private rather than public funds, which was the case with fourteen of the sixteen existing programs in 1999 (seven-to-one ratio).[64] Some believe that vouchers used as tuition, or partial tuition, to the school of choice would force the public schools to improve in order to be competitive with each other as well as with private schools.

The premise of *choice* makes vouchers attractive to parents. Those against vouchers cite reasons such as creating a system of private schools that pursues individual agendas at public expense, and operating without accountability to taxpayers while draining scarce resources from public schools. Many feel the end result will be racial, ethnic, and economic segregation. Chase believes vouchers don't address the real problems of city schools, but rather abandon them. He advises bringing schools, community, and business together to transform the struggling public schools.[65] Phi Delta Kappa suggests some additional issues to be considered concerning vouchers.[66] Currently, more than 5,800,000 students attend private schools in the United States. If vouchers were made universally available, parents of these children would undoubtedly claim them to help pay the tuition in the schools where their children are already registered. Where would we find the $3 billion for vouchers for these parents? How will we make education equitable for the lower socioeconomic class? Vouchers are of greatest benefit to middle- and upper-class children whose parents can provide the additional money for the cost of an education. It is interesting to note that in California, in 1993 voters defeated a voucher proposition 70 percent to 30 percent with income and education of voters not being a significant factor in the outcome.[67] Further, how will the cost of transportation be covered for those students who can't provide their own? Will the value of the voucher increase for the handicapped child who requires more funds for a basic education?

Research from the Cleveland, Ohio, and Milwaukee, Wisconsin, voucher programs reveal four tentative patterns: (1), parents whose children attend such programs are pleased; (2), programs can be structured for children who are at risk of school failure; (3), only a small portion of eligible families apply for vouchers; and (4), evidence does not clearly indicate that voucher programs improve students' academic achievement.

The charter school concept has been much more attractive than vouchers to legislators and the general public for several reasons. First, charter schools must be nonsectarian. In 1993–94, 78.7 percent of private schools were religious and such schools would be eligible for vouchers.[68] Second, charters do not allow schools to pick and choose among applicants as voucher schools could do. If schools become oversubscribed, schools must select students by lot. Third, charter schools cannot charge additional tuition beyond the state allocation as voucher schools could do. Fourth, charter schools must document improved student achievement while voucher schools do not impose performance contracts.[69]

Magnet Schools

Public schools with *specialized curricula* are magnet schools. They are designed to bring together particular students from throughout a school district in such areas as art or physical education. More than half of secondary magnet schools and about a quarter of elementary magnet schools have some kind of admissions test. In addition, magnet schools are often given extra resources.[70]

School Site Management

With school site management, responsibility is delegated from district or state offices to individual schools with decisions to be made by faculty and, in some cases, parents and students, on site. Usually, schools are headed by principals or led by teachers with a clear vision of what they want their school to be. Lilly feels that schools must set themselves up as independent contractors, making the schools themselves responsible for their own destiny.[71] They should be functioning on individualized contracts, removing regulations, but leaving oversight of public money in the hands of elected school-board members. However, Nathan reports that very few such programs include any consequences, either positive or negative, for schools, and the results have not been especially encouraging.[72]

One thing is clear, "educational choice will continue to be the most contentious issue in U.S. education for the foreseeable future. More and more families will be afforded more and more alternatives for their children's education."[73]

School Partnerships

Many colleges and universities have formed productive partnerships with K–12 schools. For success there must be total commitment, an inclusive mission statement, and thorough planning in order for both faculty and students at both institutions to benefit from such an arrangement. For example, the rural Ithaca College forged a partnership with Harlem's inner-city School No. 10, turning it into the very successful Frederick Douglass Academy. When the partnership began, the school was known for low test scores, student violence and drug problems, and low faculty morale. The building was broken down and covered with graffiti. Most of the students came from households earning less than ten thousand dollars a year.

The main objective of the revitalized school was to prepare its students for college. The first graduating class achieved that dream with 94 percent being admitted to college, most in competitive institutions. Students at Ithaca corresponded with academy students via e-mail and helped students with homework. Future plans include Ithaca student-teaching assignments being made at the academy. College faculty members teach classes at the academy.[74] This partnership brought about benefits for both sides as a change in perspective resulted.

Partnerships such as the one Brigham Young University has with the surrounding school districts in Utah include joint planning and implementation of programs so that what is taught at the university is meaningful in the public schools. Students and faculty on both sides of the partnership become collaborators and benefactors in the process of education.

The Saber-Tooth Project is an ongoing reform effort involving the University of Nebraska–Lincoln and a local school district in a collaborative partnership designed to improve physical education for middle-school students. The focus is on curriculum improvement. The university navigated the vision of participating teachers with daily interaction over the space of a year due to the realization that teachers often do not have the knowledge to engage in curriculum planning. Results were rewarding as a major theme emerged—"improvements in reform may come about as the result of the cessation of 'business as usual.' "[75]

Improved School Facilities, Smaller Class Size

Chase informs us that a surprising number of students in America today still attend schools constructed in the first half of the twentieth century. Time has taken its toll on these buildings, and many a school district has scrimped on maintenance. The U.S. General Accounting Office (GAO) estimates that some 60 percent of America's 80,000 K–12 schools need "extensive repair, overhaul, or replacement of at least one major building feature."[76]

Recent studies confirm that smaller classes increase student achievement. Students who had attended small classes in grades K–3 were at least one full grade ahead of their peers academically. Small classes in these early years lead to higher high school graduation rates, higher grade point averages (GPA), and higher scores on college entrance exams. Those who gain the most academically are poor, minority, inner-city, and rural children. The NEA supports an optimum class size of fifteen in the primary grades, and a proportionately lower number in programs for students with exceptional needs. Efforts to reduce class size are discouraging. Despite twenty years of local efforts across the country, the average class size has decreased by only one student. As late as 1996, the average elementary school teacher still had twenty-four students in class; more than one-fourth of teachers reported classes of twenty-eight to twenty-nine students; and over 10 percent reported classes of thirty or more.[77]

Teacher Salaries, Teacher Shortage

The average salary for teachers, as reported by the American Federation of Teachers in 1997–98, was $39,347 for all teachers and $25,735 for first-year teachers. This compared with $40,862 for new engineering graduates, $40,920 for new computer scientists, and $34,843 for accountants. This is one of the reasons the AFT reports a teacher shortage for most subjects. Bracey reports even though teachers' salaries are low compared with other professions with similar education, teachers measure up well on literacy tests.[78] Low salaries often mean that districts resort to hiring marginally qualified people to staff classrooms. The percentage of teachers with neither a major nor a minor in the subjects they teach rises above 50 percent in some disciplines, such as physics. More interns are being hired by schools because they come for less salary and usually no benefits. We must ask if it is worth it to pay high-quality teachers more money. Texas found that teacher quality, as measured by education, experience, and test scores on licensing exams, accounted for 43 percent of the variance in student achievement. It seems we get what we pay for.[79]

America's schools will need at least two million new teachers over the next ten years to meet the demand caused by school enrollment increases and retirement of teachers. It is hoped that Congress will take action to assist states and localities in recruiting, preparing, and retaining qualified teachers for our nation's public schools.[80] This is encouraging to physical education teachers, but new graduates should have a viable second area of teaching expertise to make them employable. Secondary schools will always be looking for qualified coaches, but may not need additional physical education teachers. A graduate who is qualified to coach and teach another academic subject is a more qualified prospective teacher.

Review Question: Do you think we need to increase the salaries paid to beginning teachers? Why or why not?

Corporate Management of Public Schools (Privatization)

Is it appropriate for corporations to take over and run America's public schools? The corporate model for public school education usually means a corporation develops the ideas for teaching and then hires teachers to implement those ideas. Programs like the Edison Project in Boston claim they will improve student learning, renovate deteriorating school buildings, and provide computers to families and classrooms. As a result, the Boston Renaissance Charter School was developed using a curriculum the Edison Co. developed, which conformed to charter school legislation. Accountability was a part of this privatization project. However, cautions include a lack of responsibility for student achievement (which was a big part of the Edison Project), and loss of motivation by teachers whose insight, creativity, and talent may be lost to rigid parameters of corporate programs.[81]

Dropouts, Illiteracy

The good news is that high school dropout rates today are lower than they were in the early 1970s and 1980s, with a slow but steady decrease since 1972. The most marked decline is found among black youth (7 percent in 1996 from 21 percent in 1972). Hispanic youth continue to have the highest rate (29 percent in 1996 from 34 percent in 1972). Lewis attributes the higher dropout rate among Hispanic students to their finding employment more easily than members of other minority groups. The rate for white youth is also encouraging (7 percent in 1996 from 12 percent in 1972). It seems we are doing a better job of meeting student needs and retaining fewer students in a grade. Grade retention provides few remediational benefits and may place students at risk for dropping out.[82] Those without a high school education are unlikely to secure well-paying jobs.[83] The bad news is that schools are still failing a large number of adolescents who do drop out. Attention must be paid to urban inner-city schools where standards for academic and social conduct are often lower. Society must be more effective in meeting children's social, human, and health needs to ensure students are physically and psychologically ready to meet the demands of the classroom.

We must continue to strive for a higher standard of excellence in our schools. It is still reported that our top high school seniors—those taking the toughest math and science courses—performed far worse on international tests than similar students in most other countries. Of twenty-one nations, Americans scored significantly lower than students in fourteen other countries, mostly European, but including Australia and Canada. Asian countries did not participate. In science, eleven countries scored significantly higher. In physics, the United States ranked at the bottom with Austria. Fourteen other countries had scores that were significantly higher. Education secretary Richard Riley blamed a dearth of qualified teachers and easy graduation requirements for the results. Bracey and Wang challenge these results, saying the TIMSS study is not a true reflection of student achievement.[84] Phi Delta Kappa also reports student math achievement in 1994 had risen since 1982.[85] A substantial achievement gap persists between white and minority students, but the most dramatic progress occurred among black and Hispanic students.

In September 1993, the U.S. Department of Education released a detailed report on the condition of literacy in the nation. Compared with results from the 1985 study, it is clear that illiteracy is on the increase in the United States. Those adults at the lowest level were 23 percent of the population (forty to forty-four million). Those at the second lowest level were 25 percent to 28 percent of the population (fifty million adults). The literacy proficiencies of young adults were found to be somewhat lower, on average, than those in 1985.[86] All disciplines, including physical education, must incorporate activities to increase reading skills.

Inner-City Schools, Private Schools, and Home Schooling

While most students educated in the United States attend public schools, over 1,100 independent schools and associations in the United States belong to the National Association of Independent Schools (see *www.nais.org/hmbody.html*). Today the largest growing segment of education is the home school. The Internet has made it easier for students to learn at home with the aid of a computer.[87] More than half a million children are home schooled—up from ten thousand just two decades ago. That's only about 1 percent of all K–12 students, but these home schoolers are the leading users of educational technology in the United States.[88] A recent study reports that home schoolers did well on standardized tests, mostly in the range of the seventieth to eightieth percentiles. However, home schoolers do not represent a typical school population. While 21 percent of the general public had annual incomes under twenty thousand dollars, for home schoolers the figure was 4.5 percent. Almost two-thirds of home-schooler fathers, and more than half of the mothers, had at least a bachelor's degree. Further, 98 percent of participants came from two-parent homes. Given these demographics and the small class size, it could be argued that these students are underachievers. One psychologist wonders about the psychological health of the home schoolers and would like to see how they function as adults.[89]

While home schoolers are scoring well on standardized tests, urban (inner-city) students are still below the national average on ACT scores. While that national average score remained at 21.0 in 1998, students from the big-city districts had an average score of 18.8. ACT-tested urban students differ considerably in ethnicity from the total population of ACT-tested high school graduates. In 1998, 71 percent of all test takers in the nation were white, while 75 percent of all urban test takers were students of color. Ninety-six percent of Americans polled believe it is important to improve inner-city schools.[90] Sixty-six percent of the public say they would be willing to pay more taxes to improve the quality of the nation's inner-city schools as compared with 47 percent of teachers who say they would.[91]

Lewis reflects on the depersonalization of schools. When communities and schools were smaller, more parents were involved on school boards. At the end of World War II, this country supported more than two-hundred thousand school districts. Fewer than fifteen thousand operating school districts now exist. About one-third of the K–12 students are enrolled in less than 1 percent of the school districts, meaning one-third are in 150 very large districts. Charter schools, along with private schools and home schools, are returning the student to the more personal small-school atmosphere. More than one hundred studies dealing with school size found superior student performance in small schools. In small schools, there is more flexibility and individual attention. The small "school within a school" movement and *true* middle-school programs are also attempting to personalize learning.[92]

Bilingual Education

There continues to be much debate about how to educate the increasing numbers of students who are English language learners, often termed ESL (English as a second language). When polled, the public feels students should be required to learn English in public schools before they receive instruction in any other subject (37 percent). The least-supported option is to provide instruction in the the student's native language while the student is learning English (27 percent).[93]

Whether you believe the schools are in trouble, put on alert, or given a bad rap for being in crisis, these are issues the schools will have to deal with now and in years to come. Schools of the twenty-first century will reflect the thorough contemplation of these issues and the formulation of resultant programs.

Toffler's goals of education, formulated in the 1960s, are still relevant in preparing students to meet the demands of a changing society.[94] He said the students must

1. *Learn how to learn.* Education must turn out men and women who are capable of educating themselves and their families as circumstances change.
2. *Learn how to relate with others—to make and maintain rewarding human ties.* One of the goals of American education is to facilitate the fullest possible growth and development of each individual regardless of race, religion, sex, or ability.
3. *Learn how to choose—to make decisions in an environment of too many choices.* Coping with change demands that students explore possible alternatives for the future, incorporating critical thinking and problem-solving skills in conjunction with contemplating consequences for the decisions they make.[95]

The Role of Physical Education

The first part of this chapter discussed education in general. The last section will discuss the role physical education can and should play.

Physical education is the study, practice, and appreciation of the art and science of human movement. It is a part of the total process of education. Movement is natural and basic to existence for most human beings. "Children . . . are prewired for movement at birth."[96] Although movement itself is spontaneous, the refinement and perfection of movement is an educational process that is often entrusted to physical educators. This charge must not be taken lightly. The body, that magnificent instrument that enacts movement, should be highly esteemed. "The human body is sacred. . . . [I]t is a solemn duty of mankind to protect and preserve it from pollutions and unnecessary wastage and weakness."[97]

Physical education does not take place in isolation. The changes occurring in society, technology, health care, and education will have an impact on a quality program.[98] Physical educators today face the challenge of legitimizing physical education content in American public school curriculums, although it has been a regular part of such courses of study for many years. The national goals of education listed in Table 1.1 relate both directly and indirectly to outcomes attained through physical education courses. In 1974 the National Association of Secondary School Principals stressed the importance of physical education classes in the maintenance of a healthy body:

> Today's physical educational programs are aimed at helping students acquire constructive concepts and desirable habits regarding the preservation of our environment's most prized natural resource: the well tuned, efficiently functional human body and all its healthy competitive components. . . .
>
> Furthermore, physical education has earned a role as one of the essential elements in any curriculum designed to educate the whole person.[99]

What was expressed so eloquently by this administrative body more than thirty years ago could not be improved upon today. However, educators are often ignoring the importance of daily physical education. We need to justify the inclusion of physical education in such a way that it will not be pushed out of the curriculum in favor of math, science, or English. The specific values of physical education are not always reflected in national goals of education and need to be explicitly defined. These values of physical education, while appreciated by the professional, often need application and clarification for the student and public as well.

The Values of Physical Education

In 1986, Seefeldt and Vogel formulated twenty values of physical education deemed important by the National Association for Sport and Physical Education, creating a solid scientific foundation for the profession.[100] Recently, the U.S. Department of Health and Human Services incorporated these values in two reports issued from the surgeon general and the Centers for Disease Control, which stressed the benefits of physical activity.[101] These reports became controversial due to the following view of physical activity:

- People who are usually inactive can improve their health and well-being by becoming even *moderately active* on a regular basis.
- Physical activity *need not be strenuous* to achieve health benefits.
- *Greater health benefits* can be achieved by increasing the amount (duration, frequency, or intensity) of physical activity. (Italics added)

The idea of *moderate activity* and *activity that is not strenuous* challenges long-standing traditions of exercise. Examples of moderate amounts of activity included washing windows or floors for 45–60 minutes, gardening for 30–45 minutes, walking 1 3/4 miles in 35 minutes, raking leaves for 30 minutes, doing water aerobics for 30 minutes, shoveling snow for 15 minutes, and bicycling 5 miles in 30 minutes. Given the numerous health benefits of physical activity, and the hazards of being inactive, moderate activity levels will improve the health of those who are usually inactive.[102]

This surgeon general's report highlighted the benefits of exercise stating, "regular physical activity that is performed on most days of the week reduces the risk of developing or dying from some of the leading causes of illness and death in the United States." Regular physical activity improves health in the following ways:

- Reduces the risk of dying prematurely
- Reduces the risk of dying from heart disease
- Reduces the risk of developing diabetes
- Reduces the risk of developing high blood pressure
- Helps reduce blood pressure in people who already have high blood pressure
- Reduces the risk of developing colon cancer
- Reduces feelings of depression and anxiety
- Helps control weight
- Helps build and maintain healthy bones, muscles, and joints
- Helps older adults become stronger and better able to move about without falling
- Promotes psychological well-being.[103]

The second report from the Centers for Disease Control and Prevention (CDC) highlighted recommendations about physical activity for young people. It stated, "young people can build healthy bodies and establish healthy lifestyles by including physical activity in their daily lives. However, many young people are not physically active on a regular basis, and physical activity declines dramatically during adolescence. School and community programs can help young people get active and stay active."

The CDC lists five benefits, substantiating the surgeon general report, of regular physical activity in *childhood and adolescence:*

- Improves strength and endurance
- Helps build healthy bones and muscles
- Helps control weight
- Reduces anxiety and stress and increases self-esteem
- May improve blood pressure and cholesterol levels.[104]

The Surgeon General's Call to Action to Prevent and Decrease Overweight and Obesity lists the following problems of overweight children and adolescents:

1. In 1999, 13 percent of children aged six to eleven years and 14 percent of adolescents aged twelve to nineteen years in the United States were overweight.
2. Risk factors for heart disease, such as high cholesterol and high blood pressure, occur with increased frequency in overweight children and adolescents compared to children with a healthy weight.
3. Type 2 diabetes, previously considered an adult disease, has increased dramatically in children and adolescents. Overweight and obesity are closely linked to type 2 diabetes.
4. Overweight adolescents have a 70 percent chance of becoming overweight or obese adults. This increases to 80 percent if one or more parent is overweight or obese. Overweight or obese adults are at risk for a number of health problems including heart disease, type 2 diabetes, high blood pressure, and some forms of cancer.
5. The most immediate consequence of overweight as perceived by the children themselves is social discrimination. This is associated with poor self-esteem and depression.[105]

Strong support for the value of physical education has not been enough to stop the reduction of physical education requirements and programs in the schools. The worth of exercise is not in question, but the priority or rank of courses in the curriculum most certainly is. Given the climate in schools for more academics, and the emphasis on athletics and winning teams, it is understandable that the regular physical education program is suffering.

"School-based interventions have been shown to be successful in increasing physical activity levels. With evidence that success in this arena is possible, every effort should be made to encourage schools to require daily physical education in each grade and to promote physical activities that can be enjoyed throughout life."[106]

The atmosphere today is right for dedicated physical educators to make a difference. As detailed by the surgeon general's report, nearly half of young people aged twelve to twenty-one are not vigorously active on a regular basis, physical activity declines dramatically with age during adolescence, and female adolescents are much less physically active than male adolescents. In addition, high school enrollment in daily physical education classes dropped from 42 percent in 1991 to 25 percent in 1995; and only 19 percent of all high school students are physically active for twenty minutes or more in physical education classes every day during the school week. The surgeon general also reports that the percentage of young people who are overweight has more than tripled in the past two decades.[107]

Current patterns and trends in physical activity among adolescents and young adults include the following:

1. Only about one-half of U.S. young people (ages twelve to twenty-one years) regularly participate in vigorous physical activity. One-fourth report no vigorous physical activity.
2. Approximately one-fourth of young people walk or bicycle (i.e., engage in light to moderate activity) nearly every day.
3. About 14 percent of young people report no recent vigorous or light to moderate physical activity. This indicator of inactivity is higher among females than males and among black females than white females.
4. Males are more likely than females to participate in vigorous physical activity, strengthening activities, and walking or bicycling.
5. Participation in all types of physical activity declines strikingly as age or grade in school increases.
6. Among high school students, enrollment in physical education remained unchanged during the first half of the 1990s. However, daily attendance in physical education declined from approximately 42 percent to 25 percent.
7. The percentage of high school students who were enrolled in physical education and who reported being physically active for at least twenty minutes in physical education classes declined from approximately 81 percent to 70 percent during the first half of this decade.
8. Only 19 percent of all high school students report being physically active for twenty minutes or more in daily physical education classes.[108]

These behaviors in young people lead to unhealthy lifestyle practices as adults. It is reported that more than 60 percent of adults do not achieve the recommended amount of regular physical activity, and 25 percent of all adults are not active at all. Inactivity and poor diet cause at least 300,000 deaths a year in the United States. Only tobacco use causes more preventable deaths. Adults who are less active are at greater risk of dying of heart disease and developing diabetes, colon cancer, and high blood pressure. Inactivity increases with age and is more common among women than men and among those with lower income and less education; it is more common among African American and Hispanic adults than whites, and among older rather than younger adults.[109]

To combat these issues and concerns, *Healthy People 2010* has set the following goals for adolescents and young adults:

22-6 Increase to 35 percent the proportion of adolescents who engage in moderate physical activity for at least 30 minutes on 5 or more of the previous 7 days.

22-7 Increase to 85 percent the proportion of adolescents who engage in vigorous physical activity that promotes cardiorespiratory fitness 3 or more days per week for 20 or more minutes per occasion.

22-8 Increase to 25 percent in middle and junior high schools and 5 percent in high schools the proportion of the Nation's public and private schools that require daily physical education for all students.

22-9 Increase to 50 percent the proportion of adolescents who participate in daily school physical education.

22-10 Increase to 50 percent the proportion of adolescents who spend at least 50 percent of school physical education class time being physically active.

22-11 Increase to 75 percent the proportion of adolescents who view television 2 or fewer hours on a school day.[110]

Physical educators can make a difference if they dedicate themselves to doing so. Vogel indicated that physical education can serve a unique role in a child's education: "Physical education, like no other curriculum area, lends itself to a student's total development."[111] Staffo concurred when he stated, "Physical education *if it is taught properly,* is just as important as any other subject in the curriculum and can make just as valuable a contribution to the total growth and overall development of the student."[112] The CDC stated that physical education "can increase student participation in moderate to vigorous physical activity and help high school students gain the knowledge, attitudes, and skills they need to engage in lifelong physical activity."[113] The aim of every physical educator today should be to provide the skills and incentive for each child to engage in *lifelong physical activity.*

Promoting Lifelong Physical Activity

Several key principles are stressed to physical educators by the CDC to ensure that activity programs for young people are most likely to be effective:

TABLE 1.3 Definition of the Physically Educated Person and Outcome Statements

A Physically Educated Person:

- HAS learned skills necessary to perform a variety of physical activities
  1. Moves using concepts of body awareness, space awareness, effort, and relationships
  2. Demonstrates competence in a variety of manipulative, locomotor, and nonlocomotor skills
  3. Demonstrates competence in combinations of manipulative, locomotor, and nonlocomotor skills performed individually and with others
  4. Demonstrates competence in many different forms of physical activity
  5. Demonstrates proficiency in a few forms of physical activity
  6. Has learned how to learn new skills
- IS physically fit
  7. Assesses, achieves, and maintains physical fitness
  8. Designs safe personal fitness programs in accordance with principles of training and conditioning
- DOES participate regularly in physical activity
  9. Participates in health-enhancing physical activity at least three times a week
  10. Selects and regularly participates in lifetime physical activities
- KNOWS the implications of and the benefits from involvement in physical activities
  11. Identifies the benefits, costs, and obligations associated with regular participation in physical activity
  12. Recognizes the risk and safety factors associated with regular participation in physical activity
  13. Applies concepts and principles to the development of motor skills
  14. Understands that wellness involves more than being physically fit
  15. Knows the rules, strategies, and appropriate behaviors for selected physical activities
  16. Recognizes that participation in physical activity can lead to multicultural and international understanding
  17. Understands that physical activity provides the opportunity for enjoyment, self-expression, and communication
- VALUES physical activity and its contributions to a healthful lifestyle
  18. Appreciates the relationships with others that result from participation in physical activity
  19. Respects the role that regular physical activity plays in the pursuit of lifelong health and well-being
  20. Cherishes the feelings that result from regular participation in physical activity

Source: National Association for Sport and Physical Education, Physical Education Outcomes Committee, Definition of the Physically Educated Person: Outcomes of Quality Physical Education Programs, 1990.

- Emphasize *enjoyable* participation in physical activities that are easily done throughout life.
- Offer a *diverse range* of noncompetitive and competitive activities appropriate for different ages and abilities.
- Give young people the *skills* and *confidence* they need to be physically active.
- *Promote* physical activity through all components of a coordinated school health program and develop links between school and community programs.[114] (Italics added)

These recent principles are the guidelines that accomplish the steadfast purpose of physical education set forth in 1970:

> Physical education is that integral part of total education which contributes to the development of the individual through the natural medium of physical activity—human movement. It is a carefully planned sequence of learning experiences designed to fulfill the growth, development, and behavior needs of each student.[115]

Professionals should strive to develop physically educated students as set forth in the Outcome Statements of the National Association for Sport and Physical Education (NASPE) in Table 1.3.[116] The five areas include physical skills, physical fitness, regular participation in activity, knowledge about activity, and attitudes about activity. Leaders in the profession have generally accepted these outcomes as the basic goals of physical education.

Physical Skills

The development and refinement of neuromuscular skill essential for efficient everyday movement (posture and body mechanics), as well as for efficient movement in a variety of activities, lead to less energy wasted in skill performance and more enjoyment in activity. Basic movement (fundamental) skills, sport skills, and skills in rhythmic activities are all important components of this outcome.

Physical Fitness

President John F. Kennedy once said, "Fitness is the basis for all other forms of excellence."[117] The development of physical fitness and health contributes to effective living and enjoyment of life. Fitness needs to be taught with two goals in mind. Students should be expected to achieve fitness, and acquire the knowledge and desire to make it a lifelong pursuit. An important aspect of physical fitness is health-related fitness, including such components as muscular strength and endurance, flexibility, cardiovascular endurance, and body composition. Motor fitness expands the definition to include such areas as balance, agility, coordination, and speed, which may or may not be enhanced over time.

Participation

Physical skills remain sharp and health is enhanced through regular physical activity. Meaningful physical education programs provide successful experiences and instill joy and motivation for physical activity, leading to lifelong participation.

Knowledge

A knowledge and understanding of the importance of physical activity and how it relates to one's health and well-being is essential. Knowledge of scientific principles related to physical activity, exercise, and health must be included in the physical education instructional program.[118] Dr. Ernest Wynder of the American Health Foundation said, "It's as important to teach kids about the body as about math and science."[119] Such an understanding must include skills in designing and implementing a fitness or weight-control program, evaluating fitness, and safe participation in activity. Knowledge about game rules, strategies, and techniques of participation enhance participation in a variety of physical activities. Game play can also increase one's ability to solve problems in highly emotional situations. Students also need to learn the processes for acquiring physical skills and the basic principles of movement, such as equilibrium and absorption of force, that are common to all activities.

Attitudes

The attitudes students have toward physical activity and toward their feelings of successful accomplishment in activity influence future participation. We need to ensure that only positive attitudes and appreciations result from physical education classes. Not only do students need to see the value in what they are doing, but also they need to derive joy and pleasure from doing it. Desirable social values—such as cooperation, commitment, leadership, followership, sportspersonship, and courtesy—can be taught through participation in physical education activities.

Physical activity also provides an opportunity for releasing emotional tension through appropriate channels. When participation occurs in a supportive environment, students can increase their feelings of self-esteem, release tension, and develop initiative, self-direction, and creativity. Hellison suggested that "our profession needs to achieve some balance between helping people and developing and promulgating the subject matter (skills, fitness, strategies, etc.)."[120]

According to Hellison, "the affective domain is not getting enough attention in today's schools, because kids are facing more personal and social problems than ever before."[121] Affective goals in physical education include

Well-planned and implemented physical education programs help students improve existing skills and experience success.

"(1) social conventions such as appropriate dress and language; (2) appreciation and affections for physical activity and its benefits; (3) psychological constructs such as self-esteem, self-efficacy, courage, motivation, and independence; (4) moral qualities such as respect for the rights of others, compassion, and justice; and (5) aesthetic qualities such as playfulness and gracefulness."[122]

The question that remains to be answered is whether the outcomes deemed important for physical education are realized in actual practice. The priority that individual teachers give each outcome determines whether it is planned for and incorporated. Placek did a study to discover what influences determine planning by physical education teachers. She concluded that teachers did not view student learning or achievement to be as important as classroom environment. Teachers seemed to equate success in the classroom with keeping students *busy, happy,* and *good.*[123] At this time, when programs are on the chopping block, physical educators must promote lifelong physical activity and incorporate these five outcomes into class planning.

Ensuring High-Quality Physical Education Programs

The CDC has set forth the following ten guidelines to promote lifelong physical activity among young people:

1. *Policy.* Establish policies that promote enjoyable, lifelong physical activity.
   - Schools should require daily physical education and comprehensive health education (including lessons on physical activity) in grades K–12.
   - Schools and community organizations should provide adequate funding, equipment, and supervision for programs that meet the needs and interests of all students.
2. *Environment.* Provide physical and social environments that encourage and enable young

people to engage in safe and enjoyable physical activity.
  - Provide access to safe spaces and facilities and implement measures to prevent activity-related injuries and illnesses.
  - Provide school time, such as recess, for unstructured physical activity, such as jumping rope.
  - Discourage the use or withholding of physical activity as punishment.
  - Provide health promotion programs for school faculty and staff.

3. *Physical education curricula and instruction.* Implement sequential physical education curriculums and instruction in grades K–12 that
  - emphasize enjoyable participation in lifetime physical activities such as walking and dancing, not just competitive sports.
  - help students develop the knowledge, attitudes, and skills they need to adopt and maintain a physically active lifestyle.
  - follow the National Standards for Physical Education.
  - keep students active for most of class time.
4. *Health education curricula and instruction.* Implement health education curricula that
  - feature active learning strategies and follow the National Health Education Standards.
  - help students develop the knowledge, attitudes, and skills they need to adopt and maintain a healthy lifestyle.
5. *Extracurricular activities.* Provide extracurricular physical activity programs that offer diverse, developmentally appropriate activities—both noncompetitive and competitive—for all students.
6. *Family involvement.* Encourage parents and guardians to support their children's participation in physical activity, to be physically active role models, and to include physical activity in family events.
7. *Training.* Provide training to enable teachers, coaches, recreation and health care staff, and other school and community personnel to promote enjoyable, lifelong physical activity to young people.
8. *Health services.* Assess the physical activity patterns of young people, refer them to appropriate physical activity programs, and be an advocate for physical activity instruction and programs for young people.
9. *Community programs.* Provide a range of developmentally appropriate community sports and recreation programs that are attractive to all young people.
10. *Evaluation.* Regularly evaluate physical activity instruction, programs, and facilities.[124]

Siedentop believes these guidelines cannot be developed and sustained without an infrastructure of school, community, and family. He states, "Evidence suggests that the lower the socioeconomic status one is born into, the more likely one is to be at risk for problems associated with physical inactivity and poor nutrition."[125] His suggestion is a three-prong approach of holistic tactics, including families, community, and school. He suggests reconceptualizing physical education as more than a school curriculum, and further, that early intervention is necessary to combat problems, emphasizing the middle childhood years as crucial.[126] McKenzie reports that over 80 percent of a child's physical activity occurs outside of school education, and the school physical education classes alone cannot provide children with the amounts of physical activity recommended by national standards.[127] He also reports that recommended amounts of daily physical activity are not made available through current programs, and that time in these classes needs to be increased. In doing this he points out there is likely to be little carryover from a physical education program that emphasizes only team sports.

It seems clear that not only must school programs be improved and given more time, but the community and family must also be drawn into the mix for improving the health and wellness of our young people. These strategies are crucial to the well-being of our nation because these young people are soon to become the adults of tomorrow.

PHYSICAL EDUCATION TODAY

The cries of "crisis in education" heard in the 1980s had a resounding and deeply felt effect on physical education programs in the schools. The *Nation at Risk* report questioned the inclusion of physical education courses in the school curriculum and recommended that school boards include more "academic" subjects in course requirements at the expense of physical education and certain other subjects.[128]

The reverberations of this report are still felt today. In the 1990s physical education fought for its life. Programs continued to be cut and athletics became the avenue of credibility for the profession. Professionals realized that a change of focus was necessary for survival. As we moved into a new century, the cry was lifetime activity. Martens stated:

> As physical activity professionals our objective is to turn young people on to physical activity for a lifetime. We want our children and youths to be *knowledgeable* about physical activities, we want them to have the *skills* to engage in a wide variety of physical activities, and we want them to *appreciate* the lifetime benefits of being active. We want all these things because we hope that with knowledge, skill, and appreciation they will be active and therefore healthy, both as children and adults.[129]

The *Shape of the Nation Report* released by NASPE in mid-1998 disclosed that most states are not living up to recommendations of the U.S. surgeon general's and CDC reports to require daily, quality physical education for all students in K–12. Illinois is the only state that mandates students K–12 meet a daily physical education requirement and forty-six other states have varying requirements. Colorado, Mississippi, and South Dakota have *no* requirements for physical education. The majority of high school students take physical education for only one year between ninth and twelfth grades. At the secondary level, 42 percent of the states allow substitutions for physical education for medical and religious reasons, varsity athletics, ROTC, and marching band.[130]

This report brought a statement from NASPE to "educate the whole child, physically, mentally and socially," emphasizing our future depends on our children becoming productive citizens.[131] In order to do this, a full comprehensive physical education program enabling students to become and stay healthy and fit must not be compromised.

NASPE recommends the following eight actions:

That—

1. All students K–12 receive quality, regular physical education.
2. Elementary schoolchildren receive a minimum of 150 minutes per week of instructional physical education; middle and high school students receive a minimum of 225 minutes per week of instructional physical education.
3. All states require comprehensive physical education as part of their core curriculum and set minimum standards of achievement for each grade level.
4. Meeting standards for physical education be a requirement for graduation.
5. Other courses and activities that may include physical exercise not be substituted for instructional physical education.
6. Teachers who are specially trained in physical education deliver physical education instruction at all levels.
7. All sport coaches be certified/licensed teachers and have additional education and certification for coaching.
8. Physical education programs be designed to facilitate achievement of the national standards for physical education.[132]

The CDC has provided money to states to promote the development of Coordinated School Health Programs (CSHP) in all schools. Figure 1-5 illustrates the eight interactive components of the program. The program is designed to address the nation's most serious health and social problems by systematically involving families, health care workers, the media, religious organizations, community organizations that serve youth, and young people themselves. Below is the working description for the physical education component.

> A planned, sequential K–12 curriculum that provides cognitive content and learning experiences in a variety of activity areas such as basic movement skills; physical fitness; rhythms and dance; games; team, dual, and individual sports; tumbling and gymnastics; and aquatics. Quality physical education should promote, through a variety of planned physical activities, each student's optimum physical, mental, emotional, and social development, and should promote activities and sports that all students enjoy and can pursue throughout their lives. Qualified, trained teachers teach physical activity.[133]

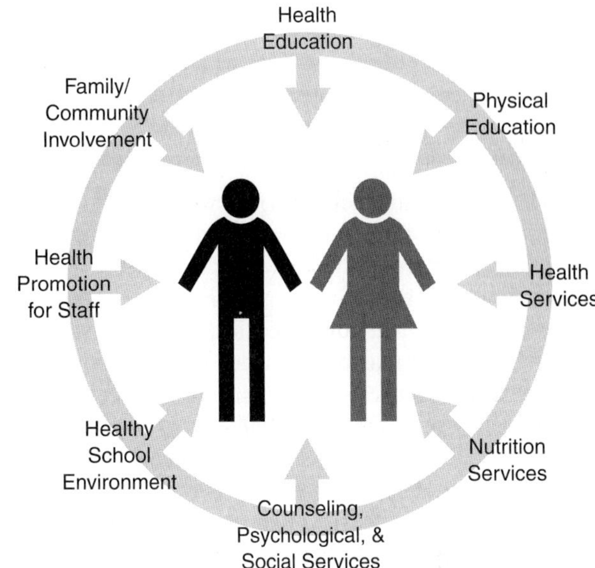

Figure 1-5 Model of Coordinated School Health Plan

A *School Health Index* has been created to evaluate the program. Module 3 provides an instrument for evaluating physical education and other physical activity programs. The instrument can be obtained from the Internet.[134]

The National Federation of State High School Associations (NFHS) also reemphasizes the idea of teaching and nurturing *citizenship* in our schools and our curriculum through the medium of sports and activities. This means grasping opportunities to teach students the positive traits, rewards, and responsibilities that accompany citizenship.[135]

Review Question: What support is available to build a case for daily physical education?

Physical Education in the Future

The physical educators of the future will have to offer programs that meet the needs of a changing American society. They will have to overcome the perception that physical education is recreation and is not needed in the school curriculum. "Physical education programs must teach students the value of physical activity as a key component of health."[136]

If students are going to see the value of physical education, educators should make sure students enjoy participation in physical activities. Their self-esteem needs to be bolstered and they should have fun. Martens suggests that feeling like competent, successful, worthy persons is a powerful motivating force in humans.[137] If children have positive, successful experiences when being physically active, the potential for future participation is enhanced. Children are motivated to have fun. They should feel things are going just right, being neither bored nor anxious. He suggests letting children play without constant instruction and evaluation, emphasizing that their goals are not performance oriented, as are those of most adults, but rather to have fun. He also advocates more enjoyable ways to be active and fit than calisthenics and he discourages using physical activity as punishment for misbehaving. At the same time students are having fun, they need to be benefiting from activity. *Healthy People 2010* recommends that 50 percent of class time be spent in being physically active. The 1999 Physical Best program of the American Alliance for Health, Physical Education, Recreation, and Dance (AAHPERD) stresses being fit while having fun.[138]

Ewing and Seefeldt studied ten thousand young people, age ten to eighteen, and found the number one reason for both boys and girls to play school sports is to have fun. The boys listed "to win" as number eight, while the girls listed it last at number twelve. Among the top five reasons for boys to play were (2) to improve skills, (3) the excitement of competition, (4) to do something I'm good at, and (5) to stay in shape. The girls listed (2) to stay in shape, (3) to get exercise, (4) to improve skills, and (5) to do something I'm good at.[139] We as physical educators must certainly capitalize on this desire of young people to have fun while engaged in physical activity, be it in class or on a competitive team.

Review Question: What would you do in your program to assure young people have fun while developing fitness?

Young people today are often opting out of elective physical education courses. It has been reported that 73 percent of high school seniors surveyed chose to avoid taking physical education as an elective. The main reason for this decision was "other courses were more important for college." The next most important reason (32 percent) was "I do not like PE." However, 52 percent of the students agreed with the statement, "If I had more time I would take more physical education." Further results indicated that 31 percent of the students agreed with the statement, "too much emphasis on winning." Further, 35 percent agreed that they "Did the same things over and over." Other areas of dissatisfaction included these: "Athletes get preferential treatment" (42 percent); "Males try to dominate" (31 percent); "Showering is a hassle" (32 percent); and "Do not like to dress out" (30 percent). Strand and Scantling also found that the most desired attributes on which to base grades were participation, effort, and attitude, whereas the least desired were tests of skill, knowledge, or fitness.[140] These findings need to be acknowledged by educators and they "must become creative thinkers and find ways to address student concerns."[141] Innovative programs and schedules along with far-reaching public relations efforts should be the foundation of such efforts.

Future programs that are successful will do the following:

1. Provide *quality* daily physical education. The NASPE standards are 150 minutes per week for elementary, and 225 minutes for secondary students.[142]
2. Make sure these programs are safe and convenient for all young people.[143]
3. Teach lifelong physical activity schemes.
4. Provide curriculum determined by the National Standards.[144]
5. Provide qualified, certified instructors and coaches.[145]
6. Point out that physical education and athletics are not synonymous.[146]
7. Teach effective goal-setting strategies.[147] In this way students will be prepared for lifelong physical activity.
8. Include activities that are fun.
9. Be wary of (fitness) testing. Use such results in the goal-setting process. Students should not be evaluated on improvement of test items only.[148]
10. Ensure that all students are successful in some way.[149] Inculcate mastery-oriented strategies[150] so that students will become proficient in some area of activity.
11. Include choice for students so they become responsible for their own behavior.[151]
12. Ensure gender and ethnic balance.
13. Involve school, community, and family in activities.

According to Staffo, "It is not too late to not only correct our past mistakes and re-establish our lost respect but to stand up, state, and justify the need for health and physical education taught K–12 by people degreed and certified in these areas. Too much is at stake if we don't . . . the health and fitness of a nation."[152]

Siedentop likewise has indicated the need to revitalize American secondary physical education. He stated, "School physical education is still the only process that has the *potential* for educating and socializing all children and youth toward lifespan activity involvement. Schools in our society are not now achieving that potential, nor is physical education. It is time to create a new American physical education."[153]

McKenzie and Sallis point out that a major barrier to improving physical education is the concern by administrators that spending more time in physical education will take time away from scholastic work.[154] They report a Canadian study showing that when more time is allocated for physical education in the school day, it does not result in a decline in academic performance. We, as professionals, must make every effort to point out the values of what we do while substantiating that the concerns of administrators are not justified.

Review Question: How will you accept the challenge to promote *lifelong physical activity* with the youth of America?

Technology is playing an important role in physical education and will only increase in the years ahead. It is critical that teacher education programs systematically include training in the use of technology in physical education. A question often asked during interviews is "How will you use technology in physical education?" Responses can include a variety of things beginning with the use of heart rate monitors to maintain safe exercise levels, to determine effort, to motivate students to increase physical activity, and to determine the effectiveness of instruction. Software is available to save the data so it can be shared with students, administrators, and parents. Other activity monitors such as pedometers are being used by many schools.

Handheld PCs and wireless formats make administrative tasks easier, from taking attendance to recording scores in class assessments. Software can evaluate dietary habits and activity levels. Many different types of devices are available to evaluate overall fitness, and body composition can now be obtained without "pinching" students. Digital cameras can be used by teachers and students to evaluate student performance and can increase student accountability for learning. The ease of digital editing programs has made the development of student electronic portfolios much easier. Videoconferencing makes it possible for students to learn new games from students in other countries. Teachers can use web pages and mass e-mails to keep parents more informed about activities in physical education. The role of technology in enhancing learning in physical education will continue to increase. The amount of use and types of uses are limited only by the creativity of teachers.

NOTES

1. By permission. From *Webster's New Collegiate Dictionary* (G. & C. Merriam Co., 1981).
2. J. I. Goodlad, *Teachers for Our Nation's Schools* (San Francisco: Jossey-Bass, 1990), 196.
3. H. Gardner, *The Disciplined Mind* (Englewood Cliffs, NJ: Simon & Schuster, 1999).
4. D. Goleman, *Emotional Intelligence: Why It Can Matter More Than IQ* (New York: Bantam Books, 1995).
5. *6seconds* (1999), 316 Seville Way, San Mateo, CA 94402.
6. P. K. Komoski, *The 81 Percent Solution,* 1994, www.edweek.org/ew/1994/18komo.h13.
7. H. Spencer, *Education: Intellectual, Moral, and Physical* (New York: Appleton, 1860), 31.
8. F. R. Krajewski and G. L. Pettier eds., *Education: Where It's Been, Where It's At, Where It's Going* (Columbus, OH: Merrill, 1973), 134; J. A. Peddiwell, *The Saber Tooth Curriculum* (New York: McGraw-Hill, 1939).
9. U.S. Department of Education, Office of the Secretary, Office of Public Affairs, *A Guide to Education and No Child Left Behind* (Washington, DC: 2004).
10. L. C. Rose and A. M. Gallup, The 36th annual Phi Delta Kappa/Gallup poll of the public's attitudes toward the public school, *Phi Delta Kappan 86* (2004): 41–56.
11. National Commission on Excellence in Education, *A Nation at Risk* (Washington, DC: United States Department of Education, 1983).
12. National Commission on Excellence in Education, *A Nation at Risk.*
13. P. G. Altbach, The great education "crisis," in P. G. Altbach, G. P. Kelly, and L. Weis, eds., *Excellence in Education: Perspectives on Policy and Practice* (Buffalo: Prometheus, 1985), 19–20.
14. S. M. Elam and A. M. Gallup, The 21st annual Gallup poll of the public's attitudes toward the public schools, *Phi Delta Kappan, 71* (1989, September): 42–54.
15. G. W. Bracey, The second Bracey report on the condition of public education, *Phi Delta Kappan 74* (1992): 104–17.
16. G. J. Cizek, Give us this day our daily dread: Manufacturing crises in education, *Phi Delta Kappan 80* (1999): 737–43; R. E. Ishler, How bad are America's public schools, really? *Phi Kappa Phi Journal 76,* no. 2 (1996): 4–5.
17. G. W. Bracey, The second Bracey report on the condition of public education, 104–17; B. Chase, Still "a nation at risk," 12 April 1998, www.nea.org/publiced/chase/bc980412.html.
18. G. W. Bracey, The second Bracey report, 104–17.
19. H. A. Lawson, School reform, families, and health in the emergent national agenda for economic and social improvement: Implications, *Quest 45* (1993): 293.
20. E. Jensen, *Brain-Based Learning* (Del Mar, CA: Turning Point, 1996); Jensen: *Teaching with the Brain in Mind* (Alexandria, VA: Association for Supervision and Curriculum Development, 1998).
21. *6seconds* (1999), 316 Seville Way, San Mateo, CA 94402.
22. B. S. Mohnsen, *Teaching Middle School Physical Education* (Champaign, IL: Human Kinetics, 1997), 3–5.
23. Jensen, *Teaching with the Brain in Mind,* 2.
24. Jensen, *Teaching with the Brain in Mind,* 1.
25. Jensen, *Brain-Based Learning;* Jensen, *Teaching with the Brain in Mind.*
26. *6seconds* (1999), 316 Seville Way, San Mateo, CA 94402.
27. Jensen, *Brain-Based Learning.*
28. D. A. Kolb, *Experiential Learning: Experience as the Source of Learning and Development* (Englewood Cliffs, NJ: Prentice-Hall, 1984).
29. Jensen, *Teaching with the Brain in Mind,* 63–64.
30. Jensen, *Teaching with the Brain in Mind,* 65.

31. Jensen, *Brain-Based Learning,* 273.
32. Jensen, *Teaching with the Brain in Mind.*
33. A. Chen and P. W. Darst, Confirming situational interest in physical activity: Testing the theoretical construct in a middle school participatory setting, *American Educational Research Association 1999 Conference Proceedings,* Special Interest Group Research on Learning and Instruction in Physical Education. Montreal, April 18–23, 1999, 33.
34. Jensen, *Brain-Based Learning,* 45.
35. *Deseret News,* 28 July 1998, C1–2.
36. Jensen, *Brain-Based Learning,* 41.
37. D. Hales, *Just Like a Woman* (New York: Bantam Books, 1999), 250–51.
38. Hales, *Just Like a Woman,* 251.
39. M. P. Driscoll, *Psychology of Learning for Instruction,* 2nd ed. (Boston: Allyn and Bacon, 2000), 90–91.
40. Jensen, *Teaching with the Brain in Mind,* 82–87.
41. S. Silverman, Student characteristics, practice, and achievement in physical education, *Journal of Educational Research 87,* no. 1 (1993): 54–61.
42. Jensen, *Teaching with the Brain in Mind,* 87.
43. Jensen, *Teaching with the Brain in Mind,* 88–89.
44. E. Miles, *Tune Your Brain: Using Music to Manage Your Mind, Body, and Mood* (New York: Berkley Books, 1997).
45. D. Niehoff, *The Biology of Violence* (New York: The Free Press, 1999).
46. National Association for Sport and Physical Education, *Moving into the Future: National Standards for Physical Education* (St. Louis: Mosby, 1995).
47. National Association for Sport and Physical Education, *Moving into the Future: National Standards for Physical Education,* 2nd ed. (Reston, VA: Author, 2004).
48. J. G. Bishop and S. G. Aldana, *Step Up to Wellness: A Stage-Based Approach* (Boston: Allyn and Bacon, 1999), xxii.
49. U.S. Department of Health and Human Services, *Physical Activity and Health: A Report of the Surgeon General* (Atlanta, GA: USDHHS, 1996).
50. Mohnsen, *Teaching Middle School Physical Education,* 61.
51. B. Chase, *Protecting Precious Lives,* 6 September 1998, www.nea.org/publiced/base/bc980906.html.
52. Rose and Gallup, The 36th annual Phi Delta Kappa/Gallup poll, 41–56.
53. B. Mohnsen, *The New Leadership Paradigm for Physical Education: What We Really Need to Lead* (Reston, VA: NASPE, 1999).
54. A. Evans and K. Bosworth, Building effective drug education programs, *Phi Delta Kappa Research Bulletin 19* (1997, December): 1.
55. K. K. Metcalf and P. A. Tait, Free market policies and public education: What is the cost of choice? *Phi Delta Kappan 81* (1999): 66–67.
56. D. Lilly, *Remedy for What Ails Nation's Public Schools,* 25 May 1997, www.seattletimes.com/extra/browse/html97/althill_052597.html.
57. J. Nathan, *Charter Schools: Creating Hope and Opportunity for American Education* (San Francisco: Jossey-Bass, 1999).
58. P. E. Peterson and B. C. Hassel, eds., *Learning from School Choice* (Washington, DC: The Brookings Institution, 1998), 41.
59. J. Nathan, *Charter Schools: Creating Hope and Opportunity for American Education,* 2; Peterson and Hassel, *Learning from School Choice.*
60. R. Mesenbrink, *National Association of Secondary School Principals, Curriculum Report 4,* no. 2 (1974, December).
61. Rose and Gallup, The 36th annual Phi Delta Kappa/Gallup poll, 50.
62. A. J. Menendez, Voters versus vouchers: An analysis of referendum data, *Phi Delta Kappan 81,* no. 1 (1999): 76; Metcalf and Tait, Free market policies, 65–75.
63. S. M. Elam, Florida's voucher program: Legislating what can't be done by referendum, *Phi Delta Kappan 81,* no. 1 (1999): 81–88.
64. Metcalf and Tait, Free market policies, 65–75.
65. B. Chase, *Why Not Vouchers,* 13 October 1996, www.nea.org/publiced/chase/bc961013.html.
66. L. C. Rose and A. M. Gallup, The 30th annual Phi Delta Kappa/Gallup poll of the public's attitudes toward the public schools, *Phi Delta Kappan 80* (1998): 41–56.
67. Menendez, Voters versus vouchers, 76–80.
68. Peterson and Hassel, *Learning from School Choice,* 45.
69. Nathan, *Charter Schools;* Peterson and Hassel, *Learning from School Choice.*
70. Nathan, *Charter Schools,* 7.
71. Lilly, Remedy.
72. Nathan, *Charter Schools,* 9.
73. Metcalf and Tait, Free market policies, 75.
74. J. Basinger, Building a partnership: Ithaca forges ties with school in Harlem, *The Chronicle of Higher Education,* 3 July 1998, A7.
75. The Saber-Tooth project: Curriculum and workplace reform in middle school physical education, *Journal of Teaching in Physical Education 18,* no. 4 (1999).
76. B. Chase, More Than Bricks and Mortar, 9 November 1997, www.nea.org/publiced/chase/bc971109.html.
77. NEA, *Issues* (1999), www.nea.org/issues/.
78. G. W. Bracey, A tale of two studies, *Phi Delta Kappan 80* (1999): *789–90; Deseret News, 23–24 June 1999, B4.*
79. B. Chase, Why Not the Best Teachers, 20 September 1998, www.nea.org/publiced/base/bc980920.html.
80. NEA, *Issues* (1999).
81. Nathan, *Charter Schools,* 8.
82. M. Roderick, Grade retention and school dropout: Policy debate and research questions, *Research Bulletin, Phi Delta Kappa 15* (1995).
83. Rose and Gallup, The 31st annual Phi Delta Kappa/Gallup poll, 41–56.
84. G. W. Bracey, Tinkering with TIMSS, *Phi Delta Kappan 80* (1998): 32–36; J. Wang, A content examination of the

TIMSS items, *Phi Delta Kappan 80* (1998): 36–38; *Deseret News,* 24–25 February 1998, A9.

85. Rose and Gallup, The 31st annual Phi Delta Kappa/Gallup poll, 41–56; *http://indian-river.fl.us/living/services/als/scope.html* (1999).
86. *http://indian-river.fl.us/living/services/als/scope.html* (1999).
87. Mohnsen, *Teaching Middle School Physical Education,* 9.
88. Mohnsen, *Teaching Middle School Physical Education.*
89. Bracey, A tale of two studies, 789–90.
90. L. C. Rose and A. M. Gallup, The 30th annual Phi Delta Kappa/Gallup poll of the public's attitudes toward the public schools, 41–56.
91. C. A. Langdon, The fifth Phi Delta Kappa poll of teachers attitudes toward the public schools, *Phi Delta Kappan* Vol. 81 (2000): 611–18.
92. A. C. Lewis, Listen to the children, *Phi Delta Kappan 80* (1999): 723–24.
93. Rose and Gallup, The 30th annual Phi Delta Kappa/Gallup poll, 41–56.
94. A. Toffler, *The Schoolhouse in the City* (New York: Frederick A. Praeger, in cooperation with Educational Facilities Laboratories, 1968), 367–69.
95. C. E. Silberman, *Crisis in the Classroom: The Remaking of American Education* (New York: Random House, 1970), 116.
96. R. M. W. Travers, ed., *Second Handbook of Research on Teaching* (Chicago: Rand McNally, 1973), 1210.
97. S. L. Richards, *Where Is Wisdom* (Salt Lake City, UT: Deseret Book, 1955), 208
98. Mohnsen, *Teaching Middle School Physical Education,* 1.
99. Mesenbrink, *National Association of Secondary School Principals, Curriculum Report 4.*
100. V. Seefeldt and P. Vogel, *The Value of Physical Activity* (Reston, VA: American Alliance for Health, Physical Education, Recreation, and Dance, 1986), 1–2.
101. U.S. Department of Health and Human Services, *Physical Activity and Health: A Report of the Surgeon General;* U.S. Department of Health and Human Services, *CDC's Guidelines for School and Community Programs: Promoting Lifelong Physical Activity* (Atlanta, GA:CDC: 1997).
102. National Association for Sport and Physical Education, *Speak II: Sport and Physical Education Advocacy Kit II* (Reston, VA: NASPE Publications, 1999).
103. U.S. Department of Health and Human Services, *Physical Activity and Health.*
104. U.S. Department of Health and Human Services, *CDC's Guidelines.*
105. *www.surgeongeneral.gov/topics/obesity/calltoaction/fact_adolescents.htm* (2004).
106. U.S. Department of Health and Human Services, Center for Disease Control and Prevention, *Physical Activity and Health Summary.* *www.cdc.gov/nccdphp/sgr/summ.htm* (2004).
107. U.S. Department of Health and Human Services, *Physical Activity and Health.*
108. U.S. Department of Health and Human Services, *Physical Activity and Health.*
109. U.S. Department of Health and Human Services, Center for Disease Control and Prevention, *Physical Activity and Health Chapter Conclusions.* *www.cdc.gov/nccdphp/sgr/chapcon.htm* (2004).
110. U.S. Department of Health and Human Services, *Healthy People 2010.* *www.healthypeople.gov/document/html/volume2/22physical.htm*
111. P. R. Vogel, Crisis in youth fitness and wellness, *Phi Delta Kappan 73* (1991): 154–56.
112. D. F. Staffo, A national K–12 health and physical education mandate is needed: But changes should be made first, *The Physical Educator 47* (1990): 2–6.
113. Center for Disease Control and Prevention, Morbidity and Mortality Weekly Report (MMWR). *Participation in High School Physical Education—United States, 1991–2003,* 17 September 2004, *www.cdc.gov/mmwr/preview/mmwrhtml/mm5336a5.htm.*
114. U.S. Department of Health and Human Services, *CDC's Guidelines.*
115. American Association of Health, Physical Education and Recreation, *Guidelines for Secondary School Physical Education* (Washington, DC: Author, 1970).
116. National Association for Sport and Physical Education, *Moving into the Future: National Standards for Physical Education,* (Reston, VA: Author 2004).
117. *USA Today,* 16 May 1986, 14A.
118. National Association for Sport and Physical Education, *Guidelines for Secondary School Physical Education: A Position Paper* (Reston, VA: American Alliance for Health, Physical Education, Recreation, and Dance, 1986).
119. *USA Today,* 16 May 1986, 14A.
120. D. Hellison, *Beyond Balls and Bats: Alienated Youth in the Gym* (Washington, DC: American Association for Health, Physical Education, Recreation, and Dance, 1978), 1.
121. D. Hellison, Evaluating the affective domain in physical education: Beyond measuring smiles, in J. E. Rink, ed., *Critical Crossroads: Middle and Secondary School Physical Education* (Reston, VA: National Association for Sport and Physical Education, 1993), 126.
122. D. Hellison, Evaluating the affective domain, 126.
123. J. H. Placek, Conceptions of success in teaching: Busy, happy and good? in T. J. Templin and J. K. Olson, eds., *Teaching in Physical Education* (Champaign, IL: Human Kinetics, 1983), 49.
124. *CDC's Guidelines for School and Community Programs to Promote Lifelong Physical Activity Among Young People* can be reproduced and adapted without permission. Copies of the guidelines can be downloaded from the Internet at *http://www.cdc.gov.*
125. D. Siedentop, Physical activity programs and policies: Toward an infrastructure for healthy lifestyles, *Journal of Physical Education, Recreation, and Dance 70,* no. 3 (1999): 33.
126. Siedentop, Physical activity programs, 35.

127. T. L. Mckenzie, School health-related physical activity programs: What do the data say? *Journal of Physical Education, Recreation, and Dance 70,* no. 1 (1999): 16–19.

128. National Commission on Excellence in Education, *A Nation at Risk.*

129. R. Martens, Turning kids on to physical activity for a lifetime, *Quest 48* (1996): 303.

130. National Association for Sport and Physical Education, *Speak II: Sport and Physical Education Advocacy Kit,* III 7.

131. NASPE, Shape of the nation report, *Academy Action* (1997–98): 5,12.

132. National Association for Sport and Physical Education, *Speak II: Sport and Physical Education Advocacy Kit,* III 8.

133. Center for Disease Control and Prevention, *Coordinated School Health Program.* www.cdc.gov/HealthyYouth/index.htm (2004).

134. Center for Disease Control and Prevention, *School Health Index: Middle and High School Module 3.* http://apps.nccd.cdc.gov/shi (2004).

135. NASPE News (1998). Shape of the nation report, 50, 1, 14.

136. M. P. Ernst, R. P. Pangrazi, and C. B. Corbin, Physical education: Making a transition toward activity, *Journal of Physical Education, Recreation, and Dance 69,* no. 9 (1998): 29.

137. Martens, Turning kids on, 303–10.

138. U.S. Department of Health and Human Services. *Healthy People 2000: National Health Promotion Disease Prevention Objectives,* DHHS Publication Number PHS 91-50212.

139. American Footwear Association (1988), *American Youth and Sports Participation,* 200 Castlewood Drive, North Palm Beach, Florida 33408.

140. B. Strand and E. Scantling, An analysis of secondary student preferences toward physical education, *The Physical Educator 51* (1994): 119–29.

141. S. Silverman, Why do high school students drop out of physical education? *The Journal of Physical Education, Recreation, and Dance 68,* no. 2 (1997): 16.

142. NASPE, Shape of the nation report, 12.

143. NASPE, Shape of the nation report, 12.

144. National Association for Sport and Physical Education, *Moving into the Future.*

145. Martens, Turning kids on, 303–10.

146. G. Graham, Physical education in U.S. schools, K–12, *Journal of Physical Education, Recreation, and Dance 6,* no. 2 (1990): 39.

147. T. J. Martinek, Fostering hope in youth: A model for explaining learned helplessness in physical activity, *Quest 48,* no. 3 (1996): 409–21.

148. Graham, Physical education in U.S. schools, 39.

149. Martens, Turning kids on, 303–10.

150. Martinek, Fostering hope in youth, 409–21.

151. Martens, Turning kids on, 303–10.

152. Staffo, A national K–12, 2–6.

153. Siedentop, Physical activity programs and policies, 10.

154. T. L. McKenzie and J. F. Sallis, Physical activity, fitness, and health-related physical education, in S. J. Silverman and C. D. Ennis, eds., *Student Learning in Physical Education* (Champaign, IL: Human Kinetics, 1996), 230.

T1.1 American Association of School Administrators, *Imperatives in Education* (Washington, DC: Author, 1966); E. L. Boyer, High school: *A report on secondary education in America* (New York: Harper & Row, 1983); B. F. Brown, *The Reform of Secondary Education* (New York: McGraw-Hill, 1973): 32–35; *Call to Action* (1997), NASPE News, no. 48; *Goals 2000 Educate America Act,* 21 March 1994, Congressional Record, U.S. House of Representatives, www.ed.gov/updates/PresEDPlan/; R. E. Gross, Seven new cardinal principles, *Phi Delta Kappan 60* (1978): 291–93.

CHAPTER

2

The Responsibilities of the Physical Educator

Study Stimulators

1. Would you advise someone to enter the teaching profession today? Why or why not? What would you tell new teachers to do to sell themselves to prospective employers?
2. What teaching characteristics do effective teachers possess?
3. What is a code of ethics? Of what value is it to a physical educator?
4. What responsibilities to the profession of education do physical educators have?
5. What causes teacher stress and how does one deal with it?
6. Is it possible to be an effective teacher of physical education and at the same time succeed as an interscholastic coach?
7. Why is public relations an important role of teachers?
8. What methods can be used to enhance public relations?

The role of a physical educator may include any of the following responsibilities: (1) teaching; (2) coaching; (3) advising and counseling students; (4) administration of instructional, intramural, and extramural programs, budgets, facilities, and equipment; (5) supervision; (6) service to school and community; (7) membership in professional organizations and professional development; and (8) public relations.

In addition, physical educators have a responsibility to be role models for a physically fit, active lifestyle. Brandon and Evans found that 77 percent of physical education teachers sampled exercised three or more times a week for at least twenty minutes per session. Even so, the majority of the respondents (57 percent) considered themselves to be overweight.[1] Studies have shown that teachers who are overweight or inactive have a negative effect on their students and on physical education programs.[2] However, Bishoff, Plowman, and Lindenman found no differences between fit and unfit teachers in terms of teacher-student interaction and on-the-job performance.[3]

The Physical Educator as a Teacher

What is a teacher? In response to that question, a fourth-grade student replied, "A teacher is someone who knows that you can do what you never did before."[4] A good teacher not only has the vision to see what the student is capable of doing or becoming but also can help the student achieve that goal. Most of us are aware that the mediocre teacher *tells,* the good teacher *explains,* the superior teacher *demonstrates,* and the great teacher *inspires.* Someone once said, "Your students deserve more than your knowledge. They deserve and hunger for your inspiration."

What is teaching? In one sense it is the business or occupation of teachers. In another sense it is the act of helping (inspiring) students to do what they never did before. If teaching is an occupation, those entering the profession must make a decision to become teachers and go through the training process necessary to become qualified. Part of this qualification is realizing "good teaching cannot be reduced to technique; good teaching comes from the identity and integrity of the teacher."[5]

The role of a teacher has changed recently as more is expected of teachers and schools than previously. One of the changes teachers must face is the ethnic mix present in our schools today. Whites make up 142.6 million citizens, while blacks represent 21 million citizens, Hispanics represent 10.9 million citizens, and Asians and Pacific Islanders, 3.9 million citizens.[6] A Virginia suburb of Washington, D.C., reports its students are from 182 countries and speak more than one hundred languages.[7] Teachers are now interacting with many cultures, languages, and attitudes that should cause them to ponder ways of creating success for each student.

A teacher often serves as a role model, counselor, substitute parent, disciplinarian, instructor, and supporter. Each of these roles is vital to the survival of the individual student. A teacher who provides an equitable, effective learning environment, which provides each student with equal access and equal opportunity to learn, will fulfill all the expected responsibilities. Palmer reminds us "students who learn, not professors who perform, is what teaching is all about: students who learn are the finest fruit of teachers who teach."[8]

Not only the role of the teacher has changed, but also the portrait of the teacher. Many states are certifying professionals to teach in the public schools. Oftentimes, people who have retired from occupations requiring capabilities that would enhance the school curriculum have geared up to enter the teaching ranks. Usually the requirement for such reentry is a baccalaureate degree from an accredited institution in a subject taught at the secondary level, with at least five years of experience related to the subject area. Most candidates come from business, industry, or the military.[9] Coaching positions are sometimes filled by such individuals. The problem with this type of teacher could be a lack of pedagogical skill, and school districts need to provide such training. This is one of the creative plans that has been devised to meet the teacher shortages in some fields. Several states are finding that the shortage has caused less-qualified candidates to seek employment as teachers. Massachusetts reported in 1998 almost 60 percent of two thousand would-be teachers did not pass the state's new Teachers Test, an exam that tests English and mathematics skills.[10] The time is right for new teachers, who are effective, to make an impact.

Teaching: An Art and a Science

Part of teaching is an art rather than a science. Thomas states that as such it cannot be quantified, qualified, or conveniently duplicated:

> Teaching is an art. One becomes a good teacher in the same way one becomes a good actor, a good poet, a good musician, a good painter. One develops a unique style, a personalized method, a way of teaching that cannot be mass produced or even replicated.[11]

When the ingredients of teacher, student, and environment come together in the right mix, an educational "happening" may be the result. DeFelice calls this "magic." An individual can be a competent teacher, in that the mechanics of teaching are done well, but not inspire students. When the "magic" is present, it is a "sense of vitality that seems to energize everything and everyone in the classroom. Sometimes it's a bubbling, exuberant kind of energy. Other times it's a powerful, quiet kind of energy. Either kind transforms lessons into learning and creates the charged atmosphere in which we also become transformed. . . . The teacher who is not afraid to make mistakes and who has a genuine respect for other people's ideas is filled with the energy from which magic is made. That teacher is alive, and others can't help but be affected by that vitality."[12]

Review Question: What abilities do you have that you think will make you an effective teacher?

Characteristics of Effective Teachers

The effective teacher has students who produce good results on measures of achievement. Shulman identified seven areas of knowledge required for good physical education teaching: (1) content or subject knowledge; (2) general pedagogical (teaching) knowledge; (3) curriculum knowledge; (4) pedagogical content knowledge (specific methods for physical education); (5) knowledge of learners and characteristics; (6) knowledge of educational contexts (community, district, school, classroom); and (7) knowledge of educational purposes, history, and philosophy.[13] Effective teachers put all this together to facilitate student learning. So, what makes some individuals more effective at teaching than others?

The AAHPERD 1998 Teachers of the Year shared eight characteristics for effectiveness: (1) in-depth content and pedagogical knowledge, (2) problem-solving ability, (3) use of self-evaluative procedures, (4) use of high rates of verbal feedback, (5) maximizing of motor time while minimizing management time, (6) a passionate belief in their work, (7) a love for teaching and young people, and (8) active participation in professional organizations and workshops.

In the past, research on teaching has not answered the question, What makes an effective teacher? The first researchers isolated certain teacher personality *characteristics,* such as being *loving, caring,* or *involved,* as criteria for judging teacher effectiveness.[14] Later, researchers focused on teaching *methods,* which led them to a certain *climate* in the classroom, based on teacher-student interaction, as being the key to effective teaching.[15] Researchers next developed a model that determined effective teachers had a large repertoire of *competencies*

Teachers who communicate interest and concern for students encourage student learning.

from which to draw, such as ability to motivate, or management skills.[16] Studies fail to confirm any of these approaches as documenting teacher effectiveness. However, research has shown that student achievement is significantly related to such teacher attributes as experience and educational attainment.[17]

To further complicate the issue, teacher behaviors ultimately appear to be situation specific; that is, they are directly related to the subject matter, environment, and characteristics of students. Research substantiates the individual teacher's role as a decision maker in producing effectiveness in the classroom. Teacher behavior and decisions that maximize student achievement have also been identified as elements of effectiveness, including: (1) quantity and pacing of instruction, (2) whole-class versus small-group versus individualized instruction, (3) giving information, (4) questioning students, (5) reacting to student responses, (6) handling seatwork and homework assignments, and (7) context-specific findings.[18] Some other characteristics associated with successful teachers are (8) teacher warmth, (9) a positive classroom atmosphere, (10) teacher expectations, and (11) classroom management. However, even these can be situation specific.

Quantity and Pacing of Instruction

The amount learned is related to opportunity to learn, which in part is determined by the length of the school day and the number of days of instruction. Achievement is maximized when teachers emphasize academic instruction and expect students to master the curriculum, with less "free time" spent in such activities as "student choice" or "throw out the ball." Student achievement is influenced by classroom organization and management that results in increased student *engaged* time (the amount of time the student is actively involved in instruction). Engagement rates depend on teachers' abilities to make academic activities run smoothly; orchestrate brief, orderly transitions; and spend little time getting organized or dealing with inattention or resistance. Students who learn efficiently experience success. If students are to work on assignments with high levels of success, teachers must be effective in diagnosing learning needs and prescribing appropriate activities. Finally, teachers must actively teach. Students achieve more in classes where teachers actively teach and supervise rather than expect students to work on their own.

Whole-Class, Small-Group, Individualized Instruction

Whole-class instruction is usually more effective because it is simpler and doesn't tie the teacher to a specific group. Individual instruction and small groups are more difficult to organize, but grouping may be most effective in heterogeneous classes.

Giving Information

Achievement is maximized when teachers effectively structure lessons. They begin with overviews, advance organizers, or review objectives; they outline content and signal transitions between lesson parts; they call attention to main ideas; then they summarize subparts and review main ideas. See Table 2.1.

Questioning Students

Questioning can be used as a check for understanding and to get students involved in the learning process. Questioning can also be used as a problem-solving strategy (see Chapter 9 for an extensive discussion of this strategy). Effective teachers master the ability to question students. Teaching styles such as guided discovery depend upon good questioning to be effective. Good questions require students to recall information, analyze information,

TABLE 2.1 Effective Lesson Structure

- Stated objectives and value of lesson
- Anticipatory set (questions/assignments to stimulate thinking)
- Lesson focus that includes input and modeling
- Checking for understanding
- Guided and independent practice
- Effective organization and transition techniques
- Summary and review of key concepts
- Allowing wait-time for concepts to sink in
- Effective closure calling attention to lesson focus and the next class period

and/or synthesize responses to the information provided. All students are given an opportunity to formulate a response but none are embarrassed. "Call outs" are monitored and all students are encouraged to participate.

Reacting to Student Responses

Good teachers monitor student responses, such as answering a question, by acknowledging a correct reply. On the other hand, they also indicate when a response is not correct without being critical or probing for a better response.

Handling Independent Work and Homework Assignments

When students are asked to accomplish tasks more independently (often termed *seatwork*), 100 percent success rates are expected. Effective teachers thoroughly explain to students what to do, what work they are accountable for, how to get help, and what to do when they finish. Teachers or aides then circulate to provide help when needed. To be successful, students who need help must receive assistance as quickly as possible.

Context-Specific Findings

Teachers must structure different learning experiences for various groups of students. For example, in the early grades, classroom management involves a great deal of instruction in desired routines and procedures. Small-group instruction is more prevalent in early grades, whereas whole-class instruction, involving application, is more typical in later grades.

Socioeconomic status (SES) is an important factor. A wise teacher will distinguish between high- and low-SES students. Low-SES, low-achieving students need more control and structure, more active instruction and feedback, more redundancy, and smaller steps with higher success rates. High-SES students are more likely to be confident, eager to participate, and responsive to challenge. They usually do not require a great deal of encouragement or praise and thrive in a somewhat demanding atmosphere. Low-SES students are more likely to require warmth and support and need more encouragement. The successful teacher will remember that what constitutes appropriate instructional behavior will vary with the objectives.

Teacher Warmth

One often-mentioned characteristic of effective teachers is teacher warmth. Earls demonstrated that distinctive physical education teachers love children, suggesting that the key difference between effective and ineffective teachers may be the intention and commitment to helping students learn. In spite of how logical it seems that teacher warmth makes for good teaching, "data do not support the notion that efficient learning requires a warm emotional climate."[19] Negative indicators such as teacher criticism or student resistance usually show significant negative correlations with achievement, but positive indicators such as praise usually do not show significant positive correlations.

A Positive Classroom Atmosphere

Teachers create a positive classroom atmosphere by learning students' names, getting to know students as individuals, sharing experiences with students, and inviting students' responses. Students don't care how much teachers know until they know how much they care.

The teacher who can communicate concern for each student creates a feeling of mutual respect, encouraging students to want to learn and achieve in school. Such feelings are engendered by showing courtesy and avoiding criticism, ridicule, or embarrassment. Acceptance of individual differences in backgrounds, abilities, and personalities tells students the teacher is interested in them as human beings and that they are essential to the success of the class. A willingness to listen to students and incorporate student ideas into the curriculum, when appropriate, are important factors in establishing student/teacher rapport.

Teacher Expectations

Effective teachers expect students to achieve, and they provide a firm foundation for this to occur. Teachers who expect a lot from their students tend to spend more time working with students on on-task behavior and push students to work to their full capacities.

Classroom Management

We also know that "teachers who are better classroom managers are more likely to produce students with better achievement test scores."[20] Physical educators are notoriously bad managers. Metzler points out that they spend from 25 percent to 50 percent of their time in management, passive observing, and organizing during class.[21] This time could be better spent in teaching for achievement gains. As it is, students are more likely to be waiting, listening, or performing unplanned tasks.

To reduce management time, effective teachers spend time during the early part of the school year discussing, practicing, and reviewing classroom rules and procedures. Administrative tasks are handled in a routine fashion and students are involved whenever possible. The teacher has clear stop-start signals and allows student input into the selection of the signals. Procedures for disseminating and collecting equipment are carefully planned for maximum efficiency.[22]

Developing a Personal Philosophy

The qualities of good teachers just discussed have a research foundation. Mastering these qualities and the remaining content in this book embodies the science of teaching. The art of teaching surfaces as a teacher develops his or her own teaching style. People's teaching style will depend upon their personalities as well as their philosophy. The development of a personal philosophy of education and physical education is critical to effective teaching.

A philosophy is a composite of knowledge, attitudes, beliefs, and values that forms the basis for a person's actions and provides central direction or purpose to his or her activities. Oberteuffer and Ulrich indicated that

> to understand anything one must relate all of the parts, episodes, or individual actions to the "grand plan," the overall purpose. This is sometimes called the point of view—or the philosophy underlying the effort. Without an overall plan, direction, or philosophy, a physical education program, or anything else, becomes nothing more than a series of disconnected and unrelated activities, having no unifying purpose.[23]

A sound philosophy is the basis for a sound program and effective teaching. In essence, philosophy dictates what is taught, how it is taught, and how it is evaluated. For example, a teacher whose philosophy stresses physical fitness will have a strong school physical fitness program. The philosophy of a very effective teacher of physical education should include a conviction that all students will get *turned on* to physical activity today and remain active for life. He or she has determined, before stepping into the gymnasium, that students will achieve psychomotor, cognitive, and affective skills while in class. A plan for determining such outcomes has been formulated and curriculum has been planned based on the National Standards.

A philosophy is the result of continuously changing knowledge and experience. It is dynamic, always evolving, and never static. However, all physical educators should have a current philosophy written down and filed in their professional portfolio.

Daughtrey suggested that prospective teachers defining a philosophy ask themselves the following questions:

1. Do I know where I am headed? What is my aim?
2. Can I scientifically justify the activities I wish to teach?
3. Am I willing to abandon the teaching of certain activities if they are shown to be educationally unsound?
4. Is my program self-centered or student-centered?
5. Are the activities safe?
6. Is my program a play program or is it a teaching program?[24]

Further, is this program relevant for the twenty-first century for me as both a teacher and a coach?

The development of a philosophy in physical education takes time to contemplate. It involves the following steps:

Step 1. *Sort out what is really important to you as a teacher and coach of physical education.* This should be done as courses are taken, new publications are read, and leaders are listened to. Focus on your professional heros. Determine whether they are impacting lives and making a difference for good. If so, learn about their philosophy and adapt their meaningful ideas into your own.

Step 2. *React to what is happening around you.* Through reacting and questioning why things are as they are and how they should be, you can get an idea of your own feelings regarding physical education, education, and even life itself. Through struggling to define your philosophy you will also gain valuable insight into what you really believe. Write down thoughts as they come to you. You may want to keep a journal for just such ideas and inspiration. You could also file your ideas in your portfolio. However you keep track of your thoughts, at some point you will want to pull them all together and formulate a concrete philosophy.

Step 3. *State your philosophy.* Discuss what you have formulated with others and articulate your philosophy about your chosen profession often. Stating your philosophy orally or in writing to others, and defending it, will help you see areas that you have neglected to consider. You will need to reconsider what you believe over and over again as you gain knowledge and experiences throughout your life. Discussion, diversity, and disagreement should be accepted and appreciated as one's philosophy is constantly emerging. Now let others know what you are about and stand behind your philosophy with conviction. Be willing to champion good programs and fight for the reinstatement of those that are being eliminated.

Following are some general rules for philosophy development:

1. Always write in third person. No "I", "My," or "Me" statements.
2. Avoid being wordy; this should be a concise statement.
3. Avoid repetitive statements.
4. Keep it clean—the look of the document itself should make it easy to read.
5. Be creative—with today's technology you should not have a problem "dressing up" the document.
6. Be honest—don't state anything that you do not believe.
7. Check terminology—be sure that the wording used is professional. You are attempting to impress someone: does your wording do so?

Some questions that might be answered within the philosophy statement include these:

1. What is it you believe to be true about physical activity for children? For adults?
2. What do you know to be true about the health benefits of physical activity?
3. What type of lifetime fitness skills do you feel should be presented in a quality physical education program?
4. What type of non-physical life lessons do you feel children learn from physical education?
5. How do you feel these can be integrated into the physical education curriculum?
6. What would you hope that parents understand about an effective physical education program?

There are no specific rules for organizing a philosophy statement but the following is one possible way:

1. Philosophy—What do you believe?
2. Purpose—Why do you believe this?
3. Goal—How will you go about accomplishing this? (Don't get too specific.)

Remember that a philosophy will change with time and experience. It is important to review your philosophy on a regular basis to be sure it still fits your current belief system and your current program. Overall, what you are doing is justifying what you believe, why you believe it, and why what you do is important to the child's learning process. Be professional; take this seriously. A high-quality program requires hard work. Put your philosophy into writing and back it up with your actions.

Employment Issues

Employment centers around three major aspects: (1) getting a job; (2) starting the job, especially as a beginning teacher; and (3) keeping the job. The material that follows is intended as a partial discussion of each of these. The professional portfolio has become an effective tool for providing evidence of the quality of a person's performance as a teacher. The first year of teaching can be exciting as well as extremely difficult and time consuming. Keeping a job depends upon being an effective teacher who operates as a professional and is able to minimize the stress that will definitely occur.

Getting a Job

This section will discuss professional portfolios and planning ideas for seeking employment.

Your Professional Portfolio You need to formulate a philosophy that you are willing to state, and also showcase your professional competence as you move along the road of teaching and/or coaching. The portfolio is an *authentic assessment* of you, or a comprehensive look at you, as a preprofessional. It is a purposeful collection of your professional work, gathered over time, representing a wide range of products and performances that demonstrate or provide *evidence* of what you have learned and what you can do. "Portfolios are not made up of anything and everything: appropriate item selection is key to a portfolio's success."[25]

a. Types of portfolios
   1. Working portfolio—A file for each standard, with evidences of your knowledge and ability.
   2. Presentation portfolio—A three-ring binder with dividers for each standard, including selected evidences and reflective statements for each standard and a self-assessment for each standard.
   3. Employment portfolio—A refined presentation portfolio, with additional evaluations of your teaching, licensing documents, student teaching evaluations, recommendations, and so on.
b. Mode of presentation
   1. Paper—easiest to use during a job interview.
   2. Electronic or digital—could be web-based or presented on a CD or DVD. The CD or DVD could be left with the potential employer for further review.
   3. Portable file—the least effective means of presentation; it is more effective as a storage and organizational tool.
c. Organization—A portfolio can be organized around NASPE's National Standards for Beginning Physical Education Teachers. With credit to Melograno, here are the standards with some examples of portfolio materials:[26]

   1. Content Knowledge
      - Transcripts
      - Readings list organized around courses taken
   2. Growth and Development
      - Research paper on child growth and development
      - Progressions for various age groups
   3. Diverse Learners
      - Anecdotal notes from field experiences in multicultural school settings
      - Learning contracts for children who are physically challenged
   4. Management and Motivation
      - Written rules and procedures for conducting a high school physical education class
      - Videotape of a teaching experience
   5. Communication
      - Log of activities during student teaching
      - Bulletin board materials
   6. Planning and Instruction
      - Lesson plans
      - Teacher-made materials
   7. Learner Assessment
      - Examples of assessment materials
      - Awards and certificates

8. Reflection
    - Journal of field experience observations
    - Essay written on an issue
9. Collaboration
    - Letter of appreciation for conducting intramural program
    - Letter to parents

d. Implementation
1. You are ultimately responsible for selecting and judging the quality of your own work.
2. Mentors facilitate, guide, and offer choices; provide time for reflection and decision making; model expectations.
3. Peers give valuable feedback.

e. Item categories
1. Baseline samples
2. Balance of items you produced, items from peers, and items from students as evidence of their learning
3. Something that was hard for you to do
4. Something that makes you feel really good
5. Something you would like to work on again
6. Best pieces—examples of work over a period of time—exams, videos, logs, and other items
    (a) What makes this your best piece?
    (b) How did you go about writing it?
    (c) What problems did you encounter?
    (d) How did you solve them?
    (e) What makes your most effective piece different from your least effective piece?
7. Work in progress with plans for revision
    (a) Progress assessment of works
        (1) What goals did you set for yourself?
        (2) How well did you accomplish them?
        (3) What are your future goals?
    (b) Drafts of a final product as it evolved and improved over time.
    (c) Anecdotal record of observations over time

f. Possible items (Melograno)[27]
1. Anecdotal records (observation notes on students' skills), article summaries or critiques (reflect on an article read on your own)
2. Assessments (items you developed)
3. Awards and certificates (volunteer recognition)
4. Bulletin board ideas (photograph)
5. Case studies (show knowledge of an anonymous child's development)
6. Classroom management philosophy (written summary including citations)
7. Computer programs (programs incorporated into teaching)
8. Cooperative learning strategies (copy of lesson plan)
9. Curriculum plans (thematic units)
10. Evaluations (on-the-job performance assessments)
11. Goal statements (outline perceived role as a teacher)
12. Individualized plans (show how lessons or units have been adapted for diverse learners)
13. Journals (observations during field experiences)
14. Lesson plans (copies of all components)
15. Letters to parents (weekly newsletters)
16. Management and organization strategies (summary of system for grouping students)
17. Media competencies (examples of forms of media used in teaching)
18. Meetings and workshops log (reaction paper with program)
19. Peer critiques (rating sheets from presentations)
20. Philosophy statement (brief position paper)
21. Pictures and photographs (show special projects/learning centers)
22. Plans (see item 14)
23. Portfolio, student (sample artifacts from a student's portfolio)
24. Position papers (scholarly defense of an educational issue) and professional materials, i.e., (list of future workshops to attend, list of memberships, involvements and journals received)
25. References (statements from supervisors)
26. Rules and procedures descriptions (written guidelines)
27. Schedules (show format for events in a day)
28. Seating arrangement diagrams (reflect on a particular management strategy)
29. Self-assessment instruments (questionnaire results)
30. Student contracts (samples of agreement with students)
31. Teacher-made materials (games, videotapes, teaching aids)
32. Theme studies (lessons that show integrated curriculum)
33. Transcripts (copy of official transcript with personal analysis)
34. Vita or resumé

The storage options for collecting artifacts is a matter of personal preference. Possibilities include notebooks, expanding and accordion files, large file box, folders, satchels, pockets for electronic documents, large notebook divided into sections, and file drawers in a cabinet.[28]

It is important that feedback be given on the portfolio, both formal and informal. If the certifying institution does not do that, each person should seek out others to help in finalizing the professional portfolio.

Seeking Employment Although competition for positions in physical education may be keen, an ambitious person can enhance his or her opportunities by incorporating definite strategies in securing a position. Lambert outlined the following systematic planning techniques for seeking employment:

1. Explore job possibilities early. Find a job or volunteer, working at as many different jobs as you can.
2. Stay current about job opportunities. Consult the school placement office regularly. Check library resources.
3. Maintain a 3.0 GPA.
4. Prepare a portfolio including resumé
   a. List all previous jobs by year.
   b. List educational background.
   c. List activities you have done that enhance credibility (i.e., Sunday School teacher, camp counselor, recreation leader, etc.).
   d. Collect letters of recommendation.
   e. Write a personal philosophy.
5. Inform relatives, friends, acquaintances, and former employers you are job hunting.
6. Follow up on all leads and advice.
7. Keep names of important contacts.
8. Start interviewing.
   a. Be positive.
   b. Find out all you can about the organization before going.[29]

Starting the Job

Beginning teachers in all fields have similar concerns. When these concerns are known, steps can be taken to diminish or alleviate first-day and first-year jitters. Houston and Felder listed the following concerns of new teachers.[30]

1. Expectations about them by their principal and fellow teachers
2. Classroom management and discipline
3. Planning and preparing for the day

Despite these concerns, when beginning teachers believed in themselves as teachers, they looked forward to working with students and entered the classroom with enthusiasm. Beginning teachers must be well prepared before school starts. Textbooks must be read, materials collected, policies formulated, and a support group of caring people found. Teachers need also to recognize that once teaching has begun they will be fatigued, may develop other somatic symptoms, may become emotionally drained, or may feel they are just surviving. These symptoms will usually dissipate after three to four months. New teachers can cushion this process by anticipating it and by surrounding themselves with a support system of persons with whom experiences can be discussed. Fellow teachers should be part of one's social experiences. More and more school districts realize the trauma of first-year teachers and are surrounding them with a support system and easing them into full-time teaching gradually. Some states have an organized mentor program for first-year teachers. If this is not true in your case, seek out a mentor, an experienced teacher you feel comfortable consulting about local practices and ideas for teaching. The beginning teacher and physical educators in any stage of professional development need to pay attention to stress.

Keeping the Job

Keeping a job depends on how well the beginning teacher is socialized into the school and the culture and behavior of teaching. A teacher's effectiveness should be measured against accepted standards for effective teaching but most importantly on how much students have learned. Ways to assess each of these are discussed in later chapters. To maintain a teaching job individuals also need to demonstrate honesty, integrity, empathy, and fairness. Generally this means the teacher is following a professional code of ethics.

A Professional Code of Ethics A code of ethics is a statement of conduct that governs individuals within a profession. It refers to all of the relationships that occur among people and between people and institutions in the educational environment. It deals with what is right and wrong or good and bad in human conduct. Ethics deals with values as it attempts to answer the question "Why?" For the physical educator, a code of ethics includes such ideals as sportspersonship, tolerance, understanding others, loyalty, fair play, cooperation, support of others, and sacrifice of self for the welfare of others. Because ethics involves conduct, a code of ethics is not complete without the decision-making process of what ought to be.[31]

Physical educators are confronted with ethical decisions on and off the playing field, and they must be prepared to take a stand and be an example for students forming their own set of values. Educators must also accept responsibilities that include belonging to professional organizations; attending conventions, workshops, clinics, and in-service meetings; acquiring and reading appropriate books and periodicals; and continuing their education. The American Alliance for Health, Physical Education, Recreation, and Dance endorses the code of ethics of the National Education Association. This code consists of the expected commitment of the teacher to the student, the public, the profession, and the employer.

Commitment to the Student

The teacher must be committed to the optimum development of every student, regardless of skill level, gender, race, or disability. "Physical education should be adapted for those students who have special needs."[32] Bain indicated that "teachers have an ethical obligation to act on the student's behalf when it is in the student's best interest"[33] Williamson discussed what is needed to provide an equitable environment for students. She defined equity "as creating a supportive atmosphere where students have the opportunity for successful participation and exposure to instruction regardless of gender, race, ethnicity, religion, sexual orientation, social class, or motor ability."[34] She presented six ideas to consider to establish a more equitable learning environment:

1. The teacher must believe that each student has the capacity to learn. Since one approach will work for one student but not for another, many different teaching styles need to be used.
2. The teacher needs to consider how groups are organized. Are different groups encouraged to work together? Are students needlessly categorized by sex?
3. Does the teacher interact with one group more than another? Videotaping lessons and analyzing the tapes will help determine if this is true. Also consider the use of language, using terms such as *sportspersonship* and *player-to-player* defense rather than *sportsmanship* and *man-to-man* defense. Rules can be modified according to ability level and not sex.
4. Does the curriculum offer a broad range of activities with equal opportunities for all students to participate?
5. Different standards for fitness tests for boys and girls indicate that one group is better than the other. A study of ten- to thirteen-year-olds indicated no differences between boys and girls.
6. To be successful in physical education the entire school must also be practicing the same values.[35]

Another issue related to commitment to the student is the establishment of a friendly but professional relationship with students. When a student and teacher become too familiar, the teacher-student link is weakened and the nature of the educational relationship is impaired. Information of a personal nature must be kept in strictest confidence and all students protected from unnecessary embarrassment.

Meaningful instructional opportunities should be available to all students. It is recommended that elementary school students have a *daily* instructional period of at least thirty minutes. The minimum instructional period for students in secondary schools is a *daily* standard class period.[36]

Commitment to the Public

Everyone in the profession must assume the role of promoting a positive image in the eyes of the public. An *exemplary job of teaching* must be done to sell physical education programs to the taxpayers. Those involved in athletics must work tirelessly to be sure practices are completely ethical. Crawford stressed the ethical commitment that physical educators must demonstrate:

> Physical educators have a moral responsibility to speak up, speak out, and speak at young people to stress that difficult "right" and "wrong" decisions have to be made if sport is to remain as an expressive and dramatic facet of human experience dependent on ethical behavior.[37]

Outstanding teachers participate in community affairs, promote good community-school relationships, and refrain from using school affiliation for personal gain.

Commitment to Professional Employment Practices

Once a contract has been signed with a school district, the teacher is legally and ethically committed to complete the term of service specified with high-quality work and integrity in employment practices. If the contract must be terminated because of reasons beyond control, then the teacher and the district arrive at a mutually agreed upon solution to the situation.

Adherence to ethical policies and practices of the employer must always be standard procedure for teachers. Likewise, employers are expected to adhere to the same policies. Professional organizations can often assist members experiencing unethical behavior by employers.

Commitment to the Profession

A professional person is dedicated to providing a service to other people. Outstanding educators strive to provide a service that is highly esteemed. In education, more often than not, students have no choice of which teacher's class to take. Moreover, tenure laws, which originated to protect teachers, now protect incompetent teachers from termination.

Physical educators must never forget that they are educators and that the purpose of all programs in the school is to educate students. As such, physical education teachers and coaches share the concerns of other teachers in the school and must work together with them to promote total school unity. They can show their concern by attending general faculty meetings; serving on faculty committees; upholding school policies; and taking turns with hall, cafeteria, or bus duty. Cooperation with the school staff—secretaries, custodians, nurses, business personnel, and so on—is also essential because of the many and varied facilities necessary for physical education programs. Further, teachers must make every effort to sell themselves and the program by personal appearance, manner of speech, and enthusiasm about the program and the entire school. This cannot be done while hiding out in the gym.

Teachers need to maintain relationships with other members of the profession that are based on mutual respect for one another. Teachers have an obligation to be objective, honest, and fair; to respect and defend the rights of their associates; and to hold in confidence information shared by colleagues. However, professionals also have a responsibility to confront associates who are acting unethically or are incompetent. Moreover, they also have the responsibility to follow proper administrative channels and be willing to listen to the other person's point of view.

Commitment to Professional Organizations

Professional organizations exist to help members of a given profession work together to achieve common goals. The American Alliance for Health, Physical Education, Recreation, and Dance (AAHPERD) is the national affiliate for the profession. Physical educators need to join this organization at the state, regional, and national levels and other organizations whose goals are to help its members achieve the goals of the profession.

Education associations and professional organizations catering to specialized groups capitalize on collective bargaining while enhancing communication among individuals. These organizations include the National Education Association (NEA) and the American Federation of Teachers (AFT), as well as those for only coaches, teachers, athletic trainers, or administrators. Helpful publications are often a benefit of belonging to such organizations. Members of professional organizations can benefit by sharing ideas with one another, speaking at conventions, writing articles in professional journals, serving on committees; holding office; or just attending, listening, reading, or helping in other ways. These groups also help with employment needs by publishing job openings and providing opportunities at conventions for potential employers and employees to get acquainted.

Good teachers constantly improve their effectiveness through ongoing professional development. Physical education teachers show a varied record of participation in professional organizations, and could most certainly benefit by being more involved. One-third of the teachers polled attended a state Health, Physical Education, Recreation, and Dance (HPERD) conference during a two-year period. Elementary and junior high school physical education teachers were twice as likely as senior high school teachers to attend state conferences. Women teachers were also more likely than men (41 percent versus 26 percent) to be in attendance. Attendance by these professionals at regional conferences dropped to 6 percent, and at national conventions attendance was 2 percent. Teachers in this survey were more likely to attend clinics and workshops sponsored by local school districts or organizations (56 percent). The lowest attenders at local meetings were the least-experienced teachers.[38]

Minimizing Stress Stress is a common concern for all of us operating in a busy, hectic lifestyle. Common symptoms of stress include fatigue, nervousness, frustration, and sleeplessness. These can lead to serious illnesses, as well as to many psychological disorders.

To prevent stress, teachers need to plan a personal lifestyle that can alleviate the stresses of teaching. Proper nutrition, exercise, and sleep are essential. Developing hobbies and interests separate from physical education is also important. Attending cultural events, engaging in interior decorating, woodworking, or other activities can release built-up tension. Involvement with people from many other walks of life is also valuable.

Pajak and Blase reported that the personal lives of teachers influenced what they did in the classroom and how they interacted with colleagues. Negative outcomes with students resulted from aspects of teachers' personal lives that took time, energy, and attention away from classroom responsibilities. They became distant from students and experienced feelings of guilt. The issues of finances (salaries, etc.) and status (poor respect for the teaching profession) were not identified as major issues in effective classroom performance.[39]

Time management techniques are a must for busy teachers who desire to avoid stress. Within the school environment, teachers must learn to use time efficiently so that they do not need to work longer than necessary. Knowing school policies and procedures in advance of an emergency helps one to be calm in the face of adversity. Allowing students and paraprofessionals to help also saves time and effort. The following time-management techniques will increase efficiency and release time needed to pursue high-priority goals:

1. *Plan.* Use a large yearly calendar for school as well as personal activities. Make a list of daily tasks in order of importance and try to complete the high-priority items. Plan lessons efficiently.
2. *Put an end to putting it off.* Reduce procrastination.
3. *Get organized.* Organize and simplify your work space, filing system, materials, and so on. Develop specific class procedures that students know and follow.
4. *Consider time constraints.* Remember that it's okay to say no. Avoid the paper avalanche by setting aside a time to go through correspondence, saving only vital items.
5. *Modify teaching routine.* Team-teach by planning with other teachers and sharing facilities and equipment. Organize a physical education club that trains students to assist. Maintain a lesson plan for substitutes taking over the class.
6. *Exercise with the class.* Time to do this outside of school may not materialize.
7. *Guard against interruptions.* Shut the door or find a hideout to unwind. Play the ball; don't let the ball play you.
8. *Take time to be yourself.* Engage in recreational or social activities that are enjoyable.
9. *Develop a support system.* Ask yourself, "Who can help? How can they help?"[40]

Many of the preceding suggestions will help a teacher avoid "burnout." Burnout is real, and to avoid it prospective teachers must understand thoroughly the demands of the profession. Teacher burnout has been described as a response to a circuit overload—a result of unchecked stress on the physical, emotional, or intellectual system of the teacher.[41] Teacher burnout has neither a single cause nor a single solution. Physical education teachers must be alert to the reality that the dual roles of teacher-coach may lead to burnout. "Teachers must recognize the problem, look to its sources, and plan for correction."[42]

Other strategies to minimize burnout include focusing on the positive aspects of the job and allowing fellow workers to complete their share of the responsibilities.[43]

The teaching profession today offers many challenges, yet many exciting and creative opportunities. The prospective teacher can be optimistic about a bright future.

The Physical Educator as Teacher-Coach

Though physical education and athletics are not the same, many physical education teachers also coach. Typically, the coach deals with relatively small numbers of highly motivated students of advanced ability who participate voluntarily. The teacher usually transmits knowledge to large numbers of students with a wide range of abilities who are required to be in class and are sometimes unmotivated or hostile.[44] Chelladurai, Kuga, and O'Bryant found that males prefer to coach and females prefer to teach.[45] Schempp determined that physical education was valued less than coaching and that a coach was viewed first as a coach and second as a teacher.[46] More time was spent preparing for athletics than teaching. It is not surprising that the role of coach might be preferred to that of teacher. The challenge of producing a winning team, the added financial gain, and the higher public credibility attributed to the coach often cause coaches to neglect physical education classes and place more importance on coaching. Begly viewed this as the rule rather than the exception, thus causing a role conflict.

> The crux of the teacher/coach role conflict is not that educators occupying both roles concurrently perceive them as totally different, and therefore choose the one they prefer as the dominant role. Rather . . . the core of the difficulty is mostly a matter of time. . . . The impossibility of meeting the demands of both roles simultaneously is often compounded by powerful social and personal incentives to make the coaching role pre-eminent.[47]

Physical educators involved in both teaching and coaching will need to make both of equal priority, and set and meet goals that manage their time to be successful at both. They will also need the help of administrators such as athletic directors and principals. These key people must take the initiative to schedule classes, practices, and competition to aid the coach in fulfilling commitments, while providing an atmosphere of support. Both teaching and coaching programs are needed, and although physical educators are better trained to wear both hats, they must not allow their responsibilities of coaching to overpower those as educator, if they are hired to fulfill both roles.

While many physical education programs are being cut, athletic programs usually remain robust. Schools are staffing coaching positions while sometimes using interns to teach, or they are giving larger classes to physical education teachers rather than adding more qualified teachers. Undergraduate teaching-coaching majors should be prepared to teach another academic subject, such as mathematics or English, to expand their possibilities for future employment. They must also be committed to teaching all students in the school to be physically active for life. Any physical educator who is dedicated to having all students learn skills that enable them to enjoy an active, healthy lifestyle, will usually strive to work out a conflict. This may be difficult, but it is possible.

Both roles are vitally important, but their aims, goals, and objectives may be different, and often in conflict. If physical educators are hired to teach both the regular student as well as the athlete, and the commitment for serving both populations is not there, our present system, including a complete physical education curriculum, cannot survive.

Review Question: What is your commitment to *teaching* and/or *coaching*? It is necessary for you to determine this before going into the job market.

Physical educators need to answer the question, "Do I want to be a teacher, or a coach, or both?" Once the decision is made, they must then perform with excellence. Ethical conduct on the part of the teacher-coach often solves the problem of role conflict.

The Physical Educator's Role in Public Relations

One of the activity and fitness goals established by *Healthy People 2000*[48] was daily physical education for all students K–12. Illinois was the last state to require daily physical education.[49] Thus, physical educators need to improve the public image of physical education.[50] A marketing strategy can be used to justify to the public the need for a physical education program.[51] Marketing includes advertising, communication, and public relations.[52] A high-quality physical education program is the first requirement. Without an excellent program that meets the needs of students, all marketing strategies will fail.[53] Schneider suggests four steps for marketing physical education programs:

1. Know the product.[54] The American Alliance for Health, Physical Education, Recreation, and Dance (AAHPERD), through the National Association for Sport and Physical Education (NASPE), has developed position papers, press releases, and other materials to assist the physical educator.

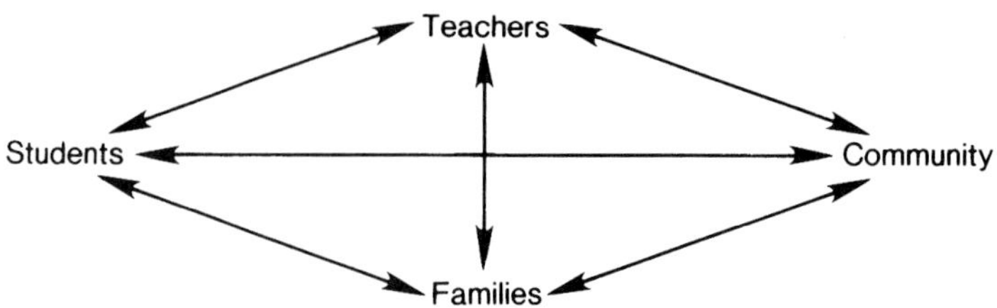

Figure 2-1
The interrelationships among the various publics of the school.

2. Project a good image. A physical educator's practices must be consistent with the message being presented.
3. Plan the work. Specific plans must be formulated for each target audience.
4. Work the plan. This includes being alert to new ideas and each week concentrating on a particular strategy. Personally getting to know people and meeting with as many people as possible face-to-face is very beneficial.[55]

All the various publics in the school must be part of the marketing plan. Figure 2-1 shows the interrelationships among these groups. Some ideas for motivating students, families, teachers, and the community are presented next.

Review Question: What is marketing?

Influencing Students

Students are the most important public in that they are the only ones teachers see from day to day. When students experience a sound instructional program, they will "sell" it to their parents through their enthusiasm. Therefore, physical educators must plan lessons based on sound educational goals and objectives that address cognitive, psychomotor, and effective domains. They must concentrate on "constructive, positive, observable student results."[56]

The teachers who have the most influence on students provide a high-quality educational experience and genuinely care about their students. They respect their students and as a result the students respect their teachers. These teachers understand the worth of each student. Expectations are high but all students are provided with the tools necessary for success.

Students grow up to be community and school leaders and will have an influence on physical education in the future. Students who have a positive experience in physical education will be more supportive of it in the future. A number of ways to enhance student learning will be discussed in Chapter 8. Additional ideas for student motivation are discussed in Chapter 13.

Some other events that can promote public relations with students include demonstrations of physical activities in school assemblies, interdisciplinary units with teachers of other subject areas, field days such as the Super Kids' Day presented in Chapter 10, and contests for the entire school.

Working with Administrators, Faculty, and Staff

Far too often, physical education teachers divorce themselves from the total school environment. Effective teachers make the effort to emerge from the gymnasium to share experiences with the rest of the faculty. They help administrators understand physical education and its importance by regularly communicating with the principal about the physical education program including an overview of the program, goals for the year, changes that have been implemented, achievements, and new trends or ideas.[57] Committed physical educators also attend faculty meetings and volunteer to serve on faculty committees, from which they gain new ideas and through which they have a positive effect on the rest of the school. They attend professional workshops and become involved in professional organizations.

Physical educators need to be aware of opportunities to integrate physical education concepts with other subject areas in the curriculum. Implementing interdisciplinary units with teachers of mathematics, foreign languages, home economics, health, and physiology can be effective in promoting student and faculty interest in physical education activities. These are discussed in Chapter 10. Additional goodwill can be initiated by inviting administrators, faculty, and staff to participate in faculty fitness programs, clinics to learn new skills, tournaments, and free-play activities. One's personal appearance, manner of speech, and enthusiasm can affect the entire school.

Promoting Parent and Family Participation and Interest

A number of methods can be used to help parents understand what is happening in physical education classes. A schedule of courses to be offered is helpful for parents. A "back-to-school night" is held in many schools. Teachers could take this opportunity to point out the objectives of physical education and provide an outline of activities in which students will be involved. Samples of the students' work and minidemonstrations by students could also be provided along with a schedule of future events. Parents

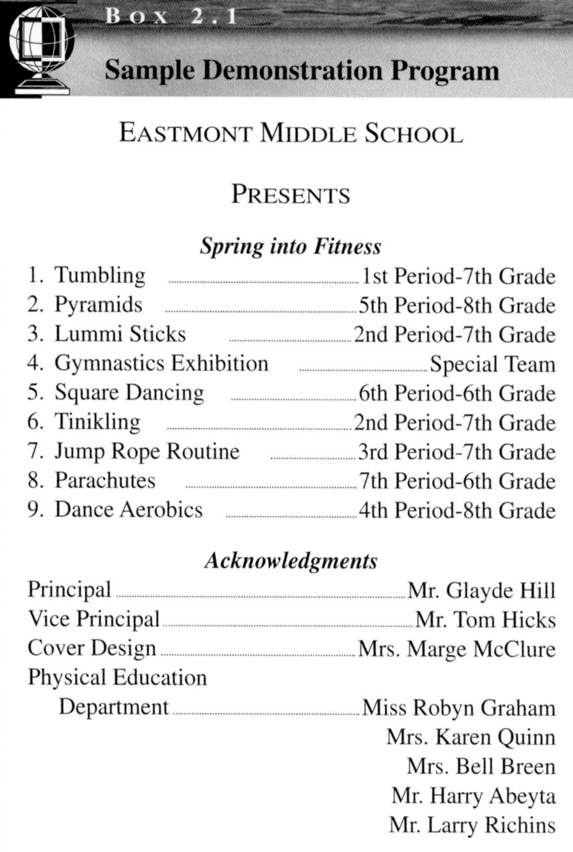

BOX 2.1

Sample Demonstration Program

EASTMONT MIDDLE SCHOOL

PRESENTS

Spring into Fitness

1. Tumbling	1st Period-7th Grade
2. Pyramids	5th Period-8th Grade
3. Lummi Sticks	2nd Period-7th Grade
4. Gymnastics Exhibition	Special Team
5. Square Dancing	6th Period-6th Grade
6. Tinikling	2nd Period-7th Grade
7. Jump Rope Routine	3rd Period-7th Grade
8. Parachutes	7th Period-6th Grade
9. Dance Aerobics	4th Period-8th Grade

Acknowledgments

Principal	Mr. Glayde Hill
Vice Principal	Mr. Tom Hicks
Cover Design	Mrs. Marge McClure
Physical Education Department	Miss Robyn Graham
	Mrs. Karen Quinn
	Mrs. Bell Breen
	Mr. Harry Abeyta
	Mr. Larry Richins

Source: Spring into Fitness program, Eastmont Middle School, Sandy, Utah

could also be invited to visit classes during a back-to-school day or week. Parent-teacher conferences are helpful in discussing mutual problems and goals for individual students and for the program as a whole.[58]

Halftime Shows and Demonstration Nights

Demonstrations are valuable in showing what students are learning and are generally well attended when all of the students participate in some way (see Box 2.1). These can be as simple as two teams playing speed-a-way or team handball during halftime at a football or basketball game, or as complex as a demonstration night for parents in which every student in the school participates. The important thing to remember is to let all students participate regardless of skill level or disability. Each class can be asked to demonstrate some aspect of the program. This provides parents with a realistic view of physical education in contrast to that of athletics. Posters in downtown stores, notices to parents, and announcements in the local paper can be used to invite the public. A public-address system is essential in most cases. The principal welcomes parents and introduces the physical education faculty, who can take turns introducing the various groups and explaining what they are demonstrating.

Family Participation

Parent or family participation in student homework can stimulate families to become more involved in outside activities, such as bike riding or jogging, and to be more supportive of student involvement in completing extra-class assignments or activities. Inviting families to participate in contests in which students earn points by participating in family recreational and fitness activities has also been very effective in some areas.

Parent-student participation nights can include everything from movement education to sports to fitness activities. McLaughlin reports a "Chip-N-Block" bowling tournament in which a parent and student form a team and compete against other teams.[59] Fitness assessment nights are popular in many areas. Likewise, aerobic activities have become increasingly popular in recent years. Other possibilities include mother-daughter, father-son, father-daughter, and mother-son activities.

Newsletters and Websites

A brief newsletter to parents or an article in the district newsletter several times a year can be valuable in describing school and community programs and promoting parent and family involvement in these programs. The newsletter might contain a description of the physical education program, objectives, evaluation, and grading; physical fitness goals and achievements; extra-class programs; programs for students with physical and mental disabilities; and special events for parents. A portion of the newsletter could provide tips for better performance in a particular activity such as tennis, bowling, or physical fitness. Newsletters that represent the best effort of the department in terms of spelling, grammar, layout, and use of pictures cast a positive image on the profession of physical education, as well as on the teachers involved. Consult with the English faculty for help if needed. In some locales the newsletter should be printed in both English and local native languages such as Spanish or Native American.

This same information can be posted on a physical education web page within the school's web page. Pictures of upcoming events, announcements, and students involved in physical education class activities will add interest, but permission to post any pictures of students should be obtained from the parents/guardians and the student prior to posting.

Direct Parental Communications

In addition to newsletters, letters can be sent to parents describing the physical education program,[60] the specific fitness test results of their children and what they mean, or progress in learning other skills. An example appears in Box 2.2. Schuman mentioned sending home red, green, or yellow cards each week for extremely unmotivated students to indicate their improvement. Green meant "great work," yellow meant "caution," and red said "stop and

BOX 2.2

Sample Letter to Parents

Dear Parents:

One of my primary goals as a physical educator is to teach children—from the physically gifted to the physically challenged—how and why they should keep themselves healthy and fit throughout their lifetimes. In our physical education program, we provide learning experiences that are developmentally appropriate and that will teach each child how to be physically active in ways that increase physical competence, self-esteem, and joy through lifelong physical activity. Here's how we achieve that goal:

1. Our physical education curriculum includes a balance of skills, concepts, game activities, rhythms, and dance experiences designed to enhance the cognitive, motor, affective, and physical fitness development of every child.
2. We provide experiences that encourage children to question, integrate, analyze, communicate, apply cognitive concepts, and gain a wide multicultural view of the world.
3. Throughout the year we teach activities that allow children the opportunity to work together to improve their emerging social and cooperation skills. These activities also help children develop a positive self-concept.
4. Ongoing fitness assessment is used as part of the ongoing process of helping children understand, enjoy, improve, and maintain their physical health and well-being.
5. Children are taught exercises that keep the body in proper alignment, thereby allowing the muscles to lengthen without placing stress and strain on the surrounding joints, ligaments, and tendons.
6. Grade decisions are based primarily on ongoing individual assessments of children as they participate in physical education class activities, and not on the basis of single test score.
7. Finally, our class is designed so that ALL children are involved in activities that allow them to remain continuously active.

I would like to invite you to come and visit our physical education class. By working together to encourage fitness, I am certain we will be able to help your children enjoy a lifetime of physical activity! I welcome your support.

Sincerely,

Your Name and Title

Source: A letter to parents. Based on material from SPEAK with permission of National Association for Sport and Physical Education, 1900 Association Drive, Reston, VA 22091.

change your work habits." On the cards she listed all tasks completed during that week. Parents were asked to sign the cards and return them each Monday. Cards were stopped when students no longer needed them.[61] When students know that they will be "paid" each week, they seem to work harder.

Letters or phone calls to parents can also be used to point out students' accomplishments. The following story is told about a boy who had not had much success in school. The teacher sent home a letter to the boy's parents commending something he had done. Later the teacher asked, "Did you give the letter to your mother?" "Yes," the boy responded. "What did she say?" "Nothin'," he replied. "Nothing? Why, it was a lovely letter—and your mother said nothing?" The child nodded, "She didn't say nothing! She just bawled."[62] Generally, parents who have never heard anything good about their children are so happy to hear praise that they will do anything to cooperate with such a teacher or principal.

Junk Days

Herman suggested another practical way of gaining parents' support: have a junk day in which parents contribute items such as old tennis rackets, golf clubs, or shuffleboard sets. Parents get rid of these space-wasters and the school gains some usable equipment. With the approval of the principal, a note can be sent to parents on which they list what they are donating. Parents sign the note to indicate that they know what their children are contributing.[63] One school's teacher asked for old brooms for broom hockey and was surprised to discover that many parents purchased new brooms just so they could help out.

Including the Community

Two factors are involved in community-school relations. They include (1) getting the school involved in the community and (2) getting the community involved in the school.

Getting the School Involved in the Community

Teachers can take the lead in community involvement by participating in institutional, civic, and neighborhood activities or projects. Educators often participate in local business-education exchanges by touring various commercial institutions. Students can also be encouraged to participate in community-oriented projects and in work-experience programs. Youth sports provide an excellent opportunity for service in the community.

To carry out a lifetime sports curriculum, many schools must rely on resources within the community. The first step is to survey the community facilities to see what is available and appropriate for an instructional situation. The cost of a facility and the cost of transportation must then be determined. Once permission from the school and district administration is obtained, a specific legal agreement is drawn up to clarify the dates and times the facility is to be used, the cost, the roles of the school and the institution with regard to the instructional situation, and legal liability. The legal implications of transportation to and from the facility must also be considered. The use of community facilities is one more way in which schools and community can develop a better understanding of one another.

Getting the Community Involved in the School

Passive involvement of the community in the schools generally occurs through the mass media, speeches, and exhibits. The Sport and Physical Education Advocacy Kit II (SPEAK II) developed by the National Association for Sport and Physical Education contains materials and sharing techniques for use in the public relations and advocacy efforts.[64] Another organization that has played a prominent role in public relations is the President's Council on Physical Fitness and Sport. Both groups have produced films and television spots that have been well received.

Publishing articles in school and local newspapers about intramural activities, fitness projects, and class activities can stimulate community interest in physical education just as it has in athletics. The administration should approve all news articles to prevent embarrassment to the school from improper timing or undue controversy. Whenever possible, action photos should accompany the articles. Another way to inform the community about the physical education program is by speaking to parent-teacher organizations and civic groups. Talks can be accompanied by slides, videotapes, or actual performances by students. Exhibits in local stores, the public library, or other community buildings can be used to draw attention to special events. A CD could be burned for distribution.

The use of school facilities for adult education and family-oriented recreation programs is increasing in many areas. Programs range from supervised recreation to instructional programs in physical fitness and skill development. They may be sponsored by the city recreation department or the school district. Adults who become involved in these programs appear to be more supportive of school programs.

Another possible service to the community is a fitness or sports fair in which booths are set up to show what the students have learned in the various areas of sports or physical fitness. Fitness evaluation activities can be conducted at such events. It is often fun for children to test their parents. Legislative fitness days have been sponsored in Washington, D.C., as well as in individual states. Participants are tested and the results are presented in terms of actual scores as well as prescriptions for maintenance and improvement.

Just as many community groups contribute to athletics through booster clubs, a number of service clubs, commercial institutions, and government agencies, along with many lay citizens, contribute to school programs either financially or by donating their time and resources. These groups have sponsored demonstrations, health and fitness fairs, safety clinics, and many other programs. For example, Clay described an "adopt-a-school" program in which various businesses each adopted a specific school and helped them with facility and equipment needs.[65] Government and other public-service agencies have donated innumerable hours teaching first aid, safety, and health skills to students.

Invitations to prominent athletes, sportscasters, sports journalists, and commercial recreation leaders to speak to physical education classes, parent-teacher organization meetings, and other school groups can extend the relationship. A file can be kept on citizens who possess skills needed by the department. Foster grandparent programs provide a double benefit by helping senior citizens to serve in useful endeavors and through providing needed services to the schools. Parents and other citizens can also serve as paraprofessional aides.

No one public relations technique works for every situation. By understanding a variety of techniques, the best one can be found for each situation. Maggard emphasized that "physical educators everywhere should unite behind a banner of pride and energy, and work together to upgrade our national image."[66]

Review Question: Give some examples of how each of the following publics might be reached in a public relations or marketing program: (a) students, (b) administrators, (c) faculty and students, (d) parents and families, and (e) community.

NOTES

1. L. J. Brandon and R. L. Evans, Are physical educators physically fit? *Journal of Physical Education, Recreation, and Dance 59,* no. 7 (1988): 73–75.
2. D. S. Melville and B. J. Cardinal, The problem: Body fatness within our profession, *Journal of Physical Education, Recreation, and Dance 59,* no. 7 (1988): 85–87; D. S. Melville and J. G. G. Maddalozzo, The effects of a physical educator's appearance of body fatness on communicating exercise concepts to high school students, *Journal of Teaching in Physical Education 7,* no. 4 (1998): 343–52; J. D. Whitley, J. N. Sage, and M. Butcher, Cardiorespiratory fitness: Role modeling by

P.E. instructors, *Journal of Physical Education, Recreation, and Dance 59,* no. 7 (1988): 81–84.

3. J. A. Bischoff, S. A. Plowman, and L. Lindenman, The relationship of teacher fitness to teacher/student interaction, *Journal of Teaching in Physical Education 7,* no. 2 (1988): 142–51.
4. E. Fisher, What is a teacher? *Instructor,* May 1970, 23.
5. P. J. Palmer, *The Courage to Teach: Exploring the Inner Landscape of a Teacher's Life* (San Francisco: Jossey-Bass, 1998), 10.
6. *USA Today,* 29, July 1999, 8A.
7. *USA Today,* 24, August, 1997, 1A.
8. Palmer, *The Courage to Teach,* 6.
9. *Deseret News,* 10, August 1998, C1.
10. *Deseret News,* 2–3, July 1998, A17.
11. D. Thomas, in L. O. Pellicer, Effective teaching: Science or magic? *The Clearing House 58* (October 1984): 53.
12. L. DeFelice, The bibbidibobbidiboo factor in teaching, *Phi Delta Kappan 70* (1989): 639–41.
13. L. S. Shulman, Knowledge and teaching: Foundations of the New Reform, *Harvard Educational Review 57,* no. 1 (1987): 1–22.
14. D. M. Medley, The effectiveness of teachers, in P. L. Peterson and H. J. Walberg, eds., *Research on Teaching: Concepts, Findings, and Implications* (Berkeley: McCutchan, 1979), 12.
15. D. Siedentop, *Developing Teaching Skills in Physical Education,* 3d ed. (Mountain View, CA: Mayfield, 1991), 19.
16. R. J. Shavelson, N. M. Webb, and L. Burstein, Measurement of teaching; and J. Brophy and T. L. Good, Teacher behavior and student achievement, both in M. C. Wittrock, ed., *Handbook of Research on Teaching,* 3d ed. (New York: Macmillan , 1986), 52, 339.
17. R. W. Eberts, Union effects on teacher productivity, *Industrial and Labor Relations Review 37* (April 1984): 347.
18. Brophy and Good, Teacher behavior, 360–65.
19. Brophy and Good, Teacher behavior, 336–37.
20. K. McCartney and E. Jordan, Parallels between research on child care and research on school effects, *Educational Researcher 19,* no. 1 (1990): 25.
21. M. Metzler, A review of research on time in sport pedagogy, *Journal of Teaching Physical Education 8* (1989): 93.
22. S. K. Lynn, Create an effective learning environment, *Strategies 1* (1994): 14–17.
23. D. Oberteuffer and C. Ulrich, *Physical Education: A Textbook of Principles for Professional Students,* 4th ed. (New York: Harper & Row, 1970), 6.
24. G. Daughtrey, *Effective Teaching in Physical Education for Secondary Schools,* 2nd ed. (Philadelphia: Saunders, 1973).
25. V. J. Melograno, Preservice professional portfolio system (Reston, VA: National Association for Sport and Physical Education, AAHPERD, 1999).
26. Melograno, Preservice professional portfolio system.
27. Melograno, Preservice professional portfolio system.
28. Melograno, Preservice professional portfolio system, 10.
29. C. Lambert, Career directions, *Journal of Physical Education, Recreation, and Dance 55,* no. 5 (1984): 40–43, 53.
30. W. R. Houston and B. D. Felder, Break horses, not teachers, *Phi Delta Kappan 63* (March 1982): 457–60.
31. E. J. Shea, *Ethical Decisions in Physical Education and Sport* (Springfield, IL: Thomas, 1978), 4–8.
32. The Society of State Directors of Health, Physical Education, and Recreation, *The School Programs of Health, Physical Education, and Recreation: A Statement of Basic Beliefs* (Kensington, MD: Author, 1985), 8.
33. L. L. Bain, Ethical issues in teaching, *Quest 45* (1993): 73.
34. K. M. Williamson, Is your inequity showing? Ideas and strategies for creating a more equitable learning environment, *The Journal of Physical Education, Recreation, and Dance 64,* no. 8 (1993) 15.
35. Williamson, Is your inequity showing?
36. The Society of State Directors of Health, Physical Education, and Recreation, *The School Programs.*
37. S. A. G. M. Crawford, Values in disarray: The crisis of sport's integrity, *Journal of Physical Education, Recreation, and Dance 57,* no. 9 (1986): 42.
38. D. Zakrajsek and J. L. Woods, A survey of professional practices—Elementary and secondary physical educators, *Journal of Physical Education, Recreation, and Dance 54,* no. 9 (1983): 65–67.
39. E. Pajak and J. J. Blase, The impact of teachers' personal lives on professional role enactment: A qualitative analysis, *American Educational Research Journal 26,* no. 2 (1989): 283–310.
40. S. J. Virgilio and P. S. Krebs, Effective time management techniques, *Journal of Physical Education, Recreation, and Dance 55,* no. 4 (1984): 68, 73.
41. L. Horton, What do we know about teacher burnout? *Journal of Physical Education, Recreation, and Dance 55,* no. 3 (1984): 69.
42. Horton, What do we know, 71.
43. A. J. Figone, Teacher-coach burnout: Avoidance strategies, *Journal of Physical Education, Recreation, and Dance 57,* no. 8 (1986): 60.
44. T. J. Templin and J. L. Anthrop, A dialogue of teacher/coach role conflict, *Physical Educator 38* (December 1981): 183.
45. P. Chelladurai, D. J. Kuga, and C. P. O'Bryant, Individual differences, perceived task characteristics, and preferences for teaching and coaching, *Research Quarterly for Exercise and Sport 70,* no. 2 (1999): 179–89.
46. P. G. Schempp, Constructing professional knowledge: A case study of an experienced high school teacher, *Journal of Teaching in Physical Education 13,* no. 1 (1993): 2–23.
47. G. Begly, The role of the teacher/coach, *NASPE News 17* (Winter 1987): 6.
48. U.S. Department of Health and Human Services, *Healthy People 2000: National Health Promotion Disease Prevention Objectives* (DHHS Publication Number PHS

91-50212) (Washington DC: U.S. Government Printing Office, 1990).

49. National Association for Sport and Physical Education, *Shape of the Nation: A Survey of State Physical Education Requirements* (Reston, VA: Author, 1998).
50. R. E. Schneider, Don't just promote your profession—market it! *Journal of Physical Education, Recreation, and Dance 63,* no. 5 (1992): 70–73.
51. Schneider, Don't just promote; M. Mize, Marketing elementary physical education, *Strategies 3,* no. 6 (1990): 15–18; D. B. Moore and D. P. Gray, Marketing—The blueprint for successful physical education, *Journal of Physical Education, Recreation, and Dance 61,* no. 1 (1990): 23–26.
52. Mize, Marketing elementary physical education; P. Kotler and A. R. Andreasen, *Strategic Marketing for Educational Institutions* (Englewood Cliffs, NJ: Prentice-Hall, 1987).
53. Mize, Marketing elementary physical education.
54. Schneider, Don't just promote.
55. Schneider, Don't just promote.
56. N. J. Maggard, Upgrading our image, *Journal of Physical Education, Recreation, and Dance 55,* no. 1 (1984): 17, 82.
57. E. Giles-Brown, Teach administrators why physical education is important, *Strategies 6,* no. 8 (1993): 23–25.
58. H. L. Henderson and R. F. French, The parent factor, *Strategies 5,* no. 6 (1992): 26–29.
59. R. D. McLaughlin, Chip-n-block for parental involvement, *Journal of Physical Education, Recreation, and Dance 52,* no. 8 (1981): 22–23.
60. National Association for Sport and Physical Education, *Sport and Physical Education Advocacy Kit (SPEAK) II.* (Reston, VA: Author, 1999).
61. M. E. Schuman, Enrich the curriculum and your own style, *Today's Education 70* (November–December 1981): 36.
62. K. D. LaMancusa, *We Do Not Throw Rocks at the Teacher!* (Scranton, PA: International Textbook, 1966), 80.
63. W. L. Herman, Have a junk day, *Journal of Physical Education and Recreation 46,* no. 8 (1975): 35.
64. National Association for Sport and Physical Education, *Sport and Physical Education Advocacy Kit (SPEAK) II.*
65. W. B. Clay, First class and getting better, *Journal of Physical Education, Recreation, and Dance 52,* no. 8 (1981): 19–21.
66. Maggard, Upgrading our image.

CHAPTER

3

Physical Education and the Law

Study Stimulators

1. What is tort liability? How can teachers defend themselves in a tort liability case?
2. What steps can teachers take to reduce the likelihood of being sued?
3. What is the connection between students' safety and planning, organizing, and managing instruction?
4. What actions are expected of a reasonably prudent physical educator?
5. What civil rights are protected by the First, Fourth, and Fourteenth Amendments to the Constitution?

Michelle Landers was fifteen years old, measured 5′6″ tall, and weighed 180 pounds. She was in a class of forty students. Because of her size, she expressed fear in her ability to successfully execute a backward roll. She was given only a brief demonstration of the backward roll. The teacher told Michelle to practice the skill with the help of another student; Michelle suffered a neck injury that required surgery. She sued her teacher for improper instruction.[1] Michael Mantague had successfully executed a vault thirty-three times, including five or six vaults one day prior to falling and fracturing his arm. He sued the instructor for negligence, and the suit was decided in favor of the teacher.[2]

It is estimated that children and adolescents receive 10 percent to 20 percent of their injuries in and around schools. An analysis of 1,558 cases reported to the National Pediatric Trauma Registry indicated that 49 percent of these injuries occurred in recreational areas rather than in the school building. Of the cases studied, 524 happened during a sports activity. The causes of these injuries included falls; being struck by a ball or another piece of equipment; hazards related to asphalt surfaces, playing fields, bleachers, and concrete gymnasium walls; and lack of protective equipment. The most common sports connected with the injuries were football, basketball, wrestling, soccer, track and field, and gymnastics.[3]

In a survey of more than four hundred recent lawsuits in recreation, instruction, and organized sports, 24 percent of the cases involved accusations of faulty supervision, 40 percent were due to the selection and conduct of activities, and 36 percent resulted from accusations of failure to provide a safe environment. In the instructional area, 65 percent of the cases were due to the selection and conduct of activities. Supervising, selecting and conducting activities, and providing a safe environment are all duties of a physical educator.[4] The nature of physical education presents an environment in which the risk of potential injuries resulting in legal action is great. Physical educators must be familiar with issues of law to provide an environment that is as risk-free as possible.[5]

This chapter explains legal liability and discusses practices that will provide a safer environment and reduce the likelihood of a lawsuit. Also included is a discussion of other law issues of importance to physical educators.

LEGAL LIABILITY

Liability refers to a legal responsibility that can be enforced by a court of law in a civil action, which is an action involving a relationship between citizens or between citizens and an institution such as a school or district. Physical educators need a basic understanding of the laws governing liability in physical education; this can be essential to the preservation of physical education programs in the schools.

The past two decades have seen an increase in the number of lawsuits involving physical education classes. Baley and Matthews suggested several reasons for the increases.

1. Increased emphasis on lifetime sports. Teachers are teaching and supervising activities in which they have limited training or knowledge.
2. People more attuned to their individual rights. Actions once considered reasonable are now considered negligent by a court of law.
3. Increased accessibility of legal services.
4. Awareness that schools and most individuals are insured.
5. Increased valuing of individual rights.[6]

A journal titled *Sports and the Courts: Physical Education and Sports Law Quarterly* emerged in 1980 to inform professionals of actual cases and court settlements. Each issue documents an average of twenty cases. The Summer Law and Sports Conference came into being in the early 1980s to prepare physical educators to deal with the issues of legal liability.[7] In the past, researching court cases required access to a law library. The Internet now allows quick searches for court cases on any topic. The use of any search engine and the key words "court cases" will provide a list of several sites on which searches for specific cases can be undertaken.

Settlements now reach millions of dollars, and a single case can wipe out a school district's entire year's budget.[8] In light of these facts, some states have passed legislation limiting awards to the maximum amount of insurance coverage. With this turn of events have come escalating insurance costs for school districts. Many districts report that the price of insurance is prohibitive.[9]

Review Question: Use the Internet to find a court case in physical education or sport related to one of the following subjects: Title IX, supervision, proper instruction, corporal punishment, searches.

A Legal Liability Case

The parents of a senior high school student filed a one million dollar lawsuit against her physical education teacher and the board of education for injuries the young woman suffered in a physical education class–related accident. (The student had disobeyed the teacher's orders and was jumping on a trampoline between classes.) In the suit, the parents complained that she was required to take the class to graduate and that reasonable safety precautions were not taken to prevent injury.[10]

In the preceding incident, the injured girl and her parents were the *plaintiffs*—the person or group initiating the action against another party. The teacher and school board were the *defendants*—the person or group against whom the action is brought. The complaint summarized the reasons the plaintiff felt she was entitled to compensation for her injury. As the legal process continued, the defendant (the teacher) filed an answer stating why she felt she was not at fault. After a period of time, the case came before the court. The entire case was based on the assumption that a wrong had been committed, resulting in an injury. In this case, the parents charged the teacher with the commission of a tort.

Tort

A *tort* is a civil or legal wrong, an action that results in injury to another person or to that person's reputation or property. A tort can be caused by an act of *omission,* or the failure to perform a legal duty, such as failure to close the outside doors during a fire drill when previously instructed to do so. A tort can also be caused by intentional interference, or *commission.* There are various types of intentional tort:

1. *Negligence* is the failure to act as a reasonably prudent person would act under the same circumstances.
2. *Assault* is a threat to inflict harm on someone.
3. *Battery* is the unlawful use of physical force against another person.
4. *Defamation* involves a malicious intent to injure a person's reputation through (a) *slander*—the spoken word, or (b) *libel*—the written word.

Negligence

Most liability cases involving the schools are based on negligence. Negligence may be caused by any of the following:

1. *Nonfeasance* involves failure to do what is required, such as failure to instruct the students properly in the use of the trampoline or failure to administer first aid to an injured student.
2. *Misfeasance* involves doing something incorrectly, such as moving an injured student when it is improper to do so, thereby further injuring the young person.
3. *Malfeasance* involves doing something illegal, such as using corporal punishment in a state where it is against the law.

Negligence involves a comparison of the situation with an acceptable or established standard of conduct for persons in similar situations. To determine negligence, the courts generally ask four questions:[11]

1. Duty—Did one person owe a duty to another?
2. Breach—Did that person fail to exercise that duty?
3. Harm—Was a person actually injured?
4. Cause—Was the failure to exercise due care the direct or proximate cause of the injury?

A *duty* is a legal responsibility to act in a certain way toward others to protect them from physical or mental harm. It includes the expectation that a teacher will provide appropriate instruction and supervision, and a safe environment in which students can learn. A *breach* is failure to exercise a standard of care equal to the risks involved. However, the breaching of a duty does not constitute negligence. Cause and harm must also be shown. A causal relationship must exist between the breach of duty and the injury of another person. *Foreseeability* is involved when a teacher could have anticipated or foreseen a potential danger and failed to eliminate the danger. If a person was injured as a result, the teacher is liable. In the case just cited, the teacher could have seen that leaving a trampoline available for student use would result in students jumping on it even when advised not to do so. As another example, when teachers know that a student has exhibited violent behavior in the past, they should foresee that such acts are likely to be repeated in the future.[12]

Finally, an actual injury or loss must occur as a result of the breach. *Harm* can exist in many forms. Physical injury is most often the result, such as a broken bone, but sometimes the end result of a condition initiated by negligence is the harm. For example, permanent paralysis, death, or emotional distress may not be evidenced until a later time. These conditions are still grounds for court action.

To establish negligence, the plaintiff must demonstrate that the teacher's actions were the direct or *proximate* cause of the injury. In the case just cited, the fact that the trampoline was left out by the teacher could be considered the proximate cause of students' jumping on it and, therefore, of the accident.

Review Questions: Define the following terms using the text or another source:

legal liability	malfeasance	defamation
defendant	breach	libel
negligence	harm	*in loco parentis*
foreseeability	slander	misfeasance
cause	plaintiff	duty
attractive nuisance	tort	battery
nonfeasance	assault	proximate

What four questions are asked to determine negligence? Explain negligence by omission and negligence by commission.

Defenses against Negligence

When defending a case involving possible negligence, lawyers generally rely on one or more of the following defenses.

Governmental Immunity Governmental immunity is based on the English common law premise that "the king can do no wrong" and is therefore immune from suit. In a few states, the government still enjoys this privilege. Therefore, even when a school district is negligent, no damages or money can be awarded. However, beginning in 1959, when an Illinois state court abolished governmental immunity in a school transportation case,[13] most of the states have lost their immunity through legislative or court action.[14] Unlike boards of education, individual administrators, teachers, or other employees of the districts have never been immune from tort liability.

Contributory Negligence Contributory negligence occurs when the injured person directly contributes to the injury. No damages are allowed in cases of contributory negligence. In the case discussed earlier, the student contributed directly to her injury by jumping on the trampoline despite knowing that she was violating the safety rules the teacher had established and repeatedly emphasized. Participants must act for their own protection as a reasonably prudent person of their age would act.

Comparative Negligence Comparative negligence happens when both the injured person and the defendant are jointly responsible for the accident. The court generally determines the percentage of responsibility held by each person and distributes the money accordingly. For example, in the case involving the trampoline, the student, the teacher, and a medical doctor could be held responsible for 50 percent, 25 percent, and 25 percent of the injuries, respectively. If an award is determined, the defendants would be required to pay the percentage for which they are held responsible.

Comparative negligence has replaced contributory negligence. In most cases of contributory negligence, if the court determined the plaintiff's actions had contributed in any way to the injury, no award for damages could be given. Comparative negligence allows an award even if the plaintiff's actions did contribute to the injury. The award is reduced by the amount of the plaintiff's responsibility.

Assumption of Risk Assumption of risk occurs when a person understands and accepts that participation in the activity involves a certain amount of risk of injury that a teacher or supervisor cannot prevent. The defense of assumption of risk can be used only when the participant knows and understands the risks involved and voluntarily participates in the activity. If coercion is present in any form, an assumption of risk by the participant has not occurred. This defense can rarely be used in physical education classes because participation in class is generally not voluntary as it is in interscholastic athletics or intramurals.[15] However, a person never assumes the risk of negligent behavior of another person in any activity.

Act of God An act of God is an unforeseeable or unavoidable accident due to the forces of nature. If a student were suddenly struck by lightning while playing softball, the accident would be considered an act of God. However, a teacher allowing students to remain in an outdoor swimming pool during an electrical storm is undoubtedly negligent.

Legal Precedents Legal precedents are court decisions made previously in similar cases. They are used by both the plaintiff and the defendant to defend their particular points of view. Cases often depend on previous legal decisions for their solutions.

Review Question: What six possibilities exist for a defense of negligence?

Preventing Negligence

Because of large settlements occurring in court cases, more and more lawsuits involving physical education are being settled out of court. However, when these suits do come to court, the courts are showing less tolerance for mistakes by teachers and demanding greater responsibility than ever before.

Negligence generally arises from one of five sources. They are (1) failure to supervise students properly; (2) failure to instruct students properly; (3) unsafe facilities, grounds, or equipment; (4) failure to take proper first aid measures in an emergency; and (5) failure involving transportation. By increasing their awareness of these five areas, teachers can considerably decrease their chances of becoming a defendant in a lawsuit and the damages awarded if such a case occurs.

Review Question: What are the five sources of negligence?

Supervision

More than 50 percent of all lawsuits involving physical education and sports are a result of improper supervision.[16] Henderson stated, *"By far the most crucial responsibility of physical education teachers is that of supervision."*[17] Berryhill and Jarman listed two basic questions frequently asked by the attorney for the plaintiff in a suit involving supervision:

1. If the supervisor had been present, would the accident have occurred?
2. Did the supervisor perform his assigned duties or abide by the rules and regulations?[18]

Dougherty, Auxter, Goldberger, and Heinzman defined supervision as

> the quality and quantity of control exerted by teachers or coaches over the individuals for whom they are responsible. Therefore the number of supervisory personnel assigned to a group must be sufficient to effectively control the group in question, and the supervisors must have the training and skills necessary to fulfill their assigned duties.[19]

Teachers are expected to be where they are assigned on time and to provide active rather than passive supervision. Hart and Ritson stated that active supervision requires more than mere presence. Physical education personnel are expected to

1. monitor and keep activities within the skill level of individual students and athletes;
2. keep students from participating in unsafe activities;
3. enforce class and school rules;
4. keep records and be aware of the health status of individual students;
5. provide spotting and other specific supervision in activities of elevated risk, such as gymnastics, wrestling, and football.[20]

Student discipline is a critical element of supervision. Effective practices and policies must be initiated. Class and school rules, especially safety rules, must be established, communicated both in written and oral form, and enforced. Failure to enforce rules when reckless behavior occurs implies approval of the behavior.[21] Results of court cases indicate that teachers who use corporal punishment will be vulnerable to litigation. Always avoid the use of physical contact of any kind in disciplining students.[22] California and Oregon include exercise used for punishment, such as laps and push-ups, in their definition of corporal punishment, which is prohibited by law.[23]

The quantity and quality of supervision needed depends on the circumstances, including the (1) age and maturity of the students, (2) amount of risk inherent in the activity, (3) skill level of the students, and (4) previous preparation of the students.

Proper instruction and supervision help to prevent lawsuits.

Age and maturity Younger, less mature students need more supervision; older, more mature students generally need less. However, teachers should consider the tendency of older students to engage in horseplay.[24]

Amount of risk in the activity Activities that involve greater risk—such as gymnastics, wrestling, swimming, archery, and initiative activities—require closer supervision and fewer students per teacher than activities with less risk. Avoid supervising two high-risk activities at one time, such as the high jump and shot put in track and field, as well as many gymnastic activities.[25]

Skill level Students who are just beginning to learn a new skill need more direct supervision than advanced students.

Preparation of students The teacher should gradually prepare students to assume responsibility for their own behavior. Students should earn the opportunity to participate in student-directed styles of learning.

Responsibilities of administrators and teachers Administrators have the responsibility to (1) assign qualified teachers for each activity taught in the curriculum, (2) communicate to teachers what is expected of them, and (3) supervise teachers to determine whether the expectations have been met. They also have the responsibility to regulate class sizes to meet the needs of the students.

Teachers have a responsibility to remain with their classes at all times. This includes positioning such that the entire class is in view at all times. When an emergency occurs, a student should be sent to the physical education or administrative office for help. The teacher should not leave the room to assist an injured student unless a second, qualified teacher is in the room. Never dismiss a class early or late without supervision. Locker rooms are one of the more potentially dangerous rooms in a school and should be supervised when in use and locked at all other times.[26] Teachers are liable for unsupervised students in gymnasiums, dressing rooms, halls, or on the school grounds. Table 3.1 provides guidelines for the behavior expected of a reasonably prudent physical educator.

Sample Court Cases Related to Supervision

Football Game on School Grounds Prior to Start of School A junior high student broke his leg during an informal football game on school grounds prior to the start of classes. The student fell over a sprinkler pipe. The suit stated inadequate supervision, improper storing of sprinkler pipes, failure to properly maintain the grounds in a safe condition, and failure to warn of the potential dangers. In regard to supervision, the ruling of the courts stated that the school had a duty to supervise the football game and that when the principal and faculty were on duty and students had arrived, the school day had begun.[27]

Teacher Asked to Cover Two Classes at the Same Time—Inadequate Locker Room Supervision An eighth-grade student, Daniel, was involved in an incident in the locker room. Another student, Steve, stepped on his heels as the two headed to the gym. Daniel elbowed Steve in the genitals in retaliation. Steve picked Daniel up and Daniel fell on his head. Daniel asked and was granted permission to see the nurse. The nurse did not see any signs of injury and returned Daniel to class. Daniel began to feel worse and returned to the nurse's office. His parents were summoned and Daniel was taken to his physician. He died shortly thereafter from a massive cerebral hemorrhage from a skull fracture. Normally the teacher remained in the locker room until all students left but since the teacher was responsible for two classes, he sent his normal class to the gym first and left the locker room to join his class. The others were to follow when everyone was dressed. The injury occurred when no one was in the locker room to supervise. The courts ruled in favor of the plaintiff.[28]

Large Number of Students in the Gym Due to Inclement Weather A fourteen-year-old eighth-grade student was injured during a physical education class. Due to inclement weather, three physical education teachers brought their classes to the gym and provided them with a free day. Sixty-three students were in the gymnasium. Students were allowed to use several pieces of athletic equipment. The plaintiff, with several others, practiced tumbling moves on a six-to-eight-inch-thick crash pad. On one of the attempts to complete a running front flip, the student lost control and received an injury resulting in the student's becoming quadriplegic. The court in this case ruled in favor of the defendants on the grounds of contributory negligence but said the teachers should not have allowed a dangerous activity to take place without a spotter and with so many students in the area.[29]

Review Question: What are some supervision practices undertaken by a responsible, prudent physical education teacher?

Instruction Several principles apply when designing the instructional situation. They relate to (1) the selection of the activity, (2) safety precautions, (3) planning, (4) direct instruction, and (5) grouping.

Selection of the activity Potential activities must be evaluated for their educational value and their appropriateness for students. Educational value is determined by the ability of the activity to help students meet the objectives of physical education. The courts have considered activities such as killer ball or war ball to be hazardous for students.[30] Appropriateness for students is determined by the age, maturity, skills, and fitness levels of students. Carefully screen students for such high-risk activities as combatives and gymnastics and for fitness activities in which students might be

TABLE 3.1 Supervision Guidelines

The Reasonably Prudent Physical Educator

1. Develops comprehensive class, team, and locker-room rules and procedures and effectively communicates those to students and athletes. Establishes clear rules relative to all equipment use.
2. Strictly and consistently enforces all established class, team, and school rules.
3. Provides active supervision required within the scope of his/her employment whether in the gym, on the field, in the locker room, or in the hall. The teacher is where he/she is assigned and on time. Provides general as well as specific supervision.
4. Does not unnecessarily absent him/herself from classes or practice sessions. Gives consideration to age and composition of the group, past experience with the group, the nature of the activity and the equipment being used, and the reason and duration for any temporary absence before leaving the group for any reason.
5. Assigns only qualified personnel to conduct and supervise activities.
6. Does not allow students to engage in unreasonably dangerous activities.
7. Is aware of the health status of all students under his/her charge and provides modified activity or exclusion from activity where appropriate.
8. Carefully matches students and athletes in any activity involving potential contact, giving consideration to age, size, skill, and experience differences.
9. Keeps activities within the ability level of individual students.
10. Refrains from all use of physical discipline and punishment, including the use of exercise as punishment.
11. Does not attempt to supervise more than one area at a time.
12. Immediately attends to any dangerous situations.

Source: J. E. Hart and R. J. Ritson, *Liability and Safety in Physical Education and Sport* (Reston, VA: American Alliance for Health, Physical Education, Recreation, and Dance, 2002) 115. Reprinted with permission of the National Association for Sport and Physical Education, 1900 Association Drive, Reston, VA 22091.

compelled to push themselves beyond their limits.[31] Running backward in a relay race is highly questionable for many students, although learning to move backward to reach a high clear might be acceptable in a sport like badminton.[32] A sound educational practice would be to individualize instruction for all students, not just students for whom Individualized Education Programs have been written.[33]

The use of stations is a common and appropriate practice in many situations. Extra planning is required, though, to be sure all stations are adequately supervised. If only one teacher is present, only one station should be an activity in which the risk is elevated. The teacher must be able to supervise or spot at the station of elevated risk and still maintain general supervision of the entire class. The teacher must be positioned to see all students at all times.[34]

Evaluate health problems and prevent students from participating in activities that are beyond their abilities. Do not allow students to participate in activities following a serious illness or injury without medical approval. Physical education teachers must be aware of medical conditions of all students in their classes. A student who complains of an illness or injury should be believed.[35]

Safety precautions Warn students of the possible dangers inherent in the activities in which they participate and caution them not to try things that they have not yet been taught. This is especially true in gymnastics, in which the plaintiff has usually been favored in court cases.[36]

Carefully formulate and teach safety rules and regulations to students. Rules should be few in number and well enforced. To ensure that students have learned them, safety rules can be distributed to students, reviewed with students, and posted as reminders. Test students to determine their knowledge of the rules before allowing them to participate in the activity. Do not allow students who have been absent to participate in activities until they have learned the appropriate safety rules.[37] Failure to follow the rules should result in exclusion from that activity.

Safety equipment—such as fencing masks and body protectors, catcher's masks and chest protectors, helmets, and other game-related safety equipment—should be required of all participants. Eyeglass protectors should be strongly encouraged when not required by policy or law. Check to make sure all equipment is used properly and safely. Ground rules can be used to help students learn safety rules, such as requiring softball players to lay the bat in a marked area on the way to first base or be called out.

Students should be taught that they have a responsibility to be careful, to respect possible dangers, and to prevent accidents from occurring by using appropriate means of prevention. Provide a handout and review it with the class that explains the responsibility of participants to report bad equipment, to rest when fatigued, and to ask for help when experiencing difficulty in performing a new skill. Remind students that instructors cannot be present at all times to help individuals, and therefore they must accept some responsibility for their own safety.

Sufficient space must be allowed between playing boundaries and walls or other obstructions. When the space is minimal, the walls and obstructions should be padded. A wall should never be used as a boundary,[38] or be used to touch as part of a relay race.

Planning Teachers should follow accepted procedures for instruction contained in state, district, or school courses of study or in a recognized text. Deviations from such procedures must be based on sound reasons, such as research demonstrating that the previous procedure was unsound or that a new procedure is better.

Unit and lesson plans are essential to ensure that proper progressions are followed and specific concerns regarding safe participation are provided (see examples in Chapter 7). Failure to carefully plan each unit and lesson can not only result in poor teaching but will also provide no evidence to defend, in a court of law, the progressions used.[39] Careful planning of lessons and units can do much to decrease the potential for an injury and a resultant lawsuit.[40]

Never leave substitute teachers in charge of a class unless the teachers have a lesson plan. A substitute is at a distinct disadvantage because the individual does not know the students as well as the teacher does. Provide the substitute with information about the health status of the students, including those who are excluded from activity due to injury or illness. Also supply information about chronically disruptive or physically aggressive students, safety procedures, and the names of individuals who could help in case of an emergency. The substitute should be informed of known hazardous conditions within the facilities or grounds. Activities with an elevated risk of injury should not be planned.[41]

Direct instruction Instruction in proper techniques and progressions should precede participation in any activity. Students should progress gradually from less strenuous and simple tasks to more demanding, complex, and higher-risk activities. Include proper techniques for the performance of the activity, the proper use of equipment, the inherent dangers in the activity or the equipment, and information on how to avoid those dangers.[42]

Grouping To prevent unnecessary injuries in contact sports or combative activities, group students for competition by similar characteristics such as height, size, skill, or sex; however, students cannot be grouped *solely* by sex. "Counting off" and other such methods of grouping are convenient but may result in mismatches. Teachers participating with their classes can result in the greatest mismatches and should be avoided. Failure to properly match participants has resulted in awards to students who are injured.[43]

Lehr has provided some recommendations for properly classifying students into groups.

1. Document all planning strategies.
2. Know the skill and experience levels before the student is asked to perform a skill.
3. Do not segregate on the basis of sex.
4. Do not pair/match by convenience.
5. Know the physical or emotional conditions of a student that may restrict participation.
6. Determine the most appropriate method of matching. Pair students by matching characteristics, and match the student to the activity.[44]

Table 3.2 provides guidelines for the behavior expected of a reasonably prudent physical educator in regard to instruction.

Sample Court Cases Related to Instruction

Coercion to Perform a Gymnastic Skill A fifteen-year-old girl was injured doing a backward roll in physical education class. She was a large girl at 5′6″ tall and weighing 180 pounds. The day prior to the accident the student had gone to the teacher's office and indicated a fear of doing backward rolls because of her size. She said she had tried them before and the attempts resulted in a sore neck. The teacher offered to help her after school but the student could not stay because she rode the bus and would not have a ride home. The next day the teacher asked the student if she could do the backward roll and the student said no. The teacher told her to practice with the assistance of another student and the teacher left to work with other students. The student suffered a subluxation of her vertebrae requiring a cervical fusion, grafting bone from her hip onto four vertebrae in her neck. The courts ruled in favor of the plaintiff. Teachers should not second-guess a student with fears or with possible injuries. Coercion is a risky strategy that may easily lead to injury and a case of negligence.[45]

Insufficient Safety Instructions in Soccer The class was playing line soccer. Each member of the two teams was given a number. The teacher would call out one or more numbers and the appropriate individual(s) from each team would run to the center and attempt to kick the ball. The class was not instructed as to what to do if two individuals got to the ball at the same time. The plaintiff was injured by running into another student while trying to kick the ball. A lower court dismissed the case of negligence but the Supreme Court of the State of New York reversed the ruling and remanded the case for a jury trial.[46]

Failure to Properly Match Students for Competition In another line soccer game in which boys on each side were randomly given a number, when a particular number was called two boys ran to the center of the gym. One boy was much taller and heavier than the other, the plaintiff. The plaintiff was kicked in the head by the larger boy, suffered a cerebral concussion, and was hospitalized for four days. The court awarded $2,500 in damages because the teacher failed to match students according to height and weight. Though counting off and other random systems of dividing into groups is fast and efficient, these systems do not consider height, weight, strength, and experience differences in the selection of teams and can increase the risk of injury. Participation by the teacher results in the greatest mismatch and potential for injury.[47]

TABLE 3.2 Instruction Guidelines

The Reasonably Prudent Physical Educator

1. Selects activities appropriate for the age of the student being instructed and is familiar with any existing district or state scope and sequence documents.
2. Develops written unit plans for each unit of study or sport season to ensure that proper progressions and safety are built into each activity unit.
3. Develops daily written lesson plans that allow for adequate warm-up, instruction, and practice, with both classroom management and safety considerations included.
4. Gives proper instructions, for both skill and safety, that conform to recognized standards employed in the professional field.
5. Provides adequate instruction before requiring student or athlete participation in any activity, including verbal instructions as well as teacher and/or student demonstrations.
6. Analyzes his/her teaching or coaching methods not only for their effectiveness but also for their attention to student and athlete safety.
7. Provides adequate safety instructions prior to any activity.
8. Provides clear warnings to students and athletes as to the specific risks involved in any activity or in the use of equipment, facilities, or grounds.
9. Provides adequate and proper modifications to activity, where appropriate, for special needs students or those returning from injuries or illness.
10. Avoids teaching to the masses and individualizes instruction wherever appropriate.
11. Teaches or coaches only those activities with which he/she is familiar and qualified to teach/coach.
12. Does not coerce students to perform.
13. Follows all guidelines related to program that are set forth by the school, district, state, or activity association.
14. Requires an adequate amount of practice before competition.
15. Does not attempt to instruct or supervise an excessive number of students or athletes, especially in activities involving elevated levels of risk.
16. Continues to upgrade both skill and knowledge through participation in workshops, continuing education, and other in-service opportunities.

Source: J. E. Hart and R. J. Ritson, *Liability and Safety in Physical Education and Sport* (Reston, VA: American Alliance for Health, Physical Education, Recreation and Dance, 2002), 52–53. Reprinted with permission of the National Association for Sport and Physical Education, 1900 Association Drive, Reston, VA 22091.

Exercise as Punishment A thirteen-year-old fifth-grade special education student was ordered to do a "gut run" as punishment for talking in line at recess. The teacher who ordered the run was the student's teacher and was aware that the student was born with a congenital heart defect and had contracted meningitis, which left him with mental and physical disabilities including legs of unequal length. He wore a brace to stabilize one ankle and was under doctor's orders not to participate in competitive contact sports or forced exertion. The gut run was a 350-yard sprint that had to be completed in less than two minutes. The student suffered cardiac arrhythmia and died. The courts ruled for the plaintiff.[48] Even though this may appear to be a severe case, any use of exercise as punishment is risky. In some states that ban corporal punishment, exercise as punishment is considered corporal punishment. Other means of discipline are more appropriate (see Chapter 13).

Review Question: What are some instructional practices undertaken by a responsible, prudent physical education teacher?

Safe Facilities, Grounds, and Equipment Essential components of accident prevention are safe facilities, grounds, and equipment. Administrators should set policies and make plans for periodic inspection of facilities, grounds, and equipment to determine possible hazards and defects. The line of responsibility must be clearly delegated to a specific person.[49] Records listing the inspector, date, condition of the equipment, and recommendations for repair should be retained. Maintain complete inventories of equipment, including the dates of purchase and repair.

Physical educators should inspect facilities, grounds, and equipment frequently and take note of any potential hazards. Report hazards promptly to the principal and follow up with a written letter to the principal (and superintendent, if necessary) stating the date and the nature of the problem. Retain a copy of the report. Administrators are responsible for maintaining facilities and grounds and correcting defects.

While waiting for the defect to be corrected, use temporary measures to protect students from injury: post signs warning of the danger; warn students to stay away from the area; close off or lock the area; or station a supervisor nearby to keep students away. Never use a facility while unsafe conditions exist. Appenzeller sums up one of the major problems with equipment: "Too often teachers try to get by just one more day with obsolete and outdated equipment that should have been discarded years ago. These teachers are either indifferent to the needs of their pupils or are totally unaware of the serious consequences that may lie ahead."[50]

Physical education departments provide equipment for the use of students in their physical education classes. Brown listed four general responsibilities of individuals who provide equipment:

1. When providing equipment without charge, make sure that the equipment is safe. Inspect all new equipment for defects.
2. Select equipment that is appropriate for the participants' height, weight, skill, and overall competence.
3. Ensure that equipment is used only for its intended purpose. A school could be liable if a participant is injured while being allowed to use equipment in ways other than were intended by the manufacturer.
4. Teach all participants how to use the equipment properly.[51]

An *attractive nuisance* is a dangerous situation that attracts the attention of children or youth. Swimming pools, gymnastics apparatus, jumping pits, and excavation areas are all attractive nuisances. To prevent injuries, teachers and administrators have a responsibility to keep such areas and equipment locked up when not in use.

Table 3.3 provides guidelines for the reasonably prudent physical educator in regard to safe equipment, grounds, and facilities.

Sample Court Cases Related to Facilities, Grounds, and Equipment

Inadequate Locker Room Facilities A high school student was injured from a fall while running to take a shower after class. There were forty-five girls in the class with only six showers available. The girls had five minutes to shower and get ready for class. As the plaintiff attempted to get to the locker room quickly, her feet got entangled with those of other girls and she fell. As a result of the fall she suffered a broken left femur and a cracked right elbow. She spent considerable time in the hospital and home in bed. The suit alleged the teacher and school were negligent because too many girls were in the class, shower facilities were not adequate, and insufficient time was allowed for forty-five girls to shower. The courts ruled for the defendant but the result might have been different if the fall had occurred in the locker room.[52]

Lack of Protective Equipment in Floor Hockey A tenth-grade student was participating in a floor hockey game and was hit in the eye with a hockey puck. As a result he suffered a detached retina and eventually lost the eye. The game was being played on only half the gym and though safety glasses were available, they were not required to be worn. The courts ruled in favor of the plaintiff.[53] A responsible, prudent physical education teacher has

TABLE 3.3 Equipment, Grounds, Facilities Guidelines

The Reasonably Prudent Physical Educator
1. Does not allow students to use any equipment prior to receiving instruction on the safe use of that equipment.
2. Regularly inspects equipment, facilities, and grounds used by students. Does quick visual check daily with a detailed inspection monthly.
3. Keeps all inspection reports on file.
4. Reports all hazardous facility or grounds conditions immediately and refrains from using hazardous areas until these conditions are remedied.
5. Does not use defective, overly worn, or broken equipment.
6. Refrains from using equipment for purposes other than those for which it was intended.
7. Provides all necessary safety equipment in those activities where appropriate such as soccer, hockey, softball, football, in-line skating, rock climbing, and gymnastics.
8. Purchases equipment of high quality; does not supply equipment that is dangerous for other than its intended use.
9. Does not modify factory-purchased equipment.
10. Properly secures and/or stores all equipment when not in use.
11. Does not turn an otherwise safe facility into a dangerous one by improperly arranging equipment and materials for student or athlete use (e.g., placing equipment too close to walls, bleachers, or other obstructions or crowding).
12. Does not use common boundary lines but provides a safe buffer zone between all play and competition areas and between play areas and all obstructions.
13. Follows all school and district rules and guidelines relative to equipment use.
14. Instructs students and athletes to also check for common safety hazards involving equipment, facilities, and grounds.
15. Posts appropriate warnings and rules relative to equipment and facility use.
16. Disinfects all equipment and facility surfaces whenever exposure to possible blood-borne pathogens and other communicable diseases occurs.
17. Exhibits caution in the use of homemade equipment.
18. Keeps locker rooms clean and orderly.

Source: J. E. Hart and R. J. Ritson, *Liability and Safety in Physical Education and Sport* (Reston, VA: American Alliance for Health, Physical Education, Recreation and Dance, 2002), 172–73. Reprinted with permission of the National Association for Sport and Physical Education, 1900 Association Drive, Reston, VA 22091.

two choices when considering the inclusion of activities that are potentially dangerous in the curriculum: either safety equipment must be available and required by all participants or the activity is not included in the curriculum.

Review Question: What are some safe practices undertaken by a responsible, prudent physical educator relating to facilities, grounds, and equipment?

First Aid versus Medical Treatment The law both requires and limits the medical treatment of students to first aid—the immediate and temporary care needed to preserve the student's life or prevent further injury until medical care is available. This legal duty is imposed because the teacher stands *in loco parentis,* or "in the place of the parent," and also because physical education teachers are expected to be qualified to administer this aid.

Two common errors occur in giving first aid—doing too much or doing too little. An example of doing too much is moving an injured student before medical help has arrived. Cases of spinal injury and paralysis have resulted from this particular error. On the other hand, failure to obtain medical help for students suffering from heat exhaustion, a broken bone, or other injury can also be harmful. All head injuries should be considered serious. Any delay in treatment can be life-threatening.[54]

To help prevent accidents, proper medical examinations are often required of students at various school levels. Physical educators should take note of students who have medical problems or handicaps and may need close supervision or adapted instruction. Require students who have been seriously ill or injured to obtain a doctor's release before resuming normal physical activity.

If an accident does occur, administer first aid while sending a student to summon medical help and inform the principal. An emergency plan should be formulated and reviewed frequently so that it can be followed quickly and without further mishap. Keep an accurate report of each accident including a detailed report of the activity and the circumstances of the accident, the nature of the injury, the first aid treatment given, medical attention obtained, the names of persons rendering service, and the names of witnesses. A sample accident report form is shown in Box 3.1.

Appenzeller summarized the expectations of the court regarding first aid:

> As a coach, the court expects you to handle emergencies when they arise. The court will set a much higher standard of first aid for the coach than the average classroom teacher. The court will demand emergency treatment but nothing more. Do not go beyond the emergency stage; avoid attempting to treat your players; *let the professional do this!*[55]

Medical treatment includes the dispensing of any medication. Teachers and coaches should be extremely cautious in this regard and should not give students even aspirin.

Sample Court Case Related to Administration of First Aid

Improper First Aid for Heat Stroke A high school student became ill during a football practice at about 5:20 P.M. and was transported to the high school. A heat injury was suspected, so the boy was laid on the floor and covered with a blanket. Attempts were made to give him salt water, which were unsuccessful. His mother was called at 6:45 P.M. and she called the doctor who arrived at 7:15 P.M. The boy died at 2:30 P.M. the next day with heat stroke listed as the cause of death. The doctor indicated that if the boy had been given proper treatment immediately, he probably would not have died. The courts ruled in favor of the plaintiffs. Whenever activities are conducted in heat, the severity of the workout, the number of rest breaks, and the availability of water must be adjusted for the heat.[56]

Review Question: How will first aid be administered by a responsible, prudent physical educator?

Transportation and Field Trips When transportation is necessary to and from off-campus facilities or during a field trip, school officials should approve all travel arrangements. The preferred arrangement is to use school buses or commercial vehicles. However, in an emergency situation when these are unavailable, several precautions should be taken.

When teachers or adults drive their own cars, administrators should ensure that they have adequate liability insurance in case of student injury. They should also be aware that many automobile insurance policies do not protect the car owner who is paid for transporting passengers, even if the pay is only reimbursement for gas and oil. An insurance rider on the policy must be purchased to provide this protection.[57] Only 1 school or district transportation should be used by teachers except in emergency situations.

Extreme caution should be used when allowing students to drive to and from school functions. Only when drastic circumstances arise should this be allowed. Administrators must then examine the student drivers' reputations and records for safe and careful driving and the cars for freedom from defects that might make them unsafe when student drivers are used. Such drivers should also be cautioned to obey all traffic laws and not to overload their cars or to allow students to drive who have not been approved by the administration. The students' insurance policies should be checked for adequate coverage.[58]

School boards would be wise to protect their students by establishing rules and regulations for student transportation and by securing liability insurance for their employees who transport students. It is also good public relations to let parents know exactly what is and is not covered.

Consent forms are often sent home to parents before students are allowed to go on field trips. Consent forms are not the same as waivers. Permission to attend an event is given with a consent form. A waiver is designed to release

BOX 3.1

Accident Report Form

INJURED PERSON

Name (last, first, middle)

Telephone Number

Address

Age

Sex ☐ Female ☐ Male

Classification ☐ Student ☐ Faculty ☐ Visitor

ACCIDENT

Date and Hour of Accident

Severity ☐ Nondisabling (loss of less than a full day of normal activity)
☐ Disabling (loss of one or more full days of normal activity)

Department Supervising Activity

Jurisdiction ☐ On school property
☐ Off campus in school-conducted activity

Type of Facility
☐ Athletic or physical education
☐ Instruction
☐ Exterior walk or sidewalk
☐ Other, specify _____
☐ Street or highway
☐ Service or maintenance
☐ Undeveloped area

Activity at Time of Accident (e.g., driving auto, diving from low board, lifting crate, etc.).

Location
☐ Gymnasium
☐ Sports arena or play field
☐ Swimming pool
☐ Bath, shower, or locker room
☐ Interior stair or ramp
☐ Interior hall or corridor
☐ Classroom, lecture hall
☐ Auditorium or library
☐ Laboratory
☐ Shop (mechanical)
☐ Home economics
☐ Storeroom
☐ Food preparation/service
☐ Cafeteria or dining room
☐ Public transportation
☐ Private transportation
☐ Bldg. exterior or grounds
☐ Water area
☐ Farm, field, or woods
☐ Other, specify ________
____

Details of Accident (Describe fully the events, conditions, factors that contributed to the injury)

Action to Prevent Similar Accidents (Indicate if taken)

INJURY

Nature of Injury
☐ Amputation
☐ Bruise
☐ Burn, scald
☐ Concussion
☐ Open wounds
☐ Dermatitis, infection
☐ Other, specify
____
____
☐ Exposure, frostbite
☐ Fracture
☐ Foreign body
☐ Heat exhaustion, sunstroke
☐ Inhalation (dust, fumes, gases, etc.)
☐ Internal injury
☐ Poisoning, internal
☐ Shock, electrical
☐ Shock, fainting
☐ Sprain, strains, dislocation
☐ Suffocation, drowning, strangulation
☐ Rupture, hernia

Part of Body Injured
☐ Generalized
☐ Skull or scalp
☐ Eye
☐ Nose
☐ Mouth
☐ Jaw
☐ Other head
☐ Neck
☐ Spine
☐ Chest
☐ Other, specify ____________
☐ Abdomen
☐ Back
☐ Pelvis
☐ Other trunk
☐ Shoulder
☐ Upper arm
☐ Elbow
☐ Forearm
☐ Wrist
☐ Hand
☐ Finger
☐ Hip
☐ Thigh
☐ Knee
☐ Lower leg
☐ Ankle
☐ Foot
☐ Toe

Continued

BOX 3.1 *Continued*

Accident Report Form

WITNESSES	**Witnesses and Their Addresses**	
TREATMENT	**Emergency Care & Patient Status** ☐ First aid only, not at hospital or by doctor ☐ Treatment by school nurse ☐ Treatment at hospital ☐ Confinement at hospital or at residence	This report prepared by (signature) ______ Title or status ______ Address ______ ______ Date ______

DISTRIBUTION: White, Principal Yellow, Originating Department

someone from responsibility for injuries which might occur while participating in an event. A waiver does not remove responsibility from an individual who is guilty of negligence. Box 3.2 shows a sample waiver form.

A parent cannot waive the rights of a child who is under twenty-one years of age; the parent is merely waiving the parent's right to sue for damages. The child can still sue the individual, however, at the time or at a later date. Although waivers do not stand up in court,[59] they serve a valuable purpose of informing parents and receiving parental permission for a trip. They may also reduce the possibility of a lawsuit.[60] Teachers who are transporting students should have an emergency treatment authorization form with them for each student, which includes the student's name; family physician's name; parent's name and signature; and information regarding the student's insurance, allergies, and current medications.[61]

Table 3.4 summarizes behaviors expected of a reasonably prudent physical educator.

Review Question: What will a responsible, prudent physical educator do to reduce lawsuits related to transporting students and going on field trips?

Protection against Legal Liability

Study the guidelines for protection against legal liability presented in this chapter and apply them to your own environment. Because of the abrogation of governmental immunity, more students are now able to recover damages for injuries caused by the negligence of school employees. Although this is a positive outcome for the injured person, it also means that teachers may be involved in more nuisance suits with resulting stress, professional embarrassment, and financial loss. School districts will also pay higher rates for insurance and sports equipment.[62] The result is a higher cost to the taxpayers for the support of their schools.

The fact that physical education teachers are held legally responsible for their actions should not cause prospective or practicing educators to throw in the towel. Rather, it should make them take their responsibilities as educators seriously and use common sense in their interactions with others. Teachers should become acquainted with the tort liability laws as they apply to their particular states.

In addition, the prudent physical education teacher will also obtain liability insurance to protect against catastrophic personal loss. In some states, *save-harmless* legislation requires or permits districts to provide teachers with protection against financial losses resulting from a job-related liability suit. Personal liability insurance is available from some local or state education associations, the American Alliance for Health, Physical Education, Recreation, and Dance; or the National Education Association.

Departmental and class procedures must be legal and safe. Policies and procedures for supervision, instruction, care of equipment, emergencies, and transportation must be documented (see Chapter 12).[63] Units and lessons must be thoughtfully and carefully planned, and student welfare should be of prime concern.

Review Question: What protection is available against the costs of defending a court case?

CIVIL RIGHTS OF STUDENTS

Clement stated, "To create a quality learning environment, professionals must foster freedom without disruption, secure individual rights without infringing on the rights of others, and establish gender equity."[64] These are protections of civil rights provided by the First, Fourth, and Fourteenth Amendments to the United States Constitution.

BOX 3.2

Sample Waiver Form

WAIVER AND RELEASE OF LIABILITY

DISCLAIMER: STATE UNIVERSITY IS NOT RESPONSIBLE FOR ANY INJURY (OR LOSS OF PROPERTY) TO ANY PERSON SUFFERED WHILE PLAYING, PRACTICING, OR IN ANY OTHER WAY INVOLVED IN THE RUGBY CLUB FOR ANY REASON WHATSOEVER, INCLUDING NEGLIGENCE ON THE PART OF STATE UNIVERSITY, ITS AGENTS, OR EMPLOYEES.

In consideration of my participation, **I hereby release** State University, State University Board of Trustees, The Sports Club Federation, The Rugby Club, and any of their employees, instructors, agents, **from any and all present and future claims resulting from negligence on the part of State University or others listed** for property damage, personal injury, or wrongful death, arising as a result of my engaging in or receiving instruction in Rugby Club activities or any activities incidental thereto, wherever or however the same may occur. **I hereby voluntarily waive any and all claims resulting from negligence,** both present and future, that may be made by me, my family, estate, heirs, or assigns.

I am aware that rugby is a vigorous team sport involving severe cardiovascular stress and violent physical contact. I understand that rugby involves certain risks, including but not limited to, death, serious neck and spinal injuries resulting in complete or partial paralysis, brain damage, and serious injury to virtually all bones, joints, muscles, and internal organs and that equipment provided for my protection may be inadequate to prevent serious injury. I further understand that rugby involves a particularly high risk of knee, head, and neck injury. Furthermore, I understand that participation in The Rugby Club involves activities incidental thereto, including, but not limited to, travel to and from the site of the activity, participation at sites that may be remote from available medical assistance, and the possible reckless conduct of other participants. I am voluntarily participating in this activity with knowledge of the danger involved and hereby agree to accept any and all inherent risks of property damage, personal injury, or death.

I further agree to indemnify and hold harmless State University and others listed for any and all claims arising as a result of my engaging in or receiving instruction in Rugby Club activities or any activities incidental thereto, wherever or however the same may occur.

I affirm that I am of legal age and am freely signing this agreement. **I have read this form and fully understand that by signing this form, I am giving up legal rights** and/or remedies which may be available to me for the ordinary negligence of State University or any of the parties listed above.

(Signature of Participant)	Date	(Signature of Parent if Participant is Under 18)	Date

TABLE 3.4 Transportation Guidelines

The Reasonably Prudent Physical Educator

1. Refrains from using anything other than district vehicles to transport students and athletes.
2. Never overloads a vehicle.
3. Makes sure each rider has a designated seat and uses a seat belt if one is provided.
4. Completes a visual check of a vehicle as well as a check of all lights, blinkers, tires, and wipers whenever a vehicle other than a school bus is used. Does not use any vehicle that is not well maintained.
5. Immediately reports any maintenance or safety needs of any district vehicle that he/she uses to transport students.
6. Makes sure any vehicle is equipped and supplied with adequate warning devices such as markers and flares.
7. Equips any vehicle used to transport students or athletes with a first aid kit.
8. Never arranges for students or athletes to drive.
9. Provides adequate supervision within the vehicle.
10. Makes sure any vehicle used is properly insured and that all drivers are properly licensed. In a number of states, a large passenger van full of riders requires the driver to have a chauffeur's license.
11. Follows district guidelines and all reasonable standards for total driving time as well as total on-duty time within any given work day. Does not attempt to transport students when overly tired.

Source: J. E. Hart and R. J. Ritson, *Liability and Safety in Physical Education and Sport* (Reston, VA: American Alliance for Health, Physical Education, Recreation, and Dance, 2002), 170, 201. Reprinted with permission of the National Association for Sport and Physical Education, 1900 Association Drive, Reston, VA 22091.

The First Amendment

The First Amendment allows for freedoms of speech, press, and privacy. The amendment protects an individual's right to express ideas either in speech or writing. Any language that is obscene, libelous, or slanderous is not protected. The learning environment must be protected and anything that disrupts the learning environment is prohibited. The courts will balance the needs of the public against the rights of the individual.[65] Freedom from invasion of privacy will be discussed as a part of the Fourth Amendment.

The classic case cited for freedom of speech is *Tinker v. Des Moines School District* (1969).[66] Tinker and two other students wore black armbands to protest the Vietnam War. Knowing that students were contemplating the wearing of black armbands, the school adopted a policy against the wearing of black armbands. The three students decided to wear the armbands anyway. The students were asked to remove the armbands and refused. They were then suspended from school until they were willing to return without wearing the armbands. The students sought an injunction. The District Court upheld the decision by the school. The United States Court of Appeals reversed the decision stating that neither students nor teachers relinquished their rights to free speech as they entered the school and that there was no evidence that the wearing of the armbands disrupted the educational process. Therefore, the ban was unconstitutional.[67]

The Fourth Amendment

The Fourth Amendment provides protection against unreasonable searches. This also includes drug testing. In recent years, random drug-testing policies have been established in many schools. Typically, the students included in random drug testing are those who drive to school and/or are involved in extracurricular and cocurricular activities. The courts have allowed random drug testing of these individuals because it can be proven that the use of drugs while driving or in activities such as sports can be dangerous. Also, each of these activities is a privilege and not a right and if the student does not wish to participate in the random drug testing, the student can choose to be excluded. As a result of the choice made, the student no longer is allowed to participate in the activities. The student's education has not been impaired in any way. In drug-testing cases, the students must be made fully aware of the procedures that will be followed and should be required to sign a form indicating their willingness to participate and an understanding of the procedures. Students should be told how the tests will be conducted, how information about the results will be distributed, and what happens in the case of a positive result.

Searches of students' purses, lockers, and clothing have been the subjects of litigation. In each case, the searches are allowed if a reasonable suspicion exists that the search will reveal evidence to support the claim of violation of a rule.[68] The standard for school officials is different than for law enforcement professionals. Again it is important that policies be established and made known to the students and parents prior to the start of school or a specific school activity.[69] This includes indicating to students that lockers may be subject to search at any time.

The classic case cited to guide search and seizure cases is *New Jersey v. T.L.O.*[70] T.L.O. was a high school student who, along with five other young women, was caught smoking in a restroom by one of the teachers. The young women were asked about their smoking. One confessed that they had been smoking. T.L.O. did not and said that she had never smoked. As a result of the information supplied by the teacher and the one student who confessed, the assistant principal decided to search T.L.O.'s purse. In it he found a package of cigarettes. He also saw some papers that might be used for rolling marijuana. As a result of this discovery he more thoroughly searched the girl's purse. He found marijuana, a large sum of money, lists of debts, and two letters implicating the involvement of the young woman in the selling of drugs. In making its ruling in this case the Supreme Court indicated the need to balance the need for a search with the invasion of privacy that would result. If there is reason to believe that the search will produce evidence that a law or school rule has been broken, school officials may do a search. The second test suggested by the Supreme Court was that the means of searching must be appropriate. In the above case a strip search would not be appropriate but in a case described below the courts ruled that the strip search was considered appropriate.

A sixteen-year-old male student was thought to be "crotching" drugs. Several teachers and the past history of the student suggested that this was a possibility. As he was beginning to board a bus to go home, the student's teacher in the behavioral disorder program in which he was enrolled and the dean of students requested the student to come to the dean's office. Both individuals were males. The two adults confronted the student with the accusation. The student became agitated and requested that his mother be called to seek consent for the search. She refused consent. The two men decided to continue the search anyway and escorted the student to the boy's locker room. The room was checked to be sure it was empty and the door was locked. The two men stood twelve feet from the student on either side when he was asked to remove all of his clothes and then put on a set of clothes that was provided for him. The two men visually inspected the student from a distance as he undressed and physically inspected his clothes as he was putting on the other clothes. No drugs were found. The search was ruled constitutional by the courts. There was sufficient reason to believe that drugs would be found and the method of the search was reasonable.[71]

In another search and seizure case, a business teacher returned to his classroom after a few minutes' absence to find two girls yelling obscenities to each other. He told them to take their seats and be quiet. One sat down but the other approached her and the first girl stood up again. One girl took a swing at the other one. The teacher stepped between them and told the other girl to get her books and leave the room. She began to leave but very slowly. The teacher grasped the girl by the elbow to speed her exit from the classroom. She stopped and told the teacher to release her, which he did. Later that day the two girls did get into a fight and were suspended from school for three days. The student alleged that grasping her arm was an unreasonable seizure. The courts ruled that since schools must maintain discipline and to do so must restrict student movement and allow movement only at specified times, that this was not an unreasonable seizure.[72] Even though the seizure was considered reasonable in this case, teachers should be wary of ever touching a student for any reason other than to provide assistance in the performing of a skill.

The Fourteenth Amendment

The Fourteenth Amendment includes procedural due process and equal protection, which also includes Title IX. "Procedural due process is the provision of an opportunity for an individual to be heard, to defend personal actions, and be assured of fair treatment before a right or privilege is taken away."[73] The right of a student to explain or defend actions must be considered whenever punishment or discipline is implemented. The minimum requirements for due process include (1) a statement of the violation, (2) a notice of the intended punishment, and (3) an opportunity to respond.

More severe cases require more formal procedures including written notification of the violation and opportunities to call witnesses and cross-examine witnesses as well as legal representation to be present at all hearings. Most cases of wrongdoing in a school fit the minimum requirements just listed.[74]

The Fourteenth Amendment and Title IX provide protection against discrimination. Title IX will be discussed in Chapter 4 but it is important to note that monetary compensation for lost opportunities may now be awarded.[75] Prior to *Franklin v. Gwinnett,* complaints of violations of Title IX resulted in an investigation. If a violation was found, then the institution was required to make the necessary changes in policy, procedures, and practices. No monetary damages were allowed. Title IX cases generally occur in the area of athletics.

The Constitution of the United States protects the rights of students as well as teachers. These include a safe learning environment; freedoms of speech, press, and privacy; protection from unreasonable searches; due process; and equal protection. If efforts are made to ensure that these rights are protected in the school, they are less likely to need to be settled in court.

Review Questions: What civil rights are protected by the First, Fourth, and Fourteenth Amendments to the Constitution?

What does Title IX have to do with the civil rights of students?

NOTES

1. *Landers v. School District No. 203,* O'Fallon, 66 Ill. App. 3d 1978 383 N.E. 2d 645.
2. *Montague v. School Board of Thornton Fractional Township North High School District,* 215.57 Ill. App. 3d 828 (1978).
3. Children's Safety Network at Education Development Center, Inc., *Injuries in the School Environment: A Resource Guide,* 2nd ed. (Newton, MA: Education Development Center, Inc., 1997).
4. N. J. Dougherty, D. Auxter, A. S. Goldberger, G. S. Heinzmann, and H. A. Findlay, *Sport, Physical Activity, and the Law* (Champaign, IL: Human Kinetics, 1994).
5. J. H. Conn, The litigation connection: Perspectives of risk control for the 1990s, *Journal of Physical Education, Recreation, and Dance 64,* no. 2 (1993): 15.
6. J. A. Baley and D. L. Matthews, *Law and Liability in Athletics, Physical Education and Recreation* (Dubuque, IA: Wm. C. Brown, 1989).
7. *Sports and the Courts: Physical Education and Sports Law Quarterly,* Box 2836, Winston-Salem, NC 27102.
8. H. Appenzeller, *From the Gym to the Jury* (Charlottesville, VA: Michie, 1970).
9. H. Appenzeller and T. Appenzeller, *Sports and the Courts* (Charlottesville, VA: Michie, 1980).
10. *Smith v. Vernon Parish School Board,* 442 So. 2d 1319 (La. Ct. App. 1983), is similar to the case described here.
11. H. C. Hudgins, Jr., and R. S. Vacca, *Law and Education: Contemporary Issues and Court Decisions* (Charlottesville, VA: Michie, 1979); *Waechter v. School District N. 14-030,* 733 F. Supp. 1005 (1991).
12. L. J. Carpenter, Guns, knives and fists—Campus violence by third parties, *Journal of Physical Education, Recreation, and Dance 61,* no. 5 (1990): 13–14.
13. *Molitor v. Kaneland,* 163 N.E. 2d 89 (Ill. 1959).
14. D. E. Arnold, Positive outcomes of recent legislative and case law developments which have implications for HPER programs, *Physical Educator 37* (March 1980): 25.
15. J. E. Hart and R. J. Ritson, *Liability and Safety in Physical Education and Sport* (Reston, VA: National Association for Sport and Physical Education, 1993).

16. L. Berryhill and B. Jarman, *A History of Lawsuits in Physical Education, Intramurals and Interscholastic Athletics in the Western United States: Their Implications and Consequences* (Provo, UT: Brigham Young University, 1979).
17. D. H. Henderson, Physical education teachers: How do I sue thee: Oh, let me count the ways! *Journal of Physical Education, Recreation, and Dance 56,* no. 2 (1985): 44.
18. Berryhill and Jarman, *A History of Lawsuits.*
19. Dougherty et al., *Sport, Physical Activity.*
20. J. E. Hart and R. J. Ritson, *Liability and Safety in Physical Education and Sport* (Reston, VA: National Association for Sport and Physical Education, 1993).
21. Hart and Ritson, *Liability and Safety.*
22. Hart and Ritson, *Liability and Safety.*
23. Hart and Ritson, *Liability and Safety; Metzger v. Osbeck,* 841 F. 2d 518 (1988).
24. J. N. Drowatzky, Liability: You could be sued! *Journal of Physical Education, Recreation, and Dance 49,* no. 5 (1978): 17–18.
25. *Merkley v. Palmyra—Macedon Central School District,* 515 N.Y.S. 2d 932 (N.Y. 1987).
26. Hart and Ritson, *Liability and Safety.*
27. Hart and Ritson, *Liability and Safety; Bauer v. Minidoka School District No. 331,* 778 P. 2d 336 (1989).
28. *Kersey v. Harbin,* 591 S.W. 2d 745 (1979).
29. Hart and Ritson, *Liability and Safety; Harrison v. Montgomery County Board of Education,* 456 A. 2d 894 (1983).
30. *Cook v. Bennett,* 288 N.W. 2d 609 (Mich. Ct. App. 1979).
31. Appenzeller, *From the Gym.*
32. K. R. Barrett and L. P. Gaskin, Running backwards in a relay race: *Brown v. Burlington City Board of Education, Journal of Physical Education, Recreation, and Dance 61,* no. 1 (1990): 33–35.
33. Hart and Ritson, *Liability and Safety.*
34. Hart and Ritson, *Liability and Safety.*
35. Hart and Ritson, *Liability and Safety.*
36. Appenzeller, *From the Gym.*
37. Hart and Ritson, *Liability and Safety.*
38. *Brahatcek v. Millard School District No. 17,* 272 N.W. 2d 680 (Neb. 1979).
39. *Larson v. Independent School District No. 314,* 289 N.W. 2d 112 (1979).
40. G. R. Gray, Risk management planning: Conducting a sport risk assessment to enhance program safety, *Journal of Physical Education, Recreation, and Dance 62,* no. 6 (1991): 29.
41. Hart and Ritson, *Liability and Safety.*
42. Hudgins and Vacca, *Law and Education.*
43. C. Lehr, Proper classification, *Journal of Physical Education, Recreation, and Dance 64,* no. 2 (1993): 24–25, 63.
44. Lehr, Proper classification.
45. Hart and Ritson, *Liability and Safety; Larson v. Independent School District No. 314,* 289 N.W. 2d 112 (1979).
46. Hart and Ritson, *Liability and Safety; Darrow v. West Genesee Central School District,* 342 N.Y.S. 2d 611 (1973).
47. *Brooks v. Board of Education of the City of New York,* 189 N.E. 2d 497 (1963); Hart and Ritson, *Liability and Safety.*
48. Hart and Ritson, *Liability and Safety; Waechter v. School District N. 14-030,* 733 F. Supp. 1005 (1991).
49. Appenzeller, *From the Gym.*
50. Appenzeller, *From the Gym.*
51. S. C. Brown, Selecting safe equipment—What do we really know? *Journal of Physical Education, Recreation and Dance 64,* no. 2 (1993): 33.
52. Hart and Ritson, *Liability and Safety; Driscol v. Delphi Community School Corporation,* 290 N.E. 2d 769 (1972).
53. Hart and Ritson, *Liability and Safety; Sutphen v. Benthain and the Vernon Township Board of Education,* 397 A. 2d 709 (1979).
54. *Barth v. Board of Education of City of Chicago,* 490 N.E. 2d 77 (1986); Hart and Ritson, *Liability and Safety.*
55. Appenzeller, *From the Gym.*
56. Hart and Ritson, *Liability and Safety; Mogabgab v. Orleans Parish School Board,* 239 So. 2d 456 (1970).
57. Appenzeller, *From the Gym.*
58. Appenzeller, *From the Gym.*
59. R. A. Kaiser, Program liability waivers, *Journal of Physical Education, Recreation and Dance 55,* no. 6 (1984) 55.
60. R. V. Acosta, I promise I won't sue! *Strategies 2,* no. 5 (1989): 5–6.
61. Hart and Ritson, *Liability and Safety.*
62. Arnold, Positive outcomes.
63. A. Clement, *Law in Sport and Physical Activity* (Dubuque, IA: Brown & Benchmark, 1988).
64. A. Clement, Civil rights—The First, Fourth, and Fourteenth Amendments, *Journal of Physical Education, Recreation, and Dance 64,* no. 2 (1993): 16–17, 62.
65. Clement, Civil rights.
66. *Tinker v. Des Moines School District,* 393 U.S. 503 (1969).
67. Clement, *Law in Sport.*
68. Dougherty et al., *Sport, Physical Activity.*
69. Clement, Civil rights.
70. *New Jersey v. T.L.O.,* 105 S. Ct. 733 (1985).
71. *Cornfield v. Consolidated High School District No. 230* (1993), www.kentlaw.edu/7circuit/1993/92-1863.html
72. *Wallace v. The Batavia School District 101* (1995), www.kentlaw.edu/7 circuit/1995/94-3943.html
73. Clement, Civil rights.
74. Clement, *Law in Sport.*
75. Clement, Civil rights; *Franklin v. Gwinnett County Public Schools,* 117 L. Ed. 2d 208 (1992).

CHAPTER

4

Understanding the Learner

Study Stimulators

1. What common characteristics do adolescents of various ages have? What differences do they exhibit?
2. What effect do student similarities and differences have on learning and teaching?
3. How can a teacher best meet the needs of all students?
4. What effect have laws that have been enacted had on the physical education classroom?

Ralph Waldo Emerson once said, "The secret of education lies in respecting the pupil."[1] Respect comes from getting to know someone and appreciating that person's worth. By getting to know students, teachers can design instructional programs to help them become successful, contributing members of society. Teachers who become familiar with the characteristics of their students have a considerable advantage in planning their teaching. The investment of time in getting to know the characteristics of a learner population and students as individuals yields a generous return in the classroom. Three areas to consider when learning about students are (1) common characteristics of children and youth, (2) significant differences among students, and (3) social forces that affect students. Educational programs must be planned that meet the needs identified in these three areas.

Common Characteristics of Children and Youth

Much research has been conducted in child and adolescent growth and development and is available in textbooks of educational and developmental psychology. A summary chart of the characteristics of upper-elementary-age children is shown in Table 4.1, with a corresponding chart for adolescent characteristics in Table 4.2. Many middle schools include children from groups represented in both tables.The tables are organized by domain. The *cognitive domain* includes learning and application of knowledge. The *psychomotor domain* incorporates the development of the physical body and neuromuscular skills. The *affective domain* involves the acquisition of attitudes, appreciations, and values. Chapter 5 includes an in-depth discussion of each domain.

TABLE 4.1 Characteristics and Interests of Children in Fourth, Fifth, and Sixth Grades

Characteristics and Interests	Program Guidelines
PSYCHOMOTOR DOMAIN	
Steady growth. Girls often grow more rapidly than boys.	Continue vigorous program to enhance physical development.
Muscular coordination and skills improving. Interested in learning detailed techniques.	Continue emphasis on teaching skills through drills, lead-up games, and free practice periods. Emphasize correct form.
Differences in physical capacity and skill development.	Offer flexible standards so all find success. In team activities, match teams evenly so individual skill levels are less apparent.
Posture problems may appear.	Include posture correction and special posture instruction; emphasize effect of body carriage on self-concept.
Sixth-grade girls may show signs of maturity. May not wish to participate in all activities.	Have consideration for their problems. Encourage participation on a limited basis, if necessary.
Sixth-grade boys are rougher and stronger.	Keep sexes together for skill development but separate for competition in certain rougher activities.
COGNITIVE DOMAIN	
Want to know rules of games.	Include instruction on rules, regulations, and traditions.
Knowledgeable about and interested in sport and game strategy.	Emphasize strategy, as opposed to merely performing a skill without thought.
Question the relevance and importance of various activities.	Explain regularly the reasons for performing activities and learning various skills.
Desire information about the importance of physical fitness and health-related topics.	Include in lesson plans brief explanations of how various activities enhance growth and development.
AFFECTIVE DOMAIN	
Enjoy team and group activity. Competitive urge strong.	Include many team games, relays, and combatives.
Much interest in sports and sport-related activities.	Offer a variety of sports in season, with emphasis on lead-up games.
Little interest in the opposite sex. Some antagonism may arise.	Offer coeducational activities with emphasis on individual differences of all participants, regardless of sex.
Acceptance of self-responsibility. Strong increase in drive toward independence.	Provide leadership and followership opportunities on a regular basis. Involve students in evaluation procedures.
Intense desire to excel both in skill and physical capacity.	Stress physical fitness. Include fitness and skill surveys both to motivate and to check progress.
Sportspersonship a concern for both teachers and students.	Establish and enforce fair rules. With enforcement include an explanation of the need for rules and cooperation if games are to exist.
Peer group important. Want to be part of the gang.	Stress group cooperation in play and among teams. Rotate team positions as well as squad makeup.

Source: Victor P. Dauer and Robert P. Pangrazi, *Dynamic Physical Education for Elementary School Children* (New York: Macmillan, 1986).

The secondary school years consist of a constantly evolving period of growth and development in which the characteristics change only in degree.[2] Exercise caution, however, in defining all students in terms of these norms. Since students are continuously growing and developing, all students do not fit the norm for a particular grade level. Students in one grade level may be as much as eleven months different in age, not counting older students who have been held back. Even students of the same age mature at different rates; therefore, seldom are all children or youth of a given group at exactly the same stage of growth and development. Common characteristics of children and youth serve as a general guide for making curriculum decisions for the school.

Review Question: What are the common characteristics of children and youth?

TABLE 4.2 Characteristics and Interests of Adolescents in Middle or Junior High School and High School

Middle or Junior High School

Characteristics and Interests	Program Guidelines
PSYCHOMOTOR DOMAIN	
Widely differing maturation levels among students:	Adjust activities for dramatic differences in sizes and skill levels of students.
Maturation of girls about 1.5 years before boys.	Distribute players to teams based on size or height.
Emergence of secondary sex characteristics.	Be aware of self-consciousness of students. Avoid awkward situations.
First girls and then boys are taller and heavier.	Consider differences in boys and girls when evaluating progress.
Differences in strength, flexibility, balance, and endurance between boys and girls.	Students must be helped to accept the dramatic differences in physical maturation they possess and understand that they are normal. Provide activities to develop health-related fitness.
Poor coordination, low strength and endurance, a greater need for sleep, and increased appetite as a result of growth spurts.	Provide opportunities for developing coordination and skill in a variety of activities. Avoid calling attention to awkwardness.
Bone ossification not yet complete.	Provide supervision to avoid injuries.
Posture affected by peer pressure.	Teach correct posture and body mechanics. Guard against fatigue.
Growth rapid and uneven. Energy absorbed in growth process.	Test for structural deviations such as kyphosis and scoliosis.
COGNITIVE DOMAIN	
Increased attention span and ability to handle complex concepts and abstract thinking.	Teach the *why* of concepts regarding biomechanics, motor learning, exercise physiology, etc. Promote creative thinking and problem solving.
Increased interest in possible career options.	Teach the importance of physical activity throughout life.
Increased interest in societal problems.	Promote leadership and followership through cooperative, democratic living.
Wide range of experiences due to travel, TV, and family mobility.	Avoid talking down to students.
AFFECTIVE DOMAIN	
Desire for independence from adults. Often critical of adults.	Help students learn responsibility, leadership and decision-making strategies, and the value of rules in their lives. Help students develop self-confidence and feelings of personal worth.
Vacillation between adult and peer-group values.	Provide approval from both peers and adults. Emphasize high ethical standards.
Interest in impressing the peer group and opposite gender.	Provide social interaction in classes and extracurricular activities to help students develop social and leadership skills. Provide success experiences in basic skills.
Interest in and self-consciousness about own bodies, appearance, and abilities.	Help students understand physiological changes, capacities, and limitations and provide help with grooming, clothes, appearance, weight control, physical fitness, weight training, and nutrition. Be aware of student self-consciousness and embarrassment dressing in front of peers.
Moody and easily angered or upset.	Help students learn strategies for emotional control and stress reduction.
Eager to try new things.	Introduce new activities. Satisfy need for adventure in socially acceptable ways.
Competitive.	Provide a balance between cooperative and competitive activities.

TABLE 4.2 Continued

High School	
Characteristics and Interests	**Program Guidelines**
PSYCHOMOTOR DOMAIN	
Physical maturity results in higher levels of motor ability and fitness, with boys ending up bigger, faster, and stronger than girls.	Use different evaluation standards for boys and girls.
Large appetites continue, but some girls restrict intake.	Be aware of incidence of anorexia nervosa and bulimia among girls.
Coordination improves. Interest in personal development continues.	Develop increased specialization in lifetime activities.
COGNITIVE DOMAIN	
Reaching full intellectual potential. Increased knowledge and experience base.	Teach concepts regarding the *why* of biomechanics, motor learning, exercise physiology, etc. Promote creative thinking and problem solving.
Continued interest in societal problems.	Promote leadership and followership through cooperative, democratic living.
Narrowing of career options and lifetime choices.	Teach the importance of physical activity throughout life. Provide opportunities to develop increased specialization in activities of their own choosing.
AFFECTIVE DOMAIN	
Peer-group and dating activities dominate social lives of students.	Provide appropriate social activities with opportunities to learn leadership and social-interaction skills.
Continued conflict between youth and adult values; highly critical of adults and peers.	Provide both peer and adult approval. Help students develop a personal value system.
Interest in personal appearance and social skills.	Help students with ways to improve themselves and to impress others.
Interest in new activities, adventure, and excitement.	Help students choose appropriate risk activities; avoid drugs, etc.
Emotional conflicts continue.	Help students learn stress-reduction techniques.
Increased competitiveness in dating, grades, and athletics.	Provide activities that involve a balance between cooperation and competition.

SIGNIFICANT DIFFERENCES AMONG STUDENTS

Considerable differences exist among students both within and across age and grade levels with regard to (1) physical growth and development, (2) intellectual development, (3) emotional development, and (4) social development. At the elementary-school level, a span of four to five years can exist in student achievement in a single class. Greater variability exists at the secondary school level.[3]

Students are becoming increasingly diverse. A majority of students in the largest school districts are minority students.[4] In one large city, students speak eighty-two different languages. There is an increasing spread between the rich and the poor. The number of children with disabilities is also increasing. Much of this growth is due to an increase in the diagnosis of learning disabilities.[5] Approximately 10 percent of students have disabilities.[6] During the decade of the 1990s, the practice became inclusion and acceptance of all students as much as possible.[7] A knowledge of individual differences is essential to teachers planning to individualize instruction in their classes.

Physical Growth and Development

Growth and development depend on heredity and environment. Because of improved nutrition and better health care, today's children grow up faster. Both boys and girls are taller and heavier and mature earlier than children of previous generations. They can expect the longest life expectancy ever known.

Adolescence is a "clash between culture and biology." Adults try to pass on the culture to children who are struggling with maturing bodies and childlike emotions.[8] Although adolescence begins earlier than it used to, the economic and educational requirements of a technological

The goal of education is to provide a quality educational experience for every student, as different as those students are.

society force it to end later. As a result, activities that used to be reserved for older students are now handed down to younger students. This leaves older students frustrated because nothing new is left for them to try, and yet they are not allowed to assume the privileges and responsibilities of adulthood. Teachers face the challenge of trying to help students cope with the physical and emotional changes that affect them.

Adolescents differ widely in physical growth and capacity. Some children are early bloomers; others mature much later. They vary widely in body build and physical capacity. Although boys and girls at the elementary school level have no significant physiological differences, great variability exists between the sexes and within each sex during the middle and junior high school years. Griffin and Placek summarize these differences as follows:

> Girls have begun or are completing puberty and are growing and maturing rapidly. Most boys have not begun their growth spurt and in the early junior high years most still possess late childhood characteristics. Thus, in all the physical categories described for 7–9 graders, teachers will see a wide range of characteristics in their students. Height and weight, aerobic capacity, and body proportions will vary depending upon each individual student. With the onset of puberty girls will gain additional body fat. Hip width will also increase in girls, while boys' shoulder width will increase. In effect, boys end up with wider shoulders and narrower hips than girls, whose proportions are the reverse, with wider hips and narrower shoulders. Boys will begin to attain additional muscle mass toward the latter part of junior high.[9]

Because of the variability among students, they should not be automatically grouped by sex for physical education activities. Griffin and Placek summarize the data about students at the high school level as follows:

> At this age level (14 to 18 years) most girls are physically mature and boys are rapidly growing toward adult size. Therefore, most boys will be taller and heavier and have more muscle mass. Boys' heart and lung sizes are larger than the girls', thus increasing their aerobic capacity. Most girls again have a greater percentage of body fat, wider hips, and narrower shoulders in relation to boys. Boys have longer leg length in proportion to trunk length. As adults, the average female has about 2/3 the strength of the average male. . . .
>
> This information gives teachers guidelines about what to expect of students at different developmental levels. However, these studies also show that there is great variation within each gender from the average for each gender. Moreover, there is overlap between the comparisons of girls and boys. This means that even though there may be *average* differences between the genders on physical characteristics, in any physical education class there will also be a full range of variation and overlap in physical characteristics. There will be tall girls, short boys, strong girls, weak boys, strong boys, heavy girls and thin girls. It is important for teachers concerned with equity to teach *individual* students regardless of gender, not *average* boys or girls.[10]

Motor ability factors—such as agility, balance, coordination, flexibility, strength, and speed—predispose some students to success in some motor activities and others to success in other activities. Body build, muscle composition, and respiratory capacity help some students to be better long-distance runners and others to be better sprinters or jumpers. Other factors that vary include visual and auditory acuity, perception, and reaction time. Physical disabilities enlarge the differences among students.

Because of the wide variety of individual differences among students, excellent physical education programs include a variety of activities so that students will find some commensurate with their individual abilities. By providing different levels of activity, students are challenged to extend their abilities, yet they experience success during the learning process.

Intellectual Development

Today's youth are better informed than ever before. Preschools; television; books, newspapers, and magazines; and widespread travel have increased the information available to today's adolescents. As a result, children and adolescents are not easily impressed. They have seen it all. However, young people have so much information and so many choices in dress, lifestyle, courses, occupations, and values that they are confused about what information to process and how to make the decisions that confront them. They must be helped to develop problem-solving skills if the school is going to be of value to them.[11]

Intellectual development can be impaired by the failure of some students to take advantage of instruction. For a few students, physical or emotional disabilities disturb learning. However, even as the number of disabled students is decreasing, the number of so-called learning disabled students has nearly doubled since 1977.[12] Many of these learning disabled students may suffer from a late start, after which the self-fulfilling prophecy takes effect; that is, students who are labeled "slow learners" gradually begin to see themselves as such. Bereiter concluded that

> for any sort of learning, from swimming to reading, some children learn with almost no help and other children need a great deal of help. Children whom we have been labeling as educationally disadvantaged are typically children who need more than ordinary amounts of help with academic learning. . . . From this point of view, a successful compensatory education program is one that gives students plenty of help in learning.[13]

Social Development

Adolescence is characterized by a change in social interaction patterns and a challenging of parental and authority roles. A basic need of adolescents is to learn to accept responsibility for their actions and to demonstrate self-discipline before asking for greater freedom.[14] Early adolescents are predominantly interested in groups of friends of the same sex. They are in a process of relinquishing old ties and establishing new ones in an attempt to gain independence and a new identity. Peer approval at this stage is more important than parental approval. Peers become sounding boards for ideas and controversial topics. However, adults are still important for helping adolescents test their newly formed theories. Adolescents who transfer their dependence on their parents to dependence on the group fail to develop the independence needed for mature behavior and personal self-worth. Gangs can be detrimental due to the artificial interaction patterns of the youth involved, both the leaders and the followers, as well as the failure to learn appropriate procedures for conflict resolution. Youth who are economically disadvantaged and affluent youth whose parents lavish them with material goods rather than with personal attention and love often have more difficulty adapting to appropriate interaction patterns.

The influence of the peer group, coupled with a desire for adventure, often leads adolescents into situations incompatible with their level of judgment. A lack of judgment often results in an increase in the number of accidents among this age group.[15]

During the middle phase of adolescence, same-sex peer groups decrease in size and become cliques, which emphasize certain modes of dress and behavior. Popularity and conformity to group norms is important. In the normal development process, youth gradually discard group choices for individual selection. During this phase, teenagers often identify with the parent of the opposite sex as well as develop friends of the opposite sex. Problems arise between boys and girls of the same ages because of different rates of maturation.

During late adolescence, young adults limit friends of the same sex to a few "best" friends, and they continue to develop romantic relationships with friends of the opposite sex. In addition, they become more friendly with adults on a new level. They learn to accept the flaws of friends and adults and to understand that "nobody is perfect."

Emotional Development

A critical factor in adolescent development is the ability to build and maintain feelings of personal worth and belonging. Self-esteem and self-confidence have to do with a belief in one's own worth and positive attitudes toward one's own abilities. To understand and accept other people, individuals first must learn to understand and accept themselves. The foundation for self-esteem and self-confidence is laid in infancy. Love leads to trust and a sense of being acceptable and worthwhile.

One of the tasks of adolescence is a search for a new self. Adolescents struggle with changes in physical appearance, such as being too tall, too short, too fat, too skinny; having acne; or anything else that makes them feel different or unacceptable. Hormonal changes bring on personality and mood changes, and responses vary from excitement to depression. Students fluctuate between childlike and adult emotions and behavior in an attempt to establish a new state of independence from parents while maintaining their needs for adult approval and affection. Youth spend a lot of energy "trying on" different personalities in an attempt to find the one that suits them.[16] For example, they lose or add nicknames or change from a first to a middle name. They experiment with new styles of penmanship, dress, and behavior. Unhappiness results when they fail to match up with the ideal self they envision. All of these adjustments lead to emotional stress. Thus, adolescents need time alone to reflect on and examine themselves. When a young adult learns to accept his or her physical body, public personality, and inner self, a mature personality emerges.

Once the self-concept is formed and internalized, the person tends to nurture it by seeking experiences to validate it. For example, if John feels he is a failure, he will continue to fail, since that supports his image of himself. To change a student's self-concept, significant people in the student's life, such as family, friends, neighbors, and teachers need to provide encouragement and acceptance over a long period of time. Because the self-concept is long-lasting, even minor changes for the better should be applauded. Combs noted that students take their self-concepts with them wherever they go. Everything that happens to them affects their self-concepts. We need to ask ourselves how people can feel liked, wanted, and accepted unless somebody likes, wants, and accepts them? How can they feel they are persons with dignity and integrity unless somebody treats them accordingly? How can people feel capable unless they experience success? In the answers to those questions, he indicates, we will find the answers to the human side of learning.[17]

Adolescents are extremely concerned about social injustices. Unless knowledge and skills are related to students' attitudes, feelings, and beliefs about themselves and their fears and concerns about the community that surrounds them, education probably will have only a limited influence on their behavior. Instruction, then, becomes a matter of linking the cognitive and psychomotor aspects of the curriculum to the intrinsic feelings and concerns of the students. When these feelings and experiences are validated for students, students believe they are worthwhile.

Various personality characteristics cause students to feel more comfortable in one activity than another. Hartman developed the Color Code system to explain why people act in different ways. Red personalities are motivated by power and productivity and work hard to succeed in life. Blue personalities are committed to a strong code of ethics and are loyal, devoted, and nurturing friends. Yellow personalities embrace life as a party. They are very social and active, yet sensitive to others. Whites are motivated by peace and kindness. They like to be quietly independent and do their own thing in their own time. Learning about the personality characteristics of themselves and their students helps teachers understand how to deal more effectively with students and to help them in their relationships with each other.[18]

The aggressive, competitive, social student might prefer participation in a team sport, whereas the cooperative, passive loner might prefer engaging in a jogging or cycling program. Some students suffer from anxiety that limits their capacity for self-fulfillment and need activities to build up their confidence and help them become self-directing.[19]

Learning Styles

Learning styles refer to a learner's preferred way of attending to and absorbing information. A learning style is, in reality, a group of individual physiological, cognitive, psychosocial, and affective traits that determine how students perceive and respond to the learning environment. Physiological traits affect student preferences for noisy or quiet, bright or subdued, mobile or immobile environments, while psychosocial traits affect preferences for working alone or in groups. Most of the research relates to cognitive styles.

One system classifies learners as field-dependent or independent. *Field-dependent* individuals are socially oriented and have high levels of self-esteem. They respond to external stimuli, such as faces and social cues, and choose people-oriented professions. They prefer externally defined goals, structure, external reinforcement, and a minimum of criticism. *Field-independent* people are sensitive to internal cues, tend toward a more impersonal orientation, have less self-esteem, and choose abstract-oriented fields. They prefer to select their own goals and are intrinsically motivated.[20]

Another classification system utilizes methods of reasoning. Children who group a table and chairs together because they both have four legs are using an *analytic* style, while those who group them together because both are used for dining demonstrate a *global or relational* style. Cohen hypothesized that many low-socioeconomic-level children function with a relational style, thereby creating a cultural mismatch with the analytic style of the schools.[21] Standardized intelligence tests measure students' analytic styles.

Brain hemisphericity studies relate to cognitive style. Most students use the left hemisphere and employ a reflective, analytic style. Some, however, use a global style reflective of the right hemisphere and tend to be more impulsive and want to do things in different ways. While right-brained students learn better through visual, holistic, "hands-on" methods, the majority of teachers teach in a left-brain, structured, "one right answer" verbal mode. The implication is that all students can succeed if helped to use their own natural processes for learning.[22]

While most schools focus on linguistic and logical abilities, Gardner believes that individuals are born with different intelligence profiles and use their unique profiles to solve problems. He identified the eight intelligences shown in Table 4.3. The first two form the basis for IQ and standardized achievement tests. His purpose was to show that individuals possess different strengths and weaknesses and that schools should help students develop all of their intelligences, while also helping them reach vocational and avocational goals that are appropriate to their particular intelligence profiles.[23]

It would be difficult, if not impossible, for a teacher to match the learning styles of several hundred students a day. How can an instructor utilize information on learning styles? The answer appears to be to create an environment in which different learning styles can be accommodated and then empower the learner to become an active participant in the learning process. Gardner suggests that it is impossible to learn everything, so students should be helped to experiment with activities that utilize the different intelligences so they understand their strengths and weaknesses and preferred learning styles.[24] Then they can make informed choices about what and how to learn. The intelligences can serve as a means to acquire new information. In addition, the content itself may fit within the realm of an intelligence. Using a variety of entry points to introduce new material helps all learners move more quickly toward the desired competencies. Table 4.4 illustrates one way to involve the various intelligences or learning styles in instruction. Projects, portfolios of one's best work, and process folios that document the learning process can be used as learning experiences and to assess the results of learning. Assessment strategies are presented in Chapter 11.

Review Questions: Outline the significant differences among students—physically, socially, and emotionally.

How do differences in personalities and learning styles affect instruction?

TABLE 4.3 Gardner's Eight Intelligences

Intelligence	Examples	Preferences	Teaching methods
Linguistic—verbal	Authors, poets, speakers, reporters, attorneys, politicians	Read, write, tell stories	Verbal learners—listening, note taking, memorizing, writing
Logical-mathematical—abstract thinking	Mathematicians, engineers, physicists, astronomers, chemists	Experiment, explore, ask questions, math reasoning, problem solving	Reasoning, problem solving, categorizing, classifying, experimenting
Spatial—ability to form a mental model of a spatial world	Sailors, engineers, surgeons, sculptors, painters, architects, cartographers	Draw, build, do puzzles, read maps and charts, watch movies	Visual learners—looking at videos, pictures; designing and creating
Musical	Musicians, composers	Sing, listen to music, play instruments	Recognizing sounds and rhythms, clapping, composing
Bodily-kinesthetic—solve problems or fashion products using one's body	Dancers, athletes, surgeons, craftspeople	Moving, gesturing, sports, dance, crafts, acting	Doing, touching, moving, interacting with space; role playing; using the senses
Interpersonal—understand other people: what motivates them, how they work, how to work with them	Salespeople, politicians, teachers, clinicians, religious leaders	Socializing	Group activities—organizing, communicating, leading, sharing
Intrapersonal—capacity to form an accurate picture of one's own feelings, strengths, weaknesses, and use it to guide one's own behavior	Philosophers, psychologists, novelists	Work alone, pursue own interests	Individual projects, self-paced learning
Naturalist—absorbed in natural things in the world	Forest rangers, animal trainers, botanists, zoologists	Interact with animals; watch insects, birds, plants, fish	Hands-on in the natural environment

Source: Howard Gardner, *Frames of Mind: The Theory of Multiple Intelligences* (New York: Basic Books, 1983), 71–72, 386–89; Howard Gardner, *Multiple Intelligences: The Theory in Practice: A Reader* (New York: Basic Books, 1997), 8, 203–7, 224–26, 334; J. K. Rogers, Quadrillion Consulting, 3488 N. Foothill Dr., Provo, UT 84604.

TABLE 4.4 Teaching to Include Various Learning Styles and Intelligences

	Teaching Techniques	Learning Activities
Teach why	Introduce the subject and connect it to the students' previous experience. Tell why the students are learning this and what it has to do with their lives now and in the future. Generate enthusiasm.	Stories, experiences, class discussion, role playing, simulation, journal writing.
Teach what	Provide information in an organized manner. Provide time for thinking and reflection.	Lecture (rule of thumb: never longer than the age of the student); provide outline, study guides, copies of notes and visual aids—graphs, charts, statistics; textbook assignments; cues.
Teach how	Provide opportunity for students to apply the material. Provide opportunities to fail safely.	Guided practice, homework, labs, tests, reports, demonstrations, simulations, esthetic experiences, role playing.
Teach application to real-life context	Provide opportunity to try what they have learned in new situations.	Real-life or simulated individual or group projects.

Source: Adapted from J. N. Harb, R. E. Terry, P. K. Hurt, and K. J. Williamson, *Teaching through the Cycle* (Provo, UT: Brigham Young University Chemical Engineering Department, n.d.).

SOCIAL FORCES THAT AFFECT STUDENTS

Rapid changes in society can have a detrimental effect on youth. Increased mobility has taken families away from relatives and friends. Dramatic role changes for men and women confuse some young people as to what is expected of them. Values and morals change constantly and are no longer a stabilizing force in American society.

The following statistics are evidence of how today's students are influenced by society's changes. Three to four million children have been exposed to damaging levels of lead. From 15,000 to 30,000 children have been infected with HIV (human immunodeficiency virus). Of the 37,000 babies born each year weighing less than three and one-half pounds who will live long enough to leave the hospital, many will face substantial learning problems. Learning capabilities will be affected for the 350,000 newborns per year that are exposed prenatally to drugs, including alcohol.[25] The American Health Foundation determined that in 1992, for each 100,000 teenagers aged fifteen to nineteen there were 837 new cases of gonorrhea. About twelve children per day are victims of homicide in the United States. Mental disorders afflicted about eight million children aged eighteen and younger.[26] Surveys of adolescents twelve to seventeen years old found that in the thirty days prior to the survey, 19 percent had used alcohol, 10 percent had used illicit drugs, and 7.7 percent had engaged in binge drinking.[27] Thirty-three percent had ridden with a driver who had been drinking. In the previous two weeks, 32 percent of high school seniors sampled reported engaging in binge drinking, and 28.5 percent of high school students had smoked cigarettes one or more days.[28] Somewhere between 14 and 27 percent of all young people drop out of school prior to high school graduation. Approximately one million children and youth are homeless.[29]

Deterioration of the Family

Many of the preceding problems have resulted from the deterioration of the family, with one out of every four children being raised by a single parent.[30] Nearly half of our children will live in single-parent families before they reach age eighteen. Only about 6 percent of U.S. households consist of a "normal" family, with a working father, a housewife mother, and two school-age children.[31]

Divorce, death, and births to unwed mothers result in many mother-only households with significantly lower income than those of two-parent homes.[32] Each year 8.7 percent of all births are to single, teenage mothers.[33] This results in 500,000 children each year born to teenage mothers and 3.3 million children today living with teenage mothers. Approximately one in every five (twelve million) children is being raised in poverty.[34]

According to a study by Dornbusch and his colleagues, adolescents in single-parent households have a significantly higher level of deviant behavior than those in families with two natural parents.[35] In many other homes, both parents work outside the home, leaving the children to fend for themselves. More than half of all mothers of children under six and almost 70 percent of mothers of children between six and seventeen were working or seeking work.[36] *Latchkey* children (a term describing the house keys they often wear hanging around their necks) leave home after their parent(s) have gone to work or come home to an empty house, or both. Estimates of the number of latchkey children range from 1.8 to 15 million.[37] These children come from all socioeconomic levels.

Social consequences arising from unsupervised youth include crime (especially shoplifting) and drug abuse. Individual consequences include fear, loneliness, boredom, accidents, child molestation, rape, and teen suicide, not to mention the fear and guilt experienced by parents. Unsupervised access to the Internet increases opportunities for viewing pornography and locating ways to commit violence. Academic achievement may or may not be affected.[38]

Some solutions to this lack of supervision include programs offered by community organizations, parent groups, social service agencies, youth groups, private industry, schools, churches, private day-care centers, and worksite centers. Some employers offer flexible work times. Volunteer tutors after school hours, after-school playground programs, and phone-a-friend or tutor hotlines have all proven helpful. However, legal liability, money, and a lack of policies regarding these programs have limited their availability for all children.

Implications for teachers include the need to structure homework more carefully, to provide homework hotlines and web pages, and to take time to listen to the concerns of youth. Emergency procedures for contacting working parents and the establishment or support of extended-care programs enhance the working relationship between parents and the school.[39]

The remainder of this section will discuss drug abuse, suicide, child abuse, the current youth culture, at-risk youth, and the role of media in childhood obesity.

Drug Abuse

Many youth first experiment with tobacco, alcohol, and illicit drugs during early adolescence. Almost 74 percent of adults aged twenty-one or older started drinking prior to age twenty-one (4 percent before age 12, 15 percent between 12 and 14 years old, 33 percent between 15 and 17 years old, and 22 percent between 18 and 20 years old). Of 14 million adults with alcohol dependence or abuse, 13 million (95 percent) started drinking before age twenty-one. Those who use alcohol before age fifteen are five times more likely to report dependence or abuse than those for whom first alcohol use occurred after age twenty-one.[40] Initial drug use usually occurs between the ages of twelve and eighteen.[41] "Teenagers in the United States have the highest rate of drug abuse of any industrialized country in the world."[42] Commonly abused drugs include tobacco, alcohol, narcotics, depressants, stimulants, hallucinogens, and marijuana. Although adults have been smoking less, teenagers (especially girls) have been smoking more. If current smoking patterns continue, 6.4 million people currently younger than eighteen will die prematurely from a tobacco-related disease.[43] Other harmful practices include inhaling glue, gasoline, paint, and aerosol fumes and the use of chewing tobacco or "snuff." Synthetic drugs or analogs of controlled or illegal drugs can have potencies thousands of times those of their natural counterparts and often result in brain damage or death. Increasingly, youth are indiscriminately mixing drugs such as alcohol and barbiturates that can result in respiratory and heart failure or violent behavior.[44]

Drugs cripple or kill young people or ruin young lives, physically and emotionally. In addition to the personal harm resulting from drug use, many drug addicts steal, assault, prostitute themselves, and sell drugs to others to support their habits. Drugged and drunken drivers maim or kill tens of thousands of people each year. Drug use also can precipitate violent, senseless crimes.[45]

Precipitators of drug abuse are similar to those for other dysfunctional behaviors and include (1) stress, (2) skill deficiencies, (3) situational constraints, and (4) changes in the nuclear family. All of these factors interact with one another and can contribute separately or collectively to problem behavior.[46]

Adolescents today experience a great deal of stress, isolation, and alienation. Adolescence is a painful period, in which the body, mind, and emotions change drastically. New roles and increased expectations by teachers and parents create feelings of inadequacy. Postman and Elkind both focused attention on the disappearance of childhood from the life cycle.[47] Norwood added:

> Caught in this frustrated age of development, today's children experiment with behaviors thought to be adultlike with little ability to ascertain the good and bad of such behavior. . . . Thus, the role-modeling of adult behavior encouraged in today's society pressures children to engage in alcohol consumption, smoking, illicit drug use, sexual intercourse, and other roles they perceive to be adult. "Sooner is better" is a message received by our children. . . . The rationale behind pressuring children to achieve beyond their age and normal expectations must be re-examined.[48]

Youth have been superficially exposed to so many adult activities and privileges that by the time they are in their midteens they are already bored and have nothing to look forward to. Many respond by escaping to drugs, delinquency, or religious cults.

In addition to the factors just mentioned, stress may come from the loss of a parent or friend, rejection or failure, family conflict, or abuse. People vary greatly in their abilities to cope with stress. The more stress they can tolerate, the less likely they are to turn to drugs.[49]

Youth who have the ability to face problems realistically and attack them systematically are not likely to get involved with drugs, whereas those who deny or blame others for their problems, run away from their problems, or expect others to solve them are especially vulnerable. Skills needed to resist drug use include problem solving, realistic self-assessment, and communication skills. People suffering from feelings of inferiority or powerlessness may turn to drugs for the false sense of confidence or power they create.[50]

The medical revolution has led to the acceptance of drugs as chemical "miracles" and the widespread availability of prescription drugs to "cure" the ills of society. People encounter drugs everywhere they look—television, movies, newspapers, sports, and music. Television commercials and programming sell youth on drugs and alcohol and the need to look better, feel better, or escape from their humdrum lifestyle. The "me"-oriented generation focuses on pleasure, leisure activities, and winning. The need to be first in everything can result in the use of drugs to stay awake, lose weight, or ward off stress. The widespread availability and the casual acceptance of drugs place people in situations in which drug use seems desirable. At-risk youth find themselves in many situations in which drug use is expected and supported.[51]

Children who grow up in well-adjusted, happy homes are less prone to use drugs than those who come from troubled environments. Parents who use alcohol and other drugs are poor role models for their children. Changes in the family unit have forced many youth into early independence and precipitated feelings of loneliness. These youth passively accept a way of life they see as meaningless, with a constricted expression of emotion, a low threshold of boredom, and an apparent absence of joy in anything not immediately consumable such as music, sex, drugs, and possessions. Youth who find no purpose in life and believe that life is dull, uneventful, or boring may turn to drugs for the "thrill" it affords them.[52] Table 4.5 lists factors that might increase or decrease usage of tobacco, alcohol, and illicit drugs.

Although adolescents can exhibit strange behaviors without being on drugs, some signs of drug use might include a sudden unwillingness to follow parental rules, a decline in academic achievement, increased truancy and class cutting, an endless need for money, evidence of drugs or drug paraphernalia, major changes in interpersonal relationships, inappropriate clothing habits for the weather conditions, aggressive behavior, loss of interest in former activities or friends, failure to fulfill responsibilities, and physical or mental deterioration—in short, any sudden and unexplained change in behavior, appearance, or personality.[53] Evidence of drug use could include redness of the skin and eyes; burns on the thumb and fingertips; drug particles on teeth or clothing or protruding from pockets; large numbers of matches; use of excessive deodorant, aftershave lotion, gargles, and breath fresheners to disguise telltale odors; increased illness; or emotional outbursts.[54]

When teachers suspect drug use, they are obligated, if not legally then ethically and professionally, to do something about it. When school personnel act in good

TABLE 4.5 Factors Effecting Usage of Tobacco, Alcohol, and Illicit Drugs

Increased Rate of Use of Tobacco, Alcohol, and Illicit Drugs
• Lower family income[a]
• Student has run away or slept on the street
• Live in rural area
• Received grades of D or below previous semester
• Increased risk of suicide
• Live in neighborhood with following characteristics: crime, drug selling, street fights, abandoned buildings, and graffiti[b]
• Participate in violence
Less likely to use drugs:
• Those who participate in one or more school, community, church, faith-based, or other activities[c]
• Have positive school experiences
• Participated in team sports[d]

Sources: [a]Retrieved January 1, 2005, from *http://www.oas.samhsa.gov/2k4/youthIncome/youthIncome.cfm*.
[b]Retrieved January 1, 2005, from *http://www.oas.samhsa.gov/2k4/youth.htm#Drugs*.
[c]Retrieved January 1, 2005, from *http://www.oas.samhsa.gov/2k4/activities/activities.cfm*.
[d]Retrieved January 1, 2005, from *http://www.oas.samhsa.gov/2k4/youth.htm#Drugs*.

faith and show reasonable cause for concern, they are usually protected in the case of a lawsuit.[55] Towers suggested five steps that teachers can take when they suspect a student is abusing drugs:

> (1) Express concern about the youngster's failing grades, moodiness, or other observed behavior; (2) encourage the youngster to seek help and offer to assist in getting that help; (3) if the behavior is extreme or if it persists, notify the parent and similarly express concern over the observed behavior; (4) consult with colleagues about the student and refer the youngster to appropriate staff; and (5) participate in the intervention program if appropriate.[56]

However, he cautioned, if the student is currently under the influence of drugs or alcohol—glazed eyes, extreme lethargy, sleepiness, or mood swings—teachers should avoid confrontation and instead send the youth to the health room or school office.[57]

Students on some drugs may feel invulnerable to pain or injury, have delusions of great strength, or feel threatened by teachers and classmates, who may appear as monsters. In these situations they can be dangerous to themselves and others. In emergencies such as these, Towers suggested that teachers stay calm and avoid threatening the student; immediately notify the office to call for emergency help; try to keep the class quiet or remove the student to a nonstimulating environment; and speak calmly and try to reassure the student that no one intends any harm.[58]

Prevention efforts are best started in the elementary school. Towers and Swett listed three strategies for preventing drug and alcohol abuse. First, education can provide clear and accurate information about drugs and their effects on the individual and help students develop the skills needed to make responsible decisions; cope with stress, responsibility, and peer pressure; and improve self-esteem. Second, students can be helped to find alternative ways to derive pleasure in natural, more socially acceptable, and less harmful ways by engaging in adventure activities, yoga, religion, political action groups, the arts, music, or dancing. Third, school officials can deter drug use by limiting the availability of drugs and imposing stiff, consistent penalties for use, possession, and distribution. Enforcement of school policies and the law can help students accept the consequences of drug-taking activities, rather than having them absolved by caring parents or professionals.[59]

Once students are dependent on drugs, professional treatment is needed, either on a residential or outpatient basis. The sooner the treatment begins, the better the chances for success; therefore, early identification is critical.[60]

School Violence and Suicidal Behavior

School violence and adolescent suicide have become a major concern of parents and educators in the past few years. The number of reported adolescent suicides has jumped 300 percent in the past thirty years.[61] Reported suicides are now second only to accidents as the leading cause of death in youths fifteen to nineteen years of age.[62] Every ninety seconds a teenager attempts suicide, with one succeeding every ninety minutes. In addition, many suicides are not reported due to social stigma or lack of evidence. Adolescents who commit suicide tend to be highly intelligent, physically precocious, and between the ages of fifteen and twenty-four. Some are quiet and uncommunicative. Others are impulsive and delinquent. Many are driven by perfectionism.[63]

Deykin and her associates reported rates of life-threatening behaviors of all types to be similar for boys and girls, although suicide attempts were nearly three times more prevalent among females.[64] However, males are three times more likely than females to actually kill themselves and others because they choose more lethal methods.[65] The three strongest correlates of teenage violence and suicidal behavior are family breakdown, youth unemployment, and decreased religious observance among youth. Youth may be isolated, highly irritable and aggressive, or have maladaptive coping behaviors. Abused teenagers are at high risk for self-destructive behavior.[66] Jacobs proposed a five-stage model to explain adolescent suicidal behavior: (1) a history of problems beginning in early childhood, (2) an escalation of the problems with the onset of adolescence, (3) less and less ability to cope with stress and increasing isolation from others, (4) a "last straw" event (such as breaking up with a boyfriend or girlfriend or the loss of a family member or friend) that leaves few remaining social relationships or little hope for resolving the problems, and (5) a justification of the suicide by the adolescent to himself or herself.[67]

Garfinkel identified three clusters of identifying symptoms for potential suicide victims: (1) academic deterioration; (2) slowing down physically, such as physical complaints or illnesses, changes in eating and sleeping habits, or dropping out of athletics; and (3) withdrawal from peer involvement. Some students signal the intent to commit suicide with verbal remarks about death, suicide themes in writing or artwork, giving away personal belongings, or supposed "accidents" such as wrist-slashing or overdosing on medication.[68] Other behavioral clues include changes in dress and grooming, personality changes, depression, acting-out behaviors, alcohol or drug abuse, running away, sexual promiscuity, and belligerence. Physical educators are often the first ones to suspect a problem. Before death is finally attempted, the adolescent may be silent. Outside interference at this point is no longer desired.[69] Motto suggested several factors for assessing suicidal risk:

1. A prior suicide attempt
2. The degree of detail in the current suicidal plan
3. The extent of feelings of hopelessness
4. The presence of a lethal weapon
5. The presence or threat of a progressively disabling physical illness
6. The presence of a psychotic disorder (including temporary disorders induced by alcohol or drugs)
7. Clues related to termination behavior, such as giving away valued objects or dropping verbal hints about not being present.[70]

Hafen and Frandsen remind teachers, parents, and friends to never ignore threats of violence or suicide. Confront the individual immediately. Listen calmly and evaluate the seriousness of the situation. Help the adolescent realize that the feelings are temporary and will clear up with time and that death is a permanent decision that cannot be reversed. Stay with the youth, eliminate possible resources for committing violence and suicide, and get professional help immediately from a suicide prevention center or hospital. Let the youth know that you care.[71] Garfinkel emphasized establishing a support network with school counselors, psychologists, or social workers to help in this process. He also stressed the importance of teaching youth effective coping styles, including communication and problem solving.[72]

Many of the preceding problems are interrelated. Young people who smoke and drink may also experiment with sex and drugs, and these same students are prone to school failure.[73] Increasing numbers of teenagers below age sixteen are becoming sexually active with high risks of pregnancy, low birth weight infants, and school dropout.[74] Besides the risks of pregnancy, AIDS and other sexually transmitted diseases may infect 25 percent of sexually active teenagers.[75]

Hafen and Frandsen highlighted seven adolescent needs that youth leaders might consider in program planning and implementation:

1. Increased respect from adults
2. More time and involvement from adults
3. More constructive opportunities to experiment with life
4. More help in developing social competence
5. More qualified adult youth leaders
6. More opportunities for moral development
7. Help to find the meaning of life.[76]

Child Abuse

Another problem of epidemic proportions is child abuse. Although the true incidence of child abuse is unknown, estimates of abuse range into millions of cases per year. Cases involving adolescents are less likely to be reported. Child abuse occurs among people of all races, social classes, and religious beliefs. Most abusive parents were abused as children, thus perpetuating a cycle of abuse. In all fifty states, the law requires educators to report suspected child abuse. Educators who report suspected child abuse in good faith (i.e., based on reasonable information) are immune from civil or criminal liability.[77]

Signs of abuse include bruises or other physical injuries not related to normal childhood activities; pain, especially in the genital area; nervous or fearful behavior or fear of going home; inappropriate clothing for weather conditions; malnutrition; untreated sores or cuts; and lack of hygiene.[78] Behavioral symptoms may include a decline in academic achievement, increased absence from school, explicit artwork, anger and hostility, and changes in social interaction patterns. Low self-esteem, depression, and pseudomature sexual behaviors are often seen in adolescents experiencing sexual abuse. Substance abuse and running away from home are common among abused children. Most children are afraid to tell others of their experiences due to embarrassment, fear of repercussions, or fear of not being believed. Victims of sexual abuse are usually girls under the age of seventeen. However, Harrison estimated that one out of four girls and one out of ten boys have been sexually abused before the age of eighteen. Perpetrators are generally males known to the victim.[79]

If you are confronted with the evidence of child abuse, do not act surprised or horrified. Provide support, express concern, and praise the child for displaying the courage to tell about it.[80] Educators can follow the guidelines listed by Roscoe:

1. Show feelings of genuine concern for the student.
2. Make oneself available and provide opportunities to allow the student to talk freely about feelings, fears, and so on.
3. Maintain the student's normal status within the class.

4. Reassure the student that he or she is not responsible for the assault that occurred.
5. Present learning activities that enhance the student's self-concept and self-esteem.
6. Provide experiences that allow student's self-expression and facilitate the constructive venting of emotion.
7. Respect and maintain the student's privacy.
8. Present oneself as a model for appropriate adult-child relationships.
9. Help the student keep fears and anxieties from growing out of proportion.
10. Interact closely and cooperatively with professionals who have been trained to work with sexually abused children (e.g., social workers, police, school psychologists).[81]

Educators must also notify the local department of social services.

Youth Culture

How do today's youth view society and their role in it? In a study of youth culture, students wrote essays about themselves in four themes.[82] First, students search for *family stability and communication.* Students named parents as the major influence in their lives. Even grandparents outranked idols in sports and music in terms of influence. In data collected from eleven thousand eighth through tenth graders, a majority of the respondents said they rely on adult guidance to help them make important decisions about their future or about issues such as sex, drugs, and alcohol.[83] Although television ranked third in terms of influence, preferred shows dealt with family life. The second theme involved *identity problems and loneliness.* Teenagers look for connections and guidance. Third, youth live in a culture that moves at a disturbing pace. Therefore, *living with rapid change* is essential. They look forward to some stability in a changing world. The fourth theme was a *fear of failure.* With the increasing knowledge demands for employment, competition is stiff.

The effects of social forces on individual students depend on their various backgrounds and experiences. For example, ethnic groups' expectations regarding the value of education differ. Likewise, families differ in the cultural experiences they provide, as well as in their goals and interests. Friends, neighbors, and other social groups also influence values and attitudes. Thus, experiences of individual students can be so different that generalities are no longer of use in planning educational programs.

At-Risk Youth

At-risk youth are turned off to traditional school settings. Some are academically inferior students and not goal oriented, which may explain their expulsion from school. They have a low self-concept, and they also feel alienated from their family and society with its rules and regulations.[84]

At-risk students need to know they are important. When teachers take an interest in students, barriers can be broken down. Students feel good about themselves and are motivated to participate in class. Once trust is established, the students can be helped to develop responsible behavior and good decision-making skills. Sparks listed four steps for building self-responsibility and decision-making skills.[85] First, establish a positive environment. Second, help students set achievable goals. Third, provide students with alternatives and allow opportunities to make choices. Students need to commit to decisions if they are to feel responsibility for the outcomes of those decisions. Fourth, students examine the consequences and assume responsibility for their choices. At-risk students look for excuses and blame others or even society in general for situations they cannot control. If even one teacher can help them develop a sense of responsibility, the students will begin to act more responsibly. Throughout this process, the at-risk students must receive positive reinforcement, be treated with respect, and be praised for their efforts in reaching their goals. Rewards rather than punishment are preferred as motivators.[86]

Youth Obesity

In 2004, over 15 percent of six- to nineteen-year-olds were overweight. The number is 30 percent when at-risk students are included. The obesity level among children and youth has tripled in the past twenty years. By some projections morbidity and mortality from obesity may exceed that from cigarette smoking. The medical complications for overweight children include hypertension, type 2 diabetes, respiratory ailments, orthopedic problems, trouble sleeping, and depression. All of these can have an adverse effect on a child's performance in school.

The potential contributions to this problem include

- a reduction in physical education classes and after-school athletic programs,
- increase in availability of sodas and snacks in public schools,
- growth in the number of fast-food outlets,
- the trend toward "super-sizing" food portions in restaurants,
- an increase in the number of highly processed high-calorie and high-fat grocery products.

Many believe that the increase in media and computers may have contributed as well.

During the same twenty years that obesity has tripled, sources of media have increased and have targeted children with their television shows and videos, specialized cable networks, video games, computer activities, and Internet websites. In 2002 children spent five and one half hours per day using media. Much of the media includes advertising targeted at youth and promoting food. A typical child sees 40,000 ads per year on television.

Even with this evidence, a study by the Kaiser Family Foundation found no relationship between the media and obesity. The Foundation did recommend the following:

- Reduce the time children spend with media
- Reduce exposure to food advertising
- Increase the number of media messages promoting fitness and sound nutrition[87]

Review Question: Summarize the social forces that affect students and their families.

MEETING THE NEEDS OF ALL STUDENTS

The goal of education in a democracy is to provide a high-quality educational experience for all students, regardless of their differences. There are boys and girls, low-skilled and highly skilled, slow learners and gifted, nondisabled and disabled, and a large number of different cultural and ethnic backgrounds, including many non-English-speaking students. Added to these are those students labeled "at risk." As students mature, differences among them escalate. Not only must opportunities be provided, but programs must increasingly demonstrate that all students achieve the goals of instruction. At the same time, students have needs in common. Table 4.6 summarizes the ten basic needs of youth.

School statistics show a decline in self-esteem and liking for school as children mature into adolescents. Decreases in academic achievement and increases in nonattendance and disciplinary cases caused teachers and administrators to rethink how schools could be restructured to meet the needs of young adolescents. The result was the introduction of middle schools. In contrast to junior high schools, which consisted of high school schedules imposed on preteens, middle schools were designed to include small learning communities with stable, close relationships with adults and peers. Large schools were divided into smaller schools-within-schools, with teams of students and teachers staying together for longer periods of time and with small groups of students assigned to advisors to ensure that every student is known well by at least one adult. A core academic program focuses on literacy, learning how to think critically, and direction for leading a healthy life, behaving ethically, and assuming the responsibilities of citizenship in a pluralistic society. Instruction focuses on achieving success for all students through flexible instructional time, active and cooperative learning, and provision of adequate resources. Teachers, hired for their expertise in teaching young adolescents, assume control over the instructional program and have greater responsibilities for student performance. Schools work with the community and individual families to improve academic performance through fostering the health and fitness of their students by access to health care and counseling services, and a health-promoting school environment. In return, students often are expected to perform service in their communities.

Communities have adopted the concept of middle schools differently. Some districts place sixth- and seventh-grade students into middle schools and eighth and ninth graders into junior high schools, while others place sixth through eighth graders into middle schools and leave ninth graders in high schools. A few have even tried to change existing junior high schools into middle schools. However, some of these are changed in name only, without adopting the characteristics of high-quality

TABLE 4.6 Ten Basic Needs of Youth

1. **Positive Social Interaction.** Youth want to belong and need opportunities to form positive social relationships with adults and peers.
2. **Safety, Structure, and Clear Limits.** Expectations, structure, and boundaries are important for youth so that they feel secure and also have a clear picture of the areas that they can or cannot explore.
3. **Belonging and Meaningful Involvement in Family, School, Community.** Youth have a desire to be a part of and to participate in activities related to their families, their schools, and their communities.
4. **Creative Expression.** Youth need opportunities to express to others who they are and how they feel. Music, writing, sports, cooking, or other activities help to achieve this goal.
5. **Self-Worth/Giving to Others.** Involvement in meaningful and worthwhile efforts related to larger goals is extremely important to youth.
6. **Physical Activity.** Youth have tremendous energy and require a great deal of physical activity and time for fun.
7. **A Sense of Independence, Autonomy, and Control.** Youth have a desire to mature, become more independent, and exert some control and influence over their lives.
8. **Closeness in Relationships.** Youth need opportunities to form close relationships with peers and adults. They also have a need for relationships with caring adult role models.
9. **A Sense of Competence and Achievement.** It is important for youth to have opportunities to achieve success and to receive recognition.
10. **A Sense of Individualism, Identity, and Self-Definition.** Youth need to have opportunities to become individuals and to define their sense of identity and self-concept based on positive input from others.

Source: Reprinted with permission from the *Journal of Physical Education, Recreation & Dance* 68, no. 9, 1997, p.17. JOPERD is a publication of the American Alliance for Health, Physical Education, Recreation, and Dance, 1900 Association Drive, Reston, VA 20191.

middle schools that are essential to meet the needs of students. Some middle schools have been so successful that junior high and high schools have adopted similar characteristics, such as the "school-within-a-school" concept or block plans, which result in fewer students per teacher.

In the past, physical education programs have perpetuated "a method of teaching that supports a singular learning concept for all students based on one kind of motivation, one style of learning, and one set of learning needs."[88] Physical growth and development, intellectual and emotional development, social forces, and personality factors all suggest that excellent instructional programs must consider various styles of learning. Some principles to consider when planning educational programs include the following:

- Each student is unique, a result of both heredity and environment.
- Each student learns at his or her own rate regardless of how the teacher paces the instruction.
- Students learn many things simultaneously.
- Students learn different things from identical experiences.
- Learning is not a smooth, continuous process. It involves intermittent periods of growth followed by plateaus.
- Students must learn for themselves. The teacher cannot learn for them.
- Students learn best when
  - the learning process involves experiencing and doing;
  - learning is positively and immediately reinforced by success or positive feedback;
  - a wide variety of relevant, meaningful learning experiences are provided at the appropriate level for the maturity of the student;
  - new learning is connected with previous learning;
  - they make choices about how to learn and how to demonstrate the products of learning.

Each of these principles will be discussed in more detail in the following chapters.

There is no room for teachers to maintain stereotypes about certain groups of students. Lack of opportunities for girls, for students of some racial or ethnic groups, and for low-skilled students may have hindered their performance. As Dodds indicated, "No law protects students with less motor ability against the implacable laws of nature which guarantees that in the gym, as in the wider world, the rich simply get richer and the poor get poorer."[89] Programs that equalize opportunities for all students could see a decrease in performance differences.

Mizen and Linton advocated six steps to consider when designing programs to meet the needs of all students.[90] Guidelines for specific populations will be presented at the end of this section.

Prepare an Environment in Which Individual Differences Are Respected and Valued

This is achieved by acknowledging differences among students through class discussions and experiences in which people who are different from each other work together. Students can be taught that teasing is often caused by anxious or insecure behavior around those who are different. Wearing blindfolds or earplugs, looking through petroleum jelly smeared on glasses, or playing with the nondominant hand or foot can help students understand the challenges others face. Focus on what the students can do rather than on what they cannot do.

Eliminate Established Practices That Unwittingly Contribute to Embarrassment and Failure

By adapting activities to meet the needs of all students, the teacher will help students learn faster and experience positive attitudes toward physical activity. Beware of practices that contribute to the failure or embarrassment of some students, such as elimination games, in which the unskilled children who need the most practice sit on the sidelines, or activities in which obese or disabled students cannot compete on equal terms with other students. Do not choose teams in front of the class. Post most-improved scores, rather than just the top scores, so low-skilled students have an equal opportunity for recognition. Change grading policies to meet the needs of the students. "Learn three new skills" would challenge all students in gymnastics, whereas "perform a somersault dismount off the balance beam" might discourage all but a few. Consider a combination of factors rather than just skill alone. All students can improve their physical fitness.

Build Ego Strength

Help students develop self-esteem and self-confidence by providing successful experiences, helping students set realistic expectations, and allowing students to participate at appropriate levels for their abilities. Help students to develop an awareness of their personal strengths.

Teachers communicate their interest in students as individuals not just by words but also through feelings. Within every student lies an inner self that can be reached only when the student extends an invitation. This occurs when the student feels the sincere, unselfish concern of a caring teacher. A teacher who listens to a student sends the student a message, "I care about you. Your feelings are important to me." Listening is different from hearing. It involves putting oneself in the other person's shoes and paying attention with the heart. Listening involves patience and compassion. Encourage the student to express feelings. Note the student's facial expressions, posture, and tone of voice as well as what is said. Hanks wrote:

> The time to listen is when someone needs to be heard. The time to deal with a person with a problem is when he has the problem. . . . Every human being is trying to say something to others, trying to cry out, "I am alive. Notice me! Speak to me! Listen to me! Confirm for me that I am important, that I matter."[91]

Other ways to demonstrate an interest in students include calling them by name and recognizing each student in some way each day. Photos or videotapes of students can be helpful in learning names. Let the students know you want to learn their names and you want them to help you learn them. Jot down identifying characteristics in your roll book. Use games to help learn names. For example, in the name game, students introduce themselves using an adjective that begins with the letter of their name. Each student repeats the names of the previous persons and adds his or her own, for example, "Jumping Miss Jones, Singing Sally, Typing Terry, and I'm Caroling Carolyn." Another way to get acquainted is to have students create name tags. Some ideas include a collage, a personal coat of arms, or a self-commercial, such as a guitar for a student who plays the guitar. When all else fails, assign students to a given court or team and learn the names of one group each day.

Learn something about each student—interests, achievements, hobbies, favorite subject, favorite sport, or family life. Get feedback from students on how they would like their class to be run. A file card or form handed out at the beginning of the year or unit could solicit answers to such questions as these:

1. Most of all, what do you like to do?
2. What is your favorite game, sport, or hobby?
3. What are your expectations of the class? The teacher? Yourself?
4. How would you like the class to be run? How will you help?
5. What would you like me to know about you?

Another technique is to ask students to pair up with a student they do not know and interview their partners for a specified period of time, then take one minute or less to tell something that impressed them about their partners, or to tell about their similarities and differences.

Make it your business to be in strategic places at strategic times—such as the school play or a band concert when a student of yours is participating. Seek opportunities to say "hello" when you see students in the hall or on the street. Compliment students when deserved and appropriate. Emphasize their positive qualities. Sit with students at football games or in the cafeteria. Notice their achievements in other curricular areas such as the school newspaper; music, theater, or dance productions; or in out-of-school service to the community. Share student successes with students, other teachers, and administrators.

One teacher sends a Sunshine Gram home with each student during the first six weeks of school telling something positive about the student. Items such as acts of kindness, improvement, special achievements, and taking responsibility are then noted throughout the year to both students and their parents.[92]

When teaching, adjust the content to student needs and interests. Encourage student involvement and sharing. Make it easy for students to ask questions and make comments. Counsel with individuals regarding fitness and skill test scores so students know where they stand with regard to class goals. Focus your attention on both the skilled and the unskilled. All of them deserve equal time and attention.

Give students an opportunity to accept leadership positions, and rotate positions often. Do not do for students what they can do for themselves. Students can be assigned to greet visitors, demonstrate skills, lead exercises, and issue and set up equipment. Know the current needs and interests of your students. Provide each student with the opportunity for success and recognition.

Sigmund Freud's niece once recalled a mushroom hunt her uncle had during a family outing. By the end of the activity each child had a prize—for the biggest, oddest, smallest, first, last, or other mushroom. Similar awards or recognition could be given to students in physical education or intramural programs. Possibilities include participant of the month, best equipment monitor, best sport, best official, most-improved player or official, or best scorer. Recognition before the class may carry more weight than individual recognition because of the need for peer approval.

One teacher names a most valuable player each day (students are selected in alphabetical order so all have an opportunity), with an appropriate interview about such items as the student's characteristics, talents, cultural characteristics, and favorites, with recognition by teacher and students during the period.[93]

Since self-esteem is linked to body image and skill in physical activities, a program that helps students develop physical fitness and proficiency in activity skills can increase self-esteem and enhance the development of positive attitudes toward physical activity. Since body concept is an important part of self-esteem, students can be taught to define and accept realistic body concepts and to modify factors that can be affected through physical education activities. They can also be helped to respect themselves and others, regardless of appearance.[94] When teachers occasionally engage in skills for which they have little competence or expertise, students learn that other people also have difficulty learning new and unfamiliar skills.

One of the main goals of physical education is to get students to incorporate physical activities into their lifestyles. When students experience successful participation in physical activities in a warm, supportive, positive environment with teachers who care, they are more likely to continue to participate outside of the school setting. A number of different needs stimulate interest in physical activity. These needs may take the form of social affiliation, energy-release, health and well-being, or self-fulfillment. As needs change, so do interests.

Provide Individual Assistance and Keep Students Active

Teachers and parents have the task of helping adolescents direct their energies into socially acceptable activities that also enhance their personal worth. Adults do this by acting as positive role models, with clearly defined values. They establish limits and define procedures so students have the emotional security that comes from knowing what is expected. Gradually, students must learn to accept responsibility for their own actions, to set personal goals, and to learn self-discipline. Adults can facilitate this process.

The buddy system and peer tutoring are excellent ways to help special-needs students. Peer tutors significantly increase academic learning time, physical fitness, and attitudes toward physical education. Peer tutoring creates the best environment for enhancing motor performance for moderately mentally handicapped students. Student aides improve in their understanding and appreciation of disabled students. The Physical Education Opportunity Program for Exceptional Learners (PEOPEL) teams fifteen student aides and fifteen exceptional learners in a one-to-one ratio in physical education classes. The peers are trained to understand the problems of exceptional learners and to help their partners learn. A second method of peer tutoring uses reciprocal teaching, along with modeling and task and criteria sheets. All students serve as tutors and tutees regardless of ability level. This enhances the social interaction skills of both students. Using peers as tutors, rather than teacher assistants, helps students develop social skills with their classmates. Peers can also rotate over to help a student with enrichment or corrective activities. A whole class can act as buddies to a particular student, helping with instruction as needed.[95]

Traditional demonstration and practice strategies may not be appropriate for all students. Teachers can learn to use a variety of teaching styles and activities to meet the diverse learning styles, needs, and interests of students. Student differences are more adequately considered by including both competitive and noncompetitive activities in the curriculum.

Teachers can use one teaching style with the class, such as a practice style, and a different style with an individual student, such as command style. Students with visual impairments could be asked to help demonstrate, with the teacher placing the student's hands on the bat correctly. Students with attention deficits could be assigned a buddy and get started on an activity while the teacher continues with instructions for the class as a whole. Using hand signals along with a whistle helps deaf students start and stop activities. Students can raise their hands to pass the signal along. One way to teach cross-lateral throwing and bowling patterns uses red sweatbands on the throwing arm and red tape on the opposite shoe. The student is taught to step with the red foot to a red line on the floor and to throw with the red arm.[96]

Presenting skills in a developmentally sequential manner enhances opportunities for success. In addition, engaged learning time can be increased by using all balls and equipment available or utilizing alternative teaching stations.

The I CAN program is a published, individualized instructional management system for teaching physical education and associated classroom skills to all children, disabled and nondisabled. It includes a set of sequential performance objectives, assessment instruments, instructional activities, games, class and individual records, and a teacher's implementation guide. These diagnostic and prescriptive teaching resource materials are divided into four program skill areas: associated, primary, sport-leisure, and social.[97] Eight activity notebooks and accompanying films are provided to teach fundamental skills, health, fitness, body management, and aquatics.

Project Active was developed by the Township of Ocean School District, Oakhurst, New Jersey, under the direction of Thomas M. Vodola. Materials assist teachers in the assessment, prescription, and evaluation of the physical and motor needs of disabled students.[98]

Group Students by Ability to Allow for Mastery Teaching

A challenge for every physical educator is to help each student experience success by planning small, sequential steps so that all students can succeed as often as possible. Although this takes time, it is rewarding because students progress more rapidly than they would without the sequential steps, and there are fewer discipline problems. For a discouraged student, even a small success can be a boost, since these students often feel they have never experienced success before. As skills are learned and small successes become big successes, self-esteem begins to increase. Once students begin to experience success, they show a willingness to try new skills, they put forth greater effort, they obtain more success, and the circle continues as shown in Figure 4-1. Conversely, failure results in an unwillingness to try and little or no effort.

Activities can be provided on various skill levels. It is sometimes advisable to group students by ability level within classes to help low-skilled students experience success while at the same time providing a challenge for the more highly skilled. Make sure skills are learned well before moving on to new skills. Provide remedial or challenge activities for students to practice the skills they are learning.

Levels of participation for the same skill can be color coded so the student is working at the red level, then the blue level, and finally the gold level, with improvement

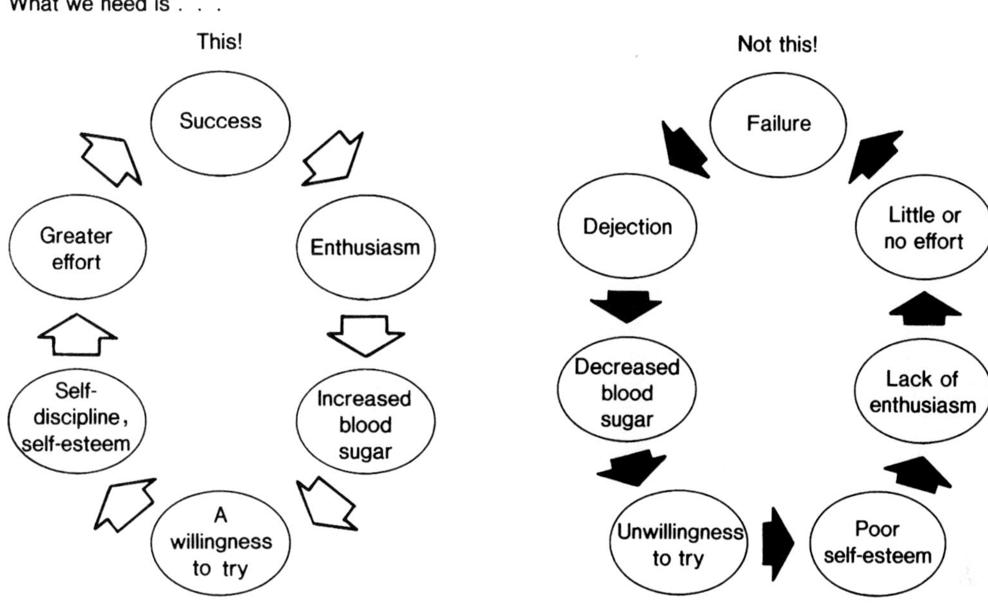

Figure 4-1

Failure and success cycles in students.

Source: Health, Physical Education and Recreation Newsletter, Utah State Office of Education.

leading to success within each level as well as in moving to higher levels. This works especially well for physical fitness and individual sport skills.

Mastery learning, described in Chapter 9, is an excellent way to meet the diverse needs of students while giving all students an opportunity to achieve at a higher level. Individual contracts or units can also be used to individualize instruction.

Alter and Adapt

Most activities can be adapted to meet the needs of students of varying abilities by decreasing time periods; modifying courts, fields, and equipment; and changing the rules. Some activities are more readily adapted than others. The best activities are those in which success or failure does not depend on the ability or performance of another person. Since many secondary schools now offer selective or elective programs, students have the opportunity to select the activities that best meet their needs. Winnick suggested seven ways in which activities can be adapted so that disabled students can participate effectively with their peers.[99] (See Table 4.7.)

Other modifications might include the following:

1. Emphasize cooperative rather than competitive games.
2. Remove elimination games from the curriculum.
3. Decrease the duration of the activity.
4. Increase or decrease the size of game objects (such as balls) or game implements (such as rackets or bats).
5. Increase or decrease the size of the target or hoop.
6. Require that players guard or block only players of the same size.
7. Require that every player on the team touch the ball before a goal is scored.
8. Allow players to choose the implement with which to hit and the object to be hit (softball-type games).
9. Make the pitcher (in softball) a member of the team at bat.
10. Organize tasks into a sequential progression and post them or hand them out to students. Students then choose the tasks to work on based on their levels of readiness and move to the next higher tasks when ready. Teachers can also step in and verbally direct individuals or groups of students to move to higher-level tasks.[100]

Encourage students to modify activities to ensure fair play. For the mentally and/or physically disabled student select games with simple rules and strategies. Rhythms and dance, swimming, and other individual activities are popular with these students.

Since awareness is one of the principal ways for teachers to change, Colvin suggested that teachers videotape themselves, tally skill and behavior feedback to each member of the class, and then ask themselves:

- Am I leaving out some children or groups of children?
- Are most of my interactions related to behavior rather than to skill development?
- Are one or two students demanding my attention?
- Is each student receiving the same information?
- Do I play favorites?
- Do I stay in one area?
- Do I notice students who are not trying?[101]

TABLE 4.7 Seven Ways to Adapt Activities

1. Modify activities to equalize competition by (a) creating "handicaps" for students, as in golf and bowling; (b) changing distance, height of basket, and so on (see inclusion style in Chapter 9); or (c) reducing skill complexity (i.e., kicking a stationary rather than a moving ball).
2. Permit "courtesy" runners (or partner runners for the blind) for students who need them.
3. Include activities in which contact is maintained with a partner, small group, or object (such as square dancing, wrestling, tug-of-war, a rail for bowling). Contact helps some disabled students know what is expected.
4. Modify the activity to require nondisabled students to assume the impairment of the disability (such as using only one leg in a relay or playing blindfolded in a game).
5. Assign positions according to the abilities of the disabled students. (Field hockey goalies and softball pitchers do not have to move quickly and are good position choices for individuals with one leg. Catcher can be a good position for persons with one arm because they do not have to throw quickly.)
6. Limit the size of the playing area by reducing the court size or increasing the number of players on a team.
7. Use audible goals, such as a horn or drum, to allow visually impaired students to compete in relays, basketball, archery, shuffleboard, or softball.

Source: Adapted from J. P. Winnick, Techniques for integration, *Journal of Physical Education and Recreation 49,* no. 6 (1978): 22.

Review Question: How can teachers meet the needs of all students in their classes?

GUIDELINES FOR SPECIFIC POPULATIONS

The Individuals with Disabilities Education Act and Section 504 of the Rehabilitation Act

The education of children with identified disabilities is protected by law. In 1975, PL 94-142 (The Education for All Handicapped Children Act) was passed. This law was renamed and updated under the Individuals with Disabilities Education Act of 1990 (IDEA), PL 101-476, and reauthorized in 1997 and again in 2004. The principal parts of PL 94-142 are maintained in IDEA, along with the mandates of PL 99-457, the Education Amendments of 1986.

One of the main guarantees of all the legislation for disabled students is that all children, regardless of their disability, are entitled to a free, appropriate public education in the least restrictive environment under the direction of a highly qualified teacher. This means that every disabled child must be assured a public education that will meet his or her special needs alongside nondisabled children (as much as possible) at no cost to the parents or guardian. School districts cannot deny services because of the severity of a child's disability. One key factor to remember here is that the child's individual needs, not those of a grouping of students with the same disability, are to be considered in determining the education of the child.[102]

Within IDEA, the only specific subject mentioned is physical education. The act states that "the term special means specially designed instruction, at no cost to parent or guardians, to meet the unique needs of a child with a disability, including . . . instruction in physical education."[103]

According to the law, physical education includes the development of (1) physical and motor fitness; (2) fundamental motor skills and patterns; and (3) skills in aquatics, dance, individual and group games, and sports (including intramural and lifetime sports). In addition, students receiving special education and related services must have access to extracurricular activities, including athletics, that are comparable to those received by their nondisabled classmates. Related services—such as recreation and school health services—or supportive services—such as athletics, physical therapy, or dance therapy—*must* be provided by the district or school or contracted from some other agency if such services are required to assist a disabled student to benefit from special education.

A second federal law that affects physical education programs and facilities is Section 504 of the Rehabilitation Act of 1973 (PL 93-112); the final rules and regulations came out in 1977. This law provides that "no otherwise qualified handicapped individual . . . shall, solely by reason of his handicap, be excluded from participation in, be denied the benefits of, or be subjected to discrimination under any program or activity receiving federal financial assistance."[104]

This law requires schools to provide equal opportunities for the disabled to participate in *all* programs offered by the school, including physical education, intramurals, clubs, and interscholastic athletics. Accommodations, adaptations, and adjustments expected so that individuals with handicapping conditions can participate in regular physical education programs and activities include the following:

1. Accessible buildings and other facilities
2. Appropriate transportation
3. Appropriate curricular adjustments, such as changing competency requirements, eligibility requirements, and rules that discriminate
4. Appropriate adaptations for activities, such as a bowling ramp or beeper balls

The major impact on the schools as a result of the two laws dealing with the disabled is to modify existing curricula to include a wide spectrum of activities for the disabled. In addition, architectural, administrative, and instructional barriers must be removed to allow disabled students access to all programs offered by the schools. Eichstaedt and Kalakian suggest that schools make sure that (1) individuals with disabling conditions are not separated from those without a disabling condition and that (2) individuals with a disabling condition are not indiscriminately placed in special or segregated programs and activities. Doing so violates federal laws and can jeopardize federal funding for the school district.[105]

The Individualized Education Program and the Individualized Transition Program

By law, every student with an identified disability receiving special education and related services must have an Individualized Education Program (IEP). The IEP is used throughout the school year as a guide for teachers (and administrators) to follow in working with individual students with an identified disability. It includes the following:

1. The student's present levels of educational performance
2. Annual goals (long- and short-term) and instructional objectives for that student
3. Specific special services to be provided to the student and the extent to which the student will be able to participate in regular educational programs
4. Projected dates for initiation of and anticipated duration of services
5. Objective criteria and evaluation procedures and schedules
6. Services needed to assist the student in making the transition from school to postschool activities. This may be called an Individual Transition Program (ITP).

IEPs vary in form, length, and detail from one school district to another and from one student to another. A multidisciplinary team writes the IEP. The physical education teacher should be a part of the team when it is apparent that a particular child will need a specially designed physical education program. The physical education teacher can suggest goals, modifications, and other items that need to be addressed in developing a physical education curriculum for the student.

The Individualized Transition Program (ITP) identifies goals for assisting the student in making the transition to postschool activities and the methods for achieving them. Examples include helping the student identify community resources for recreation and fitness and making the necessary arrangements for the support or equipment needed to participate effectively. Since these goals coincide with the content standards for physical education, students can help each other in making this transition to out-of-school activities.[106]

Alternative Placement Possibilities

The *least restrictive environment,* mandated in the law, refers to the education of disabled students with their nondisabled peers when the environment is conducive to helping students reach their full potentials. If a student cannot participate successfully in a regular class program, then that student can be placed in a special class or school. Most disabled students can be successfully integrated into regular physical education if their individual needs are considered.

Advocates of *total inclusion,* a term not found in the law, believe that disabled students should be placed in regular classes in the school they would regularly attend, with the needed services brought to the student.[107] Miller states that inclusion is important because

1. Separation causes stigmatization.
2. Separation leads to lowering of expectations, self-fulfilling prophecy.
3. Inclusion provides for the benefits of peer interactions: language, social, and academic role models.
4. Inclusion provides benefits to general school population: tolerance, acceptance, the valuing of differences in people.[108]

Mainstreaming, another term not found in the law, involves that portion of the continuum in which disabled students are educated in the regular classroom along with their nondisabled peers, rather than in special education classes. Many of the same reasons are given for inclusion and mainstreaming.[109]

Placement of *all* disabled students into regular physical education classes or into adapted physical education classes violates the principles upon which the law was based. Placement in the least restrictive environment must be made according to individual needs. Students must not be grouped by disabling condition (i.e., learning disabled students assigned to a class together). Physical educators must take the initiative to see that placement flexibility is maintained in IEPs so each student participates in regular physical education activities where possible and in specially designed programs as necessary. The courts commonly use the following tests to determine where a student should be placed:[110]

- a comparison of the academic benefits to the student in the various placements
- a comparison of the nonacademic benefits (social, role modeling, language skills) to the student in the various placements
- the effects of inclusion on other students in the classroom, including the probability of physical harm and educational disadvantages
- the probability of harm to the individual with a disability
- whether the costs of inclusion would be so great as to inhibit the education of other students

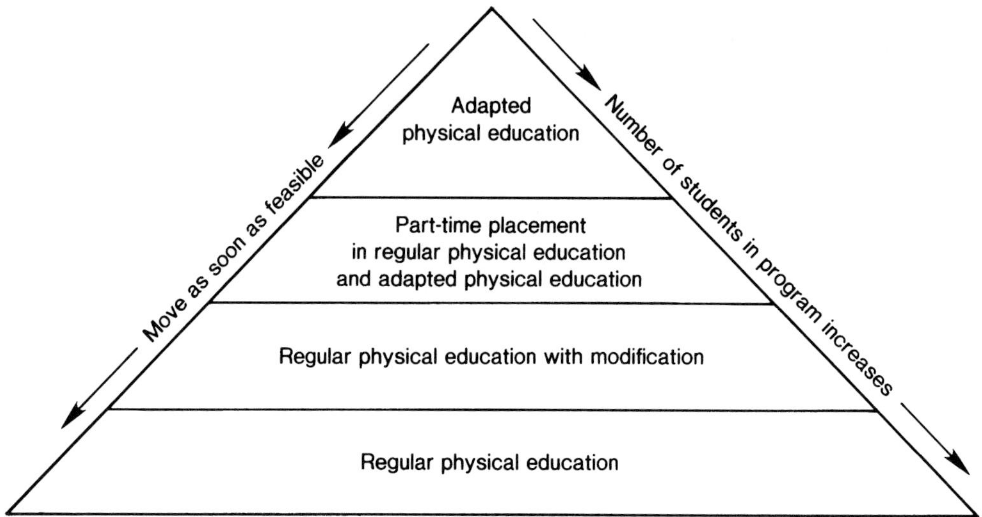

Figure 4-2

A continuum of physical education placement possibilities.

The burden is on the school to demonstrate that the conditions in a regular classroom are not appropriate. This is difficult to do if the student has not been allowed to experience a regular physical education program with appropriate supportive services.

Since schools are now required to enroll students who possess a wide range of individual abilities, a continuum of physical education services must be provided, including the following (see Figure 4-2):

- *Regular physical education.* Students who can safely and successfully participate in the regular physical education program should be encouraged to do so.
- *Regular physical education with modification.* Some disabled students can participate with their nondisabled peers if appropriate modifications are made such as (1) a buddy or peer-tutoring system, which pairs a disabled student with a nondisabled partner for specific activities as in the PEOPEL program described earlier; (2) circuit or station organizational patterns; (3) contract-learning techniques; (4) team-teaching, involving regular and adapted physical education teachers, resource teachers, or paraprofessional aides; or (5) preteaching certain activities to students with special needs. Students with special needs might work on such needs a specified amount of time each period, with the remaining time being devoted to regular activities with other members of the class.
- *Part-time placement.* Part-time placement is an arrangement in which students spend specified days each week in an adapted physical education class, where they concentrate on special needs as delineated in the IEP, and other days in regular classes. This type of placement may be especially useful in helping students gain the skills and confidence necessary to make the transition to a regular physical education program.
- *Adapted physical education.* Students with severe or multiple disabilities may need to be placed in an adapted physical education class to receive corrective therapy or remedial help. Only in this setting can activities be adapted enough for students with severe handicaps to participate freely and successfully. Adapted physical education can occur as a separate class within the school, in a special school, in a home, or in a hospital.

Review Question: Define: IDEA; Section 504 of the Rehabilitation Act; IEP; mainstreaming; least restrictive environment; adapted physical education.

Multicultural Education

Multicultural education is education designed to promote understanding and appreciation of cultural diversity. It recognizes differences in human behavior as they are influenced by language, race, gender, and national origin or culture. The United States is a multicultural society. The number of Asian, Hispanic, African American, Native American, and Asian American citizens is increasing. By the year 2020, 48 percent of school-age children in the United States will be ethnic minorities, many of them living at or below the poverty level.[111] Gorski provides the following working definition of multicultural education:

> Multicultural education is a progressive approach for transforming education that holistically critiques and addresses current shortcomings, failings, and discriminatory practices in education. It is grounded in ideals of social justice, education equity, and a dedication to facilitating educational experiences in which all students reach their full potential as learners and as so-

> cially aware and active beings, locally, nationally, and globally. Multicultural education acknowledges that schools are essential to laying the foundation for the transformation of society and the elimination of oppression and injustice.[112]

Federal legislation and Supreme Court decisions require *equal educational opportunities* for all students regardless of gender, physical condition, socioeconomic level, racial or ethnic background, religion, or language. However, equal opportunity does not mean that all students should be treated the same. Sometimes equity requires different treatments to meet the differing needs of individual students. Multicultural education implies that teaching will capitalize on the strengths of student differences rather than on their weaknesses. This means that teachers must learn to view cultural values from each group's perspective rather than from their own. This can be done by asking questions about family life, interpersonal interaction styles, health and hygiene, and similar items. Problems arise when the interaction style of the culture differs from the style of the school. For example, the culture of Native Americans may tend to emphasize cooperation rather than competition; Mexican American children tend to learn with a global rather than an analytical cognitive style; some Asian children tend to hold the teacher in high esteem. All of these styles may differ considerably from those of other children.[113]

A multicultural perspective must also exist in schools where intergroup contact is absent. Students need to examine stereotypes and misunderstandings that can result from no contact with other groups as well as from books and media.[114] Culturally responsive teachers adopt a multicultural approach to instruction as shown in Table 4.8.[115]

Physical education is often one of the first classes in which students in the English as a Second Language (ESL) program are placed. These students, as well as their level of English proficiency, need to be identified for the physical education teacher. Glakas suggested some communication techniques to use with ESL students:

1. Do not ask an ESL student to speak in class immediately.
2. Have another bilingual student help translate.
3. Use simple language with basic vocabulary.
4. Use examples, gestures, and demonstrations.
5. Do not correct ESL students who give appropriate answers in imperfect English.
6. Allow sufficient time for ESL students to respond.
7. At first ask simple yes/no-type questions, then gradually increase the difficulty of questions as the student's English improves.
8. Have essential written material such as departmental policies, course outlines, and form letters to parents translated.[116]

Other suggestions included teaching sports and games with which ESL students are familiar. Do not give timed tests to ESL students and encourage the use of bilingual dictionaries.[117]

Cultural differences also exist between students growing up in poverty versus affluence. "These differences grow out of the many ways in which the daily world of the adolescent is structured by relationships that begin in the family and spread out from there into other social environments in the community."[118] Students with a low-income background are more likely to have learning disabilities and lower educational achievement. "They are also more likely to drop out of school, to experience teenage pregnancy and early parenthood, to become involved in criminal and delinquent acts, to be arrested and incarcerated, to be unemployed, and to continue their working lives on the lowest rungs of the work force."[119] Students from suburbia may experience strong pressures to excel in areas such as sports, music, and academics. Both groups require a stable and consistent environment in which to grow and develop.[120]

Robinson stated:

> More multicultural education takes place when the white kid and the black kid sitting next to each other start making friends than in all the multiculturalist lectures in the world. The teacher is often in a position to facilitate that kind of connection, by having students work together on projects, by steering students toward projects that disturb but also strangely fascinate them, by creating an atmosphere of fun and tolerance in the classroom. Teachers who listen to their students as whole people learn from them; and when learning starts flowing in both directions, student to teacher and back, and then in all directions, everybody to everybody, barriers soon come crashing down, both inside our own heads and in society at large.[121]

Above all, teachers who accept student differences communicate to students that these differences are not problems to be remediated. Swisher and Swisher conclude that multicultural education is an attitude that communicates to students "that diversity is desirable and to be different is okay."[122]

Review Questions: What is multicultural education?

What can teachers do to adopt a multicultural approach to teaching?

Gender Equity and Title IX

Historically, physical education programs were segregated by sex. The intent of Title IX of the Education Amendments of 1972 was to provide equal educational opportunities for males and females. With regard to physical education classes, the law provided that

1. Students may be grouped by ability using objective standards of individual performance developed and applied without regard to gender.

TABLE 4.8 Suggestions for Adopting a Multicultural Approach to Instruction

Become culturally literate.

- Learn about students' cultural backgrounds—traditions, interaction styles, social values, foods, fashions, holidays.
- Get to know students and families in nonschool and extracurricular activities.
- Learn to speak even a few words in their language, especially pronouncing names correctly.
- Recognize differences between students' cultures and the culture of the school.
- Learn how social inequities have influenced attitudes throughout history.
- Be aware of the different ways in which students of different cultures pay attention (i. e., eye contact or no eye contact).
- Be aware of your own biases.

Create an environment of trust and mutual respect.

- Treat students as individuals, not categories. Don't assume certain abilities or disabilities based on genetics or culture.
- Learn students' names and pronounce them correctly.
- Accept students' native languages, while patiently helping students develop proficiency in English.
- Let students know their efforts are valued and will be rewarded.
- Build self-esteem.

Use alternative teaching styles that allow for differences in students' learning styles.

- Expect all students to succeed.
- Vary instructional approaches to meet different learning styles of students.
- Ensure equal opportunity among all groups.
- Use effective questioning techniques to promote critical thinking.
- Use problem-solving approaches to master physical challenges—adventure, etc.
- Include games that reflect the cultural heritage of students.
- Analyze instructional materials to ensure perspectives from different groups—cultural, racial, gender, disability.

Become a community of learners, not isolated individuals.

- Provide a strong knowledge base in students that emphasizes understanding of various cultural differences in the world and that it is okay to be different.
- Give individuals opportunities to work together in small heterogeneous groups.
- Develop student communication and interaction skills.
- Help students set goals for inclusion and consequences for racial slurs or disrespectful behavior.
- Help students develop sensitivity to the needs of individual students.
- Use cooperative games and stress cooperation rather than competition.
- Have students explain differences of opinion.

Establish positive home-school relations—invite input from adults representing different groups.

- Encourage students to research their family background and share their genealogy or "coat of arms" with the class.
- Encourage students to share customs, games, dances, etc. with the class.

Eliminate discriminatory and embarrassing practices (your own and students).

- Model appropriate behavior.
- Avoid language such as "black mark," "Indian style," "white" lie.
- Ban discriminatory clothing, such as Nazi symbols, offensive language, or pictures on T-shirts.
- Avoid choosing teams during class time.
- Avoid calling attention to individual students in front of their peers.
- Ensure that all students receive effective feedback—specific and concrete.
- Allow flexibility in uniforms due to differences in cultural dress customs.

2. Students may be separated by gender within physical education classes during participation in contact sports—wrestling, boxing, rugby, ice hockey, football, or basketball.
3. Portions of classes dealing exclusively with human sexuality may be conducted separately for males and females.
4. When use of a single standard of measurement has an adverse effect on members of one gender, then appropriate standards may be used, such as in skill and fitness test norms.[123]
5. Students whose religion prohibits coeducational physical education may be offered gender-segregated classes.[124]

In a 1984 decision by the Supreme Court (*Grove City College v. Bell*), Title IX was limited to specific programs within an institution that received federal funds. However, the Civil Rights Restoration Act of 1988 reversed the decision and restored coverage to all programs in institutions receiving any type of federal financial assistance.[125] However, implementation of Title IX has not yet reached the desired goal. Girls continue to receive a less positive experience in physical education and athletics than boys.[126]

Some would also argue that athletic opportunities for boys have been decreased as a result, particularly at the college/university level. As the NCAA and other athlete governing bodies have enforced equity requirements and in an age of decreasing budgets, some men's activities have been dropped at the collegiate level.

Even when programs meet the requirements of the law, gender-role stereotypes are often reflected in differing teacher expectations for males and females. In a study by Geadelmann, 54 percent of the boys and 44 percent of the girls thought the teacher expected more of the boys. According to Griffin, teacher expectation differences appear in programs in four ways: (1) class organization strategies, (2) teacher-student interaction patterns, (3) teacher language, and (4) teacher role modeling.[127]

With regard to *class organization,* studies have consistently demonstrated that participation styles of boys and girls differ, even when the teachers' purposes favor nondiscrimination. Boys tend to dominate team play and girls tend to give scoring opportunities to boys. Girls and boys perceive boys as more highly skilled, even when objective tests show the girls to be more talented. Boys have more contacts with the ball and tend to see girls' events, such as in gymnastics, as of lower status. Boys tend to sit in front of girls in squads, and boys have longer active learning time. Boys tend to dominate class discussions and interrupt more frequently. Low-skilled students have fewer opportunities to practice skills.[128]

However, as Griffin pointed out, "A generalized description of student interaction and participation by sex . . . can ignore or minimize differences in participation among students within the same gender group." She concluded, "To rely on gender differences in describing participation styles . . . would have presented an inaccurate picture ignoring the variety of action and attitude among the boys and among the girls observed."[129]

Even when teachers adapt games to increase participation by girls, the changes may be discriminatory. These changes favor the girls over the boys. Geadelmann emphasized, "Without raised expectation levels regarding the physical performance of girls, it is unlikely that the girls will receive the necessary encouragement and assistance to reach new performance levels."[130]

Studies on *teacher-student interaction* patterns show that teachers interact differently with males and females. They interact more with boys in the areas of class management, discipline, physical contact, informal talk, feedback, and criticism. Teachers praise boys more for their performance and girls more for their effort. Boys were chosen more often as class leaders, demonstrators, role models, and equipment managers. Teachers rarely corrected gender stereotyping by students in language or behavior.[131]

Studies on *teacher language* showed that teachers occasionally made stereotyped comments about "girls'" push-ups or throwing "like a boy," but they rarely made comments about girls being equal to boys. Although teachers generally used inclusive language to refer to students as a group (i.e., people, students), some stereotypical activity terms, such as "man-to-man," were used. Occasionally girls were called "ladies," but boys were rarely called "gentlemen." Some teachers used boys' last names and girls' first names.[132]

Research demonstrates that *teacher role modeling* is stereotyped in that male teachers rarely teach activities such as dance and gymnastics, whereas female teachers teach a wide variety of activities. Few teachers team-teach activities. A predominance of male athletes were pictured on bulletin boards and mentioned as role models by teachers.[133]

Sex equity depends on teachers' awareness of sex stereotyping patterns, their commitment to change, and specific action to change.[134] Effective teachers have learned that a wider range of motor abilities exists within each sex than between the sexes. Grouping students by ability can resolve the problems of students being intimidated or held back. Teachers can experiment with rules to find the best ones for both sexes. In fact, students can be challenged to experiment to find the best solution to the problem of appropriate rules.

Two additional areas in which gender inequities occur are in student-to-student interactions and in assessment of student learning. Most physical educators have noted that males' interactions with other males are more physical and public, including hassling and clowning, while males hassle females, both verbally and physically. Females, on the other hand, tend to interact with other females privately, cooperatively, and verbally. They interact with males only as a reaction to males' interactions with them.[135] Suggestions for increasing gender equity in physical education classes include activities to counteract the tendencies listed here, as shown in Table 4.9.[136]

Teachers can also elicit anonymous feedback from students about their feelings, preferences, and assessment of the results of instruction. In short, when sex makes no relevant difference, boys and girls can be treated similarly; however, where relevant differences exist, boys and girls should have different, but equally valuable, opportunities. Classes should be individualized according to ability level and not by sex.[137] In individualized instruction, students select different instructional programs to meet their various needs.

Griffin listed the factors necessary for successful coeducational programs as follows:

> In programs where coeducation is a success, where boys and girls are learning and enjoying physical activities together, students participate in a variety of

TABLE 4.9 Suggestions for Increasing Gender Equity in Physical Education

Class organization and instruction

- Use a broader repertoire of instructional styles to meet differences in learning styles.
- Change game rules to include all students, such as in three-on-three basketball or seven-player soccer, or by having every player touch the ball before scoring.
- Use a variety of ways to divide students into teams.
- Group students for instruction by skill level or interests, with opportunities to work with both same-sex and other-sex partners.
- Help students become aware of and overcome gender stereotyping and sexual harassment and learn to appreciate themselves and each other in physical education activities.
- Since variations in abilities within gender are greater than between the genders, base activities on individual needs rather than arbitrary male/female standards.
- Rather than segregate by gender for contact sports, reduce the contact in such activities so all students can participate.
- Provide sufficient practice time for all students to master skills, with additional help to students who need it.
- Schedule equal numbers of boys and girls into physical education classes, thus permitting equal numbers of each gender on each team. This promotes equality and fairness in participation styles.
- Allow students to make choices about their learning.

Teacher-student interactions

- Encourage females to talk more in class discussions.
- Praise performance, effort, and appearance equally for boys and girls.
- Choose boys and girls equally as class leaders, role models, skill demonstrators, equipment managers, and referees.

Teacher language

- Avoid words and phrases containing *man, lady,* or *you guys.* Consciously use inclusive language such as *the student, player, fair play, player-to-player* defense.
- Use equivalent terms when referring to boys and girls, males and females, men and women. Avoid the use of *girls* for women age fourteen and over. Use *young women.*
- Avoid reference to activities or equipment as *boys'* or *girls',* such as *girls' push-ups.*

Gender-equitable role modeling by teachers

- Develop competencies in activities traditionally associated with the opposite gender.
- Team-teach activities traditionally associated with the opposite gender.
- Include male and female models participating in a variety of nontraditional activities on instructional materials such as bulletin boards.

Gender-equitable student-to-student interactions

- Use cooperative activities to encourage positive interaction between females and males.
- Encourage appropriate verbal and physical interactions between students.
- Praise positive interactions and turn positive and negative interactions into teachable moments.
- Establish and enforce class guidelines to eliminate name-calling, teasing, and physical harassment.

Gender-equitable assessment of student learning

- Place the same expectations on males and females. Adjust for differences by skill level.
- Give feedback equally to females and males.
- Consider all aspects of performance—agility, balance, flexibility, form, speed, strength.

competitive and noncompetitive activities, teachers spend as much time as they can helping students improve their skills, teachers step in to eliminate destructive student interactions and to change unfair game participation, and teachers frequently use ability grouping to even up competition and to match instruction to student needs. Teachers who have made coed physical education a success are enthusiastic about teaching, their students, and trying something new. They have a sense of their own power to change student behavior in their classes and know specific strategies to use in addressing problems they encounter.[138]

When planning coed programs, it is important to teach many activities in which competition is not a critical factor. Lifetime activities, such as tennis, golf, badminton, fitness, and swimming can be enjoyed on an equal basis by both boys and girls. Interest surveys will make teachers aware of students' desires for instruction in specific activities.

As Dodds indicated, "Equity is a way of looking at the world."[139] She said:

> Creating physical education classes where all children join a team without being subjected to humiliation or stress; where Blacks, Hispanics, Asians, and Whites play

> together peacefully; where the norms are cooperation, sensitivity to others, and appreciation of differences; and where each individual can learn in an atmosphere of encouragement and joy for every achievement is a vision held up for every teacher willing to pay the price to be fair and affirmative to all students.[140]

To implement all at once the suggestions offered for meeting the needs of all students would require a super teacher. Although it is true that excellent teachers seriously attempt to improve their teaching, they do so by tackling a few ideas at a time rather than trying to implement everything at once. Wessel noted that "Individualizing instruction does not necessarily require major changes in the class or school. Teachers can adjust existing instructional approaches to students' learning . . . within their own classrooms and within existing constraints," through the use of a variety of instructional cues, different groupings for different activities, and the modification of games and activities. Students can be given the responsibility of helping to assess, monitor, and record learning outcomes.[141]

Although the design of instruction attempts to establish conditions to facilitate learning, it is up to the learner to take advantage of them. Teachers cannot learn for their students. More and more of the responsibility for education must be placed on the learners. One seldom observes signs of friction or disorder in a classroom where the students are interested and actively engaged in meaningful school activity related to their needs and interests, especially if that schoolwork is a part of their own planning.

Review Question: What is Title IX? How does it affect physical education class instruction?

STUDYING STUDENT NEEDS

Getting to know students implies taking the time to find out what the similarities and differences are among students in a particular school. Some of this information will be available in the form of school and student records. School records include data about the entire school population such as total enrollment, age and sex distributions, race or ethnic backgrounds, dropout rates, and other essential information needed for developing educational programs. Student records include health and medical status, intelligence and achievement test results, grades, results of interest and attitude inventories, and other information.

The Family Educational Rights and Privacy Act of 1974 (PL 93-380) withholds federal funds from any school denying parents (or students aged eighteen or over) access to student educational records or permitting third-party access to personally identifiable data in the records without prior consent. Persons permitted access to the records include teachers and school officials with legitimate educational interests and local, state, or national officials specified in the law. Parents have a right to challenge the content of the records.[142]

Observation of students in the school setting also can be a valuable source of data. Parent-teacher conferences and back-to-school nights can be helpful in getting acquainted with family backgrounds. The following questions could be used to direct your observation of students in a selected class to better meet individual needs:

1. What would you guess to be the range in height in the class? In weight? Have you observed any students for whom size may be a source of potential problems? What problems do you foresee? Record ideas for dealing with these problems.
2. What is the age range of students in the class? Does it appear that age may be a problem for any student in this class? Explain.
3. Identify the student whom you consider to be the most aggressive in the class; then identify the least aggressive student. As you think about these two and observe them, do you see a basic difference in the way they approach learning activities at school? Explain.
4. Which student, in your judgment, comes from the most affluent home? The least affluent? What implications do you see for instruction and learning?
5. What is the performance range of students in the class? The range in physical fitness? How would you adapt the instruction to meet the needs of each level?
6. Identify students who are disabled physically, culturally, or otherwise. What would you do to help them achieve success?
7. List as many other ways as you can think of in which students differ. Which of these might affect the way a student learns? Try ranking them in order of importance.

Observation of students in nonschool functions can also provide insights into student activities, interpersonal relationships, and leadership abilities. The following questions might be used as a guide:

1. Who was the group leader? How could you tell?
2. Were the leaders in these activities also leaders in school activities? Why or why not?
3. How did the boys react to the girls and vice versa?
4. Who directed the activities officially? Unofficially?
5. How was attention shown? To whom was it shown?
6. How were the students' behaviors different from their behaviors in school?
7. What motivating factors influence students when they are not in school?
8. What group or individual values were in evidence?
9. How did the group values influence the individuals?
10. How were decisions made among the students?
11. What learning was taking place?
12. What was the nature of the activity (constructive, destructive, social, religious)? How did this help determine the type of behavior considered appropriate for the situation?

13. Why were these particular students together?
14. What methods of influence did you notice being practiced?
15. How will knowing this information about students change your behavior in the classroom?
16. How do students behave differently in adult company? With different teachers?

Questionnaires can provide insight into the actual interests, attitudes, and values of students. Some possible questions are given here.

Directions: Do not write your name on this paper. Answer the questions below in the best way you know how.

1. How do you feel about yourself? I am:
2. How do you rate yourself as a student?
3. Do you have a job? If so, what kind?
4. What do you do in your free time?
5. What are your favorite sports or activities?
6. Do you play a musical instrument? Take private lessons in dance, music, sports? If so, what kind?
7. Do you have a lot of friends? A few friends? Are they close friends? Casual friends? Both?

Of course, teacher-student interaction before, during, and after classes provides one of the best opportunities for teachers and students to get to know each other on a more informal basis.

In summary, Hill indicated that as a teacher it is important to never forget:

- that failure hurts;
- that being forced to do something in front of others—particularly something "simple"—can be humiliating;
- that failure prompts impulses to escape, distract, cheat, and attack;
- that failure can come from simply not knowing how to think about a task;
- that wanting to learn and being able to learn are two different things;
- that being forced to do something is painful but may be a necessary first step if you are going to start to improve;
- that, when you are thinking poorly, it helps if people try to understand how you are thinking;
- that taking time to talk about the way you think can change the way you think;
- that learning different specific strategies for thinking is motivating;
- that success and learning cross-fertilize one another;
- that nothing is more important than being accepted and affirmed for who you are.[143]

NOTES

1. D. Pratt, *Curriculum: Design and Development* (New York: Harcourt Brace Jovanovich, 1980), p. 270.
2. C. E. Willgoose, *The Curriculum in Physical Education,* 4th ed. (Englewood Cliffs, NJ: Prentice-Hall, 1984), 255.
3. J. A. Wessel and L. Kelly, *Achievement-Based Curriculum Development in Physical Education* (Philadelphia: Lea & Febiger, 1986), 56.
4. L. Tyson, Context of schools, in S. J. Silverman and C. D. Ennis, *Student Learning in Physical Education: Applying Research to Enhance Instruction* (Champaign, IL: Human Kinetics, 1996).
5. Tyson, Context of schools.
6. K. P. DePauw, Students with disabilities in physical education, in S. J. Silverman and C. D. Ennis, eds., *Student Learning in Physical Education: Applying Research to Enhance Instruction* (Champaign, IL: Human Kinetics, 1996).
7. K. P. DePauw, Students with disabilities; K. Swisher and C. Swisher, A multicultural physical education approach: An attitude, *Journal of Physical Education, Recreation and Dance 57,* no. 7 (1986): 35–39.
8. L. J. Chamberlin and R. Girona, Our children are changing, *Educational Leadership 33,* no. 4 (1976): 301–5.
9. P. Griffin, and J. Placek, *Fair Play in the Gym: Race and Sex Equity in Physical Education* (Amherst: University of Massachusetts, 1983), 53–54.
10. Griffin and Placek, *Fair Play in the Gym.*
11. Chamberlin and Girona, Our children are changing.
12. T. Armstrong, How real are learning disabilities? *Learning 14,* no. 2 (1985): 44–47.
13. C. Bereiter, The changing face of educational disadvantagement, *Phi Delta Kappan 66,* no. 8 (1985): 538–41.
14. C. A. Bucher and C. R. Koenig, *Methods and Materials for Secondary School Physical Education,* 6th ed. (St. Louis, MO: Mosby, 1983), 42, 57.
15. Willgoose, *The Curriculum in Physical Education.*
16. Bucher and Koenig, *Methods and Materials.*
17. A. W. Combs, The human side of learning, *The National Elementary Principal 52,* no. 4 (1973): 38–42.
18. T. Hartman, *The Color Code* (Salt Lake City, UT: Color Code Communications, 1998).
19. Pratt, *Curriculum.*
20. P. Grippin and S. Peters, *Learning Theory and Learning Outcomes: The Connection* (New York: University Press of America, 1984), 125–26.
21. R. Cohen, Conceptual styles, culture conflict, and nonverbal tests of intelligence, *American Anthropologist 71* (1969): 828–56.
22. C. P. Jenkins, Brain research leads to new teaching methods, *BYU Today 40,* no. 1 (1986): 4–5.

23. H. Gardner, *Frames of Mind: The Theory of Multiple Intelligences* (New York, Basic Books, 1983), 71–72, 386–89; Gardner, *Multiple Intelligences: The Theory in Practice: A Reader* (New York: Basic Books, 1993), 8, 203–7, 224–26, 334.
24. Gardner, *Frames of Mind;* Gardner, *Multiple Intelligences.*
25. L. J. Stevens and M. Price, Meeting the challenge of educating children at risk. *Phi Delta Kappan 74,* (1992): 18–20, 22–23.
26. American Health Foundation, *Youth Get a Poor Grade on Their Health Report Card* (New York: Author, October 4, 1993).
27. Healthy People 2010, Chapter 26, Substance Abuse, retrieved January 1, 2005, from http://www.healthypeople.gov/document/html/volume2/26substance.htm.
28. Center for Disease Control and Prevention Report, retrieved January 1, 2005, from http://www.cdc.gov/tobacco/ issue.htm and http://www.cdc.gov/tobacco/research_data/youth/smke.htm.
29. M. A. Lawson, School reform, families, and health in the emergent national agenda for economic and social improvement: Implications. *Quest 45,* no. 3 (1993): 289–307; P. Woodring, A new approach to the dropout problem, *Phi Delta Kappan 70,* no. 6 (1989): 468–69.
30. Lawson, School reform.
31. W. Duckett, Using demographic data for long-range planning: An interview with Harold Hodgkinson, *Phi Delta Kappan, 70,* no. 2 (1988): 166–67.
32. M. Verzaro and C. B. Hennon. Single-parent families: Myth and reality, *Journal of Home Economics 72,* no. 3 (1980): 31–33.
33. American Health Foundation, *Youth Get a Poor Grade.*
34. American Health Foundation, *Youth Get a Poor Grade.*
35. S. M. Dornbusch, J. M. Carlsmith, S. J. Bushwall, P. L. Riter, H. Leiderman, A. H. Hastorf, and R. T. Gross, Single parents, extended households, and the control of adolescents, *Child Development 56,* no. 2 (1985): 326–41.
36. William T. Grant Foundation, Commission on Youth and America's Future, (1988). *The Forgotten Half: Pathways to Success for America's Youth and Young Families.* Washington, DC: Author.
37. J. McCurdy, Schools respond to latchkey children. *The School Administrator 42* (March 1985): 16–18.
38. L. P. Campbell and A. E. Flake, Latchkey children—What is the answer? *Clearing House 58,* no. 9 (1985): 381–83; McCurdy. Schools respond; A. Pecoraro, J. Theriot, and P. Lafont. What home economists should know about latchkey children. *Journal of Home Economics 76,* no. 4 (1984): 20–22; D. B. Strother. Latchkey children: The fastest-growing special interest group in the schools. *Phi Delta Kappan 66,* no. 4 (1984): 290–93.
39. Strother. Latchkey children.
40. Retrieved January 1, 2005, from http://www.oas.samhsa.gov/2k4/ageDependence/ageDependence.cfm.
41. J. D. Hawkins, D. Lishner, and R. F. Catalano, Childhood predictors and the prevention of adolescent substance abuse, in C. L. Jones and R. J. Battjes, eds., *Etiology of Drug Abuse: Implications for Prevention,* National Institute of Drug Abuse (Washington, DC: U.S. Government Printing Office, 1985), 85; C. L. Jones and R. J. Battjes, The context and caveats of prevention research on drug abuse, in C. L. Jones and R. J. Battjes, eds., *Etiology of Drug Abuse: Implications for Prevention,* National Institute on Drug Abuse (Washington, DC: U.S. Government Printing Office, 1985).
42. R. L. Towers. *How Schools Can Help Combat Student Drug and Alcohol Abuse* (Washington, DC: National Education Association, 1987), 18–19, 26–27, 29–30, 45, 61–65, 71, 76, 186.
43. Retrieved January 1, 2005, from http://www.cdc.gov/tobacco.
44. R. L. DuPont, Jr., *Getting Tough on Gateway Drugs* (Washington, DC: American Psychiatric Press), cited in Towers, *How Schools Can Help;* Towers, *How Schools Can Help.*
45. Towers, *How Schools Can Help.*
46. A. Norem-Heibesen and D. P. Hedin. Adolescent problem behavior: Causes, connections & contexts of drug abuse, in B. Q. Hafen and K. J. Frandsen, eds., *Addictive Behavior: Drug and Alcohol Abuse* (Englewood, CO: Morton, 1985), 39–48.
47. D. Elkind. The hurried child. *Instructor, 91* (1982), 40–43; N. Postman. Disappearing childhood. *Childhood Education 58,* no. 2 (1981): 66–68.
48. G. R. Norwood. A society that promotes drug abuse: The effects on pre-adolescence. *Childhood Education 61,* no. 4 (1985): 267–71.
49. B. Q. Hafen and K. J. Frandsen, Drug behavior: The factors behind drug abuse, in B. Q. Hafen and K. J. Frandsen, *Addictive Behavior: Drug and Alcohol Abuse* (Englewood, CO: Morton, 1985), 52–64; Norem-Heibesen and Hedin, Adolescent problem behavior: Causes, connections & contexts of drug abuse. In Hafen and Frandsen, *Addictive Behavior: Drug and Alcohol Abuse* (Englewood, CO: Morton, 1985), 39–48.
50. Hafen and Frandsen, Drug behavior.
51. Hafen and Frandsen, Drug behavior; Norem-Heibesen and Hedin, Adolescent problem behavior; Norwood, A society that promotes.
52. P. Zimbardo, quoted in B. Q. Hafen and K. J. Frandsen, Preventing drug use and abuse, in B. Q. Hafen and K. J. Frandsen, eds., *Addictive Behavior: Drug and Alcohol Abuse* (Englewood, CO: Morton, 1985), 363–76.
53. Hafen and Frandsen, Drug behavior; Towers, *How Schools Can Help.*
54. Towers, *How Schools Can Help.*
55. Towers, *How Schools Can Help.*
56. Towers, *How Schools Can Help.*
57. Towers, *How Schools Can Help.*
58. Towers, *How Schools Can Help.*
59. W. E. Swett, Helping young people survive in a chemical world, in B. Q. Hafen and K. J. Frandsen, *Addictive*

Behavior: Drug and Alcohol Abuse (Englewood, CO: Morton, 1985): 359–69, reprinted from *Family & Community Health,* August 1984; Towers, *How Schools Can Help.*
60. Towers, *How Schools Can Help.*
61. J. Frymier, Understanding and preventing teen suicide: An interview with Barry Garfinkel, *Phi Delta Kappan 70,* no. 4 (1988): 290–293.
62. B. Q. Hafen and K. J. Frandsen. *Youth Suicide: Depression and Loneliness* (Provo, UT: Behavioral Health Associates, 1986).
63. Hafen and Frandsen, *Youth Suicide.*
64. E. Y. Deykin, R. Perlow, and J. McNamarra, Non-fatal suicidal and life-threatening behavior among 13- to 17-year-old adolescents seeking emergency medical care, *American Journal of Public Health 75,* no. 1 (1985): 90–92.
65. Hafen and Frandsen, *Youth Suicide.*
66. Frymier. Understanding and preventing.
67. J. Jacobs. *Adolescent Suicide* (New York: Irvington, 1980).
68. Frymier. Understanding and preventing.
69. M. M. Wellman, The school counselor's role in the communication of suicidal ideation by adolescents, *The School Counselor 32,* no. 2 (1984): 104–109.
70. J. A. Motto, Assessment of suicide risk, *Medical Aspects of Human Sexuality 18* (October 1984): 134, 153.
71. Hafen and Frandsen. *Youth Suicide.*
72. Frymier, Understanding and preventing.
73. J. G. Dryfoos, *Adolescents at Risk: Prevalence and Prevention* (New York: Oxford University Press, 1990).
74. S. L. Hofferth, J. R. Kahn, and W. Baldwin. Premarital sexual activity among U.S. teenage women over the past three decades, *Family Planning Perspectives 19,* no. 2 (1987): 46–53.
75. C. D. Hayes, ed., *Risking the Future: Adolescent Sexuality, Pregnancy, and Childbearing* (Washington, DC: National Academy Press, 1987).
76. B. Q. Hafen and K. J. Frandsen, Preventing drug use and abuse. In B. Q. Hafen and K. J. Frandsen, *Addictive Behavior: Drug and Alcohol Abuse* (Englewood, CO: Morton, 1984), 373–376.
77. B. Beezer, Reporting child abuse and neglect: Your responsibility and your protections, *Phi Delta Kappan 66,* no. 6 (1985): 434–36; B. D. Hurwitz, Suspicion: Child abuse. *Instructor 94,* no. 8 (1985): 76–78; G. Solomon, Child abuse and developmental disabilities. *Developmental Medicine and Child Neurology 21,* (1979), 101–8; M. A. Straus, R. J. Gelles, and S. K. Steinmetz, *Behind Closed Doors: Violence in the American Family* (New York: Doubleday, 1980), 73.
78. Hurwitz, Suspicion.
79. R. Harrison, How you can help the abused child. *Learning 14,* no. 2 (1985): 74–78; B. Roscoe, Sexual abuse: The educator's role in identification and interaction with abuse victims. *Education 105,* no. 1 (1984): 82.
80. Hurwitz, Suspicion.
81. Roscoe, Sexual abuse.
82. B. Workman, Dear professor: This is what I want you to know, *Phi Delta Kappan 67,* no. 9 (1986): 668–71.
83. William T. Grant Foundation, Commission on Youth and America's Future, *The Forgotten Half: Pathways to Success for America's Youth and Young Families* (Washington, DC: Author, 1988).
84. W. G. Sparks, Promoting self-responsibility and decision making with at-risk students. *The Journal of Physical Education, Recreation and Dance 64,* no. 2 (1993): 74–78.
85. Sparks, Promoting self-responsibility.
86. Sparks, Promoting self-responsibility.
87. The Henry J. Kaiser Family Foundation, 2400 Sand Hill Road, Menlo Park, CA 94025, report released February 24, 2004, *Role of Media in Childhood Obesity.* Available at www.kff.org.
88. D. Zakrajsek and L. Carnes, *Learning Experiences: An Approach to Teaching Physical Education* (Dubuque, IA: Wm. C. Brown, 1981), 5.
89. P. Dodds. Stamp out the ugly "isms" in your gym, in M. Piéron and G. Graham, eds., *Sport Pedagogy* (Champaign IL: Human Kinetics, 1986), 141–50.
90. D. W. Mizen and N. Linton, Guess who's coming to physical education: Six steps to more effective mainstreaming. *Journal of Physical Education, Recreation, and Dance 54,* no. 8 (1983): 63–65.
91. M. D. Hanks, How to listen. *Improvement Era 72,* no. 3 (1969): 16–19.
92. E. McHugh, Going "beyond the physical": Social skills and physical education, *Journal of Health, Physical Education, Recreation, and Dance 66,* no 4 (1995): 18–21.
93. McHugh, Going "beyond the physical."
94. K. M. Haywood and T. J. Loughrey, Growth and development: Implications for teaching, *Journal of Physical Education and Recreation 52,* no. 2 (1981): 57–58.
95. J. L. DePaepe, The influence of three least restrictive environments on the content motor-ALT and performance of moderately mentally retarded students, *Journal of Teaching in Physical Education 5,* no. 1 (1985): 34–41; C. Houston-Wilson, L. Lieberman, M. Horton, and S. Kasser, Peer tutoring: A plan for instructing students of all abilities, *Journal of Health, Physical Education, Recreation and Dance 68,* no. 6 (1997): 39–44; PEOPEL, 2526 West Osborn Road, Phoenix, Arizona 85017, is sponsored by the United States Education Department National Diffusion Network and National Inservice Network, Washington, DC, and the Phoenix Union High School District, Phoenix, AZ; M. E. Block, Use peer tutors and task sheets, *Strategies 8,* no. 7 (1995): 9–11; M. E. Block, Don't forget the social aspects of inclusion, *Strategies 12,* no. 2 (1998): 30–33; Zimbardo, quoted in Hafen and K. J. Frandsen, Preventing drug use.

96. M. E. Block, Modify instruction: Include all students. *Strategies,* 9, no. 4 (1996): 9–12; J. E. Johnston, P. Gregory, and T. Roberts, Keep it simple: Teaching tips for Special Olympic athletes, *Strategies 9,* no. 7 (1996): 10–12.
97. J. A. Wessel (ed.), *Planning Individualized Education Programs in Special Education with Examples from ICAN Physical Education* (Northbrook, IL: Hubbard, 1977).
98. A. A. Annarino, C. C. Cowell, and H. W. Hazleton, *Curriculum Theory and Design in Physical Education,* 2d ed. (Prospect Heights, IL: Waveland, 1980): 333.
99. J. P. Winnick, Techniques for integration. *Journal of Physical Education and Recreation 49,* no. 6 (1978): 22; M. M. McCarthy, Severely disabled children: Who pays? *Phi Delta Kappan 73,* no. 1 (1991): 66–71.
100. B. Everhart, Back to the basics of individualizing instruction for all learners, *Journal of Health, Physical Education, Recreation and Dance 67,* no. 9 (1996): 12–16.
101. A. V. Colvin, Learning is *not* a spectator sport: Strategies for teacher-student interaction, *Journal of Health, Physical Education, Recreation, and Dance 69,* no. 2 (1998): 61–63.
102. McCarthy, Severely disabled children.
103. Individuals with Disabilities Education Act of 1990, P. L. 101-476, Section 602 (a)(16)(20 U.S.C. 1401(a)(16).
104. *Federal Register,* vol. 42, May 4, 1977, 22676.
105. McCarthy, Severely disabled children.
106. C. K. Piletic, Transition: Are we doing it? *Journal of Health, Physical Education, Recreation and Dance 69,* no. 9 (1998): 46–50.
107. J. U. Stein. Total inclusion or least restrictive environment? *Journal of Health, Physical Education, Recreation and Dance 65,* no. 9 (1994): 21–25; M. M. McCarthy, Inclusion and the law: Recent judicial developments, Research Bulletin No. 13 (Bloomington, IN: Phi Delta Kappa, 1994).
108. D. Pratt, *Curriculum: Design and Development* (New York: Harcourt Brace Jovanovich, 1980), 270; S. E. Miller, Inclusion of children with disabilities: Can we meet the challenge? *The Physical Educator 51,* no. 1 (1994): 47–52.
109. Stein. Total inclusion; McCarthy, Inclusion and the law.
110. McCarthy, Inclusion and the law; R. French, H. Henderson, L. Kinnison, and C. Sherrill, Revisiting Section 504, physical education, and sport, *Journal of Health, Physical Education, Recreation and Dance 69,* no. 7 (1998): 57–63.
111. N. Postman, Disappearing childhood, *Childhood Education 58,* no. 2 (1981): 66–68; D. C. Rittenmeyer, Social problems and America's youth: Why school reform won't work, *National Forum: The Phi Kappa Phi Journal 67,* no. 1 (1987): 34–38; W. Duckett, Using demographic data for long-range planning: An interview with Harold Hodgkinson, *Phi Delta Kappan 70,* no. 2 (1988): 166–67.
112. P. Gorski, *Defining Multicultural Education—McGraw-Hill Multicultural Supersite,* retrieved January 12, 2005, from http://www.mhhe.com/socscience/education/multi/define.html.
113. K. Swisher and C. Swisher, A multicultural physical education approach: An attitude, *Journal of Physical Education, Recreation and Dance 57,* no. 7 (1986): 35–39.
114. Swisher and Swisher, A multicultural physical education approach.
115. Swisher and Swisher, A multicultural physical education approach; P. Lyter-Mickelberg and F. Connor-Kuntz, Stop stereotyping students, *Strategies 8,* no. 6 (1995): 16–21; S. E. King, Winning the race against racism, *Journal of Health, Physical Education, Recreation and Dance 65,* no. 9 (1994): 69–74; W. G. Sparks, III, Culturally responsive pedagogy: A framework for addressing multicultural issues, *Journal of Health, Physical Education, Recreation and Dance 65,* no. 9 (1994): 33–36, 61.
116. B. A. Glakas, Teaching secondary physical education to ESL students, *The Journal of Physical Education, Recreation and Dance 64,* no. 7 (1993): 20–24.
117. Glakas, Teaching secondary physical education.
118. F. A. Ianni, Providing a structure for adolescent development, *Phi Delta Kappan 70,* no. 9 (1989): 673–82.
119. Ianni, Providing a structure.
120. Ianni, Providing a structure.
121. D. Robinson. Teaching whole people. *National Forum: The Phi Kappa Phi Journal 74,* no. 1 (1994): 34–36.
122. Swisher and Swisher, A multicultural physical education approach.
123. *Federal Register,* vol. 40, 4 June 1975.
124. E. J. Vargyas, Title IX today, *Strategies 2,* no. 4 (1989): 9–11.
125. Vargyas, Title IX today.
126. P. L. Geadelmann, Physical education: Stronghold of sex role stereotyping, *Quest 32,* no. 2 (1980): 192–200; J. C. Young, Teacher beliefs and behaviors concerning coeducational physical education, *Abstracts of Research Papers 1986* (Reston, VA: American Alliance for Health, Physical Education, Recreation and Dance, 1986).
127. Geadelmann, Physical education; P. S. Griffin, One small step for personkind: Observations and suggestions for sex equity in coeducational physical education classes, *Journal of Teaching in Physical Education 1,* no. 1 (1981): 12–17.
128. S. Brown, D. Brown, and K. Hussey, Promote equality in the classroom, *Strategies 9,* no. 6 (1996): 19–22; P. S. Griffin, Gymnastics is a girl's thing: Student participation and interaction patterns in a middle school gymnastics unit, In T. J. Templin and J. K. Olson, eds., *Teaching in Physical Education* (Champaign, IL: Human Kinetics, 1983), 71–85; Griffin, One small step; H. H. Solomons, Sex role mediation of achievement behaviors and interpersonal interactions in sex-integrated

team games, In E. A. Pepitone, ed., *Children in Cooperation and Competition* (Lexington, MA: Heath, 1980), 1–64; J. C. Young, Teacher beliefs and behaviors concerning coeducational physical education, *Abstracts of Research Papers 1986* (Reston, VA: American Alliance for Health, Physical Education, Recreation and Dance, 1986); B. M. Wang, An ethnography of a physical education class: An experiment in integrated living (Doctoral dissertation, University of North Carolina at Greensboro, 1977), *Dissertation Abstracts International* 38, 1980A.

129. P. S. Griffin, Girls' and boys' participation styles in middle school physical education team sport classes: A description and practical applications, *Physical Educator 42,* no. 1 (1985): 3–8.
130. P. L. Geadelmann, Physical education: Stronghold of sex role stereotyping, *Quest 32,* no. 2 (1980): 192–200.
131. Geadelmann, Physical education; Griffin, One small step; Solomons, Sex role mediation; Young, Teacher beliefs.
132. Griffin, One small step.
133. Griffin, One small step.
134. Griffin, One small step.
135. P. S. Griffin, Gymnastics is a girl's thing.
136. S. Brown, D. Brown, and K. Hussey, Promote equality in the classroom, *Strategies 9,* no. 6 (1996): 19–22; J. Bischoff, Equal opportunity, satisfaction and success: An exploratory study on coeducational volleyball, *Journal of Teaching in Physical Education 2,* no. 1 (1982): 3–12; Carolyn B. Mitchell, *Gender Equity through Physical Education and Sport* (Reston, VA: American Alliance for Health, Physical Education, Recreation, and Dance, 1995); V. Melograno, *Designing Curriculum and Learning: A Physical Coeducation Approach* (Dubuque, IA: Kendall/Hunt, 1979), 216.
137. Bischoff, Equal opportunity; A. Knopper, Equity for excellence in physical education, *Journal of Physical Education and Recreation 59,* no. 6 (1988): 54–58.
138. P. Griffin, Coed physical education: Problems and promise, *Journal of Physical Education, Recreation and Dance* 55, no. 6 (1984): 37.
139. Dodds, Stamp out the ugly "isms."
140. Dodds, Stamp out the ugly "isms."
141. J. A. Wessel, ed., *Planning Individualized Education Programs in Special Education with Examples from I CAN Physical Education* (Northbrook IL: Hubbard, 1988).
142. *United States Statutes at Large, 93rd Congress, 2nd Session, 1974,* vol. 88, part 1, pp. 571–74 (Washington, DC: U.S. Government Printing Office).
143. D. Hill, Tasting failure: Thoughts of an at-risk learner, *Phi Delta Kappan 73,* no. 4 (1991): 308–10.

CHAPTER

5

Understanding Learning

Study Stimulators

1. What is cognitive learning? Affective learning? Psychomotor learning?
2. What is a taxonomy? Of what advantage is it to physical educators?
3. How do the methods differ for teaching cognitive information, skills, and strategies?
4. How can attitudes toward physical education, self-esteem, self-efficacy, and moral education be influenced?
5. What is the best strategy for teaching motor skills?
6. What is ALT-PE? Why is it important in instruction? How can ALT-PE and practice trials be increased for each student?

This chapter is divided into two sections. The first part explains the three learning domains. It is followed by strategies for increasing learning and development in these three domains.

The Three Learning Domains

Bloom and his associates are well known for dividing learning into three categories, or *domains*—cognitive, affective and psychomotor.[1] The *cognitive domain* includes the learning and application of knowledge. The *affective domain* involves the acquisition of attitudes, appreciations, and values. The *psychomotor domain* incorporates the development of the physical body and neuromuscular skills. The learning outcomes in each area were arranged by Bloom and his colleagues into levels they considered hierarchical in nature. That means that the performance of behaviors at each level would be prerequisite to the behaviors at a higher level.

A *taxonomy* is a system for classifying something. An educational taxonomy classifies the behaviors that students can be expected to demonstrate after learning. Perhaps the most commonly known taxonomy is the cognitive taxonomy of Bloom and his associates shown in Table 5.1. Their taxonomy for the affective domain, which is shown in Table 5.2, was developed later and has also been widely accepted, although rarely implemented in physical education.[2] Bloom also constructed a psychomotor taxonomy, although he preferred to omit it in later editions of his work (see Table 5.3).[3] Several other efforts have been made to develop taxonomies in the psychomotor domain.[4] The one proposed by Jewett and associates is shown in Table 5.4.[5] Corbin outlined a separate taxonomy for physical fitness,[6] and Singer and Dick proposed one for the personal-social area of physical education.[7] Annarino proposed an operational taxonomy for all areas of physical education—physical, psychomotor, cognitive, and affective.[8] None of these taxonomies has been adopted as a standard for the profession.

The Cognitive Domain

The cognitive domain includes knowledge, comprehension, application, analysis, synthesis, and evaluation, as shown in Table 5.1. Each category on the taxonomy contains some elements of previous categories. Attempts to validate the hierarchical nature of the cognitive taxonomy have not been successful past the application level, at which point the taxonomy may split into a Y shape, with synthesis and evaluation on one side and analysis on the other.[9] However, the taxonomy has been useful for curriculum design and test construction.

Knowledge

The first level on the taxonomy is knowledge—the ability to recognize or recall specific facts, methods for organizing information, or theories. This level is often referred to as memorization or rote learning. Physical education content that fits into the knowledge level of the taxonomy includes

1. game rules and strategies,
2. terminology,
3. history and current events, and
4. body systems.

Comprehension

Meaningful learning includes more than just facts. Students must understand what they have learned. Comprehension is evidenced by the ability to translate or paraphrase information; to interpret or explain why something is occurring; or to summarize, extrapolate, or use facts to determine consequences and implications. Examples of items that students must comprehend include

1. game rules and strategies in specific game situations,
2. the effects of exercise on the body,
3. the benefits of exercise,
4. factors affecting exercise, and
5. social and psychological factors affecting sports participation.

Application

Once students comprehend verbal information, they are ready to use or apply the information in new problems and situations. Students use formulas, principles, theories, ideas, rules, procedures, and methods in particular situations to solve problems. For example, in physical education students must apply

1. game rules and strategies,
2. biomechanical principles to produce effective body movement,
3. processes for learning new skills,
4. techniques for relaxation and stress management,
5. safety principles, and
6. game etiquette.

TABLE 5.1 Bloom's Cognitive Taxonomy

Levels of Behavior
1. *Knowledge*—Involves recognition and *recall* of the following: —specific facts, terms, definitions, symbols, dates, places, etc. —rules, trends, categories, methods, etc. —principles, theories, ways of organizing ideas
2. *Comprehension*—Involves ability to use learning: —translating, paraphrasing —interpreting, summarizing —extrapolating, predicting effects or consequences
3. *Application*—Involves ability to use learning in a variety of situations: —using principles and theories —using abstractions
4. *Analysis*—Involves breaking down the whole hierarchy of parts: —identifying or distinguishing parts or elements —discovering interactions or relationships between parts —relating organizational principles (parts to whole or whole to parts)
5. *Synthesis*—Involves combining elements into a new whole: —identifying and relating elements in new ways —arranging and combining parts —constructing a new whole
6. *Evaluation*—Involves judgments of value of material and methods for a given purpose: —judgments in terms of internal standards —judgments in terms of external criteria

Source: Concepts from Benjamin S. Bloom, ed., *Taxonomy of Educational Objectives, Handbook I: Cognitive Domain* (New York: McKay Co., 1956).

Analysis

Breaking down information into its components or parts to see their relationships is called analysis. Students learn to organize, classify, distinguish, discriminate, and clarify information by demonstrating or making explicit the relationships among ideas. Knowledge, comprehension, and application are all involved in analyzing information. Examples of analysis include relating hypotheses to evidence, relating assumptions to arguments, or creating systematic arrangements of structures and organizations. In physical education, students analyze

1. game strategies for effectiveness in specific situations,
2. articles on physical fitness for effectiveness and accuracy of information distributed,
3. the muscles stretched or strengthened by a specific exercise,
4. the reasons a particular exercise is harmful,
5. the principles involved in producing more force in skills like the volleyball or tennis serve, and
6. skills to determine whether they are performed in the most efficient way.

Synthesis

Another cognitive process based on knowledge, comprehension, and application is synthesis. It involves creating something by arranging or combining elements into patterns to form a whole, a structure or pattern not clearly there before. In synthesis, there is no "right answer." Students use their creativity to

1. create exercise programs to attain physical fitness,
2. invent new games or game strategies, and
3. choreograph dance and gymnastics routines.

Evaluation

Evaluation includes both quantitative measurements and qualitative judgments about the value of ideas, solutions, methods, or materials. It is used to determine whether methods or materials satisfy the criteria or standards specified for appraisal. Either internal or external evidence may be used to evaluate such things as policies and situations in terms of their accuracy, precision, or conclusions. Evaluation appears to involve synthesis. Students in physical education evaluate

1. the quality of sports-related consumer goods,
2. exercise programs,
3. rules and strategies and their effects on game play, and
4. how equipment affects game play.

The Affective and Social Domain

Affective learning refers to the emotional aspects of learning. It deals with how students feel about the learning experience, how they feel about the subject, and how they feel about themselves. It considers their interests, appreciations, attitudes, values, and character. Since attitudes and appreciations cannot be measured directly, they are inferred from people's tendencies to engage in certain behaviors when they have positive attitudes and in certain other behaviors when they have negative attitudes toward some subject. For example, Greta has a positive attitude toward sports. This attitude is demonstrated by the fact that she talks about sports, attends every sporting event she can, and learns the names and characteristics of each player. Once she even took her radio to a club meeting so she could listen to a championship game. In general, people who like something keep going back for more experiences with the subject. They seek opportunities to be involved with the subject in preference to other activities. The stronger their attraction, the more obstacles they will overcome to get involved and stay involved. People who don't like something try to avoid it by changing the subject, inventing excuses, or walking away from it. When forced to become involved in instructional situations they dislike, they threaten never to have anything to do with the subject in the future. Once such an attitude has developed, the chances are slim that it will be reversed, since the opportunities to influence these people become fewer and fewer as time goes by.

The taxonomy of affective behaviors developed by Krathwohl, Bloom, and Masia describes levels on a continuum of internalization of behaviors as shown in Table 5.2.[10] It will be illustrated with an example from physical education.

Receiving

Receiving involves passive attention to the activity or event. Adam first becomes aware of what physical fitness is, begins to listen to material concerning fitness activities, and even selects and reads articles about fitness to the exclusion of other reading materials.

Responding

When a person does something about the activity it is called responding. Adam responds to his information by forming an opinion about physical fitness, initially only by complying with a teacher-initiated fitness program. He participates voluntarily in a school-sponsored fitness program and begins to feel some satisfaction in doing so.

Valuing

When Adam is seen trying to convince his friends of the importance of a fitness program, he is beginning to place worth on the activity, or he is valuing it.

Organization

Adam internalizes his conviction of the importance of physical fitness and incorporates it into his hierarchy of values. His own beliefs rather than the opinions of others

TABLE 5.2 Bloom's Affective Taxonomy

Levels of Behavior

1. *Receiving*—Involves passive attention to stimuli:
   —awareness of a fact, occurrence, event, or incident
   —willingness to notice or attend to a task
   —selecting stimuli
2. *Responding*—Involves doing something about stimuli:
   —complying, following directions
   —voluntarily involves self
   —satisfaction or enjoyment
3. *Valuing*—Places worth on something; involves display of behavior consistent with values:
   —expressing strong belief in something
   —expressing preference for something
   —seeking activity to further something and convert others to own way of thinking
4. *Organization*—Organizes values into a system:
   —seeing how the value relates to other values held
   —establishing interrelationships and dominance of values
5. *Characterization*—Acts consistently with internalized value system:
   —acting consistently in a certain way and can be described by others in terms of actions or values
   —developing a total *consistent* philosophy of life, integrating beliefs, ideas, and attitudes

Source: Concepts from David R. Krathwohl, Benjamin S. Bloom, and Bertram B. Masia, *Taxonomy of Educational Objectives, Handbook II: Affective Domain* (New York: David McKay Co., 1964).

now guide his actions. This step involves seeing how the values relate to other values the individual holds and weighing these values to determine which ones are more important.

Characterization

When a person acts consistently with an internalized value system, the particular behavior is said to be characteristic of him or her. Adam becomes so committed to the importance of physical fitness that he may even decide on a career in the fitness area or do volunteer work instructing others about physical fitness.

A close relationship exists between the affective domain and the other two. By having students learn about something (cognitive) or do some activity (psychomotor), instructors can help to produce attitudinal changes in students. When students' positive attitudes toward physical education increases, they can be motivated to learn cognitive or psychomotor skills.

Singer and Dick's social domain is closely related to the affective domain and is concerned with personal adjustment and social interaction skills. These researchers included the following areas in the social domain:

1. Conduct (sportspersonship, honesty, respect for authority and rules)
2. Emotional stability in competitive situations (control, maturity)
3. Interpersonal relations (cooperation, competition)
4. Self-fulfillment (confidence, self-actualization, self-image).[11]

Teachers must ensure that positive rather than negative social skills are outcomes of physical education.

The Psychomotor Domain

Psychomotor learning involves learning physical or neuromuscular skills. One characteristic of psychomotor learning is that it is possible to identify distinct stages or phases that all learners seem to experience as they learn skills. Think of how a baby learns to walk. Once the baby gets an idea of what is required and has the prerequisite skills—strength, maturity, and so forth—the child makes crude attempts that are gradually refined through constant feedback from the environment—door sills, falls, carpet textures, and parents' "oohing" and "aahing." Finally, a skilled performance emerges that is unique to that particular toddler.

Graham and his colleagues classified skills into four levels: precontrol, control, utilization, and proficiency. The *precontrol* level is characterized by lack of ability to control an object or the body. Every time the skill is performed, it looks different. Preschool and kindergarten children are usually at this level, although aptitude and experience determine execution, not age. The *control* level is characterized by the ability to reproduce a movement, often with intense concentration, that becomes increasingly efficient and consistent. Elementary school children are examples of performers at this level. In the *utilization* level, movements become more automatic, can be combined with each other, and can be used in different contexts, including simple games. The *proficiency* level is characterized by seemingly effortless, automatic, and flowing movements in games or

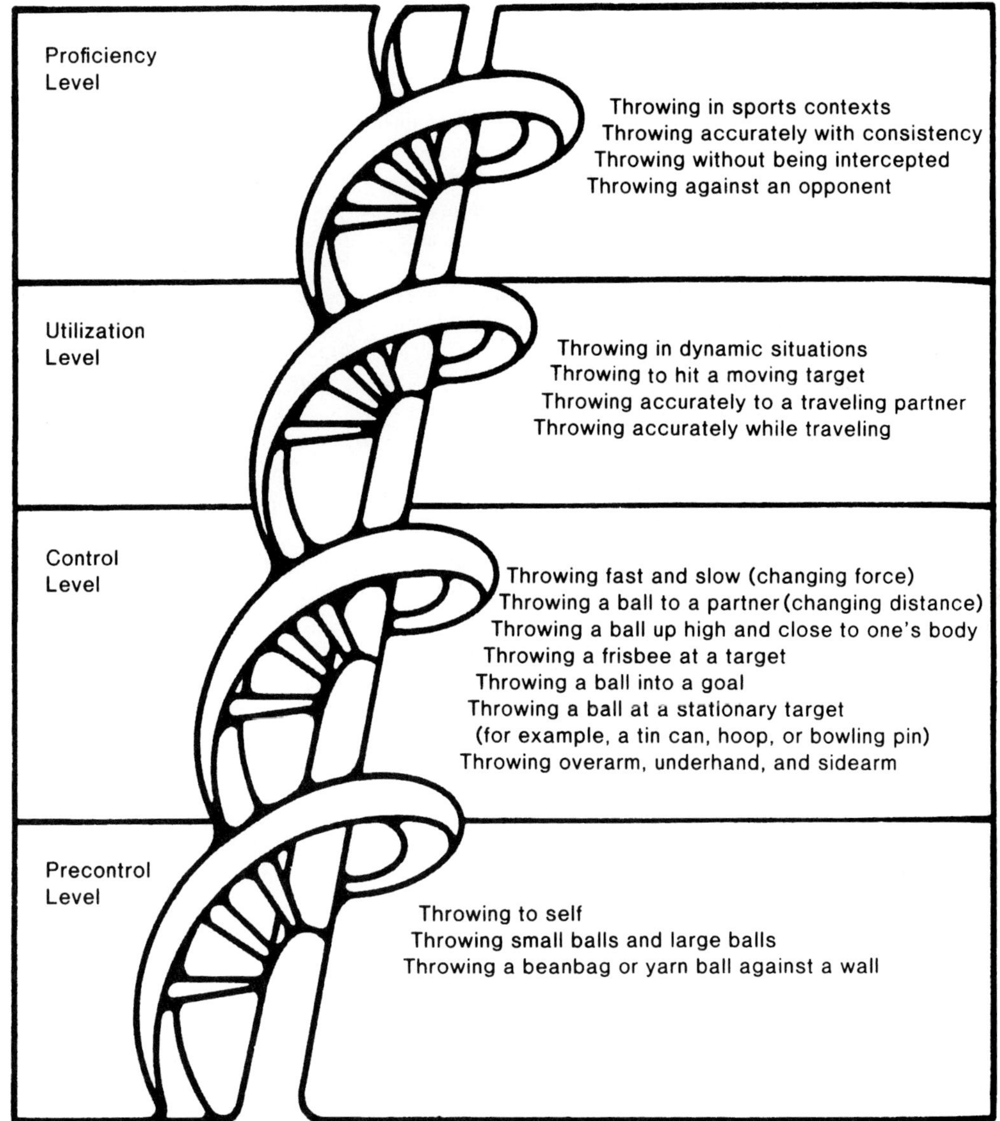

Figure 5-1

An example of a progression for throwing in a spiral curriculum.

Source: From *Children Moving: A Reflective Approach to Teaching Physical Education,* 4th ed., by George Graham, Shirley Holt-Hale, Melissa Parker. Copyright © 1998 by Mayfield Publishing Company. Reprinted with permission of the publisher.

activities that require adjustments to the environment or repeated exacting movements. This level is not often seen in regular physical education classes, although it should be seen more often. Older children and adolescents may be at one level in one skill and at a different level in another, depending on their experience with different activities. As they grow older, the variation in performance among children widens. Figure 5-1 is an example of a progression for throwing using these four levels.[12]

Fitts and Posner classified psychomotor skill learning into three overlapping phases: (1) cognitive—an attempt to understand the skill to be learned, (2) fixation or associative—an attempt to refine the movement by eliminating errors, and (3) autonomous—an automatic movement.[13] Gentile divided skill learning into two stages: (1) getting the idea of the movement—the cognitive stage—and (2) fixation or diversification of the movement—an attempt to refine or increase the variety of response possibilities.[14]

In 1971, Jewett and her colleagues introduced the psychomotor taxonomy shown in Table 5.3.[15] Bressan reformulated the taxonomy into a model to aid teachers in designing and sequencing psychomotor learning experiences.[16] She renamed Jewett's three stages of skill development, calling them (1) skill construction, (2) skill stabilization, and (3) skill differentiation, as shown in Table 5.4. Understanding these developmental stages is essential when planning the instructional sequence in physical education. Unless the teacher understands the higher levels of the taxonomy, the tendency is to stop too soon and omit some very important learning skills.

TABLE 5.3 A Psychomotor Taxonomy

Learning Behavior	Definition
1.0 Generic movement	Movement operations or processes, which facilitate the development of human movement patterns.
1.1 Perceiving	Recognition of movement positions, postures, patterns, and skills by means of the sense organs.
1.2 Imitating	Duplication of a movement pattern or skill as a result of perceiving.
1.3 Patterning	Arrangement and use of body parts in successive and harmonious ways to achieve a movement pattern or skill.
2.0 Ordinative movement	Meeting the requirements of specific movement tasks through processes of organizing, performing, and refining movement patterns and skills.
2.1 Adapting	Modification of a patterned movement or skill to meet specific task demands.
2.2 Refining	Acquisition of smooth, efficient control in performing a movement pattern or skill as a result of an improvement process, e.g., a. elimination of extraneous movements. b. mastery of spatial and temporal relations. c. habitual performance under more complex conditions.
3.0 Creative movement	Processes of inventing or creating skillful movements that will serve the unique purposes of the learner.
3.1 Varying	Invention or construction of unique or novel options in performing a movement pattern or skill.
3.2 Improvising	Extemporaneous origination or initiation of novel movements or combinations of movements.
3.3 Composing	Creation of unique movement designs or patterns.

Source: Ann E. Jewett, L. Sue Jones, Sheryl M. Luneke, and Sarah M. Robinson, "Educational Change through a Taxonomy for Writing Physical Education Objectives," *Quest* 15 (January 1971): 35–36.

TABLE 5.4 Bressan's Adaptations

Bressan's Adaptations
Skill Construction
Perceiving
Patterning
Skill Stabilization
Accommodating
Refining
Skill Differentiation
Varying
Improvising
Composing

Source: Adaptations made by E. S. Bressan, "A Movement Processing Paradigm and the Curriculum in Physical Education." *Journal of Teaching in Physical Education 6* (1987): 335–43.

Skill Construction

Skill construction, or acquisition, includes the initial processes of receiving information and transforming it into a motor pattern. It requires establishing new or revised muscle synergies—muscles working together to create a movement pattern. The brain (cerebral cortex) incorporates the muscle synergies into motor programs that can be controlled at lower neurological levels by the brain stem (cerebellum) and spinal cord.

Perception is the basis for all learning. The student must be helped to perceive, or focus on, the important aspects of the skill to be learned. This requires active, conscious effort by the learner. The brain creates temporary neurological connections so the learner can approximate the desired performance. An example might be how a child explores throwing patterns, trying different ways of throwing, with different forces, directions, and distances. An older learner might attempt an overhead throw, again with a variety of forces, directions, and distances. The teacher must provide a balance between the efficiency of learning a prescribed pattern and the flexibility necessary for later adaptations to various sport contexts.

Patterning is the process of acquiring a specific movement pattern to create a consistent, automated motor program of muscle synergies. To achieve this, the teacher displays a model of the skill, provides for repetition through practice, and gives feedback and knowledge of results. Practice results in a permanent motor program, regardless of whether it is biomechanically correct. Therefore, the selection of the specific skill to pattern is critical for the next two stages of skill development.

Skill Stabilization

Skill stabilization involves generalizing the motor pattern so that it can be performed efficiently, effectively, and consistently in a variety of environmental conditions. This

TABLE 5.5 Two Examples of the Movement Behaviors Described in the Psychomotor Taxonomy

Movement Process	Balance Beam	Soccer
Perceiving	The child walks on the balance beam hesitantly, stops frequently to maintain balance; may hang onto partner or teacher. Experiments with body and arm positions. Child may use a shuffle step or slide step.	After a demonstration, the student replicates a kicking pattern. A fundamental striking pattern (swing) with the foot is the goal of performance. Neither accuracy nor distance is brought into focus.
Patterning	Child walks on the balance beam using an alternating step pattern with a well-balanced body position. Some hesitancy or slowness in performance may still exist.	The student executes a kicking pattern. The force, point of contact, and follow-through is the focus.
Adapting	Child walks on a balance beam with an alternating step pattern. He/she walks over a wand and through a hula hoop. May lack smoothness in performance.	The student adjusts his/her kicking pattern to perform an instep kick.
Refining	Each time the child walks on the balance beam, he/she performs the task smoothly with an alternating step pattern and good body position. He/she is able to move over the wand and through the hula hoop with no hesitation or loss of body control.	The student performs the instep kick efficiently in soccer. The pattern of the kick is performed smoothly with the same force and accuracy each time.
Varying	The child while walking on the balance beam varies the walk by adding a hop. The child is trying to perform a movement in a different way.	The student alters his/her kicking pattern to perform several variations. The student tries to perform the soccer kick from varying distances and positions from the goal.
Improvising	The child while walking on the beam uses a leap to go over the wand instead of a step.	The student in a game of soccer modifies the pass pattern to take advantage of his/her opponent's being pulled out of position.
Composing	The child designs and performs a series of moves on the balance beam.	The student designs an offensive strategy (kick at goal), responding to a set pattern of play developed with teammates.

Source: Sheryl L. Gotts, unpublished paper, Purdue University, 1972, 1976, cited in Ann E. Jewett and Marie R. Mullan, *Curriculum Design, Purposes and Processes in Physical Education Teaching-Learning* (Washington, DC: American Association of Health, Physical Education and Recreation, 1977).

involves the formulation of rules or principles that can be applied flexibly for different environmental conditions.

Accommodating or *adapting* consists of modifying a skill to meet the needs of a variety of conditions, such as shooting from different distances at archery targets or adapting to an opponent's movements on a basketball court. Accommodating results in a motor schema, which can be compared to a computer program that governs the use of various motor programs. Lead-up games can be used to promote accommodation.

Refining a skill involves practicing a specific skill, usually with skill drills, until it becomes smooth, efficient, accurate, and automatic, so that the learner can concentrate on game strategy rather than on the skill itself. Some skills, such as archery, require mostly refining; others are probably learned best with a combination of accommodating and refining.

Skill Differentiation

Skill differentiation includes creating and changing movement patterns to serve the unique needs of the individual performer. At this level of skill acquisition, the learner can selectively retrieve movement or motor patterns, or even schemas, to initiate and create changes in the environment rather than reacting to the environment.

Varying occurs when the performer changes force, speed, effort, shape, or other variables to make the movement unique to the learner. Advanced players create their own grip on the racket or club, their own free-throw variation, or even a new way to perform a skill.

Improvising utilizes spontaneous movements to create new or previously untried movements or combinations of movement, such as when a student must recover from an error in a gymnastics routine or when the ball must be saved from traveling out-of-bounds.

Composing makes use of consciously planned movements to create a new movement or a movement unique to the individual performer. This occurs when a learner choreographs a dance or synchronized swimming routine or creates a new game or movement skill. Two examples of each process just identified are presented in Table 5.5.

Review Questions: Define the three learning domains: cognitive, affective, psychomotor. What other learning domains might exist?

Define taxonomy.

Importance of the Taxonomies in Teaching Physical Education

In spite of the classifications determined by learning theorists, it is difficult to divide outcomes of learning into *solely* psychomotor, affective, or cognitive learning. For example, driving a car may involve mental and physical skills and attitudes and values such as courtesy and respect for the rights of others. Skills can be classified on various continuums, in terms of their cognitive, affective, or psychomotor involvement.[17]

Physical fitness involves all of the taxonomies. The skills involved in physical fitness are psychomotor skills. A knowledge of concepts and principles is necessary to assess fitness, write fitness programs, and evaluate progress. Maintaining a health- and fitness-enhancing lifestyle involves attitudes and values and is optimized by social interaction. Each of these areas is included in the following sections. In addition, Chapter 10 suggests strategies for teaching and assessing fitness.

The purpose of each taxonomy is to encourage physical educators to include in instruction a progression of learning outcomes from those lower on the taxonomy through the higher-order objectives listed at the top of each taxonomy. In this way the taxonomy can be used as a checklist to ensure that the entire range of behaviors is included in the curriculum or learning situation.

Corbin listed three common errors that result in failure to include the entire range of behaviors in the taxonomies. They are (1) trying to teach advanced skills and information without teaching essential prerequisites, (2) overemphasizing lower-order objectives, and (3) sacrificing higher-order objectives in the process of achieving lower-order objectives.[18] Teaching the higher-order problem-solving skills is essential so that students can learn to apply their knowledge and skills to real-life problems. The challenge, then, is to help students develop the capabilities to meet a full range of learning outcomes in each of the learning areas—cognitive, affective, and psychomotor.

A well-rounded physical education program helps students acquire a variety of physical skills, knowledges, and attitudes that contribute to students' enjoyment of physical activity and development of positive attitudes toward the body. The following sections will provide several practical strategies for developing teaching skills in each of the three learning domains.

Cognitive Learning

Traditionally, physical education teachers have emphasized skills and activities as the content of physical education. However, "being physically educated means having understandings about the body and physical activity that prepare each individual to want to live and be capable of living a physically active lifestyle."[19] Simplified concepts can be taught in elementary school with more in-depth analysis occurring in secondary schools.

Teaching the cognitive aspects of physical education is not easy. Planning is required to integrate concepts with psychomotor activity. Knowledge gained through relevant experience lasts longer than that gained merely through reading or listening, and psychomotor learning occurs faster when students understand the principles involved in skill performance. Many concepts can be integrated with physical activity to enhance understanding and save time. Concepts such as exercise heart rate can be taught during rest between periods of intense activity. Others can be taught when outdoor activities must be canceled during inclement weather, including concepts related to the activity itself or to the body of knowledge in physical education. Preservice teachers learn valuable concepts about principles of movement, motor learning, and exercise physiology that can be shared with students.

Cognitive Content

The knowledge explosion has dramatically increased physical education knowledge. The *Basic Stuff Series* was produced by AAHPERD to help physical educators communicate that knowledge to students in physical education classes. This series was updated and enhanced by a book entitled *Concepts of Physical Education: What Every Student Needs to Know.*[20] Using the content standards for physical education as a base, the book delineates the concepts that each student should know in order to become physically educated. Each discipline in physical education is featured in a chapter with a definition of the discipline, a brief statement about its importance, the standards to which it is linked, and the concepts related to that discipline that will help students reach the standards. Following an explanation of each concept, ideas are provided for the teacher to integrate the concepts into instruction for each grade level specified in the standards (in two-year intervals) and to assess student learning. For example, the following concepts are included in the chapter on social psychology, which is linked to the standards on personal and social behavior, enjoyment, challenge, self-expression, and social interaction:

- How do people feel about themselves when participating in physical activity?
- How can people improve their sense of self through physical activity?
- How can people continue to develop toward their full potential through physical activity?
- How do people learn to understand and respond to individual and group diversity?
- What kinds of social skills must people learn in order to perform successfully with others?

- How do people achieve the social skills needed to perform successfully with others?

A number of textbooks have emerged for students in middle and secondary schools that emphasize physical education content. The physical education content standards delineate several outcomes that students should achieve. For example, cognitive content such as rules, strategies, and an understanding of how to perform skills is required for students to demonstrate competency in movement forms. Students learn how to learn skills in the standard on applying movement concepts and principles to the learning and development of motor skills. The fitness outcomes require students to be able to assess their own fitness and to construct programs to achieve their desired goals. Underlying responsible personal and social behavior is an understanding of etiquette in activity settings and an understanding and respect for differences among people. An understanding of various physical activities can help students select those that will provide opportunities for enjoyment, challenge, self-expression, and social interaction.

Cognitive Learning Skills

Gagné listed three types of cognitive learning outcomes: (1) verbal information, (2) intellectual skills, and (3) cognitive strategies. *Verbal information* is knowledge or facts. *Intellectual skills* allow the learner to use the information to interact with the environment. The former are things learners can *tell,* while the skills reflect things students can *do.* Facts may be provided by the teacher prior to learning, recalled by the learner from previous learning, or learned just prior to the task at hand. When both facts and intellectual skills have been mastered, the learner is said to have the appropriate readiness for learning.[21] *Cognitive strategies* are skills used by learners to manage their own "learning, remembering, and thinking." They are used to help the learner decide what past knowledge and skills are to be used and how. During early learning experiences, the strategies are cued by the teacher. As the student's experience increases, the teacher may expect the strategies to be self-activated by the learner.[22]

Verbal Information

Verbal information includes memorization or rote learning and meaningful verbal learning. Teachers should become adept at teaching methods appropriate for both types of learning. Much information can be acquired through verbal learning in relatively short time periods.

Memorization Behavioral psychologists emphasize associating items to be learned with familiar items. Repetition of paired events is assumed to create a bond or association between them. For example, the acronym FITT is used to remember the components of an aerobic fitness program—frequency, intensity, time, and type of activity. Another method is using a key word, phrase, or mental image to remind the learner of the idea to be learned. Examples of mental images are the "backscratch" position in the tennis serve, the heart-shaped pull in the breaststroke, or the S pull in the freestyle. Learner-generated memory devices are generally more effective than teacher-generated devices.[23]

A common practice method is the progressive part method. The student learns part one, then parts one and two, and then one, two, three, and so forth. For example, when learning the bones in the body, start with the foot, review the foot and learn the ankle, review the foot and ankle and add the leg, and so forth. Another practice method is to respond to the entire task on each trial by using prompts such as crossing out parts of the material until the whole sequence has been learned. A third method is to use questions spaced periodically throughout the practice to increase student attention to the material. An example is to stop students during a game and have them identify the rule infraction. Reinforcement or confirmation of correct responses is essential so the learner knows that the material has been learned correctly. Feedback must be specific so students know whether the response is correct or, if incorrect, how to change it to make it correct. Rote learning has only specific transferability. Identical elements must occur in the new situation in order to trigger retrieval.[24]

Meaningful Verbal Learning Although memory devices are adequate for learning facts, they are not effective for comprehension. According to Ausubel, the key to comprehension is actively connecting new material to previously learned material to form a meaningful relationship.[25] Learning is enhanced by (1) presentation of an advance organizer, (2) presentation of the material to be learned, (3) anchoring new ideas to the existing cognitive structure, and (4) mastery of the new ideas.

An *advance organizer* is a verbal or visual expression that clarifies the relationship of knowledge to be learned with previously learned material. There are two kinds of advance organizers. An *expository organizer,* such as the one shown in Figure 5-2, is used when unfamiliar material is to be presented. It shows the relationship of parts to the whole. A *comparative organizer* shows the relationship of new and previously learned concepts by pointing out the similarities and differences between the two. A comparative organizer might compare the football throw to a softball throw. To facilitate learning, the teacher must refer to the previously learned skill, summarize the new material, and point out similarities and differences. The best advance organizers are often diagrams illustrating the relationships among content variables.

Content may be presented by lectures, demonstrations, class discussions, films, readings, or experiments. An outline can facilitate student organization of the material, and help students understand logical relationships and maintain their attention. General information should be presented

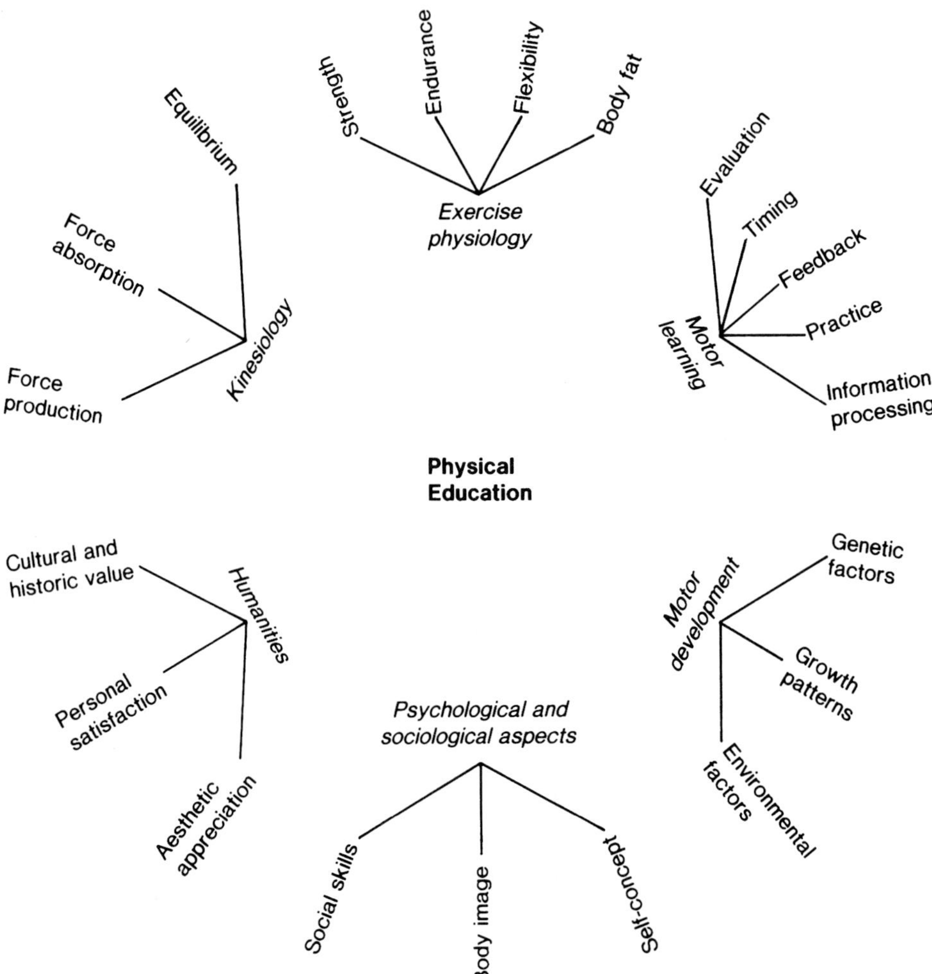

Figure 5-2
An advance organizer. The relationship of the various components of physical education.

first, followed by the details. Studies show that meaningful verbal material is learned more rapidly and retained more readily with less interference than rote learning and has the potential for general transfer to many situations.

Intellectual Skills

Intellectual skills use verbal information to help the learner interact with the environment. They include concept and discrimination learning, rule learning, and problem solving. *Concept* learning involves organizing environmental input into categories for storage in the brain. *Discrimination* involves perceiving features in an object or event that are the same as or different from features in other objects or events. A *rule* is a meaningful relationship between two or more concepts. *Problem solving* uses rules to help the learner interact with the environment.[26] Each skill will be reviewed briefly in the discussion that follows.

Concept and Discrimination Learning A *concept* is an idea or picture in the brain that helps to aid understanding, as diagrammed in Figure 5-3. It consists of perceptions, the meanings given them, feelings about them, and the words or symbols with which one discusses them. Most school learning involves concepts or the rules and principles created when concepts are linked together. Concept learning entails classifying objects and experiences into a category of elements that share certain essential characteristics. The essential features of a concept are shown in Table 5.6.

Concept learning involves the ability to *discriminate* between the relevant and irrelevant characteristics of examples and nonexamples. Concepts can be taught by using the following steps:

Step 1. Present a variety of labeled examples that incorporate all essential characteristics of the concept—"Jogging, stationary cycling, and walking are aerobic activities."

Step 2. Compare examples and nonexamples (see definitions in Table 5.6) to identify essential characteristics and develop a hunch or hypothesis. Within the examples and nonexamples, vary the irrelevant attributes.

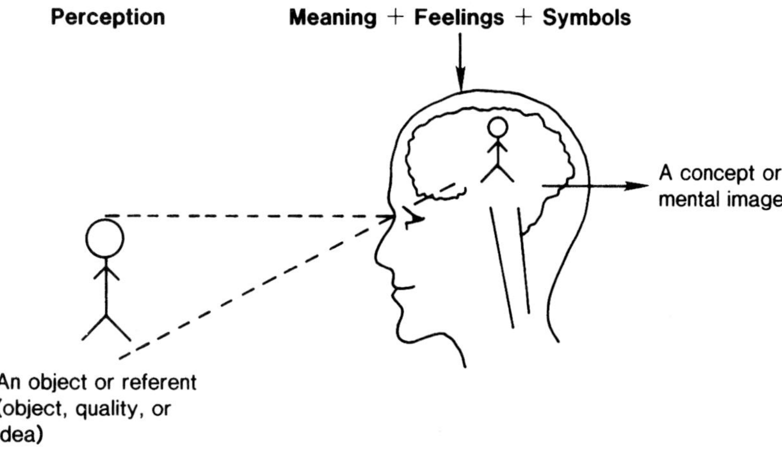

Figure 5-3
The origination of a concept.

TABLE 5.6 Features of a Concept

Name: Aerobic activities	
Definition—a Statement Specifying Essential Concept Attributes: Activities that develop oxygen transportation and utilization without incurring an oxygen debt are called aerobic activities.	
Essential or Shared Attributes:	**Irrelevant Attributes—Features That Often Accompany, but Are Not a Required Feature of, an Element Included in the Concept:**
The constant use of oxygen without incurring an oxygen debt	When or where a person runs
Examples Containing All Essential Characteristics:	**Nonexamples of the Concept—Examples with None or Only Some Essential Characteristics:**
Jogging	Sprinting
Walking	Calisthenics

Start with examples that are least similar, with the fewest shared characteristics. Ask "Is this an aerobic activity?": rowing—yes; sprinting—no; folk dance—yes.

Step 3. Verify the hypothesis by asking for several new examples of the concept. "List several aerobic activities."

Step 4. Have students state a definition of the concept in their own words. Check to see that the definition includes all essential characteristics of an aerobic activity.

Step 5. Reinforce correct answers.

Step 6. Apply the concept to choose appropriate examples.

Step 7. Test the concept. Can students generate examples with the essential characteristics and distinguish examples from nonexamples (e.g., aerobic from anaerobic activities)?

Concepts become more meaningful as students accumulate more experience with them. Laboratory experiences and demonstrations help students gain the experiences needed. Other ideas for teaching concepts include omitting some important feature of a skill, like stepping in the direction of the throw, to help the students see what a detrimental effect this has on the force of the throw, or conducting informal experiments by comparing conditions, such as heat, cold, or smog, as they affect exercise on different days.[27]

Rule Learning Concepts can be linked to form rules or principles, which are taught best by application. Students who apply rules retain them more easily than those who only learn to say or write them. Rules and principles are best taught by the following steps:

Step 1. Inform the learner of the expected performance. "Traveling is a violation in basketball."

Step 2. Recall the component concepts. "Traveling is . . . A violation is . . ."

Step 3. Provide verbal cues that explain the relationships of the concepts. "Traveling is an unfair advantage with no body contact and is therefore a violation."

Step 4. Ask each student to demonstrate one or more instances of the rule (e.g., show various examples of traveling such as taking more than a two-step stop or moving the pivot foot).

Step 5. Ask each student to state the rule.

Step 6. Apply the rule in more complex situations (e.g., play a game and identify traveling).

Students should be taught concepts and rules at the same time the psychomotor skill is learned. For example, rules involving the volleyball serve should be taught while students are learning the serve. Principles relating to force production should be taught or recalled when hitting a tennis serve or throwing a ball. Following are some ways to teach rules:

- Give the rule and an example. Ask students to supply a second example.
- Give one or more examples. Have students formulate the rule.
- Give an example. State the rule. Ask students for a second example.
- Give the rule and ask students for an example.
- Give the rule and ask students to restate the rule.
- Give an example. Ask students for a second example.[28]

Problem Solving Problem solving is the capacity to solve previously unencountered situations by combining old rules and principles into new higher-order ones. A problem is solved when previous knowledge or behavior is combined into a new relationship or added to new information to form an insight that resolves the new situation. Problem solving can be used to develop game strategies, create new games, compose gymnastic routines, choreograph dances, and for a host of other creative endeavors. Problem solving involves the following steps:

Step 1. *Present students with a worthwhile problem.* Design problems to help students apply recently learned principles. Problems must be worth solving and be capable of resolution with the time and resources available. Students should understand the problem and the expected performance. Essential features of the problem could be in the form of questions as simple as "How do I move my bowsight in archery?" or as complex as "Why are some people better performers in some activities, while others are better in other activities?"

Step 2. *Recall previously learned knowledge and behavior.* Teach or recall knowledge and skills that relate to the problem. For example, have students shoot at thirty yards and ask them where they think they should place the bowsight based on their previous shooting at twenty yards.

Step 3. *Provide assistance to channel students' thinking.* Teaching problem-solving strategies leads to better problem solving. Students differ in their abilities to solve problems. Bloom and Broder discovered a number of differences between successful and unsuccessful problem solvers.[29]

Unsuccessful solvers

- had low reading comprehension and failed to understand the problem. Often the problem they solved was not the one presented.
- were unaware they possessed the knowledge necessary to solve the problem.
- approached problems as if they had pat solutions.
- lacked confidence in their ability to solve problems.

To help students understand the problem, break it down into manageable components, recall relevant knowledge and skills, and reinforce the possibility of several solutions. The greater the ability to recall and apply previously learned knowledge and skills, the greater the chances of solving the problem. Listen to students' exploration of possible alternatives or provide students with cues to channel their thinking.[30] For example, ask, "What happened when you moved your bowsight up? Try moving it another direction to see what happens." Group discussion and participation appear to be superior to individual problem solving.

Step 4. *Reinforce both the process and the solution.* Let students know you have confidence in their ability to solve problems, and establish an environment of acceptance and self-worth in which students feel free to explore alternative solutions to problems. Make sure students have time to solve problems without pressure.

Cognitive Strategies

Learning strategies are behaviors designed to influence the manner in which the learner selects, organizes, and integrates new knowledge with already existing knowledge.[31] Helping students develop effective ways to handle information should be a major educational goal. Goals should be concerned with the products, as well as with the processes, of learning. Teachers can help students recognize the correct strategies for given situations. A relative newcomer in the research arena is *metacognition,* which refers to one's knowledge about his or her own cognitive processes. Flavell wrote:

> I am engaging in metacognition . . . if I notice that I am having more trouble learning A than B; if it strikes me that I should double-check C before accepting it as a fact; if it occurs to me that I had better scrutinize each and every alternative in any multiple-choice type task situation before deciding which is the best one; if I sense that I had better make a note of D because I may forget it.[32]

Metacognition involves knowing *when* you know something and when you do not, *what* you need to know and what you already know, and *how* to use learning strategies to acquire the information needed. Metacognition also helps you decide what information should be stored, how much information can be handled at a time in short-term memory, and how to link the new information with previously stored information. Metacognition increases as children mature.[33]

Learning strategies range from the basic association strategies used for rote learning, such as key words or mental images, to complex strategies for organizing material, such as paraphrasing, summarizing, creating analogies, using advance organizers, underlining, listing, note taking, question asking or answering, outlining, diagramming, and comprehension monitoring.[34]

Students should be encouraged to make a conscious effort to apply learning to life's problems. Cognitive work can be done in learning centers, at which students work individually or as teams to discover psychomotor or cognitive principles and skills related to sport and fitness.[35] Students should rotate into games or other activities at planned intervals. Homework assignments might be used to apply school learning to problems in the home or community. Homework can inform the family about physical education and even involve them directly in physical education activities. It can be used to practice skills, to learn or apply concepts, to increase physical fitness, to solve problems, and to develop self-discipline. Students can be encouraged to work together to complete assignments. French, Arbogast and Misner, and Docheff listed a number of possibilities for homework in physical education:[36]

- Practicing skills using task sheets or mental practice
- Attending sports events or watching them on television
- Coaching or officiating youth sports
- Tutoring another student in a skill
- Watching films or other media in a learning resource center
- Studying for tests and quizzes or completing take-home tests or quizzes
- Interviewing well-known sports figures
- Reading books on sports and physical activities and writing book reports
- Reporting on current events
- Participating in fitness or activity programs
- Completing study guides, worksheets, or concept games (such as crossword puzzles or scrambled word games)
- Completing a fitness journal
- Charting skill improvement on a progress chart
- Reacting to situations involving sportsmanship, feelings, or attitudes

As one objective of physical education is to encourage people to exercise on their own, why not reward students who make a habit of self-directed fitness activities?[37] Cameron tried a bonus incentive plan with extra-credit points earned for an optional out-of-class assignment each week. A maximum of three points could be earned based on the level of the problem selected. Problems consisted of self-testing and problem-solving activities, concept-related experiences, analysis of readings, and the interpretation and design of learning materials.[38]

Table 5.7 shows some examples of activities involving the various aspects of cognitive learning in physical education. Other examples, including how to assess individual and group projects involving cognitive learning, are provided in Chapter 11.

Review Questions: What differences exist between rote learning and meaningful verbal learning? Which type of cognitive learning is best for learning facts? For learning principles?

What is an advance organizer? How should it be used to increase student learning?

List some concepts you might teach when explaining a sport or game.

List some examples of problem solving that might help students learn the principles of biomechanics in sport activities.

Why is it important to teach the "why" along with the "how" of physical activity? How can this be accomplished?

AFFECTIVE AND SOCIAL LEARNING

Affective strategies are used to focus attention, maintain concentration, establish and maintain motivation, manage anxiety, develop self-esteem, and learn ethical and social behavior.[39] The primary purpose of teaching in the affective domain is to help students learn how to deal with their emotions and attitudes toward physical activity and toward others.

Compared with cognitive and psychomotor learning, little affective learning has been deliberately introduced into the curriculum because it is much easier to teach knowledge and skills than to influence attitudes, feelings, and character.

Developing Positive Attitudes toward Physical Activity

One's tastes, preferences, attitudes, and values will ultimately affect how one chooses to behave. Because students are both thinking and feeling beings, no learning can possibly occur without feelings being involved—feelings about themselves, the subject matter, and the situation. These feelings and values are powerful forces that sometimes block learning and on other occasions enhance it. When teachers are aware of students' feelings about physical education, they can provide appropriate learning situations. When teachers ignore the affective domain and pressure students to learn apart from their feelings and interests, students often end up disliking physical activity.

Since activity enjoyment is prerequisite to continued engagement in activity, teachers should help students

TABLE 5.7 Examples of Cognitive Learning Activities

	Teaching Strategies	Learning Activities
CONCEPTS AND RULES	• Use cues to teach skills. • Teach related rules when teaching skills. • Use bulletin board displays or worksheets to teach concepts and rules. • Have students make appropriate officiating calls from written descriptions of game situations. • Show video clip excerpts of game play, stopping at intervals and asking students to make the call, first as a group and later individually. • Use heart rate monitors to help students understand cardiovascular endurance.	• Look for examples of concepts and rules in videos or on TV. • Look for examples of the use of skills in one's own or a partner's performance. • Read books or newspaper articles and find examples of good or bad etiquette, racial or gender discrimination, etc. • Diagram or define a rule or strategy (such as offsides). • Interpret fitness data, supported by reasons or evidence for the interpretation. • Create a bulletin board or poster using concepts learned about fitness, etc. • Collect fitness articles and look for concepts about fitness. • Perform lab experiments involving fitness principles and write a report of your findings.
PROBLEM SOLVING	• Encourage students to study their own performance and the performance of their opponents and to change their performance to match changes in the environment. • Ask students questions that demand application to various situations and encourage students to ask and answer their own questions. • Make sure problems are worthwhile. • Recall information and skills needed to solve problems. • Provide resources for student projects. • Express confidence in students' abilities to solve problems.	• Plan a practice session for your team. • Write a newspaper article or a newsletter to mail home. • Create an advertisement or television commercial for a sport-related product. • Compare and contrast tennis shoes and work shoes. • Compare two methods of high-jumping. Use biomechanical principles to explain your answer. • Make up a lead-up game incorporating your assigned skill and other required components. • Choreograph a dance, jump rope routine, aerobics, or gymnastics routine. • Develop a way to collect game statistics for each team and player during a class tournament. Collect the statistics. Use the results to assess how well your team is performing. • Create a web page or video that teaches rules and strategies for basketball. Share your production with the class. • Design nutritious meals. Use a computer software program to evaluate your meals.
LEARNING STRATEGIES	• Lead a discussion about students' effectiveness in working together on projects.	• Students write about their experiences in physical education and reflect upon their learning and about their interactions with others.

develop favorable attitudes toward physical activity. To achieve this it is imperative that when students are in any physical education instructional or extracurricular activity, they are at the same time (1) in the presence of positive conditions and consequences and (2) in the presence of as few negative conditions and consequences as possible. This does not mean that all instruction should be fun, but it does mean that students will work harder and learn more when given the appropriate conditions. Although it is not always possible to determine whether a given condition is positive or negative for a certain student, Mager suggested a number of conditions or consequences that are generally considered to be positive or negative.[40] Examples are shown in Tables 5.8 and 5.9.

A supportive classroom environment is one in which students are treated as individuals and in which they know that help is available. Brophy summed up the research by saying:

TABLE 5.8 Positive Conditions and Consequences

Content-Oriented Conditions

1. Providing challenging instruction that leads to success most of the time
2. Helping students know what the course objectives are and where they are in relation to the goal
3. Preassessing students and providing instructional tasks that will help students achieve course objectives
4. Providing immediate, specific feedback in a positive way
5. Helping students develop confidence in their performance by overlearning skills
6. Keeping verbal instruction to a minimum
7. Using only relevant test items for the specified objectives
8. Allowing students to select some learning activities
9. Basing grades on each student's achievement, not on how well the other students performed

Student-Oriented Conditions

1. Expressing genuine interest in the students and in their individual successes
2. Treating each student as a person
3. Acknowledging students' responses as legitimate learning attempts even when incorrect
4. Allowing students to learn without public awareness of errors

Environment

1. Providing an environment in which students feel accepted, supported, and trusted
2. Providing a wide range of activities in which students can choose to involve themselves with appropriate counseling
3. Focusing on what students can do rather than on what they cannot do

> Effective teachers maintain a strong academic focus within the context of a pleasant, friendly classroom. Highly effective teachers clearly stress . . . objectives, but they do not come across as slave drivers, and their classrooms do not resemble sweatshops. They maintain high standards and demand that students do their best, but they are not punitive or hypercritical. Instead, students perceive effective teachers as enthusiastic and thorough instructors whose classrooms are friendly and convivial.[41]

Improving Self-Esteem

Felker developed five keys for improving students' self-concepts based on helping students develop the language necessary to enhance and maintain the self-concept.[42] They include (1) adults, praise yourselves, (2) help students evaluate realistically, (3) teach students to set reasonable goals, (4) teach students to praise themselves, and (5) teach students to praise others.

Because students learn by imitating a model, teachers must learn to praise themselves. Express how good it makes you feel that you accomplished something. Later, expand to praise of your personal qualities. Try to use a variety of phrases for praising. Students need to learn to evaluate realistically in terms of actual achievement. One way to help students do this is to have them check off skills or grade and record test scores. See Chapter 11 for examples of useful assessment techniques.

Research shows that students with poor self-esteem tend to set goals too high or too low. They perceive themselves as failures when they fail to achieve goals that are too high or when they achieve a goal that anyone, even they, could reach. When students are taught to set realistic goals, their commitment to reaching them is increased. Goals should be set slightly higher than prior performances for effective learning. Short-term goals geared toward success lend themselves to appropriate praise and reward for achievement. Students should then move step-by-step up the ladder toward long-term goals.

By teaching students to praise themselves, the teacher is released from the role of behavior reinforcer. Teachers can help students learn to reinforce their own behavior by beginning with group praise, such as "Didn't we do well at . . .?" and then moving to "Don't you think you did a great job on . . .?" Students could also be helped to evolve from such self-encouraging statements as "I am trying hard" or "I am improving" to such self-praise as "I did a good job" or "I am a good sport." As students praise themselves, they attach the label of "worthwhile" to themselves and their behavior, and their self-esteem rises.

Felker pointed out that self-praise and praise of others are positively correlated. Praising others tends to result in satisfying responses from others, but students should be taught how to handle the few negative responses that might result. They also should be taught how

TABLE 5.9 Negative Conditions and Consequences

Pain (Physical Discomfort)

1. Forcing students to overdo in a physical fitness program, resulting in nausea, sore muscles, etc.
2. Failing to provide adequate safety, with resulting injury
3. Making students sit for long periods of time when dressed for activity
4. Allowing the classroom to be too hot or too cold or forcing students to participate outside when the temperature is too hot or cold, on wet grass, or when it is smoggy
5. Forcing students to rush from one class to another or to dress more quickly than is reasonable
6. Using subject matter as an instrument of punishment

Anxiety (Mental or Emotional Discomfort or Anticipated Unpleasantness)

1. Being unpredictable about what is expected or how it will be graded
2. Expressing that the student cannot possibly succeed
3. Using vague, threatened punishment

Frustration (Interference with Goal-Directed Activities)

1. Presenting information or skills faster or slower than the student can learn them or forcing all students to learn at the same pace
2. Teaching one thing and testing another
3. Failing to provide immediate and/or adequate feedback
4. Stopping an activity just as the students are beginning to enjoy and be absorbed in it
5. Overemphasizing competition during class time

Humiliation and Embarrassment (Lowered Self-Respect, Pride, or Painful Self-Consciousness)

1. Making a public spectacle of a student, such as making the student do push-ups while the class watches or belittling the student's attempts to do well
2. Allowing repeated failure
3. Labeling students—"special ed.," "handicapped," etc.

Boredom

1. Repeating instructions that students have already had
2. Failing to challenge students
3. Failing to use variety in presenting course content

to receive praise sometimes, by praising in return and sometimes by a simple "thank you."

Developing Self-Efficacy

Self-efficacy is a person's belief in his or her ability to execute the behavior needed to produce a specified outcome, or, in simpler terms, it is situation-specific self-confidence. Efficacy expectations determine a student's activity selection, effort expenditure, and task persistence. Teachers should focus on developing competence, which in turn develops self-confidence. Romance suggested three ways teachers can detect students who lack confidence in physical education:

1. Performer uses extraneous or protective movements.
   a. Performer spends an inordinate amount of time warming up before trying a gymnastic trick.
   b. Performer goofs around—does not perform seriously—so as to mask unconfidence.
   c. Novice diver constantly reverts to a jump into the water at the moment of execution.
2. Performer uses inappropriate choice of tempo for moving.
   a. Performer rushes through a dance step, not staying with the music.
   b. Performer walks through the hurdling motion again and again.
3. Performer fixates on single element in environment.
   a. Performer continues to measure his or her jump rope and trade for new one.
   b. Performer is constantly tying shoe.
   c. Performer complains about condition of equipment (balls too slippery).[43]

Students who possess self-confidence persist in activities even when not directly supervised by the teacher.

Confident performers believe they can handle new tasks and that the tasks will be satisfying, whereas those who lack confidence anticipate unpleasant consequences. Students who think they can accomplish a task may achieve tasks the teacher thinks are too difficult. However, students who think they cannot do something may avoid a task they could easily do. Dangers arise when students try activities beyond their capacities, resulting in injury or defeat.[44]

According to Feltz and Weiss, self-efficacy can be increased through (1) ensuring performance success, (2) communicating effectively, (3) modeling techniques, (4) encouraging positive talk, and (5) reducing anxiety-producing factors.[45] Performance accomplishment results from challenging activities at a level that permits student success early in the learning experience. Success yields motivation; therefore, teachers should choose activities for which students have the prerequisite skills and ensure a progression of activities from simple to complex. If tasks are too easy or performed with outside help, students attribute success to outside forces, resulting in boredom and a lack of self-efficacy. If tasks are too difficult, anxiety and failure may occur. Only success attributed to student effort results in self-efficacy.

Personally selected, specific, challenging but realistic goals result in self-efficacy. Process-oriented goals under the learner's control, such as the ability to use specified strategies in a game situation or perform a certain skill in a gymnastics routine, should be emphasized rather than winning, over which the learner may have no control. Teachers and coaches should evaluate communication to determine if it is positive and equitable for all students. One means of effective communication involves complimenting correct technique, then providing feedback on how to improve, followed by encouragement to keep trying. This "sandwich" technique was developed to the pinnacle of success by Coach John Wooden at UCLA.[46]

Modeling is important for developing self-efficacy, especially when the models are similar in age, sex, and athletic ability, and when they demonstrate the ability to achieve success through effort. To promote task persistence, however, models must exude confidence. Appropriate role modeling by teachers and coaches wins student respect, encourages confidence in teachers' abilities to help students learn, and encourages students' desire to achieve the modeled behavior.

Positive self-talk by students should be directed toward effort rather than winning. Students who perceive that effort yields success persist longer than those who focus on ability. Mental imagery can be used to envision successful performance in sport situations.

Promoting Moral Development

Phi Delta Kappa/Gallup polls show that a majority of the American people want schools to teach values and ethical behavior.[47] As an agent of society, the school is obligated to transmit societal values to the young. Historically, values cherished by the American people include loyalty, self-discipline, honesty, and hard work. The existing morality of a society is called the *moral consensus.* Each individual must develop a personal value system by applying rules and principles to moral situations and making decisions that result in a *moral sense.* Oser, paraphrasing Durkheim, stated that "values like the protection of life, the procedural forms of a democracy, and the dignity of a person cannot be reconsidered in such a way that everybody is free to choose or not to choose them."[48]

Oser concluded that moral education has been greatly neglected in the schools.[49] He said, "The inescapable reality is that the school setting is always a moral enterprise; the inescapable fact is that social and political life is filled with moral content, and that history encompasses millions of moral decisions with which we as educators have to deal."[50]

Oser found conflicting strategies for moral learning.[51] Values education usually refers to helping people become aware of their own values. Moral education commonly refers to a Kantian concept of justice. According to Rest, morality includes behavior that internalizes social norms, helps others, puts their interests ahead of one's own, arouses guilt or empathy, or includes reasoning about justice.[52] One must base decisions on the universal principles that guide moral behavior.

Kohlberg's *cognitive development approach* is probably the best-known moral development model. He proposed six levels of moral judgment, and he encouraged teaching moral judgment by stimulating a moral crisis or disequilibrium to guide the person to the next higher stage of moral judgment. This procedure is called a *plus-one strategy.*[53]

Moral discourse is the common denominator of moral learning. Members participate in discussions about problems of justice, through which each person learns to develop a personal point of view and, at the same time, consider the point of view of others.[54] Any solution to a moral problem must be understood in terms of the following four principles governing moral discourse: (1) justification of one's course of action, (2) fairness, (3) the consequences of actions and omissions, and (4) universalization, which is a desire to take the role of a concerned person.[55]

A moral educational situation is created for an educational purpose. It demands a moral decision and has real consequences. The situation must look at the circumstances, needs, motives, and interests of the person involved and apply the four principles just outlined. Hersh, Paolitto, and Reimer described a nine-year-old boy with cerebral paralysis whom the other students teased. One day when Brian was absent the teacher explained that some people are born with conditions that prevent them from using their muscles in a normal way. She wondered what it would be like to be Brian. The children empathized and reacted. When Brian returned, they were much more receptive and helpful.[56]

The discussion helped students evaluate previous actions in terms of what was just, and the children changed their behavior as a result. The interaction allowed the children the freedom to react openly and listen to the point of view of someone else. Students need to consider a justification for the correct action, the means for carrying out the action, the responsibility they are willing to accept, the psychological and social obstacles they might confront, and the social consequences of the action.[57] To accomplish the goals of moral education, students must have a warm, accepting atmosphere in which conversation rules are maintained and aggression is minimized. Students should be led to analyze their own values and then the values of their peers, families, schools, and places of employment.

Physical education is an especially appropriate place to teach moral education. A position statement by the American Academy of Physical Education urged physical educators to encourage and support the following:

1. That the development of moral and ethical values be stated among the aims of the physical education program
2. That the educational preparation of physical education teachers and athletic coaches emphasize moral and ethical values
3. That the emphasis on the teaching of moral and ethical values by physical education teachers and athletic coaches be encouraged
4. That the profession of physical education establish criteria for the selection of appropriate ethical and moral values, develop formal plans of instruction, and methods for the assessment of results[58]

Values that physical education can teach are cooperation and teamwork, tolerance and respect for others, loyalty, fairness, integrity, dependability, unselfishness, self-control, responsibility for the consequences of one's behavior, and friendliness.

Several research studies have shown that the use of moral dilemmas in physical education classes can effectively promote moral development. Preston used the Kohlbergian process to teach moral education in once-a-week sessions in health and physical education with positive results. Romance, Weiss, and Bockoven used moral dilemmas and other techniques successfully with fifth graders. Bredemeier, Weiss, Shields, and Shewchuk used Bandura's social learning principles and moral dilemmas in physical education classes and found both to be effective. Giebink and McKenzie utilized three strategies (instruction and praise, modeling, and a point system) to promote sportspersonship in a softball class. They demonstrated that sportspersonship can be taught in physical education classes, with unsportspersonlike behaviors decreasing dramatically. Since the phases followed each other, the three techniques undoubtedly had a cumulative effect. The learned behavior, however, did not transfer to a recreational basketball setting. They concluded, therefore, that sportspersonship training must occur over a long period of time and in a variety of settings.[59]

Wandzilak suggested five steps for constructing a social learning and moral development model to affect values through physical activity. The steps are (1) identify and define the specific values to be developed in terms of the behavior to be observed; (2) identify the physical activities and the dilemmas most appropriate for achieving the values and place them in a sequential order in terms of difficulty; (3) reward higher stages of moral reasoning with extra playing time, a sportspersonship trophy, or other reward rather than winning; (4) evaluate by using various observational techniques (see Chapter 14); and (5) use the evaluation data to evaluate the success of the model.[60]

The following techniques have proven useful to promote moral or character development:

Moral dilemmas—real or hypothetical.[61] Sport provides its own moral dilemmas in which disequilibrium exists between the actual and desired behavior of students. Physical educators acting in a warm, accepting environment can guide or facilitate student discussions about these dilemmas. Interacting with an individual, small group, or class, the teacher can help students understand (1) why the action was taken, (2) alternative behaviors that might have been used, (3) the feelings of all persons involved in each of the alternative solutions, and (4) the most just solution to the situation the students are ready to accept. Real dilemmas can be created by allowing students to form their own teams for a game or relay, play as long as they want before substituting themselves out of a game, or by teacher-imposed rules that are unfair. Help students discuss and change the rules or procedures to improve the situation for all concerned.

Game creating.[62] Interpersonal communication, learning to consider the perspective of others, cooperation, and problem solving are involved in creating games. The teacher might prescribe a limited amount of equipment, space, skills to be used, and safety procedures and ask students to develop a game in which all players have an equal chance to succeed. Games can be cooperative or competitive.

Class rules.[63] Students in each class can participate in a discussion at the beginning of the school year to establish class rules and the consequences for nonconformance to rules. As part of this process, students can be asked to make a list of their rights and responsibilities.

Challenge and initiative activities. Students work together to solve problems and achieve specified goals (see Chapter 10).

Sharing.[64] Students are given a task and some of the resources necessary to complete the task. They must bargain with other groups for the resources they are missing. A time limit is imposed.

Listening bench.[65] When two students disagree, send them to a specified place to discuss their feelings and come up with potential solutions. A time limit and specific dialogue instructions can facilitate the process. Students should report their results to the teacher before resuming activity.

Review Questions: How can you tell whether a student feels good about physical education? How can you increase the chances of a student feeling good about physical education?

Why is self-efficacy important in learning motor skills? How is it acquired?

How can moral and character education be increased? What values might best be taught in physical education?

Activity: Attempt to incorporate the use of higher-order cognitive learning into your lessons using some of the ideas presented in this chapter. Design lessons to promote a positive affective environment each day.

PSYCHOMOTOR LEARNING

Although physical education has the same concerns relative to the domains of learning as do other subject areas, the unique contribution of this field is in the psychomotor area. Skills can be taught by creating environmental conditions in a microcosm of the total game or by learning the most basic skills, then playing the game and teaching related skills as they arise. For example, a simple game of soccer can be played with the dribble and pass, with throw-ins, goalkeeping, corner kicks, and other skills, rules, and strategies added as the need arises. Telling students what will be encountered is less effective.

Psychomotor development depends on several factors. Three of the most important factors, determined from research on psychomotor learning, are perception, practice, and feedback.

Perception

Perception is the process of entering information into the brain.[66] The sense organs receive information from the environment that is processed in terms of its relationship to previously learned data. Only a small part of the information received by the senses is processed.

A model of the skill is extremely important so that students gain a correct perception of the desired performance. A good demonstration is worth a thousand words. Complete demonstrations, performed several times (three to five) from different angles, enhance their effectiveness. The demonstration may be done by the teacher, a student, a film, or a videotape. Factors that interfere with the learner's visual, auditory, or internal attention on the model include poor lighting, sighting into the sun or against a similarly colored background, background activities, yelling or talking by other students, sleepiness, fatigue, boredom, or discouragement. "Formulating an accurate motor plan may be the most important stage of skill learning" next to motivation.[67] Students must perceive what the skill should look like and feel like while they are performing it.

Two or three short verbal cues help the student perceive the demonstration's key points without being distracted by nonessential movement. Too much verbiage or too many cues can be distracting. Verbal directions or cues help learners recognize or recall facts, skills, or strategies needed for current learning. Cues are a guide to learning during the cognitive phase as described by Fitts and Posner.[68] Appropriate cues are selected by analyzing the learners and biomechanics related to the skill and determining the most common errors. The cues focus the learner's cognitive processes on the part of the performance that may be more difficult. Concentrating on cues one at a time facilitates absorption by the learner. Some cues for the volleyball set might be (1) look through the triangle, (2) keep your seat down, and (3) extend. For the badminton clear, the cues might be (1) scratch your back, (2) reach for the shuttle, and (3) make the racket whistle. Fronske has written two books that include possible cues for several activities.[69]

Students must also be helped to identify and attend to regulatory stimuli such as ball direction, speed, height, spin, angle or distance from the goal, or the location of other players. With skills like golf, the focus is on the position of the body and the implement and the learner's kinesthetic awareness. Students need to know such items as where to position themselves in relation to other objects, where to look for relevant cues, how to discriminate the object from the background, and how to use the cues to predict changes in the environment. At the same time, learners need to learn to disregard irrelevant aspects such as the spectators, environmental conditions, and anxiety. Although learners may be told this information, a demonstration or guided discovery is more effective.

Review Questions: Why is perception important in all kinds of learning? What is the purpose of cues, and how are they selected?

Practice

Following the demonstration, students should practice the skill in the most appropriate environment. Motor skill practice is essential for skilled movement. In general, motor learning and field-based research have shown that practice is highly related to achievement. The following are factors that teachers should consider when designing practice for the psychomotor domain: (1) learner involvement, (2) type of skill, (3) task appropriateness, (4) whole versus part practice, (5) massed versus distributed practice, (6) mental practice, (7) transfer, and (8) retention.

Learner Involvement In the mid-1970s researchers conducted the Beginning Teacher Evaluation Study

(BTES). The research team concluded: "Teachers who find ways to put students into contact with the academic curriculum and to keep them in contact with that curriculum while maintaining a convivial classroom atmosphere are successful in promoting achievement."[70]

From these findings, the research team identified and studied three measures of time, each of which correlated more closely with academic achievement.[71] *Allocated time,* the amount of time provided for instruction in a given subject area, depends on the district, school, or department philosophy and on school finances. *Engaged time,* the amount of time the student attends to instruction in a given subject, primarily depends on the teacher's goals and managerial skills. *Academic learning time* (ALT) is the number of minutes the student is engaged with activities and instructional materials at an easy level for that student (generally an 80 percent success level). Although the BTES study showed a strong correlation between ALT and achievement, it varied for different subjects, objectives, grade levels, and teachers.[72]

Metzler modified the BTES instrument to measure ALT in physical education; he then measured ALT-PE in a variety of contexts.[73] He defined ALT-PE as "the amount of time students spend in class activity engaged in relevant overt motor responding at a high success rate."[74] Far less ALT was found in physical education than had been imagined and much of it was cognitive rather than psychomotor.

In 1989 Metzler reviewed the research on time in physical education. He concluded that teachers (1) spend 25 to 50 percent of class time in noninstructional activities, (2) conceptualize time for classes, not individual students, (3) do not plan for maximum student participation, and (4) are inconsistent in their use of time during a class period or from lesson to lesson. He also noted a relationship between what teachers do and how students spend time in classes. With regard to students, he summarized that (1) students spend only about 20 to 50 percent of their time in activities that contribute to intended learning outcomes; (2) students differ in the amount of time they spend on achievement-related learning; (3) student time varies with the activity in which students are engaged; and (4) student ALT is low regardless of who the teacher is. Although boys and girls get approximately equal amounts of ALT, elementary pupils get more than secondary students, and college students get more than twice that of younger students. Students in individual sports get more time on-task than those in team sports. Time also varies with student ability, with students with disabilities in regular physical education classes receiving the least of all.[75]

ALT-PE was used for many years to evaluate teacher effectiveness. ALT-PE research was based on the assumption that ALT in physical education correlates with student achievement as it does in academic subjects. Metzler noted at least eleven studies in physical education that reported correlations between practice time on the criterion task and increased student learning. Although ALT-PE is essential for learning, it is not sufficient by itself to cause learning. For example, when students are engaged in playing a full six-versus-six-player volleyball game, the players may be actively participating, but receive relatively few opportunities to actually "practice" the skill.

Silverman found that the number and appropriateness of practice trials correlated significantly with student achievement. Buck and Harrison suggested that ALT-PE might not exist under Siedentop's definition, which required successful student engagement about 80 percent of the time. Students *appeared* to be motor appropriate, but videotape analysis of learning trials showed that very few students achieved an 80 percent success level.[76] Buck and Harrison further showed that game play did not increase the performance level of students; in fact, student skill levels regressed during game play. Contrary to popular belief, sport skills are not acquired merely by playing games.[77] Neither the number of contacts per serve nor the percentage of correct trials improved. As the emphasis turned to strategies, the level of play decreased. Regression occurs when students have not learned basic skills or when they are unable to apply the skills in a game setting. Finding themselves unsuccessful, some students become "competent bystanders" like Griffin's invisible players and lost souls. They develop "a strategy for appearing to be involved in game play without actually coming in contact with the ball."[78] They back off and expect someone else to step in and hit it. The high-ability students are aggressive and take over for the low-skilled students. Low-skilled students talk to the teacher about how to perform the skill rather than actually practicing it.[79]

This discussion leads to one conclusion—*physical education teachers need to increase the number and quality of learning trials if students are to become proficient in motor skills.* Research indicates that instruction should be provided in a way that allows maximum participation by each student. Some relatively simple changes in teacher behavior have been shown to increase ALT-PE. Programs that teach teachers to reduce management and student nonengagement time and to increase feedback to students result in more engaged skill learning time. Teachers increase motor appropriate responses by using additional equipment and facilities to decrease waiting, clearly communicating class procedures, and challenging students with more demanding instructional objectives.[80]

Reductions in funding for education forces teachers to creatively manage large classes in limited spaces with inadequate equipment. The organization of time, space, equipment, rules, and group size all affect the amount of time each student has to participate in the activity and, therefore, to achieve success. Table 5.10 provides some suggestions for dealing with these variables. The book *Changing Kids' Games* also outlines different ways to modify activities to increase learner involvement.[81] A games approach can also be used to teach wall/net games, target games, invasion games, and striking/fielding

TABLE 5.10 Guidelines for Increasing Learner Involvement

I. Time
   A. Keep talk short and provide demonstrations/cues.
   B. Eliminate unnecessary showering or dressing. Reduce roll-call time.
   C. Keep waiting in lines to a minimum.
   D. Plan drills to minimize transition time (i.e., three-player drill to a six-player drill).
   E. Use inactive time to work on study sheets; learn rules or fitness concepts; take written, skill, or fitness tests; study films or videotapes; work on skill checklists, etc.

II. Space
   A. Use alternative teaching areas (hallways, multipurpose rooms, community facilities) when feasible.
   B. Teachers could share a gym and a classroom and take turns teaching concepts and activities.
   C. Adjust class sizes among instructors when facilities are small (i.e., sixty students in soccer, twenty in tennis).
   D. Provide alternative activities (fitness) for those waiting for turns.

III. Equipment
   A. Use modified equipment (i.e., lighter balls and implements, shorter net heights and baskets, shorter serving distances).
   B. Increase the number of equipment pieces so all students have access to equipment.
   C. Design drills that involve learners in different roles at the same time—dribbling and guarding in basketball.
   D. Use one piece of equipment for every two or three students and have one student tutor or one toss and one retrieve.
   E. Use stations at which students practice using different pieces of equipment or apparatus.

IV. Rules
   A. Design games to increase trials—require three hits on a side; use underhand volleyball serves; have softball pitchers pitch to their own team; eliminate jump balls and free throws.
   B. Change nature of drill or game from competitive to cooperative (award points for the highest number of volleys, pass-set-spike sequences, lay-ups, etc.).
   C. Use a games approach to teach wall/net games, invasion games, and striking/fielding games.

V. Group Size
   A. Keep teams small so the number of contacts with equipment is increased.
   B. Keep playing areas small.
   C. Use both homogeneous and heterogeneous grouping patterns to motivate students to improve skills.

games. Games are adapted so students can play real games at their level of competence and then play at progressively more complex levels until the official game is played.[82]

Type of Skill While a learner is acquiring the motor pattern of a movement, the teaching emphasis and practice environment should differ depending on the type of skill to be learned. Gentile, who adapted a system used in industry to classify skills into open and closed skills, indicated that skills actually exist on a continuum.[83]

A *closed skill* is done in a relatively stable environment. Examples of closed skills are archery, bowling, gymnastics, golf, the basketball free throw, the place-kick in soccer, and hitting a ball from a batting tee. For closed skills, fixation of the motor skill is the goal. Learning involves concentrating on the identical elements in the body and the environment and striving for consistency in executing the motor plan. Closed skills are not necessarily easier than open skills because they require extraordinary kinesthetic awareness. Students should learn to "feel" the correct movements through kinesthetic perception.

In an *open skill,* the environment is unpredictable, the players keep changing places, and objects move through space. Adjustments must be made in speed, timing, and space, such as in the height and speed of a softball pitch or the interaction of players on a basketball court. Other examples include tennis, racquetball, soccer, and the martial arts. Skill diversification is required to meet a multitude of environmental conditions. Decisions must be made in split seconds. Therefore practice must include a variety of situations and the learner must be informed about the range of possibilities. At first, combinations of two or three variables may be practiced, but later practice must include all possible variables. If only three speeds, three directions, three ball heights, and three distances were considered, eighty-one different combinations must be rehearsed. Imagine how many might exist in an actual game. Practice for open skills should not consistently occur with any particular combination or a fixation might occur. Schmidt indicates that learning tasks under different conditions from those required in the actual game situation requires a shift in ability. Thus, the complex nature of many games almost ensures a regression to less desirable movement patterns.[84]

With both open and closed skills, practice should be as gamelike or competition-like as possible, with a changing, unstable, unpredictable environment for open skills or a stable, predictable environment for closed skills.

Review Questions: Define allocated time, engaged time, academic learning time (ALT), and ALT-PE.

What did Buck and Harrison discover about learning trials in physical education classes?

How can teachers maximize student involvement in instruction?

Explain Gentile's model for teaching motor skills.

Task Appropriateness Effective teaching requires the selection of appropriate learning tasks. Students should possess prerequisite knowledge and skills, and activities should challenge students to improve existing skill levels. Instruction must be adjusted to challenge students who have high skill levels or to correct deficiencies so that poorly skilled students can benefit from instruction. Unit and lesson plans should include skill progressions from simple to complex. Harter proposed using *optimum challenges* to match task difficulty with learners' developmental capabilities.[85] Tasks that are too easy are boring, whereas tasks that are too difficult produce learner anxiety. Neither results in learning.

Fitts classified psychomotor skills into difficulty levels based on the degree of body involvement and the extent of external pacing of the activity. The simplest skills and activities are done with the body at rest. Intermediate skills and activities would involve movement of the body or an external object, but not both. The most complex skills and activities involve simultaneous movement of the individual and the external object.[86] Merrill divided skills into four areas as shown in Table 5.11,[87] but there appears to be no difference in difficulty between types II and III.[88] An example of a type I skill is a placekick in soccer. In a type II task, a stationary player kicks a moving ball, and a type III task consists of a moving player kicking a stationary ball. The most difficult task involves a moving player receiving and redirecting a moving ball.

Students should begin with skills at their present level and gradually move to higher skill levels. This requires preassessing current performance levels and starting instruction at the appropriate level for each learner. In Table 5.12, Rink lists ways to increase task difficulty. A successful skill progression will increase one aspect of the performance at a time.

Once the concept of the skill has been acquired, the learning environment should include as many situations as possible in which students will actually use the behavior (e.g., a moving rather than a stationary ball, as close to the real speed as possible). In activities involving a ball, speed and accuracy should be stressed rather than just speed or just accuracy. In most situations, the movement should be practiced at a moderate speed.[89]

A major mistake that is made while teaching skills is to jump directly from practice drills into competitive games before students have had time to refine their skills. According to Earls, few teachers really make a difference in skill development, because they present an ideal model that students cannot or do not follow and because they ask students to participate in complex games before students are ready.[90]

Barrett emphasized that the development of game-playing ability is in reality a three-phase process, in which constant flow between adjacent phases is essential. Phase 1 focuses on the development of game skills, phase 2 on the

TABLE 5.11 Merrill's Task Classification System

		Object	
		At Rest	**In Motion**
Learner's Body	**At Rest**	Type I task	Type II task
	In Motion	Type III task	Type IV task

Source: From M. David Merrill, "Psychomotor Taxonomies, Classifications, and Instructional Theory," in Robert N. Singer, ed, *The Psychomotor Domain: Movement Behaviors* (Philadelphia: Lea & Febiger, 1972), 385–414.

TABLE 5.12 Ways to Increase Task Difficulty

1. Increasing the size of the "whole" to be handled by the learner
2. Adding movement to a stationary skill
3. Increasing the force requirements, such as the height or distance involved in producing or receiving force
4. Receiving an object at different levels or from different directions, such as to the side of the receiver
5. Decreasing the size of the target or goal
6. Requiring a higher degree of accuracy in the placement of a hit or throw
7. Involving more interaction with other people (e.g., offensive or defensive players)
8. Using larger or heavier equipment (e.g., bowling ball, racquet, bow)
9. Increasing the speed of the object to be received or redirected
10. Involving sideways or backward movement
11. Receiving an object from one direction and redirecting it to another direction
12. Increasing the speed of the body movement or the tempo
13. Combining skills
14. Using the skills in competitive or self-testing situations

Source: J. E. Rink, *Teaching Physical Education for Learning,* 3d ed. (Boston: McGraw-Hill, 1998), 59, 112, 117, 297–99.

transition from skill development to actual game play, and phase 3 on game playing. Phase 2 "is the most critical phase and one which is often missed entirely or passed through so quickly as to have no effect."[91]

To make the transition from skill drills to game play, students need to practice in gamelike conditions early in the learning sequence. Gamelike practice increases the success of low-skilled students and results in increased student confidence to attempt skill trials in game settings. Young discussed ways to improve practice drills to make them more gamelike. She suggested cones at random rather than in straight lines for dribbling practice, with several players moving at a time so that students learn to adapt to changing circumstances. Play games called 3-on-3 or Bonus Ball rather than "lead-up games," which make students feel incapable of playing the real game. For Bonus Ball, award points for using the skill in game situations.[92]

Teachers can choose or create drills and lead-up games that force students to move to the ball, to direct the ball to a moving target, or to practice under the innumerable conditions that occur in game play. For example, rather than have students hit a volleyball back and forth to a partner, a threesome forces students to direct the ball to a place different from the point of origin. Students should not set the ball over the net or hit the ball and run under the net; neither situation occurs in a game. Team strategies should not be introduced before students feel secure with the basic skills and individual offensive and defensive tactics, such as marking or guarding, playing one's position, or shooting without being guarded have been taught.

The use of modified games before students play the full game may help bridge the gap between skill drills and game play. Games with fewer players per team force low-ability students to be involved and provide more opportunities for contacting the ball. Siedentop, Mand, and Taggart observed, "The games students play must be developmentally appropriate in terms of skills required, complexity of strategy, and opportunity for participation."[93] The final result of skill learning is accurate, consistent, adaptable, coordinated motor responses. Automatic skill execution enables the learner to devote attention to the game plan and strategy. Rather than paying attention to each part of a skill, the elements are "chunked" into a skill or even a combination of skills. Performers learn where to look and what to look at, how to differentiate relevant and irrelevant information, and how to predict outcomes from cues. In essence, students learn to integrate movements and information into schemas that help them to select appropriate movement responses for a wide variety of conditions, to monitor outcomes, and to guide their own learning.[94] This occurs because the information processing system improves its ability to process information. By integrating information from the environment and the body, a rule or principle emerges to guide future behavior.

Bressan and Weiss proposed an optimal challenge model to combine the teaching of skill with psychosocial education. The optimal challenge model requires teachers to observe the needs of their students and design learning experiences at the appropriate level of difficulty, with appropriate educational support for students to gain self-confidence in movement. Observation is the central process of the model. Observing for *competence* requires concentrating on the student's proficiency in managing the activity's motor, fitness, and cognitive demands. Observing for *confidence* demands focusing on students' feelings about their perceived ability to meet the challenges at hand and their anticipation of pleasant or unpleasant sensations. Observing for *persistence* involves noting the student's ability to sustain participation under various circumstances. Confidence and persistence are psychosocial or affective components. These three sources of information become the basis for teachers' instructional decisions.[95]

Teacher behavior can modify task difficulty or the degree and type of educational support provided to the learner. Task difficulty should consider the student's competence—motor, fitness, and cognitive. Feltz and Weiss identified four instructional strategies for increasing competence: (1) Sequence activities according to the students' development, (2) break skills into meaningful practice units, (3) use appropriate performance aids, and (4) provide appropriate physical or verbal guidance. Educational support relates to the learner's confidence and persistence. Helping students set performance goals, reinforcing effort and persistence, emphasizing correct rather than incorrect performance, and selecting appropriate teaching styles for maximum learner involvement in decision making can be used to provide educational support. To be true professionals, teachers must reflect on their own performance and evaluate their teaching to determine ways to increase their abilities to educate the whole student.[96]

Practice drills used with interscholastic teams are generally not appropriate for physical education classes in which students are developing rather than refining skills. Research by Earls demonstrated a regression in skill development when students were challenged to move on to more complex patterns before their skills were sufficiently rehearsed.[97] Since most skills are learned best in a positive atmosphere, with low muscle tension, a stressful learning situation should be avoided.

Students also need help applying movement principles to a variety of situations. This can be achieved by pointing out activities in which the concepts apply and do not apply. Worksheets, such as the biomechanics task sheet (Box 5.1), can help students generalize concepts to various activity situations. Just prior to skill execution, the teacher might direct the student to focus on specific feedback processes and how they can be used to improve the skill. Through analyzing the learning process, students will learn how to learn, as well as acquire the skills themselves.

Review Questions: What is an optinum learning task for students? How can a task be adjusted to increase or decrease its level of difficulty?

BOX 5.1

A Biomechanics Task Sheet

DEFINITION:
Absorption of force
Force can be reduced efficiently by increasing the surface area and the distance or time over which it is received.

LEARNING ACTIVITIES:
1. Catch a ball with your arms stiff.
2. Catch a ball, bringing it in toward your body as you catch it.

Question:
Which way was easier? Why?
3. Have your partner throw a ball to you. Put one hand up and stop it. Repeat the throw with two hands used to stop it.
4. Cross your hands over your chest and block a ball thrown to you by your partner.

Question:
Which throw hit you with the least force? Why?

Question:
Why do softball and baseball players use a glove to catch the ball?
5. Jump off the floor and land stiff-legged. Do it again and bend your knees.

Question:
Which one was easier? Why?

Question:
A soccer ball is flying through the air toward you. How would you use the principle of absorption of force (distance and surface area) to control the ball so that you can dribble it?

Question:
If you were diving over an object and landing on your hands, how would you use the principle of absorption of force (distance and surface area) to prevent injury?

Source: An example of a worksheet (written by Marilyn Buck, George Bayles, and Hilda Fronske).

What are Barrett's three phases of development of game-playing ability? Which is the most important phase and why?

Identify skills in a sport activity and develop a progression using Merrill's task classification system and Rink's ways of increasing task difficulty.

Summarize the guiding principles for developing a skill progression.

Whole versus Part Practice *Whole practice* is practice of a whole task, as opposed to practice of its parts. For example, in the breaststroke in swimming, the whole method is to demonstrate the stroke and have the students imitate and practice it. In *part practice* the whole is broken down into parts, each of which is mastered separately before putting them all together. For example, the kick might be taught first until it has been mastered. Then, the arms and breathing are taught and practiced. Finally, the coordination of the entire stroke is demonstrated and practiced.

To overcome the difficulty the student experiences when putting the parts together, the *progressive part* method was developed. It consists of learning part one, then learning and adding part two, then part three, and so on until the whole is completed. When learning the breast stroke, for example, the student begins with a glide, then adds the arm stroke, then breathing, and finally the kick.

The majority of thirty studies reviewed by Nixon and Locke found some variation of the whole method to be superior.[98] This is in agreement with the cognitive theory of learning in unitary wholes. The basic problem seems to be in the definition of the "whole." In practical teaching situations, an instructor rarely would present the whole game of basketball at once. Instead, combinations of skills, such as throwing, catching, dribbling, passing, and shooting, are combined to form play patterns. In sports that require no interaction with others, such as archery or bowling, the sport itself may be considered to be a whole for the purposes of instruction.[99] Seagoe described the characteristics of a whole as follows: "(1) It should be isolated and autonomous, an integrated entity. (2) It must have 'form' quality, a functional, coherent unit. (3) It must be more than the sum of the parts; it must be a rational structure in itself."[100]

TABLE 5.13 Factors That Influence Choice of Whole or Part Practice

Practice Should/Can Emphasize:

	WHOLES	PARTS
If the task:	Has highly dependent (integrated) parts	Has highly independent parts
	Is simple	Is made up of individual skills
	Is not meaningful in parts	Is very complex
	Is made up of simultaneously performed parts	If limited work on parts or different segments is necessary
If the learner:	Is able to remember long sequences	Has a limited memory span
	Has a long attention span	Is not able to concentrate for a long period of time
	Is highly skilled	Is having difficulty with a particular part
	Cannot succeed with the whole method	

Source: Anne Rothstein, Linda Catelli, Patt Dodds, and Joan Manahan, *Basic Stuff Series I: Motor Learning* (Reston, VA: American Alliance for Health, Physical Education, Recreation, and Dance, 1981), 38.

Even though use of the whole has been shown to be advantageous, the evidence does not mean that the whole method should be used exclusively. Rather, the selection of a method should be based on the characteristics of the learner and the task and the instructional style of the teacher. Table 5.13 shows how the first two factors influence the choice of whole or part practice.

Older and more mature learners can comprehend larger units of instruction than can younger or less-skilled students. Intelligence and cognitive style also influence the learner's ability to handle relationships in complex tasks. Several researchers have found that students with a global cognitive style learn better with whole learning, whereas students with an analytical cognitive style learn better with the part method. Meaningful, connected activities are best taught with the whole method, whereas complex, independent tasks can be taught with part practice. When practices are distributed, the whole method appears to work better.[101]

Implications for teaching are that the learner should begin with a whole that is large enough to be meaningful and challenging but simple enough to achieve success. This may involve understanding a concept of the whole skill or game and the relationship of the parts to the whole. As skills are practiced, students should understand how the skills fit into the total activity. Modified games are "small wholes" that help learners join parts into meaningful wholes without becoming overwhelmed.[102] Meaningfulness is increased when the skill approximates the final objective sought. Work to improve portions of the performance can occur readily during practice of the whole movement. When the complete action is too complex for the beginner to handle, such as in activities in which a chance of injury exists or the learner is afraid, or the amount of information overloads the processing capability of the learner, it should be broken into the largest subwhole that the learner can handle.

A combination of wholes and parts, including alternating from one to another, is often the best approach. Variations include *whole-part* and *part-whole* methods and the *whole-part-whole* method in which students learn the whole, then practice the parts and then put them back together into the whole.[103] In the breaststroke, the whole-part method involves practicing the whole stroke and then working on the arms, legs, and breathing. The part-whole method, in contrast, requires teaching the arms, legs, and breathing separately until they are learned and then combining them into the whole stroke. The whole-part-whole method consists of teaching the entire stroke, then working on each part, and then again practicing the whole stroke.

Massed versus Distributed Practice *Massed practice* is a practice or a series of practice sessions with little or no rest between. An example is teaching one skill for the entire physical education period. *Distributed practice* is practice interspersed with rest or alternative activities. This can be done by practicing several skills for a brief period of time during each class session.

Research findings about the advantages of each type of practice are contradictory because of inconsistencies in the terminology used. With verbal skills, most research concludes that distributed practice is best except when the material is simple or can be learned in its entirety in one session.[104] Research on motor skills shows that skill learning generally occurs better with many short, distributed practice sessions rather than longer and less frequent sessions. However, on discrete tasks when boredom and fatigue are not factors, massed practice is equally effective with distributed practice, assuming that the number of practice trials is the same.[105] Massed practice has the advantage of reaching the goal sooner under these conditions (i.e., three hours on Monday versus one hour on Monday, Wednesday, and Friday).

Factors to consider when planning the frequency and length of practice sessions include (1) the learner's age, skill level, and experience; (2) the type of skill; (3) the purpose of the practice; and (4) circumstances in the learning environment.[106] These factors are presented in Table 5.14. Distributed practice is defined in the table as shorter and more frequent, and massed practice is longer and less frequent.

TABLE 5.14 Factors That May Influence Your Choice of Massed or Distributed Practice Organizations

	Shorter and More Frequent	Longer and Less Frequent
If the task:	Is simple, repetitive, boring	Is complex
	Demands intense concentration	Has many elements
	Is fatiguing	Requires warm-up
	Demands close attention to detail	Is a new one for the performer
If the learner:	Is young or immature (unable to sustain activity)	Is older or more mature
	Has a short attention span	Is able to concentrate for long periods of time
	Has poor concentration skills	Has good ability to focus attention
	Fatigues easily	Tires quickly

Source: Anne Rothstein, Linda Catelli, Patt Dodds, and Joan Manahan, *Basic Stuff Series I: Motor Learning* (Reston, VA: American Alliance for Health, Physical Education, Recreation, and Dance, 1981), 40.

Younger students and students with low ability levels fatigue easily and have shorter attention, or concentration, spans and lower interest levels. Distributed practice sessions in which several skills are practiced during a class period are usually preferred for these students. This results in less boredom, fatigue, and frustration when learning new skills. When students take turns practicing, a built-in rest interval also occurs. Older, more highly skilled students possess higher levels of concentration and motivation and can tolerate longer practice with less fatigue.

Strenuous activities often must be scheduled for shorter periods of time due to the effects of fatigue. An overview of an activity may require a different scheduling pattern than intense practice for competition or performance.

Weather conditions, such as heat, cold, smog, and rain, and school activities, such as assemblies, may interfere with a practice session. With distributed practice less time is lost when one practice must be canceled or interrupted than when a massed practice is canceled.

The time schedule for practice sessions is not nearly as important as the amount of time spent in actual activity or the number of practice trials. Too often, instructors expect a beginner to learn an entirely new activity in a two-week unit (ten days with thirty minutes of instruction per day = three hundred minutes), but they spend two hours every day for months coaching talented students in the same basic skills.

Mental Practice Mental practice is sedentary practice in which the learner imagines performing a skill and the muscles receive stimulation, but no overt movement occurs. This technique is based on the work of Kwhler, in which insight plays an important role in learning. Since studies have shown that mental rehearsal increases skill performance, instruction might well include mental practice in addition to physical practice in order to efficiently use the crowded facilities and inadequate equipment in many schools. A good time for mental practice is when a student is waiting for a turn or a piece of equipment. Mental rehearsal can also be used advantageously to practice perfectly after an error and before the next response, to warm up, to increase concentration during the performance, or to practice while watching a film or videotape of a skill. Mentally rehearsing what to do in certain game situations can be helpful in developing appropriate reactions during game play. For example, in softball, students can imagine that the bases are loaded and the ball goes to third base and determine what should be done. *Reminiscence,* improvement between practice periods, may be the result of mental practice.[107] To be effective, students must understand the skill and have practiced it overtly prior to mental practice. Encourage students to *feel* the movement during practice and then during mental rehearsal.

Review Questions: What kind of practice is best for beginners? For advanced players?

a. Massed versus distributed
b. Whole versus part
c. Progressive part
d. Mental practice

Transfer Transfer is the effect that learning one skill has on the learning or performance of another skill. Transfer can be positive or negative. Positive transfer occurs when previous learning has a favorable effect on new learning. With negative transfer, prior learning interferes with learning new information or skills (proactive transfer) or new skills interfere with previously learned tasks (retroactive transfer).

Transfer theories include (1) the theory that only identical elements (i.e., specific elements common to both tasks) transfer and (2) the theory that transfer occurs as a result of the ability to apply previously learned principles and insights or problem-solving strategies to new situations.[108] Laboratory research shows that very little transfer is seen from one task to another. However, the transfer of general problem-solving and learning strategies is supported when more complex tasks are studied. Transfer is probably a result of several factors, including those specific to the task and those inherent in the learning environment.[109]

An understanding of the conditions affecting transfer is essential for planning instruction. Singer listed five conditions that affect transfer: (1) similarity between the tasks, (2) amount of practice on the first task, (3) motivation to transfer, (4) method of training, and (5) intent of transfer. Cratty added a sixth condition—the amount of time between tasks. The amount of transfer depends on the complexity of the task and the capacity of the learner.[110]

Similarity between tasks The most important of the six conditions is the similarity between the tasks. The greater the similarity between the tasks, the greater the transfer. If there were no similar elements, there would be no transfer (either positively or negatively). In many tasks, however, some elements will yield positive transfer and others will elicit negative transfer. Thus, Cratty indicated that "the degree to which negative or positive transfer is measured depends on whether the *summation* of the negative transfer elements equals, exceeds, or fails to exceed the total of the common elements likely to produce positive transfer."[111]

Similar or identical elements can be found in the student's perception of the stimulus or in the response. Negative transfer occurs when the students are asked to respond to the same verbal or visual perception with a different response. For example, if students have practiced rebounding by batting the ball continuously against the backboard during practice, and then are expected to rebound the ball into the basket during a game, negative transfer will occur. Negative transfer may also result when the weight of an object changes, such as when changing from tennis to badminton, or when the speed of the object differs, such as in rallying a tennis ball off a backboard rather than over a net. Similar movements, such as the overarm softball throw and the overhead volleyball serve, differ in that one is a throwing pattern and the other a striking skill.

Positive transfer occurs when the two tasks have a number of identical elements, such as the names of the players in softball and baseball. Some positive transfer occurs when the same response is expected to a number of related situations. Examples include shooting at different target sizes or distances in archery, or throwing a ball fielded from many different directions to first base.

When two tasks have many elements that are similar, but not identical, negative transfer results. An example is in the rules and scoring of soccer, speedball, speed-a-way, and field hockey. Tennis, badminton, and racquetball have similarities in eye-hand coordination and agility. However, differences in wrist action and the weight of the object struck can cause negative transfer.

Amount of practice on the first task Greater positive transfer occurs when the first task is well learned. Less practice on the first task may result in negative transfer. Skills involving similar movement patterns, such as tennis and racquetball, should not be taught at the same time if the learner is a beginner in both activities.

Motivation to transfer When motivation toward the transfer of skill or knowledge to a new task is high, greater positive transfer occurs. Increasing the motivation of students should also increase the effects of positive transfer.

Method of training The highest positive transfer seems to occur when the whole task is practiced rather than when the parts are practiced separately. For this reason, many current experts discourage the use of drills and progressions to teach skills. Nixon and Locke stated: "Progression is a near sacred principle in physical education, and is taken most seriously in teacher education. Evidence indicates that the faith . . . may be misplaced . . . progressions generally appear not to be significant factors in learning many motor skills."[112] On the other hand, research on teaching in physical education by Rink and her colleagues supports the concept of breaking down complex skills into manageable components to facilitate learning.[113]

Progressions are especially valuable when fear, danger, or lack of self-confidence are present. Drills that are not well planned may introduce elements that do not transfer to the game situation. Therefore, drills should be planned so that the environment and movement relationships are as gamelike as possible. Evaluation should also be in gamelike settings.

Intent of transfer When the teacher points out the common elements in the two tasks, the learner will probably make greater transfer to the second task of principles and skills learned in the first task. Often, general problem-solving and learning strategies will transfer to the new situation. Understanding the principles of biomechanics should transfer to new situations, as should principles of learning.[114]

Amount of time between tasks As the amount of time increases between the learning of two tasks, both negative and positive transfer decline until negative transfer disappears entirely. Since negative transfer decreases faster, a point occurs at which positive transfer is at its optimum, before it too disappears. For this reason, skills may be best learned during distributed practice sessions.

Retention Retention, often called memory, is the persistence of knowledge. Forgetting is the opposite of retention. Behavioral psychologists believe that memory is affected by the original association of two events with each other and by the association of an event with a reward. Forgetting may be caused by lack of use over a period of time, by unlearning due to lack of reinforcement, or by interference from other learned events, such as the learning of Spanish after French.

Information-processing research differentiates between short-term memory and long-term memory. Events are held only for a short period of time unless they are rehearsed and transferred to long-term storage. Short-term memory is limited to about seven digits, as in the ordinary telephone number. By chunking, more information can be attended to, as when phone numbers are changed to letters to form words like *car-loan.*[115] Using cues to chunk information also can help learners avoid an information overload. Once the information is encoded into long-term memory, it can be very persistent, as in the case of some motor skills, which have been known to last for many years.

Factors influencing retention include (1) the nature of the task, (2) the meaningfulness of the task, and (3) the amount of overlearning that has occurred. Tasks differ in terms of their outcomes—cognitive, affective, or psychomotor; their complexity—simple to difficult; and their effect on the learner—pleasant versus disagreeable. Fundamental skills, such as walking and bicycling and higher-order mental processing skills are relatively permanent, whereas facts are difficult to remember.[116] Pleasant tasks are more easily learned, as when an exercise series is done to music. The complexity of some learning tasks can be reduced by chaining concepts to each other, as in learning a dance, or organizing concepts into chunks of information, such as a grapevine step, which consists of a number of side and crossover steps.

Meaningful, well-organized material is remembered longer than unorganized facts. Teachers can enhance long-term memory by teaching students mental imagery, chaining concepts, and problem-solving and information-processing skills and teaching the principles underlying performance, such as the effects of ball spin and air resistance or the principles for applying and receiving force. When students know they will be held accountable for certain material, retention is also increased.[117]

Review Questions: What conditions are necessary for positive transfer?

What can you do to promote transfer? Retention?

Feedback

Feedback is information about the learner's performance or the results of performance available during or immediately following performance. Feedback may be verbal, such as "Good serve" or "Your spike is getting better," or it may be nonverbal, such as a nod, smile, glance, or merely continuing on to the next part of the lesson. Of course, visual and verbal feedback can be used simultaneously.

Feedback helps the learner decide what to do differently on the next practice trial.[118] It can also help students determine how well they are progressing toward a course objective. Information provided to the learner that tells about the quality of a performance, such as the contact position with the ball or correct arm action, is called *knowledge of performance.* Information about the outcome of the performance, such as where the ball lands on a tennis court, is called *knowledge of results.* Studies show that little or no learning occurs without knowledge of performance or results. In fact, Bilodeau and Bilodeau stated, "Studies of feedback or knowledge of results show it to be the strongest, most important variable controlling performance and learning."[119] However, it should be noted that feedback effects have not been shown to be as significant a learning variable in field-based research.[120]

Feedback can occur from the performance itself, from the performer's kinesthetic awareness of body position, or from visual or verbal cues from the teacher. Feedback directly from the task is called *intrinsic* feedback. It can be produced internally by proprioceptors in the muscles, joints, and tendons, or by the effects of the performance on the environment, such as a strike in bowling or a bull's-eye in archery. *Extrinsic or augmented* feedback is provided by an outside source such as a teacher, a coach, other student, or a videotape. Extrinsic feedback may be verbal or nonverbal. *Concurrent* feedback occurs simultaneously with the performance and may be intrinsic or extrinsic. *Terminal* feedback occurs after the performance and may result from the effects of the performance (a made basketball shot) or from an external source.

The ability to provide meaningful feedback at appropriate times is one of the most important abilities a teacher possesses. Feedback is most helpful when it is specific and meaningful. Feedback should be delayed briefly until the learners have had time to analyze their performances and should be matched to the individual learner's comprehension and ability to use it in subsequent practice. Too much feedback can cause an information overload and confuse the learner. Teachers can speed up the knowledge of results by cuing during the performance using verbal, kinesthetic, or visual assistance. For example, having bowlers aim at a spot on the lane rather than at the pins provides feedback much sooner. Placing a hand just behind the wrist of the archer's shooting hand can keep the student from jerking the hand away from the face. Moving a student's arms in the correct swimming pattern can be useful with some students. A rope could also be strung over a badminton net to encourage correct serving technique, or a videotape replay could be provided for the student.[121] Another valuable feedback technique is a redemonstration of the skill following the students' initial skill attempts. The students' attention should be directed to the essential aspects of the skill (perhaps using the verbal cues that accompanied the initial skill demonstration) to help them correct the attempt. Gradually, as the students' skills approximate the model, patterning is complete and the cues should be changed to promote accommodation and refinement of the skill performance.

Checklists of the most important aspects of performance help students and teachers focus on skill essentials. Gentile proposed that the learner answer two questions about the response: "Was the goal accomplished?" and

TABLE 5.15 Four Possible Outcomes for Evaluating Skill Learning

Type of Evaluation	Was the Movement Executed as Planned?		
	OUTCOME	Yes	No
Was the Goal Accomplished?	Yes	Got the idea of the movement	Surprise!
	No	Something's wrong	Everything's wrong

Source: A. M. Gentile, "A Working Model of Skill Acquisition with Application to Teaching," *Quest 17* (January 1972): 9.

"Was the movement executed as planned?"[122] The possible answers are shown in Table 5.15. If the answer to both questions is yes, then the learner should continue to use the same motor plan. If a "surprise" is obtained, the learner must make a decision. Either the original motor plan or the incorrect but successful movement may be tried. Perhaps both plans will be tried and compared. If the "something's wrong" response is obtained, the learner may need to reevaluate the regulatory conditions to determine whether some stimuli have been ignored and establish a new plan. If the "everything's wrong" response occurs after several tries, the learner's motivation may suffer. Possible strategies include revising the motor plan, reevaluating environmental conditions, or altering the goal. Ainsworth and Fox found that students taught to use this technique to evaluate their performance learned skills as well as those taught using a traditional teacher-oriented technique. The advantage was that these students had learned *how* to learn as well as learned skills.[123] Lichtman suggested that helping students develop the ability to evaluate movement errors can speed up learning.[124] This is verified by the fact that students who controlled their own schedule of videotape feedback on their throwing form performed better and retained skills better than those given the same feedback on a structured schedule of every five trials or those who only had a knowledge of the results of their trials on a target. In addition, they required less feedback than the other groups.[125] Pease emphasized the importance of teaching students to evaluate and interpret kinesthetic awareness or feelings during performance and performance results by comparing them with the desired results and the motor plan. In this way students can obtain immediate feedback, which would be impossible to obtain from the teacher when there are thirty or forty or more students in a class.[126]

Review Question: Summarize the various kinds of feedback and their effects on learning.

a. Knowledge of performance
b. Knowledge of results

NOTES

1. B. S. Bloom, ed., *Taxonomy of Educational Objectives, Handbook I: Cognitive Domain* (New York: McKay, 1956).
2. D. R. Krathwohl, B. S. Bloom, and B. B. Masia, *Taxonomy of Educational Objectives, Handbook II: Affective Domain* (New York: McKay, 1964).
3. B. S. Bloom, Personal communication, 1982.
4. C. B. Corbin, *Becoming Physically Educated in the Elementary School,* 2nd ed. (Philadelphia: Lea & Febiger, 1976), 52–66; A. J. Harrow, *A Taxonomy of the Psychomotor Domain: A Guide for Developing Behavioral Objectives* (New York: McKay, 1972); E. J. Simpson, The classification of objectives, psychomotor domain, *Illinois Teacher of Home Economics 10* (1966/1967): 110–44; M. M. Thompson and B. A. Mann, *An Holistic Approach to Physical Education Curricula: Objectives Classification System for Elementary Schools* (Champaign, IL: Stipes, 1977).
5. A. E. Jewett, L. S. Jones, S. M. Luneke, and S. M. Robinson, Educational change through a taxonomy for writing physical education objectives, *Quest 15* (January 1971): 35–36.
6. Corbin, *Becoming Physically Educated.*
7. R. N. Singer and W. Dick, *Teaching Physical Education: A Systems Approach* (Boston: Houghton Mifflin, 1974), 105–107.
8. A. A. Annarino, Operational taxonomy for physical education objectives, *Journal of Physical Education and Recreation 49* (January 1978): 54–55.
9. W. G. Miller, J. Snowman, and T. O'Hara, Application of alternative statistical techniques to examine the hierarchical ordering in Bloom's taxonomy, *American Educational Research Journal 16,* no. 3 (1979): 241–48; G. M. Seddon, The properties of Bloom's taxonomy of educational objectives for the cognitive domain, *Review of Educational Research 48,* no. 2 (1978): 303–23.
10. Krathwohl, Bloom, and Masia, *Taxonomy Handbook II.*
11. Singer and Dick, *Teaching Physical Education.*
12. G. Graham, S. A. Holt/Hale, and M. Parker, *Children Moving: A Teacher's Guide to Developing a Successful Physical Education Program,* 2nd ed. (Palo Alto, CA: Mayfield, 1987), 38–41.
13. P. M. Fitts and M. I. Posner, *Human Performance* (Belmont, CA: Brooks-Cole, 1967).
14. A. M. Gentile, A working model of skill acquisition with application to teaching, *Quest 17* (January 1972): 3–23.

15. A. E. Jewett and M. R. Mullan, *Curriculum Design: Purposes and Processes in Physical Education Teaching-Learning* (Washington, DC: American Association for Health, Physical Education, and Recreation, 1977).
16. E. S. Bressan, A movement processing paradigm and the curriculum in physical education, *Journal of Teaching in Physical Education 6* (1984): 335–43.
17. J. B. Oxendine, *Psychology of Motor Learning* 14–15 (Englewood Cliffs, NJ: Prentice-Hall, 1984), 154, 164, 176–79, 185, 280–99, 304–6, 310–13.
18. C. B. Corbin, First things first, but, don't stop there, *Journal of Physical Education, Recreation and Dance 52,* no. 6 (1981): 12–13.
19. B. D. Lockhart, The basic stuff series: Why and how, *Journal of Physical Education, Recreation, and Dance 53,* no. 7 (1982): 18–19.
20. B. Mohnsen, ed., *Concepts of Physical Education: What Every Student Needs to Know* (Reston, VA: National Association for Sport and Physical Education, 1998).
21. R. M. Gagné, *The Conditions of Learning and Theory of Instruction,* 4th ed. (New York: Holt, Rinehart & Winston, 1985), 47–48.
22. C. Gabbard, Teaching motor skills to children: Theory into practice, *Physical Educator 41* (1984): 69–71.
23. P. Grippin and S. Peters, *Learning Theory and Learning Outcomes: The Connection* (New York: University Press of America, 1984), 137, 177, 179, 194–97, 208.
24. Grippin and Peters, *Learning Theory.*
25. D. P. Ausubel, *The Psychology of Meaningful Verbal Learning: An Introduction to School Learning* (New York: Grune & Stratton, 1963), 16.
26. Grippin and Peters, *Learning Theory.*
27. D. R. Mohr, Identifying the body of knowledge, *Journal of Health, Physical Education, Recreation 42,* no. 1 (1971): 23–24.
28. J. E. Rink, *Teaching Physical Education for Learning,* 3d ed (Boston: McGraw-Hill, 1998), 59, 112–17, 27–99.
29. B. S. Bloom and L. J. Broder, Problem-solving processes of college students: An exploratory investigation, *Supplementary Educational Monographs,* No. 73, (Chicago: University of Chicago Press, 1950), 25.
30. B. B. Hudgins, *Problem Solving in the Classroom* (New York: Macmillan, 1966), 43.
31. C. E. Weinstein and R. E. Mayer, The teaching of learning strategies, in M. C. Wittrock, ed., *Handbook of Research on Teaching,* 2nd ed. (New York: Macmillan, 1986), 315–27.
32. J. H. Flavell, Metacognitive aspects of problem solving, in L. B. Resnick, *The Nature of Intelligence* (Hillsdale, NJ: Erlbaum, 1976), 232.
33. Grippin and Peters, *Learning Theory.*
34. C. E. Weinstein and R. E. Mayer, The teaching of learning strategies, in M. C. Wittrock, ed., *Handbook of Research on Teaching,* 2nd ed. (New York: Macmillan, 1986), 315–27.
35. J. K. Espiritu and T. J. Loughrey, The learning center approach to physical education instruction, *Physical Educator* 42, no. 3 (1985): 121–128; D. M. Miller, Energizing the thinking dimensions of physical education, *Journal of Physical Education, Recreation, and Dance 58,* no. 8 (1987): 76–79.
36. G. Arbogast and J. Misner, Homework "how-to's": Guidelines for designing out-of-class assignments, *Strategies 4,* no. 1 (1990): 12, 15. D. Docheff, Homework . . . in physical education? *Strategies 4,* no. 1 (1990): 10–11, 13–14. R. French, The use of homework as a supportive technique in physical education, *Physical Educator 36,* no. 2 (1979): 84.
37. L. A. Klappholz, ed., Half the PE grade is based on outside activity, *Physical Education Newsletter* (November 1980).
38. D. A. Cameron, Who plays basketball? Bonus incentive plans—A learning stimulus, *Physical Educator 42,* no. 3 (1985): 151–55.
39. Weinstein and Mayer, The teaching of learning strategies.
40. R. F. Mager, *Developing Attitude toward Learning* (Palo Alto, CA: Fearon, 1965), 50–57.
41. J. Brophy, Successful teaching strategies for the inner-city child, *Phi Delta Kappan 63* (1982): 527–30.
42. D. W. Felker, *Building Positive Self Concepts.* (Minneapolis: Burgess, 1974).
43. T. J. Romance, Observing for confidence, *Journal of Physical Education, Recreation, and Dance 56* (1985, August): 47–49.
44. E. S. Bressan and M. R. Weiss, A theory of instruction for developing competence, self-confidence and persistence in physical education, *Journal of Teaching in Physical Education 2* (Face 1982): 38–47.
45. D. L. Feltz and M. R. Weiss, Developing self-efficacy through sport, *Journal of Physical Education, Recreation, and Dance 53* (March 1982): 24–26, 36.
46. R. G. Tharp and R. Gallimore, Basketball's John Wooden: What a coach can teach a teacher, *Psychology Today 9,* no. 8 (1976): 74–78.
47. S. M. Elam, L. C. Rose, and A. M. Gallup, The 25th annual Phi Delta Kappa/Gallup poll of the public's attitudes toward the public schools, *Phi Delta Kappan 75,* no. 2 (1993): 145. L. C. Rose and A. M. Gallup, The 31st annual Phi Delta Kappa/Gallup poll of the public's attitudes toward the public schools, *Phi Delta Kappan 81,* no. 1 (1999): 51.
48. E. E. Durkheim, *Moral Education: A Study in the Theory and Application of the Sociology of Education* (New York: Free Press of Glencoe, 1961), cited in F. K. Oser, Moral education and values education: The discourse perspective, in M. C. Wittrock, ed., *Handbook of Research on Teaching,* 3d ed. (New York: Macmillan, 1986), 144.
49. F. K. Oser, Moral education and values education: The discourse perspective, in M. C. Wittrock, ed., *Handbook of Research on Teaching,* 3d ed. (New York: Macmillan, 1986), 917–41, 935–36.
50. Oser, Moral education.
51. Oser, Moral education.

52. J. R. Rest, Morality, in J. H. Flavell and E. M. Markman, eds., *Handbook of Child Psychology, Volume 3: Cognitive Development* (New York: Wiley, 1983), 556–629.
53. L. Kohlberg, The just community approach to moral education in theory and practice, in M. W. Berkowitz and F. Oser, eds., *Moral education: Theory and application* (Hillsdale, NJ: Erlbaum, 1985), 27–87; J. S. Leming, Curricular effectiveness in moral/values education: A review of research. *Journal of Moral Education 10,* no. 3 (1981): 147–164.
54. A. L. Lockwood, The effects of value clarification and moral development curricula on school-age subjects: A critical review of recent research. *Review of Educational Research 48,* no. 3 (1978), 325–364; Oser, Moral education.
55. M. Keller and S. Reuss, The process of moral decision-making: Normative and empirical conditions of participation in moral discourse, in M. W. Berkowitz and F. Oser, eds., *Moral Education: Theory and Application* (Hillsdale, NJ: Erlbaum, 1983), 109–23.
56. R. H. Hersh, D. P. Paolitto, and J. Reimer, *Promoting Moral Growth: From Piaget to Kohlberg* (New York: Longman, 1979), 4.
57. Oser, Moral education.
58. American Academy of Physical Education, *The Academy Papers: Reunification* (Reston, VA: American Alliance of Health, Physical Education, Recreation, and Dance, 1981), 107–8.
59. M. Bredemeier, M. Weiss, D. Shields, and R. Shewchuk, The development and consolidation of children's moral reasoning in response to three instructional strategies (unpublished manuscript, 1984); M. P. Giebink and T. L. McKenzie, Teaching sportsmanship in physical education and recreation: An analysis of interventions and generalization effects, *Journal of Teaching in Physical Education 4,* no. 3 (1985): 167–77; D. Preston, *A Moral Education Program Conducted in the Physical Education and Health Education Curriculum,* Doctoral dissertation, University of Georgia, Athens, 1979. T. J. Romance, M. R. Weiss, and J. Bockoven, A program to promote moral development through elementary school physical education. *Journal of Teaching in Physical Education 5,* no. 2 (1986), 126–36.
60. T. Wandzilak, Values development through physical education and athletics, *Quest 37,* (1985): 176–85.
61. G. E. Figley, Moral education through physical education, *Quest 36* (1984): 89–101.
62. R. Horrocks, Sportmanship moral reasoning. *Physical Educator 37,* no. 4 (1980): 208–212; T. J. Romance, Promoting character development in physical education. *Strategies 1,* no. 5 (1988): 16–17.
63. C. Morrison, J. Reeve, and D. Mielke, Teaching ideas for the affective domain. *CAHPER Journal 55,* no. 5 (1989): 13–16; affective Romance, Promoting character development.
64. Morrison, Reeve, and Mielke, Teaching ideas; Romance, Promoting character development.
65. Romance, Promoting character development.
66. R. M. Travers, *Essentials of Learning,* 4th ed. (New York: Macmillan, 1977), 25.
67. D. A. Pease, A teaching model for motor skill acquisition, *Motor Skills: Theory into Practice 1,* no. 2 (1977): 104–12.
68. Fitts and Posner, *Human Performance.*
69. H. A. Fronske, *Teaching Cues for Sport Skills for Secondary School Students,* 3rd ed. (San Francisco: Benjamin Cummings, 2005); H. A. Fronske, *Teaching Cues for Basic Sport Skills for Elementary and Middle School Students* (San Francisco: Benjamin Cummings, 2002).
70. D. C. Berliner, Tempus educare, in P. L. Peterson and H. J. Walberg, eds., *Research on Teaching: Concepts, Findings, and Implications* (Berkeley, CA: McCutchan, 1979), 120–35.
71. J. E. Brophy, Teacher behavior and its effect, *Journal of Educational Psychology 71* (1979): 733–50.
72. C. Fisher, N. Filby, R. Marliave, L. Cahen, M. Dishaw, J. Moore, and D. Berliner, *Teaching Behaviors, Academic Learning Time, and Student Achievement: Final Report of Phase III-B, Beginning Teacher Evaluation Study* (San Francisco: Far West Laboratory for Educational Research and Development, 1978).
73. M. W. Metzler, *The Measurement of Academic Learning Time in Physical Education,* Doctoral dissertation, Ohio State University, Columbus, 1979 (University Microfilms No. 8009314).
74. M. W. Metzler, Adapting the academic learning time instructional model to physical education teaching, *Journal of Teaching in Physical Education 1* (1982): 44–55.
75. M. Metzler, A review of research on time in sport pedagogy, *Journal of Teaching in Physical Education 8* (1989): 87–103.
76. M. Buck and J. M. Harrison, Improving student achievement in physical education, *Journal of Physical Education, Recreation, and Dance 62,* no. 7 (1990): 40–44; D. Siedentop, *Developing Teaching Skills in Physical Education,* 3d ed. (Mountain View, CA: Mayfield, 1991), 25; D. Siedentop, M. Tousignant, and M. Parker, *Academic Learning Time—Physical Education Coding Manual* (Columbus: Ohio State University, 1982); S. Silverman, Relationship of engagement and practice trials to student achievement, *Journal of Teaching in Physical Education 5* (1985): 13–21.
77. D. Parkin, Comments on skill development and competition by Mandle and Pang, *Australian Journal of Health, Physical Education, and Recreation 65* (1981): 7–8.
78. P. S. Griffin, Girls' and boys' participation styles in middle school physical education team sport classes: A description and practical applications, *Physical Educator 42,* no. 1 (1985): 3–8.
79. Buck and Harrison, Improving student achievement.
80. D. K. Landin, A. Hawkins, and R. L. Wiegand, Validating the collective wisdom of teacher educators, *Journal of Teaching in Physical Education 5* (1986): 252–71.
81. G. S. D. Morris and J. Stiehl, *Changing Kids' Games* (Champaign, IL: Human Kinetics, 1989).
82. P. Werner, Teaching games: A tactical perspective, *Journal of Physical Education, Recreation, and Dance*

60, no. 3 (1989): 97–101; L. L. Griffin, S. A. Mitchell, and J. L. Oslin, *Teaching Sport Concepts and Skills: A Tactical Games Approach* (Champaign, IL: Human Kinetics, 1997).

83. A. M. Gentile, A working model of skill acquisition with application to teaching, *Quest 17* (January 1972): 3–23.
84. N. F. Earls, Research on the immediate effects of instructional variables, in T. J. Templin and J. K. Olson, eds., *Teaching in Physical Education* (Champaign, IL: Human Kinetics, 1983), 254–64; A. Rothstein and E. Wughalter, *Basic Stuff Series I: Motor Learning* (Reston, VA: American Alliance for Health, Physical Education, Recreation, and Dance (1987): 30, 50, 77; R. A. Schmidt, *Motor Control and Learning: A Behavioral Emphasis* (Champaign, IL: Human Kinetics, 1988).
85. S. Harter, Effectance motivation reconsidered: Toward a developmental model, *Human Development* 21 (1978): 34–64.
86. P. M. Fitts, Factors in complex skill training, in R. Glaser ed., *Training Research and Education* (Pittsburgh: University of Pittsburgh Press, 1962), 177–97.
87. M. D. Merrill, Psychomotor taxonomies, classifications, and instructional theory, in R. N. Singer, ed., *The Psychomotor Domain: Movement Behaviors* (Philadelphia: Lea & Febiger, 1972), 385–414.
88. S. J. Hoffman, C. H. Imwold, and J. A. Koller, Accuracy and prediction in throwing: A taxonomic analysis of children's performance, *Research Quarterly for Exercise and Sport 54,* no. 1 (1983): 33–40.
89. Rothstein and Wughalter, *Basic Stuff Series.*
90. Earls, Research.
91. K. R. Barrett, Games teaching: adaptable skills, versatile players, *Journal of Physical Education, and Recreation 48* (September 1977): 21–24.
92. J. E. Young, When practice doesn't make perfect—Improving game performance in secondary level physical education classes, *Journal of Physical Education, Recreation, and Dance 56,* no. 8 (1985): 24–26, 93.
93. D. Siedentop, C. Mand, and A. Taggart, *Physical Education: Teaching and Curriculum Strategies for Grades 5–12* (Palo Alto, CA: Mayfield, 1986), 201.
94. Young, When practice doesn't make perfect.
95. Bressan and Weiss, A theory of instruction; M. R. Weiss and E. S. Bressan, Connections—Relating instructional theory to children's psychosocial development, *Journal of Physical Education, Recreation, and Dance 56,* no. 9 (1985): 34–36.
96. Feltz and Weiss, Developing self-efficacy.
97. Earls, Research.
98. J. E. Nixon and L. F. Locke, Research on teaching physical education, in R. Travers, ed., *Second Handbook of Research on Teaching* (Chicago: Rand McNally, 1973), 1217.
99. Oxendine, *Psychology of Motor Learning.*
100. M. V. Seagoe, Qualitative wholes: A re-valuation of the whole-part problem, *Journal of Educational Psychology 27* (1936): 537–45.
101. Oxendine, *Psychology of Motor Learning.*
102. Oxendine, *Psychology of Motor Learning.*
103. Oxendine, *Psychology of Motor Learning.*
104. Travers, *Essentials of Learning.*
105. R. Magill, Augumented feedback in skill acquisition, in R. N. Singer, M. Murphey, and L. K. Tennant, eds., *Handbook on Research in Sport Psychology* (New York: Macmillan, 1994).
106. J. D. Lawther, *The Learning and Performance of Physical Skills,* 2nd ed. (Englewood Cliffs, NJ: Prentice-Hall, 1977), 139, 144.
107. Oxendine, *Psychology of Motor Learning.*
108. Magill, Augumented feedback.
109. B. J. Cratty, *Movement Behavior and Motor Learning,* 3d ed. (Philadelphia: Lea & Febiger, 1975), 364, 387, 389, 396–98.
110. Cratty, *Movement Behavior;* Oxendine, *Psychology of Motor Learning;* R. N. Singer, *Motor Learning and Human Performance: An Application to Motor Skills and Movement Behaviors,* 3d ed. (New York: Macmillan, 1980), 421, 471.
111. Cratty, *Movement Behavior.*
112. Nixon and Locke, Research on teaching.
113. Rink, *Teaching Physical Education for Learning.*
114. Oxendine, *Psychology of Motor Learning.*
115. Oxendine, *Psychology of Motor Learning.*
116. Oxendine, *Psychology of Motor Learning.*
117. Oxendine, *Psychology of Motor Learning.*
118. Rothstein and Wughalter, *Basic Stuff Series I.*
119. E. A. Bilodeau and I. M. Bilodeau, Motor-skills learning, *Annual Review of Psychology 12* (1961): 243–80.
120. Magill, Augumented feedback; P. DelRey, Appropriate feedback for open and closed skill acquisition, *Quest, 17* (1972):42–45.
121. S. Melville, Process feedback made simple, *Physical Educator 40,* no. 2 (1983): 95–104.
122. A. M. Gentile, A working model of skill acquisition with application to teaching, *Quest 17* (January 1972): 3–23.
123. J. Ainsworth and C. Fox, Learning to learn: A cognitive processes approach to movement skill acquisition, *Strategies 3,* no. 1 (1989): 20–22.
124. B. Lichtman, Motor schema: Putting theory into action, *Journal of Physical Education, Recreation and Dance 55* (1984, March): 54–56.
125. C. M. Janelle, D. A. Barba, S. G. Frehlich, L. K. Tennant, and J. H. Cauraugh, Maximizing performance feedback effectiveness through videotape replay and a self-controlled learning environment, *Research Quarterly for Exercise and Sport 68,* no. 4 (1997): 269–79.
126. D. A. Pease, A teaching model for motor skill acquisition, *Motor Skills: Theory into Practice 1,* no. 2, (1977): 104–12.

U N I T

II

Planning the Instructional Program

CHAPTER

6

Basic Principles of Curriculum Design

Study Stimulators

1. What is a curriculum? What is the relationship between curriculum and instruction?
2. What is curriculum design? Why is it important?
3. List the steps for designing a curriculum.
4. What is the role of administrators in curriculum design? Of teachers? Of students? Of other resource persons? Why are all of these important on a curriculum committee?
5. What information should be considered before designing a curriculum?
6. Describe the influence of government legislation on curricular decisions.
7. Name the common physical education curriculum models and give an example of each. How are the models used to build physical education programs?
8. What resources are of most value in designing a curriculum for a particular school?
9. Explain what is included in a balanced curriculum.
10. Identify the methods to use in selecting content for a specific curriculum.
11. Should physical education credit be awarded for nonphysical education activities?
12. Describe how sequence relates to teaching activity skills or content.
13. Describe appropriate objectives and activities for each grade level.
14. Describe each of the steps in the scheduling process. Tell why scheduling is so difficult to do.

What Is a Curriculum?

Jewett, Bain, and Ennis described the physical education curriculum as follows: "Broadly defined, the school curriculum includes all experiences conducted under school auspices, from formal classroom instruction to interscholastic athletics. More specifically, the curriculum is defined as the planned sequence of formal instructional experiences presented by the teachers to whom the responsibility is assigned."[1] The curriculum should reflect the society and its philosophy. The teacher becomes the intermediary to translate the curriculum (the blueprint) into the instructional strategies (the delivery system) that influence student learning. Teachers' personalities and abilities influence their capacity to transpose curricular content into student learning. Students' interests and abilities, in turn, influence their input into the instructional system. Figure 6-1 demonstrates how this interaction occurs.

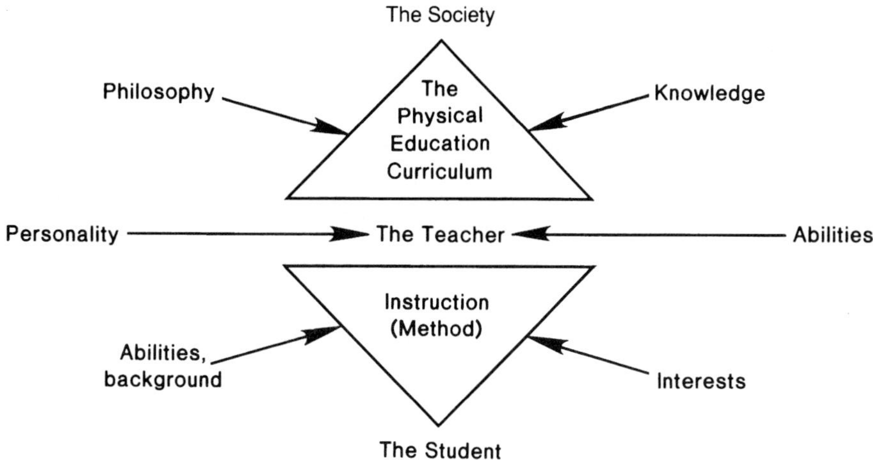

Figure 6-1
The relationship of curriculum and instruction.

The Importance of Curriculum Design

Curriculum design involves the creation of a set of operating principles or criteria, based on theory, that guide the selection and organization of standards-based content and the methodology used to teach that content. With the accelerated rate of social change, schools are preparing youth for adulthood in a society not yet envisioned by its members. Hawley's words still ring true: "It's not a question of whether or not to change, but whether or not we can control the way we are changing. We are living in an *Alice in Wonderland* world where you have to run just to stay where you are. To get anywhere you have to run even faster than that. The pieces on the chess board keep changing and the rules are never the same."[2]

Progress is impossible without change. Changes in financial resources, facilities and equipment, student populations, faculty availability and expertise, student needs and interests, and other environmental and technological advances force curriculum change. However, all change does not result in improvement. In fact, some changes may be worse than none at all. On the other hand, when schools lag behind in curriculum development, changes are imposed from the outside. The move to national standards for content areas is an example of the push for accountability from outside the schools.

Curriculum change should be based on a well-informed evaluation of past, present, and future, including the best thinking of professionals who have researched and tested each proposal. Effective ideas should be retained, ineffective ones discarded. New ideas ought to be tried on a small scale prior to adoption. Planning and preparation are keys to a successful and meaningful program. Traditionally, educators make two mistakes with regard to curriculum design. They either attempt to maintain the status quo and not make change or they look around for a good curriculum and adopt it, regardless of whether it fits their particular needs. Curriculum designers must carefully merge cultural elements, old and new, into a curriculum that fits the students, school, and community. The constantly changing American society requires a continuous, systematic process of evaluating and redesigning the curriculum to achieve program objectives.

Review Questions: What is a curriculum? What is curriculum design? Why is it important?

Models of Curriculum Design

An effective curriculum must be built on a solid philosophical foundation that answers the question of what educational purposes the school should seek to achieve. The classical model for curriculum design, proposed by Tyler in 1949, asked four questions of curriculum planners: (1) What educational purposes should the school seek to attain? (2) What educational experiences can be provided that are likely to help attain these purposes? (3) How can these educational experiences be effectively organized? and (4) How can we determine whether these purposes are being attained?[3] Tyler's steps for curriculum design included stating objectives, selecting learning experiences, organizing the experiences, and evaluating results. Tyler's model is most closely aligned with the educational purposes of preserving the social order and teaching skills and competencies needed to function effectively in society.

Tyler's model of evaluating curriculum did not define the process used to develop curriculum but did include an evaluative component that required curriculum designers to select measurement techniques to determine whether program goals were being met. Too often today's curriculum designers overlook this component as they focus on identifying content without regard to how the content will be used to reach programmatic objectives. In the current educational climate of standards-based curriculum, evaluating curriculum effectiveness is an important component that must be addressed during curriculum development. Chapter 15 of this book contains several different ways to measure curricular effectiveness.

Review Questions: What are Tyler's four questions for curriculum design?

Why is evaluation an important component of curriculum change?

The Curriculum Design Process

The steps of the curriculum design process presented here are based primarily on Tyler's classical design for curriculum development.

1. Establish a curriculum committee.
2. Study information needed to make curriculum decisions.
3. Identify the philosophy, aims, and objectives of the school.
4. Decide how to measure whether objectives were met.
5. Determine the program's scope and sequence.
6. Establish the schedule.
7. Implement the program.
8. Evaluate and revise.

Figure 6-2 shows a diagram of the curriculum design process. After evaluation, the designers should follow the feedback loops back to the beginning of the cycle and reexamine the objectives and instructional programs to determine how to improve them using the new information gained.

Activity: Form a curriculum committee, choose a school (real or imaginary) with which to work, and follow the steps to design a curriculum while studying this chapter.

Review Question: What are the steps in the curriculum design process?

Establish a Curriculum Committee

People responsible for curriculum decisions include administrators, teachers, students, parents, and community leaders. Most major innovations in the public schools are introduced by teachers and administrators. Colleges and universities that train teachers, state boards or departments of education, and textbook publishers and instructional materials producers indirectly provide educational leadership.

The Administrator's Role in Curriculum Design

The instructional program is the most important responsibility of school administrators. They must (1) oversee the planning of instructional programs that contribute to the intellectual, physical, and emotional growth and well-being of all young people, (2) select and assign competent teachers, and (3) hold programs accountable for reaching curricular objectives and standards. They provide leadership for curriculum planning, implementation, evaluation, and revision. Direct leadership occurs when department chairs, principals, or district supervisors help teachers with curriculum development. Once a decision is made to develop or revise a curriculum, the administrator selects a curriculum committee and proposes goals and guidelines for action. This process is more formal at the district level or in a large department, whereas in a smaller district all teachers in a department might compose such a committee. Administrators work closely with the committee, providing input, reviewing proposals for new programs, and providing resources. Administrators are also responsible for helping to implement approved programs and hold them accountable for reaching standards established by the state or discipline for the program area.

Indirectly, all administrators, and especially principals, have the responsibility to provide a climate for personal and group growth. This requires effective communication, time and resources for personal and group study, opportunities to attend conferences or visit innovative schools, and freedom to experiment with new ideas. Teachers with time and resources to study and experiment with new ideas and practices generally are more innovative.

The Teachers' Role in Curriculum Design

Although instructional supervision is an administrative responsibility, teachers' insights are critical for developing a successful curriculum. Teachers are the first to notice a need for change. Their intimate knowledge of learners, classrooms, and the school environment puts them in a position to make and implement practical curriculum changes. In fact, many changes occur, almost unnoticed, as teachers work together to revise course content and schedules. Regular meetings to discuss issues related to the curriculum play an important role in curriculum effectiveness. Many schools assign curriculum leaders, master teachers with additional training in curriculum development and leadership skills, to help teachers make curriculum decisions.

Physical educators have more flexibility for curriculum development than other teachers because of their unique facilities. Students can be grouped and regrouped by ability levels or interests more easily than in intact classrooms, and class sizes can be altered to fit the activity to be taught and the facilities available. Sound development principles and practices will keep the curriculum viable and dynamic. Teachers who attend conventions and in-service meetings, visit other schools, read professional journals, serve on school or district committees, and discuss ideas with other teachers are able to keep abreast of changes in physical education curriculums.

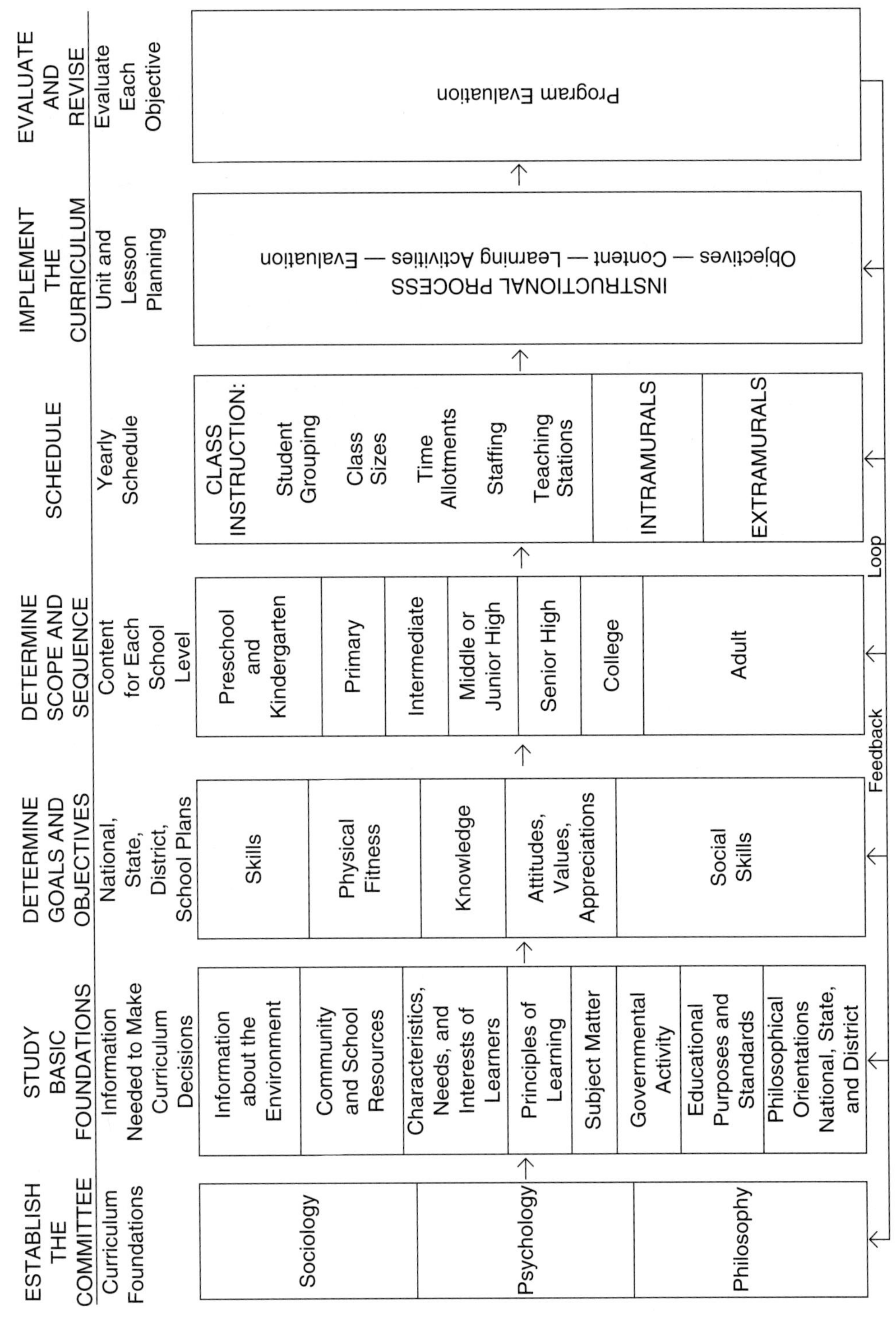

Figure 6-2
The curriculum design process.

Program development should be a cooperative effort of all those involved in its implementation.
©Tracy Pellet

The Curriculum Committee

The number and kinds of curriculum committees depend on the extent of the curriculum project. A school curriculum project might include a coordinating committee, with subcommittees for each grade level. On a smaller level, each member of the physical education staff might serve on the committee. The coordinating committee acts as a clearinghouse for ideas and suggestions. The coordinating committee or the smaller committee establishes the overall physical education philosophy for the district or school, explores satisfactions and dissatisfactions with the present program, and schedules meetings and establishes the work sequence.

Although program development can be a product of individual teachers, administrators, or supervisors, experience shows that a curriculum cooperatively planned by all those involved in its implementation yields the best results. Teachers are more likely to "buy into" a curriculum that they helped develop.

- *Administrators* provide insights into time schedules, budgets, facilities, resources, and other administrative details.
- *Teachers* interact daily with students and know what will or will not work.
- *Students* provide information regarding their own interests, learning obstacles, relevance of learning experiences, and recommended extra-class programs.
- *Parents and community leaders* provide varied, fresh ideas based on their experiences with school and life and their aspirations for children. They provide valuable insights when consulted during the planning stages.
- *Recent graduates* can be especially helpful in evaluating the curriculum's relevance to real life.
- *Curriculum specialists* provide expertise in curriculum design and ideas that have worked well in other schools.
- *Clerical assistants* can record, type, copy, collate, and distribute information.

People chosen to serve on curriculum committees should represent and have the respect and support of their peers and the administration. Small committees can achieve consensus and get the work done more effectively. Periodically rotating committee memberships avoids fatigue and promotes a fresh attack on the problems at hand. When several people from various backgrounds join together in a group effort, synergy occurs; that is, the result is greater than the sum of its members. To show respect for their time and expertise, released time or pay for extra work should be given to committee members.

Review Questions: Who should serve on a curriculum committee?

What is the role of each of these persons?

Resources for the Curriculum Committee

People responsible for curriculum design should be aware of the resources available, which include people and organizations, publications, curriculum guides, facilities, and media. Collaborative arrangements in which teachers work with curriculum and instruction specialists and researchers to identify and investigate problems and solutions make their findings more applicable to public school settings.

A large number of national associations and societies and government agencies also have materials or journals of value to physical education. Check your university or local library for addresses and publications or check the Internet. A few of them include the American Cancer Society, the American College of Sports Medicine, the American Medical Association, the American Heart Association, and the Centers for Disease Control.

Two national organizations with tremendous resources are the American Alliance for Health, Physical Education, Recreation, and Dance (AAHPERD), and the President's Council on Physical Fitness and Sports. AAHPERD has excellent position papers outlining guidelines for physical education. It also publishes several journals and a number of other pertinent publications. The President's Council provides speakers, public relations help, bulletins, and films on various areas of interest to physical educators. State departments of education often provide consultants, in-service activities, conferences, clinics, and workshops. State education associations and state associations of health, physical education, recreation, and dance can be of inestimable service. The local chamber of commerce can provide information about the resources and makeup of the local community. Resources are also available on the Internet. The number of professional journals relating to physical education has increased dramatically in the past few years. An excellent list of the scholarly periodicals in physical education appeared in the *Journal of Physical Education, Recreation, and Dance.*[4]

State departments of education and local school systems publish curriculum guides detailing the course of instruction and requirements for specific subject areas. Curriculum guides generally include some or all of the following: (1) philosophy, goals, objectives, and standards; (2) characteristics and needs of students; (3) program scope and sequence with suggested units of instruction for each grade level; (4) sample schedules; (5) administrative guidelines; (6) instructional activities; (7) assessments for determining whether program goals and standards (district, state, or national) have been met; and (8) resources. Curriculum guides enhance the articulation between programs at different school levels and assure proper progression and development in the three domains of learning—cognitive, affective, and psychomotor.

Review Question: What resources are available for curriculum designers?

Study Information Needed to Make Curriculum Decisions

To make effective curriculum decisions, the committee must learn all it can about the environment, the school, the learners, and the subject matter and how it is learned. Then it must attempt to integrate this information and its implications with the educational philosophy espoused by the district and school. Governmental activity also has an influence on curriculum decisions.

Information about the Environment

A large number of social forces that affect students' lives and therefore the school curriculum were discussed in Chapter 3. Curriculum developers must consider local attitudes and values as well as national ones. Most communities share certain values, attitudes, and beliefs. Local resources and interests influence the selection of learning activities. The current emphasis on physical fitness and lifetime sports reflects a general commitment to the ideal of preparing students for effective adult living. Thus, schools in many areas have adopted Fitness for Life or similar courses. The curriculum must allow equal opportunity for learning and participation by all students, from those who are motor challenged to those who excel in psychomotor sports and activities. Needs and priorities can be identified through brainstorming, observation, interviews, questionnaires, surveys, inventories, public hearings, and available statistics. Asking people to indicate priorities as critical, important, or desirable can be helpful, as can asking them to classify needs as long-range or immediate. A community survey can provide information concerning the following:

- The community's historical background.
- The philosophy of community members and their willingness to support education and physical education programs.
- Economic and tax base factors of the community, such as major employers; average family income; incidence of unemployment; and educational, recreational, health and other services.
- Social, cultural, and political factors, such as population and prospective changes in population, age distribution, ethnic and racial makeup of the population, social and cultural attitudes, religious orientation, educational background, crime, political pressures, and form of government.
- Geographical and locational factors, including such regional factors as climate, altitude, and the availability of lakes, mountains, and seashores, that affect students' activity interests and the time that can be spent out-of-doors; and the environment (urban, suburban, or rural), which affects the activities students can engage in outside of school.
- Community resources, including colleges and universities, private and parochial schools, public libraries, parks and playgrounds, swimming pools, tennis courts, golf courses, cultural programs, government agencies, citizens' groups, and commercial ski resorts, bowling lanes, and equestrian clubs.

Learning more about the community increases one's understanding of its organization and lifestyle. The analysis of social forces leads to implications for curricular needs. After obtaining information about the factors listed above, the committee must evaluate each one for its potential impact on the physical education curriculum. This information should be used during the curriculum planning process.

Information about the School

School resources that influence the physical education curriculum include finances, facilities and equipment, staff, school and department policies, and the total school curriculum. Most school monies are spent for building construction and maintenance and salaries. When finances are low, teachers may be left without essential facilities and instructional materials. School facilities can be supplemented by community resources such as bowling centers, skating rinks, ski slopes, and gymnastic studios. State and national parks and forests provide resources for adventure and outdoor education activities. Government, community, business, and philanthropic agencies often aid schools in obtaining resources. Some communities are developing multi-use facilities that include a library and recreation center when they build new schools. Physical education programs have access to these facilities during the school day and the community can enjoy them during evening hours. Since students have the opportunity to become familiar with these resources during classes, a potential barrier to regular participation in physical activity is lessened. The school's organizational structure and school policies stifle or encourage creativity in curriculum planning. Administrators' values, attitudes, and policies toward learning, student behavior, and faculty freedom impact decisions about the scope of a curriculum. The number, age, gender, socioeconomic background, interests, and expertise of physical educators directly affect what is taught. The school curriculum pattern and schedule dictate the limits within which the physical education program must operate.

Student interests and needs play an important part in the selection of curriculum content.
©Tracy Pellet

Information about the Learners

Educational goals and curricular objectives arise from student needs, which are generally of two types. The first kind arises from needs within the organism itself. To achieve physical and psychological safety, students need self-efficacy and skill in basic movement skills and a safe progression of curricular activities. Selecting developmentally appropriate activities that take into account differences in skill and emotional readiness will lead to greater participation as students are more likely to experience success with them. Low-skilled students or those facing social rejection will often refuse to participate if they sense that they will fail. Using cooperative activities, adapting activities so students with a wide range of abilities experience success and enjoyment, and counseling students to select those activities best suited to their individual needs and interests increase student self-esteem. According to Maslow, the school environment should help students satisfy their basic needs so they will be free to move on to self-actualization. To develop self-actualization in physical education, students need to learn how movement affects their health and well-being in adulthood and how to take responsibility for their decisions.[5]

The second type of needs is determined by comparing the learner's current status with the status expected by society. The gap between these two levels defines an educational need. For example, if a society expects its members to be able to swim and students cannot swim, then a need exists. Some educational needs are common to children or adolescents of a particular age level, no matter where they live, while other needs are specific to the local environment. Youth in Hawaii may need to be adept at swimming and surfing, while children in Colorado may need to be good snow skiers. With today's mobile society, all students need to develop basic motor skills and be open to learning new activities so that if their environment changes as an adult (e.g., the skiers move to Hawaii), they still can find physical activities in which to participate.

Students who differ dramatically from group norms, including potential dropouts, bilingual students, the mentally and physically disabled, and the gifted also should be considered. In fact, the courts have ruled that schools must meet the needs of *all* learners. Programs must be flexible enough to adapt to learners' individual differences. Students' interests and purposes for enrolling in physical education must be considered. Curriculum designers should plan for a variety of learning modes to accommodate students' individual personalities and learning styles.

Data concerning both the whole student population and individual students are essential. Curriculum designers must consider the nature of the student body—the number of students, their ages, gender, grade levels, socioeconomic levels, racial composition and ethnic background, personal and family characteristics, interests, achievements, talents, and goals. Data from physical fitness, knowledge, skill, and attitude tests can describe students' past achievements. Health assessments provide essential information about students. Questionnaires to determine student interests can help determine readiness for learning specific activities. Other methods for studying learners include observations, questionnaires, interviews, and school and community records concerning attendance, delinquency, health, social status, discipline, and participation in extracurricular and recreation activities. Hass listed questions curriculum planners can ask to test how well programs have been planned to meet students' needs:

1. Does the planned curriculum provide for the developmental differences of the learners being taught?
2. Does the planned curriculum include provisions so that learning may start for each learner where he or she is?[6]

Data about students are compared with desirable norms and deviations noted as possible concerns for school attention. The curriculum committee must decide which needs can be appropriately met by the school and which are best met by coordination with other social agencies.

The Subject Matter and How It Is Learned

The trend toward outcome and standards-based education at the national and state levels makes it imperative for physical educators to design curriculums that help students achieve the specified outcomes. The *Goals 2000: Educate America Act* in March 1994 established a national council to help professional organizations develop standards specifying what students should know and be able to do. In response to the national call for standards, the National Association for Sport and Physical Education (NASPE) developed content standards for physical education that were published in 1995. These *content standards* describe the knowledge and skills of each discipline, while the *performance standards* stipulate "how good is good enough." Once assessments of student work or performance have been accumulated over time, *performance benchmarks* can be used to describe the students' progress toward the performance standards. Table 6.1 lists the revised content standards for physical education.[7]

All students should be expected and helped to meet the content standards of physical education before graduating from high school. This can occur only when the curriculum is carefully planned and instruction carried out at each level to lead toward the standards.

Curriculum planners use a backward design technique when planning curriculum.[8] By starting with the exit standards (what students are expected to know and be able to do at the twelfth-grade level or after graduation), planners divide this content among the various grades so that students learn a little each year and by the time they graduate, they have achieved the standards. Goals and objectives must be written for every grade level. It is very important that students achieve or master what is expected for them every year so that they have the necessary skills to accomplish what is expected in the next grade. Starting with the end in mind helps to focus a curriculum as planners have a target for which to aim. Assessments are developed to measure whether students are achieving the goals set for them. Teachers must carefully select units of study that will meet the expectations set by the standards. Although many different activities are possible, curriculums that have mainly a team sport focus will not be able to meet the expectations set by the NASPE Physical Education Content Standards.

TABLE 6.1 Physical Education Content Standards

A Physically Educated Student
1. Demonstrates competency in motor skills and movement patterns needed to perform a variety of physical activities.
2. Demonstrates understanding of movement concepts, principles, strategies, and tactics as they apply to the learning and performance of physical activities.
3. Participates regularly in physical activity.
4. Achieves and maintains a health-enhancing level of physical fitness.
5. Exhibits responsible personal and social behavior that respects self and others in physical activity settings.
6. Values physical activity for health, enjoyment, challenge, self-expression, and/or social interaction.

Source: From National Association for Sport and Physical Education, *Moving in the Future: National Physical Education Standards: A Guide to Content and Assessment,* 2nd ed. (Reston VA: Author, 2004).

Curriculum designers must consider each of the standards and the learning domains—cognitive, affective, and psychomotor—that relate to those standards. Students should be helped to discover how physical education relates to them and how they can use the information gained to solve their own problems. Some questions to consider when planning the subject matter and instructional methodology include the following:

- What does a physically educated student know? Do? Table 1.3 lists what a physically educated person has, is, does, knows, and values.
- What should students know and be able to do at the high school level, the junior high school level, the middle school level, or the elementary level? (These are called benchmarks.)
- What should students know and be able to do at the specific grade level to meet the school level outcomes?
- What instructional units will help students achieve these objectives?
- What lesson objectives will help students achieve the unit objectives?

The curriculum should allow students to develop at all levels in each learning domain and help learners to identify and organize the key concepts and principles of physical education and use them to solve personal problems, now and in the future. To accommodate individual learning styles, it should also provide alternative approaches to learning.

Research in educational psychology and motor learning, in exercise physiology, and in other areas of education also have implications for curriculum development. A knowledge of educational psychology and adolescent development helps educators select objectives that are attainable at certain age levels and the conditions and amount of time necessary for learning. Time greatly influences achievement of the objectives. It is better to have fewer objectives and teach them well than to have a large number of unattained objectives.

Governmental Activity

Federal and state legislation; judicial decisions such as those on legal liability, integration, and busing; and government regulations and supervision, including the power to allot or withdraw funds, play a major role in the educational process. Federal laws that have had a tremendous effect on school programs include PL 94–142 (The Education for All Handicapped Children Act) and its sequel, The Individuals with Disabilities Education Act of 1990 (PL 101–476); Section 504 of the Rehabilitation Act;

Title IX; and No Child Left Behind. These laws, with implications for physical education, were discussed in Chapter 4. Policy constraints often dictate what can be done, leaving little latitude for innovation. The National Association for Sport and Physical Education lists current articles on its website to help physical educators change public opinion and influence political decisions that affect physical education.[9]

Philosophies, Aims, and Objectives of Education and Physical Education

When developing a curricular philosophy, physical educators must align with both the philosophy and goals of the district. If physical education programs fail to establish links with the purpose of education in the district, they may be viewed as unessential to the education of children and therefore be subject to elimination. Boards of education are typically responsible for establishing the overall philosophy of a district. An alternative to governance by a board of education is the establishment of a site-based management committee that has jurisdiction over the school and is, in a sense, the school board for the school. The logic behind having a school governed by a school committee composed of the various stakeholders in a school (e.g., administrators, teachers, students, parents, support staff) is that individual schools within a district might be very different and have very different needs. Since members of the site-based management committee have a personal interest in the school, decisions about the school are made only after careful deliberation by the entire group. Regardless of the type of governance system used, physical education teachers should link program philosophies and goals to those of the school and/or district.

To form a philosophical base on which to build a meaningful program, teachers must become aware of their own philosophies. To accomplish this, they should wrestle with questions like the following:

- What is the purpose of education?
- What is the purpose of physical education? To teach concepts, sport skills, fitness? Personal and social skills?
- How does physical education fit into the purposes of education?
- What is the role of a teacher?

Local social and environmental forces and the philosophies of educators and physical educators directly influence the purposes of education and the value orientations that are selected as the bases for local curricula. As social forces change, the demands placed on schools also change. Decisions about social implications must take into account the following purposes of education:

1. To preserve and maintain desirable social features by transmitting them to the young.
2. To teach skills and competencies needed to function effectively as an adult member of society.
3. To help the individual function within society to the fullest extent possible, both now and in the future, through intelligent self-direction, group deliberation, and action.
4. To teach the individual to constructively evaluate social issues and influence the social order by contributing to ordered, purposeful change.

Jewett, Bain, and Ennis described five value orientations for curriculum development that match the purposes described above.[10] They are disciplinary mastery, social reconstruction, learning process, self-actualization, and ecological integration. The chosen value orientation should be stated in the philosophy of the curriculum guide.

Disciplinary mastery emphasizes the transmission "of the cultural heritage from one generation to the next." The "back to the basics" movement reflects this emphasis, as does the traditional emphasis on physical fitness and mastery of basic movement and sport skills in physical education.

Social reconstruction stresses instruction for "creating a better society," and emphasizes interpersonal and problem-solving skills. Social reconstructionists include nontraditional activities such as outdoor and adventure education and "new games," with emphasis on cooperation rather than competition, in an attempt to broaden community recreational interests.

The *learning process* emphasizes learning how to learn and the importance of learning the skills needed to deal with rapid changes in knowledge and technology. Content includes basic physical education knowledge, as well as learning how to acquire sport skills.

Advocates of *self-actualization* provide opportunities for students to explore many activities and then develop expertise in one or more chosen activities. Experiences that lend themselves to each student's quest for personal excellence and satisfaction include outdoor pursuits and adventure activities.

In the fifth orientation, *ecological integration,* self-actualization is sought as a means toward a holistic interaction between the individual and the environment. This orientation focuses on the global interdependent society and emphasizes health-related fitness, skillful movement, self-confidence, creativity, outdoor education, and leadership skills designed for optimum personal development.

These value orientations should be useful when developing the curriculum philosophy. Writing objectives is the next step in the curriculum development process. These objectives must reflect and help define the intent of the philosophy. Grant Wiggins encourages curriculum planners to picture the graduate of the program when developing a program philosophy and objectives related to it. What skills, knowledge, and attitudes should every student possess both now and twenty years from now? Brainstorming this perspective with colleagues will help curriculum planners focus on the most essential knowledge, rather than creating a curriculum that is so complex it would be impossible to accomplish even if the amount of time spent in schools was doubled.

Once the objectives have been selected, they should be stated as observable student behaviors and in a way that educators, parents, students, and other interested persons can understand what behaviors are intended. Hass listed some guidelines for evaluating goals and objectives as follows:

1. Have the goals of the curriculum or teaching plan been clearly stated, and are they used by the teachers and students in choosing content, materials, and activities for learning?
2. Have the teachers and students engaged in student-teacher planning in defining the goals and in determining how they will be implemented?
3. Do some of the planned goals relate to the society or the community in which the curriculum will be implemented or the teaching will be done?
4. Do some of the planned goals relate to the needs, purposes, interests, and abilities of the individual learner?
5. Are the planned goals used as criteria in selecting and developing learning activities and materials of instruction?
6. Are the planned goals used as criteria in evaluating learning achievement and in the further planning of learning subgoals and activities?[11]

For learners to achieve curriculum goals and objectives, learning experiences must be selected and organized to reinforce concepts, values, and skills.

No one curriculum is adequate to serve the varied populations of all schools. Curriculum designers must study curriculum models as a basis for intelligent action and then select and combine elements from several models to develop a curriculum that suits the needs of the particular school or system within which they are working. This requires knowing the elements of each model and possessing the creativity to adapt them to the needs of the situation.

In physical education, curriculum models have evolved from either a subject-centered or a student-centered approach. Subject-centered curriculum models include the traditional activity-based and the more recent movement-based and concepts-based models. They are generally chosen to promote the purposes of transmitting the culture to young people to prepare them for effective living in society. They emphasize disciplinary mastery and learning how to learn. Student-centered curriculums include the developmental-needs and the student-centered curriculum models. These patterns tend to reinforce the purposes of self-actualization and social change, along with their respective value orientations.

Review Question: What should be considered in each of the following areas before making curriculum decisions?

a. community
b. school
c. learners
d. subject matter
e. trends, innovations, research
f. governmental activity
g. philosophy

Activity-Based Curriculum Models

In the most common pattern, the activity-based curriculum is organized around activity units, including dance, fitness, and sports. Participation in activities is the goal. Since all activities cannot be included, a percentage of the total time is established for each activity category. Local considerations influence specific selections within each category. Progression is from basic skills in the elementary grades to specialization in a few selected activities at the high school level. Although the multiactivity pattern is easy to administer, many programs are inadequately planned and implemented resulting in boredom, repetition, and failure among students to develop skills beyond the basic level. When implementing multiactivity models, some teachers develop an "exposure" mentality, meaning that they want to expose students to as many activities as possible. Instead of offering units that have sufficient time for students to develop mastery of the activity, students are given minimal instruction on skills and then play regulation games for which they have not developed the skills in order to be successful. Games tend to be dominated by players with prior experience, and those with little skill or background become disenchanted with and alienated from the benefits of physical activity. These programs are difficult to justify to administrators and taxpayers.

Other types of activity-based curriculum models provide positive experiences for students. Sport education is an activity-based model developed by Siedentop that values the use of play in teaching physical activity. Siedentop stated that "physical education derives from play, is best understood in reference to play and best defined as playful motor activity, and in its mature form is institutionalized in culture as sport and dance."[12] Play is seen as an important part of human existence. Students need instruction to develop the fundamental motor patterns needed for participation in all activities and counseling to help them match their interests and abilities to suitable activities. *Sport education* seeks to develop competent, literate, enthusiastic sportspersons. Instruction mirrors sport in society, with modifications to fit the educational setting. Six features make this model unique from other curricular models.

1. *Seasons:* Students participate in seasons that are long enough for them to achieve the goals of the model. This is similar to the season a sports team would experience. Practice dominates the beginning of the season. Game play is the dominant learning experience as the season comes to a close.
2. *Team affiliation:* Instead of new teams being chosen every day, students are assigned to a team at the beginning of a season and work with that group of players until the season is completed.

3. *Formal competitions:* Competitions are scheduled in advance, giving teams the opportunity to prepare for playing an opponent. Competitions involving small-sided games (e.g., two v. two) might be played at the beginning of the season to reinforce some of the concepts learned during practice while larger teams are used as players' skills increase.
4. *Culminating event:* The season concludes with some type of a tournament, meet, or competition much like a varsity athletic team. However, winning the culminating event does not mean that the team won the season; other items such as practice minutes and fair play are used to calculate the final winner.
5. *Record keeping/statistics:* Records and statistics provide important feedback for players regarding their improvement. These statistics might also be used to decide which team actually won the final competition.
6. *Festivities and rituals:* Competition is celebrated with team names, colors, logos, banners, opening ceremonies, and award ceremonies at the conclusion of the season.

Students participate in formal competitive schedules with preseason instruction, team practice sessions, a culminating event, and publicized records and standings. Games progress in difficulty, with modified games such as one-on-one, two-on-two, and three-on-three, helping all students become competent and confident in their skills and strategies. All students are involved in playing, refereeing, and scorekeeping, with roles such as coach, manager, trainer, statistician, and sports information person rotated among students. Fair play points are awarded to lead students toward appropriate personal and social behaviors. Sports education may occur in single classes, with competition between classes scheduled during the same class period or other class periods, or during intramural activity time. Guests such as parents, grandparents, teachers, and community members may serve as spectators or event managers. Sports education teaches skills, rules, strategies, appreciation for play in our society, and proper ethical principles involved in *good* sport.[13] Research has shown that students in the sport education model improve in the use of strategy, participation levels, and team play, while students in traditional models often do not.[14]

Another activity-oriented curriculum approach is outdoor education. This model includes activities conducted in wilderness settings, such as backpacking, canoeing, and scuba diving. While physical skill is the primary objective of wilderness activities, group or individual problem solving under stress is the major purpose of outdoor education. Although instruction is included in physical education classes, weekend or overnight outings are essential for skill application in wilderness settings.[15] Some activities for this approach are presented in Chapter 10.

Movement-Based Curriculum Models

The movement-based curriculum is based on the work of Laban and is used primarily in elementary school programs.[16] The curriculum is organized around themes involving the body and its interrelationship with space, time, effort, and flow. Exploration of movement concepts and a variety of movement skills in dance, gymnastics, and games are included. Students use problem solving or discovery learning to create new ways of using their bodies to achieve specified goals with various pieces of equipment. Graham and his associates produced the framework shown in Figure 6-3 for developing a movement-based curriculum.[17] Although movement-based curriculum patterns are primarily used in elementary schools, effective programs have also been implemented in middle schools and high schools.

Concepts-Based Curriculum Models

Concepts approaches based on the body of knowledge about human movement are organized around key ideas or principles, broad enough to permit instruction in a wide variety of activities and meaningful enough to justify the time and effort expended. The goal is to help students understand the what, why, and how of physical education through problem solving in laboratory and activity settings. Sport and movement skills can be used to teach concepts. Progression is from simple to more complex knowledge. Concepts approaches are based on two assumptions: (1) that concepts transfer to new skills and situations and (2) that students learn concepts better if the teacher emphasizes the concept (e.g., force production) rather than teaching the concept within an activity unit.

Concepts-based curricula are more easily justified in an academic sense and may help physical education achieve a more respected place in the school curriculum. They adapt readily to individual student differences and to different locales. Students who do not excel in physical education activities often like the concepts approach. Another advantage may be the carryover of basic concepts about health and fitness to real life. Two disadvantages are that students may not learn the skills needed to participate in each activity and that concepts may transfer to new skills and situations only when the application is made clear in the new situation.

In the late 1960s and 1970s, a group at Loughborough University in England devised a teaching model to overcome the deficiencies of the traditional activity model.[18] Their approach, which focuses on student understanding of game strategies and solving problems unique to game forms, became known as the *Teaching Games for Understanding (TGfU) Approach.* It begins with the premise that the learner must move toward cognitive dissonance to create a desire to seek solutions to problems.[19] The Games for Understanding Model involves a classification of games into types, such as invasion games (basketball, soccer, etc.), target games (golf, archery), net/wall games (volleyball, racquetball), and field games (softball). Games are taught using a cycle of six steps.[20]

1. *Introduction of the game form and the problems unique to that game.* For example, volleyball is a net game that requires the use of strategic angles for

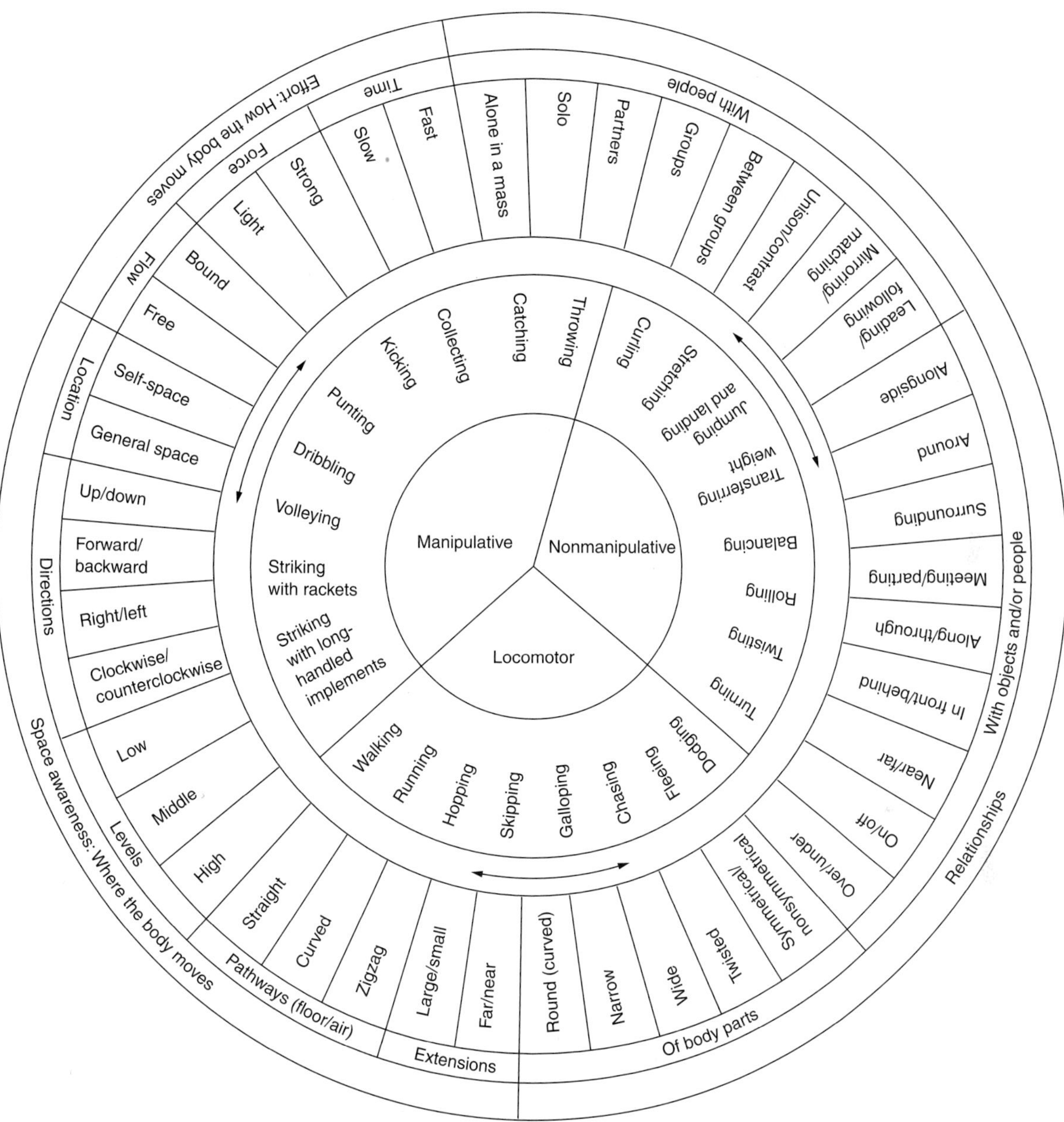

Figure 6-3

Movement analysis framework.

Source: George Graham, Shirley Ann Holt/Hale, and Melissa Parker, *Children Moving: A Reflective Approach to Teaching Physical Education,* 3d ed. (MountainView, CA: Mayfield, 1993), 24.

placing the ball into spaces on the opponent's court and for defending spaces on one's own court. Game forms are modified games such as three-on-three or two-on-three which contain the essential elements of the official game, with adaptations to meet the needs of the learners and to ensure safety.

2. *Games appreciation.* The emphasis is on students understanding the rules of the game. Players learn that rules affect the skills and strategies needed. Rules generally include the number of players on a team, the playing area, the type of equipment (modified balls, lower nets), and ways of scoring.
3. *Tactical awareness.* Game components are exaggerated to increase student awareness of the need for certain game strategies such as creating space when attacking or denying space when defending and recognizing opponents' weaknesses. The teacher's role is to observe the outcome, assess the situations that arise and the players' solutions, and then pose questions to individuals or groups that stimulate possible answers or challenge further thought. "Questions may concern the objective of the game, the selection and execution of particular tactics or techniques, [such as] What are you trying to do? What are the alternatives? How could you best achieve it? How can other team members help? How will you adjust to the opponents' play? etc."[21]

4. *Decision making.* Students gain experience in recognizing cues from game situations and predicting possible outcomes, then choosing the best outcome for the situation. Decisions include "What to do" and "How to do it."
5. *Skill execution.* Once students see the need to improve skills to accomplish their tactical goals, they are better prepared to work on skill development under the guidance of the teacher. Both skill efficiency and appropriateness in the game are considered.
6. *Performance.* Appropriate response selection and efficient technique execution ultimately result in effective game performance. In this phase, the students' abilities are assessed and the cycle returns to the beginning.

The TGfU model takes into account both learning and motivation theory, helps students see relationships and differences between games, and fosters both cognitive development and skill development. However, it requires teachers to be truly knowledgeable about game structures and to select developmentally appropriate game forms and modify games to help students understand the activities without violating the basic principles on which the games are based. Teachers must be helped to develop the pedagogical content knowledge required to implement this approach.[22]

In the *subdiscipline* approach to physical education, units are based on the subdisciplines traditionally associated with physical education—exercise physiology, kinesiology, motor development, motor learning, sport sociology and psychology, and sport history, philosophy, and art. An example of a concept-oriented instructional unit for biomechanics using the subdiscipline approach might include the following:

Week 1: Center of gravity and base of support

Week 2: Balance

Week 3: Spin and angle of rebound

Week 4: Newton's laws of motion

Week 5: Force production

Week 6: Summary of the use of biomechanics in sport[23]

Several variations of the concepts-based curriculum pattern include (1) integrating concepts with the traditional activity-based curriculum, (2) teaching a separate unit on concepts along with the traditional activity units, and (3) teaching concepts on special occasions such as rainy days and shortened periods. An example of activities in which concepts are integrated with sport skills is shown in Table 6.2.

With the current emphasis on physical fitness, wellness, and healthy lifestyles, it is no surprise that physical educators have created a *fitness-based curriculum approach.* Most programs emphasize fitness concepts, as well as activity skills for developing healthy lifestyles. A number of textbooks for teaching fitness concepts to secondary school students have been published. Most programs are supplemented with activity units designed to encourage participation in physical activity throughout life.

Developmental-Needs Curriculum Models

The *student-needs curriculum* is based on the cognitive, psychomotor, and affective developmental stages and growth patterns of children and youth. Basic skills are taught in elementary school programs; team sports are emphasized in middle and junior high school programs; and lifetime activities are taught in senior high school and college curricula, along with appropriate cognitive and affective objectives for students' developmental levels. The curriculum is often divided into activity or theme units chosen by the faculty to meet student needs. This curriculum pattern is based primarily on the assumption that students go through the same developmental stages at the same rate, although some programs attempt to provide a variety of learning experiences to allow for individual variation in developmental levels. In a survey of professionals, researchers concluded that developmentally appropriate practice involves "experiences which are adapted to the individual learner's needs, interests, skill, and confidence levels."[24] The developmental-needs curriculum is widely accepted and often combined with the activity-based curriculum under the assumption that development will occur automatically through participation in motor activities.

Student-Centered Curriculum Models

Student-centered curriculums are based on students' purposes for enrolling in physical education activities, including social interaction, adventure, emotional release, physical fitness, self-discipline, or personal expression. The assumption is that students are capable of assessing their own purposes and making appropriate choices, although counseling helps students with these choices. A wide variety of activities with beginning, intermediate, and advanced levels of instruction are required to meet student needs. Attendance, cooperation, and learning increase when students are allowed to concentrate on activities in which they have real interest and develop competence in activities in which they will participate outside of school. Some teachers may need to learn to teach new activities that are of interest to students. If students continually shift from one teacher to another, teachers may not get to know students. Some students can get lost in such a system.

Humanistic physical education stresses the uniqueness of each individual. It uses physical activity to assist students in their search for personal meaning, self-understanding, self-actualization, and interpersonal relations. Subject matter mastery is de-emphasized. Humanistic physical education requires a caring, authentic teacher who can establish a close teacher-student relationship and facilitate student learning.

Hellison developed a *personal and social responsibility* model for physical education. Its focus is on teaching and empowering students to take more responsibility for themselves and to be socially responsible and sensitive to

TABLE 6.2 Commonalities of Fundamental Movement Skills and Related Mechanical Principles

Moving the Body through Space (INITIATING MOVEMENT, LOCOMOTION, ABSORBING MOMENTUM)		+ Moving an Object through Space (ALTERING THE PATHWAY, SENDING, AND RECEIVING)			= Moving the Body and an Object through Space		
Activities	*Locomotor Skills*	*Activities*	*Manipulative Movements*		*Activities*	*Manipulative Movements*	*Locomotor Skills*
Badminton Basketball Field hockey Gymnastics Soccer Softball Tennis Track and field Volleyball	Starting (staying ready to move) Running Sliding Jumping Stopping Changing directions (flexible pathways) Landing	Softball Field hockey Badminton Tennis Golf Volleyball	Striking	Sending	Basketball	Dribbling (hands)	Starting Running Stopping Changing directions Sliding
Swimming	Propulsion	Soccer	Kicking	Sending	Soccer	Dribbling (feet)	
		Softball Basketball Field events	Throwing	Sending	Field hockey	Dribbling (stick)	
		Archery	Projecting	Sending	Basketball	Juggle (air dribble)	
		Softball Basketball Soccer	Catching Blocking and trapping	Receiving			
Control of body		+ Control of Object			= Control of Body and Object		

Source: From Beverly L. Seidel, Fay R. Biles, Grace E. Figley, and Bonnie J. Neuman, *Sports Skills: A Conceptual Approach to Meaningful Movement,* 2nd ed. (© 1975, 1980 Wm. C. Brown Publishers, Dubuque, Iowa. All Rights Reserved. Reprinted by permission).

the rights, feelings, and well-being of others. He identified the five goals shown in Table 6.3 and then placed these goals into a hierarchy of levels for developing responsibility: (0) irresponsibility, (1) respect, (2) participation, (3) self-direction, and (4) caring. Hellison proposed strategies to help youth progress through the five stages, including awareness talks, group and individual reflection, time to try out or experience the levels, group problem-solving meetings, individual counseling, and individual choice.[25] An example of a task sheet used to promote goal setting is shown in Table 6.4.

Adventure Based Learning (ABL) uses events such as trust activities, games, and problem-solving initiatives to develop students socially as well as physically.[26] These activities are purposefully chosen to be sequentially more difficult and challenging to students. Physical activity is the medium through which children learn how to challenge themselves, cooperate with others, take risks, trust in themselves and others, and solve problems with support and guidance from other members of the group. ABL uses an experiential cycle that generally begins with a problem or challenge that teachers present to students followed by a chance to reflect. Students are asked to comment about what happened during the experience as they describe and interpret the events both personally and as it relates to other members of the group. Students are next asked to generalize, answering a "So what?" question about what made the experience successful or less successful and what it meant to them personally. In the last phase in the experiential cycle, students are asked to apply what they learned in this specific experience to other settings. What students learn from this particular experience then feeds back into future experiences in the sequence of activities designed to help students reach new levels of social and physical development. In ABL, students are expected to follow a full value contract, a document created by the group to promote safe participation and discourage inappropriate behaviors. Students as a group take ownership in enforcing the full value contract rather than the leader disciplining those who refuse to follow rules. Challenge by choice, which means that an individual has the option of discontinuing participation if feeling physically or emotionally unsafe, is the final component of ABL that sets it apart from other curriculum models.

TABLE 6.3 Levels in Hellison's Personal and Social Responsibility Model

Level Zero, Irresponsibility

- Students make excuses, blame others for their behavior, and fail to assume responsibility for what they say, do, or fail to do

Level I, Respect for the Rights and Feelings of Others

- Have self-control of their attitudes and behaviors so that respect for others is demonstrated
- Resolve conflicts peacefully and democratically
- Recognize that everyone has a right to be included regardless of gender, race, skill, ethnicity, or sexual preference

Level II, Participation and Effort

- Self-motivation to complete tasks
  - Try new tasks
  - Practice or train to improve performance
  - Have the courage to persist when the going gets tough
- Develop a personal definition of success

Level III, Self-Direction

- Stay on task without supervision
- Set realistic goals to achieve
- Can set, carry out, and evaluate personal goals
- Identify unique personal interests
- Stand up for personal rights and interests against external forces

Level IV, Sensitivity and Responsiveness

- Act out of caring and compassion for others
- Contribute to their community without expectation of external rewards
- Listen and respond to others without being judgmental
- Help others when they want to be helped
- Resolve differences peacefully and democratically
- Recognize that perspectives of others may differ from their own and learn to see and feel things from the viewpoints of others

Level V, Application beyond the Gymnasium

- Students demonstrate levels of responsibility in the different settings of their lives
- Are role models for others

Source: Table created from D. Hellison, *Teaching Responsibility through Physical Activity,* 2nd ed. (Champaign, IL: Human Kinetics Publishing, 2003).

Review Question: Define each of the following curriculum patterns:

Subject-centered

a. Activity-based
   (1) Sport education
   (2) Wilderness sports
b. Movement-based
c. Concepts-based
   (1) Teaching games for understanding
   (2) Subdiscipline; fitness
d. Developmental needs

Student-centered

a. Humanistic
b. Social development
c. Adventure Based Learning

Activity: Create a unit or lesson plan from your favorite curriculum model—sport education, movement-based, other.

Building a Program from Main Theme Curriculum Models

Each curriculum model described in the previous section will address the content standards in different ways. Some models are more appropriate for meeting the intent of some standards than others. For example, Hellison's model of social and personal responsibility addresses NASPE's Content Standards 5 and 6 very well, but does not contribute strongly to meeting the other standards. The TGfU model does an excellent job of addressing the concepts and strategies necessary for satisfying the intent of Standard 2, but

TABLE 6.4 Big Ideas Sheet

My Personal Plan #1

1. Fitness: Choose at least one
   My flexibility goal is ______
   My strength goal is ______
   My aerobic goal is ______
   Today in fitness I did ______
2. Motor skills: Choose at least one skill from one activity
   My basketball goal is ______
   My volleyball goal is ______
   My soccer goal is ______
   My ______ goal is ______
3. Choose one
   The creative/expressive activity I did was ______
   I spent my "pal time" with ______ doing ______
   The stress management activity I did today was ______
   The self-defense activity I did today was ______
4. During my Level III time
   My respect for others was
   ______ good ______ OK ______ not OK
   My effort was
   ______ high ______ medium ______ low
   My plan was
   ______ my own ______ somewhat my own ______ not my own
   My self-discipline in carrying out my plan was
   ______ good ______ fair ______ poor
   I helped someone else
   ______ Yes! ______ A little ______ No!

Source: D. Hellison, *Teaching Responsibility through Physical Education,* 2nd ed. (Champaign, IL: Human Kinetics, 2003), 70.

does not deliberately address Standards 5 and 6. Since no single model will meet all of the content standards, Lund and Tannehill suggest using a multimodel curriculum that selects several of the main theme curricula when developing a K–12 curriculum.[27] The multimodel should not be confused with the multiactivity model that typically consists of a hodgepodge of activities with little regard for subject matter mastery. Rather, the multimodel uses several of the main theme curricular models that focus on specific learning goals and allow students to meet the objective of becoming physically educated in innovative and challenging ways. After selecting the models to be used in the curriculum, those developing the curriculum must remember that each school or district has unique characteristics that must be addressed and unique needs that must be met. There is no magic slipper that will automatically fit every foot in the district and meet every need. The cobblers (or in this case the curriculum designers) must adjust components of the main theme curricula so that there is a comfortable fit. Curriculum developers must also remember that what works in one district may not necessarily work in another—there is no one size that fits all. For example, a movement curriculum might be used at the elementary level, followed by a combination of TGfU and sport education at the middle school level. Ninth graders might experience a fitness curriculum followed by an outdoor education program during the rest of the high school years. Several factors will dictate the type of curricular model selected:

- School and state requirements.
- Exit goals and objectives for the program.
- Motivation of the physical education teachers to build a program that is worthwhile.
- Needs and interests of the students.
- Type and availability of facilities from the school and community during school and nonschool hours.
- Availability of equipment and supplies.
- Expertise of the teachers.
- Instructional time available.
- Ability of students to attend before or after school programs.
- Willingness of school officials to financially support a high-quality physical education program that may include compensation for time spent beyond the school day.[28]

Whatever program is selected, do it well. It may be worthwhile to implement program components in small steps and work with that portion until success is achieved before starting another part.

Documenting Learning

Once the curriculum designers have decided what is important for students to know and be able to do, they must determine how to measure whether their goals have been met. Chapter 11 contains many assessment ideas that are useful for measuring student learning. In states that have developed a statewide testing format, schools and districts will follow those guidelines. If the state or district has not developed an assessment system, schools and districts will need to develop their own. Earlier in this chapter it was suggested that objectives be written in observable terms. If this is done, the choice of assessment will be obvious. Curriculum designers should develop assessments that focus on the "big picture" rather than creating several smaller assessments. Since performance-based assessments are closely associated with the assessment process, they are preferred by many because dramatic interruptions in instruction are not required to administer them. The less obtrusive the assessment, the more likely teachers will be to accept it. In some instances, the assessments can actually be linked with instruction. For example, in a sport education unit, the goal is for students to become competent participants. Assessments in this curriculum might include rubrics for game play (if written properly they can measure competency in the psychomotor, cognitive, and affective domains), statistics gathered during the unit, officiating ratings derived from a rubric, and a written assessment (test, newspaper article covering a game) or project (analysis of a video, tape of a play-by-play game broadcast). Portfolios are another excellent way to assess whether students are reaching standards, as teachers can require components that address every domain.

Assessments should be developed for the curriculum that measure whether students are reaching the criteria specified by the standards. These assessments will play a key role in the evaluation of the curriculum (see Chapter 15). Although these assessments may also be used for assessing effectiveness of instructional units, their primary purpose is to measure student achievement of the standards.

Determine the Program's Scope and Sequence

Once the assessments for the standards are in place, it is necessary to select the content that will allow students to reach the objectives as measured by the curricular assessments. The content selected for the curriculum and the order in which it is organized for presentation are called scope and sequence. *Scope* includes *what* should be taught. Some schools have a narrow scope focusing only on a few sports. In contrast, the curriculum should be broad in scope, encompassing a variety of rich and guided experiences—instructional, intramural, recreational, and athletic—in order to meet the wide diversity of physical, intellectual, emotional, and social needs of children and youth. Too many experiences, however, can dilute the effectiveness of each experience.

Program Balance

A balanced program emphasizes a variety of learning experiences consistent with the content standards, school goals, and students' needs and interests. The curriculum model chosen should provide a logical structure for organizing learning activities. Balance among the standards can be maintained by allocating time to each one consistent with the value placed upon it within the school context and the philosophy of the curriculum committee. Additionally, to meet the standards, a curriculum must have variety with units in dance, body control, team and net sports, target activities, and other types of individual activities. Curricula in which only sports are taught are not balanced, nor are curricula that exclude instruction in fitness or knowledge. Social skills, such as teamwork and fair play, are often cited as goals but are difficult to find in the instructional program. Some teachers fail to teach the activities specified in a curriculum guide because of personal preference or lack of knowledge and/or skill. The proposed curriculum and the delivered curriculum should be the same.

Time allotted to class instruction, intramurals, and extramurals must also be balanced. Commitment should be first to class instruction, second to an intramural program, and last to an extramural program. Intramural programs and clubs extend opportunities for students to use and refine skills learned in class instruction and to learn skills not available during class time, due to the inaccessibility of facilities, such as bowling, skiing, skating, hiking, and rock climbing. Extramural or interscholastic athletics provide competition for highly skilled students. To meet educational objectives, athletic programs must be carefully designed and managed by dedicated professionals. Legislation requires equal opportunities for boys, girls, and the disabled to participate in extra-class programs.

Review Questions: Define scope, sequence, and balanced curriculum.

What activity or concept areas should be included in a balanced curriculum?

Methods for Selecting Content

Since far more activities and experiences exist than can possibly be included in the curriculum, only the most appropriate should be selected. Many programs try to do everything and therefore do nothing well. They repeat activities and content year after year, but the short units have insufficient time for students to master content. Learning experiences must be selected to meet students' needs and interests, society's needs, and the program's expressed philosophy and goals.

Activities are often selected based on the teachers' interests and abilities or the coaches' desire to develop skills involved in the athletic program. Such practices usually result in unbalanced programs based primarily on team sports. Parents and participants suggest the need for lifetime activities such as golf, swimming, tennis, bowling, and dance. Some recent innovations in the secondary school curriculum include outdoor pursuits such as cross country and alpine skiing; hiking, backpacking, orienteering, and camping; canoeing, sailing, and bicycling. Additionally, climbing walls installed in gymnasiums are becoming more popular and some teachers use circus events to teach psychomotor activities. These activities involve concerns about teacher expertise, safety, transportation, and legal liability that must be dealt with before implementing the programs. However, with appropriate planning, such activities can be safely introduced in the curriculum. Content should be selected by a curriculum committee composed of teachers and administrators who use input from parents and students. The following steps are suggested:

Step 1. Review the outcome statements in Chapter 1 and the content standards in Table 6.1 and any state or district standards. Next, the standards must be "unpacked" so that they are defined in concrete, observable terms. By unpacking the standards, you are identifying what a physically educated student should know and be able to do at the level at which you teach—high school, junior high, or middle school. *Moving into the Future: Content Standards for Physical Education* has student expectations and sample performance outcomes for grades 6–8 and 9–12 that can help you as you unpack the standards.[29] These can be further delineated for a specific grade level. Table 6.5 gives a sample curriculum plan using this process.

Step 2. Determine broad activity or concept categories and possible instructional units that will help

TABLE 6.5 A Sample Curriculum Plan Based on the National Standards and Emphases from the National Association for Sport and Physical Education

Content Standard	Tenth-Grade Emphasis	Unit Objective	Assessment
Demonstrates competency in motor skills and movement patterns needed to perform a variety of physical activities.	• Demonstrate competence (basic skills, strategies, and rules) in an increasing number of more complex versions of at least three of the following different types of movement forms: aquatics, team sports, individual and dual sports, outdoor pursuits, self-defense, dance, gymnastics.	• Uses a variety of clubs competently to play a round of golf.	• Single best "by the rules" golf score.
Demonstrates understanding of movement concepts, principles, strategies, and tactics as they apply to the learning and performance of physical activities.	• Use more specialized knowledge to develop movement competence or proficiency. • Identify and apply critical elements to enable the development of movement competence/proficiency. • Identify and apply characteristics of highly skilled performance to enable the development of movement competency/proficiency. • Understand and independently apply discipline-specific information to their own performance.	• Uses biomechanical concepts and principles, and examples of expert performance to improve performance.	• Keep a journal of various things learned about the swing, rules, and course management. • View at least two hours of a golf tournament (on TV or in person) or view an instructional golf video. • Videotape a golf outing—provide commentary on one entire hole *or* • Create a ten-minute video including at least three separate scenarios with three different types of clubs. Explain why each club is used for the particular scenario. • Develop a practice activity to improve swing consistency, ball placement, putting accuracy, chipping accuracy. Chart your results for three weeks. Include qualitative cues that improve task performance *or* • Analyze the parts of the swing. Indicate important cues. Videotape yourself each week and write about your progress.
Participates regularly in physical activity.	• Participate regularly in health-enhancing and personally rewarding physical activity outside the physical education class setting. • Seek and select physical activities from a variety of movement forms based on personal interest, meaning, and fulfillment. • Develop and conduct independently a personal physical activity program meeting their needs.	• Participates in health-enhancing activities in the community. • Identifies personal goals to improve golf fitness.	• Play three rounds of golf. Complete the Golf Play Evaluation and Playing Skill Evaluation. • Develop a stretching routine to improve flexibility. Pretest and posttest yourself to substantiate the effectiveness of your routine *or* • Develop a strength routine to improve your golf ball distance. Pretest and posttest your average driving range for ten balls.

Continued

TABLE 6.5 Continued

Content Standard	Tenth-Grade Emphasis	Unit Objective	Assessment
Achieves and maintains a health-enhancing level of physical fitness.	• Assess personal health-related fitness status. • Meet the health-related fitness standards as defined by FITNESSGRAM. • Begin to design personal health-related fitness programs based on an accurately assessed fitness profile. • Participate in a variety of health-enhancing physical activities in both school and nonschool settings. • Use principles of training for the purpose of modifying levels of fitness.	• Assesses personal fitness status and progress. • Sets and achieves appropriate fitness goals.	• Take the Fitnessgram test, record your scores, assess your progress since the last test, and set new fitness goals.
Demonstrates responsible personal and social behavior that respects self and others in physical activity settings.	• Apply safe practices, rules, procedures, and etiquette in all physical activity settings. • Act independently of peer pressure. • Resolve conflicts in appropriate ways. • Keep the importance of winning and losing in perspective relative to other established goals of participation.	• Plays by the rules. • Plays fair. • Uses appropriate etiquette.	• Create a pamphlet on golf etiquette.
Values physical activity for health, enjoyment, challenge, self-expression, and/or social interaction.	• Enjoy participating in a variety of physical activities in competitive and recreational settings. • Pursue new activities both alone or with others. • Enjoy working with others in a sport activity to achieve a common goal. • Recognize that physical activity can provide a positive social environment for activities with others.	• Identifies factors that contribute to enjoyment of golf.	• Participate in two different types of golf events. Tell which event you preferred and why. • In your journal, write daily reflections of how you felt about the activity.

Source: *Moving into the Future: National Physical Education Standards: A Guide to Content and Assessment* (Reston, VA: Author); Unit Ideas from Shawn Fluharty and James D. George.

students achieve the standards for the appropriate school or grade level. Concept category suggestions appear in Table 6.6.

Within each category selected, list all possible units. A sample list of units for selected activity categories is shown in Table 6.7. For other categories, select units or activities that help students understand the category to be studied. For example, under self-awareness you might list risk taking and self-defense. For personal behavior, units could include goal setting, decision making, and problem solving. A unit or curriculum on kinesiology might consider the laws of motion and force, balance, and ball spin. A program on fundamental skills could include locomotor skills, throwing and catching, striking with a body part, and striking with implements.

Create scope charts for each grade or school level using the categories chosen. A scope chart shows the percentage of the total program to be spent in each broad

TABLE 6.6 Categories for Curriculum Development

Skills/Activities	Concepts	Personal/Social	Standards-Based
Fundamental skills	Exercise physiology	Self-awareness	Movement skills
Aquatics	Biomechanics	Personal behavior	Movement concepts and principles
Team sports	Motor development	Cultural understanding	Physically active lifestyle
Gymnastics	Motor learning	Joy of movement	Achieves and maintains physical fitness
Individual sports	Movement in the humanities	Cooperation	Responsible personal and social behavior
Rhythms and dance	Social and psychological aspects of movement		Enjoyment, challenge, self-expression
Physical fitness			
Outdoor education and adventure activities			
Invasion games			
Target games			
Field games			
Net games			
Rhythms/dance			

TABLE 6.7 Possible Activities Listed by Category

Fitness	Combatives/ Gymnastics/ Track and Field	Rhythms	Invasion Games	Net/Wall Games	Field Games	Target Games	Aquatics	Outdoor Pursuits
Jogging	Self-defense	Creative/ modern	**Hands**	**Net-dual**	Kickball	Archery	Safety	Hiking
Rope jumping	Martial arts	Ballet	Team handball	Pickleball (paddle tennis)	Softball	Bowling	Swimming strokes and related skills	Backpacking
Aerobic dance	Wrestling	Synchronized swimming	Basketball	Tennis	Rounders	Golf	Life-guarding	Orienteering
Cycling	Gymnastics	Folk	Flag football	Badminton	Baseball	Curling		Biking
Weight training	Diving	Floor exercise	Ultimate Frisbee	Table tennis	Cricket	Shuffleboard		Rock and wall climbing
	Stunts	Country/ square	Netball	Deck tennis		Pool		Ropes courses
	Tumbling	Social	Water polo	**Net-team**		Croquet		Rodeo
	Apparatus	Rope jumping	**Feet**	Minivolley		Lawn bowling		Fishing
	Track and field		Soccer	Volley tennis				Canoeing
			Hands and feet	Volleyball				Water skiing
			Speedball	Wallyball				Surfing
			Speed-a-way	**Wall**				Scuba diving
			Quad ball	Paddleball				Snowshoeing
				Racquetball				Cross-country skiing
				Squash				Downhill skiing
				Handball				

Note: Some activities could be included in more than one category, such as aerobic dance in fitness or rhythms.

category. These percentages should reflect the philosophies of the curriculum committee, the school district, and the teachers. They should provide a balanced program of experiences that correspond with students' needs and developmental levels. Examples of scope charts for an activity-based curriculum are shown in Figure 6-4. Note that a curriculum could be based on an entire category for one year, such as fundamental movement skills or personal and social skills. Subsequent years would then emphasize other content standards. Whatever categories are selected, students should be able to meet the performance standards for the grade level in preparation for achieving the content standards prior to graduation from high school.

Step 3. Establish a systematic method for selecting curricular experiences.

Since school time is obviously limited and only the most appropriate experiences for a given situation can be considered, a systematic method for selecting relevant

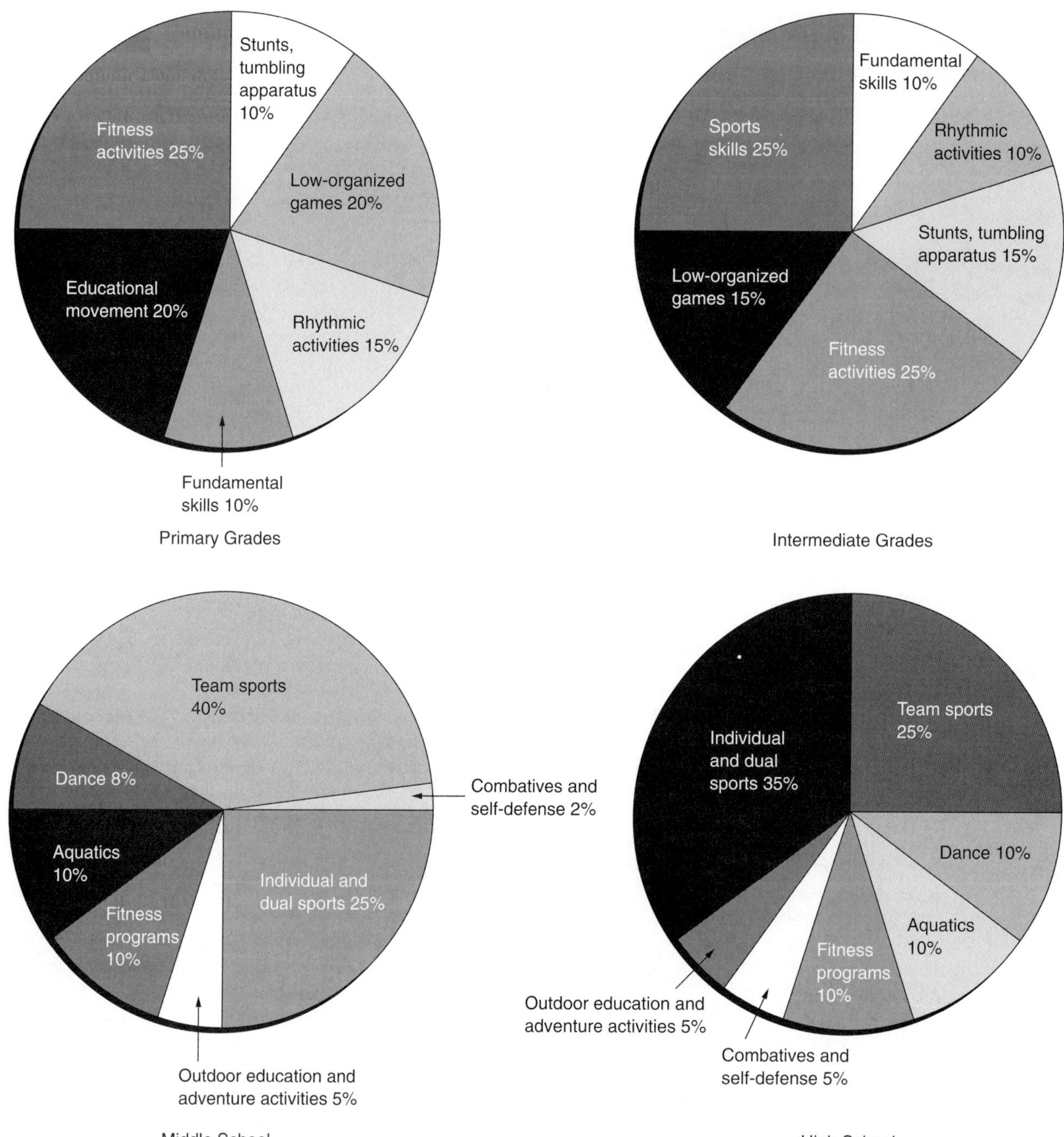

Figure 6-4

Sample scope charts.

curricular experiences must be established. List essential criteria for including an activity or unit in the curriculum. Keep criteria few in number and realistic. The following criteria are generally considered to be essential:

1. Does the experience contribute to students' meeting the content standards for physical education?
2. Is the experience consistent with students' present and future growth and developmental needs?
3. Can the activity be taught safely?
4. Is the activity feasible in terms of local considerations? Some possible criteria for determining which activities are most suitable for a particular area include these:
   a. Is the activity acceptable to the community? (For example, in some regions, dancing may be prohibited by certain religious groups.)
   b. Do students like the activity? (Regional and local factors influence students' interests and possible carryover values, e.g., surfing and snow skiing.)

c. Are the necessary resources available in the school or community, including facilities, equipment, finances, faculty expertise or availability of resource persons, time constraints, transportation, and climate?

Each criterion might be assigned a weight based upon its importance in meeting the program goals. One method involves weighing all criteria equally with each one counting a number of points. A more realistic way is to weight each criterion differently based on its importance to the selection process. Individual factors such as safety and feasibility may be considered separately. A chart like the one in Figure 6-5 could be given to each committee member for evaluation and the points could be averaged and ranked within each category as shown in the total column. Eliminate experiences that do not meet the criteria. Some activities may satisfy the physical fitness objective but be of little value in terms of social skills. Others may contribute to students' knowledge but be of little value with regard to physical fitness. By ranking experiences within the broader categories selected in step 1, the committee can determine which experiences within each category best meet the selected criteria.

Experiences that best meet the content standards and student needs are given priority. When several desirable experiences meet the criteria but cannot be included because of lack of time, two possibilities exist. First, experiences can be evaluated on the basis of local criteria. For example, tennis may command such an interest in the community as a leisure-time activity that the committee feels students need specific instruction on it. Second, teachers can organize experiences or units into categories (like those shown in Table 6.8) and select one from that category. For example, soccer, Ultimate Frisbee, basketball, and field hockey are all invasion games. By selecting one of these sports, concepts common to all these games can be emphasized in that unit. In subsequent years, different sports from that category can be taught with teachers emphasizing the same concepts. When this is done, students learn the strategies important for success in the game so the time required to learn the new activity is less (students will need to learn only the skills and features unique to the game as the strategies will remain the same). When this is done, teachers can make the units longer, which should increase student success. Building on prior knowledge, or scaffolding learning, makes it easier to learn new things. Also, because students have new units every year, they are less likely to become bored with physical education and are more likely to discover a sport or activity that they would like to pursue on their own. The activities in each category could be spread throughout the K–12 curriculum in such a way that students take some invasion sports in elementary school, others in middle school, and a different set in high school.

Extra-Class Activities

Extra-class activities such as intramurals, sports days, play days, and club activities should be chosen in a manner similar to the steps listed previously. Student interest is a major factor in selecting these activities. By using gymnasiums when athletic teams are outdoors and community facilities such as bowling centers, golf courses, skating rinks, swimming pools, and tennis courts, a wide variety of activities can be scheduled, including some that would not be possible during class time. Intramurals can be scheduled before or after school, during the noon hour, or during a scheduled activity period.

Interscholastic activities are generally specified by state high school activities associations, with regulations sent to schools prescribing seasons and game schedules. Additional activities can be added by working directly with the state association.

Should Substitute Activities Be Allowed Physical Education Credit?

In many schools and colleges, physical education credit is awarded for participation in marching band, ROTC, or varsity athletics. Is this credit justifiable? When school officials answer this question, they frequently view the fitness component of the proposed activity substitution and little else. The physical education content standards are best met through a high-quality physical education program. Although the subject matter of varsity sport falls within the content of physical education, the intent of the program is quite different and will not enable the participant to meet all of the content standards. Physical education programs must offer the variety of physical activities necessary to satisfy Standard 1 and not resemble a varsity sport program. A physical education curriculum should be designed to meet the physical education content standards and be prepared to present data showing that students have met those standards. Physical education teachers should work hard to promote district and statewide requirements to meet the content standards. When physical education content standards are included in the accountability formulas used to measure student achievement, the case for not allowing substitution of physical education for other activities is much stronger. A NASPE position statement on substitution of activities for instructional physical education programs states,

> It is inappropriate to substitute activities that occur outside of the physical education curriculum for regular participation in a well planned instructional program. The objectives of co-curricular and extra-curricular programs, as well as other academic subject areas, have distinctly different goals and objectives from curricular physical education. . . . It is clear that activities occurring outside the physical education instructional program will not enable students to meet all of the standards/outcomes set forth for a physically educated person.[30]

Activities by Category	Consistent with Program Objectives? Fitness	Skills	Knowledge	Social	Total	Student Interests	CRITERIA FOR INCLUSION Consistent with Student Growth?	Locally Feasible? Safe?	Acceptable	Carryover	Resources	Include?	Comments
	1-5	1-5	1-5	1-5	4-20	1-10	Yes-No	Yes-No	Yes-No	Yes-No	F Eq Ex Tr C	Yes-No	
Individual													
Archery	1	3	4	2	RANK (11) 10	2	Yes	WITH PROPER INSTRUCTION	Yes	Yes	✓✓✓-✓	Yes	
Badminton	5	4	4	4	(1) 17	7	Yes	Yes	Yes	Yes	✓✓✓-✓	Yes	
Bowling	1	3	4	5	(4) 13	9	Yes	Yes	Yes	Yes	✓✓✓-✓	Yes	BOWLING LANES NEAR SCHOOL
Cycling	5	2	3	2	(7) 12	9	Yes	WATCH TRAFFIC	Yes	Yes	✓-✓-✓	Yes	HAVE STUDENTS BRING BIKES
Dance	4	5	4	3	(16) 3	6	Yes	Yes	Yes	Yes	✓✓NO-✓	Yes	TEACHER WILL GET ADDITIONAL TRAINING TO TEACH
Golf	1	3	4	5	(4) 13	5	Yes	Yes	Yes	Yes	NO ✓✓ YES ✓	Yes	NEED BUS TO GOLF COURSE
Gymnastics	4	4	4	1	(4) 13	5	Yes	No	No	No	✓✓✓-✓	No	DISTRICT PROHIBITS GYMNASTICS
Racquetball	5	4	3	5	(1) 17	9	Yes	USE EYE GUARDS	Yes	Yes	✓✓✓-✓	Yes	VERY POPULAR
Skiing	3	3	3	3	(7) 12	8	Yes	WITH PROPER INSTRUCTION	Yes	Yes	NO NO ✓ REQ ✓	(Yes)	OFFER AS A CLUB SPORT
Swimming	4	4	4	2	(5) 4	8	Yes	WITH LIFE GUARD	Yes	Yes	✓✓✓ P+	Yes	TEACH IN THE FALL WHILE OUTDOOR POOL IS OPEN
Tennis	3	4	4	5	(3) 16	10	Yes	Yes	Yes	Yes	✓✓✓-✓	Yes	VERY POPULAR
Track & Field	4	3	4	1	(7) 12	6	Yes	Yes	Yes	No	✓✓✓-✓	Yes	

Figure 6-5

An example of a chart for evaluating activities for inclusion in the curriculum. *Note:* F = Facilities, Eq = Equipment, Ex = Teacher expertise, Tr = Transportation, C = Climate or geographic necessity.

TABLE 6.8 An Example of Skill Order Sequence in Volleyball

Beginning	Intermediate	Advanced
1. Skills: Overhead pass Forearm pass Underhand serve Teamwork 2. Concepts: Basic rules Scoring Basic strategy 3. Minivolley to learn skills, brief introduction to official game	1. Review: Overhead pass Forearm pass Underhand serve Teach: Overhand serve Spike Block Team strategy 2. Official rules Offensive strategy Defensive strategy 3. Official game, including tournament play	1. Review: All skills Teach: Rolls Emphasize: Advanced strategy and team play 2. Official rules Officiating Offensive strategy Defensive strategy 3. Official game, with advanced strategy and tournament play

When students are excused from physical education for four years or more, we are really saying that physical education programs are not particularly beneficial.

Review Questions: What determines which activities or concept areas to include in a curriculum for a specific school?

Should substitute activities ever be allowed physical education credit?

If you have to give a presentation defending the benefits of physical education, what sources could you use to find this information quickly?

Sequence

Sequence refers to the order in which curriculum components are taught. Appropriate sequencing depends on achieving basic movement patterns such as throwing, catching, and using space prior to engagement in game skills such as fielding and guarding. Failure to provide a graduated instructional sequence in knowledge and skills is the biggest stumbling block to quality programs in physical education. For example, the same basketball unit is often taught to the same students year after year with no increased learning. This would be equivalent to teaching students "2 + 2" or similar arithmetic skills from kindergarten through the twelfth grade. Teachers often justify this practice by saying that students have not learned the skills previously and therefore they must be re-taught. If this is the case, teachers should review their instructional practices and determine why students are not learning the skills. Deliberately planning to re-introduce the same skills year after year should be considered curriculum malpractice. This is not saying that an activity cannot be repeated during a K–12 program. If an activity is repeated, it should have increased difficulty each time it is offered in the curriculum. An example of skill sequencing for throwing is shown in Figure 5-1. A sequence for a series of volleyball units is shown in Table 6.8.

Physical education programs should be organized as a continuous flow of experiences through a carefully planned, graduated sequence of ideas and skills from preschool through college. This sequence would fulfill student needs and interests and build progressively toward the attainment of the physical education standards. Planning must be coordinated to provide a variety of activities at all grade levels, to develop skills required for later participation, and to avoid unnecessary overlap or omissions or undue repetition of instruction. Then, students will be able to progress toward an increasingly mature utilization of their knowledge and skills to solve complex problems related to themselves and to society.

Obviously, students do not learn all there is to know or develop skill proficiency in an activity in a single encounter. Teachers are often frustrated when students absorb only the smallest part of a unit of instruction. Often teachers try to do too much and so students learn nothing well. If teachers and curriculum designers planned knowledge and skill sequences throughout the K–12 program, the results would be dramatic. Too often curriculum planners divide writing tasks between elementary, middle, and high school groups. When the groups fail to plan the instructional sequences from a K–12 perspective, there frequently is overlap between the levels. The elementary teachers do not know what middle school teachers expect students to know when they reach that level and high school teachers repeat units covered previously. When a curriculum is viewed from a K–12 perspective, teachers can be selective in their choice of activities and avoid unnecessary overlap. When developing curriculums, it is essential that representatives from the various levels communicate and establish goals that are sequentially planned.

Considerations for determining skill sequence or grade placement include student characteristics, the subject matter, and safety. Students' physical, mental, and social development, along with previous fitness, knowledge, and skill competencies, are the primary considerations when placing activities into grade levels. Student interests should also be considered. Consider the complexity and amount of information to be presented and the difficulty of skills to be learned. Proper sequencing will result in safe, effective learning and successful student participation. The National Association for Sport and Physical Education has established benchmarks for the various standards presented in Table 6.1.[31]

Review Questions: What is the biggest stumbling block to quality physical education programs?

What factors should be considered when determining sequence?

Curricular Scope and Sequences for Various School Levels

Determining the scope and sequence of the curriculum from preschool through college is a complex and significant task requiring careful consideration of the correct emphases for the different developmental stages of children and adolescents. Possible scope charts are shown in Figure 6-4. A scope chart for one school system may not fit the curriculum for a different school system. Categories and percentages must be determined by following the steps presented earlier in the chapter.

Review Question: What should be the emphases at each of the following school levels?

a. Preschool and kindergarten
b. Primary grades
c. Intermediate grades
d. Middle and junior high school
e. Senior high school
f. College or university

Integration of Physical Education with Other Subject Areas

In real life our experiences rarely deal with one subject at a time. Learning, too, becomes more meaningful when subjects are taught from an integrated, real-life perspective. Mohnsen describes four models for integrating physical education with other subject areas.[32]

In the *sequenced model,* teachers rearrange the order of their units of instruction to synchronize the content of two related subject areas, thus enhancing learning in both disciplines. For example, the physical educator teaches body composition at the same time as the health educator teaches nutrition, or teaches adventure activities at the same time as students are studying medieval history.

In the *shared model,* teachers from two disciplines look for overlapping content and plan their instruction so that their lessons complement each other. Examples include a wellness unit, involving physical and health educators; or music, drama, and physical educators teaching a unit on music, dance, and theater for a particular country or during a specified time period. Mathematics and physics could be integrated into a unit on the biomechanics of movement.

The *integrated model* involves teachers from four or more subject areas working on a common unit, all contributing their own concepts and skills. One example of this involves an entire course, integrating physical education with the physical and biological sciences and English. Students spend up to one-half of the school day and some weekends hiking, backpacking, and bicycling to natural environments where they study science and then write about their findings.[33]

In the *webbed model,* instruction in the various subjects is integrated with a common theme of interest for teachers and students. Examples of themes might include taking acceptable risks, promoting personal well-being, strategies for change, or working together to achieve goals. For example, for the theme of taking acceptable risks, Mohnsen describes physical educators teaching problem-solving initiatives and ropes courses, science teachers discussing research on animals and humans, math teachers presenting units on probability and statistics, health teachers discussing risk management and insurance, history teachers teaching about military strategies, and language arts teachers teaching literature involving risks with nature.

While planning integrated activities, teachers should carefully evaluate the learning activities to ensure that students will achieve the physical education content standards. Integrating activities with other curricular areas should not interfere with students' meeting the physical education content standards. Proper sequencing of activities should also be considered so students develop the necessary skills and knowledge in earlier units to successfully participate in later units.

Establish the Schedule

Scheduling is the process of adapting the physical education program, including classes and extracurricular activities, to the individual school and its community, staff, students, facilities, and time restraints. It is a time-consuming but essential job. Physical educators must work with local school administrators to achieve the best possible scheduling arrangement for physical education within the master schedule. Computers vastly increase scheduling possibilities based on student need and subject matter requirements. The following steps are suggested as a guide toward the achievement of a workable schedule:

Step 1. Identify the most desirable grouping pattern for class assignments.
Step 2. Determine class size.
Step 3. Determine appropriate time allotments for daily, weekly, and unit instruction.
Step 4. Determine staffing patterns and teacher loads, and assign teachers.

Step 5. Identify teaching stations and equipment.
Step 6. Develop a schedule.

Step 1—Identify the Most Desirable Grouping Pattern for Class Assignments

Students can be grouped homogeneously or heterogeneously for physical education classes. Homogeneous grouping puts similar students together in the same group. In heterogeneous groups students differ from each other. The assignment of students to classes and learning groups should be made on the basis of individual learning needs. The ideal grouping arrangement would take into consideration all of the factors affecting learning—intelligence, maturity, knowledge, skill, fitness, interests, and so on. However, the inability to scientifically measure such factors has served as a deterrent to homogeneous grouping.

In most schools, students are assigned to physical education according to the period they have free in the schedule. In middle or junior high schools, students are usually assigned by grade level. Senior high school students are often scheduled in tenth through twelfth or eleventh and twelfth grade groupings, with ninth or ninth and tenth grades scheduled by grade level. Within these classes, teachers are generally free to rearrange students into homogeneous groups by students' interests, abilities, and needs. The physical education staff divides students according to performance assessments or interests. Groupings should vary as activities change, since students have different interests and skill levels in different activities. Grouping persons with similar interests and skills is believed to enhance success and therefore the social and emotional development of students. However, lower-skilled students can profit from playing with students of a higher ability, without hindering the learning of higher-skilled students if the instruction is carefully managed. Mainstreaming of disabled students and coeducational programs have considerably increased the range of abilities in physical education classes. A wide range of student abilities can be frustrating to teachers and might result in recreational rather than instructional programs.

Instruction must be provided for students with physical limitations, including those with inadequate skill development and the physically underdeveloped. Physical performance tests can be used to identify physically underdeveloped students and to assess the motor aspects of physical fitness. Students should be placed in the least restrictive environment in which an appropriate learning situation can be provided. One beneficial aspect of heterogenous grouping is highly skilled students acting as role models and peer tutors for their less-skilled classmates, thereby increasing motivation and social interaction. Teaching styles can facilitate dealing with individual differences. Peer tutoring, inclusion, task, and problem-solving activities are particularly useful when dealing with heterogeneous groups. Activities that emphasize cooperation rather than competition can also be effective with heterogeneous groups of students.

Step 2—Determine Class Size

Identify the appropriate class size for each learning group, task, and instructional method. Class size may range from very large to only one student, depending upon the aim of the instruction. For example, a film could be shown to a large group, while skills have to be practiced in smaller groups, and individual help or contract learning may be on a one-to-one basis. Team sport classes usually lend themselves to larger class sizes to accommodate competitive situations.

Class size should be consistent with the requirements of good instruction and safety. Appropriate class sizes ensure that students receive adequate teacher assistance and individual practice or study. For example, a tennis unit with four courts available would best be limited to sixteen students if the course objectives are to be met. Since it would be impossible to schedule sixteen students in a traditional class each period, a suitable alternative is to schedule a reasonable "average" class size (i.e., the same pupil-teacher ratio as for other subject areas in the school)[34] and then to adjust class sizes among the physical education teachers in terms of the units being taught. The average class size for secondary-school physical education can be determined by the following formula:

$$\text{Average class size} = \frac{\text{Total students in school}}{\text{Number of teachers} \times \text{Number of periods/day taught by each teacher}}$$

The average recommended class size is usually thirty-five.[35] Adapted physical education classes should have no more than twenty. When classes are too large, teachers may resort to a recreational rather than instructional approach to teaching, which negates the purpose of having students in physical education. Conversely, some teachers arbitrarily combine classes and designate one person as the lead instructor. This practice can jeopardize teaching positions as administrators may feel that if one person is doing all the teaching, the other positions are unnecessary.

Step 3—Determine Appropriate Time Allotments for Daily, Weekly, and Unit Instruction

In 1986 and 1987, the U.S. Senate and the House of Representatives passed a concurrent resolution supporting daily physical education for all students. However, the individual states prescribe the minimum instructional time allotment per day or per week (either by law or by suggestion). NASPE; the Society of State Directors of Health, Physical Education, and Recreation;[36] and the President's Council on Physical Fitness and Sports recommend a daily instructional period or its equivalent for secondary school students.[37]

One of the biggest concerns in curriculum planning is the failure to provide long enough instructional units for students to develop the skills and knowledge needed for participation in a given activity. Most teachers underestimate the time necessary to achieve mastery. Failure to achieve mastery of the objectives for one year results in the need to adjust the objectives for every year thereafter.[38] Units of two, three, and four weeks are inadequate for students to achieve competency in most activities. Research substantiates the fact that beginning-level learners often experience frustration in units that are not long enough to learn the skills necessary for success. The curriculum should be limited in scope so that in-depth instruction can be given in activities of particular interest to students.

How much time is needed to achieve each objective? It depends on the task to be learned, the instructor's teaching skills, and the age and ability of the students, the amount of available equipment, and the number of students in class. Younger students and beginners have shorter attention spans and fatigue sooner, and so shorter lessons distributed daily are more appropriate. Older and more advanced students can benefit from longer periods of time occurring less often. Simple skills require less time to teach than more complex skills. Wessel and Kelly reported the need to budget approximately 120 to 180 minutes to develop each fundamental motor skill, with the lower number representing the time needed for older students.[39] This translates into four to six thirty-minute periods with 100 percent on-task activity. However, since students are active only 20 to 50 percent of the time, eight to thirty class periods might be necessary per objective.[40] Obviously, this number will vary from objective to objective. Teaching the do-si-do might take only a few minutes, while the volleyball spike might take many hours. The number of objectives that can be achieved is a function of the time available and the amount of time required to achieve mastery of the objectives to be taught.[41]

Instructional units must be long enough to develop the skill levels necessary to enjoy participation in the activity, yet short enough to prevent boredom with the activity. Each unit consists of a cluster of objectives. If each unit had an average of five objectives or skills to be taught in 120 minutes per objective, that would be an average of 600 minutes per unit or four weeks minimum of daily physical education. However, at 50 percent activity rate, the unit would take a minimum of eight weeks. Once the number of objectives to be taught is known, they can be distributed over a unit or several years. Some units at the middle and junior-high school levels may be devoted to learning basic skills so that students are introduced to activities from which they will be allowed to choose later on in the curriculum. Teachers must learn to emphasize concepts that are common to a group of sports or activities (e.g., invasion games, net games, target activities) so that students can generalize the concepts and transfer this knowledge to other sports. Also when this is done, a single sport from that category can be taught for a longer period of time rather than teaching several different sports from the same category.

Scope charts with percentages of time for each area can be translated into units by multiplying the percentage by the number of weeks (or periods) in the year to get the weekly (or period) allotment for each category. Time can be allotted to specific activities or to areas for student choice within the category time allotment. However, limit the number of activities so that each unit will provide adequate time for learning to occur. Kelly suggested using the following formula to determine the number of objectives that can be achieved in each year of instruction:[42]

Number of weeks school is in session	36
Number of days per week of physical education	5
Weeks × days (5)	180
Number of minutes per period in instruction	30
Weeks × days × minutes	5,400
Subtract 10 percent of time for "lost" instructional days	540
Total time available for year's instruction	4,860
Total time divided by 600 minutes (approximate time per unit at the high school level) = the maximum number of units that could be taught	8

Yearly schedules include (1) the sequence and length of time of physical education activity units within a school year, (2) the sequence of instruction over a span of several years, and (3) the relationships of class instruction, intramurals, and extramurals. Two types of yearly plans for class instruction have emerged, the cycle and the modified cycle.

In the *cycle* plan, the course of study changes for the whole department each year as shown in Figure 6-6. This means that all students participate in the same unit at the same time. Units are usually different each year. The advantages of this system are (1) teachers have to prepare for only one class at a time and equipment can be left set up all day; (2) motivation is increased by reducing the repetition of activities from year to year; and (3) the length of time for each unit is increased, thus facilitating learning. The disadvantage of the cycle plan is that teachers become bored when they teach the same activity all day long. This system works well in small schools where teachers and facilities are limited.

The second type of yearly plan is a *modified cycle* in which all of the cycles are taught each year but to different classes. For example, the sophomores receive cycle 1; the juniors, cycle 2; and the seniors, cycle 3. Advantages are that progressions in specific activities can be built into the program and boredom is reduced since teachers generally teach more than one grade level. A disadvantage may result, however, if too many activities are taught and the program is spread so thin that students fail to learn any activity well.

Many schools have adopted some form of *block* plan, with the intent of allowing students to spend more time on fewer subjects each day.[43] One of the most popular models is the 4 × 4 plan, which consists of four classes per day for one semester, following which the students change to four new classes, making eight classes per year. The advantages of block plans are that students and teachers have fewer classes at a time to concentrate on and more innovative teaching practices can be implemented in the longer class sessions. Teachers have fewer students per se-

Cycle / *Modified Cycle*

Cycle 1 (2005, 2008)	Orientation	Flag football	Tennis	Folk and square dance	Archery	Swimming	Closing and testing	Sophomores
Weeks	1/2	7	7	7	7	7	1/2	

Cycle 2 (2006, 2009)	Orientation	Basketball	Golf	Social dance	Gymnastics and apparatus	Swimming	Closing	Juniors
Weeks	1/2	7	7	7	7	7	1/2	

Cycle 3 (2007, 2010)	Orientation	Soccer	Track and field	Wrestling and self-defense	Weight training and jogging	Volleyball	Closing	Seniors
Weeks	1/2	7	7	7	7	7	1/2	

Figure 6-6
An example of cycle scheduling.

mester and students have fewer teachers to get acquainted with, which enhances student-teacher relationships. The 4 × 4 + 1 schedule adds an enhancement period for lunch and extracurricular activities. Another option is to split the fourth period block in two, resulting in three extended classes each semester and two short classes that run all year. These options are useful for music, art, athletics, and other subjects in which a year-long class is preferred.

The second plan consists of eight blocks or classes, alternating four every other day for the entire year. This plan provides the advantage of extended periods, but teachers have the same number of students per semester and students have the same number of teachers as in the traditional plan of six or seven classes per day.

The third plan is to take only two classes at a time, one in the morning and one in the afternoon for sixty days and then to take two more classes, concluding with the last two classes, for a total of six classes per year. A variation is three classes per day for sixty days, totaling nine classes per year.

Physical educators generally schedule units of study within these blocks, just as other educators do. The extended classes allow time for fitness activities, learning activities for concept development and character development, and skill practice, with time left for dressing and showering. Facility scheduling is easier, especially in off-campus facilities. Proponents argue that massed practice also favors skill learning and retention. Problems occur when teachers fail to take advantage of the extra time that a block schedule provides and teach the content from a fifty-minute class in a ninety-minute block class.

Step 4—Determine Staffing Patterns and Teacher Loads, and Assign Teachers

Analyze existing staff strengths and assign teachers to classes on the basis of the skills and knowledge needed to teach the activity. Teachers of potentially hazardous activities with potential risk such as aquatics, gymnastics, skiing, and adventure education need specialized training to the extent that they are recognized and certified by the national agencies associated with these activities. Special qualifications, including the ability to work with students at various skill levels, or with particular phases of the instructional program, and preferences about classes, planning times, and related matters should

BOX 6.1

Scheduling Example

Total Number Students	Class Size	Periods per Day	Periods per Week	Sections Offered	Teaching Stations	Teachers Needed
1,500	30	6	5	50	10	10.0
1,500	35	6	5	43	9	8.6
1,500	40	6	5	38	8	7.6

Note: Each teacher teaches five periods. Fractions equal a part-time teacher in physical education.

also be considered. Secondary schools may be staffed by "generalists" or "specialists." Specialists are often hired for areas such as aquatics or dance because they are trained to anticipate and resolve potential learning problems with the subject matter and can usually help learners achieve higher levels of skill. Generalists have an adequate level of skill in most curriculum offerings. They see the student in a variety of activities and can anticipate the learning needs of individual students.

Consideration of the teaching load is essential to high-quality instruction. At the secondary school level, the recommendation is that class instruction per teacher not exceed five class periods or hours per day or more than two hundred students per teacher.[44]

Step 5—Identify Teaching Stations and Equipment

A teaching station is an area assigned to a teacher for a class, preferably with some physical or visual barrier between two classes to cushion sound. Distance may serve as a barrier between classes. The following method can be used to calculate the number of teaching stations and teachers needed for a *secondary school* physical education program:

1. Number of sections to be offered

$$= \frac{\text{Total number of students}}{\text{Class size}}$$

2. Number of teaching stations (classes per period)

$$= \frac{\text{Total number of students}}{\text{Class size} \times \text{Number of periods/day}}$$

Round off to the next higher whole number.

3. Number of teachers needed

$$= \frac{\text{Number of sections}}{\text{Number of periods taught/day/teacher}}$$

An example is shown in Box 6.1.

Program flexibility is increased when large numbers of students are assigned to a physical education program in which there are multiple teaching stations. Few schools possess all the facilities they need. Multipurpose rooms, hallways, auditorium stages, theaters, and leftover classrooms can provide needed facilities for physical education. Community resources can be used to supplement school facilities. For example, bowling lanes, archery ranges, skating rinks, swimming pools, ski resorts, bicycle paths, equestrian facilities, boating marinas, dance studios, golf courses and driving ranges, tennis courts, and adventure courses can often be rented by having students pay a small fee. The use of community resources can help educators bridge the gap between school and community. Transportation may cause legal problems and should be discussed with the principal for approval before adopting any off-campus program. Elective programs can help to resolve problems with fees and transportation, since the class is not required of those who cannot afford the fees for transportation. Teachers should retain control of classes taught in off-campus facilities even when an outside professional is teaching. Courses offered before or after the normal school day can take advantage of facilities out of transportation range during regular class time.

Regarding equipment, AAHPERD recommends: "Facilities, supplies and equipment should be provided for the instructional program in accordance with the needs, interests and number of students to be served. . . . The physical education program should have enough equipment to provide each student with an opportunity to actively participate throughout the entire class period."[45] Equipment can sometimes be built by industrial arts classes, parents, or teachers, or purchased by parent-teacher associations. All equipment must meet established safety guidelines, however, or schools can be subject to a lawsuit. Good teaching also requires provision of appropriate books, periodicals, media, and other teaching aids.

Step 6—Develop a Schedule

Work out a schedule that coordinates time, teachers, and facilities. Some considerations include the following:

1. Two classes must not be scheduled in the same facility at the same time.
2. Class sizes must not exceed the space available for participation.
3. A teacher must not be assigned to teach two classes at the same time.
4. Units should be assigned to teachers based on their individual skills and interests.
5. Each teacher should be assigned a preparation period.

BOX 6.2

A Possible Schedule

	Block 1		Block 2		Block 3	
Period 1						
Jones	Golf	g	Aerobic dance	b	Gymnastics	b
Garcia	Tennis	f	Volleyball	a	Basketball	a
Lungo	Flag football	g	Swimming (beg.)	e	Wrestling	h
Platero	Prep.		Prep.		Prep.	
Period 2						
Jones	Social dance	a	Cycling	i	Aerobic dance	b
Garcia	Prep.		Prep.		Prep.	
Platero	Flag football	g	Soccer	g	Swimming (beg.)	e
Lungo	Archery/Tennis	d,f	Fitness	b	Basketball	a
Period 3						
Jones	Rec. dance	a	Bowling	i	Aerobic dance	c
Platero	Soccer	g	Swimming (beg.)	e	Volleyball	b
Lungo	Prep.		Prep.		Prep.	
Garcia	Archery/Tennis	d,f	Fitness	b	Basketball	a
Period 4						
Jones	Prep.		Prep.		Prep.	
Platero	Flag football	g	Tennis	f	Aerobic dance	c
Lungo	Rec. dance	a	Swimming (beg.)	e	Volleyball	a
Garcia	Archery/Tennis	d,f	Fitness	b	Basketball	b
Period 5						
Jones	Rec. dance	a	Bowling	i	Jazz dance	c
Garcia	Tennis	f	Aerobic dance	c	Outdoor pursuits	i
Lungo	Soccer	g	Swimming (beg.)	e	Basketball	a
Platero	Badminton/Bowling	b	Fitness	b	Volleyball	b
Period 6						
Jones	Golf/Softball	g	Fitness	b	Basketball	b
Lungo	Archery	d	Basketball	a	Volleyball	a
Platero	Tennis	f	Bowling	c	Swimming	e
Garcia	Cycling	i	Flag football	g	Aerobic dance	c

Continued

6. Time should be planned for all teachers in the department to meet together for department meetings.
7. Outdoor facility use is dependent upon the weather.

Although scheduling is essentially an administrative function, the success of the program is based on its implementation by the various faculty members involved. A possible scheduling chart is shown in Box 6.2.

Review Questions: Define the following and give an example of each:

a. Scheduling
b. Homogeneous grouping
c. Heterogenous grouping

How is class size determined? What is the recommended class size for secondary school physical education?

What is the recommended time allotment for physical education in elementary and secondary schools?

How much time is needed to achieve each instructional objective according to Kelly?

What is a scope chart? How can it be translated into weeks or days?

Define and give an example of each:

a. Cycle plan
b. Block plan
c. Teaching station

BOX 6.2 *Continued*

A Possible Schedule

	Block 4		Block 5		Block 6	
Period 1						
Jones	Bowling	i	Cycling	i	Archery	d
Garcia	Badminton	a	Soccer	g	Tennis	f
Lungo	Swimming (int.)	e	Track and field	d	Softball	g
Platero	Prep.		Prep.		Prep.	
Period 2						
Jones	Badminton	b	Gymnastics	b	Golf	g
Garcia	Prep.		Prep.		Prep.	
Platero	Swimming (int.)	e	Basketball	a	Tennis	f
Lungo	Volleyball	a	Golf/Softball	g	Badminton/Bowling	a
Period 3						
Jones	Gymnastics	h	Badminton	b	Cycling	i
Platero	Basketball	a	Swimming (int.)	e	Archery	d
Lungo	Prep.		Prep.		Prep.	
Garcia	Volleyball	b	Golf/Softball	g	Badminton/Bowling	a
Period 4						
Jones	Prep.		Prep.		Prep.	
Platero	Bowling	i	Softball	g	Badminton	a
Lungo	Basketball	a	Swimming (int.)	e	Track and field	d
Garcia	Volleyball	b	Badminton/Bowling	a	Golf/Softball	g
Period 5						
Jones	Modern dance	c	Ballet	c	Social dance	c
Garcia	Volleyball	a	Badminton	b	Tennis	f
Lungo	Swimming (int.)	e	Golf	g	Track and field	d
Platero	Basketball	b	Archery/Tennis	d,f	Golf/Softball	g
Period 6						
Jones	Volleyball	b	Tennis/Archery	d,f	Badminton/Bowling	a
Lungo	Wrestling	h	Track and field	d	Softball	g
Platero	Swimming (int.)	e	Badminton	b	Tennis	f
Garcia	Basketball	a	Soccer	g	Golf	g

a—Gym A
b—Gym B
c—Dance studio
d—Track
e—Pool
f—Tennis
g—Field
h—Wrestling room
i—Community facility

Ninth-grade activities are underlined.

AN EXAMPLE OF SCHEDULING

Given: A high school (grades 9 through 12) with eight hundred students, four teachers, a six-period day, five days per week.

Step 1—Identify the Most Desirable Grouping Pattern for Class Assignments

The committee decides to implement a required program in grade 9 and a selective program (required, but with student selection of activities) in grades ten through twelve. The major advantage of the selective system is that students can develop expertise in activities in which they will participate throughout their adult lives. A second advantage is the ability to meet student needs and interests within a traditional school system.

One ninth-grade class will be offered each hour and the remainder of the student body will be scheduled into the period best fitting their schedules. All classes will be coeducational. Each student will be assigned to a specific teacher who can diagnose strengths and weaknesses and provide assistance in making choices tailored to individual needs. Since students were introduced to a variety of activities in earlier grades, they will find it easier to make appropriate choices. Students will be required to select a specified number of activities in each category during each school year, as shown in this example:

Class	Team Sports	Individual	Fitness	Aquatics
Sophomore	3	1	1	1
Junior	2	3	1	
Senior	1	4	1	

Another way to balance the program might be to require a certain number of specified activities to be taken anytime prior to graduation.

Organization and record-keeping duties for the selective program will be distributed among teachers by assigning a different teacher each period as the *master teacher.* The master teacher is responsible for all of the students for that period. This includes distributing class rolls, accumulating grades, and distributing and collecting lockers and towels.

On the first day of each unit, students all meet to select the next activity. Students will be told in advance the activities and the teacher who will instruct each activity. Seniors choose first, then juniors, followed by sophomores. When the class enrollment for an activity is reached, the class will be closed for that block. A card will be issued to each student on which the activity is marked for that block. The cards will be collected and processed by hand or by computer. Roll sheets for each teacher are made from the cards. A sample record card is shown in Box 6.3.

In a selective program, class sizes can be adapted to the facilities available for instruction. Thus, instruction can be effective in activities such as tennis or racquetball where facilities are often limited.

Step 2—Determine Class Size

The average class size is 40.

$$\frac{\text{800 Students}}{\text{4 teachers} \times \text{5 periods/teacher}} = 40$$

Since approximately one-fourth of the students are ninth graders (200), the number of sections of freshmen will be five (200 ÷ 40 = 5). The remainder of the sections will have approximately 40 students per section, but all tenth- through twelfth-grade students will be placed on one roll. The schedule looks like this:

	Ninth graders	Tenth through twelfth graders
Period 1	0 classes = 0	3 classes = 120
Period 2	1 class = 40	2 classes = 80
Period 3	1 class = 40	2 classes = 80
Period 4	1 class = 40	2 classes = 80
Period 5	1 class = 40	3 classes = 120
Period 6	1 class = 40	3 classes = 120
	200 +	600 = 800

BOX 6.3

A Sample Record Card

Name ______________________ **Sex: M/F Period** ______________

First Block	***Second Block***	***Third Block***
Tennis	Swimming	Wrestling
Soccer	Fitness	Volleyball
Flag football	Aerobic dance	Badminton
Social dance	Soccer	Jazz dance
Archery	Basketball	Basketball
Fencing	Volleyball	Aerobic dance
		Swimming

Fourth Block	***Fifth Block***	***Sixth Block***
Basketball	Fencing	Aerobic dance
Swimming	Fitness	Softball
Fencing	Swimming	Tennis
Modern dance	Ballet	Track and Field
Volleyball	Outdoor pursuits	Social dance
Gymnastics	Basketball	Modern dance
Wrestling	Track and field	Cycling
Outdoor pursuits	Social dance	Golf
		Fitness

Once the students are scheduled by period, the tenth through twelfth graders will divide up into selected activities. Class enrollments may vary according to the activity.

Step 3—Determine Appropriate Time Allotments for Daily, Weekly, and Unit Instruction

The committee voted to have six 6-week blocks per year. This fits nicely with the 36-week school year. This will give students enough time to learn the activities, but not so much time that they get bored. Ninth-grade units will vary according to subject matter. Team sport units will be longer, since students are expected to have basic skills before advancing to the selective program. Other units are introductory to give students a basis for choosing activities later on, and are therefore shorter.

Step 4—Determine Staffing Patterns and Teacher Loads, and Assign Teachers

Teachers will be assigned to classes based on expertise, personal preference, and special qualification. All swimming instructors are certified Red Cross Water Safety instructors. The archery teacher is a certified National Archery Association instructor. All teachers can teach team sports and will rotate teaching those classes. Teachers will also teach at least one ninth-grade class each. Competencies are as follows:

Teacher	Expertise
Mrs. Platero	WSI, individual sports
Mr. Lungo	WSI, bowling, wrestling, track
Ms. Jones	gymnastics, dance, individual sports
Mr. Garcia	tennis, golf, badminton

Step 5—Identify Teaching Stations and Equipment

Teaching stations include the following:

Gym A	Tennis courts
Gym B	Bowling lanes (community)
Dance studio	Golf course (community)
Pool	Field space, for three classes
Balcony	Wrestling/gymnastics room
Weight room	

Equipment is available for each student in the class sizes taught.

Step 6—Develop a Schedule

The schedule might look like the one in Box 6.2. Staff schedules are such that teachers with the competencies to teach activities scheduled for certain periods are available to teach them during the periods in question.

Notes

1. A. E. Jewett, L. L. Bain, and C. D. Ennis, *The Curriculum Process in Physical Education,* 2d ed. (Madison, WI: WCB Brown and Benchmark, 1995), 11–12.
2. R. C. Hawley, *Human Values in the Classroom: Teaching for Personal and Social Growth* (Amherst, MA: Education Research Associates, 1973).
3. R. W. Tyler, *Basic Principles of Curriculum and Instruction* (Chicago: University of Chicago Press, 1949).
4. D. Crase, and F. Rosato, Selected scholarly periodicals—A profile, *Journal of Physical Education, Recreation, and Dance 60,* no. 9 (1989):34–38.
5. L. Kehres, Maslow's hierarchy of needs applied to physical education and athletics, *Physical Educator 30,* no. 30 (March 1973): 24–25; A. H. Maslow, A theory of human personality, *Psychological Review 50,* (1943): 370–96.
6. G. Hass, *Curriculum Planning: A New Approach,* 2nd ed. (Boston: Allyn and Bacon, 1977), 234.
7. National Association for Sport and Physical Education, *Moving into the Future: National Physical Education Standards: A Guide to Content and Assessment,* 2nd ed. (St. Louis, MO: Mosby, 2004).
8. Heidi Hayes Jacobs, *Mapping the Big Picture: Integrating Curriculum and Assessment K–12* (Alexandria, VA: Association for Supervision and Curriculum Development, 1997).
9. National Association for Sport and Physical Education. www.aapherd.org/naspe/
10. A. E. Jewett, L. L. Bain, and C. D. Ennis, *The Curriculum Process in Physical Education,* 2nd ed. (Madison, WI: WCB Brown and Benchmark, 1995).
11. Hass, *Curriculum Planning,* 234.
12. D. Siedentop, C. Mand, and A. Taggart, *Physical Education: Teaching and Curriculum Strategies for Grades 5–12* (Palo Alto, CA: Mayfield, 1986), 21, 141, 185–202, 203–28.
13. C. S. Collier and W. Webb, Ideas for curricular change: Inside a sport education season, *Strategies 11,* no. 3 (1998): 22–26; D. Siedentop, Physical education and education reform: The case of sport education, in S. J. Silverman and C. D. Ennis, *Student Learning in Physical Education: Applying Research to Enhance Instruction* (Champaign, IL: Human Kinetics, 1996), 247–67; D. Siedentop, What is sport education and how does it work? *Journal of Physical Education, Recreation, and Dance 69,* no. 4 (1998): 18–20; Siedentop, Mand, and Taggart, *Physical Education.*

14. T. Ormond, G. DeMarco, R. Smith, and K. Fisher, Comparison of the sport education model and the traditional unit approach to teaching secondary school basketball [Abstract], *Research Quarterly for Exercise and Sport 66* (Suppl. 1, 1995): 66.
15. Siedentop, Mand, and Taggart, *Physical Education.*
16. R. von Laban, *Modern Educational Dance,* 2nd ed., revised by L. Ullman (New York: Praeger, 1963).
17. G. Graham, S. Holt/Hale, and M. Parker, *Children Moving: A Reflective Approach to Teaching Physical Education,* 6th ed. (Boston: McGraw-Hill, 2004), 29.
18. D. Bunker and R. Thorpe, A model for the teaching of games in secondary schools, *Bulletin of Physical Education 18,* no. 1 (1982): 5–8; P. Werner, R. Thorpe, and D. Bunker, Teaching games for understanding: Evolution of a model, *Journal of Physical Education, Recreation, and Dance 67,* no. 1 (1996): 28–33.
19. L. Festinger, *The Theory of Cognitive Dissonance* (Evanston, IL: Row, Peterson, 1957).
20. Bunker and Thorpe, A model.
21. M. Ellis, Making and shaping games, in R. Thorpe, D. Bunker, and L. Almond, *Rethinking Games Teaching* (Loughborough, Leics: University of Technology, 1986).
22. T. Chandler, Teaching games for understanding: Reflections and further questions, *Journal of Physical Education, Recreation, and Dance 67,* no. 4 (1996): 49–51.
23. H. A. Lawson and J. H. Placek, *Physical Education in the Secondary Schools: Curricular Alternatives* (Boston: Allyn and Bacon, 1981), 210–26.
24. N. Davies, *Research Quarterly for Exercise and Sport 69,* no. 1 (Supplement, 1998): A-88.
25. D. R. Hellison, *Goals and Strategies for Teaching Physical Education* (Champaign, IL: Human Kinetics, 1985); D. Hellison, ed. Physical education for disadvantaged youth, *Journal of Physical Education, Recreation, and Dance 61,* no. 6 (1990): 36–45; D. Hellison. Teaching personal and social responsibility in physical education, in S. J. Silverman and C. D. Ennis, *Student Learning in Physical Education: Applying Research to Enhance Instruction* (Champaign, IL: Human Kinetics, 1996), 269–86; D. R. Hellison and T. J. Templin, *A Reflective Approach to Teaching Physical Education* (Champaign, IL: Human Kinetics, 1991), 104–11.
26. B. Dyson and M. Brown, Adventure education in your physical education program, in J. Lund and D. Tannehill, eds., *Introduction to Standards-Based Curriculum Development* (Sudbury, MA: Jones and Bartlett, 2005).
27. J. Lund and D. Tannehill, It's not business as usual, in J. Lund and D. Tannehill, eds., *Introduction to Standards-based Curriculum Development* (Sudbury, MA: Jones and Bartlett, 2005).
28. A. A. Annarino, C. C. Cowell, and H. W. Hazleton, *Curriculum Theory and Design in Physical Education,* 2nd ed. (Prospect Heights, IL: Waveland, 1986), 220; Siedentop, Mand, and Taggart, *Physical Education.*
29. National Association for Sport and Physical Education. *Moving into the Future: National Standards for Physical Education,* 2nd ed (Reston. VA: Author, 2004).
30. NASPE Middle and Secondary School Physical Education Council, NASPE position statement: Substitution of activities for instructional physical education programs, *NASPE Supplement to the AAHPERD UPDATE* (September 1993), 4.
31. National Association for Sport and Physical Education, *Moving into the Future: National Physical Education Standards: A Guide to Content and Assessment,* 2nd ed. (St. Louis, MO: Mosby, 2004).
32. Bonnie S. Mohnsen, *Teaching Middle School Physical Education: A Blueprint for Developing an Exemplary Program* (Champaign, IL: Human Kinetics, 1997).
33. J. Kudlas, Outdoor/environment programs, in P. E. Barry, *Ideas for Secondary School Physical Education* (Reston, VA: American Alliance for Health, Physical Education, and Recreation, 1976).
34. National Association for Sport and Physical Education, *Opportunity to Learn Standards for Middle School Physical Education* (Reston, VA: American Alliance for Health, Physical Education, Recreation, and Dance, 2004), 9; National Association for Sport and Physical Education, *Opportunity to Learn Standards for High School Physical Education* (Reston, VA: American Alliance for Health, Physical Education, Recreation, and Dance, 2004), 8.
35. President's Council on Physical Fitness and Sports, *Youth Physical Fitness: Suggestions for School Programs* (Washington, DC: U.S. Government Printing Office, 1986), 76.
36. National Association for Sport and Physical Education, *Opportunity to Learn Standards for High School Physical Education* (Reston, VA: American Alliance for Health, Physical Education, Recreation, and Dance, 2004), 7; National Association for Sport and Physical Education, *Opportunity to Learn Standards for Middle School Physical Education* (Reston, VA: American Alliance for Health, Physical Education, Recreation, and Dance, 2004), 9; Society of State Directors of Health, Physical Education, and Recreation, *A Statement of Basic Beliefs* (Kensington, MD: Author, 1985), 8.
37. President's Council, *Youth Physical Fitness,* 76.
38. L. E. Kelly, Instructional time, *Journal of Physical Education and Recreation 60,* no. 6 (1989): 29–32.
39. J. A. Wessel and L. Kelly, *Achievement-Based Curriculum Development in Physical Education* (Philadelphia, PA: Lea and Febiger, 1986), 100–11.
40. M. Metzler, A review of research on time in sport pedagogy, *Journal of Teaching in Physical Education 8* (1989): 87–103.
41. L. E. Kelly, Instructional time.
42. L. E. Kelly, Curriculum design model: A university-public school cooperative model for designing a district-wide elementary physical education curriculum, *Journal of Physical Education, Recreation, and Dance 59,* no. 6 (1988): 26–32.

43. D. S. Hottenstein, *Intensive Scheduling: Restructuring America's Secondary Schools through Time Management* (Thousand Oaks, CA: Corwin Press, 1998).
44. President's Council, *Youth Physical Fitness,* 76.
45. National Association for Sport and Physical Education, *Guidelines for Secondary School Physical Education* (Reston, VA: American Alliance for Health, Physical Education, Recreation, and Dance, 1992), 8–9.

CHAPTER

7

UNIT AND LESSON PLANNING

STUDY STIMULATORS

1. What components are important in designing, implementing, and evaluating instructional programs? Where can you get help on each of these components?
2. Why is it important for teachers to write unit plans and daily lesson plans? How detailed should they be?
3. What components are included in a unit plan?
4. What components are included in a daily lesson plan that are not found in a unit plan? How should a daily lesson plan be written?
5. What is reflective teaching? How can it help you improve your teaching?

Years ago, Mager used a poem to emphasize the importance of planning the instructional program, which still has relevance to teachers today:

> There once was a teacher
> Whose principal feature
> Was hidden in quite an odd way.
> Students by millions
>   Or possibly zillions
>   Surrounded him all of the day.
> When finally seen
> By his scholarly dean
> And asked how he managed the deed,
> He lifted three fingers
>   And said, "All you swingers
>   Need only to follow my lead."
> "To rise from a zero
> To Big Campus Hero,
> To answer these questions you'll strive:
> Where am I going,
>   How shall I get there, and
>   How will I know I've arrived?"[1]

Mosston described teacher behavior as "a chain of decision making."[2] Hunter defined teaching as a "constant stream of professional decisions made before, during, and after interaction with the student; decisions which, when implemented, increase the probability of learning." Learning increases when those decisions are made on the basis of sound psychological theory and reflect the teacher's sensitivity to the student and the situation.[3] Hunter found that regardless of who or what is being taught, all teaching decisions fall into three categories: (1) the *content,* (2) what the *student* will do to learn and to demonstrate that learning has occurred, and (3) what the *teacher* will do to facilitate learning. Errors in making any of these decisions can impede student learning.

TABLE 7.1 A Model for Designing Instructional Programs

Describe the Current Status of the System	Ch. 1 The educational environment Ch. 2 The teacher Ch. 3 Legal aspects of instruction Ch. 4 The learner Ch. 5 Learning	The current status of the learning system includes the educational environment; teacher capabilities; student skills, needs, and expectations; and various constraints such as legal issues, school scheduling, and facilities. Educational psychology and motor learning provide the theory and knowledge base necessary to make sound decisions.
Planning the Instructional Program	Ch. 6 Plan the instructional program-curriculum	A curriculum pattern is chosen to meet students' needs and interests and physical education content standards within the constraints of the school environment. Curriculum content is sequenced and scheduled.
	Ch. 7 Plan the instructional program-units, and lessons	Units and lessons delineate objectives, learning activities, and assessments for achieving physical education content standards.
	Ch. 8 Write objectives Analyze content	The teacher considers ways students will use knowledge, attitudes, and skills to achieve the physical education content standards. Writing appropriate objectives for specific students requires preassessment of students' abilities and the use of content analysis to select and organize content and activities.
	Ch. 9 Select a variety of appropriate teaching styles and strategies to meet the needs of diverse children, schools, and environments	A variety of teaching styles, strategies, and activities is essential to accomplish the specified objectives. A unit may include several styles and strategies.
	Ch. 10 Choose program activities and materials and plan learning experiences for specific students	Resources are selected or developed to lead students from their current status to achievement of lesson and unit objectives. Instructional resources, materials, and activities are included for cognitive, psychomotor, fitness, and affective learning standards.
	Ch. 11 Develop assessment techniques for student performance	Assessment techniques are selected or developed to indicate when students have achieved the stated objectives and to combine these techniques into a grading system.
Organizing and Managing Instruction	Ch. 12 Classroom management	Effective classroom management, organizing the components of the classroom so that effective instruction occurs, includes department policies and procedures, classroom management techniques, and record keeping.
	Ch. 13 Motivation and discipline	A major problem of public school teachers is discipline. Teachers develop an appropriate discipline model from a variety of motivational and preventive discipline techniques and select techniques for specific situations.
Evaluating Instruction and Programs	Ch. 14 Accountability and teacher evaluation	Competent teachers must be able to analyze and reflect on their teaching.
	Ch. 15 Evaluating and revising the instructional program	One purpose of an instructional model is to provide a structure for reviewing and analyzing instruction so that it can be improved.

Beginning teachers generally use a linear model for planning instruction such as the one shown in Table 7.1. They work best from daily lesson plans. Just as a traveler uses a map to reach a certain destination, teachers use the model to plan the best route for student learning. By following the model, teachers can be sure they do not leave out an essential part of the planning process. As teachers become more experienced, they tend to visualize the outcomes of the instructional process and construct a framework designed to fit the unique circumstances of the teaching situation. Experienced teachers tend to plan in weekly intervals. They consider student needs and the context of teaching, then subject matter, and finally goals and teaching methods.

Because teachers operate in a demanding, complicated environment, decision making is difficult. Teachers must plan carefully for students to successfully reach the goals of physical education. Effective instruction and learning should be based on the needs of individual students as well as the demands of a changing environment. Teachers should avoid doing the same things year after year.

DESIGNING, IMPLEMENTING, AND EVALUATING THE INSTRUCTIONAL PROGRAM

As explained in Chapter 6, the standards movement has changed the way schools operate. Although unit and lesson plans provide road maps to help teachers reach their destinations, teachers in states that have written standards for physical education must use these plans to reach specified destinations. Some states have common standards that govern every school in the state; others allow school districts to develop their own standards. Some districts, which are governed by state standards, develop additional standards that build on or extend the state standards. Prior to the standards movement, teachers had a lot of discretion about content they would teach children. Today, in states where physical education is part of the state assessment system, teachers must develop units and lessons designed for students to achieve these standards. Although there is some latitude about which activities will be used to meet the standards, nonetheless, the standards govern curriculum selections.

Teachers in states that do not include physical education in the state assessment system may feel that standards can be ignored when planning curriculum. These teachers run the risk of losing physical education programs as core academic subjects are given higher priority and more time in the school day.

Often content standards are very broad. Many states have written benchmarks for various grade levels that provide more insight about how standards will be implemented for those students. In some states, these benchmarks are not written for every grade level. (The NASPE Physical Education Content Standards also are not constructed by grade level.) This requires teachers to write intermediate requirements that will help students progress and meet the benchmarks specified for particular grades. Teachers should pay close attention to these benchmarks when creating their yearly plans, selecting activities that will allow students to meet the requirements. Given the limited time allocated to physical education, teachers cannot afford to select activities that do not contribute to meeting state or district standards. Additionally, most state standards require balance in the selection of activities for the yearly plan. In other words, a yearly plan that consisted only of team sports or one or two individual sports would not allow students to meet the state standards. Last, when developing yearly plans, teachers must pay attention to the sequence of activities. Offering the same activities and teaching the same skills year after year will not afford students the opportunity to meet standards and thus become physically educated.

Once teachers have planned the instructional program, they are ready to implement and evaluate. Achieving the physical education content standards requires an appropriate environment. In the broadest sense, the environment is a product of many factors, such as legislation, school boards, administrators, parents, and circumstances beyond the control of the teacher. Once the general environment for learning has been established within the context of the school, however, the classroom emerges as the specific environment for learning. The classroom is the domain of the teacher, who makes many organizational and management decisions that directly affect student learning. The model in Table 7.1 shows that the actual content of any instructional program is determined by the planned learning experiences and the learning environment. Once the program has been implemented, an evaluation of the teachers and the program can determine weaknesses in each of the preceding levels of the model.

Review Question: Briefly discuss the importance of each of the steps involved in designing, implementing, and evaluating the instructional program.

A teaching plan consists of the yearly curriculum, unit plans, and daily lesson plans. Although each of these phases of planning serves a different function, they are mutually interdependent. Basically, these plans include the answers to Mager's three questions: What impact do standards have on planning and implementing the instructional program? (1) Where am I going? (2) How will I get there? and (3) How will I know I've arrived?[4]

Where am I going? The plan should specify the performance objectives of the lesson plan or unit in the cognitive, psychomotor, and affective domains.

How will I know I've arrived? Evaluation techniques must be included that will help the teacher determine whether the students have achieved the objectives.

How will I get there? The plan should delineate the learning experiences that will be used to help students meet the objectives specified.

Notice that we have changed the order in which these three questions are addressed. Assessment is a key component of the standards movement. This movement requires teachers to determine what they want students to know and be able to do prior to beginning instruction. For this reason, once the objectives are written, assessments designed to measure student performance on these objectives are developed. After teachers have a clear idea about where they are headed and how they will know that students have arrived at the destination, lessons and learning experiences are developed that will allow students to make the journey.

In this chapter, we will preview how to write unit and lesson plans. Although planning, instruction, and assessment are integral and interdependent components of teaching, it is impossible in this chapter to provide all of the information necessary for each of them. The chapters that follow provide detailed information. You may expect to return to this chapter often as you study the remaining chapters in this text.

How to Write a Unit Plan

Unit and lesson planning involve planning to teach specific content to a specific group of students. Unit and lesson planning combine two elements of effective instruction—the educational environment and the subject matter—to best meet learners' needs. The unit plan directs the teacher in providing purposeful chunks of learning for students; that is, it centers class work around a central theme until some degree of unified learning is attained. The amount of time spent on the unit and on various aspects of the unit are based on curricular objectives, as well as on the previous experience and expertise of the students. Also, some units/activities are less complex than others. Teachers can take advantage of the possibilities of transfer from previous units and from units taught concurrently. The teacher decides the teaching emphasis of each unit so that sufficient time is provided for students to learn the necessary skills to achieve competency as specified in the content standards for physical education.

Before creating a unit plan and answering Mager's questions, certain *preliminary considerations* must be identified. These are listed on the unit plan form shown in the appendix.

- Subject matter and available teaching time
- Appropriate class size
- Student characteristics, including physical limitations, non-English speakers, and low-ability students, obtained through surveys, school guidance materials, or informal assessment
- Skills and principles to be taught (see content analysis in Chapter 8)
- Facilities and equipment needed
- Instructional materials and preparations
- Preassessment techniques (teachers can determine students' interests and needs through surveys or informal assessment)
- Qualifications of faculty
- Weather and its effect on the facility and the dress requirements

Determining Outcomes

Before any learning experiences are planned, *performance objectives* are formulated. Write down what the student is expected to *do* at the completion of the unit. Objectives should be included for the psychomotor, cognitive, and affective domains and should derive from the content standards.

The teacher who fails to plan, plans to fail.
© Tracy Pellet

Objectives might include the following:

1. *Skills:* These are psychomotor skills that the student will be able to do to demonstrate competency in movement forms, such as
   - shoot three types of shots.
   - bat and bunt successfully.
   - bowl a score of 120.
   - play safely.
   - officiate a game (both psychomotor and cognitive).
2. *Fitness:* These are fitness activities that help students achieve and maintain a health-enhancing level of fitness and exhibit a physically active lifestyle, such as
   - complete Fitnessgram tests.
   - set personal fitness goals.
   - keep a log of fitness activities.
3. *Knowledge:* These are cognitive skills or ideas that the student will be able to use to demonstrate competency in movement forms or the ability to apply movement concepts and principles to the learning and development of motor skills, such as
   - select the proper golf club for each distance.
   - demonstrate a knowledge of the rules.
   - use correct strategy in game play.
4. *Personal and social skills:* These are affective activities through which students demonstrate responsible personal and social behavior that respects self and others in physical activity settings, understanding and respect for differences among people in physical activity settings, and an understanding that physical activity provides opportunities for enjoyment, challenge, self-

expression, and social interaction. Examples include these:

- Demonstrate fair play in games.
- Act as a squad or other leader when requested.
- Express a joyful feeling about participating in physical education activities.

Once the objectives have been stated, unit grading policies can be formulated. Grading and reporting procedures include what to grade, the emphasis on each area, and the process for deriving the grade. Student grades for a unit should reflect the degree to which student have met the objectives. Chapter 11 explains how to grade students in a unit of instruction.

Planning to Assess

After developing performance objectives, write down the techniques to be used to determine when the performance objectives have been achieved. Plan now for evaluating the unit and the teacher (see Chapters 14 and 15). Examples of *assessment techniques* include

- Skills tests—on skills such as baserunning, batting, throwing, and fielding.
- Teacher observation—of form, use of strategy, officiating, playing ability.
- Checklist or rating sheet—in such activities as swimming or gymnastics.
- Game scores—in individual sports, such as bowling, archery, badminton.
- Times—in activities such as track or fitness testing.
- Written tests—on rules and strategy.
- Incidence charts—recording the number of correct spikes, free shots made, or hits landing out of bounds.
- Tournament results.
- Fitness logs and journals.
- Attitude or effort inventory, questionnaire, or interview.

Planning Instructional Sequences

When preliminary considerations are complete and the objectives are identified, the teacher outlines the day-by-day decisions. Unit plans provide a big picture or overview of what will be learned, listing a meaningful progression of learning experiences stating when, what, and how. Organizational strategies and specifics for skill analysis are included later in daily lesson plans. The teacher might want to include specific activities in the plan to introduce the unit, such as a videotape replay, a demonstration by several advanced players, results of a recent college or professional competition highlighting well-known performers, or playing the game the way it was played in years past.

A block plan will show a *daily progression of content* (what and when) that provides the following:

- Progression from simple to complex that will allow students to reach exit outcomes
- Maximum student participation
- Successful learning
- Safety
- Motivation
- Pacing of instruction compatible with individual skill levels

A block plan is an overview of what is to occur on each day of the unit.

Learning activities (how) translate content into meaningful learning experiences for students. Considerations for selecting learning activities include these:

- Student needs and learning characteristics
- Subject matter to be taught
- Teacher characteristics
- Learning environment—facilities, equipment, weather
- Principles of learning
- Teaching styles
- Variety
- Safety
- Motivation

Examples of learning activities include the following:

1. Psychomotor
   - Demonstration with cues
   - Skills check-off chart
   - Drills
   - Games
   - Practice with feedback
2. Cognitive
   - Brief explanation
   - Visual aid
   - Question-answer session
   - Study sheet
   - Individual or group project
   - Quiz
3. Affective
   - Role play
   - Brainstorming
   - Case study
   - Questionnaire

A variety of teaching and learning activities will keep students involved and meet individual needs. Include a short description of each activity in the unit plan in the order of presentation. Prepare a contingency plan for inclement weather (a rainy-day plan) or an emergency situation. Units often end with tournaments, field trips, interclass games, or faculty-student activities. Students are more motivated when they know from the onset of the unit what these activities will be. Motivational techniques that enhance the day-by-day learning experience can be identified at this stage of unit planning. Such techniques might be intrinsic or extrinsic. Intrinsic motivation stresses success,

A well-planned and organized environment enhances the leaming atmosphere and increases student enthusiasm.

challenge, self-confidence, and self-fulfillment, while extrinsic motivation focuses on competition, awards, unique drills, unusual warm-ups, and challenging learning strategies. Chapters 10 and 13 contain specific ideas.

After completing the unit plan, the teacher can finalize preparations for the learning experiences. Teaching stations such as the gym, field, classroom, and community facility must be reserved or scheduled, equipment organized, and handouts and examinations prepared. With all of this preparation completed, the teacher can feel secure about the unit of instruction.

Unit plans vary in their specificity or inclusiveness. Some contain resource materials and ideas from which teachers make choices for their own unit plans. The following are generally included in a unit plan:

- Title page and introduction
- Table of contents
- Characteristics and needs of the learner
- Specific performance objectives
- Facilities needed
- Equipment needed
- Preassessment techniques
- Introductory activities
- Subject matter content
- Teaching and learning activities
- Culminating activities
- Assessment and grading techniques
- Ways to motivate learners
- Resources

Review Questions: What is the difference between a unit plan and a lesson plan?

Write a unit plan for a selected activity. Include a contingency plan (rainy-day plan).

How to Write a Daily Lesson Plan

"Teaching is an act, and teachers are actors,"[5] so it follows that teachers need a script. The script teachers use in their daily performance is an instructional plan, and the better the script, the better the performance. Thus, planning is critical. Although effective planning does not guarantee a flawless show, having a plan greatly increases the chances for success.

A lesson plan is an expanded version of a unit plan, providing a detailed analysis of the activities described for each specific day. As shown in the appendix, performance objectives are listed, along with their assessment techniques. A detailed analysis of the learning experience is the main thrust of the daily lesson plan and focuses on providing maximum student participation through efficient use of facilities, equipment, and time so the learner can achieve and retain what is being taught.

Daily lesson plans must be easy to follow and understand because teachers sometimes refer to them during class.

Determining Outcomes

The daily lesson plan contains a more detailed version of unit performance objectives that once again answer Mager's question of "Where am I going?" The teacher states what the students will be able to *do* after instruction. It is better to concentrate on only one or two objectives that can be accomplished in a class period. Although all three domains are represented in unit objectives, a daily lesson plan may focus on only one. However, over the course of the unit all three domains must be addressed. The following examples of performance objectives might be included in a daily lesson plan:

1. The student will hit three out of five balls during a pepper drill using correct form.
2. The student will use correct rules 100 percent of the time during tournament play.
3. The student will perform one lay-up with correct form during practice drills, as specified.
4. The student will refrain from arguing with the official during all class game play.

A major obstacle encountered by beginning teachers is trying to keep students busy, happy, and good, rather than having a clear lesson focus.[6] Unfortunately, this often results in a series of haphazard activities, without regard for the different learning needs of students. Without a clear objective, the teacher cannot clarify the goals of a task or provide specific feedback to students. Effective teachers plan lessons that involve students in activities that contribute significantly toward the achievement of a specific lesson objective.[7]

Preassessment techniques are included in daily lesson plans so teachers (1) know whether students have already achieved the objective or (2) have the knowledge and skills necessary to begin learning what has been planned. Preassessment provides diagnostic information that helps the teacher decide whether objectives are appropriate for the specific students and how to personalize instruction for each learner. For example, knowing whether a student can do a tennis forehand stroke from a dropped ball, a tossed ball, or a hit ball helps the teacher choose activities that are challenging yet still within the realm of success for that student. It eliminates the need for starting over with beginning basketball each year. By deciding on prerequisite knowledge and skills, students' skill and knowledge deficiencies can be diagnosed and remedial help provided. Students who already have these skills can practice skills in ways that will be challenging and motivating. Preassessment also clarifies objectives for students and helps them evaluate their own skills, knowledges, and attitudes.

Preassessment should precede each new objective in the lesson or unit. Having students demonstrate prerequisite skill such as the ability to support their body weight in a handstand is an important preassessment prior to teaching them cartwheels or roundoffs in tumbling.

To select a preassessment technique, ask "What will the students have to do or know to accomplish the objective?" For example, if the objective of the course is to play tennis at a beginning level, then teachers would probably agree that the students will be able to (1) hit a forehand stroke, (2) a backhand stroke, and (3) a serve; that they would know how to (4) score and (5) follow game rules; and that they will (6) enjoy playing tennis.

The preassessment technique utilized to determine if students have achieved the objective will often be the same technique as that used for assessing achievement of the objective. However, other less formal techniques will also be useful. Some common forms of preassessment are given here. Examples of other assessment techniques are included in Chapter 11. Because of safety factors, introductory instruction often precedes preassessment. For example, students should engage in a cardiovascular endurance program prior to taking a mile run test.

Pretest

A written test may be utilized to preassess knowledge or a skills test to check on skill achievement. These tests may be equivalent forms of a posttest or a simplified version if time is a factor. If a student passes an equivalent of the posttest, reason demands that the student not be asked to repeat the evaluation.

Teacher Observation

Students are asked to perform a skill as they have previously learned it and the teacher observes to see which students can already perform the skill according to the criterion established in the objective. This can be done informally while students are engaged in a learning activity.

Most psychomotor objectives require that students have some adjunct knowledge if they are to benefit from instruction designed to reach the objective. For example, in order to perform a tennis serve correctly, students must learn about the service court and what constitutes a foot fault when serving. As the teacher preassesses serving ability, student knowledge of a legally served ball can also be determined.

Question or Questionnaire

A questionnaire or an informal question can tell the teacher which students think they have achieved the objective. For example, if students answer negatively to the question "How many of you can do a feet-first surface dive?" it is probably unnecessary to use a more formal preassessment technique.

For safety reasons, questions or questionnaires can be better alternatives than actually asking the student to perform the skill. For example, a questionnaire revealing that a student was not a deep-water swimmer would be a better alternative than having students enter the deep end of the pool to allow you to determine that ability.

Preassessment techniques can take a few minutes or an entire class period. In either case the results are used for further instruction. For example, if the teacher finds out from a pretest that students will not put their faces in the water in swimming class, instructional strategies must begin with activities in which students learn to function with water covering their faces. On the other hand, if students are already comfortable with their faces underwater, instruction could begin with breathing drills for the front crawl. Both options would be included in the lesson plan, and the appropriate one would be selected after the results of the pretest were known.

Students who have already achieved the objective, as evidenced by preassessment results, should be allowed to practice the skill at a more advanced level or move on to other activities. For example, if the objective states that students will perform the lay-up shot in basketball successfully and with correct form, the teacher can quickly identify those students who can already perform successful lay-ups with correct form. These students can be sent to a separate court to work on left-handed or reverse lay-ups or lay-ups in a game, while the rest of the class learns to perform the basic lay-up.

Students who cannot perform the behavior specified in the objective, as determined by the preassessment technique, can be given help to develop the prerequisite skills. For example, students who do not have hand-eye coordination necessary to hit a badminton shuttle are not ready to learn the overhead and underhand clears. Special help must be given to these students so they learn to connect with the shuttle before instruction can take place on the strokes.

Preassessment techniques help instructors evaluate performance objectives. For example, suppose that the class average (mean) on a pretest is fifty-five and the mean on a posttest is sixty. If a class showed very little improvement in performance from the beginning to the end of a unit, this might indicate that the test was too hard, and that performance standards were set too high. The teacher would need to carefully analyze the results of assessment in such a situation.

Preassessment results also help teachers or administrators evaluate teaching methods. For example, after teaching an archery unit Teacher A brags that her students can shoot two hundred points at forty yards and, therefore, she is an excellent teacher. Without preassessment, no judgment of her teaching ability can be made. Since two hundred points at forty yards is a good score for a beginning student, we can assume either that she taught the class well or that she began the class with students who were already highly skilled. Teacher B, in contrast, indicates that in his class no student scored two hundred points or better on the pretest at twenty yards, yet now all students can shoot two hundred points at forty yards. Because of the pretest scores, we know that Teacher B can be pleased with the results of the teaching.

Review Questions: What is preassessment? Why is it important?

What techniques can be used to preassess?

Assessing Student Learning

Assessment of the performance objectives tells whether the teacher has achieved what he or she set out to do. A good objective includes the criteria for assessing the performance. This is easily accomplished when the behavior specified in the objective has been achieved. If more than one objective has been included, it will be necessary to include more than one assessment technique. For example:

- Skills test—The student will hit eight out of ten serves into the back of the court as scored by a partner.
- Teacher observation—The teacher will evaluate each student on lay-up form using a rubric.
- Game scores—Game scoresheets will indicate students' knowledge of how to pick up leaves in bowling.
- Written test—A written test will indicate students' knowledge of rules.
- Check-off chart—A check-off chart will be used to record negative comments to officials.

Planning Instructional Sequences

The core of the daily lesson plan methodically progresses through the learning experiences of one class period in the order they will be taught. The outline includes how the task will be presented, an analysis of the content, organization of the learning environment, motivation and safety factors, and assessment of the outcomes of the instruction. Teachers should try to include enough detail that a substitute teacher could teach the lesson. Each portion of the plan is handled as an *episode.* Anyone reading the plan should be able to read directly across the plan to see all components of each episode. The following components of the plan are illustrated in the appendix.

Teaching and Learning Experiences

Briefly state a description of what will be taught in each episode. Hunter recommends the following seven components: anticipatory set, objective, key information, model, check of student understanding, guided practice, and independent practice. Rink includes such activities as task presentation, content analysis and development, developing and maintaining a learning environment, motivation, and assessment of instruction.[8]

Warm-ups should be directed toward the activity to be taught. Exercises and/or stretches should work the muscle groups that will be used in the lesson. Students can often warm up by practicing skills taught previously in the unit. Using drills or games from the previous lesson can provide a review for students and a preassessment of what students retained from the previous lesson. Some teachers take attendance during these instant activities (little explanation is required to get students moving as they have previously done the activity or drill) to begin class.

The *task presentation* includes how you will get and maintain the attention of the students, orient the students to the objective of the day's activities, and communicate the information to be learned and practiced. Getting attention involves overcoming distractions and organizing students to be able to see and hear the explanations and demonstrations. Maintaining attention will depend on the attention span of the students. Some teachers make the mistake of letting an activity go too long without being redirected with extension or refinement tasks. Students tend to have the highest rate of on task performance in the first two to three minutes following a task. After that, boredom or fatigue can cause students to modify a task making it easier or more difficult, or go off task. Adjusting task focus can prevent this and lead to more productive student practice. A good lesson plan will anticipate this decrease in task performance and contain ways to adjust task focus.

Anticipatory set involves telling the students what they will be doing during the day's activities and how the activities will be assessed or culminated. For example, "Today we are going to learn the forehand stroke in tennis. The purpose of this stroke is to . . . We will begin with a partner and work toward hitting the ball to a target and finally over the net. For some of us that may take several days of practice." If a new skill is presented, teachers should explain to students why learning it is important. Also, student interest can be piqued if teachers relate the lesson to something of interest to students. This may be done verbally (i.e., "Remember when Sekia hit both free throws during the final 10 seconds last Friday to win the women's basketball game?") or by demonstration (i.e., teacher shows students that he or she can do back handsprings and then challenges them to participate in a gymnastics unit). Tying the new skill or concept to others previously taught or to the previous experiences of the students will help them understand the new experiences. For example, "The forehand stroke in tennis is different from the forehand strokes in badminton and racquetball because . . ."

Communicating the task to the learner can be done by verbal explanation or cues and by demonstrations, followed by feedback to the learners about their performance. Since students focus primarily on the demonstration, an accurate demonstration is important. However, students can profit from both expert demonstrations and demonstrations by their peers. Darden suggested that expert demonstrations encourage imitation rather than learning how to improve one's own performance.[9] Students can identify more readily with a demonstration by one of their peers, a person they perceive to be learning along with them, accompanied by the teacher's suggestions for improvement. Teachers should plan the type of demonstration that they will do and who they will use to demonstrate (self or student). After demonstrating correct technique, sometimes teachers can point out common errors. If this method is used, a demonstration of correct technique should follow so that the last image of performance students see is the correct form.

You should also plan how you will observe students to provide corrective *feedback.* For example, you might describe what you will look for, from what angle and distance you might observe, and the number of trials that might be necessary prior to giving feedback. Your content analysis and cues, listed in the next section, will help you in this determination.

Description of Skills and Activities

This section includes the content analysis and development (see Chapter 8). Opportunities for *student practice,* with proposed interventions to extend or manipulate the skill for student learning should also be outlined here.

When teaching skills, teachers should start with simple tasks or drills, and increase the complexity during the lesson. Skills are often introduced using an informing task typically in a closed environment (e.g., they are isolated and few environmental variables will impact performance; see Chapter 5 for a review of open and closed skills). Teachers gradually increase the complexity of the environment using extending tasks. Rink suggests several different types of task extensions:[10]

- Changing the available space
- Modifying equipment (size or weight)
- Breaking a skill into parts and then using forward or backward chaining techniques to teach it
- Changing the intent of the practice
- Changing the number of participants
- Combining a skill with another skill
- Expanding the number of different examples

Extension tasks change the difficulty of a task. Although the name implies making a task harder, in some instances teachers must be prepared to simplify a task for those who are struggling with it. Lesson plans should include a variety of task modifications to either increase or decrease the difficulty of the task. Changing too many components of the task at once may increase difficulty too fast and cause students to be unsuccessful. During lesson progressions, teachers should plan to change one factor at a time to maximize student success.

Whenever possible, teachers should plan application tasks that allow students to use the skills in a gamelike setting (i.e., small-sided game that emphasizes the skill done correctly) or a culminating task that allows students to use the skill in combination (i.e., a series of tumbling and dance moves that simulate a tumbling pass or routine). Application tasks allow teachers to observe students using the task in a more open environment (useful information for planning future lessons) and give students insight as to why the skill is important or how it fits into a game. Such games and activities are fun for students and provide opportunities for learning and assessment as well as student motivation.

This section contains an outline of the biomechanical description of the skill to be taught and the cues that will be used to help the students learn the skill. Remember to describe these in enough detail that a substitute teacher would feel confident teaching. For example:

1. Forehand drive:
   a. Starting position:
      Face net
      Racket in front of body
      Racket head up
   b. Backswing:
      Racket back
      Pivot
      Shoulder to net
   c. Contact:
      Eyes on ball
      Transfer weight to forward foot
      Contact ball even with body
      Swing, do not hit
      Keep ball on racket as long as possible
   d. Follow through:
      Face net
      Weight forward
      Racket reaches in direction of ball

For the teaching cues, write a brief (one to four words) cue for each skill or activity that expresses what the performer should do. When introducing a skill with an informing task, limit the cues to three or four per skill because most students will not be able to remember more than this at one time. For example:

1. Overhead pass—volleyball
   a. Look through the triangle
   b. Get under the ball
   c. Extend
2. Badminton—overhead clear
   a. Scratch your back
   b. Reach for the birdie
   c. Make it whistle
3. Swimming—breast stroke
   a. Pull
   b. Kick
   c. Glide

Cues may be visual, verbal, or kinesthetic. For example:

1. Moving a student's arms in front crawl motion
2. Placing a hand on the student's string hand to prevent jerking to the side in archery
3. Verbal cues during a skill demonstration
4. Visual cues for footwork drill in badminton

After introducing the task, teachers can improve the quality of the skill through the use of refinements. Refinements contain additional cues or critical elements that will decrease errors and/or increase the quality or efficiency of the performance. For example, if a teacher in an archery unit observed students dropping their bows immediately after the string left their fingertips, he or she might have students count to three prior to dropping their bows. In this instance, the refinement would be a separate task designed to increase the quality of the performance. The need for these refinements is often difficult to anticipate. When planning a lesson, teachers should have a list of additional cues that they will add if needed to improve the quality of student performance. Refinements may also be linked with an extension task to ensure student success as the task is extended.

Time Allotment

Write down the *approximate* amount of time to be spent on each teaching or learning activity. Remember to plan time for a maximum amount of activity. Students learn by doing, not by being told. For example:

1. 8:05–8:07—Roll Call
   8:07–8:15—Warm-ups

or

2. Two minutes—Roll Call
   Eight minutes—Warm-ups
   Three minutes—Demonstration

Class Organization

Chapter 12 elaborates on successful ways to manage the classroom, including such items as taking attendance, classroom formations, and transitions between activities. Some of these will be a part of your management plan. However, those aspects that deal with your day-to-day teaching will appear in your lesson plan. Some formations and the transitions between formations are more carefully planned for if you diagram them as shown in Figure 7-1. Use x's for students and T for the teacher.

a.

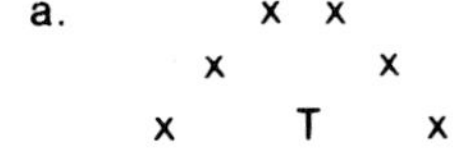

b.

c.

x x x | x x x | x x x
x x x | x x x | x x x
x x x | x x x | x x x
x x x | x x x | x x x

a.

x x x x
x x x x
x x x x
x x x x
1 2 3 4

Squad 1 go to court 1, Squad 2 go to court 2, etc.

b.

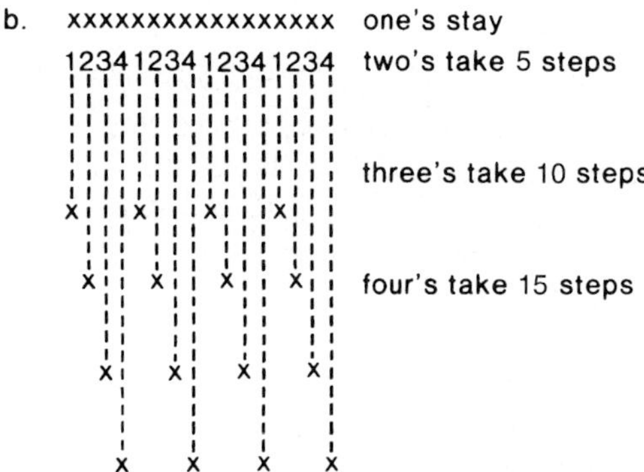

Figure 7-1 Examples of class organization.

Safety, Motivation, and Accommodations for Individual Differences

Chapter 4 described a number of ways to accommodate the needs of different learners, including gender and multicultural differences; adapting to the special needs and ability levels of students; and differences in the physical, social, and intellectual backgrounds of students. These accommodations, along with appropriate safety and motivational techniques, should be placed in this section. Examples include

1. Safety:
   - Safe spacing
   - Rules enforced
   - Surfaces free from obstacles, such as around walls that might be run into, or balls, pinnies, or other objects on the floor that might be stepped on
   - Glasses guards
   - No jewelry, long nails
   - Shoelaces tied, shoes on
   - Equipment in good repair and used properly
   - Students grouped by "handedness" when teaching racket sports

TABLE 7.2 Feedback for Student Performance That Merits Recognition

The Following Terms Link General to Specific Feedback. The *General* Terms Give *Recognition.* The *Specific Feedback* States *Why* the Performance Was Recognized.
AMAZING!—The toss was straight up rather than angled.
NO!—Work on a straight-up toss. Hang on to the ball longer.
BETTER!—You made a soft landing with knees bent.
BACK UP!—Stand three inches back and more to the side.
EXCELLENT!—You rocked over the forward leg this time.
GOOD!—Just where I wanted your arm to go on the follow-through.
CORRECT!—Feet together made the difference.
FLAWLESS!—You shifted the weight forward at the right time.
GREAT!—Looking back longer helped the weight shift.
HANG ON!—That was too slow. Speed up on the curve.
IMPROVED!—Keep the elbow at shoulder level and the wrist back.
OH, NO!—The elbow was dropped below the shoulder.
MARVELOUS!—You were on your toes all the way.
MUCH BETTER!—The follow-through made the difference.
NOT RIGHT!—The bird is almost pushed over the net. Guide it.
NEAT!—Looking to the right helped a lot.
NO!—Toes were pointed. Keep them back.
PERFECT!—Did you feel the downward extension of the wrist?
INCORRECT!—You must extend the wrist downward.
RIGHT ON!—The added speed of release increased the distance.
SUPER, JUST SUPER!—Palm position moves down and out.
STOP!—Your palm was up. It must be down on the release.
TERRIFIC!—Always release just below the hip.
TOO LONG!—You held on too long.
WAY TO GO!—You took a full step with the trail leg.
WONDERFUL!—Your head was down this time.
WRONG!—Keep your head up to correct the problem.
WOW!—A backswing made the difference.

Source: Nena Rey Hawkes, Brigham Young University.

2. Motivation:
   - Fun! (How will this be promoted?)
   - Competition
   - Grades—sometimes
   - Written or skills tests—sometimes
   - Success! (How will this be ensured?)
   - Recognition and feedback (see Table 7.2)
   - Extrinsic rewards—treats, ribbons
   - Desire for activity
   - Playing the game (not drills, but the real thing)

It may be helpful for the teacher to think of himself or herself as one of the students and write down items that would make the teacher want to participate in the learning activities if not required to do so.

3. Individual differences: Write in how individual differences will be dealt with. For example:
   - Handedness—When teaching a tennis forehand put left-handed students in front of the teacher (facing him or her) to "mirror" the stroke while right-handed students are positioned behind the teacher.
   - Disabilities—In a swimming unit, the blind student will be placed next to the outside wall (to get bearings by feel) when swimming across the pool.
   - Skill level—Students who can already do the underhand volleyball serve will move to court three and practice overhead serves.
   - Social abilities—Try to promote group acceptance of Robbie.
   - Mental abilities—Assign partners so that Mary can help Dwayne with drills.

Class Closure

Conclude the class in a meaningful way. Assignments for equipment collection and class dismissal might be given at this time. Examples of closing activities are

1. Review basic teaching cues, game rules, strategies.
2. Ask questions about activities performed.
3. Collect scores.
4. Highlight good play or performance.
5. Make assignments for participation outside class.
6. Introduce the topic or activity for the next class session.

Once the class period has been planned, several final steps are included in the preparation of a daily lesson plan. First, write in the equipment needed for that day. Be sure to plan for maximum activity for each student. For example, list the following:

- 30 balls
- 15 bats
- 24 cones
- 30 scoresheets

Next, write in the facilities or playing area that will be needed. Make a note of any special markings or preparations needed to facilitate instruction. For example:

- Three volleyball courts, tape line fifteen feet from net on north side
- Two basketball courts, no markings
- Four badminton courts, tape lines at six-inch intervals from short service line back

Finally, write in any media to be used. For example:

- Videotape, VCR, monitor
- Magnetic chalkboard, chalk, magnets
- Video camera and blank tape

Scheduling equipment, facilities, and media immediately after the unit plan is completed ensures their availability for the lesson. When the daily lesson plan is formulated, remember to double-check the availability of these items and to secure them for class.

The daily lesson plan is now complete. One final item will aid the teacher in the future. Write down *sources of information,* listing where the material for this lesson was acquired. For example:

1. Book—Allsen and Harrison, pp. 36–37
2. Handout—"Defensive Strategy: Marking" (in-service training, Sept. 2004)
3. Colleague or teacher—Ms. Jones
4. Resource file—pictures from magazine

If no sources were used or needed, write "previous experience."

With the daily lesson plan completed, the teacher should feel secure and ready to face a class of eager students.

Review Question: Prepare three daily lesson plans to be used in a formal unit plan in which skills are reviewed and taught.

Becoming a Reflective Teacher

Because teachers can never be prepared for every possible teaching situation, they must learn to become thoughtful decision makers.[11] These decisions occur during planning, in the classroom, and following the teaching experience. They occur in interactions within the school and in other professional settings. Irwin defined a reflective teacher as one who

> makes teaching decisions on the basis of a conscious awareness and careful consideration of (1) the assumptions on which the decisions are based and (2) the technical, educational, and ethical consequences of those decisions. . . . In order to make these decisions, the reflective/analytic teacher must have an extensive knowledge of the content to be taught, pedagogical and theoretical options, characteristics of individual students, and the situational constraints in the classroom, school, and society in which they work.[12]

Reflection may occur in talking with others or writing about your teaching experiences. Your first steps may be merely a description of what happened, focusing on the technical aspects of teaching—how to teach to accomplish a given objective. Reflective teachers make conscious and rational decisions based on technical and content knowledge, organized and interpreted according to their unique experiences.[13] A good reflection should begin by evaluating whether the objectives for the lessons were achieved. Rather than relying on a subjective opinion, use the lesson's assessment to provide documentation to determine this. If the objectives for the lesson were not met, reasons for this should be explored. Begin by looking at the components of the lesson plan:

- Were the lesson objectives realistic and developmentally appropriate?
- Were adequate resources available (e.g., equipment, space)?
- Was adequate time allocated for student practice during the various activities?
- Were all activities planned for the lesson completed?
- Were students grouped to maximize lesson effectiveness?
- Were transitions between learning activity sequences smooth?
- Did students understand the directions given for transitions and activities?
- Was feedback congruent with the focus of the lesson?
- Was sufficient feedback given to improve the quality of student performances?
- Did the lesson progression provide sufficient challenge and success for students?
- Were students able to apply the skills and knowledge presented in the lesson in some type of culminating activity?
- What changes or improvements to the lesson plan can be made?

Finally, you may reflect on alternative ways to do things.[14] Reflective teaching helps teachers improve their own teaching and become better and more thoughtful professionals. These reflections, and the decisions based on them, serve as guides to future action. The sample lesson plan in the appendix includes space for the teacher to write reflections on the activities in the lesson. Immediately following a lesson, teachers should record any ideas they have for increasing the effectiveness of the activity.

Teachers who have several classes on similar content often "reflect on their feet" and make refinements to lessons each time the lesson is taught. When changes improve the quality of the lesson, they should be recorded so that the next time a similar lesson is taught these changes can be implemented. Teachers who keep their lessons on a computer can actually make the changes and save the revised lesson for future reference.

Reflection should improve both the quality of lesson activities and instructional effectiveness. Teachers should compare results of the lesson assessment to determine whether students were able to achieve the objectives written for the lesson. Results of this should be used to plan the next day's lesson. If the objective was met, students are ready to move on to new skills or increased complexity for the same skills. If students did not reach the objectives, teachers must reflect in an effort to discover why: Was adequate time allotted? Were the steps in the progression too difficult? Should modifications be made in the equipment used? Should the material be presented in a different manner? Teachers could record their reflections in teaching journals designated for this purpose. If these reflections are done honestly, they should capture the teacher's professional growth. Many professional teaching evaluations now use reflection and the development of a teaching portfolio for professional development.

Strean demonstrated how teachers can use these levels to analyze their teaching in physical education.[15] He analyzed three contemporary practices of physical education—allocating playing time by aptitude or skill level, using exercise as punishment, and using skill drills isolated from game play. Students preparing to teach would be wise to analyze these and other common practices to determine if they meet the moral dimensions of teaching advocated by Goodlad.

It is the intent of the authors that teachers discuss the ideas presented in these chapters with others and expand or modify ideas to fit their own situations. Research shows that students benefit academically when teachers share ideas, cooperate in activities, and assist one another's intellectual growth. Research also points out that teachers welcome professional suggestions about improving their work, but they rarely receive them.[16]

Teachers who follow the model for designing and implementing instructional programs described at the beginning of this chapter soon realize that teaching involves both art and science. Skill in making wise decisions based on the model increases with experience and is validated by reflections on one's practice, with revisions made in the various steps of the model following the reflective process. After the completion of a lesson or unit, immediate revision of any unsatisfactory parts will make the plan more usable in the future.

Review Question: Practice reflective teaching by writing about what you are doing in a teaching assignment and why and then follow up the assignment by reflecting on what you did, what succeeded or failed, and why.

NOTES

1. R. F. Mager, *Developing Attitude toward Learning* (Palo Alto, CA: Fearon, 1969), vii.
2. M. Mosston, and S. Ashworth, *Teaching Physical Education,* 5th ed. (San Francisco: Benjamin Cummings, 2002).
3. M. Hunter, *Mastery Teaching* (El Segundo, CA: TIP, 1982), 3.
4. Mager, *Developing Attitude,* vii.
5. H. A. Lawson, Paradigms for research on teaching and teachers, in T. J. Templin and J. K. Olson, eds., *Teaching in Physical Education* (Champaign, IL: Human Kinetics, 1983), 345.
6. J. H. Placek, Conceptions of success in teaching: Busy, happy and good? in T. J. Templin and J. K. Olson, eds., *Teaching in Physical Education* (Champaign, IL: Human Kinetics, 1983), 46–56.
7. T. Ratliffe, Overcoming obstacles beginning teachers encounter, *Journal of Physical Education, Recreation, and Dance 58,* no. 4 (1987) 1:20.
8. J. Batesky, In-service education: Increasing teacher effectiveness using the Hunter lesson design, *Journal of Physical Education, Recreation, and Dance 58,* no. 7 (1987): 89–93; J. E. Rink, *Teaching Physical Education for Learning,* 5th ed. (Boston: McGraw-Hill, 2006).
9. G. F. Darden, Demonstrating motor skills—Rethinking that expert demonstration, *Journal of Physical Education, Recreation, and Dance 68,* no. 6(1997): 31–35.
10. Rink, *Teaching Physical Education.*
11. N. Tsangaridou and D. Siedentop, Reflective teaching: A literature review, *Quest, 47* (1995): 212–37.
12. J. Irwin, What is a reflective/analytical teacher? Unpublished manuscript, University of Connecticut, School of Education, in T. G. Reagan, C. W. Case, and J. W. Brubacher, *Becoming a Reflective Educator* (Thousand Oaks, CA: Corwin Press, 2000), 25.
13. J. W. Brubacher, C. W. Case, and T. G. Reagan, *Becoming a Reflective Educator* (Thousand Oaks, CA:Corwin Press, 1994), 16–25.
14. W. B. Strean, Improving instruction by thinking about your thinking, *Journal of Physical Education, Recreation, and Dance 68,* no. 4 (1997): 53–56; N. Tsangaridou and D. Siedentop, Reflective teaching: A literature review, *Quest, 47* (1995): 212–37.
15. Strean, Improving instruction.
16. U.S. Department of Education, *What Works: Research about Teaching and Learning* (Washington, DC: Author, 1986), 51–52.

CHAPTER

8

PERFORMANCE OBJECTIVES, CONTENT ANALYSIS, AND PREASSESSMENT

STUDY STIMULATORS

1. Define and give an example of a goal, an objective, and a performance objective for each of the instructional domains. Why are both goals and objectives important?
2. What three elements must be included in a performance objective? How do these differ when evaluating affective objectives?
3. What is the difference between open and closed objectives? When would it be appropriate to use each of these?
4. List at least ten acceptable verbs and ten unacceptable verbs that could be used when writing performance objectives.
5. Define and give examples of extension, refinement, and application for a sports skill. How does content analysis apply to game skills? Choose a concept or principle and analyze it.

THE CONTENT STANDARDS

In 1992, the Physical Education Outcomes Committee of the National Association for Sport and Physical Education defined what a physically educated person should know and be able to do. It delineated the twenty outcomes shown in Table 1.2. Later, NASPE created the Standards and Assessment Task Force to develop content standards for physical education based on the outcomes statements. Their work paralleled the work of a national council, established as a result of the Goals 2000: Educate America Act, designed to help professional organizations develop standards. The resulting seven *content standards* described the knowledge and skills of the discipline. *Moving into the Future: National Standards for Physical Education* also indicated several types of assessments (e.g., a test or project) that could demonstrate whether a content standard had been met. Performance standards that specify "how good is good enough" and performance benchmarks describing progress that should occur as students move toward a performance standard have been developed by several states.[1]

Objectives are relatively specific outcomes of instruction that can be achieved within a short period of time, such as in a unit or lesson. They are derived from the content standards and serve as stepping stones toward achievement of the standards. The following are examples of unit objectives:

1. Students will perform the forearm pass, set, spike, and overhand serve in six-player volleyball games with reasonable success.
2. Students will write individualized fitness plans to develop cardiovascular endurance.

Most lesson objectives are written as *performance objectives.* A performance objective is a statement of an outcome that is attainable and is stated with enough specificity to identify what the learner is to do or produce, or what characteristics he or she should possess at the end of instruction.[2] Performance objectives are always written in terms of what a student can do. An assessment that can measure student performance is included in a performance objective. The following are examples of performance objectives:

1. The student will achieve the "good" or "excellent" category on the 1.5-mile run given several opportunities to do so.
2. The student will execute three out of five tennis serves into the service court using correct form while standing behind the service line on the left service court during a skill test.

These examples emphasize that students' actions should be directly observable. Performance objectives have three characteristics:

1. A statement of behavior (what the learner will be able to do at the conclusion of instruction).
2. The situation or conditions under which the learner will perform the task, which may impact the student's performance.
3. The criteria for successful performance.

The following example illustrates these characteristics:

The student will execute three out of five tennis serves into the service court using correct form while standing behind the service line on the left service court during a skill test.

1. Behavior—*tennis serve*
2. Conditions—*behind the service line on the left service court during a skill test*
3. Criteria—*three out of five serves into the service court using correct form*

When writing the situation or conditions of an objective, people sometimes make the mistake of writing "false situations." In other words, they identify things that will not impact the performance. It is a given that the player will have a racket and a ball. However, if the racket had a shorter handle or larger face, performance might be impacted so this would become part of the conditions specified in the objective. In the above example, the students are required to serve from the left service line. Serving from the left service court requires a player to adjust the stance from that used to serve from the right service court. Also,

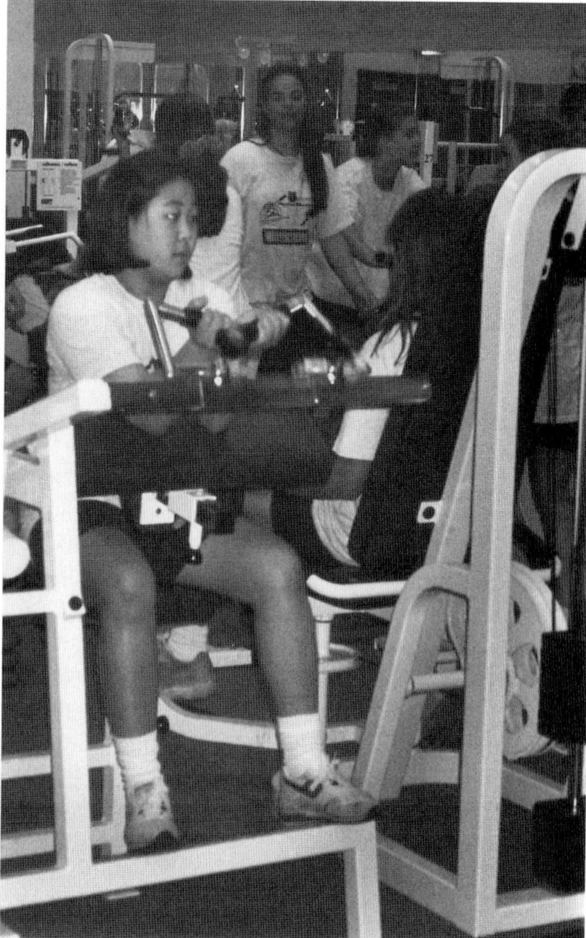

Clearly stated performance objectives help students evaluate their progress toward instructional goals.
© Tracy Pellet

serving from behind the service line will require more strength and accuracy than if the student is allowed to serve from anywhere in the court. Serving during a skills test is also different from serving during a game. In a game, the player has additional concerns about scoring, getting into position to play the ball when it is returned, and so on. A skills test represents a relatively closed situation and the player can concentrate on just the serve. Also, serving the ball several times consecutively with no game play interrupting concentration can impact performance.

Several factors can impact the conditions in physical education. Some examples might include the size and weight of the equipment, the size of the field, number of people on a team, and weather conditions.

The criterion of an assessment can specify process, product, or both. When writing objectives for beginning students, teachers will want to specify the qualitative part of the performance and focus on correct form. Using the above example, if process had been emphasized, the objective would merely have stated that the student should use correct form. Quantitative criteria identify the effectiveness of the performance or product by specifying such things as distance, speed, or a number done correctly (e.g., three out of five). If identifying product criteria, teachers must also specify that the students are to use correct form. In the previous example, if correct form was not specified, the student could satisfy the criteria with a "punch" serve rather than one with a full swing.

Review Questions: Define and give an example of a content standard, a performance standard, a benchmark, and a performance objective.

Name the three components of a performance objective and write an objective that contains all three components.

Advantages of Performance Objectives

Performance objectives serve as a base for the entire process of instructional design. Without objectives, assessment would be unnecessary and learning activities would be like a map without a destination. Expressing objectives in terms of performance provides the criteria for selecting and organizing the content and learning activities for the instructional program into a manageable, meaningful sequence. Nonessential items can be removed from lessons, providing more time to achieve the most important objectives. When a teacher has written performance objectives for a lesson or unit of instruction, clear purposes for both the teacher and students emerge.

Objectives also increase teacher accountability by focusing on specific behaviors that can be evaluated. Objectives convey to parents, administrators, students, and teachers exactly what is to be accomplished in school programs and how to gauge student progress. Clearly stated objectives help students evaluate their own progress toward instructional goals and therefore serve as a motivating factor. Students are more secure because they know what is expected and can spend more time on important items. Students who know that they are expected to reach criterion scores on serve, forehand, and backhand skill assessments have specific targets for which to practice when given the opportunity in class by the teacher. These students are able to evaluate their own performance and can concentrate on areas most needing improvement. Teachers using performance objectives are more secure because they know that what they are teaching has been carefully planned and that the assessment is appropriate. With clearly defined objectives and content, teachers can preassess student behavior in relation to the objectives, assess progress toward the objectives, and determine the extent to which students have achieved the objectives.

Concerns about Performance Objectives

Educators have some concerns about the use of performance objectives. Students and teachers often complain that writing performance objectives takes a lot of time. However, the time spent at the beginning of the planning process can save time when planning appropriate assessment activities. Both objectives and assessment are essential to achieve the content standards for physical education. Another criticism is that since writing performance objectives at the lowest levels of the taxonomies is easiest, teachers may leave out worthy objectives that cannot be easily evaluated. To avoid this, teachers can use the taxonomies to check their objectives. Some teachers complain that writing objectives in advance of instruction prevents them from taking advantage of "the teaching moment." This is especially true in the affective domain in which it is impossible to plan the teaching of such behaviors as fair play. However, specifying the objectives of instruction does not tell the teacher when something is to be taught. It can, however, make the teacher aware of the need to teach the behavior when the opportunity arises. Good teachers will continue to take advantage of "teaching moments" rather than limit themselves to those behaviors that will be assessed. In fields such as dance, it is difficult to specify measurable student behaviors. Specifying the objectives forces teachers to articulate exactly what they wish to teach. It is not enough to "know good performance when they see it." This also helps remove the mystery about the intent of instruction for students. Although critics of performance objectives say they dehumanize learning, in reality performance objectives may humanize learning by telling students what is expected. The use of open forms of objectives can also be used to individualize learning.

Review Question: Discuss the advantages and disadvantages of performance objectives from your point of view. How can some of the disadvantages be overcome?

Writing Performance Objectives

Performance objectives are generally divided into three types—cognitive (learning and application of knowledge), psychomotor (learning physical skills), and affective (concerned with interests, attitudes, appreciations, and values).

Performance objectives must describe the behavior of the learner. The key to writing objectives is the selection of the verb. Bloom recommended using verbs that are directly observable.[3] The following are examples of observable and nonobservable verbs:

***Observable* (Appropriate)**

Match (duplicate, equal, agree, fit)

Translate (decipher, interpret, explain, simplify)

Compute (calculate)

Name (identify, label, designate)

Diagram (draw, illustrate, picture, design, chart)

Classify (rank, rate, arrange, categorize)

Apply (pertain to, relate to, employ)
Construct (assemble, make, produce, build)
Identify (distinguish, recognize, associate, know)
Explain (define, decipher, illustrate)
Demonstrate (evidence, prove, be-able-to, perform)
Pass (or shoot, dribble, serve, catch, hit)
Improve (enhance, enrich, better)
List (catalog, index, enumerate, specify)

***Nonobservable* (Not Appropriate)**

Comprehend
Understand
Learn
Respect
Think
Grasp
Take an interest in
Have knowledge of

The taxonomies for each domain are reviewed in Table 8.1 along with appropriate verbs for each level of behavior.

Writing performance objectives requires practice. The following steps are designed to develop competence in properly stating performance objectives. Each step will add another piece to the soon to be completed objective.

Performance objectives should focus on skill refinement and application.

Step 1. Identify the area of instruction.
Step 2. Define what the student will be able to do (behavior) at the conclusion of instruction.
Step 3. Describe the conditions under which the student's performance will be evaluated.
Step 4. Specify the criteria for acceptable performance.
Step 5. Evaluate the objective.

Since the general principles of writing objectives apply to both cognitive and psychomotor objectives, these two types will be considered simultaneously. Affective objectives will be considered later in the chapter.

TABLE 8.1 Appropriate Verbs for Performance Objectives within Each of the Domain Taxonomies

Cognitive Domain

LEVELS OF BEHAVIOR	VERBS FOR OBJECTIVES	
1. Knowledge	Define Spell Who, what, where, when, why	Match Recite
2. Comprehension	Translate Tell in your own words Compare or contrast	Paraphrase Summarize Predict
3. Application	Solve	Apply
4. Analysis	Analyze Break down Determine	Examine Delineate Identify
5. Synthesis	Compose Design Hypothesize Create Organize	Write Invent Plan Produce
6. Evaluation	Judge Defend	Evaluate

Continued

TABLE 8.1 Continued

Psychomotor Domain

LEVELS OF BEHAVIOR	VERBS FOR OBJECTIVES	
1. Generic movement		
Perceiving	Identify Discover Imitate Duplicate	Recognize Discriminate Replicate Pantomime
Patterning	Perform (shoot) Execute (swim)	Demonstrate (pass) Coordinate (jump)
2. Ordinative movement		
Adapting or accommodating	Adjust, alter Employ	Apply Utilize
Refining	Control Improve Regulate Integrate	Synchronize Synthesize Perform rhythmically (smoothly, efficiently) Coordinate
3. Creative movement		
Varying	Alter Revise	Change Diversify
Improvising	Interpret Improvise Discover	Extemporize Anticipate
Composing	Design Symbolize Plan	Compose Create

Affective Domain

LEVELS OF BEHAVIOR	VERBS FOR OBJECTIVES	
1. Receiving	Notice Tolerate Listen	Select Be aware or conscious of
2. Responding	Comply Volunteer Be satisfied React Sympathize with Attend Accept responsibility	Follow Enjoy Agree or disagree Give opinion Demonstrate appreciation for Read
3. Valuing	Prefer consistently Pursue activities Debate Value Improve skills	Support consistently Involve others Argue Purchase
4. Organization	Discuss codes, standards Weigh alternatives against standards Base decisions on values	Formulate systems Define criteria
5. Characterization	Demonstrate consistent behavior or methods	Integrate total behavior or values

Steps for Writing Cognitive and Psychomotor Performance Objectives

As stated earlier, writing performance objectives involves a statement of behavior, conditions of performance, and criteria for successful performance. Some performance objectives are *closed* in that they demand a single correct response of all learners.[4] For example, an objective that asks the student to name the thigh bone has only one answer—the femur. Some objectives are *open*. Each learner could have a different response and yet meet the behavior specified in the objective. An example of an open objective might be to perform three new skills on a chosen piece of gymnastics equipment.

Step 1—Identify the Area of Instruction

Choose a lesson or unit of instruction that is relevant to the student population in terms of real-world utility or preparation for future educational needs. Specify the target population in terms of age, sex, and previous experience in the unit. Some examples are

1. Square dance—seventh-grade boys and girls, no previous experience.
2. Volleyball—ninth-grade boys and girls, two years' experience.
3. Physical fitness—high school, coed, varied experience.

Step 2—Define What the Student Will Be Able to Do at the Conclusion of Instruction

In clear and concise terms, state what the student will be able to *do* at the conclusion of instruction. Include only those behaviors or products of behavior that can be observed through one or more of the five senses. Some examples of behaviors are

1. Square dance
   a. The student will pass a test on square dance terminology.
   b. The student will perform two dances.
2. Volleyball
   a. The student will serve a volleyball.
   b. The student will set a volleyball.
   c. The student will officiate a volleyball game.
   d. The student will write a paper on the history of volleyball.
3. Physical fitness
   a. The student will create an aerobic dance routine.
   b. The student will improve his or her 1.5-mile run score.
   c. The student will engage in a strength and flexibility program.

Step 3—Describe the Conditions under Which the Student's Performance Will Be Evaluated

Include where, when, and with what equipment or materials and what set of rules the student's performance will be evaluated. Implicit objectives often have implied conditions. Some examples of conditions follow:

1. Square dance
   a. After learning six dances in class the student will pass a test on square dance terminology.
   b. After learning six dances in class the students will perform two dances to singing calls.
2. Volleyball
   a. While standing behind the service line, the student will perform an overhand serve into the back half of the court. (A regulation ball and court are implied.)
   b. Using a legal volley, the student will volley a volleyball continuously against the wall so that it touches above the head. (A regulation ball is implied.)
   c. The student will demonstrate knowledge of rules by officiating a 15-point volleyball game during the class tournament.
   d. The student will write a one- to three-page paper on the history of volleyball. (Handwriting is implied, since typing has not been specified.)
3. Physical fitness
   a. Given class time daily, the student will join with two or three other students to create an aerobic dance routine to any music provided by the student or teacher.
   b. Given practice time for jogging, the student will improve his or her 1.5-mile run score. (A track or running area is implied.)
   c. The student will engage in a strength and flexibility program during class.

Step 4—Specify the Criteria of Acceptable Performance

State the criterion in such a way that a qualified person could use it to successfully choose students meeting the standard. Describe the performance or the results of performance in terms of the number of trials, the number of successful completions, the number of repetitions within a given time allotment, improvement on a given scale, percent or percentile achieved, raw score, or other observable standard. Describe a subjective performance in terms of the degree or quality of performance required. The following objectives are now complete performance objectives with behavior, conditions, and criteria:

1. Square dance
   a. After learning six dances in class, the student will score at least 70 percent on a 25-question multiple-choice test about square dance terminology.
   b. After learning six dances with singing calls in class, the student will perform two of those dances to music without an error.

2. Volleyball
   a. From behind the baseline and using the correct technique for an overhand serve, the student will serve eight out of ten serves into the back half of the court.
   b. Using the correct technique, the student will volley fifteen consecutive times against the wall so that it touches above a line marked seven feet from the floor in thirty seconds or less.
   c. The student will demonstrate knowledge of the rules by officiating a fifteen-point volleyball game during the class tournament making fewer than four mistakes on rules.
   d. The student will write a one- to three-page paper on the history of volleyball that includes the origin, early rules and changes in the game, recent changes in the style of the game, and indications of current interest in volleyball.
3. Physical fitness
   a. Given twenty minutes of class time, the student will create, with two or three other students, a two-minute aerobic dance routine to music that includes activities that raise the heart rate to the target heart rate (refer to formula given in class).
   b. The student will improve his or her 1.5-mile run score by at least one level or will maintain his or her endurance at the "good" or "excellent" level.
   c. Given twenty minutes three times per week, the student will demonstrate participation in a strength and flexibility program three times a week for six weeks by turning in a log of activities on the form provided by the instructor.

Step 5—Evaluate the Objectives

Evaluate the objectives by asking the following questions: (1) Is the expected behavior attainable as a result of learning in the unit of instruction? (2) Is the objective relevant or is it included merely because it is easy to state in terms of performance? (3) Are good objectives omitted because they are difficult to state in performance terms? (4) Can another competent person understand the objective well enough to use it to evaluate learners in the unit of instruction? (5) Are facilities and materials available for the attainment of the objective? (6) Is the objective motivating to the student? (7) Are both short-range and long-range objectives included for the unit of instruction?

If some students are functioning within all levels of a domain, write objectives to include all of these levels. An example of objectives for each level of the cognitive and psychomotor domains is shown in Tables 8.2 and 8.3.

Review Questions: Choose one content standard for physical education. Write a unit objective derived from the content standard, then write at least two performance objectives for the appropriate domain(s).

Write three or more performance objectives for a lesson or a unit of instruction that are clearly stated and include the three essential components—behavior, conditions, and criteria. Include the cognitive, psychomotor, and affective domains.

Write a performance objective for each level of the taxonomy in each of the three domains for a specified unit of instruction.

Self-Check on Performance Objectives

Directions: Classify the following statements as (A) properly stated performance objectives, or (B) improperly stated performance objectives or not a performance objective. If the objective is classified as (B), identify the part of the objective that is incorrect or missing.

1. The student will bat.
2. The student will list five historically prominent persons in physical education.
3. The student will learn the rules of badminton.
4. The student should learn the reasons for using correct safety procedures in archery.
5. The Red Cross standards will be the model for student performance in swimming the five basic strokes.
6. The student will compute the percentage of body fat.
7. Given the specific data needed on a written test, the student will be able to solve six out of seven problems on body composition.
8. The student will understand physical fitness.
9. Given a pencil and paper, the student will pass a true-false quiz on the rules of bowling.
10. The student will appreciate the value of physical activity.
11. The student will shoot free throws from the foul line.
12. The student will understand basketball strategy.
13. The student will learn the overhead clear in badminton.
14. The student will demonstrate progress in weight training by keeping a progress log as specified in the handout.
15. The student will demonstrate the serve in racquetball.

Answers to Self-Check

1. B, no stated conditions or criteria.
2. A
3. B, not stated in terms of observable performance.
4. B, not stated in terms of observable performance.
5. B, not stated in terms of observable performance.
6. B, no stated conditions or criteria.
7. A
8. B, not stated in terms of observable performance.
9. B, no stated criteria.

TABLE 8.2 A Sample of Objectives for Each Level of the Cognitive Domain

Knowledge

1. Match bowling terms and definitions on a written test at the 80 percent level.
2. Given a diagram of the human body, list the names of the bones and muscles shown.
3. List the six basic rules of archery.

Comprehension

1. Given ten game situations in a specified sport, select the correct referee's decision from a criteria sheet.
2. Describe in writing (define) the meaning of "intensity" in a physical fitness program.
3. Diagram a 2-1-2 zone defense in basketball.

Application

1. List the criteria you would use to purchase a quality tennis racket for yourself based on the characteristics explained in class.
2. List the situations in which you would use a zone defense and those when you would use a player-to-player defense in basketball.
3. Write a physical fitness program for an individual who was rated "poor" after completing the fitness tests. Include specific recommendations for intensity, duration, and frequency.

Analysis

1. Analyze ten exercises in *The Readers Digest* article handed out in class. List the muscles used for each exercise and determine if the exercise develops strength or flexibility.
2. Using the criteria sheet handed out in class, analyze the offensive player of your choice by watching a videotape of the NBA championship game. List the strengths and weaknesses of this player during five consecutive plays executed by his team.

Synthesis

1. Create five new plays for flag football.
2. Choreograph a new dance lasting five minutes for three to six participants using music of your choice.
3. Create a gymnastics routine on the balance beam that includes at least five new stunts.

Evaluation

1. Using the criteria sheet, evaluate three fad diets from the following list to determine whether they meet minimum nutritional standards.
2. Judge a list of specific behaviors exhibited by the spectators at the league championship volleyball match to determine sportspersonlike behavior based on the following criteria (recognized values of society).

10. B, not stated in terms of observable performance.
11. B, no stated criteria.
12. B, not stated in terms of observable performance.
13. B, not stated in terms of observable performance.
14. A
15. B, no stated conditions or criteria.

If you had difficulty with the self-check, review the preceding pages in this chapter before proceeding. Rewrite the improperly stated objectives. Have two of your classmates analyze your objectives in terms of the three criteria for writing objectives and the questions in step 5.

Steps for Writing Affective Objectives

Performance objectives in the affective domain differ from cognitive and psychomotor objectives in that attitudes, appreciations, and values cannot be measured directly but must be inferred by the behaviors of students toward or away from the desired behavior. These behaviors are called *approach* or *avoidance* behaviors. Definitions for these behaviors are provided below. Lee and Merrill delineated a method for writing affective objectives.[5] Their ideas have been incorporated into the following steps for writing affective objectives:

Step 1. Describe the attitude the student should acquire.
Step 2. List specific student approach or avoidance behaviors.
Step 3. Describe the conditions under which the approach or avoidance behaviors will occur.
Step 4. Specify the criteria under which the approach or avoidance behaviors will occur.
Step 5. Evaluate the objectives.

TABLE 8.3 A Sample of Objectives for Each Level of the Psychomotor Domain

Perceiving

1. Identify the tumbling skills performed by the teacher.
2. Discover how the lay-up shot is performed by asking questions after a demonstration of the skill.

Patterning

1. Perform a gallop.
2. Demonstrate a backward volleyball set into the basketball hoop.
3. Execute a headstand in good form (as determined by the criteria sheet) for ten seconds.

Adapting

1. Dribble a basketball in control from one side of the court to the other while being guarded.
2. Shoot five arrows at ten yards, twenty yards, and thirty yards on the archery field.
3. Bat a pitched ball to right, left, and center field.

Refining

1. Perform a bowling approach and release until it is smooth, meeting the criteria listed on the checklist.
2. Improve a softball accuracy score at a target on the wall, until a score of fifty points in ten throws is achieved.
3. Perform a series of forward rolls in a straight line until three in good form can be executed from standing to standing.

Varying

1. Alter the forward roll until a straddle, pike, or other variation can be performed.
2. Modify the bowling stance to increase the speed of the ball three seconds from release until the pins are contacted.
3. Hit three pitched balls past the infield from the right batter's box and three from the left.

Improvising

1. Change offensive pattern #5a to involve the center more often and exploit the lack of height by the defense.
2. Add two new steps to the "That's Cool" aerobic routine.

Composing

1. Create a floor exercise routine using at least five stunts already learned.
2. Design five new flag football play patterns.

Step 1—Describe the Attitude the Student Should Acquire

Write a descriptive statement describing the attitude, including interests, desires, or appreciations.

1. Physical fitness—The student will have a desire to maintain physical fitness.
2. Dance—The student will enjoy participating in dance activities.
3. Fair play—The student will demonstrate fair play.

Step 2—List Specific Student Approach or Avoidance Behaviors

APPROACH BEHAVIORS

List the behaviors that students will most likely be expected to say or do that bring them into closer contact with the subject. These behaviors are called approach behaviors. They must be observable and serve as indicators of the desired attitude or disposition. Some examples of approach behaviors are:

1. Physical fitness
   a. Reads fitness books, articles
   b. Exercises daily
   c. Tells people how exercise can improve their lives
   d. Is always checking own heart rate during activity
   e. Tries to get others to engage in fitness activities
   f. Attends lectures about fitness
2. Dance
   a. Reads the fine arts section of the newspaper
   b. Subscribes to a dance magazine
   c. Participates in dance instruction or activity outside of class
   d. Knows the names and performance characteristics of professional dance performers
   e. Watches dance events on television
   f. Attends local dance events
3. Fair Play
   a. Volunteers to officiate intramural basketball games

   b. Reads an article or attends a lecture on fair play
   c. Calls own fouls during a competitive game
   d. Controls own temper and behavior during any sports competition
   e. Shakes hands with all opposing players after the game or match

In most school-related activities, approach behaviors are adequate for evaluating affective objectives and can be used exclusively if desired.

AVOIDANCE BEHAVIORS

List the behaviors that students will most likely exhibit that will detract from or lead them away from the desired attitude. These behaviors are called avoidance behaviors. Some examples of avoidance behaviors include

1. Physical fitness
   a. Tries to convince physical education teacher that he or she is not supposed to run but plays basketball later in the period
   b. Does not dress for activity on days that fitness activities are conducted
   c. Asks to substitute marching band for fitness unit
   d. Refuses to turn in a one-week record of eating
2. Dance
   a. Says "This is a dumb/sissy activity"
   b. Tells the teacher this is the only time the counselor is available and asks to be excused during dance class
   c. Is often tardy to class or fails to attend class
   d. Fails to study for quiz or turn in paper
3. Fair Play
   a. Gets involved in a fight during a game
   b. Refuses to come out of a game to allow other team members to play
   c. Blames others for inappropriate behavior
   d. Constantly argues with the referees

Eliminate activities that cannot be observed either directly or indirectly. Direct observation includes student activities that are actually seen. Eliminate activities that are not commonly expected to occur among students or are inappropriate.

Step 3—Describe the Conditions under Which the Approach or Avoidance Behaviors Will Occur

A testing situation for affective objectives must include a set of alternatives presented to the student that allow the student to make a free choice, unhindered by what the teacher wants the student to do. Stating the conditions or circumstances under which the behavior will take place is the hardest part of writing an affective objective. Only when the conditions are known can the behavior be interpreted as a true approach or avoidance behavior. Students should be asked to choose between two behaviors, one of which is the behavior in question.

1. Physical fitness—Each student may run a mile and a half, swim three minutes, or play basketball.
2. Dance—Each student may choose to join the square dance group or play badminton.
3. Fair Play—Each student may shake hands with the opposing team or gather up the equipment.

Another possible set of alternatives would be to ask the student to choose between an approach or an avoidance activity, for example, "Each student can choose to play basketball or fail the course." In this situation, no one would feel free to sit out. Free choice is an essential component of the testing situation. Teachers must do as little as possible to influence the alternative chosen by a student in the testing situation with affective objectives. Some other examples of teacher influence might include extra credit, praise, or special privileges. Although these might be appropriate in a learning situation, they are inappropriate in a testing situation because they cause the student to approach the subject because of the teacher rather than because of a favorable attitude toward the subject.

When using questionnaires or other direct observation techniques, allow students to express their true feelings, perhaps through anonymity or by assessing feelings after the course grades have been submitted.

Step 4—Specify the Criteria under Which the Approach and Avoidance Behaviors Will Occur

The criterion statement indicates how well, how often, or how much of the approach or avoidance behavior must occur for the objective to be achieved.

The criterion statement indicates the number of activities in which each student will participate.

a. Physical fitness—Each student will engage in a fitness activity at least three times a week for one semester.
b. Dance—The students will participate regularly (not more than three absences) in the dance class for a six-week unit.
c. Fair Play—The students will shake hands with the opposing team after a game whether they win or lose.

One advantage to using the number of activities as a criterion is that it allows students with several interests or extenuating circumstances to demonstrate approach behaviors that might not occur in a single instance. For example, a student who exhibited a large number of approach behaviors had her tonsils out and could not participate in intramural basketball, although basketball was her favorite activity.

The number indicates how much of the behavior will occur for the objective to be achieved. This number should be based on some realistic goal in terms of what is already known about students, perhaps through a preassessment of student behaviors. Do not expect miracles to occur by stating numbers that are impossible for students to achieve. Words such as *several, most,* or *often*

TABLE 8.4 A Sample of Objectives for the Affective Domain Using Hellison's Levels of Social Responsibility

Respect for the Rights and Feelings of Others

1. The student will follow the safety rules given by the teacher.
2. The student will not talk when the teacher or other helpers including students are talking or demonstrating.
3. When a dispute arises, the student will offer to replay or restart the game without gaining a personal advantage.
4. Win or lose, the student will shake hands at the end of the game.

Participation and Effort

1. When given a choice of activity units, the student will select an activity in which he or she has had no prior experience instead of selecting one in which he or she already has competence.
2. The student will stay involved with the routines even if not participating.
3. The student will engage in the inline skating obstacle course prior to the start of class without prompts from the teacher.

Self-Direction

1. The student will do a self-critique from a video and use the information to improve performance.
2. During the season, the student will work to improve skills by setting goals and then working to achieve them.
3. The student will develop a practice schedule and use it to improve skills while not in physical education class.

Sensitivity and Responsiveness to the Well-Being of Others

1. The student will accept responsibility for others by spotting them correctly.
2. The student will volunteer to help others during free skate time.
3. The student will applaud and/or congratulate others once they have finished their routine.

Applications Outside of the Gymnasium

1. The student will use skills learned in class and volunteer to officiate games in nonschool events and settings.
2. The student will practice fair play skills while participating in before- or after-school activities.
3. Following a unit on outdoor education, the student will organize a group of students for a weekend camping trip.

should also be avoided because they are too vague to demonstrate goal achievement.

Because behavior in the affective domain is evaluated on the basis of inferred behavior, teachers may not need to tell students what the performance objective says. A knowledge of the general objectives in the affective domain is usually sufficient for students.

An example of objectives for each level of the affective domain is shown in Table 8.4.

Step 5—Evaluate the Objectives

After writing several objectives, check them by referring to the following checklist, which incorporates each of the steps described by Lee and Merrill:[6]

1. Attitude
   a. Is there a descriptive statement of interest, desire, or appreciation?
2. Behavior
   a. Is a student approach or avoidance behavior specified?
   b. Can the behavior be directly or indirectly observed?
   c. Is the behavior a high-probability behavior (likely to occur often)?
3. Conditions
   a. Is a situation described in which the approach or avoidance behavior may occur and can be observed?
   b. Are at least two alternatives presented to students?
   c. Is the situation a free-choice situation in which the teacher does not directly influence the student's choice?
   d. Are cues eliminated that might indicate the expected behavior?
   e. Do students feel free to express their true feelings if direct observation is used?
4. Criteria
   a. Is a number of approach behaviors specified?
   b. Are indefinite words avoided?
   c. Is the criterion a realistic estimate of changes that can be expected in the students?
   d. Will the results indicate a trend or pattern of approach or avoidance?

Self-Check on Affective Objectives

Directions: Classify the following statements as (A) properly stated affective performance objectives or (B) improperly stated affective performance objectives or not a performance objective. If the objective is classified as (B), identify the part of the objective that is incorrect or missing.

1. The student will show responsibility by coming to class properly dressed each day of the unit.
2. The student will value dance.
3. The student will value sport by participating in at least one after-school intramural sport during the year.
4. The student will respect others.
5. The student will listen attentively to instructions.
6. The student will volunteer to help others.
7. The student will attend an athletic contest outside of class at least twice during the year.
8. The student will like others in the class.
9. The student will display fair play.
10. The student will show responsibility by collecting any equipment used by him or her after class each day.

Answers to Self-Check

1. A
2. B, not stated in terms of observable performance.
3. A
4. B, not stated in terms of observable performance.
5. B, no stated conditions or criteria.
6. B, no stated conditions or criteria.
7. A
8. B, not stated in terms of observable performance.
9. B, not stated in terms of observable performance.
10. A

Content Analysis and Development

Once instructional goals and objectives have been specified, learning activities must be selected to help students achieve these outcomes. Learning activities are determined by the skills or concepts to be learned and the readiness of the learners. The objectives state the performance standard expected of the learners at the conclusion of instruction. To help students achieve each objective, good teachers sequence learning experiences, beginning with less difficult or less complex skills or concepts and gradually add difficulty and complexity.[7] This is accomplished for each skill within a lesson or lessons, as well as for the skills within an entire instructional unit or school curriculum. This process is called content analysis and development. It includes both closed and open motor skills and games skills.

Analyzing and Developing Motor Skill Content

Skillful performance consists of effective, efficient, adaptable performance. Rink suggests that teachers analyze motor skills by asking three questions:

1. What does it mean to be skilled with this content?
2. What does a skilled performer look like?
3. What must the performer do to adjust to the conditions of the game or event?[8]

The first question deals with the student's ability to use the skill to accomplish its intended purpose, its effectiveness. After defining the desired performance, the teacher must develop a progression or sequence of learning experiences called *extension tasks,* manipulations of the movement that will lead to successful student learning at all stages of the learning environment. This is done by changing or manipulating the difficulty or complexity of the skill as shown in Table 8.5.

The second question is concerned with the quality or efficiency of the performance. Rink calls this *refinement.* The performance should be mechanically correct for the performer for the given situation. Quality of performance is important at all levels of skill development and often indicates readiness to move to higher levels of difficulty or complexity. The teacher concentrates on performance cues to refine performance.

The third question asks the student to adapt or apply the skill to a game or event. This is called *application.* It is the ability to adjust to different conditions of game play.

Content analysis begins with extension (manipulation)—a list of progressively more difficult or complex skills. These are created by adapting such factors as equipment, skill instruction, spatial arrangements, players, desired outcomes, and game play or performance (see Table 8.5). A good progression resulting in student success and learning makes increases in only one area at a time. Table 5.8 in Chapter 5 lists ways to increase task difficulty. This table can serve as a guide in building progressions and decreasing the probability of missing an important step in the progression. Table 8.6 shows content analysis for the volleyball forearm pass.

Quality of movement or skill refinement must be monitored at all levels of skill development to ensure correct performance. Students often regress to a less mature or incorrect movement pattern in order to be successful. For each task listed in the extension (manipulation) column, the expected quality of good performance is identified. These qualities clarify performance expectations for the skill and are usually used as teaching cues at each level of instruction, as cues to direct teacher observation of student success, and as feedback cues.

The application column focuses on how to use the skill in a self-testing, competitive, or performance setting. In other words, the focus is on doing the activity, rather than how to do the skill. These activities usually dominate class time. This setting must be congruent with each student's level of performance and the type of skill to be taught. These activities may be as simple as "How many consecutive hits can you have in your threesome?" or "How many free throws can you make out of ten tries?" Application activities should occur throughout skill learning, not just as a game at the end of the learning sequence.

TABLE 8.5 Techniques for Decreasing or Increasing Complexity or Difficulty of Skills

	Less Complex	More Complex	Examples
EQUIPMENT MODIFICATIONS			
Weight, size, or hardness of object	Lighter, smaller, softer ball or object (discus, shot)	Regulation ball or object hard ball or object	Volleyball, basketball, archery, bowling, tennis
Height of net or goal	Lower net or basket	Regulation height of net or goal	Volleyball, basketball
Height of equipment	Lower balance beam, etc.	Official equipment	Gymnastics, hurdles, high jump
Length of implement	Shorter racket, club, ski, bat (or choke up)	Official equipment	Tennis, golf, skiing, softball
Size of target or goal	Increased size of target or goal	Official size or decreased size	Basketball, soccer, softball
Shape of object	Round	Oblong, flat, or irregular	Football, frisbee
SKILL MODIFICATIONS			
Part vs. whole practice	Whole-part-whole, progressive part, backward chaining, etc.	Whole skills	Swimming, folk or square dance, basketball lay-up, tennis serve
Use of implement	Hand-eye coordination without implement	Use of implements (implement-eye coordination)	Tennis, racquetball, badminton
Player stationary or moving	Stationary or forward movement of performer	Sideward or backward movement of performer	Badminton, volleyball, softball, basketball
Ball or object stationary or moving	Stationary ball or object	Moving ball or object, moving performer and object	Soccer, basketball, batting
Direction of oncoming object	Receiving ball or object from straight ahead	Receiving from different directions	Volleyball, basketball, soccer, softball
Direction of intended movement	Sending ball or object straight ahead	Redirecting pass to a different space	Volleyball, basketball, soccer
Level or distance of object from body	Object in most desired position for easy play (use of ball machine or tosser)	Object on ground, overhead, or away from body (pitched or served ball)	Volleyball, softball, basketball, tennis
Speed or force of oncoming object	Decreased speed or force (hitting to fence or partner)	Increased speed or force (hitting to backboard or wall)	Volleyball serve reception, softball pitch and batting, tennis
Speed or force of intended movement	Decreased speed or force	Increased speed or force	Tennis, volleyball, racquetball, folk or social dance (with music)
Dominant or nondominant hand	Dominant hand or side	Nondominant hand or side	Basketball dribble, lay-up
Skill combinations	Isolated skills	Combinations of skills	Volleyball—pass, set, spike; Softball—field and throw; Basketball—pass, shoot, rebound
SPATIAL ARRANGEMENTS			
Distance between players or from target	Shorter distances between players or from basket or net requires less force or speed	Longer distances between players or from the target requires more force or speed	Softball, volleyball, basketball, soccer, football
Number of players in space	Playing area of moderate size for keep-away games	Smaller playing area increases player interaction, and skill difficulty	Basketball, soccer

Continued

TABLE 8.5 Continued

	Less Complex	More Complex	Examples
NUMBER OF PLAYERS			
Relationship of offensive players	One or two stationary players	Three or more requires receiving from one direction and passing or throwing to another moving player	Volleyball, softball, basketball
Relationship of defensive player or players	No defense or stationary defense	With moving defensive player(s)	Basketball, field hockey, flag football
DESIRED OUTCOME			
Direction Distance Speed Accuracy Strategy	Focus on the skill itself	Focus on placement, or accuracy, distance, speed, or an opponent	Tennis, softball, archery, bowling, golf, volleyball, track and field events, football, field hockey
GAME PLAY OR PERFORMANCE			
Simple vs. complex games	Modified games; simulated performances	Official game; actual performances	Pickleball vs. tennis; 3-on-3 vs. basketball; minivolley vs. volleyball
Use of strategies or choreography	Effective and efficient use of the skills themselves	Complex strategies and choreographies	All ball games, dance, gymnastics
Cooperative vs. competitive	Cooperative play	Competitive play	All ball games, dance, gymnastics

Several applications may be operating simultaneously to meet the needs of all students.

Analyzing and Developing Content for Closed Skills

Closed skills are done in a relatively stable environment. Examples of closed skills are archery, bowling, gymnastics, golf, the basketball free throw, the placekick in soccer, and hitting a ball from a batting tee. For closed skills, fixation of the motor skill is the goal. Learning involves concentrating on the identical elements in the body and the environment and striving for consistency in executing the motor plan. Students can learn to "feel" the correct movements through kinesthetic perception of their own body movements. Occasionally, removing knowledge of results (such as by removing an archery target or bowling pins) is valuable to force students to focus on refining the skill first. Targets can be large at first and then gradually reduced in size until students acquire accuracy. Teacher aids, such as having students dive over a stick or putting a towel on the bowling lane for students to aim at, can also be helpful.

Some closed skills must be adapted to different conditions such as the amount of oil on bowling lanes, wind or rain in archery, or spectators during a basketball free throw. Others must be adapted to different environments such as sand traps in golf, different pin set-ups in spare bowling, and defensive player positions such as for a serve in volleyball or tennis. Closed skills should be practiced until they are efficient and consistent and then practiced in the different environments in which they might be used.

To develop extension (manipulation) activities for closed skills, the identification might look like this:

VOLLEYBALL SERVE

1. To serve a volleyball
   a. to different places on the court—long or short; left, center, or right.
   b. with or without spin.
2. To decide where on the court to serve the ball and what kind of spin based on the position of the opponents and their strengths and weaknesses.

BOWLING STRIKES

1. To adjust the stance, approach speed, and release point to adjust to variations of oil on the lanes.
2. To determine
   a. whether there is too much oil on the lane or too little and where it is on the lane.
   b. whether to use the same or a different ball.
   c. whether to adjust the stance, the approach speed, the release point, or several of these factors together.

TABLE 8.6 Example of Content Analysis for the Forearm Pass in Volleyball

Extension	Refinement	Application
Develop arm position	—Back of one hand in palm of other —Forearms as flat as possible —Elbows locked and arms straight	—Proper position done on command —Do arm position with eyes closed
Stance	—Feet at least shoulder width apart —90° at hip, back at 45° to floor —Knees bent —Heel to toe position —Head up —Seat down —Weight on balls of feet	—Position on command —Move while in position (forward, right, left, back)
Hitting mechanics	—Ball will contact midforearms —"Shrug" shoulders —Contact will be made waist high at midline of body —Head still —Hands will separate after contact —Keep arms straight —Force	—Practice hitting without ball —Pretend to hit the ball to each other
Stationary hitting using Volley Lite from hold from drop from toss	—Forearm contact —Controlled straight direction of ball —Hit will be equal to height of drop/toss	—Hitter must do three in a row correctly —Tosser forms circle with arms at shoulder height and hitter will hit ball through circle seven out of ten times
Movement forward lateral backward	—Step-slide-jumpstop to ready position —Stay low	—Direction drills (teacher indicates direction of movement) —Touch floor at each step
Hitting with movement forward lateral backward	—Same as above hitting mechanics and movement —Eye contact with ball —Correct arm position, stance, and hitting mechanics (see cues for each of these above)	—Hit five out of ten back to partner

Practice of each of the skill responses suggested above will help students learn to make correct decisions about which adaptations to make in a given situation.

Analyzing and Developing Content for Open Skills

Open skills take place in unpredictable environments in which the players keep changing places, and objects move through space. Adjustments must be made in speed, timing, and space, such as in the height and speed of a softball pitch or the interaction of players on a basketball court. Skill diversification is required to meet the multitude of environmental conditions. Therefore, practice must include a variety of situations. At first, combinations of two or three variables may be practiced, but later practice must include all possible variables. Practice should not consistently occur with any particular combination, or a fixation might occur. Students can be helped to set goals for accuracy, distance, speed, quality of movement, and reduction of errors.

To develop extension (manipulation) activities for open skills, teachers must identify the skill responses and decisions that will be required in game play. For example:

TABLE 8.6 Example of Content Analysis for the Forearm Pass in Volleyball

Extension	Refinement	Application
Controlled hitting between partners	—Correct arm position, stance, and hitting mechanics —Control	—Volley six times within partners —Continuous volley 30 seconds
Hitting in a threesome	—Same as above —Face direction of receiving the ball, then angle arms on contact to redirect the ball	—Volley six times within threesome —Continuous volley 30 seconds
Pass from increased distance	—Check hitting mechanics —Stopped before contact	—Two of five tosses returned to target area
Increase speed	—Same as above	
Toss across net; decreased target area	—Eye contact with ball —Concentration	—Pass from toss across net to target. Team point scored for each pass caught by target.
Receiving serve as a team	—Communication	3 o o 2 o o 1 ⊗ ⊗ ⊗ T Teacher tosses randomly to passers who hit to target (⊗). One point for each catch.
Toss, then three forearm passes across the net	—Communication —Hitting mechanics	—Winners stay drill
Three pass game	—Communication —Hitting mechanics	—Game: Start with toss; score points for three hits on a side and hit over the net

Source: Developed by Brent Duncan, Kim Duncan, Chris Neideck, David Wagner, Tom Terlep, and Doug Haynes at Ball State University.

VOLLEYBALL FOREARM PASS

1. Receives the serve and passes it (changing direction) to the setter in the front row so that the setter can get under it for a good set.
   a. Receives ball from many directions.
   b. Moves in all directions to meet ball.
   c. Absorbs and redirects force of balls of various speeds.
   d. Moves to offensive position for next skill.
2. Decides when to play the ball and when to allow a teammate to play the ball.

Teachers have a responsibility to ensure safe and successful practice conditions and to keep students from developing bad habits. Practice makes skills permanent, whether or not they are correct. When students practice parts of skills too long, they lose the rhythm of the entire movement and have difficulty putting the parts together. Sometimes open skills are taught as closed skills, such as teaching children to bat from a tee prior to learning to bat a pitched ball. If practiced too long as closed skills, learners may not be able to adapt to the different environmental conditions of a pitched ball, since new motor patterns must be learned in the new environment. The teacher must decide whether it is better to begin with the closed skill and then spend the time to learn the skill in the open situation, or to begin with the open skill. Similarly, equipment modifications may be used to allow learners to achieve success or to overcome fear. Consideration must be given to both student success and correct performance. Rules may be adapted to increase time spent on skills, such as playing cooperative volleyball or eliminating free throws in basketball or huddles in flag football.

Analyzing and Developing Content for Games Skills

A common mistake is to jump from practice drills directly into competitive games before students have had time to refine their skills. The complex nature of the game almost ensures a regression to less desirable movement patterns because skills required in game situations require a shift in ability.[9]

Rink proposed a four-stage process to ready students for participation in games. Stage 1 involves the *ability to control the object,* including the following:[10]

1. Consistently *directs objects* (throws, strikes) to a specified place with the intended force.
2. *Obtains possession of an object* (catches, collects) from any direction, level, or speed.
3. *Maintains possession* moving in different ways with different speeds.

These activities include the following:

1. Stationary to moving performer
2. Stationary to moving object
3. Stationary to moving receivers
4. Changing levels, directions, and force of object sent or received

Stage 2 involves *combining skills and adding rules.* The focus is on controlling the object in simple gamelike play. See examples in Table 8.7. Stage 3 involves using the skills with simple offensive and defensive strategies in *less complex game situations* (lead-up games) such as keep-away games (e.g., one-on-one, one-on-two, two-on-two). Players, boundaries, scoring, and rules can be changed to gradually increase the complexity of the games. Stage 4 consists of *sport games,* modified at first to keep the play continuous by eliminating free throws, huddles, free kicks, volleyball serves, jump balls, and so on. At this level students may learn specialized player positions, rules, penalties, scoring, and out-of-bounds plays. These stages agree with Barrett's three-phase process of game playing (stages two and three are combined) and Graham's levels of precontrol, control, utilization, and proficiency. All agree that the middle stages are critical and often "missed entirely or passed through so quickly as to have no effect."[11] Table 8.7 highlights content analysis for the game skill of volleyball.[12]

Studies show that teachers often place students in game situations before they have sufficient skill to be successful. To make the transition from skill drills to game play, students should practice all possible skill combinations in less complex situations prior to using them in game play. Teachers can choose or create drills and lead-up games that force students to move to the ball, to direct the ball to a moving target, or to practice under the innumerable conditions that occur in game play. For example, rather than have students hit a volleyball back and forth to a partner, a threesome forces students to direct the ball to a place different from the point of origin. Elementary physical education textbooks often include self-testing or modified games and activities that are appropriate for the intermediate stages of learning. Examples include these:

Do correct skills.

Do correct skills (hits, shots) in a row.

How far can you throw, jump, and so on?

How long can you keep the ball in the air?

How many consecutive hits, shots, and so on can you get?

How many hits, shots, and so on can you get in the goal?

How fast can you dribble to a specified place without losing control?

Can you dribble without looking at the ball?

Maintain possession as long as possible without losing control (play dribble tag).

Move the ball to a goal with a partner without losing control.

Do the skill so quietly we can't hear you hit the ball.

Do as few elementary back strokes as possible in twenty-five yards.

See how many pass-set-spike sequences you can do.

Young discussed ways to improve practice drills to make them more gamelike. She suggested placing cones at random rather than in straight lines for dribbling practice, with several players moving at a time so that students learn to adapt to changing circumstances.[13] Modified games help bridge the gap between skill drills and game play. Games with fewer players per team force low-ability students to be involved and provide more opportunities for contacting the ball. (See Chapter 5 for more ideas on how to modify games.)

Team strategies should not be introduced before students feel secure with the basic skills and individual offensive and defensive tactics, such as marking or guarding, playing one's position, or shooting without being guarded, have been taught.

The final result of skill learning is accurate, consistent, adaptable, coordinated motor responses. Automatic skill execution enables the learner to devote attention to the game plan and strategy. Rather than paying attention to each part of a skill, the elements are chunked into a skill or even a combination of skills. Performers learn where to look and what to look at, how to differentiate relevant and irrelevant information, and how to predict outcomes from cues. In essence, students learn to integrate movements and information into schemas that help them to select appropriate movement responses for a wide variety of conditions, to monitor outcomes and to guide their own learning.[14] The teacher must continually reflect on the teaching process and make necessary corrections and adjustments. Figure 8-1 illustrates this process (see also Chapter 7).

Review Questions: Name and give examples of the three components of Rink's content analysis system.

Name and give examples of Rink's four stages of game play.

TABLE 8.7 Example of Content Analysis for Game Skills: Volleyball

Extension	Refinement	Application	Concepts
STAGE 1			
Skill: Forearm Pass			
See Table 8.6			Legal pass. Cues for pass.
Skill: Set or Overhand Pass			
(similar progression to Table 8.6)			Legal set. Cues for set.
STAGE 2			
Skills: Forearm Pass and Set			
Alternate passes and sets with movement—forward, laterally, and backward. Hit to other players.	Work on legal, accurate passes and sets to another player.	Fifteen consecutive.	Legal hits. Cues for passes and sets.
Receiving a tossed ball and passing to a setter who sets into a hoop attached to a pole.	Legal, accurate passes to center front and accurate sets to side front hoop.	Hit ball through hoop seven out of ten times.	Positions for setter and hitter in relation to passer.
Increase force of toss.			
As above, receive and pass from different positions on court.	Same as above. Face ball, angle arms.	Hit ball through hoop seven out of ten times.	Same as above.
Three-on-three, last player hits it over.	Same as above.	Start with a toss. Score one point for three hits on a side—pass, set, hit over.	Pass-set-hit sequence.
STAGE 1			
Skill: Spike			
(Teach toss, hitting action, footwork, and spike from held, tossed, and set ball on low net with Volley Lite ball.)			
STAGE 2			
Skills: All Skills Except Serve			
Spiker sets ball to setter, who sets for spiker to spike.	Work on accuracy and getting ball over net.	Ten spikes over net.	Net rules involving spike.
Toss ball over net, pass, set, spike.	Same as above.	Ten spikes over net.	Net rules.
Play three-on-three using pass-set-spike sequence.	Work on accuracy and getting ball over net on spike.	Start with a toss. Score one point for three hits on a side—pass, set, hit over.	Pass-set-hit sequence.
Increase height of net gradually to regulation height out of games and then in games.	Same as above.	Same as above.	

Continued

TABLE 8.7 Continued

Extension	Refinement	Application	Concepts
STAGE 1			
	Skill: Serve		
(Teach toss, hitting action, footwork, and serve from close, medium, and regulation distance with Volley Lite ball.)			
STAGE 3			
	Skills: Serve, Pass, Set, Spike		
Play cooperation volleyball.	Work on accuracy and pass-set-spike sequences.	Score one point for each pass-set-spike sequence. Team making an error serves. Try to score as many points as possible.	Pass-set-spike sequence.
Play minivolley on half courts (two games on each court).	Work on accuracy and pass-set-spike sequences.	Regular scoring, with bonus points for pass-set-spike sequences or spikes or whatever skill needs emphasis.	Rules.
STAGE 4: GAME PLAY			
Play official volleyball games.	Maintain accuracy of skills.	Play as above.	Official rules.
4-2 offense.	Every player must set and spike; rotate setters and spikers.	Play as above.	4-2 offense.
2-1-3 defense.	Same as above.	Play as above.	2-1-3 defense.
Play tournament.	Every player must set one full round; every player must spike successfully once a day.	Play official rules.	All listed above.

Note: In the interests of space, this table does not include all aspects of the game of volleyball.

Sources: Cooperation volleyball: G. Madden and C. McGown, "The Effect of the Inner Game Method versus the Progressive Method on Learning Motor Skills," *Journal of Teaching in Physical Education* 9 (1989): 39–48. Minivolley: J. Kessel, *Coaches Guide to Beginning Volleyball Programs,* United States Volleyball Association/Boys Clubs of America, 1988.

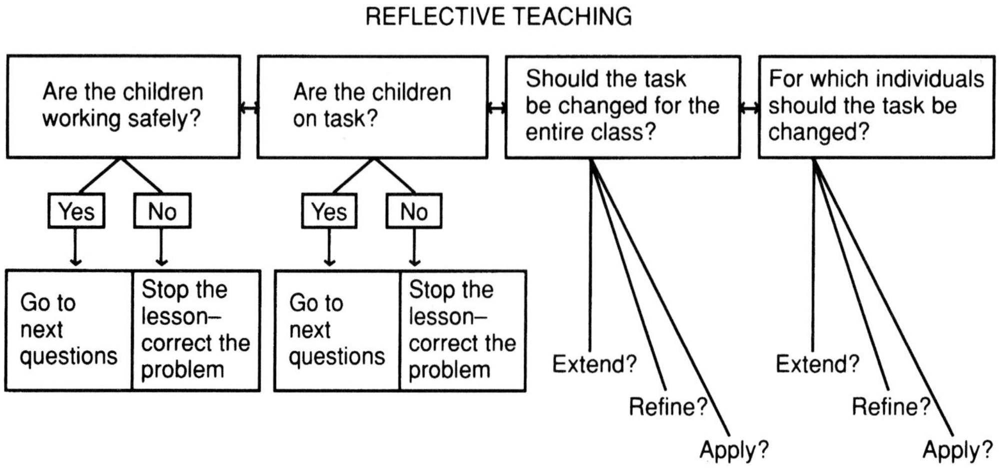

Figure 8-1

Reflective teaching.

Source: George Graham and R. Tait McKenzie, *Symposium on Sport* (Knoxville; University of Tennessee, 1989).

NOTES

1. National Association for Sport and Physical Education, *Moving into the Future: National Physical Education Standards,* 2nd ed. (Reston, VA: Author, 2004).
2. R. F. Mager, *Preparing Instructional Objectives,* 2nd ed. (Belmont, CA: Pitman Learning, 1975), 2.
3. B. S. Bloom, G. F. Madaus, and J. T. Hastings, *Evaluation to Improve Learning* (New York: McGraw-Hill, 1981), 33.
4. R. W. Burns, *New Approaches to Behavioral Objectives* (Dubuque, IA: Brown, 1972), 58–59.
5. B. N. Lee, and M. D. Merrill, *Writing Complete Affective Objectives: A Short Course* (Belmont, CA: Wadsworth, 1972).
6. Lee and Merrill, *Writing Complete Affective Objectives.*
7. J. E. Rink, *Teaching Physical Education for Learning,* 5th ed. (Boston: McGraw-Hill, 2006).
8. Rink, *Teaching Physical Education.*
9. R. A. Schmidt, *Motor Control and Learning: A Behavioral Emphasis,* 3rd ed. (Champaign, IL: Human Kinetics, 1999).
10. Rink, *Teaching Physical Education.*
11. G. Graham, S. Holt/Hale, and M. Parker, *Children Moving: A Reflective Approach to Teaching Physical Education,* 6th ed. (New York: McGraw-Hill, 2004); K. R. Barrett, Games teaching: Adaptable skills, versatile players, *Journal of Physical Education and Recreation* 48, no. 7 (1977): 21–24.
12. R. Barrett, Games teaching.
13. J. E. Young, When practice doesn't make perfect—Improving game performance in secondary level physical education classes, *Journal of Physical Education, Recreation, and Dance, 56,* no. 8 (1985): 24–26.
14. Schmidt, *Motor Control and Learning.*

CHAPTER

9

INSTRUCTIONAL STYLES AND STRATEGIES

STUDY STIMULATORS

1. What are direct and indirect instruction? When would each be used?
2. What factors influence the selection of a teaching style?
3. What is the Spectrum of Teaching? Describe a situation in which you would use each of the styles.
4. How would you incorporate individualized instruction into your teaching?
5. What is mastery learning and what are its components?
6. What is cooperative learning? How is it implemented?
7. How do problem-solving strategies fit into the physical education learning environment?
8. Which instructional strategies would you feel comfortable using in a class?

"Great instructors nourish individual differences."[1] They are aware that each student has unique aptitudes and needs that must be addressed. Teaching is said to be both an art and a science. It is an art in that each teacher decides what will best guide students to learn, while adding a personal touch to the process. It is a science in that when certain principles of learning are operating, a distinct outcome is usually the result.

Excellent teachers become experienced at making wise decisions. They select objectives at the correct level of difficulty for students; they select and use teaching activities that are directly relevant to daily objectives; they monitor student learning continuously; and they apply known principles of learning.[2] No teaching strategy or behavior has been shown to enhance learning for all students. The best physical educators develop a repertoire of styles and strategies to aid them in the teaching process. Many such options are presented in this chapter to give teachers alternatives to maximize the efficiency with which all their students achieve the desired objectives of the program.

TEACHING STYLES

Styles can range on a continuum from those designated as *direct instruction,* or teacher-centered, to those designated as *indirect instruction,* or student-centered. Direct instruction styles are used when the acquisition of basic skills is the goal.[3] Indirect instruction styles are selected to enhance creativity and independence, or change the attitudes of students.[4] Teachers most often use the direct style of teaching. Research findings have consistently substantiated that direct instruction (lecture/demonstration, drill, practice, feedback) is more effective than indirect instruction for students learning basic academic skills in elementary schools.[5] Direct instruction creates a structured teaching-learning environment that contains the following:

1. A focus on appropriate academic goals and content
2. Teacher-controlled coverage of extensive content through structured learning activities and appropriate pacing
3. Sufficient time on-task for student success
4. Monitoring of pupil performance
5. A task-oriented but relaxed environment
6. Immediate, academically oriented feedback

Selecting a Teaching Style

The selection of a teaching style depends on a thoughtful evaluation of the learning situation, including (1) the students, (2) the subject matter content to be taught, (3) the teacher, (4) the learning environment, and (5) time.

Students

One consideration in choosing a learning activity is the total educational needs of students—physical, intellectual, emotional, and social. Younger children will need a much more structured learning environment than older students, with the teacher directing most of the activities. Sooner or later, however, the students must learn to take the initiative for their own learning. Since it is the individual student who does the learning, consideration must be given to the different ways in which students learn best. Different personalities, aptitudes, experiences, and interests combine to make each learner unique in the way he or she responds to a given style of teaching. Tyler emphasized that a teacher must have some understanding of the interests and background of students to set up the desired learning environment.[6] Rink pointed out that low-ability students, as well as those who are unmotivated, unsociable, and nonconforming, seem to perform better in unstructured environments, whereas high-ability, motivated, sociable, conforming students perform better in structured environments.[7] School demographics are changing rapidly and becoming more diverse. Different cultures and races bring different needs and require different strategies for effectiveness. Teachers must consider the variety of needs of individual students when planning both the environment of the learning situation and the learning task.

Hawley suggested that using a variety of teaching styles increases the likelihood that the learner will find one suited to his or her own learning style and will be motivated to achieve class goals. He also suggested that many students are only familiar with traditional styles of teaching and will have to be taught that learning can occur in a variety of ways.[8]

Subject Matter Content

A second consideration in planning instruction is the specific ideas or skills to be taught. Obviously, some methods work best for some activities while other methods work better with other activities. For example, teaching an idea or skill at the lower levels of the cognitive or psychomotor taxonomy (refer to Chapter 5) might require a more structured approach, whereas the upper levels of the taxonomies might incorporate student experiences utilizing creativity and problem solving. Affective behaviors suffer under some teaching styles and blossom with others. A knowledge of the concepts and skills in various activities can help the physical education instructor select appropriate teaching strategies.

Teacher

The teacher is a major consideration in the selection of learning activities. Some methods work better for some teachers than for others. Each teacher selects a comfortable teaching style in terms of his or her own personality and talents. The best teachers experiment with many styles until they are comfortable with a wide range from which they can choose as the learning situation changes. They must also learn to be sensitive to feedback from the students and the learning environment and use that feedback to modify their teaching behavior.

Learning Environment

A fourth consideration is the learning environment. A school or class that focuses on basic skills would predominantly use a direct instructional style. Brophy concluded that students who receive most of their instruction from the teacher do better than those who are expected to learn on their own or from each other.[9] Each teaching style establishes a unique social environment for a specific group of learners. The social system becomes a part of the learning experience along with the subject matter to be taught. Understanding the social system in a more diverse environment becomes critical to effective teaching and learning. Students learn competitiveness, cooperation, democratic processes, and other social skills as environments change within the school. The teaching style influences the way students react to each other, to the teacher, and to others outside the class environment.

Time

Time is the fifth consideration. Early in the school year or in a new unit of activity, the teacher may choose to use a structured teaching style. Later on, as the teacher gets to know the students' capabilities and learning styles, the teacher may choose a more informal approach. Another time variable is the allocation of practice minutes built into the teaching style. Graham substantiated that students who learned more had teachers who provided them with more time to practice the criterion skill.[10]

Review Question: What factors should be considered in the selection of a teaching style?

BOX 9.1

Preimpact, Impact, and Postimpact Decisions in Each of the Learning Styles on the Spectrum of Teaching

PREIMPACT, IMPACT, AND POSTIMPACT DECISION MAKERS

Style	Preimpact	Impact	Postimpact
Command style (A)	T	T	T
Practice style (B)	T	L	T
Reciprocal style (C)	T	D	O
Self-check style (D)	T	L	L
Inclusion style (E)	T	L	L
Guided-discovery style (F)	T	T-L	T-L
Convergent discovery (G)	T	L-T	L-T
Divergent production style (H)	T	L-T	L-T
Learner-designed style (I)	T	L	L
Learner-initiated style (J)	L	L-T	L
Self-teaching style (K)	L	L	L

T = Teacher D = Doer
L = Learner O = Observer

Source: Concepts from Muska Mosston and Sara Ashworth, *Teaching Physical Education,* 4th ed. (New York: Macmillan College Publishing Company, 1994).

The Spectrum of Teaching Styles

A useful way of classifying teaching styles according to "direct" or "indirect" is Mosston's spectrum.[11] The spectrum describes a number of alternative teaching styles that provide teachers with a knowledge of the roles of teacher and learner and the objectives that can be achieved with each style. This permits teachers to move back and forth along the spectrum as needed to meet the changing needs of students, environments, and subject matter.

Mosston described teaching behavior as a "chain of decision making." The anatomy of a style categorizes decisions as being made before (preimpact), during (impact), or following (postimpact) the interaction between teacher and learner. The teaching style is identified by specifying who—teacher or learner—makes which decisions. Each style has been identified by name and letter and is called a "landmark" style. Eleven styles have been identified so far, ranging from style A (command), which is a complete teacher decision-making style, to style K (self-teaching), which is a complete learner decision-making style. An infinite variety of other styles exhibit characteristics of two adjoining styles and fall under the "canopies" of these landmark styles.

Each style of teaching creates different conditions for learning founded on the decision-making process. Box 9.1 illustrates who makes decisions at what stage of impact. Based on who makes these decisions, the styles then appear to form organized clusters along the spectrum. The spectrum is organized into two clusters of styles on either side of the discovery threshold. Styles A to E represent reproduction styles. Styles F to K represent discovery and production of the unknown. Box 9.2 lists the characteristics of each cluster.

Research validating specific application of the spectrum is sparse and sometimes conflicts with other studies. Very little research has been conducted on the discovery and production cluster.[12] Goldberger and his associates found in studies of fifth-grade children using the direct styles of B, C, and E that all of the styles facilitated learning. In one study, style B produced the most effective results.[13] Another study revealed that average-aptitude children responded best to the conditions provided by style B, whereas exceptional children, the combination of children with above- and below-average aptitude, profited more from the conditions provided by style E. Beckett determined that style B was the most effective way to teach a soccer skill to college students.[14]

Salter and Graham found that when elementary school children were taught a novel golf task using the command, guided-discovery, and no instruction methodologies, no significant differences existed between the groups on skill improvement or self-efficacy. However, cognitive understanding improved significantly for the groups taught by the command and guided-discovery approaches.[15]

Pettigrew and Heikkinen reported that on twelve measures of achievement for students taught using a variety of spectrum styles, as compared with those taught by one style, nine measures showed significantly higher achievement by students. The authors suggested that teachers who effectively accommodate the learning needs of students use a variety of instructional styles.[16]

BOX 9.2

Characteristics of the Clusters of Teaching Styles

COMMON CHARACTERISTICS OF STYLES A–K

Common Characteristics (Objectives) of Styles A–E

1. Reproduction of knowledge and skills (known to the teacher and/or the learner)
2. The subject matter is concrete, mainly containing facts, rules, and specific skills. (Basic knowledge, Fixed knowledge)
3. There is one correct way to perform the task—by emulation of the presented model.
4. Time is needed for practicing and learning to adhere to the model.
5. The cognitive operations mainly engaged are memory and recall.
6. Feedback is specific and refers to the performance of the task and its approximation to the model.
7. Individual differences are accepted only within the learner's physical and emotional boundaries.
8. The class climate (the spirit of the learning environment) is one of performing the model, repetition, and reduction of errors.

Common Characteristics (Objectives) of Styles F–K

1. Production of knowledge and skills new to the learner and/or the teacher.
2. The subject matter is variable, mainly containing concepts, strategies, and principles.
3. Alternatives in design and performance are called for. There is no single model to emulate.
4. Time is needed for the cognitive processes involved.
5. Time is needed to evolve an affective climate conducive to producing and accepting alternatives and options.
6. The cognitive operations engaged are comparing, contrasting, categorizing, problem solving, inventing, and others.
7. Discovery and creativity are manifested through these cognitive operations.
8. Discovery by the learner is developed through convergent and divergent processes or a combination of both.
9. Feedback refers to producing alternatives and not a single solution.
10. Individual differences in the quantity, rate, and kind of production are essential to maintaining and continuing these styles.
11. The class climate (the spirit of the learning environment) is one of searching, examining the validity of alternatives, and going beyond the known.

Source: Muska Mosston and Sara Ashworth, *Teaching Physical Education,* 4th ed. (New York: Macmillan College Publishing Company, 1994).

Teachers incorporating the spectrum move freely along the spectrum as students are ready to make more and more decisions, selecting one or more applicable styles for use during each episode of a particular lesson or unit of activity. An episode is defined as "a unit of time during which the teacher and learner are in the same style, heading toward the same objective."[17] A lesson is composed of one or more episodes of varying lengths of time. Often several styles may be employed in a single lesson. Students should be involved as much as possible in the selection of methods that affect them and in the application of methods on the higher cognitive levels. Using a variety of methods provides students with different learning styles and the opportunity to find their niche in the learning experience. It also prevents boredom and the "inverted U" phenomenon that can result from overuse of a single style. (The *inverted U phenomenon* refers to a teacher behavior or strategy that has a positive effect on learning but, if continued past a certain point, has a negative effect.)[18]

The following pages present a brief description of the landmark styles of the Spectrum of Teaching. A teacher using each style should be able to incorporate the appropriate decisions of the anatomy.

The Command Style (A)

In the command style, the teacher makes all of the decisions on what, where, when, and how to teach, and on how to evaluate learning and provide feedback. The teacher should tell the class that "the purpose of this style is to learn to do the task accurately and within a short period of time."

Preimpact decisions:

1. Identify subject matter (i.e., swimming, soccer).
2. State the overall lesson objectives.
3. Design the episode (learning experience).

Impact decisions:

1. Explain roles of teacher and learner.
2. Deliver subject matter.
3. Explain logistical procedures.

Postimpact decision:

1. Offer feedback to learner about performance and role in following the teacher decisions.

The command style capitalizes on the teacher's expertise through such teaching/learning strategies as lecture

BOX 9.3

Practice Sheet

Name: ______________________

Students: Do these skills the best you can! While performing the skill, place your paper to the side out of everyone's way. After you are done with each skill, cross it out and work on the next skill. When you are done, work on the skills you had a hard time with. **WORK HARD!!!**

1. **Forward roll**
   Do 4 forward rolls
2. **Tripod**
   Do 3 tripods
3. **Tripod to headstand**
   Do 2 full tripods to headstands
4. **V-Seat**
   Balance in the V-Seat for 10 seconds. Do this 2 times
5. **Cowboy roll**
   Do 4 cowboy rolls
6. **Crab walk**
   Walk for 5 steps forward and 5 steps backward
7. **Backwards roll**
   Do 4 backward rolls
8. **Cartwheel**
   Do 3 cartwheels

☆ **STAY INSIDE THE WHITE LINES OF THE TUMBLING MAT.**

Source: Brian Strong, Ball State University, Muncie, IN.

and other verbal presentations, demonstration, and drill. Homogeneous grouping can be used advantageously during drills to individualize learning. Instructional games can also be used to drill students on such items as terminology and rules. Students are expected to respond as they have been "commanded" to do. This style achieves the objectives of precision, synchronization, and uniformity. It is especially applicable when safety, efficient use of class time, and teacher control are essential.

The disadvantages of command style are that the teacher is unable to give individual feedback and all students are required to progress at the same pace. This style is not responsive to individual differences of students, the pace is determined by the students in the middle. Slower students are left behind and higher skilled students can become bored.

The Practice Style (B)

In the practice style, the teacher determines what is to be taught and how the activity will be evaluated. The students are then given a number of tasks to practice and each learner decides which task to begin with, where to do it, when to begin and end the practice of a particular task, how fast or slow to work, and what to do between tasks. Style B is the one most often used by physical educators.[19] In style B, students are encouraged to clarify the nature of the tasks by asking questions as needed. The teacher moves around the class, offering feedback to each individual. Though quality of the performance is always important, the focus is on the quantity of trials attempted. The teacher should state, "The purpose of this style is to offer you time to work individually and privately and to provide me with time to offer you individual and private feedback."

Preimpact decision:

1. The same as style A.

Impact decisions:

1. The same as style A.
2. Student—practice tasks.

Postimpact decision:

1. Teacher—offer feedback individually to all learners.

By using a variety of tasks, including fitness activities and testing activities, and employing stations, the teacher and students can make use of all of the available space. Tasks sheets, skill checklists, study guides, workbooks, journals, and progress charts are some of the teaching/learning strategies that can be used within this style.

There are two main disadvantages of using the practice style. One is that all students are doing the same task. This style, like command, does not allow adjustments for individual differences. The second disadvantage is that feedback is limited especially if the class is large. If a class has thirty-five students and the activity time is only thirty-five minutes, a teacher will spend less than one minute with each student if some feedback is to be given to everyone. Box 9.3 and Figure 9-1 are examples of practice style task sheets.

The Reciprocal Style (C)

In the reciprocal style, students provide the feedback for each other. One student performs while the other observes and provides feedback. Then the students exchange roles. The teacher decides what tasks are to be accomplished, designs the criteria sheet that will guide the observer in giving feedback, gives the assignments to the students,

Rollerblading
Review of ready position, stances, heel stops, A-frame turn, parallel turn, and crossovers

To the student:

- Look at the *number* next to each skill. Do the skill that many times.
- You do not have to go in the order listed below.
- Try to get to all skills.
- If you finish all skills, then continue skating around the circle or work on the skills listed below.

Ready Position (3 times)

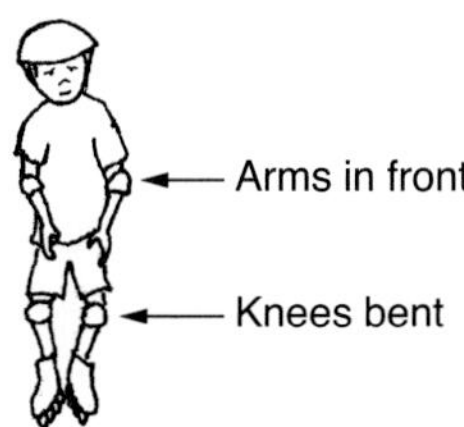

A-Stance (3 times)

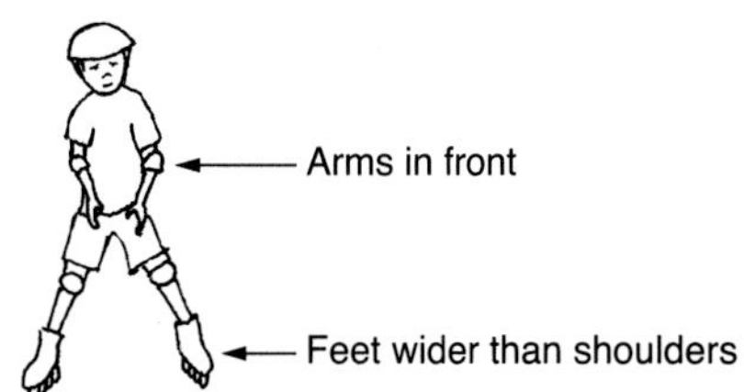

V-Stance (3 times)

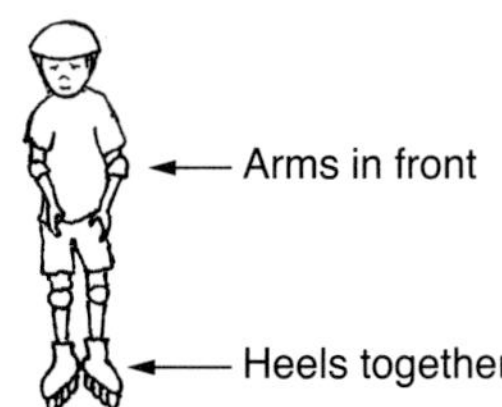

Scissors Stance (3 times)

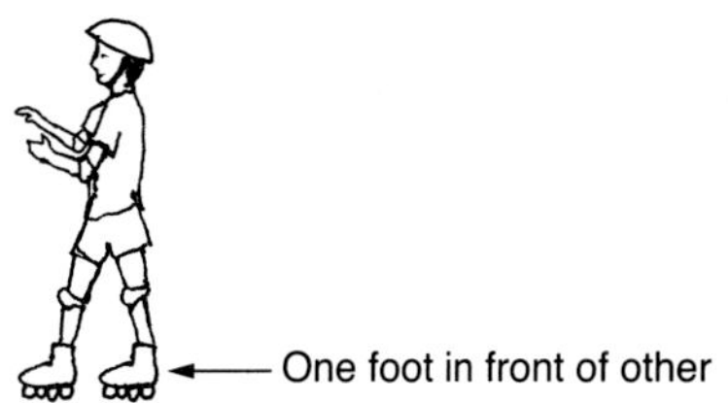

Heel Stop (15)

- Start at white line.
- Do a heel stop when you come to a cone.

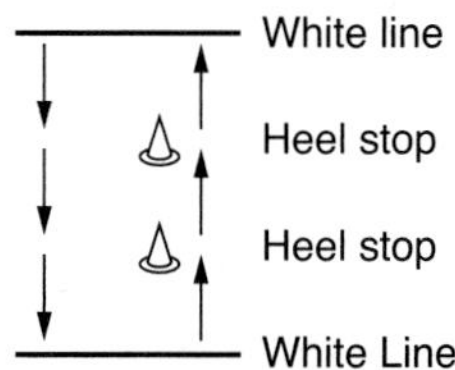

A-frame Turn (10)

- Start at yellow tape mark.
- Skate down to cone and do an A-frame turn.
- Come back and do another one.

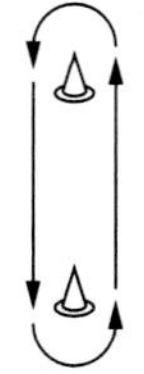

Parallel Turn (10)

- Start at yellow tape mark.
- Skate down to cone and do a parallel turn.
- Come back and do another one.

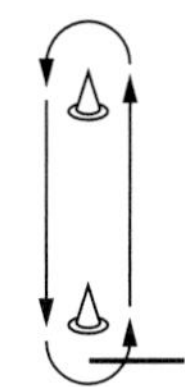

Crossover Turns (20 circles)

- Do 5 circles around a cone then rest.
- Do this 4 times for a total of 20.

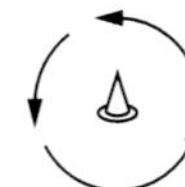

Figure 9-1

Practice style task sheet.

Source: Amber Gaskin, Ball State University, Muncie, IN.

and helps the observers improve their ability as observers and their ability to communicate with their partners. The teacher states, "The purposes of this style are to work with a partner and to offer feedback to your partner."

Preimpact decisions:

1. The same as style A.
2. Design and prepare criteria sheet for observer.

Impact decisions:

1. Teacher—set up logistics; set scene for new roles.
2. Student—understand and perform role of doer and observer.
3. Student—perform the task.

Postimpact decisions:

1. Student—(observer) receive criteria; observe doer's performance, compare and contrast performance with criteria, conclude correctness of performance; communicate results to doer; initiate communication with teacher, if necessary.
2. Teacher—answer questions of observer (do not usurp role of observer).

Socialization between students is an inherent part of the reciprocal style. Students also develop feedback skills and enhance learning in the cognitive domain. A student should receive feedback for each trial attempted. Reciprocal style contributes more to student development in all three domains than most of the other styles.

The two main disadvantages to using the reciprocal style are that feedback may be inaccurate and activity for each student is limited to only 50 percent of the available practice time. The quality of the feedback will depend upon the criteria provided and the training given to the student observer as well as the teacher's ability to move quickly around the class. When each student serves both as a performer and as an observer, only half of the activity time is available for practice.

The Self-Check Style (D)

In the self-check style, the feedback is provided by the individual learner instead of by the teacher or another student. The selection of tasks is important so that students can evaluate their own performance. Events that provide external feedback—such as making baskets, kicking a football over the goalposts, or hitting a target with an object—facilitate student self-evaluation. A student can "see" the performance through the use of mirrors or film of the performance. Software exists to compare the performance with that of an "expert." The role of the teacher is to help the students become better self-evaluators. The teacher should state, "The purpose of this style is to learn to do a task and check your own work."

Preimpact decisions:

1. The same as style A.
2. Prepare subject matter.
3. Prepare criteria sheet for self-check.

Impact decisions:

1. Teacher—set up logistics; set scene for new role; answer questions.
2. Student—understand role as a doer.
3. Student—perform the tasks.

Postimpact decisions:

1. Student—assess one's performance against criteria.
2. Teacher—offer feedback to learner about his or her role in self-check.

The self-check style can increase self-esteem for students who are comfortable working independently. A number of different teaching/learning strategies can be used within the self-check style: testing activities used as learning activities, computer-assisted instruction (CAI), individualized learning packets, and contract learning. One disadvantage of this style is that student interaction with the peer group and with the teacher is at a minimum. Another disadvantage may be the quality of the feedback. It will depend upon the student's ability to analyze errors in his or her own performance.

The Inclusion Style (E)

The major difference between the inclusion style and the styles previously discussed is that in this style the learner selects the level of performance for each task and alters it according to each self-assessment of the performance. The teacher selects the task and defines the various levels of difficulty. The learner selects a level of difficulty that is expected to lead to success. Some factors that contribute to differences in difficulty include distance, height of basket or net, size of ball or implement, weight of ball or implement, size of the target or hoop, angle of shot or kick, quantity of tasks to be done, and body positions. The task to be done must remain the same (e.g., all push-ups or all striking skills). Only degree of difficulty varies. The teacher should state, "The purpose of this style is for everyone to be successful."

The inclusion style permits all students to be successful in the task to be performed.

Preimpact decisions:

1. The same as style A.
2. Prepare the individual program for the tasks.

Impact decisions:

1. Describe the role of the learner.
2. Present the subject matter.
3. Explain logistics.

Postimpact decisions:

1. Teacher—observe class; offer feedback to individual learners.
2. Student—assess performance using criteria sheet.

The inclusion style permits all students to be successful at the task to be performed, thereby increasing each student's self-esteem and enjoyment of physical activity. For this reason, the inclusion style is especially important when teaching coed classes or classes that have students with disabilities. The inclusion style can be combined with other styles. Students choose from an inclusion skill checklist, which is a list of skills that can be performed at many levels. The checklist increases students' awareness of their own abilities and the ability to set realistic goals. Because students select their participation levels, learner anxiety is reduced. The main disadvantage of this style is that the students may be satisfied with less than their best efforts and not be willing to challenge themselves. Some examples follow:

1. Archery—Shoot 200 points in five consecutive ends at
   a. 20 yards.
   b. 25 yards.
   c. 30 yards.
   d. 35 yards.
2. Badminton—Do 10 consecutive underhand drop shots with a partner under a rope placed
   a. 20 inches above the net.
   b. 16 inches above the net.
   c. 12 inches above the net.
3. Volleyball—Volley the ball consecutively against the wall above a line 8 feet high
   a. 5 times.
   b. 10 times.
   c. 15 times.
4. Swimming—Tread water
   a. 15 seconds.
   b. 1 minute.
   c. 2 minutes.

Another example would be in basketball or soccer. The student determines how fast to dribble through an obstacle course. The criterion for success is to not lose control.

Procedures for creating the checklist are listed here:

1. Determine the tasks.
2. For each task, determine one or more factors that change the level of difficulty of the skill.
3. Make a checklist of the tasks, quantity to be done, multiple performance levels, and criteria for successful performance.
4. Have students circle or put an *X* through the starting level and the level completed.

Figure 9-2 is an example of an inclusion style task sheet.

The Guided-Discovery Style (F)

The guided-discovery style leads the learner to discover a concept by answering a sequence of questions that the teacher presents. The teacher's role is to determine the concepts and principles to be taught and the best sequence for guiding the students to the specific response. As the students are involved in these strategies, the teacher varies the size and interrelationship of the steps and the speed of the learning sequence so that students are constantly moving toward the desired objective. The teacher should state, "The purpose of this style is to evoke the correct answer or response."

Preimpact decisions:

1. Determine objectives.
2. Select concept to be discovered.
3. Design sequence of questions leading to the concept.

Impact decisions:

1. Teacher—present questions or clues to elicit the desired response; never tell the answer; maintain a climate of acceptance and patience.
2. Student—respond to sequential questions or clues.

Postimpact decisions:

1. Teacher—provide feedback.
2. Student—discover correct response.

The guided-discovery style requires a warm, accepting environment in which students are allowed time to think through their questions or responses and are helped to experience success in the discovery process. This style also requires a certain amount of risk on the teacher's part. The teacher must be able to trace backward from the desired objective to get the first question and the sequence from which to proceed. Whenever a student response deviates from the desired response, the teacher must be able to ask a question that brings the students back into the desired sequence. The advantage of the discovery style is its ability to help students understand the basic concepts of physical activity. A disadvantage of guided discovery is the time required for students to discover an answer. A teacher could provide the answer in much less time but the depth of understanding would be sacrificed. The quality of the guided discovery experience depends upon the ability of the teacher to ask questions that guide the students to discover the answer themselves. Box 9.4 is an example of a guided discovery script. The teacher, not the students, would use this script.

Name ____________________

Rollerblading/Rollerskating—Jumping

To the student:

- There are four (4) different levels of jumping heights.
- Choose a level where you think you want to start and circle that picture below.

Level 1	**Level 2**	**Level 3**	**Level 4**
Line	Noodle	Small cone	Large cone

- Perform the jump.
- Decide if you want to stay at that level, move up a level, or move down a level.
- Before each jump, circle the level that you chose to do.
- Do a total of **20 jumps**.

BEFORE DOING A JUMP, PLACE PENCIL AND PAPER ON THE FLOOR, OFF TO THE SIDE.

	LEVEL					LEVEL			
1.	1	2	3	4	11.	1	2	3	4
2.	1	2	3	4	12.	1	2	3	4
3.	1	2	3	4	13.	1	2	3	4
4.	1	2	3	4	14.	1	2	3	4
5.	1	2	3	4	15.	1	2	3	4
6.	1	2	3	4	16.	1	2	3	4
7.	1	2	3	4	17.	1	2	3	4
8.	1	2	3	4	18.	1	2	3	4
9.	1	2	3	4	19.	1	2	3	4
10.	1	2	3	4	20.	1	2	3	4

After you have finished all 20 jumps:

- Put a **star** by the level you feel you did best.
- Give task sheet and pencil to teacher.
- Continue to work on jumping.

Figure 9-2

Inclusion style task sheet.

Source: Amber Gaskin, Ball State University, Muncie, IN.

The Convergent Discovery Style (G)

In the convergent discovery style the teacher presents a question or problem and the student—through the use of logic, reasoning, critical thinking, and trial-and-error—discovers a single answer or solution. This style is different from guided discovery in that the student rather than the teacher determines the questions to be answered in solving the problem.

Preimpact decision:

1. Design the problem.

Impact decisions:

1. Teacher—observe learners.
2. Student—search for solution to problem.

Postimpact decisions:

1. Student—verify solution.
2. Teacher—ask questions to assist in verification.

The teacher's role is much different in the convergent discovery style. The teacher must have patience and allow the learner's ideas to evolve. This process takes time and the teacher must not interfere with the process.

The convergent discovery style is not appropriate when a specific performance is desired. Each student or group will be creating a different solution to a problem that has been outlined by the teacher. Each solution, even though all are very different, is correct if the parameters that were established with the problem have been met. Box 9.5 is an example of a convergent discovery task sheet.

BOX 9.4

Guided Discovery Script

GUIDED DISCOVERY

"Dead Ball"

For the teacher:

- Allow students to play the game for a while and then call them in. Most likely it won't go smoothly the first time they try to play it.
- The main question to be answered is, "What should we do to make scoring points easier?" The main answer should be, "Your classmates must get open in various ways in order to touch the ball before a score can be made."

The game is three-on-three, played in a small area with one goal. One team has the ball, and players must use soccer skills to score a goal. Everyone on the team must touch the ball before they can score. After three dead balls are made (counting goals as a dead ball), then they switch offense to defense and vice versa.

Q: Was it hard to score any points?
A: Yes

Q: Why?
A: The other team kept getting the ball. Or
A: Everyone on the team didn't touch the ball.

Q: Why did the other team keep getting the ball? Or
Q: Why couldn't everyone on the team get the ball?
A: We couldn't control it, or I don't know.

Q: What should you do so someone on the other team doesn't get the ball?
A: Pass it to our teammate.

Q: Right, now what should your classmates do to get the ball?
A: Get open.

Q: How can they do that?
A: Come to the ball.

Q: Good, what are some kinds of passes you can use to get the ball to your teammate?
A: Pass it behind you.

Q: What else?
A: Pass it around the person who is guarding you.

Q: Great, what else?
A: Pass it next to you.

Q: So what are the three directions you can pass the ball to your teammate?
A: Behind you (drop), around other team (possibly angle), and next to you (square).

Source: Susan Setlak, Ball State University, Muncie, IN.

The Divergent Production Style (H)

In the divergent production style, the student is encouraged to find multiple solutions to a given problem. The teacher selects the subject and designs the problem. The student discovers alternative solutions to the problem and evaluates them in terms of their effectiveness in solving the problem. In some situations in which the quality of the movement is part of the solution, verification must be done by the teacher. The teacher should state, "The purpose of this style is to engage in producing multiple responses to a single question. There is not one correct answer. It is all right to produce different responses." Individual problems can be offered to students, or problems can be clustered in groups. Finally, students can be allowed to select from a list of problems those that are relevant to their own interests. The disadvantages of using the divergent production style are the same as the convergent discovery style.

Preimpact decisions:

1. What is the general subject matter (i.e., tumbling, golf, modern dance)?
2. What is the specific topic (i.e., headstand, putt)?
3. What is the specific problem or series of problems that will elicit solutions (variations, downhill lie, in groups)?

BOX 9.5

Convergent Discovery

Name: __________
Class: __________
Trail # Chosen: __________

Today you will be hiking. There are a number of trails that you can choose from in order for you to accomplish your goal of being successful. You are free to choose whichever trail you like, and you have 45 minutes. Be sure to read about the trails and figure out how long it will take you according to what you already know about trail markings and terrain.

You are free to go on your trail as soon as you have decided what you want to do.

Once you have completed your trail, meet your instructor at the starting point.

Source: Sally Northcroft, Ball State University, Muncie, IN.

Impact decisions:

1. Student—discover alternative answers to the problem.
2. Student—decide which multiple and divergent solutions are applicable to the problem.

Postimpact decisions:

1. Teacher—observe solution.
2. Student—evaluate the solution by asking, "Is my solution answering the question?"
3. Teacher—offer feedback about the learners' role in producing divergent ideas.

The divergent production style requires an environment in which the teacher feels secure enough to accept a wide variety of alternative solutions to problems. The teacher should respond to the *process* of discovery, not to the *value* of the particular response. Students must have time and a supportive environment in which to work out solutions. The major advantage of the divergent production style is its ability to help the student develop creativity. Social development depends on whether the student is working in a group or individually.

Styles I, J, and K

These styles increase the creativity of the student by allowing the learner to choose the problem and design the learning activities. These styles can be used only with individual students who are ready to take the initiative for their own behavior. The teacher's role is to facilitate the student's formulation of the problem, the learning activities, and the final presentation and evaluation. During learning, the student checks in periodically to keep the teacher up-to-date on the learning process.

In the learner's individual designed program, style I, the teacher selects the general subject matter area; the learner designs, develops, and performs a series of tasks in consultation with the teacher. An example would be a fitness unit in which the students design, conduct, and evaluate their own fitness programs. The learner-initiated style, style J, could occur when a student has a schedule conflict with physical education class and requests an alternative. The learner would select an activity, design the experiences, perform them, and then evaluate the experiences with the teacher's assistance. Style K, self-teaching, is rarely, if ever, used in school. The learner takes full responsibility for the learning process without input or consultation with the teacher. An example of the self-teaching style would be a student who goes to a golf course and learns to play golf from the local teaching professional.

Review Question: Describe Mosston's spectrum of teaching styles. Give an example of each "landmark" style:

Command (A)
Practice (B)
Reciprocal (C)
Self-Check (D)
Inclusion (E)
Guided-Discovery (F)
Convergent Discovery (G)
Divergent Production (H)
Learner's Individual Designed Program (I)
Learner-Initiated (J)
Self-Teaching (K)

Teaching Strategies

As teachers utilize teaching styles in the classroom they also incorporate various teaching strategies or instructional delivery systems to enhance the process of learning. The word *strategy* originally described the placement of an army in an advantageous position in relation to the enemy. As adopted by business and industry, strategy means the advantageous relationship of an organization to its environment. An instructional strategy is a particular arrangement of the teacher, learner, and environment to produce desired learning outcomes. Hurwitz defined an instructional strategy as "a plan for a pattern of actions aimed at one or more students achieving and demonstrating mastery of a specific goal or objective."[20]

Since learners respond differently to various strategies and since distinct strategies produce diverse outcomes, a number of strategies are presented to help in selecting the appropriate one for the subject, the learner, the teacher, and the instructional environment.

Review Question: What is the difference between a style and a strategy?

Selecting a Teaching Strategy

There is no one best strategy for any one teaching style on the spectrum. Thus teachers should select strategies that

The best teaching strategy is one that "pulls" the learner toward greater capacity without overstressing the capabilities of the learner.
© Tracy Pellet

best meet the needs of the instructional situation, and adapt each strategy to the parameters of that particular style. When selecting strategies to amplify the learning process, the prime consideration is high engaged time and large numbers of correct learning trials for students (refer to Chapter 5). Consideration must be given to selecting appropriate strategies for students who lack self-motivation or discipline and for situations in which large classes are taught in limited facilities.

Many strategies fit nicely into the physical education instructional process. Included for further discussion will be (1) lecture, (2) individualized instruction, (3) cooperative learning, (4) simulation, (5) problem solving, and (6) affective learning strategies.

Lecture

A lecture is a verbal presentation to an audience of a defined segment of information by one or more persons. Lectures include special reports, outside speakers, and panel discussions. A teacher might use a lecture to present rules, a panel discussion to elaborate on health concepts, or a police officer to speak on the dangers of drugs. A good source of material that might be taught using a lecture strategy is NASPE's *Concepts of Physical Education: What Every Student Needs to Know.*[21] Lectures can introduce, summarize, explain, or create interest in a topic. They can be used to impart information to a large group of students in a short time. When classes are large, limited student-student and student-teacher interactions may result in students misunderstanding the information. When using the lecture method in the classroom, prepare in such a way that the experience is meaningful and not limited to memory learning.

Procedures

1. Know the material.
2. Define the segment of material to be presented.
3. Organize the material to fit the time available.
4. Proceed from simple or familiar to complex or abstract.
5. Present the information in a motivational way.
   a. Use visual aids to support the topic.
   b. Relate the lecture to real life.
   c. Use humor.
   d. Repeat important points.
   e. Pace the material at the middle-level student.
6. Speak clearly and succinctly.
7. Be sensitive to feedback from listeners and modify the delivery accordingly.

Procedures for Special Reports or Outside Speakers

1. Make assignments well in advance.
2. Define the assignment clearly. Explain the topic and information wanted (and the ages and background of the class for outside speakers).
3. Help students make reports interesting by suggestions of topic, tips for presentation, and so forth.
4. Thank the speaker.

Procedures for Panel

1. Select and define the problem.
2. Choose and prepare panel participants in advance. All class members can be assigned to prepare and the panel can be chosen extemporaneously, or panel members can be assigned in advance.
3. Select a moderator who can stimulate questions and guide the discussion.

Review Question: What variations are possible within the lecture strategy?

Individualized Instruction

Individualized instruction programs enable each learner to progress at his or her own pace. Such programs assume that students are capable of learning independently with minimum direction from teachers. "A major goal of individualization is to promote self-directed learners who are capable of engaging effectively in the process of decision making."[22] Teachers are then free to act as consultants to students who need or desire their assistance. Educators conceiving individualized methodologies must consider what the student already knows, what the student wants to know, and what the student needs to know.[23]

Familiarity with mastery learning, task sheets, contract learning, quests, and computer-assisted instruction are helpful when teachers attempt to individualize learning in physical education.

Mastery Learning

Mastery learning, as conceptualized by Benjamin Bloom, is a theory of school learning based on the premise that almost all students can learn at a high level what the schools have to teach if given sufficient time and instructional help.[24] Bloom asserted that children in schools are being taught as "good and poor" learners rather than "fast and slow" learners, and when students are provided with favorable learning conditions most of them become very similar with regard to learning ability. Students taught using mastery learning techniques are expected to succeed. Torshen suggested that this is the case because in mastery learning individual differences are taken into account.[25] Bloom's Learning for Mastery (LFM) is a group-based teacher-paced approach. It differs from Keller's Personalized System of Instruction (PSI), which is an individual-based, student-paced model. Both systems employ many of the same components, but Bloom's model will be discussed in detail because it has been more widely used.

Mastery learning is not a new concept. Its roots go back to the Jesuit schools before the seventeenth century. Bloom and other twentieth-century theorists have structured the concepts into a well-known educational paradigm. Others have varied the model to suit their specific situations. The mastery model includes the following components:

1. *Performance objectives,* including criterion levels for student achievement that are set high enough to be demanding and challenging for all students. These objectives are made known to the students prior to instruction.
2. *Instructional activities,* including demonstration, explanation, and learning tasks that emphasize skill acquisition and application to the point of overlearning.
3. *Diagnostic assessment,* using formative tests that students repeat until mastery is achieved. Either the formative tests or a summative test administered at the end of a unit may be used for grading purposes.
4. *Feedback,* including test results so students know how they are progressing.
5. *Prescription,* including "correctives" for students who did not attain mastery and "enrichment activities" for those who did.

"Correctives" are activities engaged in by students who did not attain mastery, which enable most of them to do so on future formative tests. Such activities include practicing the tests, practicing the test skills in other ways, and receiving personalized instruction from the teacher or a peer.

"Enrichment activities" are activities provided for students who have passed mastery tests and are waiting to move on to the next task. Such activities include probing deeper and more completely into the instructional task at hand, peer tutoring between students, and independent learning.

Students engage in learning activities involving correctives and enrichment activities until a certain percentage (usually 80 to 95 percent) of the class has attained mastery before moving on to a new task. More time to learn is needed in the initial phases of instruction because some students take longer to learn than others. Block pointed out that this time is reduced by the end of the course.[26] Students use time more efficiently as they become familiar with mastery learning procedures, and they also learn more-advanced skills faster once basic skills are mastered. Short units of one or two weeks are not sufficient for mastery learning principles to take effect.

Over the years, research on mastery learning has produced an impressive legacy of positive results. A number of literature reviews have consistently reported the beneficial effects of mastery approaches on a variety of learning outcomes.[27] However, most of the research has been done in the cognitive and affective domains. There is a lack of research documenting the effects of mastery learning on the acquisition of psychomotor skills.

Both Annarino and Heitmann and Kneer have emphasized mastery learning principles in physical education; however, very few studies have been done to substantiate their theories. Edwards determined that performance standards help individuals achieve significantly higher motor-skill achievement scores. Chambless, Anderson, and Poole demonstrated that stunts and tumbling achievement for mentally retarded children was significantly higher when mastery learning techniques were used. Ashy and Lee found no significant differences on summative scores of throwing for kindergartners and first graders in mastery and nonmastery groups, although the mastery group did better. Metzler showed that students in mastery classes benefited from higher intervals of ALT-PE than those in traditional classes. Metzler and his colleagues used Keller's PSI model to teach college students enrolled in beginning tennis courses. They demonstrated that PSI students scored significantly higher than the conventional students on four measures of playing ability. Blakemore reported that students using mastery learning techniques performed better than nonmastery learners, low-aptitude students and males performed better when using mastery techniques, and male and female performance was equalized in the mastery group. She also found that the results of mastery learning did not take effect until at least the fourth week of the unit. Thus, teachers must allot sufficient instructional time for mastery techniques to be productive. Boyce demonstrated that a mastery criterion significantly influenced the acquisition and retention of a selected shooting task.[28]

Procedures

1. Complete a unit plan that is at least six weeks long.
2. Divide the unit of instruction into small teaching segments or subunits including tasks to be learned (i.e., volleyball: volley and bump, serve, spike and block). Decide on a hierarchical order to teach these tasks (see Chapter 8 for content analysis procedures).
3. Preassess students on each task to determine entry levels and mastery criteria.
4. Devise specific objectives stating performance standards (scores) for each task based on preassessment results and previous testing (if possible).

BOX 9.6

Example of a Mastery Learning Task Sheet

MASTERY LEARNING RACQUETBALL FOREHAND/BACKHAND TASK SHEET

Name ______________________________

Mastery Test Results
30 Second Wall Volley Behind Short Line

Passed:

________ A. Long Wall Volley: MASTERY is 15 points for FOREHAND (Record *score* and date)
1. ________ 2. ________ 3. ________ 4. ________ 5. ________

Date:

________ B. Long Wall Volley: MASTERY is 13 points for BACKHAND (List *score* and date)
1. ________ 2. ________ 3. ________ 4. ________ 5. ________

Date:

IF YOU HAVE PASSED A AND B, GO TO TASK 5 BELOW:
Check Off Tasks as They Are Passed

Passed:

1. Drop 20 balls; hit 15 correctly (as stated below). You or a partner may drop the balls. Catch the ball after each hit. The ball should hit the wall at the same height and straight ahead of where it is contacted. It should rebound to within an arm's length of where you are standing. An assistant should evaluate consistency/control, slicing, hooking, and height of ball.

________ 15 correctly hit balls with forehand standing mid-court.
________ 15 correctly hit balls with backhand standing mid-court.
________ 15 correctly hit balls with forehand standing 6 feet from the back wall.
________ 15 correctly hit balls with backhand standing 6 feet from the back wall.

2. Stand at the side court and move to hit 20 balls that come to center court. Hit 15 correctly (as stated below). Your partner should hit or throw the ball to the front wall so it bounces to center court. Catch the ball each time it is hit.

________ 15 correctly hit balls standing mid-court with the forehand.
________ 15 correctly hit balls standing mid-court with the backhand.

Continued

5. Design formative tests to assess student competence for each task.
6. Teach the first subunit and allow students to practice.
7. Test all students to determine who mastered (passed) the formative tests included in the first subunit.
8. Provide feedback to each student based on the results of the formative tests.
9. Prescribe correctives or enrichment activities for each student. Provide individualized corrective activities to improve skill for those who have not mastered a task. Direct students who have mastered or passed a task to expand their performance of the specific skill in game situations, in more advanced drills, and in peer tutoring circumstances.
10. Monitor students carefully as they engage in corrective or enrichment activities. Repeat the formative tests regularly for those who have not passed.
11. Teach a new subunit when 80 percent of the students have mastered the tasks of the present subunit.
12. Repeat this process of direct instruction, practice, diagnostic testing, mastery, and enrichment activities or correctives until the unit is complete.
13. If the formal model of Bloom is followed, administer a summative test.

Task sheets similar to the example shown in Box 9.6 could be used to monitor each student's progress toward mastery of the subunit tasks. The task sheet includes mastery scores and spaces to record results for several evaluations. It also includes corrective procedures (tasks 1–4), enrichment activities (tasks 5–7), and skill execution tips. Because this sheet allows the student to work independently, engaging the teacher only when specific help is needed, the teacher is free to interact with students requiring assistance.

BOX 9.6 *Continued*

Example of a Mastery Learning Task Sheet

3. Drop the ball from behind the short line and continuously hit it off the front wall as stated below.

_________ 10 continuously hit balls with forehand.
_________ 10 continuously hit balls with backhand.
_________ 25 continuously hit balls with forehand in 2 minutes.
_________ 25 continuously hit balls with backhand in 2 minutes.

4. Practice the Long Wall Volley Test using either the forehand or backhand for 1 minute. Retake the test when you are ready.

____

5. With a partner, rally the ball continuously off the front wall using either forehand or backhand 25 times. Alternate hits with your partner. _________
6. With two or three other people, rally the ball continuously, establishing a sequence of hitting that is followed each time (e.g., John, Sally, Bill; John, Sally, Bill). _________
7. With a partner, play a modified game. The server stands between the red lines and puts the ball into play by bouncing it and then hitting so it rebounds off the front wall. The ball must then bounce on the floor beyond the red lines. The receiver may stand anywhere beyond the red lines to receive the ball. The server scores a point if the receiver makes an error. The receiver becomes the server if the server makes an error. The receiver does not score points. Play continues to 15 points.

Forehand Form

1. Face side wall, with racquet arm away from front wall. The feet are a shoulder's width apart with the left foot slightly closer to the side wall (right-handed player).
2. Bend knees comfortably.
3. Hold racquet arm back and perpendicular to body with the racquet head pointing to ceiling about shoulder level.
4. Contact ball between waist and knee as you step forward (skilled players will contact the ball at the knee).
5. Snap wrists and follow through to opposite shoulder so body now faces the front wall.

Backhand Form

1. Face side wall, with racquet arm close to front wall. The feet are a shoulder's width apart with the right foot slightly closer to the side wall (right-handed player).
2. Bend knees comfortably.
3. Bring racquet across midsection of body with elbow bent to form a 90 degree angle with the upper arm (L) a few inches from the body.
4. Point the racquet head to the ceiling near the shoulder.
5. Contact the ball between the knee and waist as described above for the forehand.
6. Snap wrists and follow through to head height away from the body.

Teachers often find teaching for mastery very time-consuming at its inception but discover that the rewards in the end are worth the effort. The rewards of mastery learning include (1) individual student success, (2) student willingness to practice, (3) progress easily identified, and (4) high levels of achievement.

Teachers incorporating mastery learning or other individualized learning techniques often desire to group students homogeneously by dividing students into smaller groups of similar ability levels. The following examples point out the practical application of such a strategy and its advantages and limitations.

Example (lay-ups):

1. Demonstrate lay-ups to the class.
2. Have all students go to baskets to practice the lay-up progression.
3. As soon as it is determined that a student can do successful lay-ups, have the student put on a pinnie but continue to practice using various types of lay-ups.
4. As soon as enough students are wearing pinnies, start a half-court game with these players and move players without pinnies to other baskets.
5. Continue with 3, 4, and 5 until all players are successful.

Example (Archery):

1. Have all students shoot at twenty yards and score the best five consecutive ends.
2. Have students who score two hundred points at a given distance move the target back five yards if there is enough room to do so safely.
3. Students will soon be shooting at various distances designated by the teacher. The students at the closest distances need the most help.

BOX 9.7

A Skill Checklist—Tennis

SKILL REQUIREMENTS FOR TENNIS

Rally Rascals—C Grade Name ______________________

Exercises

________ 1. Fifty down bounces using forehand grip.
________ 2. Fifty up bounces using forehand grip.
________ 3. Twenty-five reverse bounces using forehand grip.

Wall or Backboard Practice

________ 4. Return at least ten consecutive forehands. One bounce only from baseline.
________ 5. Return at least five consecutive backhands. One bounce only from baseline.

Tossed Balls

________ 6. Return five moving forehands in a row from no man's land to no man's land without an error. Repeat three times.
________ 7. Repeat above for backhand.
________ 8. Return eight out of ten moving forehands from baseline to baseline.
________ 9. Return five out of eight moving backhands from baseline to baseline.
________ 10. Return five out of eight moving forehand volleys to no man's land.
________ 11. Return five out of eight moving backhand volleys to no man's land.

Self-Tossed Balls

________ 12. Put ten consecutive forehands into play from the baseline to the baseline.
________ 13. Put five out of ten backhands into play from the baseline to the baseline.
________ 14. Serve five out of ten fast serves into either court.

Rally Practice

________ 15. Short court rally for at least ten times.
________ 16. With an experienced player, play a pro set.

Source: Ann Valentine, Brigham Young University.

Uses:

1. To identify students needing help with skill development.
2. To enrich the learning of advanced students.
3. To enhance safety.

Advantages:

1. The teacher can work with students who need the most help.
2. Advanced students can move on to new objectives.
3. Student effort increases.
4. Student effort is rewarded.

Limitations:

1. Advanced planning is necessary.
2. Supervising many groups doing different things at the same time may be difficult.
3. The testing situation is often emphasized rather than game play.

Review Question: Describe mastery learning. What are corrective and enrichment activities?

Task Sheets Task sheets are used to motivate students to practice tasks and keep a record of learning activities. They shift some of the decisions for learning to the student, thereby involving students in on-task behavior and eliminating standing around or "goofing off." Some students require extra help to succeed in working on their own, but they will grow by doing so, and students will learn to accept the consequences for their learning decisions. The task sheets include lists of tasks to be done, with instructions for performance, such as quantity, quality, and use of equipment. Two examples of task sheets are shown in Boxes 9.7 and 9.8. Each of these is also an example of Mosston's practice style. Task sheets can be used with most of Mosston's teaching styles.

Although extra preparation is necessary to create task sheets, they can be extremely valuable for preclass activities, as well as during class time. Task sheets can be

Box 9.8

Badminton Skill Checklist

Badminton Skill Checklist

Name ____

________ 20 consecutive underhand drop shots in a rally with a partner.
________ 8 out of 10 short serves between short service line and white line.
________ Score 25 short serves on court with rope 12 inches above net and target in right court.
________ 8 out of 10 long serves on court with target in right court.
________ Score 20 long serves on court with target in right court.
________ 8 out of 10 smashes with partner setting up (shots that can be returned with some effort by the partner cannot be counted).
________ 8 out of 10 clears (overhead) with partner setting up (must land between the two back boundary lines).
________ 8 out of 10 clears (underhand) with partner setting up (must land between the two back boundary lines).
________ Read the handout on scoring and score one game.

Complete the following play patterns with a partner (you should be player A and player B in each case).

________ Player A—Serve
B—Clear to deep backhand
A—Drive down sideline
B—Clear to deep forehand
A—Clear to deep backhand
B—Drive cross court

________ Player A—Serve
B—Clear to deep backhand
A—Drop to the forehand
B—Clear to the deep forehand
A—Clear to the deep backhand
Repeat

issued to each student, and items can be checked off by partners, team captains, student assistants, or the teacher. A composite list can be maintained by the teacher. Task sheets may form part of the grade for a unit.

Procedures

1. Select appropriate instructional objectives.
2. Select activities in terms of objectives and learning problems. Tasks should be relevant to group members.
3. Create task sheets that include
   a. a description of the tasks, including diagrams or sketches.
   b. specific points to look for in the performance.
   c. samples of possible feedback.
4. Check to be sure students understand the purpose of the tasks and the criteria for correct performance.
5. Provide for facilitation of the observation by incorporating a system of:
   a. comparison of the performance with the criterion for correct performance.
   b. communication of the results to the performer during and after the completion of each task.
6. Select partners or groups. Have students select a partner they have not worked with before.

Contract Learning and Quests Contract learning is the use of an individual learning packet in which a student contracts (or agrees) with the teacher to complete specified objectives in order to receive a specified grade. Contracts individualize learning by allowing students to select different tasks or learning activities and to take responsibility for their own learning and self-assessment. They permit students to work at their own pace on clearly defined tasks. Types of contracts include (1) teacher-controlled contracts in which the teacher determines the tasks and reinforcers, (2) transitional contracting in which the student and the teacher share decision making, and (3) student-controlled contracts in which the student determines the tasks and reinforcers. If the student writes the objectives as well, the contract is called a quest. An example of a contract is the gymnastics grade contract shown in Box 9.9. Box 9.10 is an example of a basketball grade contract. Some limitations of contracts might include the necessity of using additional media and outside facilities, the time-consuming preparation involved, and the fact that some students are not ready to work on their own without constant teacher direction.

Quests allow students to set and pursue their own goals at their own pace and to take responsibility for their own

BOX 9.9

A Gymnastics Contract

Please read the following contract carefully and ask any questions you may have. Remember: Teachers do not give students grades; students *earn* the grades they receive.

Name ______________________ Period ______________

I contract for an A B C (circle one) based on the criteria below:

Starting date __________ Ending date __________
Student signature ______________ Teacher signature ______________

Requirements for an A:

1. Attend class regularly, be dressed, and participate each day.
2. Actively participate in all activities taught by your instructor.
3. Earn a minimum score of fourteen out of twenty on the written examination.
4. Learn and perform for the instructor fourteen stunts from any or all of the events at the advanced level.
5. Select and complete fourteen Learning Experience points from the class list.

Requirements for a B:

1. Attend class regularly, be dressed, and participate each day.
2. Actively participate in all activities taught by your instructor.
3. Earn a minimum score of twelve out of twenty on the written examination.
4. Learn and perform for the instructor twelve stunts from any or all of the events at the intermediate level.
5. Select and complete twelve Learning Experience points from the class list.

Requirements for a C:

1. Attend class regularly, be dressed, and participate each day.
2. Actively participate in all activities taught by your instructor.
3. Earn a minimum score of ten out of twenty on the written examination.
4. Learn and perform for the instructor ten stunts from any or all of the events at the beginning level.
5. Select and complete ten Learning Experience points from the class list.

Source: Linda Fleming and Joyce M. Harrison, Brigham Young University.

learning. They encourage individual initiative and creativity and decrease unhealthy competition between students, since each student has different goals. However, since students are doing different types of projects, teachers may find it difficult to state or measure the quality of each quest. Some teachers have difficulty letting students do their own thing. An example of a quest contract is shown in Box 9.11.

Procedures

1. Specify the performance and/or process objectives for a given unit of study. Identify levels (e.g., A, B, C).
2. Specify possible learning activities and learning materials.
3. Devise the contract. The teacher may do this, or the teacher and student may work together.
4. Develop evaluation methods and materials, including progress checks that tell students when performance objectives have been accomplished. (They also serve as reinforcers.)
5. Divide the instructional unit into blocks that provide ample time for activities to be taught, practiced, and evaluated.
6. Meet together as teacher and student or teacher and class to discuss the conditions of the contract and specify proposed dates for the completion of various phases of the contract.
7. Begin the instruction or activity phase with the teacher serving as a resource person when needed.
8. Evaluate progress with the criteria agreed upon. The teacher and student may need to revise the contract along the way. Performance that does not meet acceptable standards should either be redone or receive a lower grade.
9. Submit completed contract and award a grade based on the specified criteria.

Computer-Assisted Instruction Computer-assisted instruction (CAI) is usually used for learning in the cognitive domain. It can be used to learn material, review previously learned material, or test the level of learning. The use of CAI may occur during class time but is most beneficial when used as a required assignment to be completed outside of class. More class time is then available to work on psychomotor skills.[29]

Box 9.10

Basketball Grade Contract

Name ______________________ Period ______________

Please read the following contract carefully and ask any questions you may have.

I contract for an A B C (circle one) based on the criteria below:

Requirements for an A:

1. Complete all of the requirements for a B.
2. Analyze 4 or more skills using the steps listed below.
3. Watch a basketball game and prepare a scouting report for one team or analyze the strengths and weaknesses of one team.

Requirements for a B:

1. Complete all of the requirements for a C.
2. Analyze 3 skills using the steps listed below.
3. Design 2 offensive plays for own team to use during game play. List specific defense for which the play is designed.

Requirements for a C:

1. Analyze your own performance of 2 skills. Videotape, then digitize and analyze the performance.
   A. List errors.
   B. List tasks to be used to correct errors.
   C. Do at the beginning and end of unit and evaluate progress made.
   D. Turn in videotape or disk with performance and written analysis.
2. Officiate game play to demonstrate knowledge of rules.
3. Complete rules worksheet.

Starting Date ______________________ Ending date ______________________

Student signature ______________________

Teacher signature ______________________

CAI consists of the following characteristics: (1) Content is divided into small steps and carefully organized into a logical sequence with each step building on the preceding step; (2) the student is presented with and actively responds to one question at a time; (3) the student receives immediate knowledge of results; (4) each student can progress at his or her own rate; and (5) programs are written or created to ensure a minimum of error.

Computers encourage student responsibility for learning. Immediate knowledge of results yields higher learner motivation and confidence. Programs insist that each point be thoroughly understood; therefore, CAI works well for slower students and results in learning efficiency per unit of time.

Programs are usually written using one of two formats. In one format each student reads the same material but at a speed the individual chooses. In the other format each student begins with the same material. However, the computer selects the next material depending on the student's responses. A student who correctly answers a question will be presented with different material than an individual who needs further study of the concept. This method ensures that students have a thorough understanding of material prior to being exposed to new material. Computers can also be programmed to keep a record of each student's progress.

A current disadvantage of this strategy is the lack of computer programs available. Use of this technique requires computer programming knowledge or the availability of authoring programs.

An example of a CAI program is a software program written to review softball strategies. A situation is presented and the student must select the appropriate play from the choices provided. If an error is made, the student is provided with feedback about why the choice was incorrect and what the correct choice should have been.

Procedures

1. Define the concept, rule, or strategy.
2. List as many examples of the concept as possible.
3. List as many nonexamples of the concept as possible.
4. Create a question that tests understanding of the concept.

BOX 9.11

A Quest Contract

1. My objectives

2. My learning activities

3. My plans for evaluation
   ________ videotape recording
   ________ expert or professional
   ________ other:

4. I plan to present evidence of my achievement of each objective by
   ____
   (Date)

5. My contract is for an ________ grade.

____________________ Signature of student	____________ Date
____________________ Signature of instructor	____________ Date

5. Determine the next step depending on the answer selected.
6. Try out and revise.

Review Question: What is the purpose of a task sheet? A contract? Computer-assisted instruction?

Cooperative Learning

A current trend in the academic classroom is toward more cooperative learning strategies. In cooperative learning a team of students work together to help its members achieve a certain goal, progressing only as fast as all members have learned each skill or passed each quiz. Cooperative learning is based on the philosophy that students make no effort to learn unless schools satisfy student needs to belong. Cooperative learning "places the responsibility for learning where it belongs, on the students."[30] As students gain a greater sense of control, their attitudes toward school learning and classmates improve, and a larger percentage of students work on-task, resulting in better classroom behavior. Although more time-consuming than teacher-directed strategies, cooperative learning significantly increases student academic performances, social interaction, and group participation, communication, and leadership skills. It also makes teaching and learning more fun. All these benefits can lead to a more effective learning environment.[31]

Cooperative learning increases student involvement in learning and motivates slower learners to improve their performance while reinforcing the learning of faster learners. Heterogeneous grouping increases learning for all students. Low-skilled students benefit by observing high-skilled students. High-skilled students gain greater insight through teaching.

The physical education classroom is an ideal setting for cooperative learning. In his reciprocal style, Mosston assigned pairs of students to work cooperatively together, with each student given responsibility as either the observer or the doer. Cooperative learning can help students internalize and apply physical education principles. For example, the lesson focus may be to perform a proper free throw in basketball. The students need to understand the biomechanics of body alignment, the impact of spin on ball rebound patterns, the appropriate angle of ball projection, and so forth. The teacher provides this information using a lecture format, written materials, appropriate group work, or some combination of these. While practicing free throws in small groups the social skills needed are (1) observing student practice, (2) evaluating performance based on correct mechanics, (3) communicating to the performer what the skill looks like, and (4) providing accurate feedback to the performer for skill improvement. When students learn and teach each other, they will be more likely to apply these concepts in their own lives.

Students need time to learn how to work together, how to communicate effectively, and how to take responsibility for their own learning. Therefore, teachers should not be discouraged early in the process. The hard work the teacher does at the beginning of the learning process will pay large dividends in student performance later on. Preplanning is necessary, including planning for specific group dynamics. Students must be taught cooperation skills, just as they are taught psychomotor skills or classroom management skills, by modeling, practice, feedback, and more practice. "For true cooperation to take place, students must realize that they will sink or swim together."[32]

Procedures[33]

1. State lesson objectives clearly.
   a. Information required for students to understand and apply the concept or to understand the mechanics of the skill.
   b. Social skills necessary during group work (i.e., cooperation, listening, communicating, supporting, evaluating, giving feedback).
   c. Psychomotor skills to be mastered.
2. Group students heterogeneously into learning "teams." Make sure best friends are not grouped together, otherwise the activity may become entirely social.
3. Communicate goals and expectations clearly to enhance group skills, ensure responsible learning of materials, and attain appropriate skill performance levels. Use task sheets if desired.
   a. Model the appropriate performance.
   b. Give directions and/or task sheet, including evaluation cues. Structure activities to establish a feeling of positive interdependence among group members. To do this:
      (1) Give only one copy of information to each group (e.g., rules or strategies sheets, task sheet).
      (2) Give each group member part of the information or a specific part of the assignment to be shared with others. Each student studies his or her information with students from other groups who were assigned the same information. The student then shares what was learned with his or her own group. This is called *jigsawing.*
      (3) Instruct the group to produce one report, game strategy, and so on (e.g., the risk factors for cardiovascular disease), with each member researching one area to contribute to the final report.
      (4) Give the groups complex tasks to complete while keeping the group relatively small. Ask groups for a complex report such as identifying offensive strategies and their rationale based on their own strengths and weaknesses and the strengths and weaknesses of the opposition.
      (5) Make the group responsible for reciprocal instruction, that is, students should model for and teach each other. Teachers must model positive ways of providing feedback and provide students with specific techniques.
   c. Assign specific group roles. Keep groups small. With two to three students in a group, the student roles are performer, observer, and leader/timekeeper. Instruct students in effective group techniques. Give each student a specific group role or assignment. Roles should change regularly. For example, while practicing dribbling one student performs the dribble, one gives feedback, and one acts as the leader who makes sure everyone gets a turn. Each person has a designated time with the ball and time for specific feedback. Roles are designed to facilitate the group and give responsibility to each group member. Groups can be trained to automatically establish group roles for every group assignment. Roles can be posted on a wall for quick referral.
      (1) *Performer:* Performs the established skill.
      (2) *Recorder:* Records the number of trials, key points of the group discussion, report to be presented to class, and so on.
      (3) *Observer:* Observes and evaluates individual or group performance and gives recommendations or feedback. Makes sure all members are involved.
      (4) *Presenter:* Reports group progress or report to the class or teacher.
      (5) *Timer:* Keeps track of practice or discussion time.
      (6) *Leader:* Keeps the group on-task, makes assignments, follows through with teacher directions.
   d. Set time limits. The teacher is then free to work with problems instead of playing the role of whistle-blower or timekeeper.
4. Move throughout the class, monitoring each group's progress and giving individual instruction where needed.
5. Evaluate all objectives.
   a. Give grades or feedback based both on how the group performed as a unit and how students performed individually. Students can be held accountable for doing their share by means of the individual quiz. Encourage cooperation by giving bonus points if everyone in a group scores at least 85 percent on the individual quiz.[34] Occasionally use group quizzes, in which each person is responsible for leading the discussion for a question; the group must reach a consensus for each answer.
   b. Have each group member write a brief evaluation of the group about halfway through the project and at the conclusion of the project. If the group is not working well together, do not intervene immediately; encourage them to work together and do their own problem solving. Provide helpful hints, but do not coerce compliance. Have the group take responsibility for itself. Removal of a group member is the last

resort and should be used only when serious trouble is erupting. Reorganize groups for the next project.

Several strategies that use cooperative learning in physical education have been reported in the literature. Baseline Basketball and Class Team Tennis are two round-robin tournament strategies reported by Eason. They are described in Chapter 10. Sterne also used the team, game, tournament strategy to teach skills.[35] Glover and Midura call cooperative learning "team building." They use physical challenges, which are described in Chapter 10, to accomplish their goals.[36]

Review Questions: What is cooperative learning? How can cognitive, psychomotor, and social skills be learned through the use of this strategy?

Simulation

An excellent teaching aid is a simulation of an event. Once again the "doing" aspect of learning is built into the learning experience. Students not competing on an athletic or intramural team may never have the experience of playing with official rules, referees, and scorers. Simulation activities are selective simplifications or representations of real-life situations in game or laboratory-type settings. They can be used to promote the learning of game skills, knowledge, attitudes, strategies, and social skills. Possible experiences include a simulated track or gymnastics meet or a diving meet that also involves students in the administration of the event.

Activities not usually performed in a gymnasium can be adapted to the school site. For example, tennis and bowling can be simulated in a gym to provide students a fairly authentic experience.[37] Cross-country skiing can be taught during the winter months, utilizing both the outside playing fields and the gymnasium.[38] One teacher designed a nine-hole golf course in the locker-room areas of the physical education building by contacting local carpet stores for pieces of carpet and using discarded or broken pieces of sports equipment. A floor plan of the course was first designed and then transferred to the carpet. The carpet was then cut to fit the appropriate area. Scorecards, similar to those on a regulation golf course, were duplicated, and golf course courtesy was observed. The course design was limited only by the imagination of the individual.[39] The same type of ingenuity might create a course outside on a grassy playing area using whiffle or Cayman (short-flight) balls for safety.

Disadvantages of simulation are the increased time needed for preparation and learning and the expense involved in providing actual equipment in some instances. Some teachers complain that simulation activities oversimplify real situations.

Procedures for Simulation Activities

1. Counsel students on how to accomplish the objectives of the assignment.
2. Tell what the results have to do with real life.
3. Supervise student activities.
4. Progress from simple to complex.
5. Emphasize the meaning of the simulation activity through preassessment and follow-up.
6. Assign heterogeneous teams.
7. Allow teams to select their own positions in the group.
8. Place faculty in legitimate roles, not as advisors to teams.
9. Define rules.
10. Play the game.
11. Evaluate the results and provide feedback.
12. Discuss principles involved.
13. Allow students to create their own games.

Review Question: What is simulation? Give an example of a simulation experience in physical education.

Problem-Solving Strategies

Problem-solving strategies can be used to develop the ability to solve problems and verify solutions to problems. They can also be used to encourage the application of concepts already learned. If done in a group, they can encourage student interaction and teamwork. They encourage the use of cognitive processes other than memory and increase retention. However, they are more time-consuming than teacher-dominated instruction and can take time away from practicing psychomotor skills.

The problem-solving techniques that will be discussed further include (1) questioning, (2) inquiry learning, and (3) brainstorming and buzz sessions. Other examples of problem-solving strategies are choreographing dance or gymnastics routines, developing new games with given parameters, or thinking up and sharing new plays for games. Mosston's discovery and production styles use problem-solving strategies.[40] Most of the affective learning activities also fall into the category of problem solving. Problem solving has been discussed previously in Chapter 5.

When problem-solving strategies are used, keep in mind that it is difficult to meaningfully involve some students (e.g., slow learners, culturally disadvantaged, and students who lack the knowledge necessary to solve the problem) in problem-solving situations.

Procedures

1. Define the problem in a few words.
2. State conditions necessary for the problem to be considered solved.
3. List possible solutions.
4. Find the best solution based on the desired outcomes.
5. Evaluate success in solving the problem.

Review Question: List and give examples of problem-solving strategies.

Questioning Strategies Teachers use questions to arouse interest and hold attention, to help learners perceive the referent of a concept or discover a specific relationship or principle, to stimulate thought, develop understanding, apply information, develop appreciations and attitudes, or to emphasize a point or clarify a misconception. Questioning can also be used to evaluate student understanding and learning. Its use during a lecture increases individual student participation and understanding. Questioning requires considerable skill on the part of the teacher to accomplish the objective without embarrassing students or limiting the responses to only a few students. Some examples of questions at the various levels of the cognitive taxonomy include the following:

1. *Knowledge or fact questions:* who, what, where, when. Involves recognition or recall of facts, events, places, or names.
2. *Comprehension:* Compare the belief in (subject) of . . . and . . . Explain in your own words. Involves understanding of what was expressed.
3. *Application:* If you were . . ., what might you do? How does this apply in our lives? Involves using knowledge in new ways.
4. *Analysis:* Give evidence. . . . Explain. . . . What caused . . .? What effect was caused by . . .? Tell why. . . Involves breaking information into parts.
5. *Synthesis:* Write a journal of your reactions to your fitness program. Describe how physical education makes a difference in your life. Involves combining parts to make a whole.
6. *Evaluation:* Should people . . .? Judge whether behavior was right or wrong. Defend the . . . Involves making judgments based on standards.

Procedures

1. Preparation. Prepare questions that
   a. relate to the purpose of the lesson.
   b. are clear, definite, and easily understood.
   c. engage the attention of the whole class.
   d. relate to the students' world and interests.
   e. cause students to stretch their minds.
   f. take into account individual differences in such areas as intelligence and background experiences.
   g. avoid manipulation of student responses.
   h. build on knowledge students now have.
   i. can be answered in the time available.
   j. are phrased in such a way as to provoke a discussion rather than a simple yes or no.
2. Inform students prior to instruction that they will be expected to answer questions. To stimulate thinking, the teacher may want to introduce the discussion session with a story, diagram, chart, video, compact disc, object, case study, or a well-planned question written on the chalkboard.
3. Ask questions by
   a. directing the question to the entire class, pausing, and then calling on volunteers.
   b. directing the question to the entire class, pausing, and then calling on a specific student.
   c. directing a question from one student to another student or the entire class.
4. Encourage student involvement by
   a. pausing after each question to encourage thoughtful and meaningful responses (at least three seconds). Say, "Think carefully before you answer," wait, then call on someone.
   b. using nonvolunteers. Inform students that they will be encouraged to contribute and that they might be called whether or not their hands are raised. If a student hesitates, say, "Think about it for a minute and we'll come back to you."
   c. redirecting questions. Ask one question, then ask, "Jane, can you add anything else?" or just nod at another student. Encourage students to direct questions to other students.
   d. rephrasing. Listen to the student's answer and then restate what was heard. For example, "Barry, do you mean . . .?" Avoid inserting personal reactions into the answer.
   e. probing. Accept the student's initial response and then ask the student to extend, justify, or clarify it by asking, "Can you tell me more, Nathan?" Probing helps the student think more carefully and express a more complete answer.
5. When answers are off the subject, only partially complete or correct, or wrong, treat responses with courtesy and tact.
   a. Say something like, "That's not quite right. Let's think it through together."
   b. Avoid rejecting good ideas that were not the hoped for answer. Instead, rephrase the question.
   c. Avoid negative responses that might lower the student's self-esteem or discourage future responses. Always attempt to make the student feel good about responding.
   d. Avoid praising answers excessively. Other students may assume their answers were no good.
6. Keep the discussion organized by relating questions to previous answers or to questions students raise about the topic under discussion.
7. Summarize often to show students the progress they are making toward a solution, to focus the class on the solution, and to emphasize truths students are learning. Give credit to students who make important contributions. Use students to summarize when appropriate, and list the main points on the chalkboard.
8. Show how the solution can be applied to real life. Challenge the students to apply it.

9. Evaluate any questions against the following criteria:
   a. Did the sequence of questions display a logical development of ideas leading students directly to the heart of the problem and to its solution?
   b. Was each question related in some useful way to the problem statement?
   c. Was the question accurately stated, specific, and to the point?
   d. Was the question within the ability of the student to whom it was addressed?
   e. Was the question relevant to students?
   f. Did the question stimulate students to think and investigate?[41]

Inquiry Learning Inquiry learning is a process through which students learn how to seek out answers scientifically by asking thought-provoking questions. The most commonly used example is the game Twenty Questions. Although inquiry learning is more time-consuming than conventional learning, it tends to help students learn how to learn by putting the responsibility for learning directly on them, thereby providing more meaningful learning.

Procedures

1. Provide and introduce the focus of the lesson—a puzzling or unfamiliar object, event, or situation.
2. Define the rules of questioning.
   a. All questions must be answered by yes or no.
   b. Ask only one question at a time.
   c. One student may ask a series of questions until a train of thought has been completed.
   d. Students may confer or call for a summary at any time.
3. Answer questions to help students gather data and verify information, reminding students of the rules when necessary.
4. Help students organize the information they have obtained, identify relationships among the variables, and create hypotheses to explain the situation. For example, if x is true, then would y be so?
5. Summarize the questioning procedure and identify how it can be improved.

Brainstorming and Buzz Sessions Brainstorming means generating solutions to a defined problem by stating any relevant idea that comes to mind. For example, a small group of students might generate ideas for a new game or dance. In a buzz session, a large group is divided into small groups of people who generate ways to solve a problem. Group members can be rotated to increase the diversity of ideas. Both techniques can be used to solve a specific problem or to define creative approaches to problem solving. They can result in individual creativity, maximum group participation, and unique, creative solutions to problems.

Procedures

1. State the problem clearly.
2. Establish a time limit of five to ten minutes.
3. List ideas about the subject on a chalkboard or paper as they come to mind with no attempt to evaluate them. Try to list as many ideas as possible.
4. At the end of the time specified, the teacher restates the problem and helps students evaluate the ideas.

Affective Learning Strategies

Although attitudes are part of the teaching-learning process at all times, some specific strategies can be used to enhance the teaching of affective behaviors. Many of these activities can take time away from physical activity, but they are important to the acquisition of affective skills.

Affective behaviors can be learned during actual situations that arise during classroom interaction or during planned activities. The preferred method in physical education is to teach affective behaviors through actual experience in situations as they arise. However, some affective activities can be used on rainy days, during assembly schedules, and on other days when time does not permit dressing for activity.

Developing attitudes toward activities necessitates knowing something about the activity; therefore, students should first learn the skills and knowledge relevant to that activity. By pairing a new skill or bit of knowledge with a preferred or rewarding activity, students may acquire a liking for the new skill or knowledge. Gagné generalized that "success in some learning accomplishment is likely to lead to a positive attitude toward that activity."[42]

A number of techniques for learning affective behavior have been included with the teaching strategies in Chapter 5. Their use will be more effective in a democratic classroom environment. Additional techniques are presented here.

Reaction and Opinion Papers Reaction and opinion papers are papers submitted by students expressing their feelings, opinions, or reactions to something. They can be used to increase student awareness of their own feelings, as well as to increase teacher awareness of student feelings. Since there is no one right answer, every student can be included. However, some students may not feel free to express their true feelings when names are included on papers or when students are graded on their responses. Writing can sometimes be done as homework to decrease time spent in lieu of physical activity. Some examples of reaction and opinion papers include these:

1. "I Urge" telegrams: Send a "telegram" urging someone to do something, change something, or stop doing something. For example, "To Mother, I urge you to stop smoking. Your loving daughter."[43]
2. "I Learned" statements: Write a brief statement of what you learned by doing a specific activity, for

example, going on a field trip or participating in a challenging activity such as rappelling.[44]
3. Write reactions to a statement or quote such as "It's not whether you win or lose, but how you play the game," or "Winning is not the most important thing; it is the only thing," or "When the going gets tough, the tough get going," or "They didn't really lose the game; they only lost the score."

Procedures
1. Establish a nonthreatening, supportive environment in which students feel free to express their feelings.
2. Have students write their feelings about some specific topic.
3. Avoid grading reaction papers.

Goal Setting Students learn to set realistic goals through practice. Since students have various abilities and backgrounds, they should be helped to set goals that are challenging and yet can result in successful achievement. Students will often set goals lower than their true expectations so they will not be penalized by failure to meet their goals. Some ideas for goal setting are as follows:

1. The Goalpost:[45]
   a. Decorate the bulletin board in the form of a goalpost.
   b. Have students record goals on footballs (use 3″ × 5″ cards or create these on the computer) and post them below the crossbar.
   c. Each day students achieve their goals, they can move the football above the goalpost.
   d. Allow students time to share their successes with the class.
2. The Envelope:
   a. Have students record long-term goals.
   b. Place them in a sealed envelope for each class.
   c. Open the envelope at the end of the unit and redistribute them so students can see their progress.
   d. Allow students to share their successes.

Procedures
1. Help students think of ideas for goals using the following or other techniques:
   a. Questions.
      (1) What skill would you like to be able to do better when we complete this unit?
      (2) What talent do you wish you had?
   b. Suppose a doctor just told you that you have only one year to live. What would you do differently? How would you change your life? What is stopping you from doing these things now? Let's set a goal to achieve some of them.[46]
2. Help students clarify goals. Goals should be
   a. clearly defined.
   b. desirable, worthwhile, challenging.
   c. achievable.
   d. measurable in terms of time and quantity.
   e. controllable (goals involving another person require that person's permission).
   f. designed so that achievement results in a better self.[47]

Discussion Group consideration of a question or real-life problem can help students clarify values and concepts. Students can discuss the implications of the problem and how it is similar to and different from other problems they are familiar with. Through individual participation, students have opportunities to organize and communicate their thoughts and to learn respect for the viewpoints of others. Care must be taken, however, to encourage everyone to participate, rather than allowing a few talkative students to monopolize the conversation or reverting to a question-answer session. The following ideas can help to initiate a discussion:

1. Continuum.
   a. Draw a continuum on the chalkboard.
   b. Label 0 in the center, degrees toward the ends, and name the ends:

      Cooperative — Competitive
      Clark 40 30 20 10 0 10 20 30 40 Connie

   c. Have students place themselves on the continuum. (Do not let them position themselves in the center.)
   d. Discuss where the most popular, happiest, or capable student would be and why.
2. Priority or ranking.[48]
   a. Rank a list of three to five situations from best to worst.
   b. Think of a situation that is better than and one that is worse than the situations given.
   c. Discuss the rankings.
   d. Example: Rank the actions you might take when you see another student cheating off your paper on a test.
      (1) Do nothing.
      (2) Hide your paper.
      (3) Tell the teacher.
3. Value voting.[49]
   a. Read questions and have the class vote for or against each one.
   b. Sample questions:
      (1) Would you try rappelling?
      (2) Would you turn in a friend who cheated on a test?
      (3) Case studies or moral dilemmas. Discuss situations that require a decision and a plan of action (see example in Chapter 5).
      (4) Devil's advocate. Take a nonpopular view of an issue and encourage reactions from students.

(5) Incomplete sentences. Have students complete sentences such as the following and discuss them: Competition is . . . Winning is . . .

Procedures

1. Make sure students have the knowledge on which the discussion will be based.
2. Define the topic.
3. Work from an idea such as a visual aid, demonstration, quote, provocative question, or film.
4. Keep to the topic.
5. Involve everyone who wants to participate; avoid required participation.
6. Summarize periodically.
7. Draw conclusions.

Role Playing Role playing is an exploration of interpersonal relations problems by re-creating or acting out real-life situations and then discussing them. Problems can include social events, personal concerns, values, problem behaviors, or social skills. Some examples are the following:

1. A coach kicks a player off the team for not conforming to the rules regarding length of hair. The student threatens the coach's safety.
2. A football player fails a test in English and is ineligible for the championship game this weekend. You are the player's best friend and the English teacher is your aunt.

Sensitivity modules, such as staying in a wheelchair for a day to see what having a disability is like or swimming without the use of the legs, can increase student empathy for others. Through playing the roles of other people, students can explore and begin to understand the feelings, attitudes, and values of others in social situations, as well as the consequences of their behaviors on others. As they become more aware of the values of society, they also develop an awareness of alternative ways to solve problems. Some students are comfortable with role playing because they can act out their own feelings without fear of reprisal. Others have difficulty portraying feelings, so avoid embarrassing these students.

Procedures

1. Define the problem situation, which might include social problems, personal concerns, values, problem behaviors, or social skills. Choose easy problems first.
2. Prepare role sheets that describe the feelings or values of the character to be played (optional).
3. Introduce students to a problem through a real-life situation far enough away from the students to remove threat or stress yet close enough to draw out the relationship between the behavior in the problem and parallel behavior within the class or school. Ask students to think about what they would do under the same circumstances.
4. Select participants from volunteers. Avoid assigning roles based on peer pressure or the natural role of the student. Assign minor roles to shy individuals. Use role sheets if desired.
5. Clarify the setting, that is, place, time, situation, roles.
6. Assign observers specific things to look for, such as feelings of certain players or alternative endings.
7. Role play several times if needed to bring out possible alternative behaviors and their consequences.
8. Discuss behaviors and feelings. Relate the role-playing situation to students' actual behavior in a nonthreatening way.
9. Discuss the role-playing situation, successes and failures, and how it could be improved.

Review Question: What affective strategies can be used to affect student attitudes and values?

Summarizing and Reviewing Lessons

A carefully prepared summary at the end of a lesson ties together the loose ends and highlights the important points. It also gives the students an opportunity to ask questions and provides the teacher with an opportunity to correct any inaccuracies acquired by the students. Some ideas for summarizing a lesson include the following:

1. Summarize the main idea of the lesson with a short statement and tell what the students should realize as an outcome.
2. Assign one or two students to listen carefully and tell the class afterward what the lesson was about.
3. Have students write or tell in their own words what they think the main idea is.
4. Use a worksheet to help students summarize the main idea of the lesson.
5. Have several students in turn tell one thing learned from the lesson.
6. Divide the class into small groups. Each group in turn acts out a part of the lesson while the other groups try to guess what is being depicted (charades).
7. Present a real-life situation that could be resolved by using lesson ideas.
8. Give an oral or written quiz.
9. Use instructional games to test the information taught.

Some ways to review a lesson:

1. Have students keep records of their progress with lesson objectives.
2. Have students write briefly on a previous lesson topic.
3. Have students perform any specific skill previously taught.

The way is clear for every physical education instructor to be creative and design "new" styles and strategies for teaching in the future. The committed teacher is limited by only one criterion—is it successful in teaching students?

Review Question: How can lessons be summarized and reviewed?

NOTES

1. D. Laird and F. Blecher, How master trainers get that way, *Training and Development Journal 38,* no. 5 (1984): 73.
2. E. Francke, Excellence in instruction, *Journal of Physical Education, Recreation and Dance 54,* no. 7 (1983): 55–56.
3. N. L. Gage, The yield of research on teaching, *Phi Delta Kappan 60* (1978): 229–35; R. C. Hawley, *Human Values in the Classroom: Teaching for Personal and Social Growth* (Amherst, MA: Education Research Associates, 1973).
4. P. L. Peterson, Direct instruction reconsidered, in P. L. Peterson and H. J. Walberg, eds., *Research on Teaching: Concepts, Findings, and Implications* (Berkeley: McCutchan, 1979), 57–69.
5. M. Goldberger, Effective learning through a spectrum of teaching styles, *The Journal of Physical Education, Recreation and Dance 55,* no. 81 (1984): 17.
6. R. W. Tyler, *Basic Principles of Curriculum and Instruction* (Chicago: University of Chicago, 1949).
7. J. E. Rink, *Teaching Physical Education for Learning,* 4th ed. (Boston: McGraw-Hill, 2002).
8. Hawley, *Human Values in the Classroom.*
9. J. Brophy, Successful teaching strategies for the inner-city child, *Phi Delta Kappan 63* (1982): 527–30; P. L. Peterson, Direct instruction reconsidered, in P. L. Peterson and H. J. Walberg, eds., *Research on Teaching: Concepts, Findings, and Implications* (Berkeley: McCutchan, 1979), 57–69.
10. G. Graham, Review and implications of physical education experimental teaching unit research, in T. J. Templin and J. K. Olson, *Teaching in Physical Education* (Champaign, IL: Human Kinetics, 1983), 244–53.
11. M. Mosston and S. Ashworth, *Teaching Physical Education,* 5th ed. (San Francisco: Benjamin Cummings, 2002).
12. M. Goldberger, The spectrum of teaching styles: A perspective for research on teaching physical education, *The Journal of Physical Education, Recreation and Dance 63,* no. 91 (1992): 42–46.
13. M. Goldberger, Direct styles of teaching and psychomotor performance, in T. J. Templin and J. K. Olson, *Teaching in Physical Education* (Champaign, IL: Human Kinetics, 1983), 211–23.
14. K. Beckett, The effects of two teaching styles on college students' achievement of selected physical education outcomes, *Journal of Teaching in Physical Education 10* (1990): 153–69; M. Goldberger and P. Gerney, The effects of direct teaching styles on motor skill acquisition of fifth grade children, *Research Quarterly for Exercise and Sport 57* (1985): 215–19.
15. W. B. Salter and G. Graham, The effects of three disparate instructional approaches on skill attempts and student learning in an experimental teaching unit, *Journal of Teaching in Physical Education 4* (1985): 212–18.
16. F. E. Pettigrew and M. Heikkinen, Increased psychomotor skill through eclectic teaching, *Physical Educator 42* (1985): 140–46.
17. Mosston and Ashworth, *Teaching Physical Education.*
18. Goldberger, Effective learning, 17.
19. Goldberger, The spectrum, 42–46.
20. D. Hurwitz, A model for the structure of instructional strategies, *Journal of Teaching in Physical Education 4* (1985): 190–201.
21. B. Mohensen (ed.), *Concepts of Physical Education: What Every Student Needs to Know* (Reston, VA: American Alliance for Health, Physical Education, Recreation and Dance, 1998).
22. D. Zakrajsek and L. A. Carnes, *Individualizing Physical Education: Criterion Materials,* 2nd ed. (Champaign, IL: Human Kinetics, 1986).
23. Zakrajsek and Carnes, *Individualizing Physical Education.*
24. B. S. Bloom, *Human Characteristics and School Learning* (New York: McGraw-Hill, 1976).
25. K. P. Torshen, *The Mastery Approach to Competency Based Education* (New York: Academic, 1977).
26. J. H. Block, Mastery learning in the classroom: An overview on recent research, in J. Block, ed., *Schools, Society and Mastery Learning* (New York: Holt, Rinehart & Winston, 1974).
27. D. W. Ryan and M. Schmidt, *Mastery Learning: Theory, Research and Implementation* (Available from Ontario Department of Education, Toronto, 1979); J. H. Block and R. B. Burns, Mastery learning, in L. S. Shulman, ed., *Review of Research in Education* (Itasca: Peacock 1977); Bloom, *Human Characteristics;* K. Cotton and W. G. Savard, *Mastery Learning. Topic Summary Report,* June 1982. (ERIC Document Reproduction Service no. ED 218 279); Torshen, *The Mastery Approach.*
28. A. A. Annarino, Accountability—An instructional model for secondary physical education, *Journal of Physical Education and Recreation 52,* no. 3 (1981): 55–56; M. Ashy and A. M. Lee, Effects of a mastery learning strategy on throwing accuracy and technique, *Abstracts of Research Papers—1984* (Reston, VA: American Alliance for Health, Physical Education, Recreation and Dance, 1984), March–April; C. L. Blakemore, *The Effects of Mastery Learning on the Acquisition of Psychomotor Skills,* Doctoral dissertation, Temple University, Philadelphia, PA, 1985; C. L. Blakemore, *The Effects and Implications of Teaching Psychomotor Skills Using Mastery Learning Techniques,* Paper presented at the International Conference on Research in Teacher Education and Teaching in Physical Education, University of British Columbia, Vancouver, BC, May 1986; C. L. Blakemore, H. G. Hilton, J. M. Harrison, T. L. Pellett, and J. Gresh, Comparison of students taught basketball skills using mastery and nonmastery learning methods, *Journal of Teaching in Physical Education 11* (1992): 235–47; J. P. Chambless, E. R. Anderson, and J. H. Poole, *Mastery Learning of Stunts and Tumbling Activities for the Mentally Retarded* (Oxford: Mississippi University, North Mississippi Retardation Center, 1980); R. Edwards, The effects of performance standards on

behavior patterns and motor skill achievement in children, *Journal of Teaching in Physical Education 7* (1988): 90–102; H. J. Heitmann and M. E. Kneer, *Physical Education Instructional Techniques: An Individualized Humanistic Approach* (Englewood Cliffs, NJ: Prentice-Hall, 1976); M. W. Metzler, Analysis of a mastery learning/personalized system of instruction for teaching tennis, in M. Pieron and G. Graham, eds., *Sport Pedagogy* (Champaign, IL: Human Kinetics, 1984); M. Metzler, K. Eddlemen, L. Treanor, and R. Cregger, *Teaching Tennis with an Instructional System Design.* Paper presented at the Eastern Educational Research Association Annual meeting, Savannah, GA, February 1989.

29. T. M. Adams, G. K. Kandt, D. Throgmartin, and P. B. Waldrop, Computer-assisted instruction vs. lecture methods in teaching the rules of golf, *The Physical Educator 48* (1991): 146–50; T. M. Adams, P. B. Waldrop, and J. E. Justen, Effects of voluntary vs. required computer-assisted instruction on student achievement, *The Physical Educator 46* (1989): 213–17.
30. R. A. Smith, A teacher's views on cooperative learning, *Phi Delta Kappan 68* (1987): 663–66.
31. Gough, The key to improving schools, 656–62; Smith, A teacher's views.
32. Smith, A teacher's views.
33. D. W. Johnson, R. T. Johnson, E. J. Holubec, and P. Roy, *Circles of Learning: Cooperative in the Classroom* (Alexandria, VA: Association for Supervision and Curriculum Development, 1984).
34. Smith, A teacher's views.
35. Adams et al., Computer-assisted instruction; M. L. Sterne, Cooperative learning, *Strategies 3,* no. 5 (1990): 15–16.
36. D. R. Glover and D. W. Midura, *Team Building through Physical Challenges* (Champaign, IL: Human Kinetics, 1992); D. W. Midura and D. R. Glover, *More Team Building Challenges* (Champaign, IL: Human Kinetics, 1995).
37. L. S. Fairman and D. Nitchman, A bowling program in the gymnasium, in R. P. Carlson ed., *Ideas II: A Sharing of Teaching Practices by Secondary School Physical Education Practitioners* (Reston, VA: American Alliance for Health, Physical Education, Recreation and Dance, 1984), 66–68; M. Krumm, Tennis, despite weather and site restrictions, in R. P. Carlson ed., *Ideas II: A Sharing of Teaching Practices by Secondary School Physical Education Practitioners* (Reston, VA: American Alliance for Health, Physical Education, Recreation and Dance, 1984), 38–39.
38. J. E. Nelson, Teaching cross-country skiing, *Journal of Physical Education, Recreation and Dance 55* (1984): 58–64.
39. K. Wright and J. Walker, Rainy day golf, *Journal of Health, Physical Education and Recreation 40,* no. 9 (1969): 83.
40. Mosston and Ashworth, *Teaching Physical Education.*
41. C. R. Hobbs, *The Power of Teaching with New Techniques* (Salt Lake City: Deseret Books, 1972).
42. R. M. Gagné, L. J. Briggs, and W. W. Wager, *Principles of Instructional Design* (Fort Worth, TX: Harcourt Brace Jovanovich, 1992).
43. M. Harmin and S. B. Simon, How to help students learn to think . . . about themselves, *The High School Journal 55,* no. 6 (1972): 256–64.
44. Harmin, How to help students.
45. J. Canfield and H. C. Wells, *100 Ways to Enhance Self-Concept in the Classroom: A Handbook for Teachers and Parents* (Englewood Cliffs, NJ: Prentice-Hall, 1976).
46. Canfield and Wells, *100 Ways to Enhance Self-Concept.*
47. Canfield and Wells, *100 Ways to Enhance Self-Concept.*
48. Hawley, *Human Values in the Classroom.*
49. Hawley, *Human Values in the Classroom.*

C H A P T E R

10

Program Materials and Activities

Study Stimulators

1. What learning resources and materials should the teacher consider when planning the instructional program?
2. What media would you feel comfortable using in your program?
3. How might you incorporate technology into your teaching?
4. How might you structure a content unit on fitness?
5. What motivation techniques would you use to encourage students to perform up to their potential in a unit of movement skills?
6. Design the playing schedule for eight teams in a round robin tournament.
7. How would you encourage students to learn concepts about physical activity?
8. How would you justify incorporating a "risk activity" into your program?
9. How might interdisciplinary units or special days contribute to your physical education program?

Committed, innovative teachers have many resources available for implementing an instructional program to achieve the physical education content standards. Teachers must be willing to teach traditional activities in nontraditional ways and incorporate innovative activities such as adventure and challenge activities or integrated units into their curriculum. Teachers are always expected to make learning meaningful and motivating even on rainy days, shortened days, days before vacations, or any other circumstance that may hinder the normal operation of the class. This chapter will present numerous resources and ideas to help physical education teachers plan programs that meet the needs of all students in a variety of circumstances.

Selecting Instructional Materials

The purpose of instructional materials is to achieve instructional objectives effectively and economically. They can increase student motivation and create heightened interest and enjoyment in learning by increasing visual involvement and reducing the amount of teacher talk. They can be used to introduce a lesson, present new material, clarify a subject or discussion, or summarize a lesson. It has been said that approximately 83 percent of all learning occurs through sight, only 11 percent through hearing, and less than 6 percent through the other senses. Retention is increased fourfold over hearing only by the use of visual involvement and nearly sevenfold by combining the use of visual and auditory senses. Instructional materials accomplish these tasks by involving students in the learning process. An old Chinese proverb points this out very well. It says:

I hear, I forget.
I see, I remember.
I do, I understand.

Ideas for instructional materials can be obtained from other teachers, the Internet, students, parents, catalogs of instructional aids, or a district or school resource center. The American Alliance for Health, Physical Education, Recreation, and Dance also publishes catalogs of instructional materials. A summary of various types of instructional materials with their advantages and disadvantages is shown in Table 10.1.

Teachers should attempt to choose materials that provide experiences as close to real life as possible. Other considerations—such as student safety, money, and practicality—will, of course, restrict the selection. Costly materials should be evaluated by teachers, students, parents, and administrators so that the needs of all are considered. Educators should consider the learning potential of the materials by asking the following questions about them:

1. Do they make a meaningful contribution to the topic under study?
2. Do they develop concepts that are difficult to convey through another medium?
3. Are they accurate, and authentic?
4. Are they up-to-date?
5. Are they worth the time, cost, and effort involved?
6. Do they develop critical thinking skills?
7. Are they appropriate for the age, intelligence, and experience level of students?

Examine the technical quality of the materials to determine whether the mode of communication is adequate for the intended purpose and the message unbiased and free from objectionable propaganda or distractions. Ease of presentation is a third consideration. Often, management problems make instructional materials ineffective when, in fact, it is the management system that needs correction. These factors should be considered before purchasing equipment. The following examples of instructional aids and materials may be helpful to teachers seeking ways to enrich programs.

Examples of Instructional Materials

Three general types of aids and materials commonly used in schools are (1) media of various types, (2) personal resource files, and (3) technology.

Media

Although instructional materials can be used effectively to enhance motivation and learning, research often reveals no

TABLE 10.1 Types of Instructional Materials

Medium	Uses	Advantages	Disadvantages
Charts Posters Bulletin boards	Attract attention. Arouse interest. Reinforce and add dimension. Provide concrete meaning to abstract ideas.	Inexpensive. No equipment needed. Easy to use and store. Readily available.	Limited to two dimensions. No motion.
Chalkboards/white boards	Clarify sequence of events. Focus attention. Stimulate discussion.	Flexibility and versatility. Availability. Size.	
Overhead transparencies	Graphic presentations.	Inexpensive software. Availability. Project in light room. Flexible sequence. Base of operation at front of room. All advantages of chalkboard plus.	
Handouts	For important information: as a quiz as a guide as a reminder. To emphasize a point. For a complete explanation.	Can be prepared in advance. Can be retained for future reference and review.	

Continued

TABLE 10.1 Continued

Medium	Uses	Advantages	Disadvantages
Audiotapes Compact discs—audio	Music fitness testing. Create a mood.	Ease of production of tapes. Low cost, accessible.	
Videotapes Films CDs—visual DVDs	Evaluation of student performance. Self-evaluation of student or teacher. Magnification of small objects. Students can make own videos. Individual study. Homework. Stimulates verbal communication and creativity. Present meanings involving motion. Compel attention. Heighten reality. Speed up or slow down time. Enlarge or reduce size. Bring past or present into class. Build common denominator of experience. Influence and change attitudes. Promote understanding of abstract concepts.	Instant replay. Can save for future use. Can pre-record. Inexpensive. Portable. Ease of operation. Can be interfaced with a computer for individualized instruction.	Internally controlled pacing. Fixed sequence.
Computers	Computer-assisted instruction. Record keeping. Word processing. Information gathering.	High interest. Fast.	Equipment often limited to computer lab or resource center. Software is currently limited.
Illustrated lectures with computer or slide projector	History, geography. Concepts.	Magnification or reduction. Inexpensive software. High reality. Can be combined with audio.	Requires darkened room for slide projection.
Magnetic boards	Strategy talks.	Easy. Attention-getting.	
Objects and displays	Examples of real-life situations. Comparisons.	Enlargement or reduction. High reality—3-D.	

increase in learning. Students are media saturated. Teachers compete with the multimillion-dollar budgets of television and movies. Media used in class have to be exceptional for students to respond positively. Instructional media are of the most value when they are closely correlated with instructional objectives, so they can supplement and increase teacher effectiveness. Media must never be used just to take up time on a rainy day or when the teacher is unprepared. No medium can substitute for a concerned, well-prepared teacher.

A live demonstration is often more effective than a visual aid. However, a videotape can give the entire class the view obtained by the observer in the most advantageous position. Close-ups afford all members of a large class the opportunity to see the motion clearly. Another benefit of this type of media is that it can reproduce action that the observer rarely sees, such as an underwater view of a swimming stroke or a slow-motion view of a complex skill. Through the use of slow motion, it is possible to analyze sports skills in terms of body position, timing, and the relationship of skills to game play.

The instant replay feature of the videorecorder makes it a terrific teaching aid because players can see themselves in action. Videotaping shows learners their own mistakes or successes. By helping students compare their own performance with the performance of a model, videotape feedback can be even more valuable. Videotapes can be retained over a period of time to show achievement and progress in learning. Digital pictures can be used to provide feedback on posture.

Personal Resource File

A personal resource file is a file of instructional materials that can be easily located and replaced for future reference and use. A practical filing system is one that functions effectively in the situation in which the teacher is working. Materials might include pictures, items for lesson and unit planning, skill analyses, evaluation materials, handouts, study sheets, instructional media lists, books, and pamphlets. Labeling each item allows it to be returned to its location when not in use. Files might include community resources and lists of people willing to assist in developing or conducting learning activities, or for special reports or projects. One of the simplest methods of filing is to have a file folder for each sport or topic. This might be expanded later as in the following examples of file titles:

Archery—Unit Plans
Archery—Equipment
Archery—Skill Evaluation
Archery—Knowledge Evaluation

Of course, the filing system must agree with the teacher's personal style and use materials that are readily available.

Technology

The availability and types of technology, both computers and other electronic technologies, has been increasing at a rate that makes it difficult to keep up with all the developments. In fact schools have not kept up with the technology used in businesses, homes, and the marketplace.[1] For teachers it has the potential to increase efficiency, but it can also increase the demands upon a teacher's time. One author suggests that using technology does not increase learning nor does it diminish learning. Technology can be an effective learning tool for students with certain learning styles. Technology might actually inhibit learning for some students.[2] Another author reviewed a study in which students made significant gains in math and reading levels using computer-assisted instruction.[3]

This section of the chapter will cover present and future uses of technology in physical education and by teachers and parents, technology standards, and suggested computer competencies a beginning physical education teacher should have.

Uses of Technology Technology should be used only if it will enhance the achievement of physical education objectives.[4] Technology is being used effectively by many PK–12 physical education teachers. One such teacher is Sue Schiemer. She has created five technology developmental levels. These levels reflect different purposes for the use of technology as well as recognizing different levels of competence in technology use. Below are the five developmental levels and the purpose of technology use at each level. Table 10.2 lists examples of the technologies used at each level by students and teachers.

Level I—Complete a task more efficiently and effectively.

Level II—Learn/demonstrate mastery of skills and concepts in novel ways.

Level III—Individualized delivery of course content and personalized documentation of student learning.

Level IV—Realize the promise of integration, flexibility, and multiple network capabilities.

Level V—Does not have a specific purpose listed since this level is still in developmental stages and not clearly defined.[5]

Several articles and books have been written that explain in more detail some uses of the technologies listed in Table 10.2.[6]

Teachers need to be alert to potential problems that may exist with the use of technology in physical education. One is the ability to find technology in economically deprived areas. Use of technology can take away activity time. Teachers need to find effective ways to integrate technology use to avoid decreases in physical activity. Technology will not make a poor teacher a good teacher. The current literature does not indicate whether technology use is the best way to teach.[7]

Another potential problem is the time required initially to learn new software, develop materials, and integrate technology into instruction. Computers are often touted for their ability to save time. This is true after the initial work is completed. A better statement about computers is that they allow us to do more.

One area in which technology can save time centers around administrative tasks. Software has been written for use with handheld PCs and Palm computers. One such program is PE Manager.[8] The software can be set up to take attendance and record all activities and scores related to an assessment and grading scheme. The data are collected in the gymnasium and then synchronized with a desktop or laptop computer. If parents supply e-mail addresses, they can be sent regular updates on student progress.

Other means are also available to enhance communication with parents. Parents in some schools can check their child's grades, transcripts, and attendance records on the World Wide Web.[9] School policies and upcoming events can be posted on the school home page. E-mail allows teachers and parents to communicate successes and concerns to one another. This can be particularly effective in contacting some parents at work. The future use of technology in schools is only limited by the abilities and creativity of educators on all levels.

TABLE 10.2 Technology Developmental Levels

	Students	Teachers
LEVEL I	Body composition analyzers Digital pedometer/cyclometer Pocket-sized pulse checkers Portable wrist/finger blood pressure Monitors (heart rate and calorie counters)	Software Wireless microphones 2-way radios CD player
LEVEL II	Videos Computer-assisted instructional software Videotaping Digital cameras	Integrated software package (Microsoft Works) Internet E-mail Websites–PE Central
LEVEL III	Heart rate monitors Interactive video CD-ROMs—*Olympic Gold* Programmable exercise equipment Laser disc—*Windows on Science*	Handheld computers (Palm Pilot, pocket PC) Authoring programs Presentation software
LEVEL IV	Multimedia projects Distance learning Electronic portfolios Video conferencing Electronic field trips Digital versatile discs (DVDs)	On-line courses
LEVEL V	Virtual reality Movement tracking 3-D animation	ALT-PE Teacher observation program

Source: Developed by Sue Schiemer; used by permission.

Review Question: How might technology be used in PK–12 physical education classes?

Technology Standards In the mid to late 1990s, each curriculum area developed content standards to guide instruction in every academic field. The International Society for Technology in Education (ISTE) has developed technology standards for all students. The ISTE stated, "To live, learn, and work successfully in an increasingly complex and information-rich society, students must use technology effectively. Within a sound educational setting, technology can enable students to become the following:

- Capable information technology users
- Information seekers, analyzers, and evaluators
- Problem solvers and decision makers
- Creative and effective users of productivity tools
- Communicators, collaborators, publishers, and producers
- Informed, responsible, and contributing citizens."[10]

ISTE has developed Technology Foundation Standards for Students. These are divided into six broad categories. Table 10.3 lists the six standards.[11] Profiles for Technology Literate Students were also developed and provide performance indicators at various grade levels for the assessment of achievement of the respective standards. Schools create activities that demonstrate the accomplishment of the performance indicators. Table 10.4 is the Profile for Technology Literate Students for grades 6–8. Table 10.5 is a sample physical education activity.

Review Question: In what ways can physical education contribute to the achievement of national technology standards?

Preservice Computer Competencies Most PK–12 teachers did not receive training in the use of technology in physical education in their undergraduate training. The training they have received has been in the form of in-service training, workshops, graduate courses, and self-training. Preservice teachers who are graduating now should be receiving training in technology use as an important part of their undergraduate curriculum. Some

TABLE 10.3 National Educational Technology Standards for Students

Basic Operations and Concepts

1. Students demonstrate a sound understanding of the nature and operation of technology systems.
2. Students are proficient in the use of technology.

Social, Ethical, and Human Issues

1. Students understand the ethical, cultural, and societal issues related to technology.
2. Students practice responsible use of technology systems, information, and software.
3. Students develop positive attitudes toward technology uses that support lifelong learning, collaboration, personal pursuits, and productivity.

Technology Productivity Tools

1. Students use technology tools to enhance learning, increase productivity, and promote creativity.
2. Students use productivity tools to collaborate in constructing technology-enhanced models, preparing publications, and producing other creative works.

Technology Communications Tools

1. Students use telecommunications to collaborate, publish, and interact with peers, experts, and other audiences.
2. Students use a variety of media and formats to communicate information and ideas effectively to multiple audiences.

Technology Research Tools

1. Students use technology to locate, evaluate, and collect information from a variety of sources.
2. Students use technology tools to process data and report results.
3. Students evaluate and select new information resources and technological innovations based on the appropriateness to specific tasks.

Technology Problem-Solving and Decision-Making Tools

1. Students use technology resources for solving problems and making informed decisions.
2. Students employ technology in the development of strategies for solving problems in the real world.

Source: International Society for Technology in Education, 480 Charnelton St., Eugene, OR 97401. Available at cnets.iste.org.

TABLE 10.4 Profile for Technology Literate Students, Grades 6 to 8

Performance Indicators

All students should have opportunities to demonstrate the following performances:

Prior to Completion of Grade 8 Students Will

1. Apply strategies for identifying and solving routine hardware and software problems that occur during everyday use.
2. Demonstrate knowledge of current changes in information technologies and the effect those changes have on the workplace and society.
3. Exhibit legal and ethical behaviors when using information and technology, and discuss consequences of misuse.
4. Use content-specific tools, software, and simulations (e.g., environmental probes, graphing calculators, exploratory environments, web tools) to support learning and research.
5. Apply productivity/multimedia tools and peripherals to support personal productivity, group collaboration, and learning throughout the curriculum.
6. Design, develop, publish, and present products (e.g., web pages, videotapes) using technology resources that demonstrate and communicate curriculum concepts to audiences inside and outside the classroom.
7. Collaborate with peers, experts, and others using telecommunications and collaborative tools to investigate curriculum-related problems, issues, and information, and to develop solutions or products for audiences inside and outside the classroom.
8. Select and use appropriate tools and technology resources to accomplish a variety of tasks and solve problems.
9. Demonstrate an understanding of concepts underlying hardware, software, and connectivity, and practical applications to learning and problem solving.
10. Research and evaluate the accuracy, relevance, appropriateness, comprehensiveness, and bias of electronic information sources concerning real-world problems.

Source: International Society for Technology in Education, 480 Charnelton St., Eugene, OR 97401. Available at cnets.iste.org.

higher education accreditation agencies expect college students to have a specified level of technology literacy. ISTE has identified six technology standards for teachers (see Table 10.6). College and university professors should also be modeling the use of technology in their instruction. Table 10.7 lists a set of computer competencies that preservice physical education teachers will have upon graduation from one university.

Review Questions: Which technology competencies do you have? Which ones do you need to obtain? How will you obtain these competencies?

TABLE 10.5 Sample Physical Education Activity

Name of Activity: Personal Sport Project
Grade Level: 8
Performance Indicators: 4, 5, 6, 7, 8, 9, 10
Subject Area: Physical Education
Procedure 1: Students will use monitors to record their heart rates during specific periods of time. They will input the raw data into a spreadsheet and chart the results.
Procedure 2: Students select a sport and investigate the skills necessary to become proficient at this sport. Using a hypermedia program, students will create a skills analysis stack or a video.
Software: Hyperstudio, PowerPoint
Evaluation: Teacher observation, student reports, student presentations

Source: International Society for Technology in Education, 480 Charnelton St., Eugene, OR 97401.

SELECTING PROGRAM ACTIVITIES

The remainder of this chapter will discuss the selection of program activities in the following areas: fitness, movement skills, concepts, affective activities, interdisciplinary units, and special days/weeks. The sections include a discussion of instruction and practice, motivational techniques, and evaluation of progress related to that area.

Fitness

"Fitness is the capacity to achieve the optimal quality of life."[12] Physical fitness is defined as "the ability to carry out daily tasks with vigor and alertness, without undue fatigue, and with ample energy to enjoy leisure-time pursuits and to meet unforeseen emergencies."[13] Health-related fitness includes cardiorespiratory fitness, muscular strength and endurance, body composition, and flexibility.

Studies clearly show the health benefits of regular physical activity in reducing the risk of dying prematurely; heart disease; diabetes; high blood pressure; colon cancer; depression; stress and anxiety; obesity; and unhealthy bones, muscles, and joints.[14] Muscular strength and endurance and flexibility are generally associated with a reduced risk of low back and other musculoskeletal problems.[15]

As stated in Chapter 1, the surgeon general has reported that we are a nation that needs to improve physical fitness levels. Satcher, Lee, and Joyner explain why this is so.

> Most Americans today are spared the burden of excessive physical labor. Indeed, few occupations today require significant physical activity, and most people use motorized transportation to get to work and to perform routine errands and tasks. Even leisure time is increasingly filled with sedentary behaviors, such as watching television, "surfing" the Internet, and playing video games.[16]

With activity participation for adolescents being especially low, and many physical education programs not meeting activity standards, physical education teachers must do a better job of fitness education. Often class periods are short, but Pangrazi and Corbin stated that students must be taught the importance of fitness and the process of gaining fitness even if sufficient time is unavailable to get fitness gains in physical education classes.[17] People who are trying to reduce coronary heart disease risk factors should not have to pay professionals to learn what they ought to have been taught in physical education.

TABLE 10.6 National Education Technology Standards for Teachers

I. Technology Operations and Concepts
Teachers demonstrate a sound understanding of technology operations and concepts.

II. Planning and Designing Learning Environments and Experiences
Teachers plan and design effective learning environments and experiences supported by technology.

III. Teaching, Learning, and the Curriculum
Teachers implement curriculum plans that include methods and strategies for applying technology to maximize student learning.

IV. Assessment and Evaluation
Teachers apply technology to facilitate a variety of effective assessment and evaluation strategies.

V. Productivity and Professional Practice
Teachers use technology to enhance their productivity and professional practice.

VI. Social, Ethical, Legal, and Human Issues
Teachers understand the social, ethical, legal, and human issues surrounding the use of technology in PK–12 schools and apply those principles in practice.

TABLE 10.7 Recommended Computer Competencies for Physical Education Preservice Teachers

1. Use word-processing software to create documents and for desktop publishing.
2. Use spreadsheets for developing budgets.
3. Use the Internet to find teaching ideas and information to be used in classes.
4. Use presentation software for curriculum and promotional presentations and teaching.
5. Use database software to create and maintain student records and equipment inventories.
6. Communicate via e-mail.
7. Use videotapes to analyze teaching and student performance.
8. Digitize video to analyze student skill performance and to detect errors.
9. Do fitness assessments using various technologies.
10. Use handheld computers for grading and student records.
11. Use sport CD-ROMs for learning strategies, rules, terms, and skill development.
12. Use heart rate monitors to monitor student performance, assess fitness, and monitor teaching effectiveness.
13. Analyze food intake using various diet-analysis programs.
14. Analyze fitness and activity levels.
15. Use digital cameras for skill analysis and development of electronic portfolios.
16. Develop electronic portfolios.
17. Develop web pages.
18. Develop written tests using specialized software programs.
19. Scan pictures for use in various types of documents.
20. Create tournaments and tournament schedules.
21. Create word games and puzzles to augment teaching.

Source: Part of the School of Physical Education Computer Competency Assessment Project Report, Ball State University, Muncie, IN, prepared by Marilyn Buck, August 1999.

Recognizing that our children are neither as active nor as healthy as many believe they should be and are also below healthy levels in the areas of hypertension, serum cholesterol, and obesity, physical educators should play a major role in health and fitness promotion for the citizens of tomorrow. Teachers need to provide activities to develop and maintain fitness, at the same time teaching them why it is important to do so.[18] This will take a full-scale effort. Physical education programs must try diligently to "turn kids on" to the grandeur of the human body. All students should be given the opportunity to learn the joys of being fit and being able to perform psychomotor skills successfully. Research has pointed out what students desire from physical education programs, and teachers are urged to pay attention to these desires when designing a fitness curriculum:

- Most students like physical education and will enroll when it doesn't interfere with required college prep courses.
- More favorable attitudes are produced when students are given opportunities for making decisions.
- Many students do not like activities designated as fitness activities, such as running and conditioning exercises.
- Students prefer that grades be based on subjective measures such as participation, effort, sportspersonship, and attitude rather than objective measures of homework, written tests, and skill and fitness testing.
- Students like classes that include a variety of activities.[19]

Such insights have prompted fitness experts to evaluate physical education programs, revise fitness tests, and design fitness-specific curricula. They have created fitness tests that assess students, require individual goal setting, recognize the accomplishments of each student, and emphasize a *lifelong physical activity lifestyle.* A relevant fitness course taught today would include the areas of cardiorespiratory fitness, muscular strength and endurance, body composition, flexibility, nutrition, and stress management. Fitness testing would be a part of the class, but *authentic assessment* would be incorporated and, as such, evaluation would be much more than fitness testing. Authentic assessment techniques allow the student to demonstrate desired behaviors in real-life situations rather than in artificial or contrived settings.[20] For fitness testing to be authentic it must (1) demonstrate the desired behavior, such as muscular strength via curl-up test; (2) link directly to the curriculum, that is, be done often enough to develop abdominal strength; (3) occur on an ongoing basis, and not be just one test score; (4) make students both capable of, and likely to, apply the tests and results outside the classroom, that is, continue to maintain and develop abdominal strength after leaving the class.[21]

Past fitness tests were designed to encourage recognition of the student who performed well according to norm-referenced criterion charts. Recent performance measures highlight performance standards that when achieved, forecast health and wellness. Students can choose a variety of ways to compete against only themselves as they strive to improve fitness measures. Rather than a select few receiving fitness awards, all students can be rewarded for their

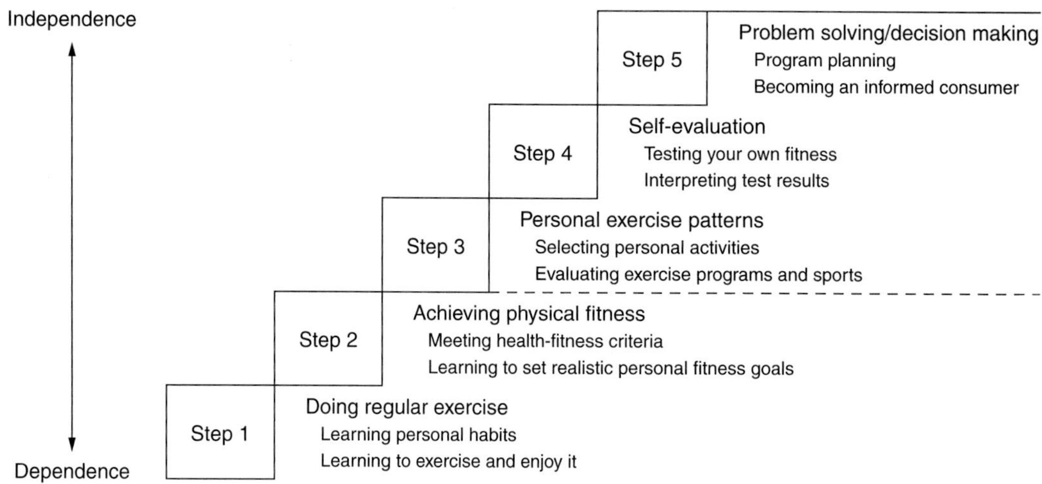

Figure 10-1

Stairway to lifetime fitness.

From *Fitness for Life: Teachers Annotated Edition* by C. B. Corbin and R. Lindsey. © 1993 by Scott Foresman. Used by permission.

efforts. The bottom line of any program should be to teach principles for *lifelong, individualized health-related fitness.* Fitness testing is one means of doing this because it aids students in knowing their current fitness status.

If fitness units taught today are going to have application for lifelong activity, and include authentic assessment, Strand et al. suggests a "concepts-based fitness course."[22] In such a course, students have a textbook, take part in lecture and lab experiences, do homework, take tests, have a variety of fitness activities, and learn how to design a personalized training program that stays with them. In such a course, there are meaningful "key concepts" and students have a sound knowledge base from which they can make applications. The components of such a course are (1) student performance standards, (2) instructional format, (3) activity/exercise program, (4) academic program, (5) assessment program, (6) personal portfolios with individual health and fitness plans, (7) incentive program, (8) exercise adherence and motivational strategies, (9) school-family programs, and (10) equipment and technology.

Concepts are taught in the classroom and often applied outside the classroom. It is vital that teachers get students involved in activities they like to do away from school. It's only when we do this that we have a chance of getting students to be active for a lifetime. Feingold substantiated this with classes he taught that only exercised in school half as much as traditional classes, yet their fitness levels improved more, because they exercised at home.[23]

AAHPERD recommends that teachers use "activities" as the foundation of a fun motivational program, and has provided activity guides for both the elementary and secondary levels.[24] In addition to students learning the cognitive and psychomotor concepts associated with fitness, they should also enjoy doing activities that increase and improve fitness levels. Such a program develops progressively and students take more and more responsibility for their own health. Corbin illustrates this concept in his stairway to lifetime fitness (see Figure 10-1).[25]

Instruction and Practice

Fitness programs must be carefully planned and structured so that they include opportunities to learn basic concepts and principles as well as to increase fitness. If students are to want to be active and fit for a lifetime, these activities need to be fun and engaging. The school of the twenty-first century has become a mecca for lifelong learning.[26] Physical education must fit into this paradigm and think of curriculum aids like climbing walls, technology that includes heart-rate monitors and exercise equipment, and stations to teach such activities as roller blading, skiing, and mountain biking. The imaginative teacher will capitalize on outside resources including the Internet, wellness centers, and community recreational opportunities by teaching students how to incorporate them into their lifestyle.

Before planning the curriculum, identify the exit outcomes you want students to have achieved when they leave the program. These would develop into program, course, unit, and lesson outcomes.[27] The foundation for such outcomes would be the National Standards for Physical Education (NASPE/AAHPERD), health education (American Health Assoc.), or dance education (NDA/AAHPERD). For example, a physical education teacher with a goal of *cardiovascular fitness* for students, and using the Content Standards in Physical Education, might have the exit outcomes listed in Table 10.8.[28]

The teacher is not left without help in developing programs and the curriculum. Fitness textbooks for students are being continually updated to aid teachers in the schools. Such texts include *Fitness Education* by Strand,

TABLE 10.8 NASPE Standards and Possible Outcomes in Fitness Unit

NASPE Standard	Outcome
1. Demonstrates competency in motor skills and movement patterns needed to perform a variety of physical activities. 2. Demonstrates understanding of movement concepts, principles, strategies, and tactics as they apply to the learning and performance of physical activities. 3. Participates regularly in physical activity. 4. Achieves and maintains a health-enhancing level of physical fitness. 5. Exhibits responsible personal and social behavior that respects self and others in physical activity settings. 6. Values physical activity for health, enjoyment, challenge, self-expression, and/or social interaction.	Will be able to correctly perform eight basic aerobic dance patterns. Will be able to list the six guidelines for safe aerobic-dance workouts. Will be able to compose an aerobic-dance routine using at least four basic patterns. Records aerobic dance workouts of at least twenty minutes, three times a week in an activity log to be turned in every four weeks. Will be able to score in the "good" category of either the Harvard Step Test, 1-Mile-Run Test, Pacer Test, 5-Mile Bike Test, or 12-Minute Swimming Test. Works cooperatively with a group of three to five others to compose an aerobic-dance routine and teach it to the class. Compose/teaches the aerobic-dance routine at both a beginning and intermediate level so all students can find success. Submits a journal once per week with entries pertaining to aerobic-dance workouts.

Scantling, and Johnson,[29] and the AAHPERD *Physical Best Teacher's Guide* and *Activity Guides.*[30]

Fitness activities may be planned for part or all of a period. Such activities might include exercise routines, circuit training, obstacle courses (see Figure 10-2), aerobic dance, jogging, cycling, swimming, or weight training. Short cognitive concepts can be given while students are warming up or performing the activity. Changes can also be made in traditional drills and games to increase the amount of vigorous activity during the physical education classes.[31] Some schools have a fitness room adjacent to the gymnasium (often a former equipment closet) and allow students to rotate to the fitness station during the period to work on those body areas that show the greatest need of improvement.

Many schools now have well-outfitted weight rooms thanks to parent-teacher groups or athletic support groups. Equipment such as that used in corporate fitness centers is sometimes donated by community businesses.[32] These options may require innovative scheduling, which might include longer periods of time achieved through block scheduling or activities outside of class. Such outside time could be found in *fitness breaks, recess, lunchtime, intramurals, after-school programs, home-based activities, cross-curricular events, and community events.* A fitness director may need to be hired to coordinate activities like family night, health fairs, Jump Rope/Hoops for Heart, and other events conducted during these activities outside class. However, when fitness activities are incorporated into the curriculum, it is suggested that *goal setting* be at the heart and soul of the program. Such a program is outlined in *The Physical Best Teacher's Guide.*[33] This program suggests the following strategies for successful goal setting with students:

1. Involve the student in the goal-setting process. Scores should be based on their efforts and not on norm-based materials.
2. Start small and progress.
3. Focus on improvements relative to an individual's past behavior. The lower the level of performance, the greater the potential for improvement, while the higher the performance, the less possibility for improvement.
4. Set specific and measurable goals.
5. Set challenging and realistic goals.
6. Write the goals down.
7. Provide students with strategies. They need to know *how* to change behavior. Provide examples.
8. Support and give feedback about progress toward goals. Write positive comments on journal entries/logs, and give personal feedback in class, such as "Keep up the good work."
9. Create goal stations. These are areas where students can work on specific goals with equipment and evaluation materials.
10. Provide opportunities for periodic evaluation. This way both you and the student will know if the goals are realistic and if progress is being made.[34]

The *Physical Best Program* suggests guidelines for activity:

1. Provide enough time for activity.
2. Let students individualize activities while exposing them to a variety of activities.

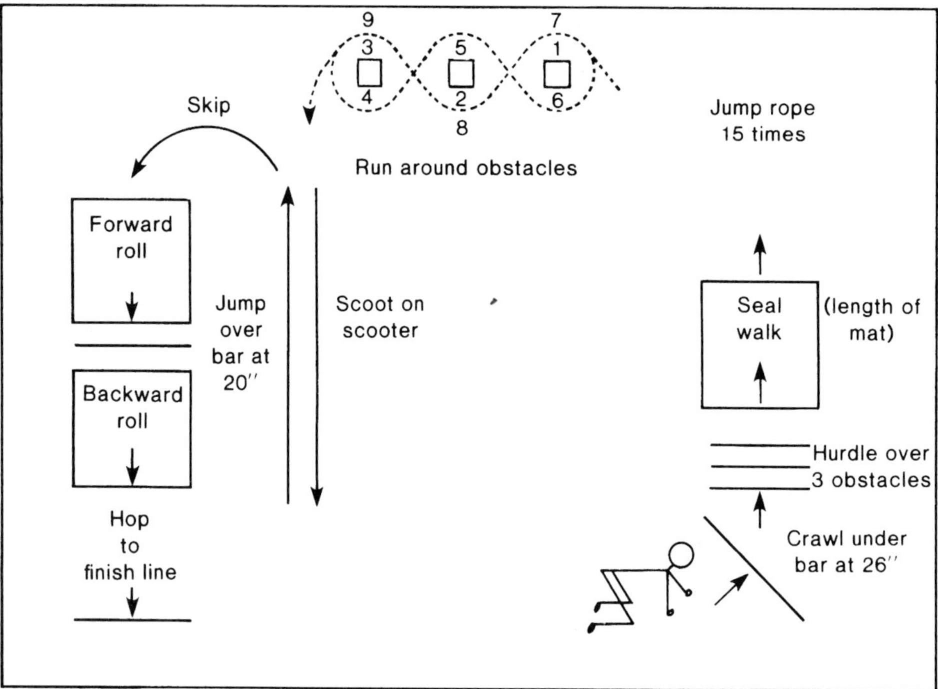

Figure 10-2

An example of an obstacle course.

3. Connect lessons to student interests.
4. Focus instruction feedback on the *process* rather than the *product.* Don't worry about how fast they run, but rather give feedback on their execution.
5. **Do not use exercise as punishment.**
6. **Do not overemphasize fitness test performances.** Focus on health criteria. Take special care not to undermine self-esteem. Always remember the dignity of the students, and use their names.
7. **Do not post fitness scores** or compare students to each other.
8. In the secondary school, be aware of social circles and help all students feel included.
9. Recognize that physical appearance is critical to teenagers.[35]

Motivational Techniques

A written questionnaire that is not graded but is used to stimulate interest and point out needed areas of instruction is an effective way to introduce a unit on fitness. Questions might include the following:

1. The emphasis in the United States today on healthy lifestyles has resulted in a more physically fit nation, especially the youth. __T__F
2. Exercising three days per week will maintain an adequate level of physical fitness. __T__F
3. Children and youth under the age of eighteen need not worry about coronary heart disease. __T__F
4. A person burns more calories jogging one mile than walking the same distance. __T__F
5. One must exercise at least sixty minutes per session to develop and maintain adequate physical fitness. __T__F
6. Performing exercises involving the hips and waist will reduce the fat in those areas. __T__F
7. Children who engage in a vigorous exercise program score higher on academic tests. __T__F
8. Exercise increases the appetite. __T__F
9. One should not exercise outside when temperatures reach zero degrees because the lungs may be damaged. __T__F
10. Golf is a good aerobic exercise for those walking the course. __T__F

As pointed out in Chapter 1, teachers themselves should be examples of fitness. This is a motivation for many students. Exercise with the students. Point out how other prominent people, such as movie stars, astronauts, and professional athletes, stay physically fit.[36] Be enthusiastic about physical fitness. The success of any fitness program lies with the teacher. "Excellent leadership can overcome poor equipment and facilities but the opposite is seldom true."[37] Nothing can substitute for the example and enthusiasm of a good teacher.

The students themselves are ultimately responsible for being fit. Each one must have *intrinsic motivation.* The teacher can aid this by providing a variety of *fun, enjoyable* activities. Another intrinsic motivator is the natural urge to learn and so there must be something for them to learn and efforts made to help them learn. If they can't perform skills successfully, they are not likely to pursue them later.[38]

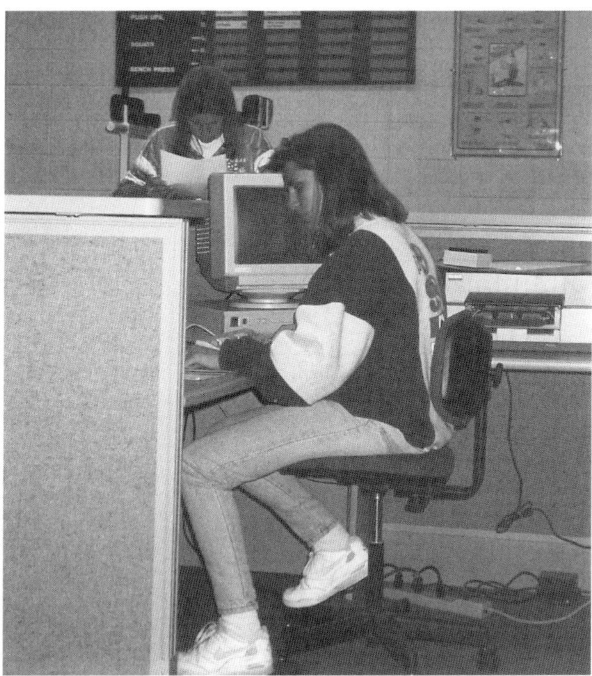

Students use the computer in the learning resource center to individualize their fitness programs.
© Tracy Pellet

Often extrinsic motivators are used such as stickers, treats, T-shirts, and certificates. As mentioned in Chapter 1, the teacher needs to be careful when using them. They may turn some children off to the activity, and they are "unlikely to promote lifetime physical activity patterns."[39] However, the chart shown in Figure 10-3 can be very motivational. Each class has a chart with a square block area for each student. Stickers or dots may be earned by students participating in acceptable fitness activities for thirty minutes outside of class. (Flexibility participation must be thirty minutes in the same week.) Students may earn stickers in any way they choose and arrange them on the chart. Other stickers may be earned in ways decided on by the class or the teacher (e.g., complete a three-day self-study of dietary habits and list appropriate changes).

Other motivational techniques include the following:

Unusual Events

1. Have a team jogging meet. Divide the class into teams of two or three people. Set a timer for a given time period, such as fifteen or thirty minutes. Team members alternate laps, one runner at a time, and report to a scorer at the conclusion of each lap. Joggers are allowed to walk, skip, run, or move as they wish, but the team with the most laps completed within the time period wins the meet.
2. Have competition among classes to see who can run the farthest in one month's time. Students record their laps each day. Awards may be given to individuals with the highest distance in each class and to all students who complete the goal.[40]
3. Have a treasure hunt in which students run from point to point as directed by a series of clues. Students can pick up a marker at each point to show that they covered the entire course.[41]
4. Sundberg suggests participation races in which students run to a given point and back, picking up a marker at the midpoint. Students are encouraged to pace themselves so they do not have to stop and walk.[42] Only those who finish are eligible for awards. Awards could be given for the fastest times as well as the team with the most finishers (divide the number of finishers by the number of starters). This type of race might be used at the end of a fitness unit after students have learned to pace themselves and have the endurance to last the entire distance.
5. Corbin suggests prediction races in which students attempt to run as close as possible to their predicted times. Individuals or teams can be used. The individual or team coming closest to its predicted time wins.[43]
6. Stein describes a "Run for Fun" in which students run a specified distance and then record their overall finish place and category on a card. Awards are given to those finishing first in each category. Although Stein suggests age and gender for the categories, many other categories could be selected, such as eye color, color of tennis shoes, or birth month.[44]
7. Elsey suggests organizing walking clubs or having class "walks out of town." The class establishes a goal and records the mileage of each class member. An announcement is made when the class arrives at its goal (i.e., walk to Disneyland).[45]

Fitness Programs Involving the School and Community

1. Fair: including displays, lectures, testing.
2. Contest: involving runners, walkers, cyclers, swimmers, wheelchair participants (e.g., Jump Rope for Heart).[46]

The family fitness program combines nutrition and fitness. Students receive points when an adult family member exercises with them. Recipes are sent home and the student gets points if his or her family uses the recipe. All family members are encouraged to participate together and T-shirts are given to each participant.[47]

It would work to substitute skipping, walking, hopping, sliding, and backward walking for running to give variety and successful experiences for all.

Evaluating Progress

With the transition from a fitness focus of *process* rather than *product,* programs now emphasize involvement by

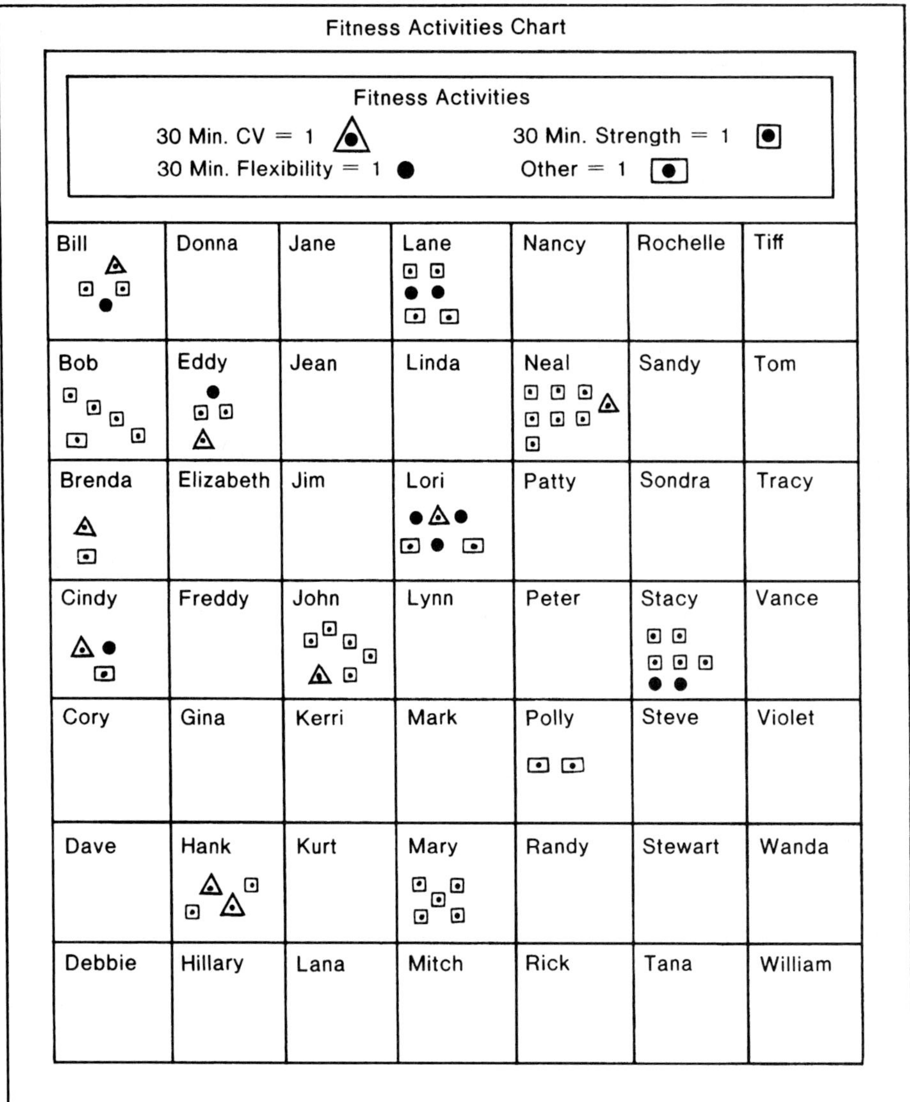

Figure 10-3

Fitness activities chart.

the individual participant. Students make choices about what they will do to become more fit and thus earn a grade. A simple *rubric* aids them in making these choices at the beginning of a unit (see Table 10.9). Instead of working for certificates of accomplishment, students are urged to complete individual goals through commitment to a contract filled out at the beginning of a unit. Fitness testing is done to aid the teacher and the student in knowing current fitness status and measurements. Materials to aid the teacher are also focusing on *process*—the process of teaching fitness. The most complete package for today's teacher comes from the American Fitness Alliance, a merger of AAHPERD, The Cooper Institute, and Human Kinetics (www.americanfitness.net). The outcome of this merger is the Physical Best Program. "Physical Best has been created specifically for the purpose of updating physical educators on the most effective strategies for helping their students gain the knowledge, skills, appreciation, and confidence needed to lead physically active, healthy lives."[48] The Alliance can provide a *Physical Best Teacher's Guide and Student Activity Guides,* testing resources for *FITNESSGRAM*® and Brockport Test, FitSmart Knowledge Exam, and other activity resources. In addition, the Alliance has introduced a certification program for physical education teachers who want to become Physical Best Health-Fitness Specialists. Two levels of certification are available through AAHPERD workshops.

1. *Physical Best Health-Fitness Specialist:* This person will know how to teach fitness and nutrition concepts through developmentally, and age-appropriate games and activities. Teacher preparation programs may want to certify their graduates to aid their employability.
2. *Physical Best Health-Fitness Instructor:* This person trains the specialist.

TABLE 10.9 Fitness Evaluation Rubric/Scoring Guide

Grade	Portfolio	Journal	Teaching	Written Exam
A (86–100 POINTS)	*50 points possible* • Exercise log/heart rate chart (Sept. 6–Dec. 6), participates at least 4 times per week (not 7) • Fitness Appraisal (4), 1 per month • Completed contract—all goals accomplished, with outline of training schedule	*25 points possible* • 1 entry per week • At least 100 words • Submit each Monday	*15 points possible* • Score of 20 or more on group evaluation—teaching of aerobics routine	*10 points possible* • Score 90% or better on exam given on Dec. 8; questions distributed on Sept. 13
B (66–85 POINTS)	*45 points possible* • Exercise log/heart rate chart (Sept. 6–Dec. 6), participates at least 4 times per week, but not each week • Fitness Appraisal (3), less than 1 per month • Completed contract—all but 1 goal accomplished, with outline of training schedule	*20 points possible* • 2 entries per month • At least 100 words	*13 points possible* • Score of 15–19 on group teaching evaluation	*7 points possible* • Score 76–89% on exam given on Dec. 8; questions distributed on Sept. 13
C (40–65 POINTS)	*37 points possible* • Exercise log/heart rate chart (Sept. 6–Dec. 6), participates at least 3 times per week, maybe not each week • Fitness Appraisal (2) • Completed contract—1/2 of goals accomplished, with outline of training schedule	*15 points possible* • 1 entry per month • Less than 100 words	*10 points possible* • Score of 10–14 on group teaching evaluation	*3 points possible* • Score 60–75% on exam given on Dec. 8; questions distributed on Sept. 13
D (15–39 POINTS)	*25 points possible* • Exercise log/heart rate chart (Sept. 6–Dec. 6), participates less than 3 times per week; incomplete heart rate chart • Fitness Appraisal (1) • Completed contract—less than 1/2 of goals accomplished, with outline of training schedule	*10 points possible* • Less than 1 entry per month • Less than 100 words	*4 points possible* • Score of less than 10 on group teaching evaluation	*0 points possible* • Score less than 59% on exam given on Dec. 8; questions distributed on Sept. 13
F—LESS THAN 15 POINTS				

The Physical Best testing tool is the *FITNESSGRAM®*. Scores on fitness tests are used for prescription and for individual goal setting. Students should perform periodic self-assessments and record progress toward personal goals. Tests are selected by the teacher from the following options and testing stations are set up so students can move quickly from station to station:

Aerobic fitness

- One-mile walk
- One-mile run
- PACER

Body composition

- Skinfold measurements
- Body-mass index

Muscular strength and endurance and flexibility

- Curl-up (abdominal strength)
- Push-up (upper-body strength)
- Modified pull-ups (upper-body strength)
- Pull-ups (upper-body strength)
- Flexed-arm hang (upper-body strength)
- Trunk lift (strength, flexibility)
- Back-saver sit and reach (flexibility)
- Shoulder stretch (flexibility)[49]

Students should be prepared in advance by doing activities designed to develop the various areas of fitness. They should understand that the testing is an aid for them to know their fitness status, to aid them in establishing fitness goals, and is *not the criteria for a grade.* In preparation for testing, the teacher may want to administer the *ACTIVITYGRAM* (Figure 10-4). This profile classifies the type of activities performed by the student based on categories from the Activity Pyramid conceptualized by Corbin and Pangrazi.[50]

The *FITNESSGRAM®* software offers a variety of options including various types of databases and reports (see Figure 10-5). These results should aid the student in filling out a fitness contract to govern activity involvement (see Tables 10.10 and 10.11).

Other programs include those developed by the President's Council on Physical Fitness (www.indiana.edu/~preschal). The tests include curl-ups or partial curl-ups, shuttle run, V-sit reach or sit and reach, one-mile run/walk or one-fourth mile or one-half mile, pull-ups, right-angle push-ups or flexed-arm hang. The Presidential Physical Fitness Award can be earned by the student in excellent fitness condition. The National Physical Fitness Award can be earned by those students in the fiftieth percentile. The Participant Physical Fitness Award can be earned by those students below the fiftieth percentile, and the Health Fitness Award can be earned by those students who reach a healthy level of fitness.

"Fitness testing that reveals whether students are healthy or at risk is a meaningful practice. It allows students to decide whether or not they need to improve their health status. Students need meaningful information to make thoughtful decisions about the quality of their lives."[51]

Pangrazi and Corbin suggest three types of fitness testing:

1. Self-testing programs: Partners work together to test each other. Each person produces his/her own fitness profile, which is private property. The student can set goals and regularly monitor her/his progress toward those goals. This approach allows testing several times a year.
2. Personal best testing programs: formal testing for the purpose of receiving awards. This testing could be scheduled before or after school or at any other time for anyone who was interested. Not everyone in the school would be required to participate.
3. Institutional testing programs: used to evaluate attainment of institutional goals and objectives. Parents could be trained to help administer these formal tests. The tests could be given at certain levels such as fifth, eighth, and tenth grades.[52]

Fitness testing is the preliminary step in authentic assessment for fitness. It is suggested that students put this information into a *portfolio* (refer to Chapter 2) so evidence of their involvement and participation is kept in an organized fashion. Other possibilities for authentic assessment include the following:

- *Journal or log entries:* Students may make daily or weekly entries in a journal expressing their feelings about the fitness experience. The teacher responds periodically in a positive way, thus getting more personally involved with the student. In addition, log entries may include nutritional information or exercise activity data.
- *Student projects:* Projects may include a report or group project such as an original aerobic dance composition taught to the class.
- *Role play:* Convince a friend not to smoke or take the role of a scientist and put on a white lab coat and discuss with parents, on *Back-to-School Night,* the information on fitness tests.
- *Written test:* Assess cognitive information that has been assimilated.
- *Interview:* Talk with a physician or fitness expert to get authentic information about participation. Write this up as a report.
- *Video analysis:* Given criteria, students may critique performance of weight-training exercises or form for running, biking, or another activity. This would usually be a self-analysis.
- *Physiological monitoring:*
  - Heart rate monitor technology: Students monitor cardiovascular system with heart rate monitors to be

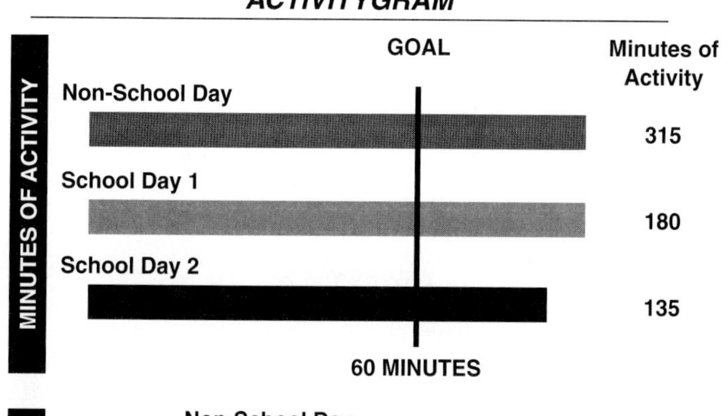

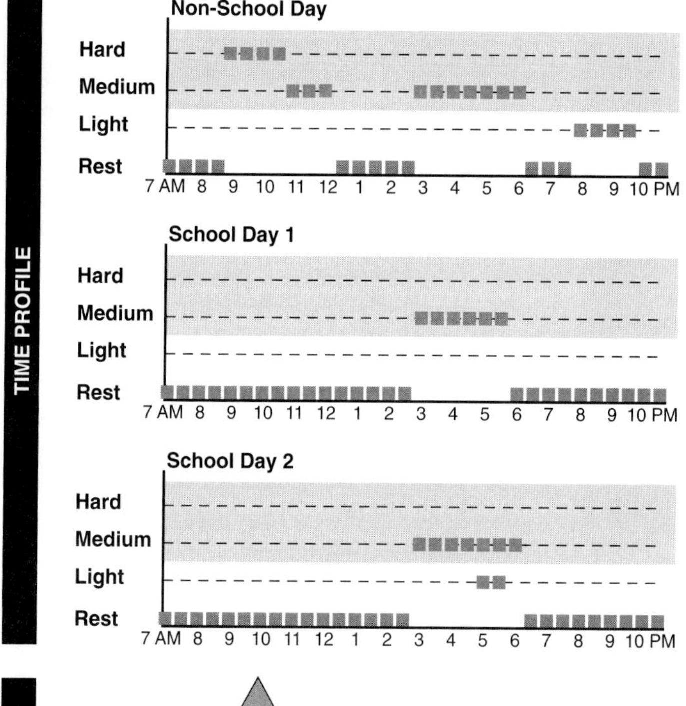

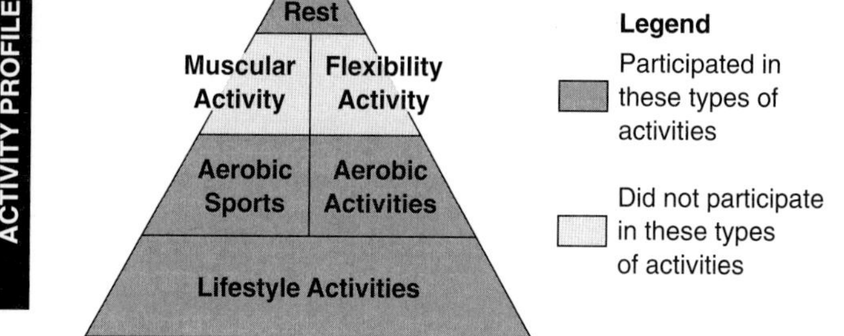

ADAM BODENSTEIN
ACTIVITYGRAM - 4/13/99
Madison County Elementary School

MESSAGES

The chart shows the number of minutes that you reported doing moderate (medium) or vigorous (hard) activity on each day. Congratulations, your log indicates that you are doing at least 60 minutes of activity on most every day. This will help to promote good fitness and wellness. For fun and variety, try some new activities that you have never done before.

The minutes of activity reported may be higher than what was actually accomplished, because there are always minutes of rest during an activity.

The goal in ACTIVITYGRAM is to find ways to include activity in levels medium and hard each day (shaded areas are medium to hard).

The time profile shows the activity level you reported for each 30-minute period of the day. Your results show that you were not active during school but that you were active after school and on weekends. If it is not possible to be active during school in PE or recess then try to be more active after school. Keep up the good work.

The activity pyramid reveals the different types of activity that you reported doing over a few days. Your results indicate that you participated in regular lifestyle activity and some aerobic activity. This is great! Try to add some additional activity from the 3rd level of the pyramid. Your results indicate that you spent an average of 2 hours per day watching TV or working on the computer. While some time on these activities is okay, you should try to limit the total time to less than 2 hours.

ACTIVITYGRAM provides information about your normal levels of physical activity. The report shows what types of activity you do and how often you do them. It includes information that you reported for two or three days during one week.

ACTIVITYGRAM is a module within *FITNESSGRAM*® 6.0 software. *FITNESSGRAM*® materials are distributed by the American Fitness Alliance, a division of Human Kinetics. www.americanfitness.net.

Figure 10-4
Sample *ACTIVITYGRAM* computer report.
Reprinted with permission of The Cooper Institute for Aerobics Research, Dallas, Texas.

FITNESSGRAM®

Charlie Brown
Grade: 5 Age: 11
Madison County Elementary School
Instructor: Kathy Read

	Test Date	Height	Weight
Current	07/15/99	5'01"	105
Past	07/13/99	5'3"	122

Needs Improvement | Healthy Fitness Zone: *Good — Better* | My Scores

AEROBIC CAPACITY

Walk Test — VO2 max (Healthy Fitness Zone: 42–52)

	My Scores
Current	**51**
Past	**42**

VO 2max Indicates ability to use oxygen. Expressed as ml of oxygen per kg body weight per minute.

Time

Current	**15:56**
Past	**16:34**

MUSCLE STRENGTH, ENDURANCE & FLEXIBILITY

(Abdominal) **Curl-Up** — Number (Healthy Fitness Zone: 15–28)

Current	**45**
Past	

(Upper Body) **Flexed-Arm Hang** — Seconds (Healthy Fitness Zone: 6–13)

Current	**49**
Past	**99**

(Trunk Extension)

Current	**INC**
Past	

If given, the flexibility test is performed on the right and left and is evaluated as 'Yes' or 'No' on both sides.

(Flexibility) **Back-Saver Sit and Reach** — R,L (Inches) (Healthy Fitness Zone: N, Y / Y, N – Y, Y)

Current	**Y,Y(9-10)**
Past	**Y,Y(8-10)**

BODY COMPOSITION

Percent Body Fat — Percent (Healthy Fitness Zone: 25–10)

Current	**16**
Past	**16**

Lower numbers are better scores on body composition measurement.

ACTIVITY

	Number of Days
On how many of the past 7 days did you participate in physical activity for a total of 30—60 minutes, or more, over the course of a day?	4
On how many of the past 7 days did you do exercises to strengthen or tone your muscles?	3
On how many of the past 7 days did you do stretching exercises to loosen up or relax your muscles?	2

MESSAGES

Charlie, your scores on all test items were in or above the Healthy Fitness Zone. You are also doing strength and flexibility exercises. However, you need to play active games, sports, or other activities at least 5 days each week.

Although your aerobic capacity score is in the Healthy Fitness Zone now, you are not doing enough physical activity. You should try to play very actively at least 60 minutes at least five days each week to look and feel good.

Your abdominal strength was very good. To maintain your fitness level be sure that your strength activities include curl-ups 3 to 5 days each week. Remember to keep your knees bent. Avoid having someone hold your feet.

Your upper body strength was very good, Charlie. To maintain your fitness level be sure that your strength activities include arm exercises such as push-ups, modified push-ups or climbing activities 2 to 3 days each week.

Charlie, your flexibility is in the Healthy Fitness Zone. To maintain your fitness, stretch slowly 3 or 4 days each week, holding the stretch 20–30 seconds. Don't forget that you need to stretch all areas of the body.

Charlie, your body composition is in the Healthy Fitness Zone. If you will be active most days each week, it may help to maintain your level of body composition.

To be healthy and fit it is important to do some physical activity almost every day. Aerobic exercise is good for your heart and body composition. Strength and flexibility exercises are good for your muscles and joints.

Good job, you are doing enough physical activity for your health. Additional vigorous activity would help to promote higher levels of fitness

Figure 10-5

Sample FITNESSGRAM® computer report.

Reprinted with permission of The Cooper Institute for Aerobics Research, Dallas, Texas.

TABLE 10.10 Fitness Goals Contract

To improve my personal fitness level, I, with the help of my teacher, have set the following fitness goals. I will participate in the activities outlined in this plan to achieve improved physical fitness. Based on my current level of fitness, I believe that these goals are reasonable.

Fitness component test item (Circle appropriate item.)	Score Date:______	My goal	Activities to improve physical fitness	Follow-up score Date:______
AEROBIC FITNESS ***ONE-MILE WALK/RUN*** ***PACER***				
BODY COMPOSITION ***PERCENT BODY FAT*** ***BODY MASS INDEX***				
MUSCULAR STRENGTH AND ENDURANCE AND FLEXIBILITY ***CURL-UP***				
TRUNK LIFT				
PUSH-UPS ***MODIFIED PULL-UPS*** ***PULL-UPS*** ***FLEXED-ARM HANG***				
BACK-SAVER SIT AND REACH ***SHOULDER STRETCH***				

Student: ________________ Date: ________ Teacher: ________________

Source: Reprinted, by permission, from AAHPERD, *Physical Best Activity Guide—Secondary Level* (Champaign, IL: Human Kinetics 1999), 222.

TABLE 10.11 Activity Goals Contract

Week of ______________________ My plans are to do:

	Activity I plan to do	**Time of day**	**Friend(s) who will be active with me**
MONDAY			
TUESDAY			
WEDNESDAY			
THURSDAY			
FRIDAY			
SATURDAY			
SUNDAY			

Student: ______________________ Date: ____________ Teacher: ______________________

Source: Reprinted, by permission, from AAHPERD, *Physical Best Activity Guide—Secondary Level* (Champaign, IL: Human Kinetics 1999), 219.

sure they are safe and working at a level to facilitate change (discussed previously in this chapter).

- Blood pressure monitors
- Body composition analysis
- Activity monitors
- Fitness equipment, such as treadmill, stationary bike[53]

Sensitive teachers hold the key to healthy lifestyles for today's youth. Have students keep accurate records of participation, both in and outside of class. If this is kept in a portfolio, it is valuable information for students to have as they continue to live an active lifestyle. It is also a convenient way to organize materials for grading purposes. Use the records as guidelines for program development, encouragement, and praise. Keep in mind that for more than a decade, "most experts . . . agree that students should not be assigned grades based upon fitness test performance."[54] Teachers, and the fitness activities they incorporate in the programs, should have a profound effect on students for a lifetime.

Movement Skills

The major emphasis of most physical education programs is the development of movement skills. Whether the thrust is sport skills or rhythms and dance, teachers spend the majority of program time concentrating on improving skill execution. In spite of this, many students fail to learn effective motor skills. Graham reviewed two studies in the United States and Canada in which experts rated students as "weak" or "marginally satisfactory" in motor skills. Both studies found girls consistently less skilled than boys.[55] Reasons given for the low skill level were the lack of time spent in physical activity, failure to perform the skills correctly, lack of specific feedback, time spent playing games instead of improving skills, and failure of instructors to teach skills for game conditions.

The skill emphasis over the past two decades has been that of "lifetime sports," primarily individual or dual activities that students can continue to enjoy after their school years. It is estimated that 75 percent of the nation's secondary schools emphasize lifetime sports, such as bowling, badminton, tennis, Frisbee, and racquetball, in their physical education programs. Although the popular activities change from time to time, the games have expanded from the traditional favorites to games like team handball, cooperative games, and modified games such as Pickle-ball.[56] Sports have also been taught using the sports-education model described in Chapter 6.

Instruction and Practice

Movement skills should be taught in an orderly teaching progression with activities chosen according to student ability. The teacher may decide to use any or all of the following activities to teach physical skills:

1. *Warm-up:* Use skills previously taught to warm up.
2. *Demonstration:* Students are shown the movements they are expected to reproduce. Demonstrations are used to create interest or to show how something is to be done, such as a sports skill or safety procedure. They help students avoid misconceptions. Procedures include the following:
   a. Plan a meaningful demonstration.
   b. Practice the demonstration or acquire a good demonstrator. Demonstrations can involve the use of live models, videotapes, or other media. When demonstrating sports skills, remember to use the mirror-image technique—that is, say "right hand" to the students and use the left hand—or face away from the students so they will see the image as they will be doing it.
   c. Assemble and set up equipment and the seating arrangement so all students can see and hear.
   d. Briefly explain the purpose of the demonstration.
   e. Demonstrate using key points to enhance perception.
3. *Drills:* Drills are contrived situations used to learn or to review skills. They provide a large number of practice trials in a short amount of time. Skills tests can be used as drills when students are allowed to repeat the tests to achieve higher levels of skill. Examples of drills are a partner volley in volleyball, a three-person weave in basketball, or a toss-and-hit drill in tennis. Procedures include these:
   a. Demonstrate and/or explain the learning activity.
   b. Organize small groups for maximum participation.
   c. Make drills as gamelike as possible to ensure transfer to game situations.
   d. Provide continuous feedback to ensure correct learning of skills.
   e. Adjust or change drills to provide for individual differences in student learning.
4. *Modified games:* Students need transitions from drill practice to game situations so they feel comfortable in game play. Modified games bridge this gap by allowing students to practice skills in gamelike settings, in which interest can be maintained while learning to refine and apply skills. Modified games involve one or more of the fundamental skills, rules, or procedures of a sport. Procedures are as follows:
   a. Use gamelike drills, then modified games.
   b. Match the games to the ability levels of the students, progressing from simple to complex.
   c. Assign teams so they are evenly matched for competition.
   d. Organize games to provide maximum participation (e.g., small teams, modified rules and equipment, rotating so all students get to play all positions).

5. *Game or team play:* Games are played using official or simplified rules. Metzler suggested a number of strategies for teaching using competitive games:
   a. Chalk talks.
   b. Walk-through on the field.
   c. Taking advantage of situations that occur in the game.
   d. "Instant replays" allowing students to play the action again.
   e. Player-coach manipulation of events forcing students to concentrate on certain skills and guiding play toward players who are not being included.
   f. Acting as a sports analyst by making observations and guiding play through questions.
   g. Making a call and then asking students to supply the reason or solution.[57]
6. *Competition:* Competitive game situations are provided with an expected winner and loser.

Graham encouraged teachers to ask themselves five questions concerning instruction for motor skill development:

1. How much time are the students spending in productive practice?
2. Am I refining the qualitative aspects of the motor skills?
3. Am I providing appropriate amounts of specific feedback?
4. How much time do the students in my classes spend playing games? Is the low-skilled student getting as much practice as the high-skilled player?
5. Am I providing the appropriate transitions so students can actually practice open skills in dynamic environments that aren't "official" games so students can try again and again without fear of penalty or harassment?[58]

Do not be fearful of straying from traditional curricular offerings. Valuable learning experiences can result for students engaged in the following nontraditional activity units:

1. *Work:* Students are taught certain tasks that facilitate the performance of work in lifting, carrying, pushing, pulling, striking, and the like. The topics of stability, force, leverage, momentum, and friction are taught through such activities as "tray relay races." In this activity students weave in and out of markers carrying various objects (an empty bottle, a bottle one-third full of water, and a bottle three-quarters full of water) on a tray to determine the differences they feel.[59]
2. *Stress Management:* The topics of stress are discussed. Students are taught relaxation responses and techniques of exercise, recreation, and diet to cope with stress.[60]
3. *Self-Defense:* Students are taught skills and strategies to protect themselves when physically attacked.[61]
4. *Movement Awareness:* Activities such as yoga, karate, aikido, or t'ai chi ch'uan are taught.[62]

Activities not usually performed in the gymnasium can be adapted to the school site. For example, tennis and bowling can be simulated in the gym. A miniature golf course could be set up using whiffle balls to ensure safety. Cross-country skiing can be taught during the winter months, both on the outside playing fields and in the gym.

Motivational Techniques

One way to motivate students to learn movement skills is to use rewards, such as the following inexpensive, easy-to-administer incentives:

1. *Recognition Clubs*—Have a Bulls-Eye Club for archery or a 100-Mile Club for swimmers or joggers.
2. *Skill Charts*—Students check off skills on the charts as they are completed.
3. *Spotlight Board*—Recognize individuals or teams for performance, sportspersonship, leadership, or honors.
4. *Awards*—Give certificates, trophies, or T-shirts, or other awards to outstanding performers.[63]

Another motivational factor is novelty or change in routine. One way to incorporate novelty is to play nontraditional games, such as team ball and quad ball, middle school games developed to teach students skills and strategies.[64] Nontraditional activities such as mountain biking, cross-country skiing, and roller skating can be included in the curriculum.

Students can create games if the teacher provides sufficient structure, such as the (1) purpose—the objectives and possible outcomes of the game; (2) grade level; (3) motor skills needed; (4) kind of game (ball, tag, etc.); (5) number of players; (6) organization—procedures, formations, boundaries; (7) rules; (8) scoring; and (9) equipment. For example, students could be told to create a new game in which each team attempts to get another team's objects, while defending its own objects.[65]

Nothing motivates students more than success, thus it is important to select instructional strategies that ensure success for all students. Instructional strategies were discussed in Chapter 9.

Review Questions: What are the guidelines that should be followed in the development of drills?

Describe motivational techniques that can be used in teaching movement skills.

Tournaments If students have attained a sufficient level of playing ability, tournaments can be motivating. Tournaments can be adapted to accomplish various instructional objectives and improve cooperation.[66] Learning communication skills and accepting responsibility can be enhanced by having students officiate games. The following types of tournaments can be incorporated into a unit of instruction or used for league or intramural play. Tournament brackets can be computer generated.

Round robin In the round robin tournament, each player competes against every other player. The victor is the player who wins the most games and loses the fewest. This structure is very time-consuming but provides maximum participation for participants. After players or teams have been ranked by previous competition, a smaller ability-grouped round robin competition is effective for participants of like ability. A round robin schedule for six teams is shown here:

1–6	1–5	1–4	1–3	1–2
2–5	6–4	5–3	4–2	3–6
3–4	2–3	6–2	5–6	4–5

This schedule was easily formulated by keeping team 1 stationary and moving every other team one place counterclockwise on the schedule. This procedure is repeated for each round until the teams rotate back to their original positions. To compute the number of games, use the following formula:

$$N\,(N - 1) \text{ divided by } 2$$

$$\frac{6(6-1)}{2} = \frac{6 \times 5}{2} = \frac{30}{2} = 15$$

Another representation of a round robin tournament illustrates the standings of each player or team. This structure allows players or teams to select the order in which they play opponents and permits longer or shorter games to be played (see Box 10.1).

Several adaptations of the round robin tournament that overcome limitations of time, facilities, absences, and scheduling were suggested by Eason. Baseline Basketball, a unit-long activity, involves earning points for acquisition of skill, knowledge, attitude, and game play. Class Team Tennis involves teams of four boys and four girls who play other teams in singles, doubles, and mixed doubles. A team wins a point for each game won by a team member. This tournament can be used for all racket sports. Computer Softball uses computer-generated teams, which change daily. An individual point system is based on the hits, runs, and defensive plays of each player during the tournament. Veal suggests playing for time and recording points scored by each player rather than wins and losses.[67]

Elimination When elimination tournaments are used, all competitors except the winner are eliminated after one or two losses depending on the type of tournament selected. Tournaments are set up with a standard number of open slots, with the total number of teams being divisible by two (e.g., 2, 4, 8, 16, 32). If the exact number of teams needed for the brackets is not available, some teams must be given a *bye* (an exemption from playing a game in a round). To determine who gets the byes, teams are *seeded* (ranked according to how they are expected to finish based on their record from previous play). Byes are placed as far apart as possible on the tournament chart so seeded players are not playing each other in the first round and byes occur only in the first round.

Single elimination. A single elimination tournament is a short tournament with half of the teams being eliminated in the first round. The winner is determined quickly, but it may not be the best team. An example of a single elimination tournament with six entries is shown in Figure 10-6. Figure 10-7 shows an example of thirteen entries.

Consolation. A consolation tournament allows teams to compete for third place after losing in the first round. When a team loses one game after the first round, it is eliminated. Winners move to the right on the bracket tournament chart and losers move to the left. An example of a consolation tournament with four teams is shown in Figure 10-8. Figure 10-9 shows an example of a tournament with sixteen teams.

BOX 10.1

A Round Robin Tournament Chart

Team	*1*	*2*	*3*	*4*	*5*	*6*	Wins	Losses	Rank
1				15–8	6–15		1	1	
2									
3									
4	8–15							1	
5	15–6						1		
6									

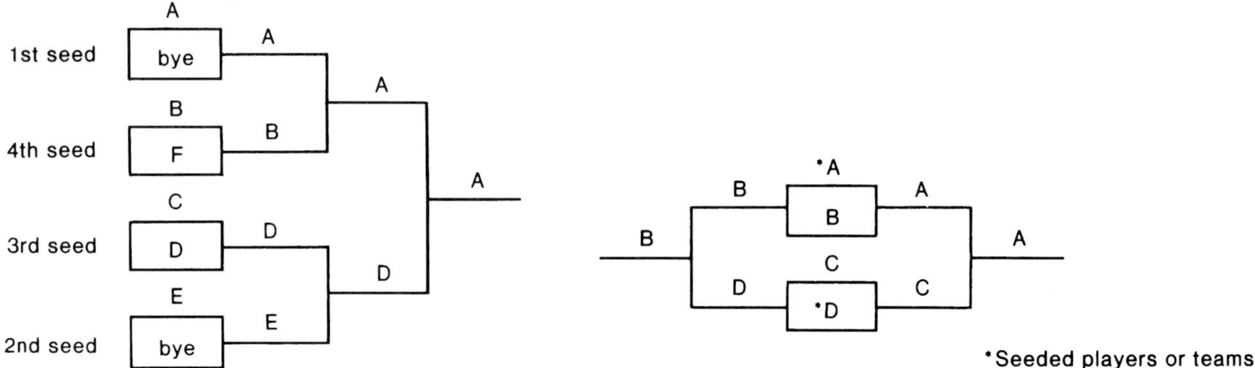

Figure 10-6
A single elimination tournament for six entries.

Figure 10-8
A consolation tournament for four entries.

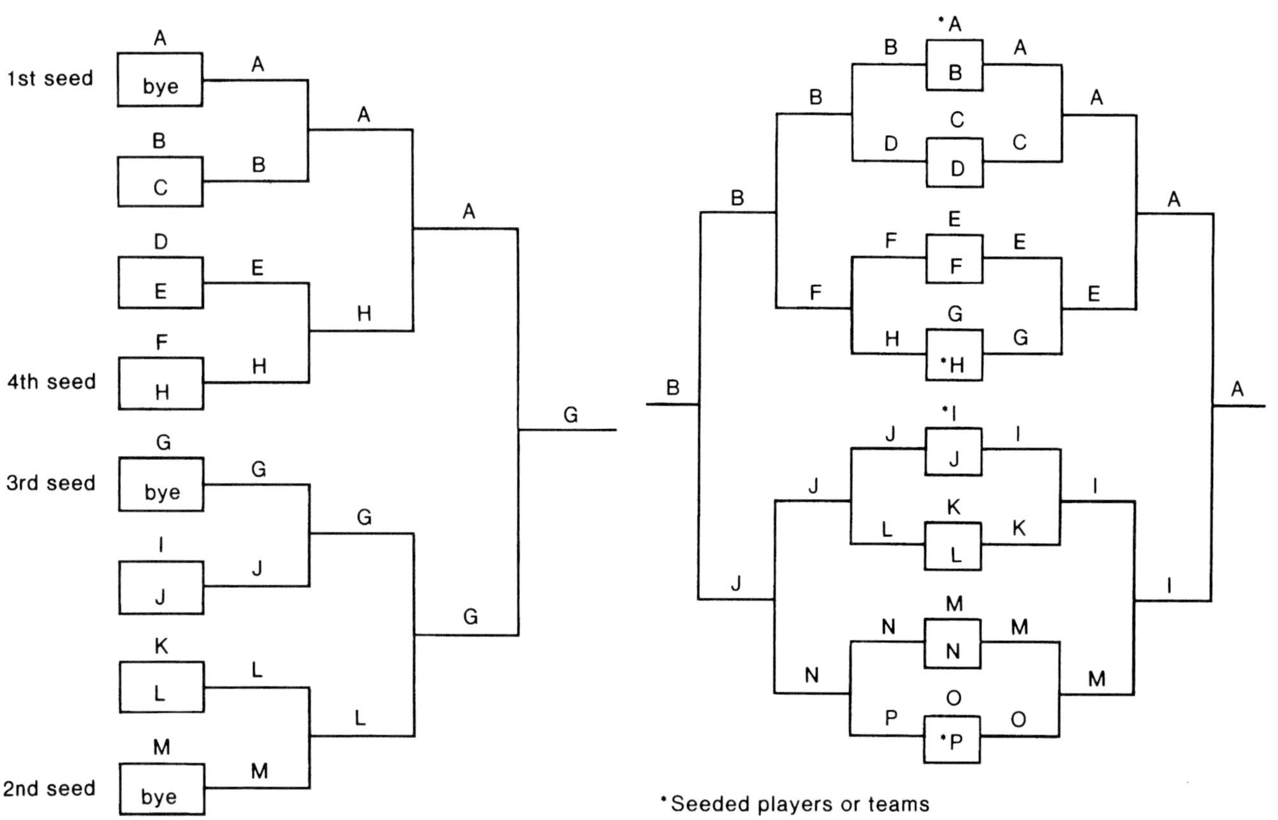

Figure 10-7
A single elimination tournament for thirteen entries.

Figure 10-9
A consolation tournament for sixteen entries.

Double elimination. A double elimination tournament requires that each team must lose two games before being eliminated. It is nearly as effective in producing a true winner as a round robin tournament and is less time-consuming. Examples of double elimination tournaments for four and fourteen teams are shown in Figures 10-10 and 10-11. Note that for fourteen teams, sixteen slots are required.

To determine the number of games to be played, compute 2N − (1 or 2). For example, 2 × 14 = 28 − 1 or 2 = 27 or 26 games.

Challenge In challenge tournaments, each student challenges as many other players as possible within the class or group. A win allows students to change places with the loser. The best players or teams move to the top of the tournament chart. Players can be placed in an initial order by a draw, seeding, or the order in which they signed up. It is sometimes fun to put the best players at the bottom of the charts so they have to win to advance to the top.

Ladder. A ladder tournament places teams directly above one another on a chart. Challenges are generally limited to one or two places above. Usually the team judged to be the best will be placed at the top of the ladder (see Box 10.2). One type of ladder tournament is a bridge or "move-up" tournament. Students are arranged

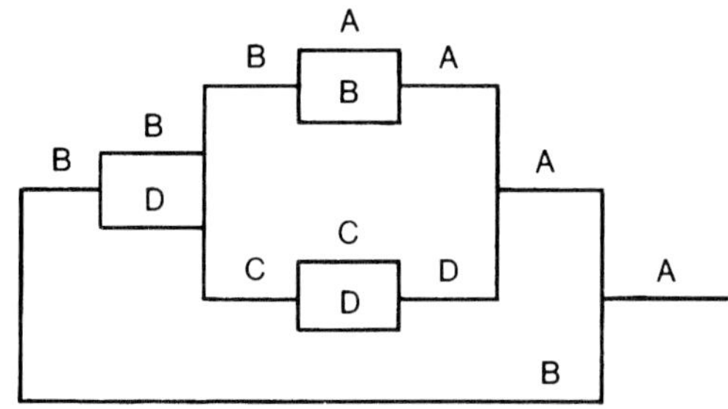

Figure 10-10

A double elimination tournament for four entries.

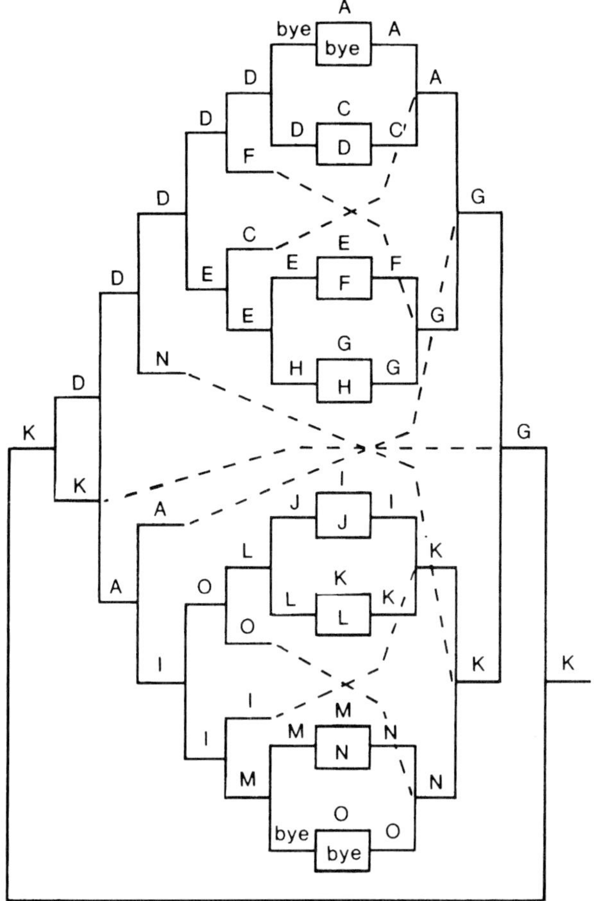

Figure 10-11

A double elimination tournament for up to sixteen entries.

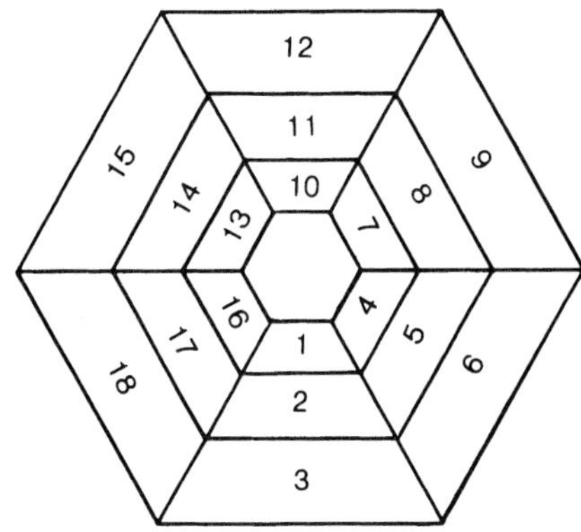

Figure 10-12

A spider web tournament.

Box 10.2

A Ladder Tournament

1
2
3
4
5
6
7
8
9
10

on adjacent courts and play timed games. The winner on each court moves up and the loser moves down. Students can play singles, doubles, or cutthroat. In cutthroat, one player plays the other two and then players rotate whenever the server loses the serve. Each player keeps his or her own score. Students or teams can also rotate in after every play.[68]

Spider web. A spider web tournament, as shown in Figure 10-12, is a unique variation of a ladder. Participants in each section of the web engage in their own challenge. Challenges are made one level above. Winners advance toward the middle of the web. On an ending date winners are placed in an elimination tournament. Participants at each level can also be placed in their own elimination tournament.

Pyramid. A pyramid tournament is designed to accommodate large numbers of participants. A team may challenge any team on the same line with it on the tournament chart as well as those to the immediate left or right on the line above. See Figure 10-13 for an example.

Funnel. A funnel tournament combines the best features of both the ladder and the pyramid by accommodating large numbers of participants while also ranking them. The lower half of the funnel is governed by the rules for a pyramid and the upper half by the rules of a ladder. An example is shown in Figure 10-14.

Clock. A clock tournament is an animated version of a challenge tournament. Participants challenge no more than two numbers ahead. The tournament ends when any player advances full circle. More or fewer numbers may be used. See Figure 10-15.

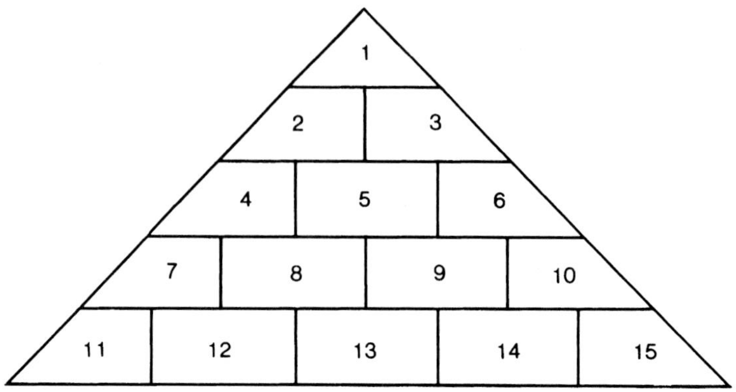

Figure 10-13
A pyramid tournament.

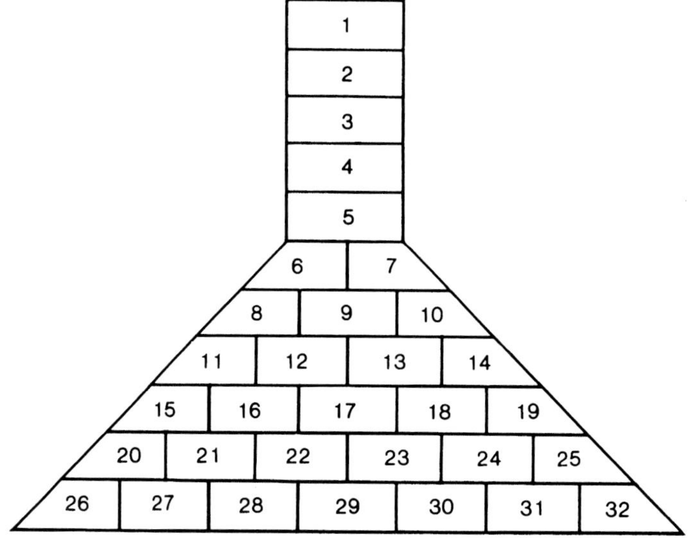

Figure 10-14
A funnel tournament.

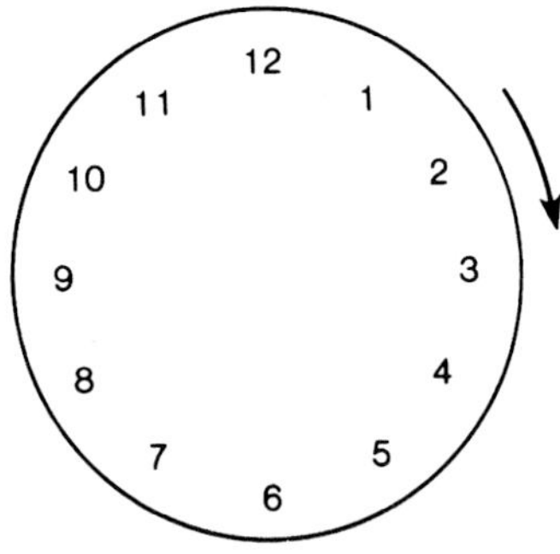

Figure 10-15
A clock tournament.

Evaluating Progress

Teacher evaluation of students' playing ability is the most accurate way to check skill performance. When skill tests are used, they should simulate the game situation as closely as possible. Students can check off specific proficiencies when they are executed or evaluate the skills or game-playing skills of their peers if given proper instruction and guidance. Box 10.3 illustrates such a checklist. A variety of assessment techniques is discussed in Chapter 11.

Review Question: Set up the following tournaments for fourteen individuals or teams: round robin, single elimination, consolation, double elimination, challenge, ladder, spider web, pyramid, funnel, clock.

Concepts

"Learning is not a spectator sport. Students must talk about what they are learning, write about it, relate it to past experiences, and apply it to their daily lives. They must make what they learn part of themselves."[69] To be physically educated means that students must understand concepts about the body and physical activity that prepare them to live a physically active lifestyle. Teaching concepts is not easy. It requires planning; however, learning

BOX 10.3

A Feedback Checklist for Evaluating Student Performance of Movement Skills

RACQUETBALL

Rally Form Task Sheet

Name ________________________________

______ Passed

The instructor will mark *YES* if student is *consistent* in doing the following:

	1		2		3		4		5	
	YES	**NO**	**YES**	**NO**	**YES**	**NO**	**YES**	**NO**	**YES**	**NO**
1. Waits for the ball to drop.										
2. Moves with the ball.										
3. Keeps opponent in view.										
4. Assumes position facing side wall before hitting the ball.										
5. Assumes the proper attack position to play the ball.										

Date:

Comments:

occurs faster when students understand the principles involved in skill performance.

Instruction and Practice

The knowledge explosion has dramatically increased knowledge in physical education. The National Association for Sport and Physical Education has published a book entitled *Concepts of Physical Education: What Every Student Needs to Know* that delineates the concepts that teachers should teach in each of the subdisciplines of physical education to help students reach the national standards.[70] Study guides, journal entries, and projects are useful in promoting cognitive learning. Students involved in completing a study sheet, a workbook assignment, or a journal entry have moved to the "I do, I understand" level of learning. An example of a study sheet is shown in Figure 10-16. Examples of projects and journal entries are presented in Chapter 11. Study guides can be used for individual study or review or as an adjunct to class instruction; they can focus student attention on important instructional points; and simplify instructions and use variety in their construction to prevent boredom. Procedures include these:

1. Use appropriate vocabulary and reading level for students.
2. Eliminate nonessential items.
3. Construct study guides so the student is actively involved in learning by filling in the blanks or working through the material to be learned.
4. Answers to study guides can be provided through class instruction, individual units, "a rule a day" bulletin boards, or individual study of text materials or media.

Some study guides can be used to help students excused from active participation to learn concepts by reading articles and answering questions pertinent to the sport or activity being taught.

Motivational Techniques

Several techniques can be used to increase student motivation to learn concepts. Colorful posters with a thought,

ARCHERY STUDY SHEET

INSTRUCTIONS: Briefly answer the following questions.

1. List two important factors about each of the following:
   Stance:
   Nock:
   Draw:
   Anchor:
   Aim:
   Release:
   Follow through:

2. Describe aiming techniques with a bowsight, including how to correct errors.

3. State how to score the following: liners, rebounds, pass-throughs, perfect end, shooting seven arrows.

4. Fill in the necessary information for the arrows shown below.

Figure 10-16

Archery study sheet.

term, or rule for the day can be posted on a bulletin board for students to read as they enter the activity area.

Instructional games add a new dimension to the learning process. They are also a viable option for involving students who do not normally like to participate. They can be used individually or in groups and are especially effective when regular lesson plans cannot be used due to bad weather, scheduling changes, or facility unavailability. Design games to meet specific course objectives and to keep the activities at the appropriate learning level of the students (e.g., vocabulary, spelling, content). Remember also that instructional games can lose their effectiveness if used too often.

The following games could be used as study sheets, as homework activities, as activities to be done after completing regular assignments, or just for fun. Instructional games can be found in resource books, magazines, or at conventions and workshops. Creative teachers will not hesitate to make up original materials.

1. *The crossword puzzle* (Figure 10-17). Computer programs (see puzzlemaker.com) are available for creating crossword puzzles. The puzzle must be proofread for accuracy before it is used. Answers can be listed alphabetically for use by students who have difficulty spelling. Students can also design crossword puzzles and word search puzzles.
2. *Pyramid* (Figure 10-18). Another puzzle-type activity is the pyramid. The longest terms for recall are placed at the bottom of the pyramid, which is built upward to the shortest terms. This works well for a test of knowledge of rules and terminology.
3. Other examples of instructional games:
   a. Soccer scrambled words (see Box 10.4).
   b. Hidden Terms (see Box 10.5).
   c. Bingo Lingo (see Box 10.6).
   d. Sports Bowl (see Box 10.7).
   e. Baseball (see Box 10.8).

Evaluating Progress

Both study guides and instructional games can be used for informal evaluation. The construction and administration of written tests is discussed in Chapter 11.

Review Question: How would you encourage students to learn concepts about physical activity?

Name ______________________ Period ______________________ Date ________

Instructions: Fill in the puzzle using the list of possible answers given below.

Across

2. The amount of force required to pull the bow to full draw.
4. The practice of shooting with bows and arrows.
9. An arrow that strikes the scoring area and bounces off the target.
10. The third ring outside the gold, counting four or three points.
11. To sight for hitting the target with the left eye closed for right-handed archers.
12. To pull the bowstring back to the anchor point.
14. Plastic "feathers" on an arrow.
15. A device that provides force for shooting arrows.
16. Six arrows shot in a row.
17. The fiberglass, aluminum,or wooden portion of the arrow.
18. A term for archery equipment.
21. The second ring outside the gold, counting six or five points.
22. Two feathers on the arrow shaftment that are not at right angles to the nock and are the same color are called ________ feathers.
23. To place the tip of the index finger of the string hand on the anchor point and hold it steady until the release.
27. The outer ring on the target face, counting two or one point.
28. A certain place on the face to which the index finger of the string hand is brought consistently (every time) on each draw (two words).
30. The round object, marked with circles, at which the arrows are shot.
31. The side of the bow away from the string.
34. The upper and lower parts of the bow, divided by the handle.
35. Colored stripes used for identification that are placed near the feathers on an arrow.
37. The plastic portion of the arrow into which the bowstring is fitted.
39. A leather protection worn on the forearm to keep the string from hurting the arm (two words).
40. The arm, the hand of which holds the bow during shooting.
41. A device for holding arrows.
42. A leather piece worn on the shooting hand to protect the fingers (two words).
43. The center of the target, counting ten or nine points.
44. The side of the bow toward the string.

Down

1. The edge of the target face beyond the white ring, counting zero points, sometimes marked "P" on the scorecard.
3. The center part of a bow that the archer grips with his or her hand.
5. The first ring outside the gold, counting eight or seven points.
6. To shoot the arrow from a position of full draw by straightening the fingers of the string hand.
7. Vanes are substitutes for this material.
8. The feather on an arrow that is set at right angles to the nock; usually of a different color from the hen feathers (two words).
13. To stand ready to shoot.
19. The middle section of an arrow.
20. Archery "games."
21. The string of the bow.
24. The part of the bow on which the arrow rests while shooting.
25. The line upon which the archer stands while shooting at a target.
26. The metal point of an arrow, on the forward end.
29. To brace the bow.
32. The object that is shot.

Figure 10-17

An archery crossword puzzle.

33. A method of recording hits and the total score on a score card.
36. The thread wrapped around the bowstring to keep the arrow or the fingers from wearing out the string where the arrow is nocked.
38. An archery ground.
40. To string a bow.

Possible Answers

Address
Aim
Anchor
Anchor point
Archery
Arm guard
Arrow
Back
Belly
Black
Blue
Bow
Bowarm
Bowstring
Brace
Cock feather
Crest
Draw
End
Face
Feathers
Finger tab
Gold
Handle
Hen
Hold
Limbs
Nock
Petticoat
Pile
Range
Rebound
Red
Release
Rest
Rounds
Quiver
Scoring
Serving
Shaft
Shooting line
String
Tackle
Target
Tip
Vanes
Weight
White

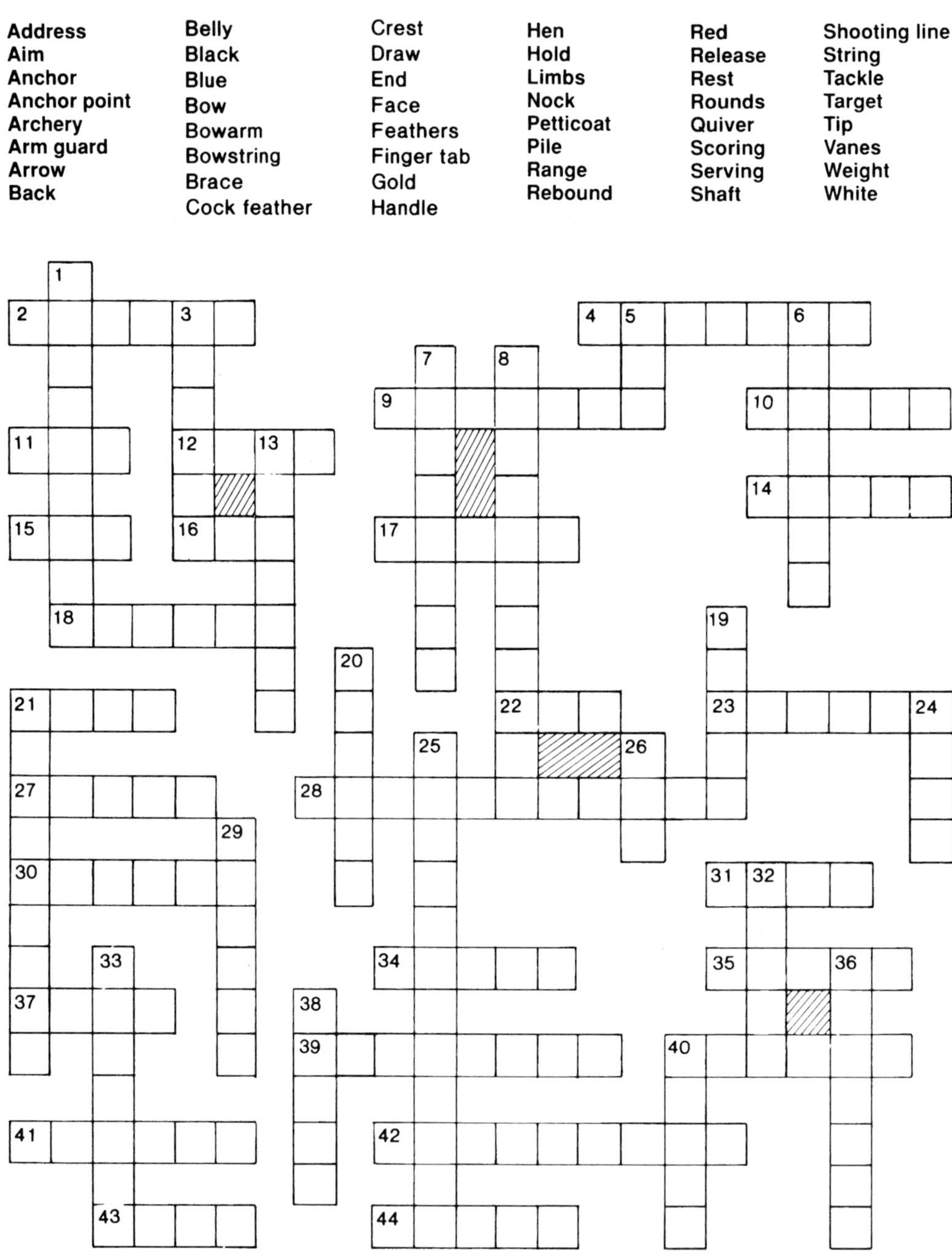

Figure 10-17
(Continued)

Pyramid Volleyball Quiz

Name ______________________

Period ______________________

Date ______________________

Instructions: Fill in the pyramid with the appropriate word or words to complete each sentence.

1.
2.
3.
4.
5.
6.
7.
8.
9.
10.

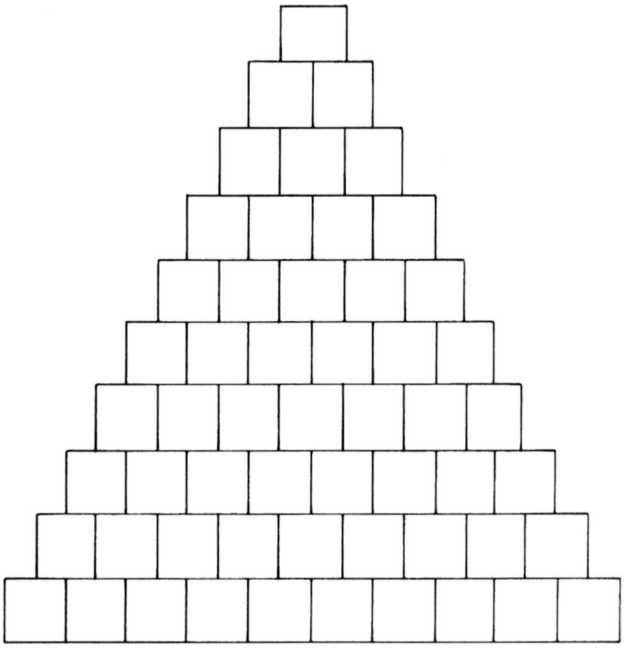

1. The winner of an official game must have at least a ____ point lead. (number)
2. The player in the ____ ____ position is the server. (initials)
3. An official team has ____ ____ ____ players.
4. A ball that lands on a court line is ____ ____ ____ ____ .
5. Except on a ____ ____ ____ ____ ____ the ball may be played out of the net.
6. To ____ ____ ____ ____ ____ ____, is the moving of all players into position to begin serving.
7. ____ ____ ____ ____ ____ ____ ____ is called when the serving team loses turn of service.
8. The plan of attack used by a team to score points is called ____ ____ ____ ____ ____ ____ ____ ____ .
9. When the ____ ____ ____ ____ ____ ____ ____ ____ ____ team loses the rally, a point is scored.
10. In playing the ball, a player may step on but not over the ____ ____ ____ ____ ____ ____ ____ ____ ____ ____ .

Figure 10-18

A pyramid test.

BOX 10.4

Soccer Scrambled Words

SOCCER SCRAMBLED WORDS

Instructions: Unscramble the following words. The circled letters will give you a message.

1. LYEARPS _ _ _ _ _ _ (○)
2. NRU _ (○) _
3. NWI _ _ (○)
4. CROES (○) _ _ _ _
5. BHACALFK (○) _ _ _ _ _ _ _
6. IKCK _ (○) _ _
7. TNPU _ _ (○) _
8. REEFIKKC _ _ (○) _ _ _ _ _
9. SSAP (○) _ _ _
10. BBELIRD _ _ _ _ _ (○) _
11. REOSCC _ _ _ _ (○) _
12. LAOG _ _ (○) _
13. SLUOF _ _ _ _ (○)
14. DFILE _ _ (○) _ _

Affective Activities/Personal and Social Development

Advocates of sport and physical education continuously tout its character-building virtues and ability to prepare its participants for life. Recent increases in illegal drug activity and violence among students and athletes, however, negate these effects.[71] How can we as educators reverse this trend? The physical education content standards 5 and 6 list two goals for personal and social behavior that are worthy of our attention:

5. Exhibits responsible personal and social behavior that respects self and others in physical activity settings.
6. Values physical activity for health, enjoyment, challenge, self-expression, and/or social interaction.[72]

Physical education is an ideal setting for achieving these goals.

Instruction and Practice

Two very successful methods for helping students develop personal and social skills are (1) to integrate opportunities for students to develop personal and social skills while focusing on sports activities, and (2) to focus on activities that specifically require students to confront and overcome personal and social obstacles. The former can be achieved through such curriculum patterns as sport education, discussed in Chapter 6, while adventure activities could be used to facilitate the second. Adventure activities meet the need for adventure and help students build self-confidence, self-reliance, and independence.[73] Through invoking the emotions of excitement, challenge, apprehension, and fear, students learn to think clearly and make wise decisions, to have the courage to act, and to control the emotion of fear.[74] Most of these activities require teamwork. Adventure activities must be geared to the level of the students so they have the necessary skills and abilities to participate safely. Some students are ready to immediately engage in risk activities, but individual students should not be forced into this type of experience.

Challenge Activities Students participating in challenge activities develop the ability to cooperate in a group, learn to solve problems, and improve individual fitness.[75] Games are one means of offering adventure and challenge to students. The New Games Foundation pioneered the use of games that equalize competition and make everybody a winner. Examples of challenge activities include the following:

1. *Knots*—Approximately twelve players stand in a circle, shoulder-to-shoulder, and place hands in the center of the circle. Everyone grabs a couple of hands of people who are *not* next to them. They cannot grab both hands from the same person. The objective of the game is to untie the knot, without releasing hands. The game is complete when all players are standing in a circle holding hands.[76]
2. *All on One Side*—A team of four or five players on one side of a volleyball court (with no one on the other side) attempts to move back and forth to the other side of the net as many times as possible without the ball touching the floor. Using a balloon for a ball, each player volleys the balloon to another player on the same side of the net and then scoots under the net to

BOX 10.5

Hidden Terms—Track and Field

Instructions: Circle the terms that have to do with track and field. Words may read horizontally, vertically, or diagonally, and forward or backward.

B R A K O S T S H O T A R T A L B U F A
T A R T A N B A U V A B A T O N A L I L
S T R O M M I N R A V E N D S Y L V N C
T J A V E L I N D U L I L I T A L S I R
E L S T R O M B L I A E X S R W S U S O
E X R I S T A H E F I I S C O N T N H S
P I T A N D R O S F H U L U N U A D A S
L E V A B E L D D A M O F S P R I N T C
E R I K M A D N U M C I T A O S D T R O
C I A M A M A D I K B A T L L I Y U I U
H U A N A K I L O L R O R O E L A T P N
A H S O C I T R O T K O N F V A R T L T
S T I A X L V Y E F H G N F A D D A E R
E L R E L A Y R G H J K L I U N S W J Y
B T A P E X S T V U O L N C L R T E U H
G N I R U S A E M Y N L O I T U T I M E
M E T E R U S P O U N D S A P S T G P J
D A M A R K E R N U O D F L A Y D H M D
S K C O L B G N I T R A T S R L C T D U

Bar
Baton
Clock
Cross Country
Discus
Distance
Finish
Hammer
High Jump
Hurdle
Javelin
Kilo
Long Jump
Marker
Measuring
Meter
Officials
Pit
Polevault
Pounds
Relay
Runway
Shot
Sprint
Starter
Starting Blocks
Steeplechase
Tape
Tartan
Time
Track and Field
Triple Jump
Weight
Yards

the other side. The last player to touch the balloon taps it over the net and scoots under. The receiving players try to keep the balloon in play on the new side of the net as they repeat the process. As the players improve, two balloons may be put into play at one time.[77]

Varying the components of an activity can cause students to perceive risk and feel a sense of fear while actually participating in a safe environment. For example, one person in each pair of students puts on a blindfold and stands behind a starting line. The partner stands ten feet behind. Other pairs are at least six feet away. On the starting signal the blindfolded persons are guided by the verbal directions of their partners around an obstacle course, or they may be guided to perform certain activities such as walking backward.[78]

Risk activities present physical and psychological challenges to participants.
© Tracy Pellet

BOX 10.6

Bingo Lingo—Diving

Instructions: The teacher draws a card one at a time and reads the definition. The first student to circle five terms in a row—either vertically, diagonally, or horizontally—wins.

Approach	Back Dive	Backward Take-off	Cutaway Dive	Degree of Difficulty
Entry	Forward Dive	Header	Hurdle	Free
Inward Dive	Jackknife	Layout	Lift	Opening
Pike	Press	Rotate	Somersault Dive	Spin
Swan	Straight	Takeoff	Tuck	Twist Dive

Source: Jack Romine and Joyce M. Harrison, Brigham Young University.

BOX 10.7

Sports Bowl

Instructions: Follow the procedure below to play "Sports Bowl."

1. Divide class into two teams of equal size.
2. Read a question.
3. The first person to raise his or her hand gets to answer the question. If the question is answered correctly, a bonus question is directed to the answering team; if it is answered incorrectly, the other team may attempt the answer (and the bonus).
4. There is a thirty-second time limit on questions.
5. The scoring is as follows:
   Correct answer—10 points
   Correct bonus answer—5 points
   Incorrect bonus—no penalty

Questions can be created from sports, history, current events, game rules, etc. Typical questions and bonus questions might be:

Q. Who holds the record for lifetime home runs?
B. What is the record?
Q. How many points can be scored on a penalty bully in field hockey?
B. When is a penalty bully awarded?

BOX 10.8

Baseball

Instructions: Follow the procedure below to play "Baseball."

1. Mark a diamond on the floor of a classroom or locker room area or use a magnetic board.
2. Write a list of questions about a sport.
3. Divide the class into two teams—designating one as the batting team and the other as the fielding team.
4. Ask the first batter a question. If correctly answered, the batter moves to first base. If incorrectly answered, the fielding team is allowed to answer. If the fielding team answers correctly, the batter is out. If not, the batter sits down and the next batter is up.
5. Continue until three outs are made or all batters have been up, then exchange teams.
6. Points are scored as runs are "batted" in.

Initiative Activities Group initiative activities are designed to provide adventure while incorporating problem-solving experiences that require a cooperative effort. Participants get to know and understand one another while developing trust and a sense of group belonging. Groups should include no more than twenty participants. Success is measured by group accomplishment rather than individual achievement. Simulation of the activity setting is stressed and little sophisticated equipment is required. The following are examples of initiative activities:

1. *Prisoners of War*—Participants are brought into a dimly lighted handball court. A five-foot-high badminton net is stretched across the court to represent a fence. A six-foot pipe or fifteen-foot rope is on the floor on the prisoners' side of the net. A mat is under the net for safety. Participants are told that guards are coming to execute them in twenty minutes. The task is to get all prisoners over the fence and up a fifteen- to eighteen-foot-high wall into the observation gallery before the guards arrive. Anyone touching the net is electrocuted. The mat may be moved to the wall for safety, but it may not be used to aid in the escape.[79] Teachers must supervise carefully and suggest safety techniques such as spotting when appropriate.
2. *River Crossing*—Participants are brought to a stream of water or a gap between two platforms, representing a fourteen-foot-wide river. Materials available are three two-inch by eight-inch planks with lengths of six, nine, and eleven feet. Participants are told the enemy is pursuing twenty minutes behind. The task is to successfully get everyone across the river using only the three planks. The water (or ground) may not be touched. The group is successful when all participants and the three planks are on the opposite bank.[80]
3. *The Chain Gang*—Participants form a circle around a stationary tetherball or volleyball standard (or a ten-foot pole set in a tire filled with cement). Short ropes or strips of cloth are used to tie team members' hands together (right hand to left hand). Mats may be placed around the base of the pole. The group is being held for ransom by international terrorists who have left momentarily, giving them time to escape. The object is to become free of the pole in the center while the pole remains upright and fixed to the ground and all members' hands remain tied together[81] (see Figure 10-19).

Active, cooperative learning helps students develop self-esteem.

Risk Activities Risk sports are characterized by physical and psychological challenges encountered by participants as they confront elements of the environment.[82] These activities usually take place in a natural setting and contain an element of perceived risk or physical danger.[83] Although some aspects of teaching these activities can be done during a regularly scheduled class period, they are often conducted after school, on weekends, and during vacations.

Activities range from low risk (fishing, cycling, orienteering) to medium risk (backpacking, cross-country skiing, horseback riding) to high risk (rock climbing, white water canoeing, winter camping).[84] Other activities of varying degrees of risk include scuba diving, cross-country cycling, rafting, field archery, high ropes courses, indoor or outdoor climbing walls, and camping.

Such activities are performed in a noncompetitive atmosphere sparked by intrinsic motivation. The activities are active and this component alone has the potential to increase physical skills and physical fitness. The development of social skills such as leadership, trust, cooperation, *esprit de corps,* and enhanced interpersonal relationships are inherent in risk activities. Knowledge of personal limits, pride in achievement, increased problem-solving ability, and enjoyment are listed as personal development benefits. Other values include an appreciation of nature, an experiential knowledge of survival and emergency care skills, as well as the application of nutrition and personal health information. The teacher must weigh the benefits against the risks of a particular activity and decide whether a safe environment can be created. Rademacher and Cruse stress that risk management is perhaps the most important key to the success of all such programs.[85] Successful protection of participants in risk activities, as well as the success of the program itself, hinges on two guidelines:[86]

1. Reduce or eliminate programs with a high potential for accidents. Activities with a high accident potential include hang gliding, ice climbing, parachuting, sky jumping, mountaineering, and spelunking.[87]

Figure 10-19

The chain gang.

From Allan C. Boyer, Brigham Young University Master's Thesis, 104 E. State Highway, Copperton, Utah 84006.

Adventure activities help build self-confidence and independence.
© Tracy Pellet

2. Maintain well-planned, carefully carried out, safe activities.
   a. Publish policies and procedures of operation.
   b. Continually analyze trip goals versus the limitations or abilities of participants and leaders.
   c. Screen participants.
   d. Provide in-service training for staff, maintaining experienced, well-trained personnel. Be committed to readiness and rescue training. Provide a carefully defined progression of activities.
   e. Inspect equipment and facilities regularly.
   f. Keep track of accidents and near misses and publish records of safety. Analyze the primary causes of accidents, such as unsafe conditions, unsafe acts, or judgment errors.
   g. Establish a program leader who provides direction and expertise (consistent, directive, nonpermissive).
   h. Repeat operations in known areas.[88]

Motivation

Feelings of personal enjoyment, challenge, self-expression, and social interaction in physical activity are derived from personal competence and the achievement of personal goals. Several methods exist for helping students accomplish these tasks.

Role Modeling One of the strongest motivational techniques is role modeling. Teachers, particularly, need to model the skills and values that they are fostering in their students. Personal reflection may help teachers realize their own beliefs, attitudes, and actions toward students and their personal and social interaction skills. Students tend to believe what they see rather than what the teacher is telling them.

Goal Setting Students can be helped to set realistic short and long-term goals for improving their skills and knowledge and, in doing so, can increase both competence and enjoyment. Lottes proposed an action plan for helping students set goals.[89] Students should

1. select appropriate long-term, short-term, and immediate goals.

2. list the costs and benefits, what they have to lose or gain, if they implement the goal.
3. assess and graph their progress.
4. create a supportive environment, such as reminders, ways to make alternatives less pleasant, and rewards and when they will be given.
5. create supportive self-messages involving personal responsibility, long-term benefits, cues, and self-confidence.
6. establish plans for maintaining progress in case of lapses and for encouragement by others.

Self-Talk Students can be taught to use cues and positive or encouraging statements to help them focus their attention on a task or activity and to motivate them to increase their efforts in difficult situations. Teachers can provide examples of cues to help students develop their own. Mercier and Hutchinson suggest that students keep a pocketful of paper clips and transfer them to a second pocket each time they give themselves a negative comment to help them realize how often they are discouraging themselves.[90]

Self-Assessment A number of techniques can help students assess their own learning. Progress logs, checklists, task sheets, journal entries, and watching videotapes of their performance can help students evaluate their progress toward their own goals. Instead of focusing on the moral dilemmas of others, students can reflect on their own habits and how they facilitate or frustrate their responsibility to do what is right and good.[91] Just as practice is important in learning motor skills, practice and reflection are also natural and essential ways to learn personal and social skills.

Conflict Resolution Students can be taught that their responses to conflict are a result of personal choice and that they can control how they react to conflict and tension, both in their own lives and in their interactions with others. Teachers can teach active listening skills, communication skills, and creative brainstorming and problem solving. Students need to reflect on their own responses to tension and conflict. Journals can provide an excellent way to do this.[92] Klemp and Hon found that participation in an open sports program during lunchtime on a middle school playground provided ways for students to gain a sense of power, status, and belonging in a positive social context and increased positive student interaction, while decreasing stress and disruptive activity.

In summary, the sports education curriculum pattern is motivating for most students because it is close to the real-life experience and yet adjustments can be made to allow students of various skill levels to excel in their own areas of expertise and not just in sport skills. Numerous opportunities exist for students to assume leadership roles, and to interact with other students, both cooperatively and competitively, to develop personal and social interaction skills. Adventure activities are highly motivating for most students. However, some students will be overwhelmed by the risk or challenge of the activity and must be carefully directed until they gain the necessary confidence, trust, and skill to participate. All students must be diligently supervised so that the apprehensive student develops trust and the fearless student learns to exercise caution. Motivation is enhanced by letting students choose the activities in which they participate. The teacher might further ensure motivation and participation by following a systematic progression. First, challenge activities would be introduced, followed by initiative activities, and finally several choices of risk activities.

Evaluating Progress A variety of authentic assessment techniques are currently being used to evaluate students' progress in the development of personal and social skills. Some of these are journal writing and portfolio construction. The use of questions to guide journal entries helps students reflect on their learning and establish control over their future learning. Journal entries can also help teachers gain insights into their students' feelings, effort, and progress.[93] Chapter 11 provides examples of these techniques. Evaluation of adventure activities is often informal and the teacher may use successful completion of the activity as the method of evaluation.

Review Question: What is the value of participating in challenge, initiative, and risk activities and including these types of activities in the curriculum?

Interdisciplinary Units

Around the turn of the twentieth century, separate disciplines became the primary means of conducting education. The separate disciplines can be a barrier to learning since the problems of the world are not divided into disciplines. Therefore, it is essential that teachers work together to create a multidisciplinary environment.

Physical education can play a vital role in the success of interdisciplinary units as well as initiate these coordinated efforts. Young worked with math, health, language arts, visual arts, and gifted and talented teachers to develop a year-long project for fifth graders. In physical education class the students learned about five health-related fitness components. They learned how to test these components and tested the first through fourth grades. The math class used these data to develop math problems. The health classes studied health-related fitness and research and developed a family fitness guide that was distributed to all families in the school. For language arts the students wrote journal entries related to their experiences and their attitudes toward personal fitness. In the visual arts class, illustrations were prepared for inclusion in the family fitness guide. The gifted and talented classes proofread, edited, and prepared the guide.[94]

Kirkpatrick developed two interdisciplinary activities.[95] For the Heart Adventure the gymnasium is set up as a giant heart. The students are the blood cells that flow through the heart and the rest of the body. In physical education the students learn about and experience how the blood circulates throughout the heart. In math class the students determine target heart rates and calculate the number of times the heart may beat during a given activity. In social studies classes the students learn what countries have the most coronary heart diseases and which ones are lowest. The differences in the cultures are then studied. Coronary heart diseases and their causes are studied in the health class. The science classes study how the heart functions. Writing assignments can be made in language arts.

In the Tropical Rainforest, students are put in groups and told they are the sole survivors of a plane crash on an island in a tropical rainforest.[96] They have several problems relating to survival to solve. All teachers in the school serve as the students' guides throughout this activity. Activities occurring in other classes include determining where the rainforests are in the world and what is happening to them, the effects of the loss of the rainforest, or how long the forests will survive at the current rate of destruction. Students can write about their feelings in language arts classes.

Another interdisciplinary idea is a time machine.[97] The gymnasium is set up with a time machine in the middle and four to eight activity modules surrounding the center. Events and subjects being studied in other classes can also be designed for inclusion. Examples of modules include the Roman Empire and the Civil War. In the Roman Empire the students participate in chariot races with scooters or flying turtles becoming the chariots. Students wear a bicycle helmet for safety. For the Civil War the students participate in the Battle of Gettysburg. Each side has different colored balls. The participants try to get their own balls into a large donut mat while removing the opponents' balls from the area. At the end the balls are counted in the various areas much as the dead and wounded were counted during the Civil War. Other types of interdisciplinary units are possible. The only limitation is the imagination and creativity of the teachers involved.

Review Question: What are interdisciplinary units and how might these units be used in a physical education curriculum?

Special Days (or Weeks)

A special theme may serve as the basis for conducting activities as a special event, such as a "Sports Day" or "Olympics." Such events might be held in the regular class or as a schoolwide project. When such events are conducted as a school activity, they become an excellent public relations tool.

A fun type of field day for students is "Super Kids' Day" in which students compete as partners rotating from one event to another.[98] Each student has a Super Kids' Day certificate (see Figure 10-20) on which the event and place—first or second—are recorded at each station.

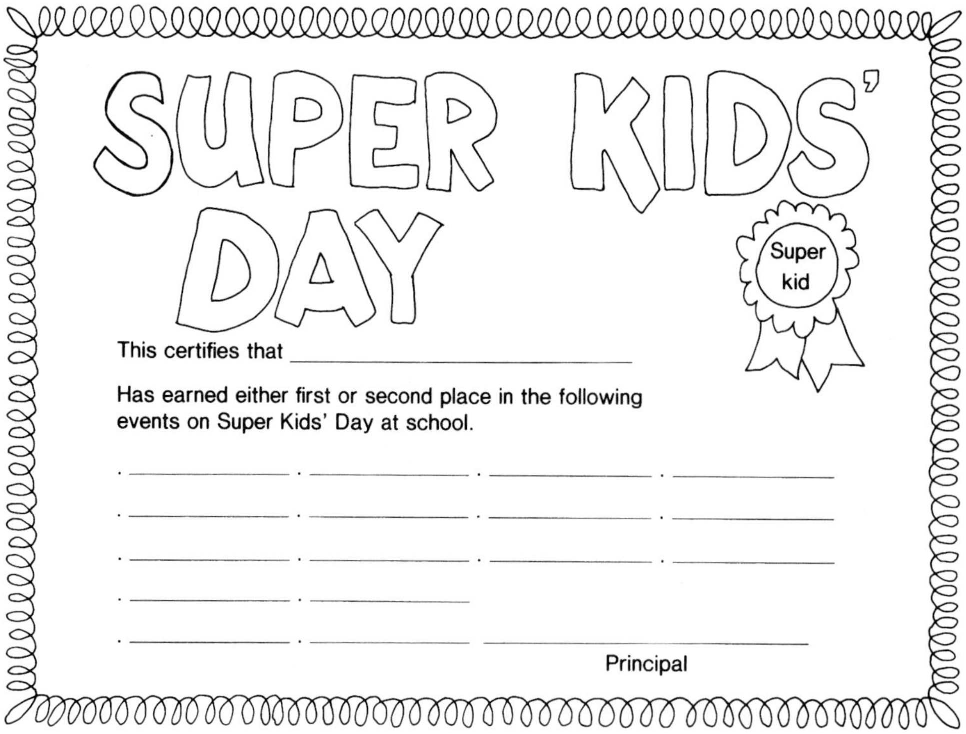

SUPER KIDS' DAY

Super kid

This certifies that ______________________

Has earned either first or second place in the following events on Super Kids' Day at school.

· ________ · ________ · ________ · ________

· ________ · ________ · ________ · ________

· ________ · ________ · ________ · ________

· ________ · ________

· ________ · ________ ______________________

Principal

Figure 10-20

A "Super Kids' Day" certificate.

From Pat Sawley, Woods Cross High School, Woods Cross, Utah.

Tenoschok listed a number of schoolwide contests that might be conducted during National Physical Education and Sport Week or at another appropriate time. He included a physical education essay contest; a poster coloring contest; a sports-in-action drawing contest; a physical education slogan contest; an invent-a-game contest; and a sports safari contest, which asks students to identify athletes by their animal nicknames. These activities can stimulate an overall school awareness of the objectives of physical education while encouraging students to achieve in other areas in the curriculum.[99] The National Association for Sport and Physical Education has developed several ideas to enhance a physical education curriculum.[100] All-school activity days or weeks can be designed to include all curriculum areas of the school. In this case they can be both fun and profitable for students and faculty alike.

NOTES

1. J. C. Isernhagen, Technology: A major catalyst for increasing learning, *T.H.E. Journal* (August 1999): 30, 32, 34, 36, 38.
2. T. L. Russell, Technology wars: Winners and losers, *Educom Review 32,* no. 2 (1997): 44–46.
3. Isernhagen, Technology.
4. M. M. Buck, Healthy alternatives for enhancing physical education and health with technology, Legacy 21 television presentation, Ball State University, Muncie, IN, 8 April 1999.
5. S. Schiemer, I'd like to use technology—but I still can't program my VCR. A paper presented at the National Association of Sport and Physical Education Technology in Physical Education and Sport Conference, Chattanooga, TN, 1999.
6. P. J. Ellery, Using the World Wide Web in physical education, *Strategies 10,* no. 3 (1997): 5–8; B. Mills, Opening the gymnasium to the World Wide Web, *Journal of Physical Education, Recreation, and Dance 68,* no. 8 (1997): 17–19; B. Mohnsen and C. Thompson, Using video technology in physical education, *Strategies 10,* no. 6 (1997): 8–11; B. S. Mohnsen, *Using Technology in Physical Education,* 2nd ed. (Champaign, IL: Human Kinetics, 1995); S. Silverman, Technology and physical education: Present possibilities and potential problems, *Quest 49,* (1997): 306–14.
7. Silverman, Technology and physical education.
8. POLAR Electro, Inc., 1111 Marcus Ave., Suite M 15, Lake Success, NY 11042-1034.
9. S. Bole, Utah parents use Web to track student work, *The Daily Universe,* BYU, Provo, UT, 8 October 1999.
10. International Society for Technology in Education, National educational technology standards for students, 1998.
11. International Society for Technology in Education, National educational technology standards.
12. E. T. Howley and B. D. Franks, *Health/fitness Instructor's Handbook* (Champaign, IL: Human Kinetics, 1986), 4.
13. United States Department of Health and Human Services, *Physical Activity and Health: A Report of the Surgeon General* (Atlanta, GA: Author, 1996).
14. United States Department of Health and Human Services, *Physical Activity and Health;* B. N. Strand, E., Scantling, and M. Johnson, *Fitness Education: Teaching Concepts-Based Fitness in the Schools* (Scottsdale, AZ: Gorsuch Scarisbrick, 1997).
15. C. B. Corbin, R. Lindsey, and G. Welk, *Concepts of Physical Fitness: Active Lifestyles for Wellness,* 11th ed. (Dubuque, IA. McGraw-Hill, 2003).
16. United States Department of Health and Human Services, *Physical Activity and Health.*
17. R. P. Pangrazi and C. B. Corbin, Physical fitness: Questions teachers ask, *The Journal of Physical Education, Recreation and Dance 64,* no. 8 (1993): 13.
18. Strand, Scantling, and Johnson, *Fitness Education.*
19. Strand, Scantling, and M. Johnson, *Fitness Education.*
20. J. J. Melograno, *Professional and Student Portfolios for Physical Education* (Champaign, IL: Human Kinetics, 1998).
21. AAHPERD, *Physical Education for Lifelong Fitnesss: The Physical Best Teacher's Guide* (Champaign, IL: Human Kinetics, 1999).
22. Strand, Scantling, and Johnson, *Fitness Education.*
23. AAHPERD, *Physical Education for Lifelong Fitnesss;* United States Department of Health and Human Services, *Physical Activity and Health.*
24. AAHPERD, *Physical Best Activity Guide: Elementary Level* (Champaign, IL: Human Kinetics, 1999); AAHPERD, *Physical Best Activity Guide: Secondary Level* (Champaign, IL: Human Kinetics, 1999).
25. Corbin, Lindsey, and Welk, *Concepts of Physical Fitness.*
26. B. Mohnsen, ed., *Concepts of Physical Education: What Every Student Needs to Know* (Reston, VA: National Association for Sport and Physical Education, 1998).
27. AAHPERD, *Physical Education for Lifelong Fitnesss.*
28. National Association for Sport and Physical Education, *Moving into the Future: National Standards for Physical Education,* 2nd ed. (Reston, VA: Author, 2004).
29. Strand, Scantling, and Johnson, *Fitness Education.*
30. AAHPERD, *Physical Best Activity Guide: Elementary Level;* AAHPERD, *Physical Best Activity Guide: Secondary Level;* AAHPERD, *Physical Education for Lifelong Fitnesss.*
31. J. E. Rink, Fitting fitness into the school curriculum, in R. R. Pate and R. C. Hohn (eds.), *Health and Fitness through Physical Education* (Champaign, IL: Human Kinetics, 1994), 67–74.
32. Institute for Aerobics Research, Around the city, *Campbell's Kids Fitness News 1,* no. 3 (March 1990): 3.
33. AAHPERD, *Physical Education for Lifelong Fitnesss.*
34. AAHPERD, *Physical Education for Lifelong Fitnesss.*

35. AAHPERD, *Physical Education for Lifelong Fitnesss.*
36. D. H. Ziatz, How do you motivate students to learn? *Journal of Physical Education and Recreation 48,* no. 3 (1997): 26.
37. J. E. Misner, Are we fit to educate about fitness? *Journal of Physical Education Recreation, and Dance 55,* no. 9 (1984): 27.
38. AAHPERD, *Physical Education for Lifelong Fitnesss.*
39. AAHPERD, *Physical Education for Lifelong Fitnesss.*
40. AAHPERD, *Physical Education for Lifelong Fitnesss;* R. Marquardt, Voluntary jog-a-thon, *Journal of Physical Education, Recreation and Dance 49,* no. 9 (1978): 68.
41. J. A. Gallery, Orienteering with a map and clues, *Journal of Physical Education, Recreation and Dance 54,* no. 5 (1983): 73–74.
42. H. E. Sundberg, A running program that works, *Alliance Update,* no. 7 (July/August 1981).
43. D. E. Corbin, Prediction races and relays, *Journal of Physical Education, Recreation and Dance 50,* no. 6 (1979): 58–59.
44. E. L. Stein, Run for fun: A program for all ages, *Journal of Physical Education, Recreation and Dance 49,* no. 9 (1978): 70.
45. S. C. Elsey, Extracurricular fitness, *Strategies 5,* no. 3 (1991): 13.
46. American Heart Association and American Alliance for Health, Physical Education, Recreation, and Dance, 1900 Association Drive, Reston, VA 22091.
47. C. Hopper, K. Manoz, M. B. Gruber, R. A. Herb, S. MacConnie, and T. Shunk, A family fitness program, *Journal of Physical Education, Recreation and Dance 63,* no. 7 (1992): 23–27; AAHPERD, *Physical Education for Lifelong Fitnesss.*
48. AAHPERD, *Physical Education for Lifelong Fitnesss.*
49. AAHPERD, *Physical Education for Lifelong Fitnesss.*
50. Cooper Institute for Aerobics Research, *Fitnessgram®*: Test Administration Manual (Champaign, IL: Human Kinetics, 1999).
51. R. P. Pangrazi and C. B. Corbin, Physical fitness: Questions teachers ask, *The Journal of Physical Education, Recreation and Dance 64,* no. 8 (1993): 13.
52. Pangrazi and Corbin, *Physical Fitness.*
53. AAHPERD, *Physical Education for Lifelong Fitnesss;* National Association for Sport and Physical Education, *Moving into the Future: National Standards for Physical Education,* 2nd ed. (Reston, VA: Author, 2004); M. L. Veal, A badminton tournament that motivates students, *The Journal of Physical Education, Recreation and Dance 62,* no. 9 (1991): 34–37.
54. B. D. Franks, J. R. Morrow, Jr., and S. A. Plowman, Youth fitness testing: Validation, planning, and politics, *Quest 40* (1988): 191; AAHPERD, *Physical Education for Lifelong Fitnesss.*
55. AAHPERD, *Physical Education for Lifelong Fitnesss;* G. Graham, Motor skill acquisition—An essential goal of physical education programs, *Journal of Physical Education, Recreation and Dance 58,* no. 7 (1987): 44–48 (p. 44).
56. AAHPERD, *Physical Education for Lifelong Fitnesss;* J. M. Curtis, *Pickle-ball for Player and Teacher,* 2nd ed. (Englewood, CO: Morton, 1989); R. P. Pangrazi and P. W. Darst, *Dynamic Physical Education Curriculum and Instruction for Secondary School Students* (Minneapolis: Burgess, 1985).
57. AAHPERD, *Physical Education for Lifelong Fitnesss;* M. W. Metzler, Teaching in competitive games—not just playin' around, *Journal of Physical Education, Recreation, and Dance 61,* no. 8 (1990): 57–61.
58. Graham, Motor skill acquisition, p. 44; AAHPERD, *Physical Education for Lifelong Fitnesss.*
59. *Adventure without Ropes* (Merchantville, NJ: C.E.C. Publishers, 1987); AAHPERD, *Physical Education for Lifelong Fitnesss.*
60. AAHPERD, *Physical Education for Lifelong Fitnesss;* G. Koehler, Teaching stress management, in R. P. Carlson (ed.), *Ideas II: A sharing of teaching practices by secondary school physical education practitioners* (Reston, VA: American Alliance for Health, Physical Education, Recreation and Dance, 1984), 108–09, 177–200.
61. AAHPERD, *Physical Education for Lifelong Fitnesss;* Koehler, Teaching stress management.
62. P. Linden, Aikido: A movement awareness approach to physical education, *Journal of Physical Education, Recreation and Dance 55,* no. 7 (1984): 64–65.
63. A. V. Carron, *Motivation Implications for Coaching and Teaching* (London, Ontario, N6G 3X7: Sports Dynamics, 1984).
64. M. Buck, J. Harrison, H. Fronske, and G. Bayles, Quad ball—A soccer, football, basketball, and pinball game, *Journal of Physical Education, Recreation, and Dance* 61, no. 2 (1990): 7; P. M. McCann, Breaking away from tradition: A new game for middle school students, *Journal of Physical Education, Recreation and Dance 58,* no. 3 (1987): 76–79.
65. R. E. Kraft, Let the students create the games, *Strategies 2,* no. 1 (1988): 27–28.
66. B. A. Glakas, Teaching cooperative skills through games, *Journal of Physical Education, Recreation and Dance 62,* no. 5 (1991): 28–30; M. Johnson, Cooperative round robin tournaments: An effective way to teach sports skills, *The Journal of Physical Education, Recreation and Dance 64,* no. 9 (1993): 10; S. Jones and K. Lamsden, The mix 'n match class structure, *Strategies 6,* no. 6 (1993): 5–7; F. Rokosz, Using cutthroat for tournament play, *Journal of Physical Education, Recreation and Dance 67,* no. 8 (1996): 4; Veal, A badminton tournament that motivates students; S. Wilkinson, Rotation play for maximum participation, *Strategies 6,* no. 6 (1993): 27–29.
67. R. L. Eason, Tournaments that work for physical education classes, *Journal of Physical Education, Recreation and Dance 61,* no. 4 (1990): 68–75; Veal, A badminton tournament that motivates students.

68. Rokosz, Using cutthroat for tournament play.
69. A. W. Chickering and Z. F. Gamson, *Applying the Seven Principles for Good Practice in Undergraduate Education* (San Francisco, CA: Jossey-Bass, 1991).
70. B. Mohnsen, ed., *Concepts of Physical Education: What Every Student Needs to Know* (Reston, VA: National Association for Sport and Physical Education, 1998).
71. D. Docheff, Character in sport and physical education—Summation, *Journal of Physical Education, Recreation and Dance 69,* no. 2 (1998): 24; C. R. Lottes, Action plan for fitness, *Strategies 10,* no. 3 (1997): 27–32.
72. National Association for Sport and Physical Education, *Moving into the Future: National Standards for Physical Education,* 2nd ed. (Reston, VA: Author, 2004).
73. J. H. Naylor, Honey & milk toast, *Journal of Physical Education, Recreation and Dance 46,* no. 7 (1975): 20.
74. *Adventure without Ropes.*
75. L. K. Smith, Using challenge activities to develop group cooperation in physical education, *Physical Education Newsletter* (August 1980).
76. A. Fluegelman, *The New Games Book* (Garden City, NY: Headlands, 1974).
77. T. Orlick, *The Cooperative Sports & Games Book* (New York: Doubleday, 1978).
78. *Adventure without Ropes.*
79. Naylor, Honey & milk toast, *Journal of Physical Education, Recreation and Dance, 46* no. 7 (1975): 20.
80. Naylor, Honey & milk toast.
81. A. C. Boyer, Initiative Activities, 104 E. State Highway, Copperton, UT 84006.
82. J. W. Tangen-Foster and C. W. Lathen, Risk sports in basic instruction programs: A status assessment, *Research Quarterly for Exercise and Sport, 54* (1983): 305.
83. D. R. Latess, Physical education and outdoor adventure: Do they belong together? *Journal of Physical Education, Recreation and Dance 57,* no. 5 (1986): 66–67.
84. *Adventure without Ropes;* Latess, physical education and outdoor adventure.
85. C. E. Rademacher and L. D. Cruse, Planning success for small college outdoor programs, *Utah Association for Health, Physical Education, Recreation and Dance Journal 18* (Autumn 1986): 12–14.
86. J. H. Naylor, *Recreation without Litigation* (Provo, UT: Brigham Young University, 1986).
87. Tangen-Foster and Lathen, Risk sports.
88. Veal, A badminton tournament that motivates students.
89. Lottes, Action plan for fitness.
90. R. Mercier and G. Hutchinson, Social psychology, in B. Mohnsen, ed., *Concepts of Physical Education: What Every Student Needs to Know* (Reston, VA: National Association for Sport and Physical Education, 1998).
91. R. W. Gough, A practical strategy for emphasizing character development in sport and physical education, *Journal of Physical Education, Recreation and Dance 69,* no. 2 (1998): 18–20, 23.
92. R. M. Klemp and J. E. Hon, An open sports program in the middle school, *Phi Delta Kappan 74,* no. 2 (1992): 187–189.
93. N. Cutforth and M. Parker, Promoting affective development in physical education: The value of journal writing, *Journal of Physical Education, Recreation and Dance 67,* no. 7 (1996): 19–23.
94. D. B. Young, Curriculum interfacing through physical education: Health, math, science, language arts, visual arts, and gifted and talented, in R. R. Pate and R. C. Hon (eds.), *Health and fitness through physical education* (Champaign, IL: Human Kinetics, 1994).
95. B. Kirkpatrick and M. M. Buck, Heart adventures challenge course: A lifestyle education activity, *The Journal of Physical Education, Recreation and Dance 66,* no. 2 (1995): 17–24.
96. B. Kirkpatrick, Tropical rainforest: Survival skills. Unpublished manuscript, 1992.
97. D. Bayer, B. Doyle, M. Loy, D. Jones, and V. Wilson. Unpublished manuscript, Ball State University, Muncie, Indiana, 1993.
98. P. Sawley, Woods Cross High School, Woods Cross, Utah.
99. M. Tenoschok, Physical education appreciation, *Journal of Physical Education, Recreation and Dance 50,* no. 9 (1979): 18.
100. National Association for Sport and Physical Education, *101 Ways to Promote Physical Activity and Sport* (Reston, VA: Author, 1994).

CHAPTER

11

Assessing Student Performance

Study Stimulators

1. How are planning, instruction, and assessment linked?
2. What is the difference between norm-referenced and criterion-referenced assessment as they relate to test selection, test assessment, and learner performance? When is each type of assessment preferred?
3. Define authentic assessment and give examples of its advantages and limitations.
4. Define the following terms: reliability, validity, objectivity, feasibility.
5. How might you go about selecting assessment materials for cognitive, psychomotor, and affective objectives?
6. What is the purpose of a rubric? How is one created?
7. What is the purpose of giving grades in physical education?
8. What is the process for determining grades in physical education?
9. What kind of grading system is best?

What Is Assessment?

Assessment is the process of gathering and organizing information from multiple sources about a student's level of achievement, which is then used by teachers, students, and parents to make educational decisions about students; to give feedback to students about their progress, strengths, and weaknesses; and to judge the effectiveness of the curriculum and instruction. *Measurement* involves the process of obtaining scores on tests. *Evaluation* involves the examination and interpretation of the information that has been collected to determine its value. When data are collected over a period of time and from a variety of contexts and situations, the judgments made can help teachers make decisions to improve instruction and learning.

Why Is Assessment Important?

The physical education *content standards* describe the knowledge and skills of the discipline, while the *performance standards* specify "how good is good enough." Together, they indicate the types of assessment tasks (e.g., a test or project) required to demonstrate that a content standard has been met and the quality of student performance that is considered acceptable for each level of achievement. Performance standards are used both for student assessment and for evaluating programs. Once assessments of student work or performance have been accumulated over time, *performance benchmarks* can be used to describe the progress that should occur as students move toward a performance standard.[1]

Assessment is done primarily for two reasons. The primary goal of assessment should be to enhance learning. Secondarily, the results of assessment are used to monitor and report student achievement. Assessment techniques should correlate directly with physical education content standards and objectives, enhance instruction and learning, provide valid and reliable evidence of student learning and performance, and enhance teacher-student relations.

The Assess-Plan-Teach-Assess Spiral

In the world of standards-based education, curriculum, instruction, and assessment are inseparable. Lambert equates them to a three-legged stool; two legs will provide some support but if one of the three is not given proper attention, the stool will lack stability.[2] Many teachers see assessment as something that is done only at the completion of instruction to determine student grades. In fact, assessment when used to its fullest potential, is integrated throughout the instructional process. Assessment prior to instruction provides the teacher with information needed to plan lessons and units. *Preassessment* reveals information about students' knowledge, skills, fitness, interests, and attitudes. From it we learn which students have already achieved course objectives and which students might need extra help. Students who already possess the skills can be directed into more challenging activities. Students who lack prerequisite skills can be given help to improve their performance and eventually achieve course objectives. Unit and lesson plans are adapted to help students achieve objectives based on the assessment information.

During instruction, assessment provides feedback to students, informing them of the course objectives and their progress toward achieving each objective. Students who are aware of teacher expectations and cognizant of their progress throughout the learning experience can longer on their own without difficulty. Well-constructed assessment activities serve as learning activities, challenging students to "put it all together." Students gain a feeling of accomplishment as they realize how much they have learned. Good assessment activities can arouse the student's interest, motivate class attendance, and require the learner to use or apply information and skills in real or simulated situations. These higher-level thinking skills are valued in education today. Students also retain skills better when learning is assessed. Teachers who predetermine what and how they will assess tend to have more focused lessons.

At the conclusion of instruction, assessment helps teachers check the effectiveness of the teaching process. It tells the teacher whether students have achieved the course objectives and the progress they made in doing so. When assessment results show that students are not performing well, the teacher must examine unit and lesson plans to determine whether the achievement of performance objectives was pursued in a meaningful way. This begins the cycle again at the next higher level of the spiral.

Assessment used to evaluate and improve instruction is called *formative assessment.* The primary purpose of formative assessment is assessment *for* learning. The data it provides allows teachers to reflect on their instruction and to formulate ways to improve student learning. Because assessment is so critical, it should be an ongoing process. As a vital component of instructional design, assessment should be both informal (assessments that are integrated into the learning process to promote student growth) and formal (assessments that may be standardized or contrived and are often associated with the grading process) and be used throughout units of instruction during the entire school year.

Monitoring and Reporting Student Achievement

The second purpose of assessment is to monitor student achievement and to report the results to appropriate persons. Summative assessments, or assessments *of* learning, are typically used for this purpose. Administered at the completion of a unit or program, they are comprehensive and allow the teacher to determine student achievement of content standards and objectives. Summative assessment is often formal, involving such instruments as skills tests, written tests, performance records, and final projects. Teachers must do more than expect students to be "busy, happy, and good."[3] They must expect students to achieve content standards and create ways for them to do so. Assessment clarifies the standards and provides a clearer vision of what students should know and be able to do at various levels of education. Assessment provides evidence to students, parents, teachers, and administrators that the standards have indeed been reached. It emphasizes the importance of the skills and knowledge being taught by expecting acceptable levels of comprehension and performance by students. When students know they will be held accountable by an evaluation of their performance, they spend more time practicing assigned tasks and less time in avoidance behaviors.[4] Students agree that active instruction, monitoring, and rewards or consequences for their performance affect their involvement in physical education classes.[5] Designing and assigning tasks with prespecified standards, and informing students of how they will be held accountable for the execution of those tasks helps students learn to take responsibility for their own behavior. A recent study showed that informing students at the beginning of a badminton unit of how they would be assessed increased the quality of student responses throughout the unit. This was true for students of all ability levels.[6] Certainly what is evaluated determines what will be taught, how it will be taught, and how students will react to instruction.[7] Teachers' responsibility for student achievement and student accountability are vital to the credibility and effectiveness of the profession. Ultimately, assessment provides information to determine appropriate amounts of time necessary for students to succeed in each unit in the curriculum.

Norm-referenced assessment refers to how well a student performs compared with others of the same age, gender, class, grade level, school, or geographic area. Standardized achievement tests are norm referenced and provide important information regarding the general school population as it relates to national norms. Norm-referenced assessment is based on the normal curve, which assumes that achievement is normally distributed around the average class performance. Because the normal curve is based on the distribution of scores in a random fashion and because education is an intentional and purposeful act, the distribution of scores should *not* be distributed randomly. Greater instructional effectiveness will lead to a less normal distribution of scores.[8] Keep in mind that norm-referenced scores tell how well students compare with their peers, but not how well any of them *should* perform. Norm-referenced scores are rank order scores. If the population to which students are being compared is skewed (very strong or very weak), teachers know how students compare to that group but do not know whether this is desirable.

Norm-referenced assessment can be used to place students into ability groups for instruction or as a baseline for establishing criterion-referenced assessment standards. Beginning teachers, not yet familiar with appropriate mastery levels for a given unit, find it easier to use norm-referenced assessment.

Criterion-referenced assessment refers to how well a student performs in comparison with a predetermined and specified standard of performance. Ideally, given enough time, all students should achieve the standards. Criterion-referenced assessment is used to determine those who are qualified to do something, such as to fly planes or perform lifesaving rescues. With increasing frequency, educators are using criterion-referenced assessment materials to measure student achievement because such measures demonstrate the extent to which a student has achieved competence in a given area of instruction. However, the complaint of grade inflation can prevent educators from adopting criterion-referenced systems. Another concern is that standards set arbitrarily by experts may be too high or too low. One type of criterion-referenced assessment is called a *mastery test.* Mastery learning is explained in more detail in Chapter 9.

Criterion-referenced assessment can be used for both formative and summative assessment. When used for summative assessment, the criteria should not change as students become more proficient. The initial criteria must be established with care. It is better to set standards too high rather than too low. Students rarely complain when standards are lowered.

Review Questions: What are the purposes of assessment? Define norm-referenced assessment, criterion-referenced assessment, summative assessment, and formative assessment.

TRADITIONAL ASSESSMENT

Traditional assessments in physical education include written tests with selected-response questions, skill tests, and fitness tests. Although not looked on favorably by everyone, they do have their role in the assessment process. The problem is not so much with the assessments as with how teachers have chosen to use them. The next section will describe the various traditional assessments commonly used in physical education.

Written Tests

Written tests are useful ways to assess students' cognitive knowledge in physical education. Selected-response items (multiple choice, true-false, and matching) are common test formats used on physical education tests. Questions requiring students to fill in the blank or short answer essay questions are also often used. When teachers have very large classes and want to know whether students have learned basic knowledge about a given activity, written tests are efficient means for determining that information. Written tests are ineffective when teachers use them to assess trivial knowledge, things that students memorize for a test and forget ten minutes after leaving the testing area. Teachers may also underutilize a written assessment when they provide students a handout of facts about a unit or activity and then develop questions based only on that handout. During a unit a wealth of information should be delivered to students. Written assessments are excellent ways to determine whether students understand this knowledge as well as holding them accountable for retaining it.

The first step in constructing a written test is to develop a table of specifications (see Table 11.1). The table should include an outline of the content to be included, as well as a breakdown of the percentage and/or number of questions in each area. The percentage of test items in each area should reflect the emphasis placed on that area during instruction and should be a representative sampling of the course content. At least some of the questions should require critical thinking skills rather than simply the recall of memorized facts. Understanding or comprehension implies that the students will be able to explain the concepts in their own words, while application involves the ability to use the concepts to do something. Sources for test questions include *Test Questions for Physical Education Activities,* textbooks on tests and measurements, and tests found in various periodicals.

Suggestions for Writing Good-Quality Test Questions

Whether you are using questions from an outside source or writing your own, questions need to be edited to ensure that they follow appropriate rules and techniques and are

TABLE 11.1 Table of Specifications for Content Validity

Content	Knowledge/Recall	Understanding/Comprehension	Application
RULES			
Violations	#2	#1	#11
Fouls	#8	#3	#12
Scoring	#9		
General play	#10		
STRATEGIES			
Offensive		#4	#13
Defensive			#14
TECHNIQUE			
Passing	#5	#6	
Shooting			#15
Dribbling		#7	
HISTORY	#16		

written at the appropriate level for your students (see Box 11.1). Organize questions in groups by item types (i.e., true-false, matching, etc.). Write instructions using clear, concise, simple wording. Underline important points. Tell how and where to record answers. Include directions concerning guessing. When necessary, include examples of how to record answers correctly. Proofread your tests before copying them for students.

Item Analysis

The purpose of item analysis is to improve test items for future use and to serve as a basis for class discussion, remedial work, and improvement of instruction. Some factors that affect validity include unclear test directions, vocabulary or sentence structure that is too difficult for students, inappropriate item difficulty, poorly constructed items, and inappropriate test items for the outcome to be measured. Testing an item that was not covered in class or using the same examples on the test that were used in class can also negatively affect the validity of a test question. Some differences exist in the manner of construction between norm-referenced and criterion-referenced tests, as explained later in this section.

The *difficulty index* is indicated by the percentage of students who answered the item correctly (the number who answered the item correctly divided by the total number of students who answered the item). The higher the difficulty index, the easier the item or the better it has been taught; thus, 100 percent is an easy question, while 20 percent is a difficult question. Guessing would normally yield a difficulty index of 50 percent for true-false and 25 percent for multiple-choice items. For a norm-referenced test, items should fall between 30 percent and 70 percent. The percentage will usually be higher for a criterion-referenced test.

Item discrimination indicates the extent to which the item discriminates between those who scored high on the test, presumably the best students, and those who scored low on the test. It ranges from −1.00 to +1.00. A 0.0 indicates that the best and worst students scored the same on the item, or that all students marked the item correctly or that all students marked it incorrectly. A positive discrimination, such as 1.00, shows that the high scorers on the test did better than the low scorers on the item, while a negative discrimination means that the low scorers on the test did better than the high scorers on the item. It indicates something is wrong with the question or the study guide or the instruction. Item discrimination indicates validity only if the test is valid. It is a measure of the internal consistency of the test—how each item measures what the test is measuring. To compute the item discrimination index for each item, use these steps:

1. Stack papers with total scores from high to low.
2. Make one stack of the highest 25 percent of the papers; make another stack of the lowest 25 percent of the papers. Disregard any papers in between.
3. Calculate the percentage of high students who answered the item correctly; then calculate the percentage of low students who answered the item correctly.
4. Discrimination index = percentage of high students − percentage of low students.

A preferred range of discrimination would be 40 percent to 100 percent, with most items closer to the high end of the range.

Items below .20	Reject or rewrite.
.20–.29	Rewrite.
.30–.39	OK, check for ways to improve.
above .40	Good items

A low index of discrimination may indicate (1) that the item tests an area of little emphasis, (2) that the item tests a

Box 11.1

Suggestions for Writing High-Quality Test Questions

True-False

1. Avoid trivial items and broad generalizations.
2. Avoid using sentences from textbooks or stereotyped phrases as items.
3. Avoid ambiguity.
4. Include an equal number of true-false items, or more false than true.
5. Randomly order items to avoid patterns.
6. Express only one idea per item.
7. Avoid negative statements.
8. Avoid words like *sometimes, usually, often, always,* and *never.*
9. Make false statements plausible.
10. Make statements clearly true or clearly false.
11. Keep true and false items about the same length.
12. Allow students to circle T or F, or if having them write the response in a blank, require that the entire word (e.g., true or false) be written out.

Multiple-Choice/Multiple-Response

1. Write short, clear items, including as much item content in the stem as possible.
2. Avoid stereotyped phrases, negative statements, and words like "sometimes."
3. Compose 3–5 well-written, plausible alternatives (i.e., the correct answer, a related but incorrect answer, an opposite or unrelated answer, an incorrect answer that sounds like the correct answer).
4. Distractors should be parallel in form, of the same length, grammatically consistent with the stem, and in random order.
5. Avoid using "none of the above" and "all of the above."
6. Have only one correct or best answer.
7. Place all distractors on the same page.
8. Use distractors designed to reveal student misunderstandings or incomplete understandings.

Matching

1. Use homogeneous items and options.
2. Place all items and options on the same page.
3. Randomly order items.
4. Have more alternatives than items or use alternatives more than once.
5. Place shorter words or phrases on the right, listed alphabetically or numerically.

Short Answer/Essay

1. The desired answer must be clear.
2. Questions should elicit responses higher than mere recall.

Essay

1. Make an answer key of what should be included, a sample response.
2. Write the question so the student knows what is required.
3. Score all responses to one question before proceeding to the next question. Score responses anonymously.
4. Students should know whether spelling, punctuation, or format will be included in the score.

Format

1. Clarity of the printed page, easily read.
2. Clear directions for each type of question.

more complex learning outcome, or (3) that there are possible technical defects in the item that need to be revised.

Item function tells the effectiveness of the distractors.

1. Create a table of the distractors for each item.
2. Eliminate or rewrite distractors that distracted the high group.
3. Eliminate or rewrite distractors that no one chose.
4. Check choices chosen by more lows than highs.

Use the item analysis to determine which items need to be eliminated or revised. Check the difficulty level for easy items, such as those answered correctly by all of the students. Giving a pretest will tell you whether the students already know the material before you teach your unit, in which case you can eliminate these items and save valuable class time. Rewrite or eliminate multiple-choice distractors with very few responses. The difficulty index could be used to arrange test items in order of difficulty, with the easiest items first.

Some schools have machines called scantrons that will score a test. Students record their answers on an answer sheet that is then fed through a machine and scored. It is possible to do a simple item analysis by marking appropriate boxes on the answer key and then feeding a summary sheet through the machine after all tests have been scored. This system is much less sophisticated than the one described above but it can provide teachers with information about which questions were missed most frequently.

Other Approaches to Testing

One-Minute Test To save class time for activity, the one-minute test is given at the conclusion of every lesson. Each student takes a piece of paper to a personal space and answers the question or questions for the day. Questions are short answer and involve such items as rules specific to dribbling, cues for the forearm drive, defensive racquetball strategies, or safety procedures for adventure activities.

Students can evaluate their own progress if answers are posted. Results give feedback to teachers on the effectiveness of instruction.[9]

True-False Test Develop a true-false test in which the students change the questions so the answers are all true or all false. Tell the students which of these conditions will exist.

Take-Home Test Students are given questions to be answered outside of class. A deadline for submission is stated when the questions are handed out. Students may use whatever resources are available to answer questions. Students can be asked to list resources on the answer sheet. Answers are expected to be comprehensive and are graded accordingly.

Nongraded Exam Students are asked to answer questions that, when completed, serve as a study sheet. Answers are corrected but not graded. Examples include crossword puzzles and other word games.

Officiating Tests Students can be taught to make calls according to the rules by presenting them with descriptions of plays and asking them to make the call. However, many students have difficulty understanding the "who is doing what" dialog. Another method would be to show video clips, stopping at intervals and asking them to make the call, first as a group and later individually.

Skill Tests

Skill tests may be appropriate for assessing beginning skill levels, since students often learn to perform skills before they are able to use them in game play. If a teacher's goal was to introduce students to the skills of a game (rather than being able to play a game), skill tests are an excellent assessment tool. They are also appropriate for measuring student achievement for activities that are best assessed by measuring discrete skills (e.g., track and field, archery, bowling, swimming). Some teachers use skill tests as learning tasks or formative assessments as they require students to perform the skill in a relatively closed environment. Students could actually use these as skill warm-ups during the beginning of class or sponge activities that encourage skill practice. Skill tests are not appropriate for assessing game-play ability. Many other factors (e.g., court movement, knowing when to use a given skill, strategy) are essential for success in game play; skill tests do not assess these.

A test can be designed to measure a specific skill or a combination of skills. Timed tests are appropriate for speed events, those measuring distance are used for jumps and field events, while tests designed for projected objects such as a tennis drive usually are concerned with both accuracy and speed. Accuracy tests often use a target on the wall or floor. AAHPERD has skill tests booklets for many activities. (These can be found on the web at http://www.aahperd.org/aahperd/aahperd-publications.html.) *Assessing Sport Skills* is another good source for skill tests.[10] Professional journals and tests and measurements textbooks also describe skill tests. To be reliable, skill tests must be carefully administered. The following suggestions may be helpful:

- Plan equipment and scoresheets in advance, mark areas prior to class time, remove equipment and markings when finished. A special floor tape is available for markings to protect the floor finish. Student assistants can help set up and take down equipment.
- Select dependable, responsible student assistants and instruct them in their specific duties (assume nothing) in writing. Arrange for their turns to take the test.
- Give all directions before beginning the test. Instructions must be clear and concise. Carefully explain trials—who, when, why, where, how many.
- Demonstrate each test. Practice in advance.
- Provide opportunities for questions. Ask questions to make sure students understand the instructions and can follow them quickly and correctly.
- Use a consistent tosser for everyone taking a test.
- Clearly mark and point out scoring areas (including values for each area) prior to beginning the test.
- Choose students who are trustworthy, accurate, dependable, efficient, and neat as recorders. Partners can record in some cases.
- No coaching should be done during the test by students or the teacher.

Discuss test results with students. Include an interpretation of the results and what they mean for each student. Remember, skill test results are only one of several ways to assess learning, *and they certainly are not very authentic.* They may be influenced by maturation as well as by factors within the tests themselves. Other assessment techniques should be used to verify student performance.

Fitness Tests

Traditionally, physical fitness has been measured by a battery of fitness tests, such as the *Fitnessgram*® test. Most of these tests assess health-related fitness and have criterion-referenced standards so students can evaluate their status and set goals toward the achievement of better fitness. The tests and standards are described in Chapter 10 and in the test booklets and software available with the various programs, which allow students and teachers to input the results and print out reports for themselves and for parents, as well as to print various summary reports for teachers and administrators. Weight training can be evaluated using an assessment like the one shown in Box 11.2. Many physical education teachers enjoy administering fitness tests. Tests are relatively easy to administer when the protocols are followed. More fit

BOX 11.2

Weight Training Assessment

As always, lift with a partner! No exceptions. The goal is to lift 10 repetitions at 75% of your maximum for each of the six required lifts. These lifts are bench press, lat pull down, leg extension, leg curl, biceps curl, and triceps press down. From your daily log take your maximum weight for each lift, write it on the chart under max weight. Then multiply it by .75 and write the answer under 75%. This is the weight you need to lift for your skills test. Do as many repetitions in a row as you can at this weight. There are 10 possible points per lift, 1 point per repetition. Write the number of repetitions you did under # Repetitions. You will have the last three days of the unit to complete the skills test. Each lift must be done at least once, but you may try up to one time per day. Your best score will be recorded for your final grade.
Example: Tom's max weight for the bench press is 150 lbs. 150 × .75 = 112.5 lbs. Tom lifts 110 lbs. for 9 repetitions, so he scores 9 out of 10 points for bench press.

Day	Lifts	Max Weight	75%	# Repetitions
Example	bench press	150	110	9
Mon	bench press			
Wed	bench press			
Fri	bench press			
Mon	lat pull down			
Wed	lat pull down			
Fri	lat pull down			
Mon	leg extension			
Wed	leg extension			
Fri	leg extension			
Mon	leg curl			
Wed	leg curl			
Fri	leg curl			
Mon	biceps curl			
Wed	biceps curl			
Fri	biceps curl			
Mon	triceps press down			
Wed	triceps press down			
Fri	triceps press down			

Source: Jennifer Roberts.

students usually enjoy seeing how they compare to the various norms or criteria established for the test. Fitness tests can time-consuming to administer. If teachers are going to spend several days administering the tests, results should be used in planning lessons for students. Too many times teachers leave the results in a file drawer or in a computer file and fail to use the information they provide to improve fitness with students. Also there is some disagreement about which tests should be included (e.g., sit-and-reach measures test hamstring flexibility, but what about flexibility in other parts of the body? Body fat composition is rife with controversy).

Other concerns with fitness testing involve the validity of the tests and the appropriate administration of the tests. Criterion-referenced standards for fitness tests are based on the latest research on health and fitness. However, since no direct connection exists between the physical fitness of children and youth and their longevity and quality of life, these standards must be based on group data, with the result that they may be inappropriate for some students. Research has shown that genetic makeup strongly influences fitness test results. For example, body weight directly influences scores on tests of upper body strength and aerobic fitness. Arm and leg lengths directly influence sit-and-reach scores. Therefore, caution should be used in grading students based on fitness-test results. This is especially true of students with low levels of fitness. Students can be graded on completing the tests, recording and graphing their results, setting personal goals, planning activities to meet their goals, and improving their scores.

One of the primary objectives of assessing physical fitness is to motivate students to engage in lifelong physical activity. This is especially important for students with minimal levels of fitness. Thus, when testing, teachers need to exercise great care to avoid embarassment by testing students in front of their peers, calling out scores, or having students record scores for others whose fragile self-image may be destroyed by these practices. Students should be given the opportunity to take fitness tests and to plot their own fitness results over time, setting and achieving goals that promote engagement in an active lifestyle.

Performance-Based Assessments

The reform movement in education advocates assessment of content standards with tools that are more congruent with the principles of effective instruction, learning, and motivation, and that provide meaningful information about student progress and achievement. The trend is toward authentic or performance-based assessments that focus on significant outcomes related to the completion of life's relevant tasks. In *performance-based assessment,* students apply skills and knowledge to solve "real-world" problems. Actually, many of these new assessment techniques are already used in physical education. Wiggins suggests that educators ask themselves "What is the equivalent of the game in each subject?"[11] Since assessments are connected to students' lives and learning experiences, they have high personal relevance and captivate student attention. Students' best work occurs when they are allowed to make choices about and control their own learning. Some examples of performance-based assessments in physical education are listed here:

1. The ability to utilize skills in a game situation.
2. The ability to assess physical fitness, develop an appropriate fitness plan, and engage in fitness activities necessary to achieve fitness.
3. The ability to use the principles of motor learning to learn new skills.

Performance-based assessments have a number of specific characteristics.

- Students perform, create, produce, or do something. They use higher-level thinking to apply concepts to a variety of significant, meaningful tasks in real-life contexts. The skills acquired are transferable to real-life social and work settings.
- Students know in advance the criteria used to evaluate performance.
- Students learn to reflect upon and evaluate their own work. Teachers serve as coaches and facilitators.
- Students are expected to present their work publicly. The intended audience is identified when the assessment is introduced. Students are more accountable and develop a higher sense of self-efficacy when their work is viewed by others as significant and they also learn presentation techniques. When assessment results are shared, advocacy for physical education programs increases and public relations improve.
- Assessment involves examination of the process as well as the products of learning. In fact, assessments are so firmly embedded in the curriculum that they are practically indistinguishable from instruction (i.e., activity logs as part of a fitness portfolio).

Performance-based assessments have a number of advantages. They measure directly what students should know and be able to do in real-life situations, employing a broad range of "intelligences" and emphasizing higher order thinking skills and collaboration. Students become actively engaged in learning and assessment. They distinguish a real audience for their work beyond the classroom. They judge their own work and understand what it means to get better.[12] Using performance-based assessments can help to satisfy the need for accountability prompted by school reform.[13] Assessments may be both self-referenced and standards-referenced.[14]

Some concerns have been expressed about the use of performance-based assessments. Valid assessments and rubrics (scoring keys) are difficult to create and more time is needed for grading. Because fewer tasks are used to sample the content, validity may suffer. The use of multiple assessments, of varying types and at different time periods, can overcome this deficiency. To improve reliability, rubrics must be very specific, and this may decrease student creativity.[15] Another problem arises because performance-based assessments do not mesh well with our current grading system.

Review Questions: What is performance-based assessment?

What are the advantages and disadvantages of traditional and performance-based assessment?

Creating Performance-Based or Authentic Assessments

Performance-based or authentic assessments require students to utilize or apply relevant knowledge and skills to address realistic or authentic problems, situations, and issues, rather than choosing responses from predetermined answers. To create these alternative assessments, do the following:[16]

1. Determine the content standard, benchmark, or objective to be assessed.
2. List possible assessment techniques for that learning domain.
3. Ask the question, "What tasks can I use so students can demonstrate their concepts, skills, and so on?" Describe the task through which students will demonstrate their understanding, including the knowledge (facts, concepts, principles) and skills (problem solving, decision making, investigation, experimentation, or synthesis) needed to complete the task.
4. Provide directions for completing the task, including
   a. Who will complete the task—individuals, small groups, or other.
   b. A timeline for completing various portions of the assessment task.
   c. Resources needed to prepare for and complete the assessment task.
   d. Suggested modifications to address the full range of students from special education to gifted and talented.
   e. Formative assessment, with feedback to guide instruction.
   f. How students will be involved in reflective activities with the teacher and peers to whom they will be able to explain and discuss their progress.
5. Provide a model of the expected behaviors.
6. Describe how the assessments will be evaluated, including how assessment data will be converted to grades.
7. Delineate instructional strategies that may be used to teach the concepts and to prepare students to complete the task, including
   a. Preassessment of prior knowledge and skills needed to complete the assessment.
   b. Opportunities to learn knowledge and skills needed or to practice those already learned, including modifications for students with various learning styles and capabilities.
   c. Ways to help students develop a positive attitude about learning and the performance task.
8. Plan how students and/or peers will assess their work.

Types of Performance-Based Assessment

The purpose of this section is to briefly introduce the reader to various types of performance-based assessments:

- Observations: teacher, self, peer
- Game play
- Event tasks
- Written assignments
- Oral presentations/demonstrations
- Individual/group projects
- Interviews and questionnaires
- Role plays
- Logs
- Open-response questions
- Portfolios

Depending on the criteria used, assessments can be designed to measure very specific learning in a single learning domain (i.e., psychomotor, cognitive, or affective) or can look at learning holistically as it applies to multiple domains. Teachers generally have fun creating these assessments for students, and students generally see them as more meaningful than traditional assessments. The caution offered here is that teachers must remember that the purpose of the assessment is to measure student learning. By developing assessments with a continual eye on the objectives they are designed to measure, frivolous or meaningless assessments can be avoided.

Observations

Because of the overt nature of physical education observations, they are among the most common forms of assessment used in physical education. Observations can be done by teachers, peers, or by the students assessing themselves. Many times teachers do these observations informally, giving feedback based on what they observe. Recording these results has many benefits. First, by recording the observation, teachers force themselves to identify the elements of the performance they feel the students should exhibit to demonstrate learning. Too often, teachers have a general idea about what they are looking for but they have not clearly defined what this is nor communicated it to their students. Second, by recording the observation, teachers will be more systematic with whom they observe. It is very easy to start watching a highly skilled athlete or help those having much difficulty with a task. While these are important parts of teaching, teachers must remember that they are there to watch every student in class. Some students are adept at avoiding activity (competent bystanders) as they may be embarrassed by their lack of skill. Systematic observation will make this apparent to the teacher. A third reason for doing written observations is to document student learning. Written observations provide proof to administrators and parents that learning is occurring in the gymnasium. The following are some ways to observe student performance.

Checklists, Task Sheets, and Self-Checks *Checklists* Some skills are relatively simple, but essential for progression in the activity. List the skills to be performed and the students' names on a card or paper and check off the skills as they are achieved or have each student carry a card to initial. Lining students up in alphabetical order

BOX 11.3

Example of a Task Sheet

Volleyball Task Sheet A Student ____________

Formation	*Activity*	*Criterion*	*Partner Initials*
Forearm Pass			
Demonstration	Cues: Arms and wrists together (thumbs parallel) Keep rear down Right foot forward		
Partners	1. Practice toss to partner's extended arms.	5 consecutive	________
X → X	2. Toss ball to partner, who forearm passes back to you.	5 consecutive	________
X<X	3. Toss ball to side of partner, who forearm passes back to you. Alternate sides.	10 consecutive	________
X ↔ X	4. Hit forearm passes back and forth with partner.	10 consecutive	________
	5. Repeat #4. Touch floor with hand between each pass.	5 correct	________
	6. Repeat #4. Turn around between each pass. Cue: Arms away from body	5 correct	________
	7. Repeat #4. Hit forearm pass to self, do 1/4 turn to the right and pass to self, do 1/4 turn to right and pass over head to partner. Cue: Face ball (angle arms to direct ball)	5 correct	________
Triangle	8. Pass ball clockwise.	15 consecutive	________
X → X \ / X	Pass ball counterclockwise.	15 consecutive	________
Shuttle	9. First person in line passes to first person in other line, then runs to the end of the other line. (Keep to the right for safety.)	10 consecutive	________
XXX⇄XXX	10. Two-hand toss over net. Forehand pass to target. Retriever rolls ball under net to tosser. Rotate.	5 consecutive	________
		Date	________
		Teacher's Initials	________

Note: Always end the drill on a good pass or a good serve, whatever the goal is for that drill.

makes it easier to use name lists.[17] Skills may be checked off by students, partners, or the teacher. Spot checks help to ensure accuracy when students check (e.g., teachers could require students to demonstrate every fourth skill on the list to the teacher). In informal assessment, students can be asked to raise their hands if they can perform a certain task, such as a cartwheel, or move to a certain court if they can already do a right-handed lay-up.

Task sheets (Boxes 11.3 and 11.4; see also Chapters 5 and 9) Student progress in learning can be assessed by noting the number of task sheets that have been completed by a student or group of students. A variation of this is to list tasks from simple to complex and mark or have students mark the highest level they are able to achieve.[18] One type of task sheet asked students to perform ten trials of a golf putt and record the number of completed trials. Success was achieved when the student performed eight out of ten trials for two out of three sets.[19]

Self-Checks In a cumulative record, students record items such as the daily distance they have run, biked, or swum, or the total number of free throws they have made out of ten shot each day. This technique is especially helpful for homework or preclass activities and can help the teacher identify student skill, endurance, and effort. Students who are doing poorly may need extra encouragement. Improvement can be recorded on a chart or portrayed on a graph.

Box 11.4

A Task List for the Basketball Dribble

Directions: Circle the Highest Level You Can Achieve While Dribbling a Basketball.

LEVEL	TASK
1	Dribble a basketball to the wall and back 5 times while walking.
2	Dribble a basketball to the wall and back 5 times while walking, using your *non*dominant hand.
3	Dribble a basketball to the wall and back 5 times while *jogging,* using your dominant hand.
4	Dribble a basketball to the wall and back 5 times while jogging, using your *non*dominant hand.
5	Dribble a basketball to the wall and back 5 times while *running,* using your dominant hand.
6	Dribble around the *cones* 5 times while jogging, using your dominant hand.
7	Dribble around the *cones* 5 times while jogging, using your *non*dominant hand.
8	Dribble to the wall 5 times and back with a *passive defender.* Switch hands on the way back.
9	Dribble to the wall 5 times and back with an *active defender.* Switch hands on the way back.

Box 11.5

Graham's Levels of Skill Proficiency

	PRECONTROL	CONTROL	UTILIZATION	PROFICIENCY
Name	Inability to control object. Tries are inconsistent.	Ability to reproduce a movement with increasing efficiency and consistency when concentrating.	Consistent execution of skills and ability to use combined skills in simple games.	Effortless, automatic movements used in games or activities.
Marcus				
K.C.				
Alysson				

Source: Concepts from G. Graham, S. Holt/Hale, and M. Parker, *Children Moving: A Reflective Approach to Teaching Physical Education,* 3d ed. (Mountain View, CA: Mayfield (1993), 24–25.

Rating Sheets Rating sheets can be constructed from a list of expected behaviors or descriptors. The teacher places a check or number beside the appropriate item. Several methods have been recommended for rating skill development. First, ratings of skill can be based on the student's *developmental level,*[20] as shown in Box 11.5. A second method involves *task complexity.* Movements arise from interactions of the person, the task itself, and the environment. Characteristics of the environment are each categorized from less complex to more complex (more authentic), as shown in Box 11.6.[21] Table 8.5 provides suggestions for the elements and levels of complexity. More information can be obtained if the person's movements are also analyzed at different levels of performance from easy to difficult. Finally, a row can be added for how well or how often the performance goal is achieved. Once the rubric is completed, the teacher merely circles what is observed. With different colored pens, several students could be recorded on one sheet or one student on various occasions.[22] Whatever scale is used, teachers should practice using it prior to testing. When several persons are using the scale, discussing the categories before use increases interrater reliability.

Student knowledge of game play and rules can be determined by observing students as they officiate games. Although being an official is common in Sport Education units, this is an excellent way to evaluate a student's ability to apply knowledge of rules, etiquette, and other information important to the game or activity. Box 11.7 is an example of a form used to assess volleyball officiating skills.

Assessments in dance and other performance-related activities such as gymnastics and rope jumping can be made more objective by defining the elements to be considered, such as the entrance, originality, quality of skills, stage poise, exit, evidence of preparation, teamwork, and the standards for each level. These also help the student discern what is to be included in the performance.

Students can assess their own performance in game play, tournaments, and simulated events—such as archery,

BOX 11.6

A Framework for Developing Progressions and Assessments for the Volleyball Forearm Pass

	ELEMENTS	LESS COMPLEX			MORE COMPLEX
Environment	Type of ball received—ball speed	Toss	Forearm pass	Serve	Hard serve
	Direction of pass received	Straight ahead	Left or right side	Behind	
	Type of pass	Hit to partner	Directed to another direction from that received	Directed to front row	Directed to setter in correct position
	Distance of pass	Short	Medium	Long	
	Focus	On skill itself			On accuracy and distance
Person	Arm action	Hits ball on hands	Hits ball on forearms	Arms and wrists together (thumbs parallel)	Faces ball, angles arms
	Leg action	None	Rear down, right foot forward	Gets under the ball	Uses legs to lift ball
Goal	Successful performance	Rarely	Sometimes	Often	Always

Sources: Ideas from David J. Langley and Amelia Mays Woods, Developing progressions in motor skills: A systematic approach, *Journal of Physical Education, Recreation, and Dance* 68, no. 7 (1997): 41–45; Kathleen M. Haywood, Authentic assessment of movement requires a developmental approach, *Missouri Journal of Health, Physical Education, Recreation, and Dance* 7 (1997): 3–15 [no issue given].

swimming, or track meets. Situations and criteria should be specified in advance and students must be helped to evaluate their own learning. In addition, students can videotape their skill performances over time and reflect on their progress, or they can keep journals of their progress. Each day could have a different point of emphasis. For example, partners could watch each other play a racquetball game and answer questions like "Did I recover to ready position in the center of the court after hitting the ball?"

Teacher Observation The third method of assessment infers student attitudes from their behavior. Teachers have almost unlimited opportunities to observe student behavior and attitudes. The fact that teachers have these opportunities does not necessarily mean their judgment will be objective and informed, however. If the assessment is to be thorough and truly useful, teachers should systematically plan both data collection and procedures for recording information. If teachers do not consciously identify the behaviors to be observed and take time to gather and record information, their impressions are more likely to be formed on the basis of extreme incidents and behavior patterns rather than by a less biased sample of the behaviors of interest. Anecdotal records should be made of approach behaviors including participation in nonrequired club, intramural, or extramural activities or volunteering to help with physical education–related activities.

Kirkpatrick tells students they will be evaluated on effort, attitude, awareness, and expectations three times during each nine-week grading period. Because students don't know when the three assessments will occur, they participate maximally every day. She also uses heart monitors to evaluate students' effort. She can read the heart monitors during the class period on a wristwatch monitor and also print out a copy on the computer.[23]

Examples of self- and peer-observation assessments used in physical education are presented later in the chapter. Teachers are reminded that it is inappropriate to use grades that students have given themselves or others in calculating student grades. Self- and peer assessments are formative and designed to make students aware of appropriate behavior and how others perceive their actions.

Game Play Assessments

Performance-based assessments of game play are excellent ways to determine whether students are able to apply

Box 11.7

Volleyball Official Rating Sheet

	Name	Name	Name	Name	Name	Name	Name	Name	Name	Name
Demonstrates knowledge of basic rules										
Demonstrates knowledge of court boundaries										
Calls the lines accurately										
Calls illegal hits										
Keeps composure under stress										
Makes consistent calls										
Demonstrated good organization skills(gets the game started, etc.)										
Calls game with confidence										
Keeps track of serve rotation and calls errors when they occur										

4 = Always demonstrating this behavior
3 = Usually demonstrating this behavior although misses some calls
2 = Demonstrates this behavior at least half of the time
1 = Demonstrated this behavior on some occasions
0 = Never demonstrates this behavior

the skills and knowledge needed to participate in various sports and activities. Games can be evaluated holistically or by using other performance indicators.

Participation in Games, Tournaments, and Culminating Activities *Tournament results* Results of a round robin class singles tournament are generally a good indication of the playing ability of individual students. To avoid grading a student on his or her team's or partner's ability or lack of ability, challenge courts can be used to assess skills. The idea is for the best players to challenge their way up to court 1. If only two players are playing on a court, after each round, players who win move up one court and players who lose move down one court. When four players are playing on a court, the players play three games with a different partner in each game. Players total their own scores for the three games. Again, the high scorers move up and the low scorers move down.[24]

Scores In activities such as bowling, track, and swimming, the score or time is the best indication of success. Fronske found that time or the number of strokes required to swim twenty-five yards were valid predictors of swimming skill.[25] In activities such as archery, raw scores on tournament rounds cannot be averaged when different rounds are shot, so raw scores must be converted into standard scores prior to averaging or summing. Electronic grading programs can do this automatically. Teachers can enter scores directly into the grading program and students can keep track of their own scores and plot them to show improvement.

Incidence charts (Box 11.8) Incidence charts list the skills performed in a given activity. The number of times each skill attempt or correct trial is used is tallied during a specified time period. The percentage of correct trials can be calculated for each student or for each team. Students can plot their progress on the number or percentage of successful trials. Incidence charts help students and teachers evaluate game performance. Team incidence charts reveal skills that need reteaching. Students who are not dressed for activity can keep data for teams or individuals. For example, students might tally the number of ball possessions, shots, and goals for a team or the number of balls received or stolen, passes, shots, goals, or turnovers by a single player.[26] Various other methods of keeping game statistics used in athletics could be adapted for use in classroom settings. Students can analyze their own statistics and set goals for improving their performance. For example, partners could record serve attempts and successful serves during a tennis game, compute and plot the percentage of successful serves, and set goals to improve performance. The number of times a player touches the ball is a good indicator of involvement in the game. Errors may demonstrate a need for more skill practice or better instruction in strategies. Incidence charts vary in complexity depending on the age and skill level of the participants.

BOX 11.8

An Incidence Chart

BADMINTON INCIDENCE CHART														
	Serve						Smash			Clear				
	Short			Long										
Name	Out-of-court	Into net	Too high	Out-of-court	Too short	Too low	Into or below net	Out-of-bounds	Missed bird	Too low	Too short	Out-of-court	Out-of-position
Diane White			I	III	I				III		IIIIII IIII	II	
Gregg Charlton				IIIIII					IIIIII		IIIIIIIIII III	IIIIII II	III

Source: Rudy Moe, Brigham Young University.

Culminating activities or performances Culminating activities require students to combine the skills and knowledge learned in a unit in a meaningful way at the conclusion of instruction in the activity is focused on giving students the skills necessary to complete the culminating activity. In a sense, game play is a type of culminating activity. In a dance unit, the culminating activity might require students to choreograph a piece that allows them to show their knowledge of the various elements of dance (i.e., pathways, levels, use of space, relationships, force). Gymnastics routines performed for the class meet would be another example. An overnight camping trip might culminate an outdoor education unit just as training for a local road race would give students the opportunity to demonstrate running ability, conditioning and training used to prepare, strategy (pacing), and participation in activities beyond the gymnasium.

Event Tasks

Event tasks are performance-based assessments that can be completed in a single class period.[27] They consist of a task that is broadly written and can be answered in a variety of ways. Event tasks are popular types of assessment for adventure education. The scenario presented to students gives them a problem to solve. Other types of event tasks can include having students create a short rope skipping or aerobic-dance routine or develop a game. Depending on the topic, event tasks could be used to assess all three learning domains.

Written Assignments

Essays in performance-based assessments are much more "real world" than having students write a term paper or book report. More authentic assignments might include the following:

- Plan a twenty-minute practice session for your team, concentrating on the skills and strategies you need to perform better. You may use practice drills from class or create your own.[28]
- Write a newspaper article or a newsletter to mail home.
- Diagram or define a rule or strategy (such as offsides).
- Interpret fitness data, supported by reasons or evidence for the interpretation.
- Design a pamphlet to distribute at Parents' Night.
- Write a critique for a dance performance seen in class (live or video).
- Create a safety manual for an upcoming camping trip.
- Compare and contrast tennis shoes and work shoes—analyze information from the shoe store. Take apart an old pair of shoes and analyze them. Make foot impressions on wet paper. Analyze how you walk in shoes—such as pronation or supination.
- Compare the hurdle and the Fosbury flop methods of high jumping. Use biomechanical principles like center of gravity and transfer of force to explain your answer.
- Analyze your running times for a half-mile; then calculate for a mile. Write splits down and analyze your strengths and weaknesses.
- Design three nutritious meals. Use a computer software program to evaluate your meals.
- Evaluate the worth of a consumer product. Support your answer with reasons and evidence.[29]
- Perform lab experiments involving fitness principles and write a report of your findings.

Reflective Writing and Journals Students can write about their experiences in physical education and reflect upon their learning. They might be asked to provide answers to questions posed by the teacher such as, "What did I learn this week?" "How do I like what we are doing?" "How will this information be useful to me outside of school?" "What am I confused about?" or "What would I like to learn more about?" They could also reflect upon an observation, a book, a movie, or a personal experience.[30] Some schools have integrated courses in English, science, and recreational activities, in which students camp out, study nature, and write about their experiences. Here is one teacher's assignment:[31]

> DAILY JOURNAL (worth 1 point per day in each unit—30 points possible in this unit) Every class day a daily journal entry must be written and put in your portfolio. Please put the date in the upper right-hand corner of the page. Answer the following questions by number.
>
> 1. What subject did we cover in class today?
> 2. What are the cues/tips for the skills we learned?
> 3. What did you learn personally?
> 4. Do you have any questions? If yes, what?
> 5. How do you feel about your performance today?

Students can write about what it means to be physically fit. They can document their efforts to live a healthy lifestyle and how they feel about their fitness program and progress. One teacher developed the following assignment:

> Each student will keep a journal and I will check it every Friday. Homework for the first day of class will be to write down what cardiovascular activity/ies you will participate in every Tuesday and Thursday. At the beginning of your journal, list the activities you might choose to participate in. There are 12 Tuesdays and Thursdays during the 6-week unit. You will receive 1 point for every journal entry completed. On Friday I will check the two journal entries for that week. I will give points for only the week we are in so don't think you can make it all up at the end of the unit. Each journal entry must be dated, have the mode of activity, how long you participated in it (at least 20 minutes) and a sentence about how you felt while doing the activity to get your point for the day. Following is an example of a journal article that would earn 2 points for that week.
>
> *Jan 5th*
>
> I rode my bike for 25 minutes today on a paved bike trail. I felt happy as I rode and the sun was shining because we are in California where there is no snow in Jan.
>
> *Jan 7th*
>
> Today I went swimming for 20 min. Swimming laps for 20 minutes did not make me very happy because I got tired really quick.
>
> This journal is easy to administer and score. All four requirements must be present to get 1 point. Each student chooses the activities to participate in. A student who chooses to walk would get the same amount of points as the student who chooses to ride a bike. One weakness of journals is that students are on their honor not to lie and make up information.[32]

Journal entries can also ask questions specific to a sport. For example, students might be asked to keep track of their heart rates to see if the sport contributes to aerobic conditioning. They might be asked to identify various types of activities, such as those involving fast twitch and slow twitch muscles and how those activities fit with their perceptions of which types of muscles might be dominant for them. They might also identify other fitness components that can improve their game playing or fitness components that might be improved by playing.

Reaction papers or journal entries are often used to evaluate the achievement of affective objectives from participation in adventure activities. Other items that might be addressed are attitudes toward physical education activities, estimations of personal effort, and student concerns.

One teacher had students write a paper delineating their personal participation goal or goals at the beginning of the course, with a progress report in the middle, and an evaluation at the end, with dated examples of contributions students had made that illustrated how they accomplished their goals. In addition, students were asked to indicate the number of points they would award themselves based on their goals and the class policy. Participation partners were assigned to review each other's goals and to observe and make notes of their partner's participation for a three-week period, after which they wrote each other a letter offering specific feedback on behaviors observed that related to the goal achievement.[33]

Oral Presentations/Demonstrations

Students can present information to their classmates, other students and teachers, administrators, or community members. Ideas include these:

- Design your own game from a list of required components. Include objectives, rules, and scoring. Teach your game to another group or give your written plan to another group to see if they can play it.
- Create a modified game incorporating your assigned skill. You will have ten minutes to organize, teach, and have students play your game. Turn in your objectives, a complete description of your game, rules, diagrams, instructions, and a list of the members of your group and their contribution to the assignment, signed by each member.
- Create a television commercial for the best brand of tennis rackit based on scientific evaluation of the various brands. Make a hypothesis, design an experiment to test your hypothesis, collect data, convert the data to a graph, analyze the data, draw conclusions, write a script, gather props, rehearse, revise, film, and evaluate your performance.

Individual and/or Group Projects

Projects are excellent ways to assess psychomotor and/or cognitive learning. The following are examples of projects:

- Create a modified game incorporating your assigned skill. You will teach this game to second-grade students at a local elementary school that adjoins your school's campus. Turn in your objectives, a complete description of your game, rules, diagrams, instructions, and a list of the members of your group and their contribution to the assignment, signed by each member.
- Design a fitness collage (an artistic composition of materials and objects pasted on a poster board), including the following topics: (i.e., cardiovascular endurance, flexibility). Organize the examples you find into some logical format and label them with the topics. You decide which items best represent your ideas of what the terms mean.[34]
- Develop a way to collect game statistics for each team and player during the tournament. Collect the statistics. Use the results to assess how well your team is performing.
- Create a bulletin board or poster.
- Create an advertisement for a sport-related product. Your ad will be evaluated on the use of a clever slogan that catches the reader's eye, artistic depiction of a logo, and appropriate spelling and grammar.[35]
- Create a web page or video that teaches rules and strategies for basketball. Share your production with the class.
- Develop a multimedia project involving heart rate monitors to determine cardiovascular responses to exercise, skill analysis, conditioning concepts, and nutritional analysis and planning.[36]
- Research folk dancing traditions in the country your group selected. Present your information to the class on the Friday of your country's week. Each member will choose one of the areas below to research for the rest of the group. Type your area as a one-page paper. Make a copy for everyone in your group so each person has each of the five subjects in his or her portfolio. You may not read your paper for the presentation. Be creative. The time limit for each person is 1–1/2 to 2 minutes. Present the content in order as follows:[37]

1. Who usually did the dances in the country and why?
2. What characteristics usually tend to be in each of the dances from that country?
3. Where did the characteristics come from?
4. Food from the country could be researched and brought to taste.
5. What kinds of costumes do they wear? Bring pictures if possible.

Following are several ideas for class projects and assignments that might be included in a fitness unit.

- Create a fitness circuit to meet your own fitness needs. State the purpose of each station. Evaluate your progress over a one-month period.
- Write a personal weight-training program. Identify three individual fitness objectives, five upper body lifts, and five lower body lifts. List the prime mover for each exercise, the body position, number of sets and reps, and days of the week.
- Evaluate your posture as shown in your posture picture. Identify concerns, spinal deviations from the norm, and body type. Design a fitness/exercise plan to improve your posture.
- Create an exercise program that will help you achieve your future fitness goals. Include frequency, intensity, duration, and type of exercise.

Interviews and Questionnaires

Interviews are excellent assessment tools when working with small groups of students or students with weak writing skills (e.g., younger children, ESL students, students with special needs). Attitudes, opinions, and social behaviors can be assessed directly by asking students to describe how they feel about something, such as in an interview or with a questionnaire. Much valuable information concerning student feelings toward physical education can be acquired through informal, unstructured discussions with individuals or groups of students. Student cognitive knowledge can also be assessed using interview assessments. Structured interviews and questionnaires involve asking students predetermined questions. The effectiveness of these techniques hinges on the trust between teacher and students. Possible questions to get to know students include these:

- List three words or phrases that best describe you as a person.
- What qualities do you possess that make you stand out from those around you?
- What are the top five priorities in your life right now?
- If all of your friends were just like you, what kind of friends would they be?
- List three goals you have for the semester.
- What sacrifices will you need to make to reach your goals?
- What extra efforts are you willing to make to help yourself reach your goals?[38]

Students can be asked to complete a questionnaire, inventory, or rating scale, and then tell what they learned about themselves. They can complete open-ended statements such as "I wish this class . . ." or "I really like this class when . . ." Other questions students might answer include these:

- If I had it to do all over again, I (would/would not) take this class. Why?
- What are the two most important things you have learned in this class?
- What do you feel were your strengths in this activity?

- What skills or strategies do you need to practice further?
- What new skills or strategies would you like to learn?
- To what extent will you use the things you have learned in this class?
- Discuss what helped you most in meeting your class goals: teacher/ practice drills/ playing games/ study sheet/ individual work on skills.
- Was the present system of grading appropriate?
- What things would you have liked more help with in this unit?
- How well do you execute the three cues of passing? Discuss how much you have improved since the beginning of this unit.

Role Plays

Teachers can develop scenarios and ask students to play various roles as they show their solution to the dilemma. There are excellent assessments tools for the affective domain and also could be used for the cognitive domain. Many times issues arise in class that need to be addressed, and role plays provide a way to both teach and assess. When using role plays, teachers should present the scenario and then give students an opportunity to discuss possible solutions with their group. Teachers might give the entire class the same problem and see how different students approach it, or give different groups different problems. Rich discussions generally follow the role plays, which also can be part of the assessment. The following are some examples of role plays:

- Students are complaining about a referee's calls and the referee is discussing with a friend what she should do.
- A highly skilled student is a ball hog and other members of the team want to curb his or her behaviors so that they can play. They are discussing this in the locker room and the highly skilled player comes in and hears the conversation.
- Tomorrow is the championship game in a sport education tournament. The captain of one of the teams approaches a person who will be refereeing the game to encouraged the referee to "help" out tomorrow.
- A Native American student is bothered by the team's choice of a mascot. What should he say to other members of the team?
- A student fell off a gymnastics apparatus and now cannot participate in a class tournament in which his team needs the score he was capable of achieving. The person who was supposed to spot this individual laughed vigorously after the fall. The two meet.
- One of the team members continually curses the play of others under her breath. This disrupts the concentration of other members of the team and they have not played as well as they should. The teacher is unaware of this and members of the team wonder what they can do to stop the person from being so unpleasant.

Logs

Teachers can use logs to track student behaviors either in class or during outside activities. Since one of the goals of physical education is to encourage regular participation in physical activity, teachers might require students to complete logs indicating that activity. Box 11.9 is an example of a log used to record fitness activities during the week. Logs can also be used to record practice trials (successful and unsuccessful) during class. They are excellent indicators to the teacher about the quality of student practice. They also can motivate students to increase levels of activity. Because honesty can be a huge factor, teachers should give more credit for completing the log than for what numbers students actually record.

Open-Response Questions

Another technique for assessing cognitive knowledge or the affective domain can be through the use of open-response questions. On the surface, open-response questions seem to resemble essay questions. The difference between the two is that essay questions are seeking specific answers for their content while answers to open-response questions typically begin with the words "it depends," which indicates that there are multiple ways to approach the response. With open-response questions students are given a real-world problem or a scenario and then asked to take information presented in class and offer a solution. From there, students are required to justify or give a rationale for their choices. In short, they are required to apply this information just as they would in real life.[39] Consider the difference between these two items:

- Compare the western roll and the Fosbury flop method of high jumping. Use biomechanical principles to explain the differences.
- You have decided to try out for the high jump in the class track meet. Your teacher has presented two different techniques for clearing the high bar (western roll and Fosbury flop). What are the advantages for each technique? Which technique will be best for you when considering your body type, jumping ability, and the fact that you only have three weeks to practice until the meet? What muscles will you need to strengthen and stretch to perform at your best in this event?

There are several different types of open-response questions. Single-dimension questions usually ask students to draw a conclusion or take a position.

- Your teacher has recently made a rule requiring all members of a team to touch the ball before someone can shoot for a goal. Do you think this rule is fair? Explain your answer.

Scaffolded questions contain a sequence of tasks that become increasingly more difficult.

BOX 11.9

Fitness Log

Your assignment is to exercise for at least twenty minutes a day, three times a week. This activity must be continuous and involve a large muscle group. You will keep a log of your progress for this six-week unit. Some of your activity choices are running, biking (stationary or outdoors), jogging, roller blading, walking, roller skating, hiking, aerobics, swimming, and jumping rope. If you have questions about alternative activities, come and talk to me ***before*** you get started. Any of these activities may be combined as long as you keep moving for the entire twenty minutes. The goal is to keep your heart rate between 60 percent and 80 percent of your maximum heart rate. After ten minutes of continuous exercise, check your pulse rate and make sure you are in your target heart rate zone.

To find your maximum heart rate (MHR), subtract your age from 220.

My maximum heart rate (MHR) is: 220 – _____(age) = _____

My target heart rate zone is: .6 × _____(MHR) to .8 × _____(MHR)

GRADING:
You will receive 3 points for each day you exercise and fulfill the minimum requirement. There are eighteen days total, for a possible 54 points.

CARDIOVASCULAR FITNESS LOG

Date	Activity	Duration

Source: Amee Sorensen and Natalie Barrus.

- Students are given a conventional athletic shoe and a track spike with long spikes. They are asked to respond to the following:
  - How do these shoes differ in construction?
  - How will these differences impact what the runner is able to do?
  - Analyze your running form (length of stride, heel strike, arm motion). How will these shoes impact the way you run?
  - You are entered in the 400 meter run during the class track meet. Explain your choice of these two shoes for this event.

Multiple independent questions give fairly independent questions that address the same prompt.

- You are the team captain for your sport education soccer team. One of your responsibilities is to prepare members of your team for the first rounds of competition (5 v. 5), which will start in five days.
  - What skills will you address that are necessary for your team's success?
  - What factors will you consider when developing your starting lineup?
  - Goal keeper is a critical position but your better athletes don't want to play there because they want to play offensive positions. How will you select your goalie? What if this person doesn't want to play this position?

Student choice questions give students the option of selecting the topic they wish to address during a question.

- You are about to begin a unit in physical education. You want to develop a weight-training and stretching plan that will take you about forty-five minutes to do at home (activities selected must be done without conventional weight lifting apparatus). Select an activity from the list below and develop your conditioning plan designed to improve your performance for that unit. Provide a rationale for the training activities you selected for your plan.
  - You may choose one of the following: soccer, tennis, golf, or swimming.

When using response to provided information open-response questions, teachers provide students with a prompt such as data tables, an article to read, or a picture and ask students to respond to a question. Articles from physical education publications can provide an excellent way to assess many affective domain issues.

Portfolios

Portfolios are purposeful collections of student work gathered over time. The reason for using portfolio assessment is to document student growth and improvement. A key component of portfolio assessment is requiring students to reflect about the pieces they include in their exhibition or grading portfolio. Since portfolios require a lot of teacher time to grade and a lot of student time to assemble, teachers often develop working portfolios for students that give students places to store various documents from class. An evaluation portfolio requires students to select a few items that represent their growth and then to write reflections about why they chose these pieces and how they represent achievement. Teachers read these reflections and use them to document and assess student learning. Reading portfolios can be very time-consuming, but if teachers require students to be selective in the items they submit for evaluation, the process becomes more manageable.

Teachers determine how portfolios will be constructed, such as in a three-ring binder or folder, and how they will be stored and accessed to ensure student confidentiality. They define the audience for the portfolio—parents, employers, and others. Parents can be involved in the development of portfolios and also be the audience to which students present their progress and achievements. Students set goals, select and judge the quality of their work, and reflect upon their learning.

Teachers need to design lessons to teach students how to select and organize selections of their work; how to use their work to document competence in the content standards; how to compare earlier and current work to show progress; and how to reflect upon their strengths and weaknesses. In addition, they provide time for students to reflect upon and evaluate their work and provide models for students that demonstrate how the expectations can be achieved. Teachers who manage portfolios regularly on a revolving schedule avoid having to grade portfolios all at once at the end of the school year. A master form, kept in the front or back of the portfolio, can be used to record items that have been submitted for each outcome, along with levels of achievement and suggestions for improvement. Dating each item as it is entered into the portfolio facilitates this process. When appropriate, students can be asked to include previous items along with the revised items so teachers need only read the new parts in depth.

Portfolios differ depending on their purposes. One type of portfolio is a synthesis of what a student has learned in a specific unit. Focusing on participation in a simulated archery, swimming, or track meet or a sport season can serve as an excellent basis for a portfolio. Examples of a portfolio assignment, a student portfolio, and a scoring rubric are shown in Boxes 11.10, 11.11, and 11.12.

Portfolios that focus on achievement of the content standards of physical education generally include a table of contents and some kind of division into outcomes or content areas. Some items are specified by the teacher, while others are selected by students. For example, students might be asked to include a section on achieving and maintaining physical fitness, which might contain copies of fitness tests at the beginning of the year, goals set, a fitness log, and results achieved. A section on movement competency might include a videotape or CD showing baseline skills in various activities, with student reflections on technique and goals for improvement, along with a section at the end of a unit demonstrating the progress made. Activities in which the student is proficient could be highlighted with video or photos. Knowledge and officiating skills for these activities would also be pertinent. Another section might include self-assessments of personal and social skills, including items that were difficult or made the student feel good, journal entries, and reflections and feelings about physical activity. Both formal and informal assessments can be included. Reflections for each item should explain why it was included, what makes it important to the student, how it was accomplished, what problems were encountered and how they were solved, what its strengths and weaknesses are, and what plans there are for revision.

As technology advances, more students will have access to CD-writers and web pages in labs or at home and can create electronic portfolios. Decisions need to be made as to what kinds of hardware and software will be needed and how the portfolios will be viewed.

Checklist for Performance-Based Assessment Tasks

Suggestions for checking your performance-based assessment tasks include the following:[40]

1. Is the task appropriate to the discipline? What content standards, benchmarks, and course objectives are linked to each task? Will the task contribute to positive attitudes toward the discipline?
2. Does the task require students to integrate knowledge from different disciplines in a meaningful form?
3. Does the task provide clear instructions in language the student will understand?
4. Does the task mirror real-life tasks or problems, asking students to use their content knowledge to address a concept, problem, or issue that is similar

BOX 11.10

Swimming and Diving Meet Responsibilities

Each student will sign up for a tournament committee in addition to participating in the meet as an athlete. This assignment is worth 50 points. You will be graded on

1. Your plan of what you will do (Due 1 week prior to the meet),
2. How well you completed your responsibilities in the swim meet, and
3. Your written reflections on what you did, what you learned, and how you felt about your participation in the meet.

Athlete:
Race other students in all four strokes. You may also choose to enter the diving competition. Congratulate other athletes and clap for them. Assist teammates with towels and getting out of the pool.

Timers:
Use a stopwatch to time a specific athlete in a specific lane. Start the watch when the starter gives the signal and stop the watch when the athlete touches the wall at the end of the race.

Scorers and Judges:
Record and post the athlete's times for each stroke and judge, record, and post the diver's marks.

Starters:
Give the athlete a warning that you will start by saying "Swimmers, take your marks." Wait until all swimmers are still in ready position then blow the whistle loud and clear. Watch all swimmers for false starts or for causing false starts. Blow the whistle three times loudly following the initial one whistle signal to alert the athletes in the case of a false start. The athletes should return to their blocks and start again.

Coaches:
Organize your athletes into lanes, the fastest in the middle lanes. Organize when the athletes will swim and what heat they will compete in. Make sure the athletes are aware of their events, heats and lane assignments. Encourage athletes, give them advice and cheer for them.

Media Personnel:
Choose a role as a sports reporter or photographer for the *Daily Herald,* a TV or radio announcer for KZXX, a video crew member, or the publisher of the event media guide/program. Arrange for the needed supplies.

Awards Committee:
Decide what awards will be given at the meet and prepare them in advance. Plan the awards ceremony, conduct it, and present the awards.

Meet Directors:
You will plan the meet, including the order of the events, construction of entry forms, assigning the athletes into heats, etc.

Source: Created by Julienne Baughman with additional ideas from Lund, Jacalyn, and Kirk, Mary F. (1998, April 8). *Integrating alternative performance-based assessments with learning activities in middle and secondary physical education classes.* Presentation at AAHPERD convention, Reno, NV.

to one they have encountered or are likely to encounter in life beyond the classroom? Do students value the outcome of the task?

5. Does the task actively engage students in researching and manipulating information and ideas by synthesizing, generalizing, explaining, hypothesizing, or arriving at conclusions that produce new meanings and understandings for them? Does the task have multiple forms of "right" answers, rather than simply correct or incorrect answers?
6. Is the task developmentally appropriate for students at the specified grade level—challenging, yet achievable? Can accommodations be made to allow *every* student to complete the task?
7. Is the task feasible? Can it be done within school and homework time? Is it safe?
8. Does the task promote student-teacher interaction and cooperative learning with other students in a way that builds improved understanding?
9. Does the task ask students to communicate their knowledge, present a product performance, or take some action for an audience beyond the teacher, classroom, and school building?
10. Does the rubric contain clear scoring criteria for evaluating performance that are directly related to the task requirements—that is, evaluation is based on what the task is actually asking the student to do or produce? Are performance standards (levels) clearly articulated in language the student will understand? How good is good enough?
11. Does the task allow a student to model, practice, and model the task again so as to gain mastery?
12. Does the task provide opportunities for student self-reflection, and self- or peer assessment of performance?
13. Does the task provide teachers with useful information for adjusting instruction?
14. Are there opportunities for student revision of tasks?

BOX 11.11

Track and Field Portfolio

TRACK MEET

Events

Running	*Field*
100 m	High Jump
200 m	Long Jump
400 m	Triple Jump
800 m	Discus
1600 m	Javelin
3200 m	Shot Put
110 m high hurdles	Pole Vault
300 m low hurdles	
Relays	

Heats

There can be as many lanes used as the track will hold; sometimes the inside lane is not used. Normally the heats are divided up by times or ranks with the fastest people together and the slowest people together.

Flights

There are as many flights as each meet decides. These are also divided by ranks. The high jump uses the five alive method, which takes five jumpers and either gets them out or to the next height.

Scoring

The team with the most points wins. The winner of the race gets the most points and the points decrease as they go down with many people not getting any points at all. The winner of the race is determined by the fastest time and not the heats.

ADMINISTRATION

—Timing begins with a visual sign and ends when the runner's torso crosses the finish line.

—When a person is doing a field event and needs to leave for a running event certain things must happen. The person needs to tell the field events staff that they are leaving for a race. Field events are to be left when a person needs to run in a race. They return immediately to the jumping event and the field events staff has them take their turn.

—The starter of a sprint race, when the racers are using blocks, says "Marks, Set, GO." For a distance event the starter says "Set, GO."

—A false start occurs when a runner begins racing before the gun goes off. They have two chances in the track meet for our class and are then disqualified. The runners know that a false start has occurred when the gun is fired again. Everyone must stop and come back to the starting positions.

—Field events are measured at the nearest mark to the foul board. Throwing events and jumping events have a foul board. High jump is measured by how high the bar is from the ground.

ORGANIZATION

I helped by:

—determining heats
—finding timers
—finding field event workers
—determining teams
—making awards

ADMINISTRATION

I helped by:

—timing
—starting the 100 m
—determining final team scores

I participated in:

—400 m with a time of 62 seconds
—high jump with a height of 5′6″
—discus with distance of 101′
—medley relay as the 400 m runner with a team score of 5:58
—110 m high hurdles with a time of 14.6 seconds
—triple jump with distance of 19′

The track meet was fun and I loved being able to compete in the things that I was good in to help the team and see how well I could do. I also liked competing in the things that I was not so good in for fun. I did not like that there were few spectators and that people did not want to watch each other and cheer. I also did not like that it was split up in two days. Maybe next year we can do it as a school or do it after school with all of the classes so that there is more competition. I think I might go out for track next year!

Continued

One of the characteristics of performance-based assessments is that the criteria for scoring the assessment accompany the assessment. In other words, when the students begin working on the assessment, they know what the teacher expects and how they will be assessed. Because students have the criteria in advance, they can self-assess as they complete the requirements of the assessment. The previous section contained many different types of performance-based assessments. The reader should understand that until the criteria used to determine their worth are included, they are not really assessments; they are simply tasks. Establishing the criteria for these assessments is probably the most difficult part of developing performance-based assessments.

A rubric is a description of the elements for judging student performance on specific outcomes or assessment tasks.

BOX 11.11 *Continued*

Track and Field Portfolio

PHYSICAL FITNESS

I did not enjoy this at all when I started, but began to enjoy it more as I did it. I also started running with Sarah and Kim outside instead of on the indoor track. My little sister is running with us also. I knew that I needed to exercise, but never thought that I had the time. I guess I had more time than I thought. Going with people makes me go regardless of whether I feel like going or not. I do not like that we get graded on whether or not we exercise because sometimes I just do not have the time and I really do not want to spend the time to go.

Fitness Log for Marie Fitt
Goal:
Exercises: Jogging and basketball

Week	Day	Date	Exercise	Time or Distance
1	1	April 1	Jogging	20 min
	2	April 3	Jogging	25 min
	3	April 5	Jogging	21 min
2	1	April 8	Basketball	23 min
	2	April 10	Jogging	30 min
	3	April 12	Jogging	20 min
3	1	April 15	Jogging	22 min
	2	April 17	Basketball	20 min
	3	April 19	Basketball	24 min
4	1	April 21	Jogging	30 min
	2	April 23	Basketball	21 min
	3	April 25	Jogging	26 min

GAME PLAY

The track and field meet in general was fun. I did not like that it was on two days and that we had to do so many events. It would be more fun if we could compete as an entire class against another class. We started out with you explaining the rules and telling us to make sure that we knew which heat or flight we were in to keep things moving quickly. The track meet then began. People were warming up along the outside of the track and people were racing and throwing and jumping. It was a lot of fun to watch and see how everything worked. It took a lot of planning to make it run so smoothly.

I did not like how hard it was for us to plan the track meet and that we had to spend class time to do it. I would have rather been practicing. I also did not like that so many people did not bother to watch the other people in the class compete. The timers that were from the class seemed to be better than the timers that were from the study hall because we understood what was going on more.

I liked that we were able to do this at all and that we had such a good time doing it. I also liked the awards that were given and that every person got one for something. (That might be because I helped make the awards.) It was a good experience and although I did not like having to set it all up it was a good learning experience and I now know how hard it can be to have a sporting event at the school.

BEHAVIOR

My Philosophy

Fair play involves cheering for everyone. Never getting down on your teammates. Playing by the rules and encouraging those around you. Don't take cheap shots and always shake hands at the end.

What I Did:

I encouraged my teammates and congratulated people on nice jumps or throws regardless of which team they were on. I also cheered for everyone at the awards ceremony. I tried to watch people when I was not personally involved in doing something for the track meet.

Some states have adopted the term *scoring guide* instead of *rubric* so that parents and other laypeople understand their function. Regardless of the term used, rubrics are a necessary component of a performance-based assessment.

Checklists are one of the most common ways used to score performance-based assessments. A checklist is simply a list of qualities that should be present in the completed assessment. People using the checklists simply indicate the presence of a trait or quality by checking it off—if the trait is present, it gets a check, if not, no check. There is no way to indicate the beginning presence of a trait or judge a degree of quality. For this reason, checklists are probably best used for simple rather than complex assessments. Teachers might develop checklists for use with peer assessments. They are excellent ways to measure the process (critical elements/cues) qualities of a skill or task and provide formative feedback. Checklists are relatively easy to create but they have no way to indicate that one trait is more important than another. Box 11.13 is an example of a checklist.

Point systems are similar to checklists as they are lists of traits or qualities, but they differ in that point values are assigned to each trait. With point systems, teachers can indicate that some items are more important than others by assigning them more value or points. Because points are awarded, teachers could use this type of scoring guide for grading purposes. Problems arise when there are subcategories to the items listed or when teachers try to give partial credit for an item that is below the desired standard of quality. The first problem can be avoided by dividing the item points among the subcategories as was done on Box 11.14. Giving credit only if the item listed on the rubric is entirely present will eliminate the second problem.

Box 11.12

Track and Field Portfolio Scoring Rubric

All areas must be included and checked off to receive full credit for the portfolio. Creativity and design will be taken into account for the final grade.

Knowledge

______ Student demonstrates a basic knowledge of the organization of a track meet. (20 pts.) Some examples of that demonstration are:
- ___ What events are involved?
- ___ How many people can be in each heat?
- ___ How are heats divided?
- ___ How does scoring work?

______ Student demonstrates ability to help administer track meet. (20 pts.) Some examples of that demonstration are:
- ___ What is the procedure for timing a track meet?
- ___ What is the procedure involving field events?
- ___ What does the starter of a race say?
- ___ What indicates a false start?
- ___ How are field events measured?

______ Student tells what he or she did to help organize the track meet. (20 pts.)
______ Student tells what he or she did to help in the administration of the track meet. (20 pts.)
______ Student tells about his or her participation in the track meet, including what events he or she participated in, times and distances, and feelings regarding the track meet in general. (15 pts)

Physical Fitness

______ The log kept for activities done outside of class is included. (50 pts; not in portfolio score)
______ Describe what you liked and did not like about this activity. (10 pts.)

Track Meet (May be included in above sections)

______ Student will describe the track meet in general. (15 pts.)
______ Student will discuss what he or she liked and disliked about the track meet. (10 pts.)

Behavior

______ Student will explain his or her theory of fair play. (10 pts.)
______ Student will cite specific examples of when he or she demonstrated or failed to demonstrate fair play during the track meet. (10 pts.)

Final Grade ______/150 possible

Box 11.13

Example of a Self-Administered Checklist Used to Assess Affective Domain

Do you exhibit good sportsmanship and fair play? Check all of the statements that apply to you while playing the game.

________ I try to follow the rules.
________ I encourage others, even if they are not on my team.
________ I help with equipment before, during, and after the game.
________ I don't intentionally foul others.
________ I do what my coach expects.
________ I respect the efforts of others, even those of opponents.
________ I work with other members of the team and don't try to be the star.
________ I accept the calls of officials.
________ After a call, I don't draw attention to myself.
________ I accept the outcome of the game, regardless of whether I win or lose.
________ I am someone others enjoy having on their team.

BOX 11.14

Example of a Point System Rubric

VOLLEYBALL PORTFOLIO

Pretest scores (5 points)	Midterm scores (5 points)	Posttest scores (5 points)
________ Set	________ Set	________ Set
________ Forearm pass	________ Forearm pass	________ Forearm pass
________ Spike	________ Spike	________ Spike
________ Serve	________ Serve	________ Serve
________ Dig	________ Dig	________ Dig

________ Goals for improvement from pretest and action plan (5 points)
________ Reflection of progress from midterm scores; adjustment of action plan (5 points)
________ Reflection of improvement and effectiveness of action plan (5 points)
________ Conditioning program based on research (10 points)
________ Game play stats (15 points)
________ Scouting reports (10 points)
________ Practice logs with graphs to show improvement (10 points)
________ Choice: Video or magazine article on history (10 points)
________ Choice: Audio play-by-play or newspaper article reporting game results (15 points)

BOX 11.15

Example of a Peer-Observation Quantitative Analytic Rating Scale

The purpose of this form is to evaluate the spirit of fair play used by your opponents. Please use the following scale to answer each question.

0 = This characteristic was not true of this person
1 = This characteristic was displayed at times but not consistently
2 = The characteristic was displayed consistently
3 = Great opponents; very competitive yet very fair in every way; we really respect this team

Your name ________________________
Opponent's name ________________________

Encourages others (says things like "nice play," "good hustle," etc.)	0	1	2	3
Accepts own errors (doesn't blame others)	0	1	2	3
Wins or loses gracefully (doesn't throw temper tantrums)	0	1	2	3
Continually tries his/her best	0	1	2	3
Correct calls were made; does not try to cheat	0	1	2	3
Demonstrated fair play throughout the game (fun to play)	0	1	2	3

Your name ________________________
Opponent's name ________________________

Encourages others (says things like "nice play," "good hustle," etc.)	0	1	2	3
Accepts own errors (doesn't blame others)	0	1	2	3
Wins or loses gracefully (doesn't throw temper tantrums)	0	1	2	3
Continually tries his/her best	0	1	2	3
Correct calls were made; does not try to cheat	0	1	2	3
Demonstrated fair play throughout the game (fun to play)	0	1	2	3

If teachers wish to give partial credit, they may decide to use a quantitative analytic rubric, discussed next.

Instead of indicating only whether the characteristic is present, analytic rubrics allow the scorer to make a judgment of quality. There are two types of analytic rubrics. A quantitative analytic rubric is similar to a checklist and a point system in that it is a list of traits that are considered important in the task being assessed. The difference is that quantitative rubrics allow the scorer to indicate the degree to which the trait is present, generally through the use of numbers that are anchored with descriptive words or phrases. Box 11.15 is an example of a quantitative analytic rubric or scoring guide. Qualitative analytic rubrics use verbal descriptions of key items. By making the categories more broad, qualitative rubrics have fewer categories for teachers to make a judgment about, but within the categories several different items can be found. For example, a quantitative volleyball rubric might list several different elements of strategy for the assessor to rate, but a qualitative rubric would consist of a paragraph that combines several of those elements (see Box 11.16). Analytic rubrics are good for use as formative assessments because students can see their level of performance for various items or traits important for the game, performance, or task being assessed. Since they involve a judgment of quality, they require more time to complete. Even though they are used for more complex assessments than checklists or traits, they typically are shorter and focus on the most important characteristics. When a rubric becomes too long, there is too much for the person doing the scoring to observe, and errors in judgment are more likely to occur. While useful for formative assessments, analytic rubrics are difficult to use in grading as there is no weighting of performance for the different traits being evaluated.

The last type of rubric most commonly used in physical education is a holistic rubric. Holistic rubrics consist of paragraphs that describe a given level of performance. The paragraphs combine the different elements found in the analytic rubrics and look at the performer or task from an overall impression rather than trying to analyze each piece. They are somewhat like the artistic impression scores that are used for gymnastics routines, but in this case the overall impression is based on criteria specified in the rubric. Holistic rubrics are used most often for summative assessments. Because only one judgment of quality needs to be made, they are faster to use than analytic rubrics. Problems arise with holistic rubrics because a performance or product is rarely entirely at a given level on the rubric. A decision must be made before the scoring begins about whether all traits must be at a given level for that level to be awarded or if only the majority of the traits need to be present. Box 11.17 is an example of a holistic rubric.

Steps in Assessing Student Learning

Although assessment is critical to effective instruction, teachers have difficulty implementing classroom testing because of large class sizes, heavy teaching loads (including coaching), lack of facilities and equipment, and peer pressure.[41] Therefore, assessment must be carefully planned for the greatest economy in time and energy.[42] The following steps can help you in this process: (1) determine the purposes of assessment; (2) select appropriate assessment techniques; (3) develop criteria for scoring; (4) administer and score the assessment tasks; and (5) evaluate and revise the assessment techniques.

Step 1—Determine the Purposes of Assessment

In 1992, the National Association of Sport and Physical Education (NASPE) published a series of statements defining what the physically educated person should know and be able to do (see Table 1.2). Following this publication, the Standards and Assessment Task Force was appointed to develop content standards for assessing learning in physical education.[43] In 2004, NASPE published a revision of this document.[44] The six standards found in the 2004 book are shown in Table 6.1 and form the basis for student assessment.

Objectives chosen for each unit should fit into one or more of the content standards, as shown in Table 11.2. Each objective should be written in performance terms, with an observable behavior, criteria, and conditions. Assessments should accurately reflect appropriate achievement expectations for students of their developmental level.

Step 2—Select Appropriate Assessment Techniques

Prior to selecting specific assessment techniques, review the unit objectives, including skills, knowledge, and other goals (see Table 11.2). Each performance objective in a lesson or unit states the specific performance that is to be observed (refer to Chapter 8 for help in writing performance objectives). If objectives have been correctly written, the verb describes what the student will be expected to do to demonstrate achievement of the objective. For example, if the objective is to throw a softball, swim a distance, shoot free throws, or improve time in running, some type of *skills assessment* to determine skill in throwing, swimming, shooting, or running would be involved. If the objective is to define bowling terms, score an archery round, or recognize correct rules of etiquette, some type of *written assessment* might be necessary. Some objectives—such as writing a paper on the history of tennis or passing a multiple-choice test on the rules of badminton—are evaluated exactly as specified, by writing a paper or passing a test. Some examples of various objectives and appropriate assessment techniques are listed below:

badminton short serve	skills test or incidence chart
archery form	rating checklist
swimming skills—dive, tread water	checklist
knowledge of rules	written test
dance composition	subjective assessment by teacher using specified criteria
challenge and risk activities	student journal about growth in personal and social skills

BOX 11.16

Example of a Qualitative Analytic Rubric

	Developing	Rookie	Right on	Awesome
Shot execution	Can use the forearm pass during game play although may misdirect ball because the arms are uneven. Occasionally plays the ball off the wrist. Setting is inconsistent. Doesn't move to the ball.	Effectively uses the forearm pass during game play. Is able to direct the ball to a target most of the time while using the set. May try to reach for a ball when out of position to make the play. Attempts to spike or dink the ball.	Uses the forearm pass when appropriate during game play. Usually is able to set the ball to the target. Moves behind the ball to make the hits. Is able to spike the ball. Uses the dink effectively to deceive opponent. Can dig a difficult to reach ball and keep it in play.	Moves quickly into position to play the ball. Judgment on the type of hit to make is always correct. Converts horizontal movement to vertical movement without drifting when playing the ball at the net. Goes after difficult shots and is able to keep the ball in play. Uses emergency techniques only when necessary.
Knowledge of rules	Knows the basic rules of volleyball about illegal hits, serving, and net play. Hesitates during game play due to limited knowledge of the rules.	Solid knowledge of the rules. Knows serving rotation and how to substitute players. Can keep score accurately.	Can answer most questions about rules. Helps others on the court. Understands the rules concerning net play.	Uses rules to the team's advantage. Other players consult this person when questions arise. Could officiate a game without error.
Strategy	Maintains a 3 front-3 back formation whether on offense or defense.	Shows different strategic formations when playing offense and defense.	Moves easily between offensive and defensive positioning during game play. Attacks the ball trying to be on the offensive. Attempts to set up a 3-hit attack strategy.	Uses player substitutions to increase team effectiveness. Has multiple offensive and defensive plans based on what the other team is doing. Is directly responsible for several kill shots.
Team work/ court movement	Attempts to cover the area within arm's reach of where he/she is standing.	Communicates with others during team play. Moves to cover the area around where he/she is standing	Moves to cover the court, rather than the area where he/she was initially standing. Is able to combine court movement with strategy for effective team play.	Takes a leadership role in communicating with other members of the team by directing players when they are out of position. Knows where other players should be and prompts court movement when necessary.
Serves	Uses an underhand serve to put the ball in play. Ball frequently ends up in the net.	Can use an overhand serve effectively during game play. Attempts to place the ball rather than merely getting it over the net.	Consistently places the ball during game play. Serve is close to the net and difficult to return.	Places the ball on the opponent's court effectively. Serve often cannot be returned.
Fair play	Rarely talks with or encourages others. May try to call plays incorrectly to gain an advantage.	Calls plays fairly. Tries to encourage others on his/her own team.	Calls the plays fairly. If there is a dispute, will replay the point. When there is an official, accepts the calls without protest. Encourages other team members to do their best. Is a good team player.	Consistently recognizes the good play of others even on the opposing team. Shows much cooperation with other members of the team. Does not try to dominate the game and show off. Calls shots honestly and fairly.

BOX 11.17

Example of a Holistic Rubric for Volleyball

AWESOME—OLYMPIC POTENTIAL

Moves quickly into position to play the ball. Judgment on the type of hit to make is always correct. Converts horizontal movement to vertical movement without drifting when playing the ball at the net. Goes after difficult shots and is able to keep the ball in play. Uses emergency techniques only when necessary. Uses rules to the team's advantage. Other players consult this person when questions arise. Could officiate a game without error. Uses player substitutions to increase team effectiveness. Has multiple offensive and defensive plans based on what the other team is doing. Is directly responsible for several kill shots. Takes a leadership role in communicating with other members of the team by directing players when they are out of position. Knows where other players should be and prompts court movement when necessary. Places the ball on the opponent's court effectively. Serve often cannot be returned. Consistently recognizes the good play of others even on the opposing team. Shows much cooperation with other members of the team. Does not try to dominate the game and show off. Calls shots honestly and fairly.

RIGHT ON!—VARSITY

Uses the forearm pass when appropriate during game play. Usually is able to set the ball to the target. Moves behind the ball to make the hits. Is able to spike the ball. Uses the dink effectively to deceive opponent. Can dig a difficult to reach ball and keep it in play. Can answer most questions about rules. Helps others on the court. Understands the rules concerning net play. Moves easily between offensive and defensive positioning during game play. Attacks the ball trying to be on the offensive. Attempts to set up a 3-hit attack strategy. Moves to cover the court, rather than the area where he/she was initially standing. Is able to combine court movement with strategy for effective team play. Calls the plays fairly. If there is a dispute, will replay the point. When there is an official, accepts the calls without protest. Encourages other team members to do their best. Is a good team player.

ROOKIE—GREAT POTENTIAL

Effectively uses the forearm pass during game play. Is able to direct the ball to a target most of the time while using the set. May try to reach for a ball when is out of position to make the play. Attempts to spike or dink the ball. Solid knowledge of the rules. Knows serving rotation and how to substitute players. Can keep score accurately. Shows different strategic formations when playing offense and defense. Communicates with others during team play. Moves to cover the area around where he/she is standing. Can use an overhand serve effectively during game play. Attempts to place the ball rather than merely getting it over the net. Calls plays fairly. Tries to encourage others on his/her own team.

DEVELOPING—JUST STARTING

Can use the forearm pass during game play although may misdirect ball because the arms are uneven. Occasionally plays the ball off the wrist. Setting is inconsistent. Doesn't move to the ball. Knows the basic rules of volleyball about illegal hits, serving, and net play. Hesitates during game play due to limited knowledge of the rules. Maintains a 3 front-3 back formation whether on offense or defense. Attempts to cover the area within arm's reach of where he/she is standing. Uses an underhand serve to put the ball in play. Ball frequently ends up in the net. Rarely talks with or encourages others. May try to call plays incorrectly to gain an advantage.

Many objectives would be more accurately evaluated by using several techniques:

lifesaving skills	skills tests, practical test, essay test, personal interview
feelings about fitness	anonymous questionnaire, observation of participation in fitness activities
tennis serve	skills test on accuracy, teacher assessment of form, successful trials in game play.

Create a class handout summarizing important content as well as instructions for the psychomotor and affective tests. Tests should reflect the emphasis placed on that area during class instruction or in study materials.

Look for appropriate tests or assessments in tests and measurements books or professional books and journals. Sample assessment activities are described in *Moving into the Future: National Standards for Physical Education.* Some specific sources for written test items include *Test Questions for Physical Education Activities* and teachers' manuals for various books on sport skills. Adapt questions to meet the specific needs of your classes. AAHPERD has skills tests booklets for many activities. (These can be found on the web at http://www.aahperd.org/aahperd/aahperd-publications.html.) *Assessing Sport Skills* is another good source for skills tests. Check to see if the norm group is appropriate for your students. If no tests are available or if the tests are not valid or practical for the teaching environment, the teacher must create the tests. In this case, list the behaviors demonstrated by an outstanding player in the activity being tested and devise a means of testing for the behavior specified. Try to keep skill assessments as close to a game situation as possible and as simple as

TABLE 11.2 Unit Objectives and Assessments for Softball

Knowledge

Students will pass a written exam on rules and techniques of softball with a score of 80 percent or better.

Assessment: Written Exam

Content Standard: #2 Demonstrates understanding of movement concepts, principles, strategies, and tactics as they apply to the learning and performance of physical activities.

Physical Fitness

Each student will participate in the Prudential "Fitnessgram" program for six weeks during the softball unit. Each student will keep a fitness journal of aerobic and strength training activities during the six-week unit.

Assessment: Fitnessgram and fitness journal

Content Standard: #3 Participates regularly in physical activity.
#4 Achieves and maintains a health-enhancing level of physical fitness.

Skill Acquisition

Each student will be able to catch and throw a softball ten times correctly. Each student will be able to correctly field ten ground balls and ten fly balls. Each student will be able to bunt and hit a softball using proper technique seven out of ten times.

Assessment: Skills tests

Content Standard: #1 Demonstrates competency in motor skills and movement patterns needed to perform a variety of physical activities.

Game Play

Students will evaluate peers during game play. Specific skills and strategies previously learned will be required of each student while playing in the tournament.

Assessment: Peer assessment of individual tournament play.
#5 Exhibits responsible personal and social behavior that respects self and others in physical activity settings.

Personal/Social Behavior and Respect

Students will attend each class period, completely dressed in uniform. All students will participate in drills. Each student will understand fair play.

Assessment: Attendance and "fair play" worksheet.

Content Standards: #5 Demonstrates responsible personal and social behavior that respects self and others in physical activity settings.
#6 Values physical activity for health, enjoyment, challenge, self-expression, and social interaction.

Source: Adapted from the work of Jessica Skiba.

Source for Content Standards: National Association for Sport and Physical Education. *Moving into the Future: National Physical Eduation Standards: A Guide to Content and Assessment,* 2nd ed. (St. Louis, MO: Mosby, 2004).

possible. Try out the tests with a few students to see how they work, and revise them as needed.[45]

Affective assessment can be used to determine student progress toward affective objectives and to assist students through individual conferences and instruction. In general, teachers attempt to assess whether student attitudes are positive or negative toward physical education or the specific activity engaged in, and how well students are applying the principles of appropriate social behavior such as good teamwork or fair play. For students to answer honestly on affective assessment instruments, they must trust that results will not be used against them.

Characteristics of Effective Tests

Selecting appropriate assessment techniques requires attention to four essential factors—validity, reliability, objectivity, and administrative feasibility. *Validity* is defined as the extent to which a test measures what it is intended to measure. A *reliable* test is one on which a student would obtain similar scores on different trials of the same

TABLE 11.3 Table of Specifications for Content Validity

Content	Knowledge/Recall	Understanding/Comprehension	Application
RULES			
Violations	#2	#1	#11
Fouls	#8	#3	#12
Scoring	#9		
General play	#10		
STRATEGIES			
Offensive		#4	#13
Defensive			#14
TECHNIQUE			
Passing	#5	#6	
Shooting			#15
Dribbling		#7	
HISTORY	#16		

test. An *objective* test is one in which a student obtains an identical score on the test regardless of who administers or scores the test. *Administrative feasibility* is enhanced by choosing tests that are low in cost and free up teacher and student time. Tests utilizing equipment already owned by the school save money, while tests easily set up by students and teachers and administered in a short period of time maximize the time available for instruction.

Establishing Norm-Referenced Validity Norm-referenced validity (sometimes called criterion-related validity) is established by comparing the *test* with a valid test of the attribute, known as a *criterion test.* In body composition, for example, the criterion test is hydrostatic weighing and a common *field test* uses skinfold calipers to estimate the percentage of body fat. Skills tests are often validated with expert ratings of performance in game play or by tournament rankings in singles or game statistics in team play. When validity is high, a Pearson Product Moment correlation coefficient, which indicates the relationship between the two variables or scores, will also be high (closer to +1.0 or −1.0). This is called *concurrent validity.* Coaches often use *predictive validity* to estimate future success, such as how well athletes will perform on a school team. To obtain predictive validity, a regression equation is calculated from athletes' scores on one or more tests and from their later success in game play. The results are then used to select future athletes. To be valid, a test must be both reliable (consistent) and relevant (testing what it is supposed to test). To determine the relevance of a test, ask, "Are the student behaviors needed for the test the same as those listed in the course objectives?" In addition to correlation, researchers use cross-validation to establish validity, using one group to determine norms and another group to see if the norms work properly.

Content validity is a type of validity used in knowledge testing. A *table of specifications* outlines how the test items directly reflect course content, and questions are written to reflect the items in each area. Tests that include a representative sample of course content encourage students to devote their attention to all areas of instruction. A sample table of specifications is shown in Table 11.3. A common error is writing the easiest questions rather than testing the content students should know. This destroys content validity. When assessing validity on a written test ask, "What might cause the student to answer incorrectly on the test when the student knows the answer when asked orally?" Some reasons might be that the test is written on an inappropriate reading level, has vocabulary or instructions that are too difficult for the student to comprehend, or has a type of question that confuses the student (such as a question that asks for an official's response). On the other hand, some test questions give verbal clues that allow students to respond correctly without knowing the correct answers. Avoid grammatical, verbal association, and placement clues. Tests given to foreign or bilingual students often create problems, but students can easily answer in oral form. Longer tests can more adequately sample the entire content area, increasing validity.

On a skills test, the teacher might ask, "What might cause the student to perform poorly on a skills test when the student performs very well in a game situation?" To establish *logical or face validity,* choose tests that test the actual elements of the activity. For example, the elements of beginning volleyball are the serve, pass, set, and spike. Tests should assess the skills as closely as possible to the way they are used in game play. Many skills tests are highly reliable but have little relationship to actual game play. For example, in the tennis backboard test, the ball returns at a much faster rate than it would in a regular tennis game. Proper test selection or construction is demanding, but teachers should always strive to use valid tests.

Construct validity is used to determine the degree to which a test measures a trait that cannot be measured directly. A construct must be measured by indicators. Physical fitness is an example of a construct. Assumptions are made as to what a physically fit person is able to do and then tests are devised to measure those components.

Establishing Norm-Referenced Reliability Reliability for norm-referenced tests demonstrates that students' scores are consistent across time. The most common form of reliability is *test-retest reliability,* in which the student takes the same test twice, with no instruction between. The time interval must be long enough for students to forget their answers on the first test, but short enough so *no* learning takes place between the tests. In *split-halves reliability* the students' scores on the odd questions are correlated with their scores on the even questions. When the split-halves method is used, the Spearman-Brown prophecy formula is needed to estimate the reliability for the longer test that results when the two halves of the test are combined into one test. When a Pearson correlation coefficient is used to determine reliability, the results are called *interclass reliability* and a small *r* is used. When Analysis of Variance and other statistical forms are used, the result is *intraclass reliability* and the correct form is *R.*

Reliability is enhanced by increasing the number of test questions or trials or the number of students taking the test. Each of these increases the range or spread of the scores. For example, if only two questions or trials appear on the test and one day the student has a perfect score and another day misses one, the scores on the two days would be 50 and 100, a difference of 50 percent. If one hundred questions or trials appear on the test, missing one would make the scores 99 and 100, a difference of 1 percent. In the same way, if ten students take the test, a particular student might change from ninth to tenth place, whereas in a group of one hundred students, a student might change in rank from ninety-ninth to one-hundredth place. Reliability is higher on tests of maximum physical effort and lower on tests with high accuracy demands. Test reliability is more accurate when the reliability was determined for students similar to yours. Tests are most reliable with high- and low-skilled students and least reliable with middle-skilled students.

A perfect positive *correlation* between two variables would be +1.00, meaning that as scores on one test increase, scores on the other test also increase. A perfect negative correlation equals −1.00, indicating that scores on one test increase and scores on the other test decrease. Many examples of negative correlations exist in physical education. Tests in which the lowest time is the desired outcome, such as in a sprint, should correlate negatively with tests in which a higher performance is better, as in the amount of weight lifted. The strength of the correlation is determined by the closeness to 1.00 or −1.00. Teachers should aim for validity and reliability coefficients for most school assessments that exceed .70.

The Coefficient of Determination (r^2) indicates the shared variance between the two variables. For example, if r equals .8 between pull-ups and push-ups, then r^2 equals .64 ($.8 \times .8$), which means that 64 percent of the variance (the spread of the scores) between the two measures involves a common element, which in this case is "arm strength."

Validity and Reliability of Performance-Based Assessment Tasks and Rubrics

The content validity of assessment tasks and rubrics is higher when they are defined by a group of knowledgeable persons. The group considers how well performance on the specified task assesses what is taught in the curriculum and meets the behavior specified in the content standard, as well as how well the behavior will predict future performance. The task must focus on important aspects of the skill, not trivial components such as the art work. Tasks must be meaningful for students, with instruction in prerequisite vocabulary and skills, adequate time to complete tasks, and appropriate adaptations to ensure opportunities for success for all students. Explicit standards for rating or judgment increase validity.[46]

Reliability is concerned with the consistency of scores among raters or within the same rater over a period of time, such as from year to year or class to class. Clearer standards and examples or models for each level produce more reliable results. Too many elements can reduce reliability as can bias among raters. The more critical the consequences of the assessment, the more reliable the scores need to be. For example, when judging future lifeguards, an error in judgment can result in a fatality for the lifeguard or the victim. Rubrics are reliable when scorers score the same students twice with the same results and when two or more trained scorers get the same scores on a group of assessments.

One way to test for rater agreement is to distribute the scoring rubric and the papers to be scored to four knowledgeable persons.[47] The first rater puts the rating in the upper-left corner and turns the corner down, then passes the paper to the next rater, who puts the rating in the upper-right corner and turns the corner down, then passes the paper to the third rater. After all papers are rated, check to see whether the ratings are consistent. Use the papers that are rated consistently among raters as examples for students the following semester (without names, of course).

Establishing Norm-Referenced Objectivity Objectivity, a form of reliability that determines the consistency among raters or scorers for a particular test, is often cited as a reason for using traditional testing formats. Because objective tests are easier to score, they lend themselves to increased reliability over essay or short-answer tests. Performance-based assessments have been criticized for their subjectivity, meaning that a judgment by the person doing the scoring is necessary.[48] When developing tests, teachers must remember that there is a degree of subjectivity or teacher choice in every type of test.[49] When teachers write tests, there is subjectivity in the content that is selected and the way the questions are written. While the scoring may be more objective, the subjectivity enters as the test is developed. Performance-based assessments have the advantage that they frequently are the actual behaviors teachers are trying to get their students to perform (i.e., playing a game, performing a gymnastics routine, demonstrating fair play and courtesy to others). The assessments are not proxies of learning, they are actual demonstrations of achievement. Although the scoring is more subjective, if the accompanying rubrics are well written and the people doing the scoring are trained to use them, there is a high degree of reliability for performance-based assessment.[50] Additionally, the teachers who create these performance-based assessments have excellent content knowledge through teaching degrees that indicate scholarly preparation, possible extensive playing experience, and experience in teaching and coaching these subjects and activities. A teacher who scores performance-based assessments exercises professional judgment, which greatly decreases the subjectivity associated with their use.[51]

Review Questions: Define validity, reliability, and objectivity. How do they differ for norm-referenced and criterion-referenced tests?

Explain how to select valid and reliable cognitive, psychomotor, and affective tests.

Step 3—Develop Rubrics and Scoring Keys

After deciding what type of assessment to use, teachers must next decide how to score that assessment. Remember, an assessment is not an assessment until the criteria for scoring it have been established. With written tests, teachers must develop a scoring key. Since established criteria accompany some fitness tests, teachers might decide to use those for classes or decide to develop their own based on the school population they are assessing. The same is true for skill tests—published skill tests typically have normative scores for assessing them. Some teachers may modify these criteria or develop their own based on adaptations made to the tests for their students and teaching situation.

How to Develop a Rubric

Performance-based assessments are scored using some type of scoring guide or rubric.

Several authors suggest methods for developing a rubric.[52]

1. State the outcome (product or task) that is to be completed.
2. Select the appropriate type of rubric for your purpose from Table 11.4. For example, if you wish

TABLE 11.4 Types of Rubrics

Type	Definition	Resulting Information
NUMERICAL OR POINT SYSTEM	Points assigned for certain features of a student's response. Often used for open-ended questions because points can reflect partial as well as full credit.	Indicates where students' performance falls within a continuum of performance levels.
CHECKLIST	Consists of a list of characteristics or behaviors scored as yes or no, present or absent. Can be applied to written work (e.g., journals) or observable behavior.	Indicates effective completion of a task or the steps in a task or demonstration.
ANALYTIC RATING SCALE	Ratings are based on multiple elements of a product or performance. Numerical (e.g., 1–7) or qualitative (with adjectives) scales show the student's score for each element on a continuum. Shows the extent to which each element of a product or performance is observed or the quality of performance. Standards for each element and level of performance are defined. Provides only partial, analytic scores rather than a total score. Is slower to use compared to a holistic rubric.	Provides diagnostic information (strengths and weaknesses) about specific elements of learning, which helps in providing feedback to learners and planning instructional improvements. Does not show performance as a whole.
MODIFIED ANALYTIC RATING SCALE	A subscore is assigned for each specific element of the student's performance. A procedure for combining the subscores into a total score is specified.	Provides diagnostic information (strengths and weaknesses) about specific elements of learning, as well as information about the performance as a whole.
HOLISTIC RUBRIC	No specific elements are identified. Student responses are compared to a series of ordered or graded models (e.g., 1, 2, 3, and 4) and assigned the score that most closely matches one of the models. They are relatively easy to create and use and faster to score than analytic rubrics.	Provides general information about student performance. Provides no instructional information about specific elements of learning. A lack of diagnostic information limits usefulness in planning improvements.

Source: Ideas from J. L. Herman, P. R. Aschbacher, and L. Winters, *A Practical Guide to Alternative Assessment* (Alexandria, VA: Association for Supervision and Curriculum Development, 1992).

to diagnose a student's level of performance and provide feedback for improved learning, you might use an analytic rubric. However, if you are determining whether a senior high school student has achieved a content standard, you might use a holistic rubric. Gather sample rubrics created by other teachers to give you ideas (see Box 11.18).

3. Analyze the performance task and list the knowledge, skills, and qualities that a person who has attained the desired outcome will possess, such as teamwork, fair play, knowledge, and application of rules, skills, and strategies in game play. Put these in the elements column on the template.
4. Determine how many levels of performance you want (see Table 11.5). Two levels will indicate whether the person achieved or did not achieve the outcome or an element of the task.
5. Write the standards for judging performance for the level you want all students to achieve first. The standards tell the student what the teacher expects for each element, including the quality of performance or skillfulness or the degree of knowledge of something.
6. Write a description of unacceptable student performance for each element. Focus on an observable behavior rather than on the absence or negative behavior of something listed above as desirable. Focus on errors or things that students may misunderstand related to the element.
7. You now have created a checklist assessment and are ready to pilot it with students. When piloting criteria in a scoring guide, use it for a low-accountability task (either not associated with a grade or with minor significance to the student). You may also want to administer the assessment on "experts" to see how they perform. Teaching colleagues can also provide feedback.
8. Use results from step 7 to revise your rubric by looking at student and expert samples that demonstrate a range of performance from ineffective to very effective. Evaluate what distinguishes the effective performance/work from ineffective. If you only wanted a checklist scoring guide you will not need the following steps. Of course, you will want to continue to refine the rubric by repeating steps 7 and 8 several times.
9. Write the standards for the other levels. Look for and eliminate overlapping descriptions between the levels.
10. Continue to try out the assessment by scoring student samples with your rubric to see if you can make reliable and accurate judgments about them. Revise the rubric as needed.
11. Select examples of student work of varying kinds and degrees of quality for raters and students to look at.[53]
12. Help students to develop rubrics and evaluate their work. By doing so they learn what good work looks like and can more effectively understand and criticize their own learning processes, as well as those of their peers. They also gain a sense of responsibility for their own learning.[54]

Checklist for Rubrics

Some suggestions for checking your rubrics include the following:[55]

1. Is it appropriate for the purpose of the assessment?
2. Does it provide a usable, easily interpreted score?
3. Are the number and complexity of the elements limited—not more than six or seven?
4. Do the elements address the desired student outcomes and no others?
5. Do the elements reflect current conceptions of excellence in the field?
6. Are the elements are appropriate for all students—developmental level, ethnic or cultural background, gender, abilities?
7. Are the elements are consistent across similar tasks in related subject areas (i.e., writing in physical education should use the same rubric as writing in other fields)?
8. Is the format easy to understand? Are spelling and grammar correct?

Step 4—Administer and Score the Assessment Tasks

Because assessment is a part of instruction, students must know what the objectives are and the criteria for success for each learning objective. Students need feedback on whether the criteria have been met and if not, how to revise and complete the task.[56]

After selecting or writing a cognitive test, proofread the test while making the answer key and correct any errors on the test. Then, make sufficient copies for class use. Number each copy to make certain that none are taken during the test administration. Provide a space on the answer sheet for students to record this number. Make sufficient copies of the test and answer sheet, and obtain extra pencils, including a red pencil or pen for correcting the tests. Be sure the answer key is in a safe place. To minimize the temptation to cheat, seat students in alternate seats or ask them to spread out through the entire room. Alternate forms of a test can also be used to discourage cheating. Review the testing procedures and the test directions orally to avoid needless questions. Include how to fill out answer sheets, how to get help if needed (e.g., raise hand or come to front desk), and what to do when finished. If possible, assign a student assistant to correct objective tests as students complete them. When students are assigned to score their own tests, the test serves as a learning activity as well as a means of assessment,

Box 11.18

A Checklist and an Analytic Rubric for Teamwork/Fair Play

Instructions: Check off items the player does in the boxes at the left, then rate each area in the boxes at the right.

Levels of Achievement

Shows respect for teammates	Rarely	Seldom	Sometimes	Usually
☐ Congratulates good play by teammate ☐ Puts team before self ☐ Plays own position—does not hog ball ☐ Assists play by teammates ☐ Talks or signals to teammates during play ☐ Does not argue with team members ☐ Demonstrates loyalty ☐ Is courteous ☐ Gets along with teammates ☐ Works with teammates to improve skills				
Shows respects for teacher, coach, and officials	**Rarely**	**Seldom**	**Sometimes**	**Usually**
☐ Follows instructions without arguing ☐ Does not argue with officials or complain about misjudgments ☐ Compliments officials				
Knows and obeys rules, even when not observed	**Rarely**	**Seldom**	**Sometimes**	**Usually**
☐ Calls own violations, fouls, liners ☐ Plays "clean"				
Shows respect for opponents	**Rarely**	**Seldom**	**Sometimes**	**Usually**
☐ Applauds or congratulates good play by opponent ☐ Is courteous ☐ Shakes hands with opponents before the contest ☐ Congratulates opponents after the game				
Maintains self-control	**Rarely**	**Seldom**	**Sometimes**	**Usually**
☐ Is punctual and in own place, does not keep others waiting ☐ Does not use profanity ☐ Puts in hard, honest practice ☐ Accepts victory without boasting ☐ Loses gracefully without complaint or alibi ☐ Does not make excuses ☐ Performs to the best of his or her ability regardless of the situation ☐ Refrains from verbal or physical abuse of others				
Shows respect for facilities and equipment	**Rarely**	**Seldom**	**Sometimes**	**Usually**
☐ Puts equipment away ☐ Respects property of others ☐ Takes appropriate care of equipment				

TABLE 11.5 Sample Terms for Rubric Levels

Knowledge/ Understanding (Maurer, 1996)	No understanding.	Responses are inaccurate or incomplete. Serious misconceptions; little is understood.	A few critical elements are understood; numerous misconceptions.	Responses show some understanding by summarizing or retelling the information or linking it with past experiences or readings. Partial or incomplete understanding; some key errors.	Substantially complete understanding with few errors.	Responses are complex and demonstrate understanding by integrating one's own experiences, past readings, and discussions with classmates. Consistently complete and in-depth understanding.
Proficiency (Baron and Boschee, 1995)	No skill is evident. Minimal achievement. Fails to meet established standards.	Novice/emerging—minimal skill, many mistakes. Rudimentary achievement. Minimally meets established standards.	Apprentice/developing/ beginner	Intermediate/ developed—meets all of the established standards.	Accomplished/ advanced/proficient Superior achievement. Exceeds established standards.	Expert/exceptional achievement.
Evidence (Herman et al., 1992)	No evidence.	Minimal evidence.	Partial evidence.			Complete evidence.
Frequency	Never	Rarely	Occasionally	Frequently	Usually	Consistently
Effectiveness	Ineffective	Minimally effective	Partially effective	Moderately effective	Effective—Purpose accomplished.	Highly effective. Results exceed expectations.
Task Completion (Hymes, 1991; Herman et al., 1992; Costa and Kallick, 1995)	Task not attempted/ no attempt or unable to begin effectively. Off task/unacceptable	Attempts to address task. Fails to complete. Inadequate response. Partial completion. Minimally acceptable.	Nearly satisfactory, but serious flaws. Minimal attention to task.	Addresses task, but no elaboration. Satisfactory, with minor flaws.	Competent/Fully elaborated and attentive to task and audience.	Exemplary/Exceptional

Sources: Baron, M. A. & F. Boschee, (1995). *Authentic assessment: The key to unlocking student success.* (Lancaster, PA: Technomic Publishing); Costa, A. L. & Kallick, B. (Eds.). *Assessment in the learning organization: Shifting the paradigm* (Alexandria, VA: Association for Supervision and Curriculum Development, 1995); Herman, J. L., Aschbacher, P. R., & Winters, L. *A practical guide to alternative assessment* (Alexandria, VA: Association for Supervision and Curriculum Development, 1992); Hymes, D. L. (with Chafin, A. E., & Gonder, P.). *The changing face of testing and assessment: Problems and solutions* (Arlington, VA: American Association of School Administrators, 1991); Maurer, R. E. *Designing alternative assessments for interdisciplinary curriculum in middle and secondary schools* (Needham Heights, MA: Allyn & Bacon, 1996).

because students learn the correct answer to the questions they missed. Make sure to collect all tests and answer sheets before dismissing the class. Plan sufficient time for students to take the test. Approximately forty-five seconds are needed for simple multiple-choice questions and thirty seconds per true-false item for English-speaking students. To increase activity time and enhance motivation, you might give several short quizzes rather than one long exam.

Before giving skills tests, devise some method of scorekeeping that allows students to quickly insert scores for each student or group of students. When administering the skills tests, demonstrate each test, read and explain the directions on the card or test sheet, and answer any questions students might have. If skill test protocols have been used previously during skill instruction and practice, this element can be shortened considerably. Carefully explain trials, scoring, and recording. Mark needed areas and set up equipment for all tests in advance. Be aware of the disadvantages of grading on a single administration of a skills test. A student might be ill, anxious about the test, or just not able to perform as well some days as others. This can be remedied by allowing the student to take the test several times and use the highest score achieved. In this way, assessment activities are also learning activities, which saves time and also increases student responses and accountability.[57]

The administration of most authentic assessments is more like the way learning activities are taught rather than like assessments. They are integrated into the regular instructional process. The physical and emotional environments should be set up to ensure success.

Step 5—Evaluate and Revise the Assessment Techniques

After using the assessment techniques with one or more classes, note how each one was implemented, whether it was effective, and why. Then, make plans to remedy any problems and to increase the efficiency, validity, and reliability of the test. Look for items such as unclear directions, complex vocabulary, poor sentence structure, poorly constructed questions, and materials that do not adequately assess course objectives. Listen to students' questions as they attempt to complete assessments and note problems with directions or test items for use in revising the assessments. Record the amount of time needed to complete each assessment. Repeat this process each time an assessment is given. Remember, assessment is a means to an end, not an end in itself.

Answer the following questions about each assessment technique or task:

1. Does the assessment agree with the performance objective stated for the activity (content validity)?
2. Are the directions and vocabulary simple enough for the students' maturity and are tasks and rubrics carefully selected or constructed (validity)?
3. Is the technique formulated so that another person with similar experience can use it for assessment and get the same results (objectivity)?
4. Does the technique consistently result in the same score or grade for a student even when given on different occasions (reliability)?
5. Does the technique contribute to improved teaching-learning practices by enhancing teacher-student relations, encouraging students to devote attention to all areas of instruction, and serving as a fair and useful measure of achievement of outcomes emphasized in instruction?

Grading Systems

Grading is perceived as one of the most bothersome of all teaching duties. Perhaps this is because there appears to be no consensus among members of the profession as to how or why it is to be done. In fact, many grading practices seem to be educationally unsound. Many years ago Dressel pointed out: "A grade [is] . . . an inadequate report of an inaccurate judgment by a biased and variable judge of the extent to which a student has attained an undefined level of mastery of an unknown proportion of an indefinite amount of material."[58] In spite of the difficulties inherent in grading, it is still a very important part of the educational process. Students, parents, employers, and institutions of higher learning all demand such accountability. Great care should be taken to ensure fairness and consistency in grading. Students are easily discouraged by the grades they receive, which can affect their desires to participate in physical activity in the future.

All criteria for the calculation of the grade should be determined and stated before beginning instruction in any activity or unit. Caution should be used in determining grades based on a few test scores because students may be incorrectly assigned to grade groupings. The more levels of grading (ABCDF = 5 levels or 4 cutoffs) that are used, the larger the chance that a student will be assigned a grade that he or she does not deserve. Validity can be increased by combining the results of several different assessments of the same factor, such as using skills tests and teacher ratings for skill grades.[59]

The Purpose of Grading

The primary purpose of a grade is to inform students, parents, and administrators of the present status and progress of students toward program objectives. Grades tend to promote positive public relations with colleges, universities, professional schools, and employers, who depend on them for admission and hiring. Grades may also serve as a motivator for teachers and students to improve the teaching-learning process. Finally, if used properly, grades help teachers evaluate the effectiveness of instruction and provide evidence that students are achieving the content standards for physical education. Under no circumstances should grades be given casually, based on the teacher's impression of the student, without evidence of student achievement.

Principles of Grading

In spite of the fact that educators have never been able to agree on how to grade, certain principles have emerged that, if followed, will make grading a more rewarding process for both teacher and student.

1. The grade should reflect individual student *achievement* as determined by declared course objectives.
2. Grades should be based on achievement of all of the physical education content standards or their benchmarks, including skills, physical fitness, knowledge, and personal and social skills.
3. Grades should reflect educational outcomes, not be an end in themselves. The stress placed on grades in conventional practice tends to cause the student to believe that getting good marks is the aim of education.
4. The school or district grading system should be developed cooperatively by teachers and school personnel so grades will be consistent with those given in other subjects in the school.
5. The department grading system should be established collectively by all physical education teachers and be applied consistently to every physical education class in the school.
6. Students should be informed in advance of the criteria and procedures used in assigning grades and receive adequate feedback on their progress toward objectives.
7. A variety of assessment instruments, both objective and subjective, should be used in the assessment process.
8. Assessment should be an ongoing process, and students should be adequately prepared for assessment. Grades should not depend on one test score or assessment session.
9. Assessment procedures should foster positive student attitudes toward physical education.
10. A grading system should be detailed enough to be diagnostic; fair as a uniform measure of achievement; and compact enough to be practical in terms of time, understandability, and ease of recording.
11. Assessment procedures should consider individual differences such as physical characteristics, maturity, background experiences, and ability.
12. Giving parents and students a voice in how the grade is reported will enhance the meaningfulness of the grade.

The Process of Grading

The process for determining grades in physical education involves the following steps:

Step 1. Select objectives and determine the emphasis to be placed on each objective.
Step 2. Select assessment instruments for each objective.
Step 3. Select a grading system.
Step 4. Measure the degree of achievement of each objective.
Step 5. Determine the grade based on the original percentage specified for each objective.
Step 6. Communicate the grade to the student.

Step 1—Select Objectives and Determine the Emphasis to Be Placed on Each Objective

List each applicable content standard and the corresponding unit objectives and determine the percentage of emphasis for each one. Boyce found that students who were graded on a combination of skill, knowledge, and participation performed better on skills than those who were graded on just skills or just participation.[60] Note that measures of social behavior are *unreliable* indicators of student performance. Grades should *not* be used as a reward for good behavior or a punishment for poor behavior. In fact, legal scholars and educators agree that assigning zeros for such behaviors as failing to bring textbooks and uniforms to class and turning in work late are most likely illegal. This could be extended to zeros or F grades for failing to take showers, cheating on tests, or failing to submit an assignment, and the use of pop quizzes to force students to read assignments.[61] A grade of zero on a major assignment greatly distorts the grading scale. Adopting a five-point scale (i.e., 0 = F and 4 = A) for recording assignments helps prevent this distortion. In summary, grades should reflect achievement of the specified course objectives. A separate mark or indicator can be used to inform parents and administrators of appropriate or inappropriate citizenship or class behavior. Misconduct is best handled by discipline and counseling.

Step 2—Select Assessment Instruments for Each Objective

This chapter contains a number of assessment techniques. Appropriate instruments should be developed to evaluate each objective. When objectives are written as performance objectives, the assessment is nearly the same as the objective. Assessments should be positive, such as earning points at completion of a performance rather than losing points for lack of performance. Both quantitative and qualitative assessments are appropriate. Avoid the practice of grading on attitude and effort, because techniques used to do so are not valid.

Step 3—Select a Grading System

In the selection of a grading system or combination of systems, consider the advantages and limitations of each.

No one method is superior in all situations; some compromises or combinations of systems may need to be made. One arrangement would be to grade all students according to prearranged standards or criteria. A second arrangement would be to group students for instruction according to skill or fitness levels and grade each group according to different criteria. The following systems of grading are presented for consideration.

Statistics Needed for Grading A knowledge of the normal, or bell-shaped, curve is essential for understanding grading techniques. An example of the importance of variability involves two bowlers, Dong Ho and Maria. Dong Ho has scores of 138, 139, 140, 141, and 142, while Maria has scores of 100, 120, 140, 160, and 180. Dong Ho is obviously the more consistent bowler since his scores concentrate around the mean. Maria was a beginner when beginning the unit but was a quick study and is now bowling better than Dong. When teachers use averaging techniques, they penalize students who have never participated in an activity and reward those who have. With performance-based assessment, it is more important to consider where students perform at the completion of the unit than how well they performed when the unit began.

Norm-Referenced Assessment Norm-referenced assessment ("grading on the curve") is the measurement of individual performance as it compares to group or class performance according to a normal probability curve. Grades are distributed at different levels, usually A, B, C, D, and F. Such a system is ideal when students must be ranked. Several disadvantages of norm-referenced assessment exist, however. First, it tends to assess the rate of learning of students rather than ability to learn; the fastest learners get A's. Second, grades are distributed over a curve whether this is appropriate or not. Small classes do not necessarily fit into a normal curve. A mark of C in one class may be the same as an A or F in another class in the same subject. When all students score very high or very low on a test, the teacher is left to wonder whether the test was too difficult or too easy and whether the students already knew the material or learned very well. Third, grading on the curve is not consistent with assessment based on performance objectives and content standards. It fails to tell whether the students have mastered the skills. In fact, some skills cannot be graded on a curve, such as "treading water" in swimming. Consequently, most grading policies do not adhere to a strict norm-referenced assessment system.

Criterion-Referenced Assessment Criterion-referenced assessments compare individual performance with a preestablished performance standard, such as a score, the number of tasks completed, or the difficulty of tasks completed. Grades can be expressed in percentage scores, as pass-fail or as letter grades of A, B, C, D, and F. Criterion-referenced assessment makes it possible for more students to earn a good grade. Grades are not influenced by the high skill levels of others, such as athletes. Criterion-referenced assessment facilitates the use of student-paced programs, competency-based instruction, and contract grading.

Contract grading specifies the performance and criteria (quantity and quality) for which each student will receive a given grade. In individual contracts, each contract specifies the performance and criteria for that student and whether the student or teacher or someone else will determine when the criteria have been met. With criterion-referenced grading, students can be told exactly what will be expected, reducing student anxiety. When students know what the objectives are, they are much more likely to achieve them.

Two major disadvantages exist for criterion-referenced assessment. First, accurate standards cannot always be specified before the activity or unit has been taught. Second, grades may reflect test difficulty rather than failure to achieve. For example, if no student got ninety or above on a test, either the students did not learn or the test was too difficult. When teaching a unit for a first time or administering a written test for the first time teachers might consider using the top student score on the test as a perfect paper and then using this to calculate grades. For example, if the highest score on the test was 90, and the range for an A was 90 percent and higher, the teacher would multiply the 90 by .9 and those students scoring 81 and above would receive an A on the test. If B work was considered 80 percent to 89 percent, any score 72 through 80 would be given a B, and so forth. In mastery grading, it is often difficult to draw the line between what is passing and what is failing and standards may vary from one teacher to another. Critics complain that criterion-referenced grading encourages mediocrity and that grade inflation occurs because too many students receive high grades. The solution is to set standards high enough that the integrity of an A grade is not in question, no matter how many students earn that grade.

Pass-fail grading can reduce student motivation to excel, when students lower their achievement to the level required for passing. Pass-fail grading does not differentiate between students of different abilities, except at a minimum level. In some classes, an A-pass-fail system is used to distinguish students who can do more than achieve the minimum specified level of performance. *Pass-no-credit* grading, a variation of pass-fail grading, reduces student cheating to get a "pass" because there is no stigma on failure. It encourages students to try activities that they might be afraid to fail. However, students must repeat the experience if they wish to receive credit. The following methods can be used for criterion-referenced grading. For ABCDF grades, four standards or cutoffs are needed. Misclassification is reduced as the validity of the cutoff scores is increased.

- *Arbitrary standards.* A common technique is to give scores by the percentage correct; thus, 60–69 percent = D, 70–79 percent = C, 80–89 percent = B, and

90–100 percent = A. This method is reliable, but may not be valid. Grades can't be compared across tests since the level of difficulty varies for each test; means and standard deviations may be very different between tests.

- *Criterion-referenced standards.* Fairly valid and reliable standards can be created by plotting the scores of about two hundred students and establishing cutoff scores for mastery/nonmastery or for each grade. This system is both valid and reliable if done properly.
- *Rubrics.* Rubrics are prepared as described earlier in this chapter to delineate the standards for each grade or achievement level.

Improvement

> It makes no sense to talk of different standards and expectations for different groups of students. A standard offers an objective ideal, serving as a worthy and tangible goal for everyone—even if, at this point in time, for whatever reason, some cannot (yet!) reach it. . . . Our task in assessment is to . . . provide students with a record of the longitudinal progress they make in emulating the standard. . . . People improve . . . by judging all their work against the exemplary performances that set the standard and by valuing the performances in question.[62]

The British national assessment scoring system provides an exemplary model for assessment. A standard of 10 indicates the desired performance for exit-level competency and students are judged throughout their career in terms of how closely they approximate that level of performance. For example, seventh graders might be expected to be at a level of 6 or 7, while high school graduates should be able to score a 10. Using such a system would give students a realistic sense of where they are in terms of the desired outcome or content standard.[63]

Grading on improvement is considered questionable at best. A grade based solely on improvement is *never* acceptable. The rationale for this is that improvement in math or science or physical education or English grammar is not worth much if the concepts needed in everyday life are missing. If students enrolled in a physical education class have not achieved the standards necessary to be considered physically educated or physically fit, grades should reflect this no matter how much improvement has occurred. Another disadvantage of grading on improvement is that many activity units do not permit adequate time for improvement to occur. Improvement scores are then unreliable. In spite of this, many physical education teachers continue to grade on improvement.

Grading on improvement is supposed to reflect individual progress, demonstrated by performance on a posttest compared with performance on a pretest. Its main advantage lies in motivating low-skilled students, especially when they are included in classes with students who have high levels of ability. It can be used to evaluate objectives where students are not compared with their peers—for example, on fitness objectives—provided that the highly fit students are not expected to achieve the same percentage of improvement or improve beyond the healthy fitness zone. Student motivation must be high enough to minimize students' purposely scoring low on the pretest. This can be avoided by counting the pretest score when it already meets the desired standard.

Grading on improvement favors the lower-skilled students over the higher-skilled students even when achievement plus improvement is included in the grade calculation. For example, a highly skilled student who scored seven baskets on ten basketball free-throws will probably not improve very much at the posttest. A score of eight on the posttest plus a score of one for improvement gives that student a total score of nine. A student who scored only two baskets on the pretest but scored six on the posttest receives a total score of ten (six plus four for improvement). The student making only six out of ten free throws has earned a higher score than the student scoring eight out of ten free throws.

Deutsch suggested two ways to consider improvement in the grading process: (1) develop separate norms for each ability group based on pretest scores, or (2) calculate an improvement score as follows:

$$\frac{\text{posttest score} - \text{pretest score}}{\text{maximum test score} - \text{pretest score}} = \text{improvement}$$

Example: The maximum possible score on the test is 100. See Box 11.19.

Thus, both students had the same amount of improvement. The use of standardized scores yields greater accuracy for this process. Deutsch suggests combining improvement with objective and subjective assessments of skill for grading.[64]

Student-Assigned Grades Teachers who think grades destroy student-teacher rapport favor student self-assessment and grading. For this type of assessment to be effective, students must be taught goal-setting techniques and techniques for assessing their own strengths and weaknesses in relation to the standards established for the unit objectives. Students might be asked to write out their goals, criteria for assessing goal achievement, ways in which the goals were achieved or not achieved, and the appropriate grade. Teachers may then add their own comments, negotiate with the student for a mutually acceptable grade, or average the student's and teacher's grades to arrive at a course grade. Student-assigned grades are often used in individualized learning programs, and student involvement in assessment is becoming more common. As long as the current method of grading is prevalent in schools, honest self-assessment by students will be difficult because of the intense pressure on students to get high grades. However, in some cases, students are harder on themselves than teachers are.

Box 11.19

Example of Calculating improvement Scores

	Pretest	Posttest	Potential improvement	Actual improvement
Student 1	80	90	100–80 = 20	90–80 = 10
	Student A improved 10/20 or 50 percent.			
Student 2	20	60	100–20 = 80	60–20 = 40
	Student B improved 40/80 or 50 percent.			

Step 4—Measure the Degree of Achievement of Each Objective

Student progress should be reported in terms of individual achievement of the unit objectives specified. Use as many different assessment opportunities as possible so students are not graded on a one-time all-out effort. Record test scores or other data for each objective in the grade book or computerized grading program. This information is essential for interpreting student progress and grades to both students and parents.

Step 5—Determine the Grade Based on the Original Percentage Specified for Each Objective

Test scores can be combined in several ways, but a student's grade and class rank can change dramatically depending on the method used to combine the scores, regardless of the original student performance. Table 11.6 gives an example of how grades can be calculated in physical education. The teacher in this example decided that grades would be based on skill, physical fitness, knowledge, and social skills. Skill and physical fitness would each be given 30 percent of the possible points while knowledge and social skills would each receive 20 percent. A total of 500 points was used for the unit and divided according to the percentages assigned to each objective.

Using Bonus Points to Motivate Students Students who have done poorly throughout a grading period may approach teachers asking for a way to improve their grade. If a grade represents a student's achievement, then awarding bonus points for this reason distorts the meaning of the grade. If teachers elect to give bonus points as a motivator for students, they should be given sparingly and to reward extra work related to the material presented in the grading period. For example, awarding a few points for students who come to help at an after-school track meet while doing a track and field unit may be appropriate. Teachers must make sure that all students have the ability to get these points; in this example, getting a ride home after the meet may be a problem for some students. Also, students who are participating in the meet could not take advantage of this offer. There have been cases in which teachers have awarded so many bonus points that the balance of the grading system was completely disrupted. The bonus points actually became a more significant part of the grade than did major student assignments.

Giving Low Grades to Motivate Students Some teachers feel that students are underperforming in physical education. In an effort to motivate these students, a teacher gives a low grade so that the student will try harder during the subsequent grading period. This practice has no place in education and frequently will backfire on the teacher. When assigning grades, teachers need to award the grade that the student earned in class. Failure to do so could cause the student to stop trying because he or she perceives that efforts in class have little bearing on a grade. The grading system should be defensible and as clearly defined as possible. If teachers are using elements like fair play and cooperation with others for calculating grades, the criteria need to be defined and the means for assessing those elements must be stated. Some teachers like to have some "fuzzy" areas in their grading system that allow them to make adjustments according to student behaviors. This practice is inappropriate and may have a negative impact on student learning in physical education.

Step 6—Communicate the Grade to the Student

Many problems are eliminated by communicating grades to the students as soon as possible after the assessment. Students are then able to see their own progress toward objectives instead of what the teacher "gave me." They can also track the grades themselves as a unit of instruction progresses. If it is possible to schedule a private moment with each student several days before the end of the grading period, the teacher can review the grades earned as well as the reasons for each grade and let the student know what grade will appear on the report card. Doing this can eliminate misunderstandings and, if necessary, changes can be made. All grades should be communicated

TABLE 11.6 Calculating Grades in Physical Education

	Category Weight	Possible Points	Assessments	Possible Points	Actual Score	Total Points for the Category	Final Grade
Skill	30%	150 points	Skill test—Pass	10	8	114	76%
			Skill test—Set	10	10		
			Skill test—Serve	10	6		
			Teacher observation of game play	80	55		
			Student self-assessment based on incident charts of game play	40	35		
Physical Fitness	30%	150 points	Complete health-related fitness tests	50	50	132	88%
			Portfolio (setting and achieving own goals)	100	82		
Knowledge	20%	100 points	Rules test	25	21	81	81%
			Officiating	15	10		
			Teacher observation of game play	60	50		
Social Skills	20%	100 points	Fair play/ teamwork rating scales	70	65	95	95%
			Journal entries	30	30		
Final Grade	100%	500		500	422	422/500	84.4% B for the unit

to the student during the course of a grading period. Nothing should come as a surprise. Increasingly, students attend parent-teacher conferences and review their own progress on achieving content standards with their parents as shown in their portfolios.

Grading in Coed and Mainstreamed Classes

After the passage of Title IX and PL 94–142, the range of abilities within each class widened considerably. When grading, equal opportunities for students to reach success are essential. Stamm discussed three possible approaches to grading in coeducational and mainstreamed classes. These include (1) grading on improvement, (2) using separate performance standards, and (3) mastery learning.[65] All of these approaches have been discussed previously. Teachers should remember that grading males and females using separate standards may result in perpetuating the stereotype that boys are capable of better performances. Perhaps a more equitable arrangement would be to group students by ability rather than by gender and set standards in terms of the abilities of each group. This plan can also meet the needs of disabled students. Once students are divided into ability groups, objectives can be written that are broad enough for all groups, such as: "Choose one piece of equipment and perform a routine on that piece (fulfilling certain criteria), in addition to checking off five new skills on each piece of apparatus." Earning tickets in track and field for meeting standards on each event, for placing in "heats," and for jogging a lap allows students to achieve regardless of their individual differences. Balancing teams by gender and ability group and awarding bonus points for team achievements on tests, sportsmanship, and game play promote achievement for all students regardless of ability.

Record Keeping for Grading

A grading system is only as good as the records of student performance that are kept. Teachers must use a record-keeping system that facilitates calculation of the final grade and keeps track of all grade input. A comprehensive system also helps the teacher explain grades to parents or administrators. Computerized grading systems are excellent for maintaining records. Many school districts adopt a specific software program to record both grades and attendance. Grade reports can automatically be transmitted to the office and printouts may be made available to students and parents on demand or at specified intervals. Handheld computers make it possible to enter data on the field for immediate feedback to students and teachers. The computer can also be available to provide student information for parent-teacher conferences. Data should be downloaded into desktop computers periodically and hard copy printouts should be produced to guard against computer error or crash. Where a specific grading program is not required, a spreadsheet can be used to record grades and related information.

Review Questions: Why do teachers give grades?

What are the advantages or disadvantages of each grading system? What grading system or combination of systems is best?

Write a letter to parents explaining the grade you would give their child in physical education. When writing your letter, put yourself in the roles of parent, teacher, and student. How would you feel about the grade given and the rationale from the point of view of each role? Is your system defensible?

NOTES

1. National Association for Sport and Physical Education, *Moving into the Future: National Physical Education Standards: A Guide to Content and Assessment* (St. Louis, MO: Mosby, 1995).
2. L. Lambert, *Standards-Based Assessment of Student Learning: A Comprehensive Approach* (Oxon Hill, MD: AAHPERD Publications, 1999).
3. J. Placek, Conceptions of success in teaching: Busy, happy and good? in T. J. Templin and J. K. Olson, eds., *Teaching in Physical Education* (Champaign, IL: Human Kinetics, 1983), 46–56.
4. M. Tousignant and D. Siedentop, A qualitative analysis of task structures in required secondary physical education classes, *Journal of Teaching in Physical Education 3,* no. 1 (1983): 47–57
5. P. A. Hastie and J. E. Saunders, Accountability in secondary school physical education, *Teaching and Teacher Education 7,* no. 1 (1991): 383–42.
6. J. Shanklin, The impact of accountability on student response rate in a secondary physical education badminton unit. Unpublished master's thesis, Ball State University, Muncie, IN, 2004.
7. J. Lund and M. Veal, Make students accountable, *Strategies 9,* no. 6 (1996): 26–29
8. D. Siedentop and D. Tannehill, *Developing Teaching Skills in Physical Education,* 4th ed. (Mountain View, CA: Mayfield, 2000).
9. L. Griffin and J. Oslin, Got a minute? A quick and easy strategy for knowledge testing in physical education, *Strategies 4,* no. 2 (1990): 6–7, 23.
10. B. N. Strand and P. Wilson, *Assessing Sport Skills* (Champaign, IL: Human Kinetics, 1993).
11. G. Wiggins, Assessment: Authenticity, context, and validity, *Phi Delta Kappan 75,* no. 3 (1993): 200–14.
12. V. Perrone, ed., *Expanding Student Assessment* (Alexandria, VA: Association for Supervision and Curriculum Development, 1991).
13. V. J. Melograno, Portfolio assessment: Documenting authentic student learning, *Journal of Physical Education, Recreation, and Dance 65,* No. 8 (1994): 50–61.
14. D. M. Neill, Transforming student assessment, *Phi Delta Kappan 79,* no. 1 (1997): 34–58.
15. J. Lund, Authentic assessment: Its development and applications, *Journal of Physical Education, Recreation, and Dance 68,* no. 7 (1997): 25–28, 40.
16. A. L. Costa and B. Kallick, eds., *Assessment in the Learning Organization: Shifting the Paradigm* (Alexandria, VA: Association for Supervision and Curriculum Development, 1995); J. Koval, K. Myers, L. V. Sande, and D. Hood, Designing assessment targets aimed at improving physical education instruction: K–5. Paper presented at the American Alliance for Health, Physical Education, Recreation, and Dance national convention, Boston, MA, April 1999; V. Melograno, Integrating assessment into physical education teaching, *Journal of Physical Education, Recreation, and Dance 68,* no. 7 (1994): 34–40; Melograno, Portfolio assessment.
17. D. Lambdin, Keeping track, *Journal of Physical Education, Education and Dance 55,* no. 6 (1984): 40–43.
18. B. Everhart, Assessing motor and sport skill performance: Two practical procedures, *Journal of Physical Education, Recreation, and Dance 67,* no. 6 (1996): 49–51.
19. M. Metzler, R. Cregger, and J. Poole, Collaboration within an ISD-based unit of instruction. Paper presented at the AIESEP/NAPEHE convention, Atlanta, GA, January 1991.
20. G. Graham, S. Holt/Hale, and M. Parker, *Children Moving: A Reflective Approach to Teaching Physical Education,* 3d ed. (Mountain View, CA: Mayfield, 1993), 24–25; T. Ratliffe, Evaluation of students' skill using generic levels of skill proficiency, *Physical Educator 41,* no. 2 (1984): 65–68.
21. D. J. Langley and A. M. Woods, Developing progressions in motor skills: A systematic approach, *Journal of Physical Education, Recreation, and Dance 68,* no. 7 (1997): 41–45.
22. K. M. Haywood, Authentic assessment of movement requires a development approach, *Missouri Journal of Health, Physical Education, Recreation and Dance 7* (1997): 3–15.
23. J. Lund, Assessment and accountability in secondary physical education, *Quest 44,* no. 3 (1992): 352–60.
24. R. L. Sweeting, Challenge courts motivate and evaluate, *Journal of Physical Education, Recreation, and Dance 65,* no. 8 (1994): 8–10.
25. H. A. Fronske, Relationship among Various Objective Swimming Tests and Expert Evaluations of Skill in Swimming. Doctoral dissertation, Brigham Young University, Provo, UT, 1988.
26. J. Gréhaigne and P. Godbout, Formative assessment in team sports in a tactical approach context, *Journal of*

Physical Education, Recreation, and Dance 69, no. 1 (1998): 46–51.

27. National Association for Sport and Physical Education, *Moving into the Future.*
28. J. Lund and M. F. Kirk, Integrating alternative performance-based assessments with learning activities in middle and secondary physical education classes. Paper presented at the American Alliance for Health, Physical Education, Recreation, and Dance national convention, Reno, NV, April 1998.
29. D. L. Hymes (with A. E. Chafin and P. Gonder), *The Changing Face of Testing and Assessment: Problems and Solutions* (Arlington, VA: American Association of School Administrators, 1991).
30. Hymes, *The Changing Face.*
31. Therese Schick, student paper, 1999.
32. Jennifer Roberts, student paper, 1999.
33. Participation problems: A solution, *The Teaching Professor 4–5* (1998, February).
34. P. Brands, Physical education for the 21st century. Paper presented at the American Alliance for Health, Physical Education, Recreation, and Dance national convention, Reno, NV, April 1998.
35. R. E. Maurer, *Designing Alternative Assessments for Interdisciplinary Curriculum in Middle and Secondary Schools* (Needham Heights, MA: Allyn and Bacon, 1996).
36. B. Mohnsen, C. B. Chestnutt, and D. Burke, Multimedia projects, *Strategies 11,* no. 1 (1997): 10–13.
37. Therese Schick student paper, 1999.
38. Brands, Physical education.
39. J. Lund and M. Kirk, *Performance-Based Assessment for Secondary Physical Education* (Champaign, IL: Human Kinetics, 2002).
40. Koval et al., Designing assessment targets; Maurer, *Designing Alternative Assessments.*
41. P. Dunham, Jr., Evaluation for excellence: A systematic approach, *Journal of Physical Education, Recreation, and Dance 57,* no. 6 (1986): 34–36.
42. T. M. Wood and M. J. Safrit, Measurement and evaluation in professional education—A view from the measurement specialists, *Journal of Physical Education, Recreation, and Dance 61,* no. 3 (1990): 29–31.
43. National Association for Sport and Physical Education, *Moving into the Future.*
44. National Association for Sport and Physical Education, *Moving into the Future.*
45. Strand and Wilson, *Assessing Sport Skills;* R. Mcgee and A. Farrow, *Test Questions for Physical Education Activities* (Champaign, IL: Human Kinetics, 1987; National Association for Sport and Physical Education, *Moving into the Future.*
46. Neill, Transforming student assessment.
47. Maurer, *Designing Alternative Assessments.*
48. L. Hensley, L. Lambert, T. Baumgartner, and J. Stillwell, Is evaluation worth the effort? *Journal of Physical Education, Recreation, and Dance 58,* no. 6 (1989): 59–62.
49. Lund and Kirk, *Performance-Based Assessment for Secondary Physical Education.*
50. J. Herman, P. Aschbacher, and L. Winter, *A Practical Guide to Alternative Assessment* (Alexandria, VA: Association for Supervision and Curriculum Development, 1992).
51. C. Danielson, Designing successful performance tasks and rubrics. Audiocassette tape #297072. Recorded live at the 52nd Annual Conference of ASCD, Baltimore, MD, March 22–25, 1997 (Alexandria, VA: Association for Supervision and Curriculum Development, 1992). Read by author.
52. T. Azwell and E. Schmar, eds., *Report Card on Report Cards: Alternatives to Consider* (Portsmouth, NH: Heinemann, 1995); M. E. Block, L. J. Lieberman, and F. Connor-Kuntz, Authentic assessment in adapted physical education, *Journal of Physical Education, Recreation, and Dance 69,* no. 3 (1998): 48–55; J. L. Herman, P. R. Aschbacher, and L. Winters, *A Practical Guide to Alternative Assessment* (Alexandria, VA: Association for Supervision and Curriculum Development, 1992).
53. Neill, Transforming student assessment.
54. Block, Lieberman, and Connor-Kuntz, Authentic assessment; Neill, Transforming student assessment.
55. Herman, Aschbacher, and Winters, *A Practical Guide.*
56. Gréhaigne and Godbout, Formative assessment.
57. Lund, Assessment and accountability in secondary physical education.
58. P. L. Dressel, Fact and fancy in assigning grades, *Basic College Quarterly 2,* no. 2 (1957): 6–12.
59. W. G. Hopkins and B. F. J. Manly, Errors in assigning grades based on tests of finite validity, *Research Quarterly for Exercise and Sport 60,* no. 2 (1989): 180–82.
60. B. A. Boyce, Grading Practices–How do they influence student skill performance? *Journal of Physical Education, Recreation, and Dance 61,* no. 6 (1990): 46–48.
61. D. J. Cotton and M. B. Cotton, Grading: The ultimate weapon? *Journal of Physical Education, Recreation, and Dance 56,* no. 2 (1985): 52–53; J. R. Hills, Apathy concerning grading and testing, *Phi Delta Kappan 72,* no. 2 (1991): 540–45.
62. G. Wiggins, Standards, not standardization: Evoking quality student work, in R. S. Brandt, ed., *Readings from Educational Leadership: Performance Assessment* (Alexandria, VA: Association for Supervision and Curriculum Development, 1992), 127–28; reprinted from *Educational Leadership, 48,* 18–25.
63. Wiggins, Standards, not standardization.
64. H. Deutsch, Sex fair grading in physical education, *Physical Educator 41,* no. 3 (1984): 137–41.
65. C. L. Stamm, Evaluation of coeducational physical activity classes, *Journal of Physical Education and Recreation 50,* no. 1 (1979): 68–69.

UNIT III

Organizing and Managing Instruction

CHAPTER

12

Classroom Organization and Management

Study Stimulators

1. What school and departmental policies, procedures, and routines are essential to a smooth operation of the department of physical education? How can these policies be communicated to students and parents?
2. What is classroom management? Why is it essential to good instruction in physical education? What governs the choice of a management technique?
3. What methods can be used to enhance classroom management?
4. Why is record keeping important? What types of records should teachers keep?

Unlike a classroom where students sit in desks during an instructional period, physical educators deal with students who typically change clothes prior to starting class, move from one activity area to another (which can involve going out of doors), and use multiple pieces of equipment during a semester. Effective physical educators stand out because of their ability to organize and manage the dozens of components that make up an effective learning environment. Since effective teachers establish policies, procedures, and routines during the first days of school to create an appropriate learning environment for the school term, many decisions are necessary prior to the beginning of school. If the department consists of several teachers, the most effective environment results when all teachers agree on these organizational components and follow them consistently. This requires teachers to carefully plan strategies for organizing and managing the department, locker room, and classroom instruction prior to the beginning of the school year. Suggestions for classroom management procedures, along with record-keeping tips to facilitate this process, are examined in this chapter.

Departmental Policies and Procedures

Departmental policies and procedures should be developed to regulate those elements that must be consistent for all students taking physical education. A departmental handout and handbook can be developed to include each of these elements, thereby reducing misunderstandings between home and school concerning the policies.[1] A creative example of a departmental handout is the work contract shown in Box 12.1.

The first few days of school are critical for establishing the tone for the rest of the year.[2] Much of the first two days in all physical education classes are spent

BOX 12.1

Work Contract

WANTED—STUDENTS
Ninety days of work available

TYPE OF WORK
Preparation for lifetime physical fitness, team sports skill development, and individual sport skill development

WAGE
One-half unit of physical education credit

PAYROLL ISSUED
After forty-five days and after ninety days

QUALIFICATIONS
Must be willing to work, be properly dressed, be cooperative, possess the ability to get along with fellow workers, and be punctual

HOURS
One hour per day at the scheduled time

SPECIAL REQUIREMENTS
A uniform will be needed each day consisting of

Shorts—White, yellow, or black—no cut-offs
Shirts—T-shirt, either white or yellow—no tank tops or bare midriffs
Gym Shoes—in good condition
Socks—preferably white

Long hair must be tied back from the face to prevent injuries
Long pants and sweatshirt for cold weather outside

SICK LEAVE AND VACATION TIME
The State of Utah requires a minimum of seventy-five class hours before credit can be issued (this would allow a maximum of fifteen days absent time). No credit will be given if exceeded.

MAKEUP TIME
All makeup work will be due *one week* after the day you return from an illness or excused absence. No makeup will be allowed if you cut (sluff) class without being properly excused.

TYPES OF OVERTIME ACCEPTED
Equal to one hour's work for the hour missed. Acceptable projects are these: (1) design a poster, (2) write a report, (3) teach a new game, (4) organize and direct a ten-minute exercise routine for class, or (5) anything else with *prior* approval of the instructor.

(Running miles, swimming, hiking, bowling are things you do for fun, *not* for makeup after you've been ill. You need recuperation time.)

Extended absence for illness is covered by a doctor's excuse, which is honored, and no makeup is required. Your grade will be based on work completed up to that time.

Failure to complete this employment will result in termination of contract.

If interested in applying for this work, please sign after carefully reading the terms of the contract. Parent or guardian should be aware of your commitment. Have them sign one copy and return it to your new employer.

____________________ Parent/Guardian

____________________ Employee

reviewing rules and procedures. Krouscas suggested the following points to consider when presenting rules.

1. State the rule.
2. Explain why the rule is important.
3. Explain the consequences of breaking the rule.
4. Provide an example of what a rule infraction looks like.[3]

Because time is so limited in physical education, most teachers are anxious to get students involved in activity as quickly as possible. Effective teachers must not only present the policies and procedures that will govern their classes but also give students a chance to practice those that will become the routines designed to decrease the time spent doing management activities.

Day 1—Introduction: Distribute handbooks and/or handouts (two copies: one to sign and return, the other to keep for reference) for parents and students. Go over policies with students. Assign students to squads for attendance and preclass activities.

Day 2—Locker-room day: Take attendance using squad formation. Record names of students who have returned their signed handout on physical education procedures. Assign students to lockers and distribute locks. Have students practice opening their locks. Use contests to see who can open his or her lock the fastest. Place locks on the appropriate lockers. Review procedure for using long lockers with street clothes and smaller lockers for storage of activity clothing.

Day 3—First day to dress: Assemble in squad formation for attendance. Gather any handouts from students who forgot them the previous day. Have permanent markers available for students who have not put their names on their activity clothing. Dismiss students to locker room to change into activity clothing. Reassemble them in squad lines for stretching activities. Teach some stretches that will be appropriate for the first activity unit. If the first unit is one that students have covered in previous physical education classes, teachers may allow students to play to preassess students' skills.

Day 4—Sponge activity (skill challenge for activity unit) for students who dress quickly: Assemble students in squads for attendance and stretching. Engage in vigorous activity. Allow a little extra time (5 minutes) at the conclusion of class for students who need to shower (15 minutes total instead of the normal 10).

No matter what system is used to inform students and their parents or guardians of the policies and procedures employed by the physical education department, requiring the student and a parent or guardian to sign a sheet indicating understanding of the policies and procedures is important. First, it eliminates the excuse of not knowing the policies and procedures. Second, it provides a parental signature to use as a comparison when parents send excuses from activity to be sure a parent actually signed the excuse. Items that might be included in a physical education student handbook are the following:

1. The department's philosophy.
2. Physical education objectives.
3. Registration procedures and course offerings.
4. Policies concerning uniforms, dressing, showers, locker rooms, and laundering uniforms.
5. Policies for medical excuses, safety, accidents, and first aid.
6. Physical education standards.
7. Activities offered in the program.
8. Grading standards and policies.
9. Policies for making up absences.
10. Physical fitness appraisals.
11. Policies concerning student leaders.
12. Extra-class activities.
13. Emergency contact information for the school.
14. Invitation to meet with parents about concerns; include school phone number and/or e-mail address on the invitation.

Policies and procedures governing such components as (1) uniforms, (2) excuses from activity, (3) locker-room policies, (4) locks and lockers, (5) towels, and (6) showers will be discussed.

Uniforms

The use of a required uniform for physical education is a controversial issue.[4] Many states now have laws restricting the use of a special uniform. Some schools have stopped requiring students to dress in a standard outfit to participate in class activities while others still require a specific uniform to be worn. Some public schools are actually returning to school uniforms to be worn throughout the school day. Whatever the policy, students should be required to change into clothing that allows active, comfortable, and safe participation. However, teachers should also realize that some low-intensity activities might not require a full change into activity clothing (e.g., changing shoes might be adequate). Not requiring students to change increases the instructional time available for that class.

Students with special needs should always be considered when establishing a dress policy. For example, students who are overweight, disabled, unable to afford a uniform, or restricted due to religious reasons should not be made to feel uncomfortable or conspicuous in class because of the uniform. It is always wise to provide several options for uniforms to teenagers who at this time in their lives are exploring their own independence.

Whatever uniform is provided should be marked with the student's name in permanent ink or on a label to facilitate recovery in case of loss. It is wise to require the uniform (whatever it is) to be kept at school and used only during the physical education class. This discourages students from participating in street clothes. Uniforms should be laundered regularly to promote good hygiene.

When a specific uniform is required by departmental policy, explain to students and parents what type of uniform is requested, why it is necessary, and possible purchase locations. A uniform can be viewed as the equivalent of school supplies needed in other classes. An example of the uniform should be available in class for students to see. A handout could be prepared to explain the uniform, marking, and laundry policies to parents.

Teachers should also dress in appropriate clothes as an example for students to follow. When teachers fail to dress for activity, students may view this as a double standard and be less willing to change into activity clothing. The teacher's clothing should be distinctive enough for the teacher to be located immediately within the activity area.

Excuses from Activity

Establish a sound policy regarding excuses from activity, and communicate the policy to students and parents at the beginning of the school year. Excuses from activity generally consist of two types: medical excuses and nonmedical excuses.

Medical Excuses

All medical excuses should be cleared through the school nurse if possible (see Box 12.2). In this way a record of the frequency of illness can be kept for each student. The nurse or the teacher should keep notes from the parent or physician for future reference. After three or four days of excuses in a row, ask the student to obtain a note from his or her physician, or contact a parent to verify the nature of the illness.

When a student brings a note from a parent or doctor asking that he or she be excused from activity, always honor the excuse and provide some alternate way of meeting physical education objectives. Often students can be scorekeepers, statisticians, equipment managers, or teacher aides. Later, teachers can telephone parents if a problem other than health is suspected. When a long-term disability exists, students are often placed in a class for those requiring modified activity or excused from the class until unhampered participation is possible. Removing a student with extended disabilities from the activity setting helps prevent that student from being injured accidentally or from distracting students participating in class. If enough days are missed, students are not getting the full benefit of a physical education class and loss of credit should result. In either case, a physician should monitor all activity. No student should return to full participation until clearance is received from a physician.

Nonmedical Excuses

When students consistently fail to dress for activity, look for the cause behind this behavior. Hardy identified three underlying causes for failure to dress for activity. They are (1) physical, (2) moral or religious, and (3) defiance of authority.[5] Discussing the reason with the student privately in a nonthreatening manner may reveal the reason the student is not dressing and allow the teacher to arrange a suitable solution, thus avoiding a power struggle with the teenager and loss of face.

Physical excuses include stomachaches, headaches, and menstrual cramps. They may also include personal embarrassment caused by, for example, obesity or peer ridicule. These excuses can often be addressed by allowing these students to dress before or after the other students or in a private area, or by allowing them to wear a different uniform, such as longer pants or a long-sleeved shirt.

A second reason students fail to dress can be moral or religious. In *Mitchell v. McCall,* a student complained that the prescribed gym shorts for her physical education class

BOX 12.2

Temporary Physical Education Excuse Form

Date ________

________________ has the following limitations for participating in physical education class:

☐ No limitations, full participation.
☐ Participate but may discontinue if feels ill.
☐ Not to participate.

Reason: ____

Recommended by:

Physician's note ________ Parent's note ________ School Nurse ________

____
School Nurse

were immodest.[6] The court ruled that she was required to take the course but that she was not required to wear the uniform. The school allowed her to choose her own uniform. Teachers should be aware of and sensitive to students' ethnic and/or religious customs.

A third reason for failure to dress is defiance of authority. Although very little can be done with some students, others will respond positively to activities they have had a part in choosing and to a teacher whom they know cares. Support from school administrators will help teachers when faced with these dilemmas. Teachers are encouraged to meet with building administrators and explain their policies and the rationales behind them prior to these confrontations.

Hardy suggested some ways to encourage students to dress for class, including (1) making classes so exciting that students will look forward to participating in them, (2) setting an example of appropriate dress, (3) exhibiting a genuine desire to understand and help students resolve self-consciousness about their bodies or their performance skills, and (4) refusing to punish students who fail to dress for activity.[7]

Explain to students why dressing for activity is important. For students whose parents or guardians cannot afford to purchase uniforms, some schools have funds that can be used to help. This is an issue that you will want to discuss with your administrator as you plan for the school year. If students have forgotten their own uniforms or desire not to dress on a particular day, a system of "loaner" uniforms often solves the problem. Suits left by students at the end of the year or uniforms donated by a parents' group can be loaned to students. With this system students know that, without a medical excuse, not dressing is not an option. Loaned uniforms can be washed and returned by the students or washed with school towels or athletic uniforms.

Students with minor excuses can be encouraged to dress and do what they can. Do not allow students who are not dressed to participate in activities or to sit on the sidelines, where they are often an attractive nuisance. Send students who are ill, idle, or disturbing to an appropriate place such as the nurse's or counselor's office. In some schools, teachers do not have the option of sending students to areas supervised by others. Students who remain should be actively engaged in the class in some way. Completing a written report or answering questions on articles related to sport or physical fitness might be done during class time to encourage learning and avoid noninvolvement. Students who fail to participate in physical education should not be rewarded by being allowed to socialize with others.

Dressing for activity is a management issue and should not be used as the chief tool of evaluation. If students fail to dress, they will usually fail to do well on written, fitness, and skills tests and in other evaluative measures. There is really no need to use dressing as a part of the evaluation system. Pease increased the percentage of students dressing for activity by rewarding students with weight training and aerobics when the percentages of students dressed reached specific goals.[8]

Locker-Room Policies

Owners of athletic clubs and fitness facilities have found that locker rooms can attract members or drive them away. Likewise, schools should make efforts to have attractive facilities that are well lighted, have adequate mirrors and electrical outlets, and are free from disagreeable odors. Clearly define locker-room policies to students at the beginning of each term, including (1) traffic patterns to ensure safety; (2) use of lockers (usually long lockers to secure clothing and books during class and small lockers to secure gym clothing at other times); (3) lost and found for locks, uniforms, clothing, and other items; (4) procedures for showering; and (5) guideline policies for locker clean-out, laundering of uniforms, responsibility to keep lockers locked, and protecting valuables. In some situations, teachers will wish to have students assist in making these policies.

Check the locker room regularly for clothing and towels left out and locks left open. One teacher or a paraprofessional aide can be assigned to supervise the locker room each period. Do not give student leaders the responsibility of supervising students in the locker room. Locker rooms should be locked when not supervised.

A number of potential liability factors exist in locker rooms where students are confined in a small space among lockers, benches, trash cans, and laundry carts. In addition, floors are often wet. Students must be supervised properly to prevent horseplay and injuries. According to Hart, proper supervision involves establishing clear rules, posting signs outlining behavioral expectations, providing written and verbal warnings of all risks, enforcing rules, locking locker rooms during class time, moving students as a group from locker room to gym and gym to locker room, providing adequate time for dressing, and quieting down students before dismissing them to shower or change. Keep locker rooms clean and orderly. When students are in the locker room, teachers must actively supervise them and be on the alert for any potential problems. Teachers who view this as nonduty time, when they can run errands or make personal phone calls, are neglecting their obligation to supervise students and thus ensure their safety. When two teachers of the opposite gender are not available to supervise both locker rooms, administrators should provide a staff member to help. Student aides can also help alert teachers to problems.[9]

Locks and Lockers

Since considerable time is spent each year managing dressing facilities, sound policies should be made to reduce management time so that instructional time can be maximized.

Locks Locks can be built into metal lockers or combination locks can be used. Although built-in locks reduce the problem of distribution, collection, and loss of locks, they can often be opened with a knife. Because they are built in, they cannot be transferred to the large locker to secure valuables during class time. They are also difficult to repair.

Box 12.3

A Master Locker List and Example of Physical Education Lockers

1A Kristi Anderson 12-6-22	1	2A Sheila Ballard 1-10-39	3A Sue Boucher 7-22-14	3	4A Lida Crowder 30-15-9	5A Shauna Foster 5-7-25	5	6A Gloria Jensen 22-38-7
1B Nancy Alexander 7-38-12		2B Sandy Andres 21-18-12	3B Dana Bergstrom 31-18-9		4B Chris Bindrup 11-36-3	5B Audree Dixon 8-26-17		6B Georgina Edwards 38-17-6
1C Karin Cardon 8-13-29		2C Barbara Durrant 16-24-6	3C Kristin Goodwin 28-2-37		4C Sharane Hepworth 3-18-9	5C Terrie Jarvis 32-11-6		6C Cindy Jemmett 17-3-26
1D Renee Baker 7-17-24	2	2D Debbie Bemis 6-4-29	3D Janis Brock 3-12-16	4	4D Kay Brown 3-22-6	5D Laura Cameron 35-9-27	6	6D Paula Campbell 20-4-33
1E Carole Brisbin 20-13-7		2E Cheri Clark 18-20-36	3E Janiece Dee 7-19-34		4E Donna Dupaix 14-33-12	5E Kelly Fredericks 2-8-16		6E Jennifer Kee 8-29-16
1F Elsie Bishop 8-23-9		2F Rosa De la Cruz 13-36-27	3F Debra Evans 29-18-26		4F Shelley Huber 18-23-9	5F Maria Vasquez 14-38-2		6F Alana Walker 3-36-15

Locks are available with combinations that can be changed from year to year to prevent theft. Combination locks are preferred over key locks because students tend to lose keys while participating in activities.

The school or the student can provide the locks. When locks are provided by the school, a lock deposit is often required to ensure that the locks are returned in good condition. Locks issued by the school allow easy access by the teacher in case of emergency because a master key is usually provided to the teacher. When students purchase locks, teacher access is more difficult unless locks are purchased that have a master keyhole built in for emergency use.

An accurate record of lock ownership, identification number, combination, and student locker number is vital for any physical education department. Locks get lost and students forget combinations. There must be a reliable file (discussed in the next section) to provide necessary information to return lost locks, restate combinations, and locate lockers. A small piece of masking tape placed on the bottom (not back—avoid covering the lock's serial numbers) with the student's name and locker number on it can help prevent the student from picking up the wrong lock when it is lying adjacent to another lock on a locker room changing bench. This also eases identification of the owner when the lock is found off the locker at the conclusion of class.

Lockers Two types of lockers are generally used for securing students' clothing possessions. The first is the wire basket, which is the least expensive and has the advantage of good air circulation for drying clothes. However, it has the disadvantage of being too small to include all of the students' possessions such as coats, boots, and books. Also, small items can be removed between the wires.

Metal lockers are often supplied in banks of six small lockers to one large locker to solve the storage problem, as shown in Box 12.3. Gym uniforms can be stored in the small lockers and street clothing can be placed in the long lockers during class time. Locating them together in this manner minimizes traffic in the locker room.

Assigning Locks and Lockers It is advisable to assign lockers to students in horizontal rows by class period. This spreads students throughout the locker room each period and prevents overcrowding with its resulting

BOX 12.4

Locker Card

Name ______________________________ Locker # ______________
(Last) (First) (Middle Initial)

Teacher ______________________________ Period ______________

Lock # ______________________________ Combination ______________

BOX 12.5

Locker Master List

Teacher ______________________________ Period ______________

Name	Locker #	Lock #	Combination

safety hazards. It also facilitates dressing quickly. If the lowest rows are assigned to the lower grades and the higher rows to the higher grades, differences in height can be easily accommodated.

A master list of lockers can be kept, showing each bank of lockers, with students' names and combinations written in pencil. Using pencil makes erasing easy when students move out.

A locker card (see Box 12.4) or master list (see Box 12.5) can be used to record the student's name, locker number, combination, and padlock number. This information should then be entered into a computer database program that is organized so a record can be found by entering any of the information provided above. A master lock book can be acquired from the manufacturer. This lists the lock serial numbers and their combinations. This information should also be entered into a computer database for easy access. Box 12.6 describes a lock distribution procedure used for many years by a veteran teacher.

Lost locks can be locked onto a towel bar placed in or near the teacher's office or on the wire screen of an issue room cage. Some teachers charge students a small fee of five to twenty-five cents for retrieving their locks or telling them their combinations. The money collected can go into a fund for purchasing loaner suits, buying equipment of student choice, or adding to funds for field trips. Give students a voice in how such monies are used.

Towels

Three decisions must be made with regard to towels. They are (1) the method of acquisition of towels, (2) the laundering of towels, and (3) the distribution and collection of towels.

Acquisition of Towels Towels can be purchased by the school or district, or leased from a towel service, or students can be asked to bring one or two towels each year for the school supply.

Laundering of Towels Towels purchased by the school are often laundered at a school or district facility. This requires purchasing laundry equipment and hiring someone to launder towels. Leased or purchased towels may be laundered by the towel service. This requires a bid by local laundries for pickup, laundry, and delivery. Students are often charged a towel fee for this service. Fees for indigent students are often paid by welfare or other community services or absorbed by the school.

In some cases, students are required to bring a towel each week and launder it at home. This generally results in mildew and odor problems as towels are left in lockers throughout the week. It also results in students missing

BOX 12.6

Tips from the Trenches: Lock Distribution

The following system used for lock distribution is informal yet effective.

1. Using the master list of locks, write the combinations of the locks on a piece of masking tape on the bottom of the lock and put the locks in a sturdy box.
2. Give every student a 3 × 5 card and have them record their name, class period, and locker number. Lockers can be assigned or allow students to go into the locker room and select a locker. If they select their own locker, make sure they spread themselves throughout the locker room to avoid crowding. Also encourage taller students to select the top lockers.
3. Once students have their locker number, they select a lock from the box and try the combination written on the lock to make sure it works.
4. After they are sure that the combination opens the lock, they should record the serial number of the lock and the combination on the card.
5. Cards are filed alphabetically by class period.
6. Students remove the combination from the bottom of the lock, record it in a secure place (student planner), and memorize the combination. Have them open the lock several times to make sure they have memorized it.
7. Give students a piece of masking tape and write with nonerasable pen their name and locker number. Put the tape on the bottom (not the back) of the lock.
8. At the end of the semester or school year, students remove the tape with their name and locker number and get a new piece of tape. On that piece of tape, they write their lock combination.
9. When handing in the lock (if done alphabetically this is much faster), the teacher checks the locker card to verify the correct combination and that the student is turning in the correct lock.
10. The next time the lock is issued to a new student, the combination is already on the lock so step 1 above is eliminated.

showers because of failure to bring a towel. Some districts, however, prohibit charging towel fees to students, and therefore a system such as this one must be used, or the cost must be absorbed into the regular budget.

Distribution and Collection of Towels
Towels can be distributed to students by their roll call numbers and checked in after showers as in this example:

Distributed 1 /2 3 /4 5 Collected 1 ×2 3 ×4 5
6 7 8 9 10 / / 6 7 8 9 10/ ×

Note that towels were distributed to numbers 2, 4, 7, and 10, but that number 7's towel has not yet been returned. This system helps to keep stray towels off the locker-room floor. Other more informal procedures are often used. For example, a towel is issued to each student at the beginning of the school year. Each time the student showers, he or she exchanges a dirty towel for a clean one.

Showers
Required showers have often resulted in negative attitudes toward physical education. This is because some teachers require showers unnecessarily and do not consider the students' feelings when developing policies for showers. Showers should not be used as a factor for determining grades. Teach students the health-related concepts about exercise and showering and help them understand when a shower should be taken and when one is not necessary. Never require showers when students have been relatively inactive during the period, such as in archery or golf.

When showering is necessary, make certain students have enough time to do it right. The amount of time will depend on the number of students in the locker room and the number of showers available, but ten to fifteen minutes is usually adequate. More time is needed for drying hair after swimming. Since students can be very self-conscious, efforts should be made to have private showers available for all students.

Emphasize safety and instruct students to dry off in a specified area to prevent them from slipping on water near the lockers. Prohibit the use of glass bottles in the locker room.

Review Question: Explain usual department guidelines for (a) uniforms, (b) excuses from activity, (c) locker-room policies, (d) locks and lockers, (e) towels, and (f) showers.

RESOURCE MANAGEMENT IN PHYSICAL EDUCATION

Effective management of resources sets the stage for high-quality instruction in physical education. This is partly due to the variety of activities provided, often in different facilities and with different equipment, and partly due to the larger numbers of students in physical education classes. The need for safety is an essential consideration in most of these activities.

Managing the Teaching Environment

Prior to teaching each day, inspect facilities and equipment for safety, proper lighting, adequate towels, and comfortable room temperature. Nets can be set up, baskets raised or lowered, apparatus arranged, and special markings put in place by paraprofessional or student aides before class begins or by students who come in before school or prior to class time. Avoid using instructional time to accomplish these tasks unless it is absolutely necessary.

A wise teacher will always check the equipment prior to starting a new unit or activity and make sure each day that enough equipment is available and that balls are pumped up, arrows repaired, pinnies washed, and other essentials attended to. Adequate teaching stations should be available for all instructors. If a specialized area is needed to show a film, administer a test, or present a guest speaker, make arrangements well before the activity. A plan of operations for inclement weather should be part of departmental procedures. Teachers can then make last-minute adjustments and present an uninterrupted teaching program. All teachers in a department should share these decisions so they feel they have a fair share of department facilities.

Storage facilities for loose equipment should include movable bins or racks. Plastic trash cans with wheels can be used for this purpose. Ball racks or bags that can be moved to and from the gymnasium allow for ease of distribution.

Managing Time

Since time is a limited resource in physical education, it is essential that class time be carefully planned to provide the maximum instructional benefit. Management time contains little, if any, instruction and learning. Additionally, it is the time when discipline problems with students are most likely to occur. As much as teachers try to avoid having management time, it is almost impossible to completely eliminate it from a class. Different coding systems use different terms for this noninstructional time. Management time with the ALT-PE (Academic Learning Time—Physical Education) coding system occurs when class begins (e.g., students changing clothing, roll call, announcements, housekeeping tasks), when class ends (putting away equipment, lining up for dismissal), when students are disciplined, when fire drills happen during class time, and so on. Another type of noninstructional time called transition occurs after class activity has begun when students move from one drill to another between instructional tasks, receive directions about the logistics of a new drill or activity (different from cognitive information), retrieve errant equipment, or relocate from one area to the next. Waiting is another type of noninstructional time. This occurs when teachers have inadequate equipment or when students must wait for a turn when elimination drills or relays are used for practice tasks. Some coding systems combine all of these noninstructional episodes under the umbrella term of management. How they are coded is immaterial. The key here is that teachers who manage time effectively work very hard to eliminate these episodes from their lessons.

Luke summarized the research on classroom management in physical education.[10] Studies of academic learning time in physical education using ALT-PE and other behavior analysis systems reveal that students spend 15 to 22 percent of class time in management activities. Waiting can be decreased through selecting appropriate activities when planning a lesson. Management and transition time can also be significantly reduced through the use of routines. Routines are class procedures that students do automatically without prompting or supervision.[11] When events occur on a frequent basis before, during, or after class, teachers should develop routines for students to follow. When teachers have established routines, classes are more orderly because students know what is expected of them and can proceed with minimal, if any, teacher talk. Routines allow the instructional flow of a class to have less interruptions, which leads to more time available for learning. Oslin identified several routines important in physical education. Routines for the locker room have been discussed previously and will be omitted from this section. Other routines important for teachers to establish include (1) distributing and collecting equipment, (2) starting class, (3) taking attendance, (4) leading warm-up and/or fitness activities, (5) getting student attention, (6) giving directions, (7) finishing an activity or class, and (8) teaching and utilizing class formations.[12]

Handling Equipment and Written Assignments

There are several routines teachers can implement for dealing with equipment. Some teachers lose considerable instructional time while distributing and collecting equipment for student use. Routines for handling equipment during teacher talk can also save time. Handling papers in physical education can also be time consuming if teachers have not established routines for their classes. The following are offered as suggestions about how to address each of these concerns.

Distributing and Collecting Equipment

A number of techniques can be used for distributing and collecting equipment. When choosing an equipment distribution and collection technique, always consider the relationship of the technique to the safety of the students and to effective learning. Timing is also another factor to consider when distributing equipment. Immature students have a tendency to "play" with equipment during teacher explanations. Novel equipment can also present problems as students want to examine it or "test it out." If the teacher feels that the equipment will be a distraction, he or she should wait until after giving directions to hand out equipment.

If equipment is not assigned to individual students, be sure to count the number of pieces you have before you start the class and make sure you have the same number when you finish. If students know that you don't keep track of the amount of equipment, they might not make as much effort to retrieve balls when they leave the immediate playing area.

The Teacher

The teacher or an aide distributes and collects equipment as students enter and leave the gymnasium or playing area. Students can sign the roll as they pick up equipment. The system should not tie up a teacher who could be helping students with other needs. Having formal class closure as part of the daily routine can provide an opportunity to collect and properly store equipment.[13]

Squad Leaders

Squad leaders acquire the equipment needed for their individual squads and return it at the end of the practice period. If using a sport education instructional model, teams may designate an equipment manager for handling equipment.

Numbers

Students are assigned equipment numbers that correspond to their roll call numbers. Student 1 picks up bow 1, arrows 1, and armguard 1. Equipment may be numbered in such a way that it would not correspond to a roll call number. In this case, the number of the assigned equipment is recorded by the roll call number. The person distributing equipment checks the roll call number of the person receiving equipment each day. Equipment can be picked up in the locker room, as students enter the gymnasium, or as they complete warm-up and fitness activities. One advantage to this technique is that students feel more responsible for returning the equipment in good condition each day. A second advantage is that students can become accustomed to a particular racket, bow, or glove.

Equipment Spots

Teachers might place equipment at various places around the gym or activity area so that students can readily access the equipment when needed. These could be placed on poly spots or in hula hoops on the perimeter of the area. If a lesson involves several different types of equipment, a "set" can be placed at each spot so that students can change pieces of equipment quickly. If using an inclusion teaching style, students would have the opportunity to select the piece of equipment most appropriate for their ability. As skill improves, students might want to change equipment to make the task more challenging. Additionally, if some drills do not require activity, teachers could have students place the equipment out of the way so that it does not interfere with student practice and learning.

Grab Bag

Students can be asked to get a piece of equipment and return to their space. This often results in students converging on a given box of equipment and grabbing out the best they can find. Chaos and loss of instructional time usually result and the less aggressive students may feel cheated by getting the worst equipment. This can be avoided by sending one squad or student at a time (changing squad order each day) and by ensuring that all equipment is in good condition. When sending a few students at a time, it is best to have students pick up or return equipment as they enter the gym or as they complete an activity in which students finish at different times, such as after jogging or completing self-check activities.

Equipment Routine during Class Instruction

Teachers should establish routines for using equipment during class. Many times this is dependent on the instructional activity and the equipment being used. For instance, when teaching basketball, having balls bounce during instructions can be a distraction to the teacher. The potential noise can also cause some students to not hear what the teacher is saying. Students who are bouncing the ball might be tuning out the teacher rather than listening. When the student loses control of the ball, he or she will frequently retrieve it, causing additional distractions to other students. To eliminate these problems, some teachers will have students "hug" the ball when receiving instruction. Others might require students to place the ball on the ground, away from their feet. Another technique might be to have students place the ball between the feet and stand at attention. Each procedure for "holding the ball" has advantages and disadvantages. The important point here is that teachers should establish a routine for handling equipment while they are giving instruction.

Handing in Assignments

Assignments can be collected very efficiently by placing a basket or box for each class in a convenient location, where students can place their assignments as they enter or leave the gymnasium. If teachers are giving handouts for an activity, unless the students will use them during class they should be given as students are dismissed to go to the locker room to change clothes or after students have changed clothes and are leaving physical education for their next class. If a student is absent, put his or her name on a handout and place it in a folder designated for the student's class period. Handouts for students who have been absent can be placed in a different colored or labeled box.

Starting Class

Students often waste a good deal of time between their arrival in the gymnasium and roll call or instruction. If this is the case, students who come in last are rewarded by not having to sit around doing nothing. When students are allowed to begin activity the minute they enter the area, they begin to dress faster and come to class earlier.

Teachers should always be close by to supervise student safety and equipment loss or damage. Teachers in larger departments can take turns supervising the locker room and the gymnasium, or a teacher aide can be used to supervise one of the two areas. At a given time or signal, students can report to roll call or to a posted or preannounced area for instruction or practice.

Taking Attendance

A fast, effective attendance system gets things started on the right track. Teachers should spend one or two minutes at the most taking attendance. When too much time is taken for roll call, students become bored and discipline problems can arise.

A number of different attendance techniques can be used depending on the class size, maturity of students, and the learning situation. The major criteria for selection of a technique are time and accuracy. Since most schools receive some funding based on the average daily attendance (ADA) of students, schools insist on accuracy in attendance taking. Five general techniques are commonly used. They include (1) numbers or spots, (2) squads, (3) student check-in, (4) silent roll, and (5) oral roll call.

Numbers or Spots

Each student is assigned a number or a spot. Students sit or stand in a specific spot, either in a line or in squad order (see Box 12.7). When numbers are painted on the floor, on a bench or bleacher, or on the wall, a blank number indicates an absent student. When no numbers are available, students can be asked to call out the numbers in sequence. Although this method is rather impersonal, it is very fast. Having students call their numbers and last names, as in "1-Allen," "2-Bacon," "3-Barr," can help teachers learn names.

Squads

Each student is assigned to a squad, and a leader is chosen for each squad. Each day the squad leader records the attendance of the squad members on a squad card. This could be done while students are participating in warm-ups or another squad activity.

Student Check-In

In this technique, students check in as they enter the gymnasium by signing their name and time of entry, by checking in with the teacher, by handing in an assignment, or by removing their name tags from a board or box and placing them in a specified location or wearing them. When name tags are used, the tags not picked up indicate absent students.

Silent Roll

In this technique, the teacher or teacher's aide takes roll silently while students are participating in activity. This permits students to remain active.

Oral Roll Call

In this technique, the teacher calls out the students' names and listens for a response. This technique is effective only when used with very small classes or to get acquainted with students during the first few days of instruction before rolls have been finalized. Another use is as an accuracy check by calling out only the names of those students who have been marked absent by one of the other methods.

BOX 12.7

Tips from the Trenches: Squads for Taking Attendance

Teachers can use squads for taking attendance. Students have a designated spot on the gymnasium floor. The teacher has a "seating" chart that has each student's name in a box on his or her clipboard. While the students are doing some preliminary stretches or stationary activities (these could be posted on a board or sheet of paper as students enter the activity area; a routine has been established so that students know what they are expected to do at the start of class) the teacher is taking attendance. Student absences are noted on the chart (S-14 means the student was absent on September 14th; circling the date the next day indicates that a student was excused; late students are noted by placing a T after the date) as are violations of the uniform requirement (S-14 ND means that the student didn't dress on September 14th; S-14 NS means that the student didn't have proper shoes/footwear for the day). At the end of the grading period, a summary of attendance is transferred to a grade book or a grading program on the computer.

The teacher keeps this clipboard handy at all times. If students exhibit good play or poor sportspersonship, these incidents can be noted on separate blank sheets or note cards. When anecdotal notes are made, these are removed and kept in a file in the teacher's office. The clipboard is much easier to carry around than a grade book and if lost, you have only lost an attendance record which can be retrieved in the school office.

Taking attendance with this method requires minimal time (often less than thirty seconds once you get to know your students) while students are engaged in an activity. It can be an effective way to learn student names at the beginning of the year as well.

Helpful hint: If you take the clipboard out doors, put a clear transparency sheet on top of your pages in case it starts to rain or the sprinklers come on without notice!

Leading Warm-Up and/or Fitness Activities

Using a variety of warm-up techniques and fitness activities will increase student motivation (see Box 12.8). Some ideas include the following:

1. Students exercise to popular music, using prechoreographed routines or "follow the leader." Music can be taped, with cues on the tapes, to free the teacher to provide individual assistance.
2. Squad leaders direct warm-up activities for their squads. Squad leaders change regularly so many students are afforded this opportunity.
3. Students warm up on their own.
4. Students rotate through a number of fitness stations.
5. Selected student leaders direct warm-up activities for the entire class.
6. Students alternate jogging and weight training at specified time intervals (e.g., every two minutes).
7. Students run three days a week and weight-train two days.
8. Students run daily with a timed run once a week.
9. Students participate in an obstacle course.
10. Students participate in relays or games to emphasize certain fitness activities.
11. Activities related to the unit are designed to provide warm-up and skill practice.

Warm-up activities can also be planned using skills from the unit. Innumerable other techniques can be invented by the creative teacher for warm-up and fitness activities (see also Chapter 10).

Warm-up techniques using game skills increase student motivation.

BOX 12.8

Tips from the Trenches

REGRESSION WARM-UP

Here is a variation for warm-ups that students enjoy.

The physical education teacher selects several activities (six to eight) and lists these on a chart. These can be generic fitness activities (e.g., jumping jacks, crunches, push-ups, squat thrusts, rope skips) or more skill oriented (e.g., finger tip push-ups, lunges, jumps at the volleyball net). The teacher designates an area where these activities are to be done (e.g., half a basketball court, area marked with cones). For our example, the teacher sets the regression at seven and students run around the activity area seven times. After completing the running, students come to the activity area and do seven of each exercise listed. At the conclusion of the exercises, students run six laps around the designated area. After running, they come to the activity area and do six of each of the exercises. The pattern concludes with the final round being one lap and one of each of the exercises. The initial number that the teacher selects is based on time available. If there isn't much time, five might be a good starting point. Starting at seven was usually good for about a ten-minute warm-up. A variation of this would be to let students select the number they feel they can do with the time allotted. This is a fun activity to do about once a month. If you do generic fitness exercises for this warm-up, you may want to put them on poster board and then laminate it for several uses.

PROGRESSION WARM-UP

A warm-up progression is similar to the regression warm-up except that all students start with running one lap and one of each exercise and then see how far they can get in a certain amount of time. This provides a challenge to highly fit students as they can see which level they can reach. Some students may compete against each other.

Since students quickly learn the exercise routine, this warm-up requires very little time to explain after it is initially introduced.

The following tips for leading exercises will aid the student leader or teacher who is directing the class.

1. Give a preparatory command, such as "ready-now-."
2. Give a command to begin, such as "GO" or "BEGIN."
3. During the exercise, repeat the sequence or cadence aloud so the group stays together (forward, side, forward, down; or 1, 2, 3).
4. Provide a model. If the leader is facing the class, try to mirror the actions (e.g., move the left arm when the class is moving the right).
5. Provide encouragement.
6. Have a sense of humor—smile, display enthusiasm, relax.
7. Give a command to stop. With exercises done to a cadence, a preparation to stop is also helpful (e.g., "and, stop").

Stretching appropriate for the activities to follow should also be part of the warm-up routine. Once students have learned how to stretch properly, an effective teacher will use this time to accomplish other educational goals. Some ideas might be to describe the activities for the lesson, to explain simple organizational arrangements to follow immediately, and to check for understanding such as reviewing previously learned concepts.[14]

Getting Students' Attention and Giving Directions

Getting student attention quickly is one of the most important routines teachers must establish. The faster students will stop what they are doing, the more quickly the lesson will proceed. Teachers actually need two different routines. The first is for having students stop what they are doing and remain in their current space. The second is for having students gather around the teacher for new directions. To avoid confusion, the same signal should not be used for both routines. Here are some verbal and nonverbal signals that have been used effectively:

- Freeze
- Stop
- Teacher says "hey" students say "ho"
- Clapping pattern by teacher; students start clapping the pattern with the teacher
- Clapping pattern by teacher; students have their own clapping pattern response
- Clapping pattern that starts slow and steady and the cadence gradually increases
- Raising a hand above the head; students raise their hands in response and are quiet
- Whistle
- Horn
- Drum beat
- Counting to five
- Music stops
- Flicking the lights on and off (effective for activities like racquetball where students are widely dispersed)

Here are some hints to remember when gaining student attention:

1. If using a whistle, do so sparingly. Don't have several different signals that mean different things. Students tend to get confused. Using a whistle as an attention signal is difficult when you are also using it to officiate a game. You might have one type of whistle for officiating and a whistle that makes a different sound for gaining student attention. Blow the whistle with authority—when you use it, mean to use it!
2. Gaining student attention when out of doors is much more difficult than when inside. The wind can cause additional problems. If trying to gain attention, always be upwind from students so that they are more likely to hear you. A nonverbal signal (raised hand) may be most effective when wind is a factor. When taking students outdoors on an open field, designate the area that you want them in with cones.
3. If your school has a signal for getting student attention, use it. It usually is much easier to reinforce something that the rest of the school is already using. Be sure students understand what system will be used during class. If the whistle is used for getting attention, use it sparingly at other times so students do not tune out the sound.
4. Teachers of physical education should develop a "gym voice" if they expect to talk all day in large classes in open spaces. Get used to speaking with a push from the diaphragm to project the voice, as singers are taught to do. Try to keep the voice pitched low. Teachers with high-pitched voices especially need to avoid raising the pitch as they try to increase the volume. The result is a piercing sound that is hard to hear and very distracting. Teachers should drink lots of water to protect the voice from damage.
5. A teacher who speaks softly yet loudly enough to be heard encourages students to listen carefully when he or she talks and also leaves room for a future increase in volume for the purpose of gaining attention. In contrast, when teachers consistently shout at students with a loud voice, they tend to increase their noise to a level that prohibits the use of verbal signals. A general rule for the teacher is to gather the students around and talk so that the student farthest away can hear clearly. If possible, try to speak with a wall behind the listeners to trap the voice.
6. Teach students what behavior is expected when the attention signal is given. For example, students can be taught to sit or kneel where they are and wait for

instructions or to gather at an appointed place for directions. Once the students learn the signal and the expected response, teachers can encourage them to shorten their response time by praising students who respond quickly or by rewarding them with extra time for activity. Feedback can also be provided on the amount of time spent, such as "You were ready five seconds faster than yesterday."

Giving Directions

It requires time to gather students in, so some teachers attempt to give directions without calling students in from their activity station. If students can be redirected quickly or the instructional area is fairly small, this is permissible. If the directions are complex or students are spread over a wide space, pull them together. They can hear you better and it is much easier to keep students focused on what you are saying if they are closer. It is also easier to tell when students aren't paying attention.

If possible, develop a listening area. When the signal is given, students know to assemble in that area. Some teachers develop a "listening circle" in the center of the gym. If doing gymnastics, students might have an instructional mat. Try to locate this listening area in the center of activity so that all students have an equal distance to travel. Distractions or acoustics might impact what you designate as your listening area. Whether you call students together in a listening area or simply give instructions where they are, develop a routine for listening. Tell students whether they are to sit or stand, what to do with equipment, and how they are supposed to behave (e.g., hands on knees, in personal space, not talking with a friend, etc.). If students know what is expected of them, you will be able to positively reinforce those who are following instructions, thus encouraging others to follow suit.

Hints for giving directions:

1. If you have lots of students, it is easier to speak to students in a group (in a semicircle or randomly clustered around you) than to spread students out on a listening line.
2. If outdoors, teachers rather than students should face the sun. The sun makes it difficult to see what is going on and can impact student concentration.
3. If other classes or "attractions" are in the activity area, have students face toward you with their backs toward the possible distractions. If outside, it is better to have students face the sun with their back to the distraction.
4. It is easier to be heard if you are facing a wall so that your voice is reflected back to students.
5. If possible, have students sit so they can see you when giving directions. Students who are sitting are less likely to "drift" over to a friend and cause a distraction. Also, it is easier to see when students are misbehaving when they are sitting and you are standing. This is not always possible or practical if outdoors or with some units.
6. Directions do not always need to be oral. Posters and demonstrations can greatly reduce the confusion. Remember: A picture is worth a thousand words.
7. Give complete instructions so that students know exactly what you expect. When giving directions think of the three parts to an instructional objective (situation, performance, criteria). If your instructions contain explicit information about all three components, students will know exactly what you expect and how well they should be doing it.
8. Avoid automatically repeating instructions. Students will learn that they don't need to listen during the initial explanation.
9. At the conclusion of your instructions, don't ask, "Are there any questions?" Ask specific questions about various procedures for the task and check randomly (not from those who have their hands raised) for understanding. Be sure to question a variety of students, especially those sitting on the sides of the group as they are the ones who are most likely not to have heard or who may have "drifted off" during your instructions.

If you have lots of student questions, you probably were not very clear with your explanation. In those situations, don't simply repeat what you have already said; try to rephrase things. A series of probing questions that go through your instructions on a step-by-step basis might reveal where the students are confused. Another indicator that instructions have not been clear is when students stand around and don't know what to do. If that happens, bring them back together to clarify what they are supposed to do.

La Mancusa listed some pitfalls in giving directions.[15] They are (1) using words that students do not understand; (2) saying the same thing over and over, instead of using a few brief statements, in hopes the students will "catch on"; (3) using extraneous words like "well" and "okay"; and (4) failing to wait until everyone is listening before talking. She stated:

> It is the wise teacher who will *not speak* until *everyone* is listening. If it means that the teacher will be forced to stop what he is saying and wait, then by all means WAIT. If it means that the teacher will have to stop a second time, or a third time, then stop and WAIT. Silent teacher disapproval and exasperated peer disapproval is too strong a factor to override. Soon enough the offenders will understand that when *their* teacher talks, *everyone listens* because *their* teacher *means it* when he says, "I will not repeat this a second time."
>
> There is nothing more to it than that. If a teacher allows himself to overlook rudeness, he will receive rudeness in return. Children will respond either to the *highest* or to the *lowest* of teacher-expectations.[16]

The key to avoiding these pitfalls is proper planning before speaking and careful evaluation of your own ability to give directions. One of the best methods for evaluating your effectiveness in giving directions is to record a class session on a tape recorder. When it is played back, ask "Would I like to be a student in my own classroom?"

Finishing an Activity or Class

Class closure is another important routine for teachers as it provides an opportunity to "bring it all together," finish class on a positive note, and have an orderly dismissal. It can provide an opportunity for the teacher to determine whether the day's objectives were met or to stretch during a cool-down. Teachers might use this time for writing in journals. Some teachers do not allot adequate time for closure either because of poor planning or because some part of the lesson required more time than initially anticipated. Include a culminating activity that capitalizes on enthusiasm and interest or reviews points taught in the lesson. This is a time when students are given an opportunity to ask questions, and it also provides the teacher with an opportunity to correct skills or reiterate important information.[17] Some ideas for summarizing a lesson include these:

1. Summarize the main ideas of the lesson with a short statement and explain what the students will be expected to realize as an outcome.
2. Ask the students questions in which responses summarize the lesson.
3. Assign one or two students to listen carefully and tell the class afterward what the lesson was about.
4. Use a worksheet to help students summarize the main ideas of the lesson.
5. Have several students in turn tell one thing learned from the lesson.
6. Present a real-life situation that could be resolved by using lesson ideas.

A teacher desiring to use activities that require more time might incorporate the following:

1. Give an oral or written quiz.
2. Use instructional games to test the information taught.
3. Have students write or tell in their own words what they think the main idea is.
4. Divide the class into small groups. Each group in turn acts out a part of the lesson while the other groups try to guess what is being depicted (charades).

Noteworthy performance and effort and team or individual winners could be recognized at this time. The stage is now set for an orderly dismissal. The teacher might request that students get ready to leave in a certain fashion. For example, "The team sitting quietly in squad order will be the first to leave."

Teaching and Utilizing Class Formations

Having students move quickly into formations for instruction is another routine that can help eliminate noninstructional time. Slow transitions destroy the pace of a lesson. Think about the time saved if a teacher can get students into the next drill in less than thirty seconds rather than spending four to five minutes doing so. Slow transitions can be frustrating to both teachers and students. Remember that the needs of the instructional situation determine the choice of a formation. For example, in the command style of teaching (see Chapter 9), formal formations are used. As instruction moves toward the less teacher-dominated styles, teachers are more apt to ask students to move out, find a partner, or find a space on the floor. A number of formations follow.

Circles and Semicircles

Circles can be formed by asking students to form a circle on a painted line on the playing surface, such as a free throw circle, and then taking three giant steps backward. In folk dancing, students can be asked to join hands to form a circle. (Avoid holding hands in other activities. It usually leads to giggling and tugging.) Circles can be used for practice drills or lead-up games and for relays. Stay on the edge of the circle when giving directions so no students are behind you. Care should be taken when circles are used for practice drills. A lack of practice time may result from improper use of circles. Also, a circle organizational pattern often does not match most game situations.[18]

The semicircle can be formed by asking students to gather around the teacher. It is often used for giving directions to small classes or for demonstrating to a group of students.

Lines and Columns

Lines are formed by asking students to line up facing the net or wall on a particular line on the floor, or between several cones or chalk marks. Lines are often used for roll call formations and for some lead-up games, such as line soccer. When teaching dances in lines, be sure to "roll the lines," rotating them so that different students have the opportunity to be in the front line. To do this, after two to three minutes of instruction, or during natural breaks between tasks, have all the students in the front line move to the sides of the room and reassemble the line in the back making line 2 the front row. All the lines behind line 2 move up, making it easier for them to see the teacher and for the teacher to see them. Teachers should watch for students who continually hide in the back line as they are probably experiencing difficulty and are too embarrassed to ask for help.

Columns are formed by selecting four to eight students as leaders and having other students line up behind one of the leaders in designated areas of the floor. Cones or other pieces of equipment can be used instead of leaders. Columns are used to create relay teams or squads.

Extended Formation

The extended formation is formed from a line. For example, students number off in fours. The ones stay where

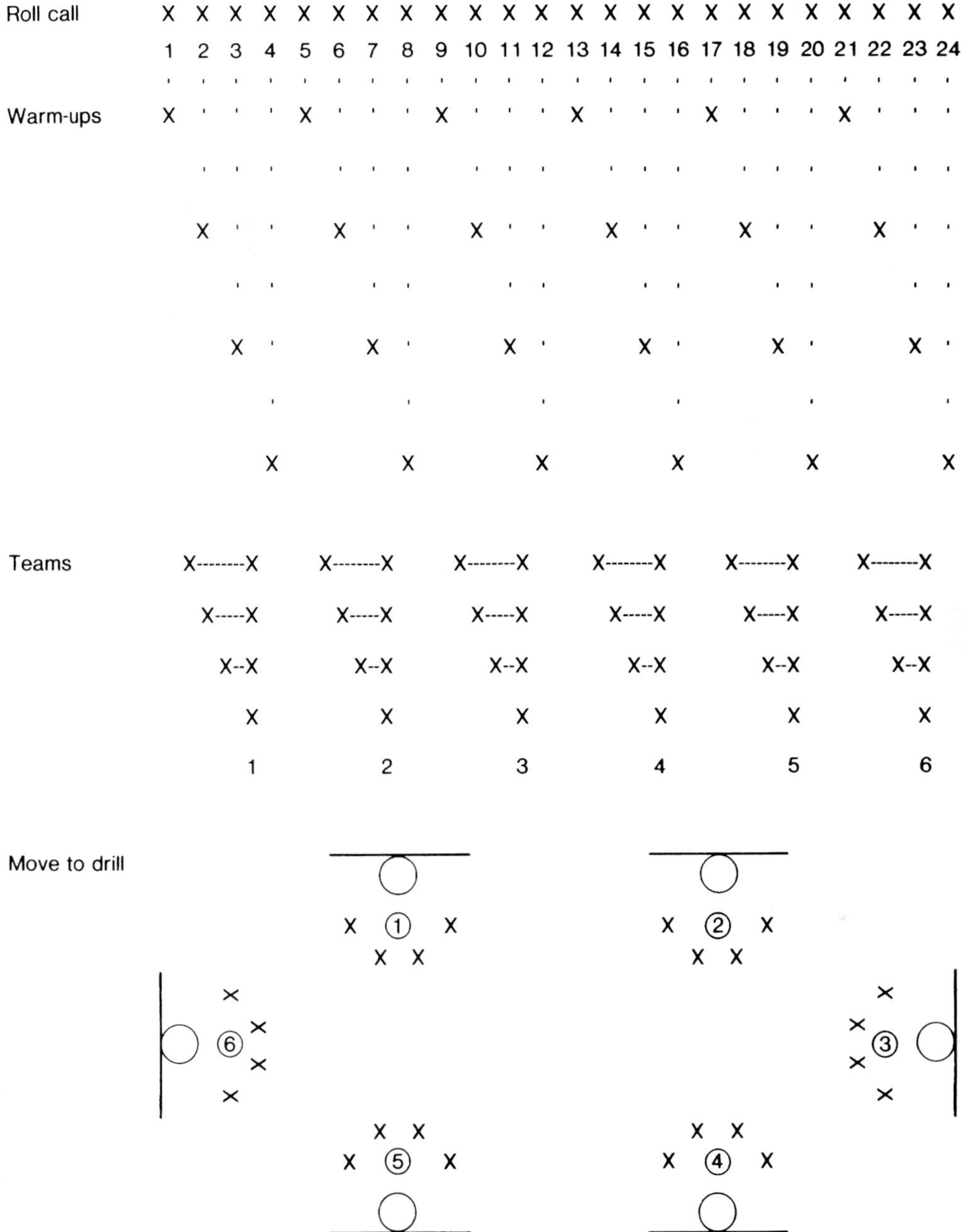

Figure 12-1
A class transition map.

they are. The twos move forward five steps, threes move ten steps, and fours move fifteen steps. The extended formation is often used for warm-up and fitness activities, for demonstrations that students cannot see when grouped close together, and for mimetic drills (pantomime). Examples of this formation are shown in Figure 12-1.

A variation of the extended formation is "waves," in which all the ones move (e.g., swim across the pool), then the twos, and so on. This technique permits the teacher to observe and give feedback to a small group of students at one time.

Partners or Small Groups

Partners and groups can be assigned, or students can be asked to simply find a partner or get in groups of three or four. Ask students to raise their hands if they need a partner or to sit down with their partner as soon as one is found. When there is an extra person, be specific on how that person is to be included. Partners and small groups are often used for warm-up and fitness activities and for practice drills or peer tutoring.

Whatever formations are used, teach students how to assume them quickly on a brief, consistent signal. Always tell students exactly where they are to be, such as on the red line; what formation they are to assume; and the direction they are to face. Painted lines and circles can be used when they are available. If there are none, chalk marks, traffic cones, or masking tape can be substituted (see Box 12.9).

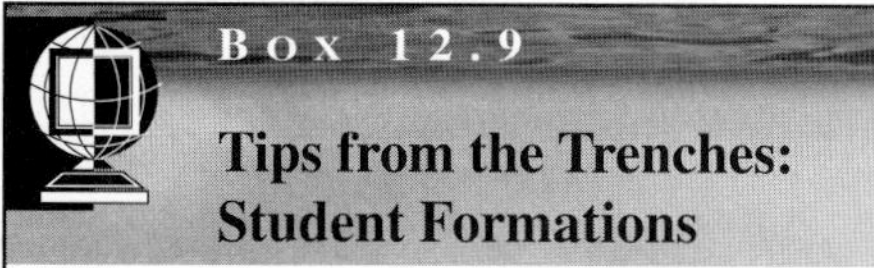

Tips from the Trenches: Student Formations

One teacher got students to move quickly into various formations by giving the formations funny names. When she wanted students to form a circle, she said, "Make an orange." If she wanted students to gather around her randomly, she had them make "grapes." which meant they were supposed to be in a cluster. When students were to be in a line, shoulder-to-shoulder, they became "celery sticks" of four or however many students she wanted in the group. "Carrots," on the other hand, meant that students were supposed to make lines but face the back of the person of the person ahead of them. Although these were used in a secondary school, some teachers might think that the words are too juvenile. That being the case, teachers might develop a different set of words for these various formations or let students develop their own. Having words that symbolize configurations frequently used in physical education can greatly reduce the time required to move from one task to the next.

Keep transitions between formations to a minimum. Transitions such as from a line to a circle to a line can be avoided by thinking through how students will get from one formation to another. Changing from groups of twos to threes can be particularly difficult and must be carefully planned if necessary to effective teaching progressions. *X's* and *O's* might be used to plot out formations and to help visualize the movement of the class from formation to formation. An example of an effective class transition is shown in Figure 12-1.

Teach students self-management skills and provide practice in using them, just as other skills are practiced. Don't try to teach every routine on the first two days of school. Introduce and teach them as the need arises. On the first day of class, teach procedures for assembly, dismissal, roll call, excuses, tardies, collecting and distributing equipment, organizing teams, and getting into formations. Tell students why each of these procedures is used. During instruction, whenever a difficulty occurs with one of the management skills, such as students getting into the proper formation, stop and review the skill or procedure before proceeding. If resistance to any policy remains, examine student feelings to determine whether modification or discontinuance would solve the problem. This attention to the problem will save instructional time in the long run and will reduce the incidence of serious discipline problems.

The true test of a successful management technique is whether the objectives of the lesson or unit in question have been realized. Whenever objectives are not being accomplished, select a new plan of action.

Using the Restroom

Having a routine for using the restroom during class can also help class management by avoiding teacher interruptions. The teaching facility (e.g., whether restrooms are available in the teaching area, only in the locker room, or outside) has a huge impact on the restroom routine, as does the level of teacher trust for the students. Some teachers prefer to know where students are at all times so they want students to ask permission before leaving for the restroom. If locker rooms are locked between classes and these are where the facilities are located, students will need a key to open the door. If theft is an issue, teachers may be unwilling to send students into the locker room without an escort.

A good restroom policy limits use to one male or one female at a time, unless there is an emergency. Some teachers have a wooden restroom pass (or one for males and one for females) hanging in the activity area. When a student needs to use the restroom, he or she simply removes the paddle and leaves class. Another student is not allowed to leave until the paddle has returned. When the routine is explained at the beginning of the semester, teachers tell students to be respectful of others and stay only as long as necessary. If a key is needed to open the locker room, it can be attached to the paddle. Another way to minimize teacher disruption is to use student aides of the same gender to escort students to the restroom.

Getting Water

A routine for getting drinks can eliminate some teacher aggravation as well. As for the restroom, the rule of thumb should be not more than one person at the drinking fountain at a time. If the drinking fountain is located away from the activity area (e.g., in the hall), a water break pass, similar to the restroom pass described above would help ensure that several people were not trying to get a drink at the same time. Bottled water carried to an activity area could eliminate the wait time that occurs when one person gets thirsty and several others decide to line up after him or her. Water bottles also help in areas where no drinking fountains are available. If a teacher allows students to bring water bottles, be sure they are not breakable and that they are marked with the student's name. If bottles brought to class are disposable, have trash receptacles available so that students can pick up after themselves.

Routines for Emergencies

Preplanning for emergencies is essential so that when they occur the teacher can act in the most efficient manner. For example, formulate plans for action when the fire alarm sounds and students are in the shower or for serious injuries occurring in class. An accident plan might include sending one student for first aid supplies, another to the office for the principal or school nurse, and a third to call the paramedics. Of course, first aid supplies, phone numbers, and so forth must be prepared in advance so they are readily available when the emergency strikes. Be prepared to give first aid if needed, wait for the paramedics, and then make sure the parents are called. Do not allow students to stand around to witness the drama of an accident or emergency situation. Devise a plan to provide supervision for the remainder of the class. This could include knowing what other teachers, administrators, or staff would be available to supervise during each period of the day and how those individuals are to be contacted.

When the emergency is over, complete an accident report as soon as possible while the incident is fresh in everyone's minds. Accident reports should be kept for many years in case of lawsuits. They should be reviewed each year to analyze problem areas that could be addressed.

Organizing Groups or Teams

There are as many ways to choose teams as there are teachers to choose them. However, many teachers resort to only one or two techniques. A little variety can be motivating. Some common techniques and ideas follow.

Counting Off

Students line up, count off by fives, and are asked to remember their number. Then all the ones become one team, the twos another team, and so on. This method takes too much time to be recommended. Also, students tend to change their numbers or position themselves to be on the same team as their friends. It can also result in mismatched teams (see Chapter 3).

Choosing Teams

Class members can elect team captains, or teachers can choose them. Rotate this responsibility among as many students as possible. Self-esteem leadership traits can be encouraged and developed in students by wise and caring teachers.

Never allow team captains to choose teams with each captain in turn picking a member of the class until all are chosen. This results in some students always being chosen last. It ruins self-esteem and wastes valuable class time. One method is for captains to choose the teams in private using the class roll as a guide. Still another method is to have captains select team members for each other or draw a team at random from teams already chosen. Teachers can then alphabetize the list for posting.

Students within a class can select teams quickly if the following system is incorporated in an orderly manner. After the captains have been chosen, students are instructed to line up behind the captain of their choice. On the command "GO" they must *walk* to form this line. No more than a designated number of persons can be a line. When the designated number is reached, students must go to another line. With this method, best friends, highly skilled players, and goof-offs tend to end up on the same team. It is wise to intersperse this method with other methods of choosing teams.

Dunn and Wilson proposed having each student write his or her name on a piece of paper, wad it up, and toss it into a pile. Team captains collect the number of wads needed for each team. For uneven numbers, have one captain pick up the extra wad.[19]

Assigned Teams

Teams can be assigned by the teacher and posted or read to the class. Squads can be used as assigned teams.

At Random

Students are told to "get in groups of four" or to stand behind a number of markers. A second method is to say, "You five go to court one, you five to count two," and so forth, while indicating certain students as they happen to be grouped around the teacher.

Ultra-Shuffle

The Ultra-Shuffle, developed by Kirkpatrick, is a system for assigning teams that results in constantly changing the composition of each team.[20] The result is reduced concern for the score and greater involvement of all students in the game play. Students are assigned to a row. The number of rows depends on the number and size of teams. The first person in each row steps forward and the group is assigned to a court, to the skill station, or to referee. When students complete the skill station, they substitute for a student in one of the games. That student goes to the skill station and when completed, substitutes into a different game. A student can substitute for a referee at any time.

Variations

Give each student a card with a color, shape, and number on it, such as the following:

Triangle	Circle	Square
Orange	Red	Blue
2	2	1

By varying the quantity of colors, shapes, and numbers, groups of different sizes can be formed. For example, if only three groups are desired, limit shapes to triangle, circle, and square. If five groups are desired, use orange, red, blue, yellow, and green. If ten groups are necessary, use the numbers one to ten. Groups can then be formed by calling out "shapes," "colors," or "numbers," and students move to join others who have the same shape, color, or number in a designated spot. Different colored wrist bands distributed to students at the beginning of class can also designate teams. Lambdin suggested using playing cards and varying groups by number, color, and suit (clubs, hearts, diamonds, spades). She also proposed assigning a permanent card and placing student names on a chart. She includes a guide for placing students on the chart by skill level and sex so that groups can be evenly balanced for activity.[21]

Other variations might include date of birth, height, eye or hair color, and right-handedness or left-handedness, depending on the size of teams wanted or the purpose for grouping students. Teachers are limited only by their ability to create other variations for special occasions.

Whatever technique is used for selecting teams, change the method often for variety and to encourage positive social interaction among students. Regularly trade leadership roles for teams so that most students are afforded this responsibility. It is also important to divide the various abilities of students as evenly as possible among the teams. When teams are used for game play, colored vests or pinnies can be used to distinguish one team from another.

Review Question: What are appropriate and inappropriate ways to choose teams?

Supervising Class Activities

Supervising is the part of teaching that occurs while students are practicing skills, playing games, or participating in other activities. Proper planning is essential for students to continue learning and to participate safely during this portion of the lesson.

The teacher must employ both vision and movement in supervising class activities when monitoring a class. Use a wide range of vision as the class is scanned and that "sixth sense" or "eyes in the back of the head." Never get so involved in the subject matter that students are forgotten.

Keep your back to the wall by moving along the edges of the class when you are not involved in direct instruction. This means you will keep all of the students in view constantly and avoid favoring students in one part of the playing area. The center of the class is not a good place for the teacher to stand. Doing so means some students will be out of view and may also have trouble hearing. When a discipline problem exists, the teacher can easily move from the perimeter toward the offenders and stand beside them and, if necessary, quietly speak to them.

Provide students with as much freedom as possible, keeping in mind the nature of the task and the maturity of the students. As the teaching style moves toward the student-directed styles of the spectrum (see Chapter 9), more and more freedom occurs, with increased student responsibility for learning. Allow students to work together as long as they work cooperatively. Keep an eye on students who cause a disturbance, separating them from other students.

Teachers are responsible for all students in the class. *Never leave students unsupervised.* Classes not working together as an entire group present problems in this regard. It is up to teachers to work out team teaching and supervising schedules or get adequate help when supervising individualized class programs.

Teachers must be sure all students are accounted for when class is in session. Some students might attempt to sneak off after roll call. If the class is a meaningful and motivational experience this should not occur, but students sometimes have behavior problems for which a teacher is not responsible. Once teachers know of such students, adequate precautions must be taken during class, or additional help from the counseling office might be secured to help with the student.

Adapting to Interruptions

A number of interruptions that reduce instructional time occur during school hours, including such things as assemblies, school dances, field trips, and testing. Some of these activities reduce the length of the instructional period, often making it impractical to dress for activity. Others take students away from physical education classes, thereby leaving the teacher with only a few students in class. Another deviation is caused by inclement weather.

Dealing with Shortened Periods or Inclement Weather

Three types of activities can be used when the planned lesson must be changed. One type includes an adaptation of the activity currently being taught to an indoor facility; a lesson on terms, rules, strategy, or other cognitive concepts related to the activity; or an evaluation activity such as a skill or written test. If the use of an activity-related lesson is not feasible, a fitness-oriented lesson could be taught. This might include teaching fitness concepts, teaching a fitness activity such as an aerobic dance or circuit training, giving physical fitness tests, or evaluating posture. A third activity is the use of a values-oriented activity from the affective domain. Chapter 9 includes several activities the teacher might use.

Dealing with a Small Class

When the teacher ends up with a small class, it is time to rejoice. This is an excellent opportunity to provide practice time for skill development, with students given individual help from the teacher. An alternative plan is to play a recreational or lead-up game using the skills that have been taught in the class.

Using Student Leaders

The physical education program should provide numerous opportunities for students to develop leadership skills. Within individual classes, students can serve as squad leaders, team captains, officials, equipment monitors, and in many other capacities. Rotate student leaders often to allow every student a chance to develop leadership skills.

In addition to these in-class leaders, student assistants can be assigned to assist the teacher with various nonteaching activities. Student assistants have proven to be an inexpensive method of improving teacher effectiveness and morale in large classes. In addition to helping teachers, student assistants can improve themselves in the following ways:

1. Develop and improve physical activity skills.
2. Develop social skills, such as leadership, followership, responsibility, and cooperation.
3. Develop improved skills in written and oral communication.
4. Learn more about the teaching profession and about physical education as a profession.
5. Grasp the significance of serving others and of working with others to accomplish stated objectives.
6. Develop a better understanding of students who are less able than others.
7. Learn how to plan and lead activities.

Select student assistants on the basis of their interest, scholarship, physical ability, character, ability to get along well with others, and willingness to do what is required. The experience afforded students is often enhanced if they can be assigned to a specific class section other than their own and if they have uniforms distinct from the other students (such as a different shirt) to set them apart.

Because student assistants are students and therefore lack professional training and experience, they must be prepared for their new role. Much of this preparation can precede the actual experience, and some of it must continue throughout the term in which the duties are performed. A leader's club or class can be used to instruct student assistants in their duties. Students should thoroughly understand the policies and procedures of the department and the duties that they will be expected to perform. The major duty of the student assistants is to assist the instructor in any way possible, consistent with their own capabilities and potential. Some other possible duties include the following:

1. Preparing the play area
2. Distributing, collecting, and caring for equipment
3. Taking roll
4. Making out squad cards
5. Checking uniforms
6. Recording tardy and absence slips
7. Leading exercises and drills
8. Demonstrating skills
9. Officiating
10. Assisting with media hardware
11. Downloading information into computers from heart rate monitors
12. Recording fitness scores on the computer
13. Turning showers on and off
14. Assisting with test administration and scoring
15. Providing individual assistance to students
16. Assisting with other duties, according to interests and abilities

Some problems have arisen from the use of student leaders. They include students being inadequately prepared for their assignments, students doing teachers' "dirty work," students being placed in situations where they "know too much," students assisting during their own physical education period and thus missing time to improve their own skills, and students losing friends by attempting to cope with grading or discipline situations. Each of these problems can be prevented by adequate preparation and by recalling that the duties of the student assistant are to assist with the class work, not to be responsible for grading or disciplining students.

Welcoming New Students

Being a new student in a physical education class can be very scary and intimidating. Physical education classes frequently take on a personality as students start working with groups and friendships are established. New students must quickly learn class procedures and routines so that they can fit in and feel comfortable participating in class rather than being alienated or not accepted. Here are some suggestions for making this happen:

- Videorecord your opening day comments. This contains much information about class expectations and requirements. When a new student arrives, give him or her an opportunity to watch this on a school VHS player or take a copy home for homework. If teachers have access to DVD burners, the student can be given a copy for future reference.
- Ask students as the year begins if they would like to volunteer to mentor new students who may join the class during the year. Try to have two to three people (preferably from both genders) who agree to help out. Mentors should be outgoing and/or accepting of others to make the new student feel welcome.
- Assign a mentor to the new student to help with locker room procedures, locks, and other equipment or routines. Have the mentor introduce the new student to others in the class. During the new student's first days in class, arrange to put the student with this mentor when assigning groups. The mentor's responsibility is to teach the student class routines and provide coaching and feedback where appropriate.
- If possible, put the new student's locker close to that of the mentor. Allow both student and mentor to leave class a couple of minutes early during the first two or three days in case the student needs assistance or extra time.

- Find someone who is in class with the new student in the period following physical education. Encourage that student to escort the new student to the next class. If lunch follows physical education, ask the mentor and his or her friends if they would be willing to take the new student to the cafeteria and each lunch with him or her.

Rewarding Good Student Behavior

Management games are generally based on Grandma's law, which states, "First clean up your plate and then you may have your dessert." Translated into physical education terminology, it states, "By accomplishing certain classroom management tasks quickly, you will have more time for play." Clearly specify a few rules that tell what is expected to earn the reward. The reward may be based on the behavior of the entire class or of each squad. For example, all squads quiet, sitting in place, and ready for roll call within five seconds from the teacher's signal earn a point. A stopwatch can be used to record the amount of time used. A variety of reinforcers to reward appropriate behaviors often set a positive atmosphere in a class. Ideas for behavior modification are discussed in Chapter 13.

Review Questions: What is Grandma's law? How can it be used in physical education?

Develop routines that you can use while teaching for the following: (1) distributing and collecting equipment, (2) starting class, (3) taking attendance, (4) leading warm-up and/or fitness activities, (5) getting student attention, (6) giving directions, (7) finishing an activity or class, and (8) teaching and utilizing class formations.

What are key points to remember when supervising students?

How can you make best use of days when time is shortened or when several students are absent?

How can student leaders make a teacher's job more efficient?

RECORD KEEPING

The main purposes of record keeping are to provide information to administrators, parents, and guidance counselors; and to help teachers evaluate students, themselves, and the curriculum. Keep only pertinent, up-to-date records, such as (1) attendance records; (2) records of achievement, including grades; (3) health and medical records; and (4) equipment and locker records.

Attendance Records

Teachers are required to keep an accurate record of the daily attendance of all students assigned to them. Keep records up-to-date each day. Because pencil tends to blur, the records should generally be kept in ink. Some teachers keep records in a book or enter them into spreadsheets on their computers. Because students change class period during the first couple of weeks of the semester, it is suggested that teachers not record names in an official grade book or on the computer until after enrollments for classes have stabilized.

Attendance Register

Box 12.10 shows a sample page from an attendance register. The top section identifies the class as Mrs. Jackson's second period physical education class at Younowhere Junior High School during the fall semester. No text is required. In the left-hand column, the students are listed in alphabetical order. Next to their names are their sex, grade, entry code, and exit code. The entry codes are as follows:

E1—Enrolled from within the state
E2—Entered from another state this school year

The exit codes are as follows:

T1—Transferred to another class
T2—Transferred to another school
D1—Dropped out of school

Attendance markings may differ from state to state or district to district. These are two common sets of markings:

Absence	–	/
Excused absence	(–)	⊘ or x
Tardy	∸	⋌
Excused tardy	(∸)	⋌: or (⋌)
Excused for another school event	Ex	Ex

Days enrolled includes the total number of days each student was enrolled in the class. Absences and tardies are also summarized for the term.

Squad Cards

Squad cards are often used to take roll and the attendance record transferred to the attendance register after class.

Records of Achievement

Records of student achievement are usually kept on class record cards and on individual permanent record cards. A discussion of each of these types of records follows.

Class Record Cards

A class record card is a record of the achievements of all students in a particular class. It provides information to the teacher and to the student on each student's progress in the class.

Individual Permanent Record Cards

A permanent record card for each student provides a valuable source of information about student progress in

BOX 12.10

An Attendance Register

Period	Instructor(s)	Course Title	Text(s)	TERM SUMMARY	YEAR-END SUMMARY
2	L. Jackson	Physical Education	None		
Fall Term	School: Younowhere Jr. High		Date Class Began: 9/8 to Date Class Ended: 1/12 Total Days Held: 80		

Ref	Pupil	Sex	Grade	Entry Code	Exit Code	Mo. Sept. Wk. 1 Day					Wk. 2					Wk. 3					Oct. Wk. 4					Wk. 5					Days Enrolled	Days Absent		Times Tardy		Days Enrolled	Days Absent	Final Mark	Credit
						M	8 T	9 W	10 T	11 F	14 M	15 T	16 W	17 T	18 F	21 M	22 T	23 W	24 T	25 F	28 M	29 T	30 W	1 T	2 F	5 M	6 T	7 W	8 T	9 F									
1	Alexander, Claudia	F	8	E1				—																		(—)					44	2		0					
2	Bishop, April	F	8	E1																											44	0		0					
3	Carter, Susan	F	8	E1											(—)												(—)				44	2		0					
4	Dixon, Lonnie	M	8	E1	T1			(—)																				[T1]			21	1		0					
5	Dove, Jim	F	8	E1																	•										44	0		1					
6	Eden, Sherron	F	8	E1																											44	0		0					
7	Giles, David	M	8	E1								(—)			(—)									(—	—	—	—	—	—)		44	8		0					
8	Herton, Giles	M	8	E1																											44	0		0					
9	Johnson, Kyle	M	8	E1											Ex																44	0		0					
10	Killian, Teresa	F	8	E1																											44	0		0					
11	Lance, Cathy	F	8	E1																											44	0		0					
12	Limb, Susan	F	8	E1	D				(—	—)					(—)		(—	—	—	—)		(—	—	—	—	—	—	—	—)		44	16		0					
13	Peery, Phyllis	F	8	E1																											44	0		0					
14	Rasmus, Jody	F	8	E1	T2										Ex												T2				19	0		0					
15	Skinner, David	M	8	E1													•														44	0		1					
16	Sousa, Pepe	M	8	E2																	[E2]						(—)				28	1		0					
17	Stevens, Jim	M	8	E1							•																				44	0		1					
18	Walden, Heather	F	8	E1											Ex																44	0		0					
19	Wardell, Mark	M	8	E1														(—)													44	1		0					
20	Wilson, Rosalie	F	8	E1																											44	0		0					
21	York, Ryan	M	8	E1						(—	—	—	—)		—	—				—			—	—							44	9		0					

Source: Marilyn Harding, Springville Junior High School, Springville, Utah.

the physical education program. It provides a record of the parents' names and phone numbers for emergencies, the students' fitness test results, all of the activity or content units completed by the student, and awards and honors in extra-class programs. File individual record cards alphabetically in the department office. The front and back of an individual permanent record card are shown in Box 12.11. The computer provides an alternative method of keeping information about student progress. A printout can be used to provide information about individual or class achievement in any area of physical education.

Health and Medical Records

In the first part of this chapter, medical excuses for temporary or long-term illness or injury were discussed and forms were presented for each of these situations. Keep each of these forms on file in the physical education department office.

Another type of record that should be kept on hand is a record of health status for each student. The school nurse can be helpful in collating this information from permanent school records. Such conditions as asthma, allergies, diabetes, heart conditions, muscular or orthopedic disorders, and many other conditions can affect student participation in the physical education program.

Equipment and Locker Records

Locker records were discussed earlier in the chapter under school policies and procedures. A record should be kept in the department by the department head, or some other faculty member, of all departmental transactions. Equipment purchases and maintenance are especially important. Equipment records include a yearly equipment inventory, copies of purchase orders, and check-out forms for athletic equipment. For further information regarding these subjects, refer to a textbook on administration.

Review Question: What kinds of records should be kept by physical educators?

BOX 12.11

An Individual Record Card (Front and Back)

AN INDIVIDUAL RECORD CARD

Name Carol Duncan Date of Birth 21 June 1982

Address 234 S. Glassell

Parents' Names Lloyd & Karen Duncan Phone 358-9308

PHYSICAL FITNESS TESTING

Grade	1.5 mile run R.S.	1.5 mile run %	% Fat R.S.	% Fat %	Flexibility R.S.	Flexibility %	Strength R.S.	Strength %
9 Pre	17:19	45	18	75	29	30	35	50
9 Post	16:34	55	18	75	30	35	35	50
10 Pre	16:14	60	17	85	30	20	35	40
10 Post	15:50	65	18	80	32	30	37	50
11 Pre	15:26	70	18	85	32	35	37	65
11 Post								
12 Pre								
12 Post								

AN INDIVIDUAL RECORD CARD

Activity	*Fitness & Skills*	*Knowledge*	*Citizenship*	*Grade*	*Year Taken*
Archery					
Badminton	B+	A	A	A-	2004–5
Basketball	B	A	A	B+	2004–5
Flag Football					
Folk Dance	A-	A	A	A-	2004–5
Golf	B-	A-	A	B+	2004–5
Gymnastics	A-	A	A	A-	2004–5
Modern Dance	A-	A	A	A-	2004–5
Soccer	B	A	A	B+	2004–5
Social Dance	A	A	A	A	2004–5
Softball					
Swimming	A	A	A	A	2002–3
Tennis					
Volleyball	B	A	A	B+	2003–3

Intramural participation—Activities and awards:

Extramural participation—Activities and awards:

NOTES

1. C. C. Cox, From handout to handbook, *Strategies 6,* no. 1 (1992): 7–8.
2. J. A. Krouscas, No substitute for the first day of school, *Strategies 10,* no. 1 (1996): 5–8; C. Summerford, Locker room boot camp, *Journal of Physical Education, Recreation, and Dance 67,* no. 6 (1996): 4–5.
3. Krouscas, No substitute.
4. Issues. *Journal of Physical Education, Recreation, and Dance 62,* no. 3 (1991): 12–15, 63.
5. R. Hardy, Dressing out in physical education: Probing the problem, *Physical Educator 36* (1979): 191–192.
6. *Mitchell v. McCall,* 273 Ala. 604, 143 So. 2d. 629 (1962).
7. J. Hart, Locker-room liability, *Strategies 3,* no. 3 (1990): 19–20.
8. P. C. Pease, Effects of interdependent group contingencies in a secondary physical education setting, *Journal of Teaching in Physical Education 2* (1982): 29–37.
9. Hart, Locker-room liability.
10. M. D. Luke, Research on class management and organization: Review with implications for current practice, *Quest 41* (1989): 55–67.
11. H. Wong and R. Wong, *The First Days of School: How to Be an Effective Teacher* (Sunnyvale, CA: Harry K. Wong Publications, 1991).
12. J. Oslin, Routines as organizing features in middle school physical education, *Journal of Teaching in Physical Education, 15* (1996): 319–37.
13. S. Aicinena, Formal class closure—An effective instructional tool, *Journal of Physical Education, Recreation, and Dance 62,* no. 3 (1991): 72–73.
14. M. F. Mitchell, Stretching the content of your warm-up, *Journal of Physical Education, Recreation, and Dance 67,* no. 7 (1996): 24–28.
15. K. C. La Mancusa, *We Do Not Throw Rocks at the Teacher!* (Scranton, PA: International Textbook, 1966).
16. La Mancusa, *We Do Not Throw Rocks.*
17. S. Aicinena, Formal class closure—An effective instructional tool, *Journal of Physical Education, Recreation, and Dance 62,* no. 3 (1991): 72–73.
18. A. M. Woods and D. J. Langley, Circle drills: Do they accomplish your goals? *Journal of Physical Education, Recreation, and Dance 68,* no. 3 (1997): 8–9.
19. R. Wilson and S. E. Dunn, Creative and fun grouping strategies, *Utah Association of Health, Physical Education, Recreation, and Dance Journal 22* (1990, Autumn): 17–23.
20. B. Kirkpatrick, *The Ultra-Shuffle: Who's Keeping Score?* (Grundy Center, IA: For Your Heart, 1993).
21. D. Lambdin, Shuffling the deck, *Journal of Physical Education, Recreation, and Dance 60,* no. 3 (1989): 27–28.

CHAPTER

13

MOTIVATION AND DISCIPLINE

STUDY STIMULATORS

1. Why are motivation and discipline studied together?
2. What is motivation? How can understanding motivational theories help teachers teach?
3. What is discipline? Why is a study of discipline so important?
4. What motivational techniques can be used to prevent discipline problems?
5. Describe several discipline models that you might like to use in your teaching.
6. What disciplinary techniques are generally considered to be acceptable? Which ones would you use and when?
7. What disciplinary techniques are generally considered to be unacceptable?
8. What factors should be considered when a disciplinary incident arises?

According to Doyle, teaching basically involves a combination of instruction and order.[1] Assuming the teacher has the expertise to model and convey subject matter, he or she must then plan the instruction to maintain order and promote learning. Inherent in this process are both motivation and discipline.

Motivation and discipline are like heads and tails of the same coin. Fewer discipline problems occur when students are motivated through active involvement in meaningful learning and when enthusiastic teachers present material in stimulating ways. On the other hand, teachers cannot motivate when students are disruptive. Teachers who punish students or attack their dignity can't increase student motivation.[2]

Hellison pointed out that physical educators and coaches are increasingly concerned with discipline and motivation.[3] He maintained that if physical education and sport leaders want to prevent or reduce discipline and motivation problems, they must adjust to the changing world in the following ways:

1. Improve control in our classes and on our teams.
2. Help students make responsible choices.
3. Help students lead more stable lives.
4. Counter the ineffectiveness of schools.
5. Accomplish these needs without minimizing participation in physical activity.[4]

Teachers working with students who lack motivation and self-discipline and teachers who want to increase these traits in students would do well to study Hellison's model. His goals are key elements of the National Association of Sport and Physical Education's (NASPE) Content Standards 5 and 6 and include teaching students to exercise self-control, to take responsibility for their own learning, to make wise choices, to develop a meaningful and personally satisfying lifestyle, and to cooperate with and support and help one another. His model for teaching involves developmental levels of progression for students involving attitudes and behavior, and interaction strategies for both teachers and students.

Teachers set the stage for both motivation and discipline. Meaningfully organizing instruction is vital to maintaining order in the classroom. Planning and consistently implementing one's plans are key elements in maintaining order. Without them teachers play a stressful guessing game in which trial and error are the dominant influences. Without some kind of systematic approach to student motivation, teachers are left not knowing what to do next.[5]

Students also contribute to maintaining or decreasing order. They come with attitudes molded by their personalities and experiences. Some live in insecure family environments in an increasingly violent society, in which they are often forced to fend for themselves. Some spend much of their time watching and listening to violence and profanity. Some students come to school with difficult temperaments. In school they may face boring lectures, powerlessness, unclear limits, attacks on their dignity, and a lack of acceptable outlets for their feelings.[6] Teachers are not responsible for students' attitudes, but they can exercise some control over the school environment.

Review Question: What is the relationship between discipline and motivation?

MOTIVATION

According to Joe Cybulski, a ten-year-old at Ballwin Elementary School in Missouri, motivation is "to convince someone he always wanted to learn something he never even knew he wanted to learn."[7] Motivation is an inner urge or desire to satisfy a need, achieve a specific goal, do one's best, surpass one's previous performance, or exceed another person's performance. It is part of the desire of humankind to improve and to excel. Achieving one's best under trying or even disappointing circumstances is a part of living one's life to the fullest. Great moments in sport, as with great moments in life, are not so much those of winning or losing but of doing one's best. Motivation is active; it is the process of initiating, sustaining, and directing activity toward a specific goal. It involves both intensity and direction toward the goal. Teachers cannot motivate students or make them learn. They can only manipulate environmental variables, which may encourage students to do something that will result in learning. Motivation is influenced both by personal factors within the student and by external environmental factors manipulated by the teacher.[8]

Motivated students engage in approach behaviors toward the activity or subject. Unmotivated students engage in avoidance behaviors and do not perform the desired responses; thus they learn slowly or not at all. The process of learning is more rapid when students are motivated. There is a positive correlation between motivation and learning.

Variables known to be related to the amount of motivation include the following:

1. *The degree of concern or tension that exists within the learner.* When tension increases to an undue degree because of excessive anxiety, anger, hostility, or compulsion, motivation decreases.
2. *The feeling tone* (pleasant or unpleasant). Pleasant feeling tones increase motivation to a high degree. Unpleasant feeling tones will also increase motivation, but to a lesser degree. The absence of or neutral feeling tones will not influence motivation.
3. *Interest.* People are motivated to do things that interest them.
4. *Success.* People are usually more successful in activities that interest them. Success in turn tends to stimulate interest. The degree of success becomes an important variable in motivation.
5. *Knowledge of results* (How am I doing?). The more specific the feedback, the more one becomes motivated to improve performance.
6. *Intrinsic (internal)-extrinsic (external) motivation.* Most examples of these are not completely one or the other, and both may be effective.[9]

THEORIES OF MOTIVATION

A number of theories have evolved in an attempt to define how intrinsic motivation develops and how it influences learners' achievements. Research has focused on (1) the need for achievement; (2) social learning theory; (3) attribution theory, locus of control, and learned helplessness; and (4) teacher expectations.

Need for Achievement

Maslow identified a hierarchy of needs as the basis for all human motivation.[10] These needs are physiological, safety (and security), love (or social), esteem, and the need for self-actualization. He proposed, in general, that lower-order needs must be satisfied before the next higher need can be activated. Thus, when physiological needs are met, the individual is concerned with safety and so on up the hierarchy until another physiological need must be attended to. For some persons, minimal satisfaction of a need is enough to progress upward, whereas others require satisfaction at a higher level. Occasionally a certain need takes precedence over all other needs regardless of its position in the hierarchy. Such is the case when a mother risks her life for her child.

Physiological needs such as food, water, sleep, exercise, and bodily elimination are essential for survival and when they are not met, students cannot learn effectively. Teachers see evidence of this in classes that meet right before lunch, in students after a morning of taking achievement tests, or in a student who is ill. Both physical and psychological *safety and security* are essential for learning. The threat of physical violence in some schools prevents effective learning, as does discrimination on the basis of race, sex, or ability. In physical education, students who are afraid to learn a new skill due to possible failure or ridicule are concerned about security. Some students have a high tolerance level for stress or physical risk while others have a low tolerance level and react strongly to situations in which their security is threatened.

When safety and security needs are met, the student seeks to fulfill the need for *love.* This need can be met in part through social approval from adults or peers, but it must be met for students to be successful in school. Most dropouts are students who lack acceptance from one of these sources. In fact a group of three male dropouts each said that if *one* teacher had indicated genuine concern for him, he would have remained in school.

Everyone needs to feel capable; therefore, each student must have some activities in which he or she feels success. Gagné emphasized the need to arrange the learning environment so students experience success and develop *self-esteem.* The best source of motivation and, therefore, a willingness to persist in an activity is "achievement, successful interaction within the learning environment, and mastery of the objectives of an educational program."[11] This fact underscores the value of adapting activities to meet the needs of students with a wide range of abilities so that each student experiences success and enjoyment. Assessments designed to measure learning and achievement will help students see their progress.

Once basic needs have been satisfied, the individual can move on to *self-actualization.* Self-actualizing persons are motivated intrinsically and have an intense desire to explore, discover, and create. They are aware of their strengths and weaknesses and those of their environment and resolve to improve them in a consistent, orderly manner. Maslow felt that only a small percentage of the population would become self-actualized. Schools need to create environments in which students can satisfy their basic needs so that they will be free to move on to self-actualization.

Social Learning Theory

Bandura, in his social learning theory, described behavior in terms of expectations of personal efficacy (situation-specific self-confidence) and estimates of behavioral outcomes.[12] Decisions involve both (1) an efficacy expectation—the person's conviction that he or she can successfully execute the behavior required to produce the outcome and (2) an outcome expectation—the person's estimate that the behavior will result in the expected outcome and will be worthwhile.[13]

Efficacy expectations differ in (1) the magnitude or level of the task perceived to be possible, (2) the generalizability of past successes to similar situations, and (3) the strength of the expectations in the presence of disconfirming experiences. Students with high expectations will try new activities and expend more effort over a longer period of time than those with low expectations.

A person is more likely to behave in a certain way if the resulting outcome is seen as positive and less likely to behave in that way if the result is perceived to be negative. Even if the outcome is considered desirable, the individual may feel unable to perform the behavior needed to achieve the outcome and so the behavior may be avoided. Since most behaviors result in both positive and negative outcomes, the person weighs the perceived outcomes and decides whether or not to engage in the behavior.

For this reason students must be given *optimum challenges.* Tasks are matched with the capabilities of the learner. The most appropriate tasks are challenging, yet achievable through practice. Students with high persistence levels sustain effort over longer periods of time, whereas their low-persistence classmates need skills that can be achieved with minimal practice.[14] Csikszentmihalyi[15] describes this as flow. For there to be flow in learning environment, there must be a balance between challenge or difficulty of the task and success. In other words, tasks that are too easy offer little challenge and will not motivate people. Conversely, tasks that are too difficult will deny students success, also failing to motivate them.

Bandura postulated that efficacy expectations can be altered by personal performance accomplishments (competence), vicarious experience (modeling), verbal persuasion, and emotional arousal. Competence is generally considered to be the strongest, most lasting source of self-efficacy. Perceived competence or self-efficacy can differ in the cognitive, social, and psychomotor domains. One student may have a high level of self-efficacy in the psychomotor and social areas and a very low level in the cognitive area; another may have a high level of perceived competence in the cognitive and psychomotor domains and feel ill-at-ease in social situations.

Modeling shows how to perform skills, which are refined through self-correction based on the consequence of the performance and feedback from others. Seeing others overcome obstacles through determined effort is more effective than viewing skilled performers who make the task look easy.

The effectiveness of verbal persuasion depends on the credibility of the persuader. Prestige, expertise, self-assurance, and trustworthiness in the eyes of the learner affect credibility. If teachers raise expectations without arranging conditions for successful learning, the resulting failure will discredit the teacher's influence and further undermine the student's self-efficacy.

Emotional arousal can reduce perceived chances of success. Emotional anxiety, increased by fear-provoking thoughts, can exceed the fear experienced in actual situations. Anxiety is best extinguished by teaching effective coping skills.

Bandura viewed self-efficacy not as a global personality trait but as dependent on the task, situation, and previous experience of the learner. According to Bandura, motivation results from personal goal-setting and evaluation.[16] Individuals prescribe self-rewards for achieving self-prescribed standards and persist in their efforts until their performance matches the standards. After accomplishing these standards, they often make self-reward contingent on the attainment of even higher achievements. To be most effective, goals should be challenging, yet attainable. Frequent failure weakens efficacy expectations and therefore motivation.

Performance accomplishments are the best predictors of self-efficacy, so teachers should ensure performance success through appropriate instructional strategies. Teachers must structure the environment so that all students can perform successfully by modeling skills, providing graduated learning tasks, and varying the severity of the threat. For example, students who are afraid of the water must be gradually introduced to feeling the water on their bodies, putting their faces in the water, opening their eyes underwater, and experiencing buoyancy. The instructor usually begins by standing nearby to provide assistance and then helps the students to rely on peer tutors and finally on their own abilities.

Realistic performance standards help students gradually increase their abilities and, in turn, their self-efficacy. Students are therefore more willing to try new skills and to persist until they have learned them.[17] High-efficacy students are more self-confident and predict success more often than low-efficacy students. In the face of failure, high-efficacy students increase persistence, whereas low-efficacy students decrease persistence. This is similar to learned helplessness.[18] (Learned helplessness is described in the next section.)

Attribution Theory, Locus of Control, and Learned Helplessness

Attribution theorists study perceived reasons for a person's success or failure. Successes and failures can be attributed to internal or external causes, which are stable or unstable over time, and are controllable or uncontrollable by the learner. Student expectations, persistence, and performance can be positively or negatively influenced by the various dimensions of attribution.[19]

Success attributed to internal causes such as ability, effort, or personality raises self-esteem and motivation, whereas attributions to external causes such as luck, task difficulty, weather, and officiating have no effect on self-esteem. Success attributed to factors over which students feel they have no control, such as the teacher's behavior, luck, or easy tasks, does not increase motivation. Success with minimal effort yields a strong sense of ability; overcoming challenging tasks through persistence results in a strong sense of self-efficacy.[20] Mastery-oriented individuals tend to take more credit for successes and more blame for failures and emphasize effort in achieving outcomes.

Failure by individuals with low perceived competence results in internal, uncontrollable, and stable attributions that lead to low expectations, a lack of persistence, and failure to improve performance. On the other hand, individuals with high perceived competence attribute failure to internal, controllable, and unstable causes, leading to increased motivation, expected performance gains, and improved performance.[21]

Research in physical education has used attribution theory to explain some student behaviors. Weinberg, Gould, and Jackson found that males displayed more positive self-talk, whereas females exhibited more negative self-talk. They suggested that failure for females may reflect on their ability, whereas males attribute failure to lack of effort. Corbin and Nix discovered that girls have lower expectations than boys for motor skills. These findings may explain why some students persist in the use of inappropriate responses "to camouflage their feelings of inadequacy."[22]

The theory of attribution helps us understand why some students persist and achieve with or without instruction and why others fail in spite of our help. Students with internal/stable attributions for failure consider themselves "helpless"; no matter what they do, they will not succeed. Even when they experience success, they attribute it to luck or easy tasks that anyone can do, so they don't expect success to occur again.

Maier and Seligman defined *learned helplessness* as the inappropriate conclusion reached by someone that controllable events are uncontrollable after experiencing uncontrollable events.[23] Learned helplessness appears to be more likely when a subject attributes failure to achieve control to stable factors such as ability or task difficulty rather than changeable ones like lack of effort or bad luck. When faced with the same situation in the future, subjects give up, whereas in new situations they may respond normally. It is important to remember that in many life situations, no control is possible and, in these instances, the best response may be to give up.[24]

Martinek and Griffith provided some questions to help teachers identify students who exhibit learned helplessness:

1. Does the student always give up quickly when presented with a learning task?
2. Does the student fail to demonstrate a variety of strategies after an unsuccessful attempt at a learning task?
3. Does the student continually attribute his or her failure to lack of skill (e.g., "I am not good at this anyway").
4. Is the student always reluctant to take credit for any success (e.g., "I was really lucky on that shot!")
5. Does the student display an "I don't care" attitude toward various learning tasks? That is, does he or she simply "go through the motions"?[25]

They also caution teachers to verify the student's "yes" responses over a period of time and with confirmation by other teachers.

Some evidence indicates that students can be taught to attribute failure to lack of effort and thus do better on future tasks than children provided only with success experiences.[26] Various researchers have attempted to increase performance expectations, persistence, and performance in sport situations when failure is present by teaching students to attribute failure to internal, controllable, and unstable factors.

The results indicate that through causal dimension training, teachers can enhance the expectations, persistence, and performance of students who would normally drop out of motor activities due to failure. Martinek and Griffith have also worked with learned helpless students and find that attributional retraining can help students succeed by trying harder.[27]

To break the cycle of failure—low expectations, helplessness—teachers must have a high sense of their own ability to influence student learning and motivation (self-efficacy), combined with high but realistic expectations for student achievement. They let students know they will be expected to achieve and that they will be taught so that they will be able to achieve.

The learning environment must be structured so that student effort yields success. Alderman listed four steps to help learners achieve success. Suggestions from Martinek and Griffith have been incorporated in the ideas listed to carry out these steps.[28]

Step 1. The first step is to set goals that are specific; hard, but attainable; and proximal (short-term). This can be accomplished by pretesting and analyzing student errors. A form that can be used to help students set goals is shown in Box 13.1. Students will need help with creating realistic goals.

Step 2. Several techniques can be used to help students select learning strategies to help them accomplish their goals. Mosston's inclusion style (see Chapter 9) requires teachers to establish different levels for the same task. Thus, students could spike an official ball or Volley Lite ball, held or moving, over a net at two meters, 7′4″ or 8′. As students experience success, they can progress to more difficult levels of the task by choosing which ball to use and where they want to practice. Students can also be allowed to choose noncompetitive self-challenge activities rather than competitive activities in which students tend to be compared with each other. Another strategy that can be very effective with low-skilled learners is mastery learning. This was discussed in Chapter 9.

A third method that appears to work with some students is the use of peer tutoring or heterogeneous learning groups, in which students help each other reach their performance goals. Whatever method is used, the teacher must be available to provide feedback and encouragement to students and helpers, and the strategy must not point out the difference of the learned-helpless student. Other teachers in the school and parents also may help students who have become "helpless" in many areas of the curriculum.

Step 3. Focus is on progress made rather than on the end result. Students might graph their performance on a progress chart. The student

BOX 13.1

A Goal-Planning Form for Learned-Helpless Students

GOAL PLANNING FORM

Make your goal as specific as possible:

Planning

1. My specific learning goals for this week (today) are:
2. I will know I have accomplished my goals by:
3. Actions or steps I will take to accomplish these goals:
4. Possible blocks, both personal and outside, that may interfere with my goals:
5. If I need help, I can go to:
6. My confidence in reaching my goal is:

   no confidence — very confident

   0 — 25

Evaluating

7. My satisfaction with my goal attainment is:

   very unsatisfied — very satisfied

   0 — 25
8. Reasons for attaining or not attaining my goal:

Source: M. Kay Alderman (1990, September), Motivation for at-risk students, *Educational Leadership 48* (1): 29.

must see that his or her own effort resulted in success (progress toward the goal). The teacher's role is to give feedback about why the student succeeded or failed.

Step 4. Once the skills have been learned well, the student may attribute success to ability. It is important for the student to see ability as something that can be learned. Once students have attributed success to effort and ability rather than to luck or easy tasks, they are on the road to increased self-efficacy—increased confidence in their ability to accomplish goals.

If failure occurs, help the student to attribute failure to an incorrect learning strategy rather than to lack of ability. Teachers can make alternative learning strategies available as students need them.

Mastery-oriented classrooms stress progress and learning rather than performance and ability. Errors are viewed as part of the learning process, not as a lack of ability. Students in mastery-oriented classrooms have opportunities to correct errors by taking tests over or revising papers and projects.

When students succeed, teachers' self-efficacy also increases. As Alderman indicated, this type of intervention takes time and patience. The focus is on progress, not miracles.

The preceding studies indicate that increased levels of self-efficacy result in higher intrinsic motivation to participate in sport activities. Students with high self-worth tend to be intrinsically motivated, whereas students with low self-worth tend to be extrinsically motivated and are unsure of the forces responsible for their successes and failures.

Review Question: Define the following terms and tell how each is applicable to teaching: (a) motivation, (b) Maslow's hierarchy of needs, (c) self-efficacy, (d) optimum challenges, (e) Bandura's social learning theory, (f) movement confidence, (g) attribution theory and learned helplessness, and (h) extrinsic and intrinsic motivation.

Teacher Expectations or the Self-Fulfilling Prophecy

Goethe is thought to have said, "If you treat an individual as he is, he will stay as he is. But if you treat him as if he were what he could and ought to be, he will become what he ought to be." The Pygmalion effect, so dramatically portrayed in George Bernard Shaw's *Pygmalion,* was demonstrated to occur in the classroom in studies by Rosenthal and Jacobson and many others. The studies discovered that students perform in agreement with the perceived expectations of their teachers. This was found to be especially true of disadvantaged children in urban schools. Brophy concluded that effective teachers perceive their students as being capable of learning and themselves as being capable of teaching effectively. They expect their students to learn and act accordingly.[29]

Studies of the self-fulfilling prophecy in physical education classes confirm that teacher expectations influence student performance.[30] They show that physical education teachers form expectations of students based on such factors as age or grade level, motor ability, physical attractiveness, perceived effort, and the presence or absence of a disability. For example, younger students tended to receive more nonverbal praise and encouragement (smiles, hugs, pats, and nods) than older students. However, teachers more readily accepted ideas from older students. Students with high skill levels received more praise, contact time with teachers, and criticism, perhaps because teachers felt they were more capable of capitalizing on the feedback than lower-skilled learners. Teachers also had higher expectations for attractive students and students who "tried hard" or were most often on task.

Although students are sensitive to teacher expectations, it appears that individual students interpret teacher behaviors differently.[31] For example, Martinek found that the perceptions of praise received by students perceived by teachers to be low skilled were similar to the number of teacher praise statements, whereas high-skilled students perceived more teacher praise than actually existed.

Martinek cautioned that when low-skilled students internalize low teacher expectations, learned helplessness may result. He added, "For some students self-perceptions may be so strong that expectations that are counter to them may have little or no effect on the student." In fact, when teachers do give help, praise, or empathy, they may reinforce the student's perceptions of incapability. Martinek and Karper found competitive environments to have a negative influence on the efforts of low-expectancy students in physical activity.[32]

Rink indicated a lack of teacher expectation for learning in physical education. She suggested that teachers communicate higher expectations to students and provide learning environments that ensure student success. She proposed three ways for teachers to communicate their expectations to students:

1. Present tasks holistically, concretely, and briefly using concrete examples, brief explanations, and cues.
2. Help students refine, extend, and apply tasks (rather than jumping from one skill to another).
3. Provide specific task-related feedback to students and modify tasks as needed to ensure student success.[33]

Hutslar pointed out that high expectations are positively correlated with achievement. Teacher expectations can be bad, however, when they negatively influence student performance or affect. She listed a number of questions teachers can ask themselves to evaluate their expectations:

1. Do I expect enough from my "low" ability students?
2. Do I present new and challenging material to my "low" as well as my "high" ability students?

3. Do I smile as frequently at my poorest students as I do at my best students, at my least favorite as much as my favorite student?
4. Do my nonverbal responses convey negative feelings to my "low" students (frowns, shrugs, rolling eyes)?
5. By creating a friendly environment, do I encourage all students to feel free to initiate a conversation with me?
6. Do I give as much corrective feedback on skill performance to my "low" ability students as my "high" ability students?
7. Do I praise and respond positively to appropriate behavior and good performance of my "low" students, or do I allow it to pass unnoticed?
8. Am I less tolerant of incorrect answers and inappropriate behavior of my "low" ability students?
9. Do I give my "low" ability students as much time to answer questions as my "high" ability students?[34]

She then suggested that teachers select several students and behavior categories and tally each interaction, and then set new interaction goals based on the findings. In this way teachers can make the Pygmalion effect work in a positive direction by setting realistic and challenging expectations for all students.

Creating a Learning Environment to Motivate Students

The learning environment in a class has much to do with what happens in a class. Although the learning environment is influenced by what students bring with them (attitudes and abilities) as well as the ethos of a school, teachers can do many things to create a learning environment that will encourage learning (see Box 13.2).

Kounin identified several principles of effective management that correlated significantly with high task involvement and low deviancy of students.[35] These were (1) "with-it-ness" and overlapping, (2) smoothness and momentum, (3) group alerting and accountability, and (4) challenge and variety.

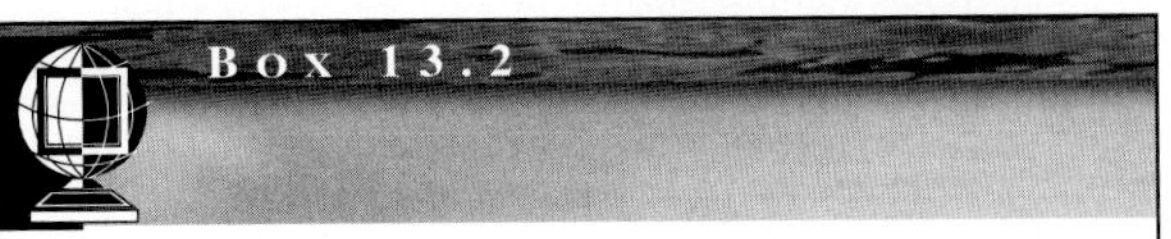

I've come to a frightening conclusion that . . . it's my personal approach that creates the climate. It's my daily mood that makes the weather . . . I can be a tool of torture or an instrument of inspiration. I can humiliate or humor, hurt or heal. In all situations, it is my response that decides whether a crisis will be escalated or de-escalated, and a child humanized or dehumanized.

—Educator Haim Ginott

Kounin's work provides excellent suggestions for preventing discipline problems. With-it-ness refers to a teacher's ability to know what is going on in the classroom at all times. Beginning teachers tend to focus their attention on the activity area rather than scanning the room and seeing everything that is happening. In physical education, being able to continuously observe the entire area is critical for teachers as so much is going on in a relatively large space. Whole-group activities are easier to monitor than station work as students should all be doing approximately the same thing. While scanning, teachers can see when students are doing things differently from others in the class. Physical education teachers must also learn to monitor with their ears as sound can alert the teachers to potential problems. It is important for teachers not only to see what is going on but also to communicate this awareness to students. Sometimes a teacher may use a certain look or move closer to the offender, and this is often enough to get students back on task without causing a disruption to the flow of the class. Kounin found that ineffective teachers were more likely to let a problem escalate into a more serious situation than were effective teachers, who tended to "nip the problem in the bud" by attending to it early. Knowing what is going on at all times is the first step in stopping misbehavior before it creates additional trouble.

When overlapping events or interruption occurs during instruction, effective teachers deal with the event and then return to what they were doing without missing a beat. Because there is so much activity in the gymnasium, physical education teachers typically deal with several interruptions during the course of a lesson that can interrupt the flow of instruction. Being able to deal with multiple events during a lesson without getting rattled can greatly enhance a teacher's instructional effectiveness.

The flow of a lesson is critical to teaching effectiveness. Pacing is important during a lesson because the teacher watches student actions and uses these as signs to redirect the activity or to move on to the next task. Some teachers will ignore minor misbehavior as correcting it interrupts the flow of the lesson. They know that if they can get the student into activity, the deviant behavior will be gone. However, misbehavior that impacts the safety of the student or others in class must be dealt with immediately. Experienced teachers have a sense of when to interrupt a lesson for discipline and when to keep moving. Teachers who are distracted by misbehavior and discipline a student far longer than the deed requires are "overdwelling" on a topic. Overdwelling can also occur during instructional episodes when teachers talk too long and fail to move students into activity. Generally, by keeping instructions simple or by using demonstrations and/or visuals to explain a task, teachers can improve the pace of the lesson and avoid overdwelling on a topic. Although it is dependent to some extent on the task, students will generally have the highest response rates in terms of quality and quantity of responses during the first two minutes after practice on a task begins.[36] Watching student performance on a task will generally signal to the teacher when it is time to change the task.

Accountability, a popular term in today's educational climate, was identified by Kounin over thirty years ago. Doyle noted that without accountability there is no task. For example, if a teacher told a group of students to go outside and run a mile, there would be no guarantee that they would do as they were told. Effective teachers know that they must set criteria for their tasks and then hold students accountable for reaching those criteria. Lund noted a hierarchy ranging from pseudo-accountability, when a teacher watched students and provided no feedback, to techniques that held students accountable for both the process and product of a psychomotor performance. Alexander[37] found grading to be a powerful form of accountability. Grading accountability can work on several days preceding a testing situation if students are aware of and reminded by teachers that they will be held accountable for their performance through skill assessments.[38]

When teachers ask a question and then wait to identify a responder, students are held accountable for academic knowledge. Since the students are unaware of who the teacher will ask to answer the question, all must formulate an answer in anticipation of being called on. This questioning technique, called group alerting by Kounin, is a form of accountability used by effective teachers.

Challenge is also an excellent way to avoid boredom for students. Students should be successful in the tasks presented. However, they should not be able to do every task without practice. Variety is another key component for avoiding boredom in a lesson.

Tomlinson[39] encourages teachers to invite students to learn by addressing five student needs. Students seek affirmation from school. They need to know that they are accepted for who they are, that people care for them and care that they succeed. Students must also feel that they make a contribution in school, bringing valuable perspectives and abilities that will make the school and class a better place. For school to be meaningful to students, they must have a sense of purpose. Teachers should take the time to provide students with reasons for learning so they will see the significance and importance of lessons. As students move toward adulthood, they are seeking independence. Giving them choices and some power to control what they do helps support the journey to becoming autonomous. The final need that Tomlinson identifies is the need for challenge. Students must see the connection between working hard and success. In an article about skateboarders, Sagor[40] outlines ideas for motivating students. Box 13.3 provides several suggestions for addressing the ideas presented in that article while teaching physical education.

BOX 13.3

Motivation for Students

Several writers[1] have provided insightful observations about students and what motivates them. After watching a group of skateboarders practice their moves, Sagor marveled that these students, who by day were disenfranchised from the learning process in schools, would work so hard at really difficult skills.[2] What was it that caused these young people to consider that learning various moves on skateboards was worthy of their time and efforts? He identified five needs that were being met: to feel competent, to belong, to feel useful, to feel potent, and to feel optimistic. The following are offered as suggestions for motivating students in physical education:

Helping students feel competent:

1. Students will participate in activities at which they feel successful. Set a goal that every day students will leave class knowing that they have learned something worthwhile and that they were successful in accomplishing it. The skateboarders know that they are successful with their activity, which is why they choose to spend hours perfecting new skills. This same attitude should be present in every physical education class.
2. Evaluate students against criterion-referenced standards. By comparing performance to others, some students will be better than others. As long as students reach the standard that you have identified, showing how a person ranks in the group really doesn't matter. The skateboarders have unwritten standards—being able to do the stunt with competence.
3. Make achievement the constant rather than time. When skateboarders learn a new skill it takes longer for some than others. This is true for any motor activity. Let students know your expectations and then provide opportunity and time to practice. When setting up units of study, be sure to allow adequate time for students to learn. Units where skills are introduced and "taught" in two or three days will not allow students who are likely to be unmotivated to experience success. Allow sufficient time for instruction and recognize that all students do not learn at the same pace.

Helping students feel like they belong:

1. Give students the opportunity to know others in the class. Spend the first few days of class doing team

Continued

BOX 13.3 *Continued*

building or cooperative activities that will allow students to get to know one another. Sitting next to someone in class is a very different experience from being in a physical education class. Mix and match the groups so that every student has many opportunities to work with different students. Do activities that require the group to work as a team rather than allowing one person to be the leader all the time.

2. In addition to working with others in the class, let students work with friends. Doing an activity with a friend often increases the enjoyment and students are more comfortable making an error with a friend than with a stranger. Sometimes working with a friend is counterproductive to learning. In these instances students may request a second chance to prove that they can work productively with a friend. Allow this opportunity with the understanding that the chance will end if their actions become inappropriate or unacceptable.

Helping students feel useful:

1. Just as the skateboarders help one another learn new skills, teachers can create this same environment in physical education to help students feel useful. Peer teaching and cooperative learning activities are just two of the many teaching strategies that can help students feel useful.
2. Students enjoy helping the teacher as well. Ask for volunteers to set up a playing area or to distribute equipment. Sport education units provide numerous opportunities for students to help the teacher as well as their teams.

Helping students feel potent:

1. Students make choices about what they want to learn. When they are learning something they want to learn, they are much more motivated. It is not enough to expect them to learn something; they must see that what you are teaching is worth their time and effort to learn it. When teaching anything, explain the importance or value of knowing it. For example, the Teaching Games for Understanding model presents new skills after students have a need to learn them. When skills are learned, they are put into the context of the game so that students can see how they fit. Regardless of the curriculum being taught or the instructional model used to teach it, students must see the importance of what you are trying to get them to learn.
2. Give students a voice in some decisions in class. Instead of offering only one activity during a class period, work with other members of the department and let students select the type of team sport or individual sport that they wish to learn. When developing class rules, let students make some of them along with the consequences of not following them. The inclusion teaching style provides students choices when selecting equipment and/or activities. If there are multiple ways to accomplish the same learning, give students the opportunity to decide which method they will choose.
3. Give them an opportunity to feel important. Leadership roles in class tell students that the teacher has trust and confidence in them. Peer teaching implies that they have the knowledge and competence to teach others.

Helping students to feel optimistic:

1. Students need a challenge when learning. Ideally, a task should require students to work to accomplish it. If students are never challenged, they will become bored. When skateboarders select new activities to learn, they are choosing activities that will provide a challenge but are within the realm of what they can achieve. Just as skateboarders add variations to increase the difficulty of skills they have accomplished, modify tasks for skilled students to keep them challenged. Students learn the value and satisfaction of working hard to meet a new challenge.
2. Encourage students to set their own goals as they move toward achieving mastery. This is another type of empowerment (potency) but students will also feel good about achieving these intermediate steps while working toward final objectives. Accomplishing their goals will provide students with a means for measuring personal growth.

Sources: [1] R. Sagor, Lessons from skateboarders, *Educational Leadership 60,* no. 1 (2002): 34–36, 38; C. Tomlinson, Invitation to learn. *Educational Leadership 60,* no. 1 (2002): 7–10; J. Raffini, *150 Ways to Increase Intrinsic Motivation in the Classroom* (Needham Heights, MA: Allyn & Bacon, 1996).

[2] Sagor, Lessons from skateboarders.

The implication for teaching is clear. Effective teachers believe that *all* of their students are capable of success and communicate that belief to their pupils. Teachers should carefully evaluate the ways they interact with students of all ability levels, all races, and both sexes.

Review Questions: What is the self-fulfilling prophecy, the Pygmalion effect? Why are teacher expectations important? How can positive expectations be communicated to students?

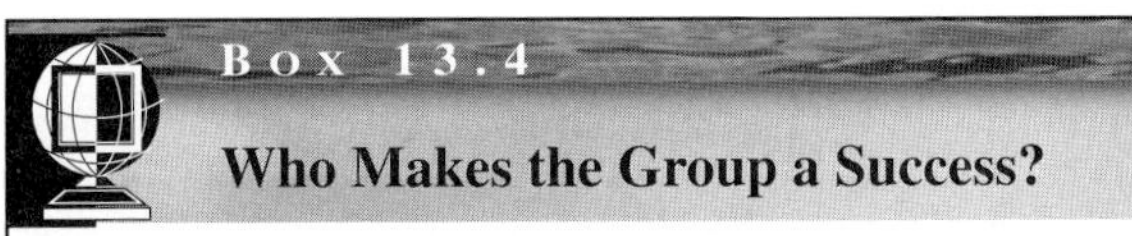

Who Makes the Group a Success?

Xvxn though my typxwritxr is an old modxl, it works quitx wxll, xxcxpt for onx or two kxys. I havx wishxd many timxs that it workxd pxrfxctly. It is trux that thxrx arx forty-six kxys that function wxll xnough, but just onx kxy not working makxs thx diffxrxncx.

Somxtimxs our group is somxwhat like my typxwritxr—not all thx kxy pxople arx working propxrly. You may say to yoursxlf, "Wxll, I am only onx pxrson, I won't makx or brxak thx group." But it doxs makx a diffxrxncx bxcausx a group, to bx xffxctivx nxxds thx activx participation of xvxry pxrson. So thx nxxt timx you think that you arx only onx pxrson and that your xfforts arx not nxxdxd, rxmxmbxr my typxwritxr and say to yoursxlf, "I'm a kxy pxrson in thx group, and I am nxxdxd vxry much."

MOTIVATION AND PREVENTIVE DISCIPLINE

The wise teacher realizes that discipline problems are most often preventable. The responsibility for discipline and motivation lies with the teacher. Preventive discipline is good teaching. It involves (1) belief in the worth of each student, (2) a warm, supportive, well-organized environment, (3) teacher modeling of mature behavior and appropriate ways to resolve problems, (4) well-planned, appropriate learning and assessment experiences, and (5) helping students learn self-direction and responsibility for their own behavior.

Belief in the Worth of Each Student

The key to classroom control comes from understanding the worth of each student and communicating that worth to them. Coloroso emphasized six critical life messages that students need to receive from teachers. They are as follows:

1. I believe in you.
2. I trust in you.
3. I know you can handle life's situations.
4. You are listened to.
5. You are cared for.
6. You are very important to me.[41]

Students need to feel self-worth and be able to say:

I like myself.
I can think for myself.
There is no problem so great it can't be solved.[42]

Teachers need to address learners' universal needs before individual differences can be attended to. One of these needs is self-esteem. Self-esteem refers to the judgment of merit or worth that an individual places on various aspects of himself or herself.[43]

Learners achieve at levels in keeping with the picture they have of themselves, even when their ability shows they are capable of achieving at near-perfect levels.[44] This occurs because all people act in ways that are rewarding and that maintain their current self as it is. Change (learning) occurs only when learners can maintain control of their lives and further support or enhance their current "self-picture." Achievement-oriented students picture themselves as capable of succeeding, whereas learned-helpless students see themselves as failures.

Self-esteem can be increased when teachers set high expectations for all students and then help them reach these goals. When teachers believe in students, students will believe in themselves. At the same time, teachers should let students know the purpose of these expectations so that students know they are accomplishing worthwhile tasks rather than meaningless busywork. When students know that they have accomplished significant types of learning, they will experience personal satisfaction. Making mistakes is often an important part of the learning experience and students need to accept their mistakes as well as their successes. Mistakes should be seen as something to learn from rather than representing failure. Teachers can model this behavior as students accept that making mistakes can be part of the learning process. A psychologically safe environment will help students accept their mistakes. Last, teachers can help self-esteem by valuing effort as well as achievements. This will help students learn the importance of effort and perseverance as they work to achieve goals set by themselves as well as teachers.[45]

Another way to help learners develop self-esteem is to look at their characteristics. Look for the best in your students. Reinforce the positive characteristics by pointing them out to the students and to others. Look for positive qualities (independence) that are currently expressed by negative behavior (stubbornness). Reinforce positive, appropriate ways to express these qualities. Ignore negative items that are merely a matter of personal taste, preference, or style.[46] Box 13.4 illustrates the importance of each individual.

Avoid comparing students with each other. Physical educators often post charts on the walls or shout out numbers during physical fitness testing. Be careful with students' fragile self-esteem. How would you feel if you were ranked number 32?

Glasser maintained that "the major problem of the schools is a problem of failure."[47] He further suggested that educators need to examine why children fail and provide schools in which children can succeed. Youth who feel the concern and acceptance of a teacher can gain self-confidence, which in turn enhances self-motivation. These factors constitute the foundation for success. A

Success in physical activities increases self-estem.

student experiencing success is much more likely to eagerly anticipate each learning activity and participate in an orderly way than a student who is not experiencing success. Once the cycle of success within each student is in operation, class control is more effective. Teachers must be committed to helping students succeed and show a genuine concern for each of them. This concern for learners involves the following:

1. Caring: helping students feel they are liked.
2. Understanding: creating an atmosphere of empathy and tolerance.
3. Identification: considering students as separate, worthy individuals.
4. Recognition: appreciating students' unique contributions.[48]

A Warm, Supportive, Well-Organized Environment

The learning climate is a result of the effects of the teacher's attitudes and behavior on the feelings and thoughts of students about their personal safety and self-esteem.[49] The personality, self-confidence, and attitudes of the teacher communicate to the students that the teacher cares about them and about the subject that is being taught.

Chandler suggested using an invitational approach to physical education in which physical educators "invite students to succeed." He defined an invitation as "informal or formal messages sent verbally or nonverbally to students, teachers, parents and others . . . to inform them that they, the recipients, are valuable, able, and responsible." Purkey suggested some things teachers could do to achieve this.[50] Some other suggestions have also been added.

1. Teach students, not sports. A psychological insight into the background, needs, and characteristics of students and the causes of behavioral problems can be helpful. Be aware of and responsive to student interests and concerns. Try to understand their world and their heroes, fads, fashions, and interests. Be a mentor and a guide for them.
   a. Learn their names, greet them at the door or in the locker room, and see them off.
   b. Create a special, caring environment.
   c. Share a thought or current event.
   d. Get to know and introduce new students.
   e. Let students know they are missed when absent from class.
   f. Tell others about good things students do.
   g. Give emotional support as needed. Praise when appropriate. Provide encouragement to attain goals.
   h. Seek out opportunities to help students succeed and then point out their successes to the class.[51]
   i. Make positive comments to them about their individual improvement, effort, sportspersonship, and teamwork.
   j. Share duties with students, such as taking roll and distributing and collecting equipment.
   k. Always treat students with dignity.
   l. Involve students in decisions.
   m. Play games with no winners or losers.
2. Listen to students in a way that indicates you care. When you listen you say, "You are important!" Listen not just for the story but also for why the student is telling you something. Respond to the feelings that are expressed. Don't try to "fix it and make it better." Rather, help the student explore alternatives if there is a problem to solve.[52]
   a. Ask for student input instead of assuming you know what they want or why they did what they did.
   b. Have a gripe box. Read the gripes to the class and get their input.[53]

3. Recognize special people and times. Activities that bring social approval to students not only increase motivation but also individual self-esteem.
   a. Remember birthdays.
   b. Post a picture and historical sketch of the student of the month.
   c. Post a "player of the week"-type award on the bulletin board for any specified behavior such as leadership, sportspersonship, effort, or skill performance.
   d. Award fun prizes for unusual accomplishments, such as the golden arrow for the most bull's-eyes (an old arrow sprayed gold) or the belle of the ball for most matches played (a tennis ball dressed in a gown) or the sneaker award (an old sneaker) to the most-improved runner on the physical fitness test.
   e. Put articles about students in the school or community newspaper.
   f. Use school assemblies to showcase student talents.
4. Send explicit, unconditional invitations supporting students, such as "I think you can do it" rather than "You can do it *if* you . . ."
5. Get to know students' families. Have a family night in which a parent and child participate in activities together.
6. Share your personal background with the students—your spouse, children, where you are from. Allow one student each week to ask you a question and ask a question of one student each week.[54]
7. Create an inviting physical environment using neat, colorful bulletin boards and posters to brighten the surroundings and attractively displayed slogans and signs politely encouraging students to do something.
8. Encourage interest in physical education.
   a. Invite students to draw posters about an activity and its history.
   b. Have students bring in little known facts.
   c. Ask students to bring their records or tapes to play during warm-up exercises (check tapes before using them).
   d. Bertel suggests starting an activity just like it might have been played by its inventors and then adding rules, skills, and strategies as the need arises. Once the students become involved, they will want to learn more. For example, basketball can be played with peach baskets or the old rules of three dribbles before passing or shooting.[55]
   e. Share inspiring sports stories.
9. Develop class spirit. Have students choose a name, motto, emblem, or color.
10. Provide opportunities for students to safely make avoidance responses and reduce aggressive behavior, such as punching a bag instead of a student or taking time out to cool off.[56]
11. Invite administrators, parents, and others to become involved in physical education by teaching special activities or skills or to be an audience for student presentations.
12. Create positive, pleasant relationships with all students. Help students develop positive interpersonal relations skills with teachers and other students. Relationships should be based on mutual respect.
13. Be professionally responsible, working through counselors and administrators to correct potential problems, confronting students professionally about their behavior, and seeing students as they *can be*, not as they are.

Motivation can also be increased by effective classroom management. When large numbers of students continually disrupt the learning environment, it typically means that something is wrong with the classroom management system. When teachers plan and implement an effective management system, students know what is expected of them and are busily engaged in achieving expectations. Some teacher behaviors that can be used to enhance classroom management are included in Chapter 12.

Review Question: How can teachers invite students to succeed in physical education?

Teacher Modeling

Teachers can model mature, effective behavior and appropriate ways to solve problems, including admitting their mistakes and accepting students' mistakes. They should also be proper role models of what they teach by incorporating good fitness practices into their lifestyles and demonstrating their enthusiasm and love for physical activity. Teachers with good discipline in their classes exhibit some similarities in their authority style, but there is no specific formula that will produce good discipline for all teachers. Effective discipline tends to emanate from teachers who are

1. Positive role models
   a. Assertive rather than aggressive
   b. Act rather than react
   c. Consistent rather than inconsistent
   d. Clearly communicate expectations rather than being vague
   e. Convey interest and enthusiasm rather than disinterest and boredom
   f. Set realistic goals rather than unrealistic goals
2. Efficient planners
3. Effective communicators
4. Thorough assessors
   a. Of their own teaching behavior, which they modify when needed
   b. Of students and their learning styles
5. Consistent in their expectations of children.[57]

Teachers should take responsibility for their own behaviors, including dressing appropriately, starting class on time, teaching in an interesting manner, returning papers in a reasonable time period, helping students learn, and ending on time.[58]

Well-Planned, Appropriate Learning and Assessment Experiences

The establishment of an interesting, relevant, challenging curriculum that is responsive to the needs of the students (e.g., love, control, freedom, fun) can be accomplished best by involving students in the planning stages. Student interests can be determined by means of a survey and the curriculum can be organized to allow students to choose between several possible units.

Students need programs that are well organized and related to their needs and abilities. A mismatch between student interests and abilities and instruction invites discipline problems. When students act out it may be to protect themselves against frustration or failure with a too difficult assignment or boredom with one that is too easy. Talking rather than doing also contributes to boredom, inattention, and deviant behavior. When learning is too easy, students find little value in it. Physical educators generally need to have higher expectations for student achievement. In 90 percent of research studies, specific, difficult goals produced better performance than easy, do-your-best, or no goals.[59] Involvement in challenging learning activities not only contributes to the opportunity for success but also keeps students busily engaged in positive behavior with little or no time or incentive for irrational, unruly behavior.

To determine learner readiness for certain skills, ask the questions, "Are students physically and emotionally ready to learn the material?" and "Do students have the prerequisite facts, intellectual skills, and strategies necessary for learning?" Introducing skills before a student is ready may result in failure and negative consequences for the learner's self-image. Therefore, readiness has implications regarding the sequencing of skills within the curriculum. Readiness for physical education activities depends on maturation, previous experience, and attitudes toward the subject. Readiness for a given activity differs among students and in the same student from time to time. Physical readiness depends on maturation; general motor development including strength, coordination, endurance, balance, speed, and agility; and prerequisite skills. Prerequisite skills include basic locomotor skills such as running and jumping and fundamental skills such as throwing, catching, and striking. Teachers can increase student readiness for future learning by providing a wide variety of activities.[60]

Students are not unmotivated. As McKeachie indicated, "They are learning all the time—new dance steps, the status hierarchy on campus, football strategy, etc."[61] Teachers need to realize this and capitalize on "what turns students on." Students are much more motivated to learn and remember material that is meaningful. Teachers must put themselves in the shoes of their students to determine what is meaningful to them.

Vary your presentation techniques. Adolescents have an attention span of about fifteen minutes, so use at least three different teaching techniques during a forty-five to fifty-minute class period (e.g., lecture, small group discussions, report back to large group, short writing assignment or review previous skill, model new skill, practice new skill using task sheets, play lead-up game).

Involve students in evaluating their own performances. Students can give input on ways to assess their behavior, what to put on tests, and how to evaluate the results. They can write questions, administer and score tests, and keep plots of their progress. With teacher evaluation, students develop an external locus of control, whereas student evaluation helps students develop an internal locus of control. Helping students evaluate their own work helps them become more responsible and self-directed.

Helping Students Learn Self-Direction and Responsibility

The right to be in school carries certain responsibilities. Students are responsible for coming prepared, not giving excuses, and doing their own work.[62] Teachers are responsible for teaching students how to be prepared, social skills for interacting with others, and how to solve problems that arise in the classroom.

Students need the guidance and security provided by well-defined rules of expected behavior and the knowledge that adults care enough about them to enforce those rules. Children raised without correction have lower self-esteem, are more dependent, achieve less, and have less control over their world. A study of appropriate behavior in a low-socioeconomic-level junior high school revealed that the teacher with discipline problems failed to enforce rules and monitor behavior of students.[63] The results substantiated Durkheim's premise that "children themselves are the first to appreciate good discipline." Teachers need to remember that it takes courage to discipline, but that students want it and they will respect and like the teacher who is a good disciplinarian.[64] Students understand that requiring appropriate behavior of everyone is a sign of respect and caring.

Rules are also necessary in a classroom as they function to prevent or encourage behavior by clearly stating expectations for students.[65] Rules differ from procedures in that they have consequences for not being followed. General rules[66] cover a wide range of behaviors and must be defined and/or explained to students. Some examples might include these:

- Respect yourself and others.
- Play fairly at all times.
- Help others when they need help.

Specific rules point precisely to one behavior[67] and might include such things as

- No swearing or use of profanity.
- Be seated in your attendance row after entering the gymnasium.
- Listen when the teacher is talking.

You should have no more than five specific rules because students and teachers have a difficult time remembering more than that. Should the need for a new rule arise, teachers should eliminate one of the specific rules, telling students that it is now an unwritten rule or including it under a general rule and adding the new rule.

Use of Rules and Consequences (Assertive Discipline—Teacher-Controlled)

Establish clear rules, communicate them to students, and teach students how to follow them. Rules for each type of activity should be explicit and posted for everyone to see, if possible. Behavior skills can be taught in the same manner as psychomotor skills—by modeling the skill and by practice, followed by positive reinforcement. Deviations from the rule might mean a misunderstanding, requiring a review. Avoid bargaining or negotiating with students. Communicate expectations at the beginning of the year and during each lesson.[68]

Tell students at the beginning of the year the consequences for misbehavior. Include a maximum of five consequences with which you are comfortable. For example: (1) a warning, (2) time-out, (3) loss of privileges, (4) call the parent, (5) go to the principal's office. Use firm, consistent negative consequences but only after ensuring that students understand and have practiced the rule. Explain consequences for inappropriate behavior.[69] Never threaten a student with consequences unless you intend to follow through. Consequences should never be physically or psychologically harmful to students. Corporal punishment, including using exercise as punishment, must never be used as discipline. Teachers should develop consequences when planning their discipline system rather than waiting until the heat of the moment to determine consequences for undesirable behavior.

Provide firm direction and structure. Avoid phrases like "Do you want to . . .?" "Would you like to . . .?" "Okay?" Use phrases like "Please do this." Make sure all students are listening when giving instructions. Do not ignore misbehavior.[70]

Be consistent and fair. Students learn to choose whether to behave or misbehave and the consequences for either choice. They learn that they control the consequences.[71] Canter emphasizes that "One day is not enough. It takes a great deal of effort and continuing training for a teacher to master the skills of classroom management."[72]

Chapter 12 presented various routines and procedures that help establish a positive learning climate. Good teachers establish clear, consistent direction, use routine procedures for recurring situations, practice skills with the class, and manage in a fair and predictable fashion using rules with clearly stated consequences.

Teacher-directed group planning, in which the scope and area of planning are predetermined, is the next step toward self-direction. Help students set their own class rules. Define a few clear, specific guidelines that define teacher and student roles and behaviors, with a range of natural or logical consequences appropriate for the age level involved. Students learn to make choices and to gain control of their own learning situation. Encourage student involvement in solving problems that arise.

Self-management through group planning is achieved only after all of the other skills and understandings needed have been achieved. Even after self-direction in known areas has been achieved, however, some students will fail to be self-directing when a new situation presents itself. For this reason, patterns of control must be applied according to the appropriateness of the situation. At times the teacher needs to provide the students with a choice between self-direction and teacher direction and let them decide which will be more valuable to them in the specific learning environment.

Student leadership can also be used to help students develop responsibility. For example, students can be asked to serve as warm-up leaders, team and squad captains, and equipment monitors. Rotate these opportunities often so all students eventually get a chance to serve. Some students who normally would be chosen last might be selected to do this early in the year. Ideally, the goal of any teacher is for students to self-manage and have enough personal responsibility to follow the routines and rules necessary for an effective learning environment. Since this is one of the National Physical Education Content Standards, physical education teachers should work hard to achieve this goal.

Review Question: What can you do to create a learning environment in which students wish to learn?

DISCIPLINE

In an ideal world, students would be highly motivated to learn and activities would be so organized that there would be no chance for off-task or disruptive behavior. Reality means that some students find it more rewarding to cause problems than learn, and this attitude leads to unpreventable managerial episodes when no learning is taking place. Teachers enter the profession wanting to teach, not discipline, students. Many leave the teaching profession when they find that they are "policing" rather than teaching.[73] Discipline isn't something that just happens naturally. It is the result of some very deliberate teacher actions designed to produce an environment in which students are safe and learning can occur. Teachers who have good discipline frequently use sound instructional practices (see Chapter 9). They know that if students are engaged in a learning activity, they are less likely to create problems. Another part of good discipline involves managing resources effectively and having well-established routines that when followed result in an orderly environment (see Chapter 12). An environment should be inviting to students and support learning. Discipline is important in teaching. Administrators expect the teachers they hire to be able to maintain order in their classes. Teacher evaluations frequently include a category involving discipline of students.

Students are critical of teachers who do not maintain adequate classroom control. They know that few teachers can teach well without establishing good class discipline. They are aware that beginning teachers often have less control than experienced teachers.

The most important concern in discipline, of course, is the establishment of a good learning environment, one in which students can grow in both knowledge and self-control. Each student has a basic right to an educational experience free from unnecessary distractions caused by a few unruly students. Good order, based on a cooperative effort of everyone involved, contributes to the teacher's goal of optimum learning and to the student's growth as a responsible member of society.

What is discipline? Is it a set of rules, controlled behavior, a systematic method to obtain obedience, punishment, or moral and ethical behavior? Discipline is difficult to define because its meaning has evolved over the years to include many aspects of behavior. We often think of discipline as cut-and-dried standards of good versus bad. However, because each individual reacts differently to his or her environment, many variations in behavior may be accepted as disciplined.

Children go through various stages as they mature and come to understand control. Preschool children are trained to follow established rules and procedures. Children learn to relate to nonpersonal objects, becoming familiar with natural laws and governing themselves so as to use those laws for their own purposes. As children enter school, they are helped to develop a certain amount of conformity to group patterns, which we might call social control. They learn to relate to the culture and its institutions and to develop the capacity for some reciprocal adjustment with their environment. Finally, children learn to interact with others through a process of self-control. They interact on a psychological level and need no extrinsic reward or punishment.

Discipline becomes a process of helping youngsters adjust to their environment and develop acceptable inner controls. For purposes of discussion, discipline will be defined as *orderly social behavior in an atmosphere that allows meaningful learning to transpire.* It involves a slow progression from the direct, authoritative control of behavior needed by some learners to a desirable level of self-control experienced by only a few. In education today, emphasis is often placed on students' natural abilities to interpret situations and react accordingly (reaping the consequences of any undesired act) rather than on a strict code of behavior for all students.

Discipline involves both students and teachers. Teachers must know when to be authoritative, when to be permissive, and when to straddle the middle ground. Classes can change dramatically from one hour to the next or one week to another. Pep rallies, assemblies, lunchtime activities, weather, or the activities of previous classes can cause normally quiet students to stampede into a room. Success or failure with homework or previous assignments can affect the attitude of students before the lesson has even begun.

As students and teacher embark upon a day's activities, many things can happen. Ideally, both teacher and students will be successfully engaged in teaching and learning activities, neither interfering with the activities of the other. However, since teachers and students often have different personalities and values, conflict might occur, resulting in behavior unacceptable to either the teacher or the student.[74] Teachers must listen to the students' problems and attempt to understand and resolve them if possible. If the problem hinders the teacher's activities, the teacher must communicate to the student how he or she feels in an attempt to resolve the conflict. For example, the teacher might say, "I'm trying to help everyone learn . . ., but I can't when I'm constantly interrupted." Sometimes the student will understand and alter the behavior. Often the school or teacher has a specific policy for handling the behavior. If not, the teacher will be forced to (1) take a stand and authoritatively decide what to do to solve the problem, (2) allow the student to continue the behavior at the expense of the teacher and often of the other students, or (3) attempt to work out a solution that is acceptable to both parties.

A typical classroom usually consists of three groups of students: 80 percent rarely break rules or violate principles, 15 percent break rules on a somewhat regular basis and need teachers to set clear expectations and consequences for them or they will disrupt learning for other students, and 5 percent are chronic rule breakers and generally out of control most of the time. Nothing seems to work for them. They have typically experienced failure from an early age and maintain no hope for success in the future.[75]

Review Question: Define discipline. How does discipline apply to teaching?

Choosing/Creating a Personal Discipline Model

In the beginning of this book, we discussed the importance of developing a personal philosophy of education and physical education. The discipline practices that you choose to implement should match these philosophies. No one procedure will work in each situation. Each discipline situation may require trying several techniques before one is successful. In all situations it is important to determine why a specific behavior has occurred. Without this information, a teacher may be able to improve the immediate situation but the problem will not have been resolved and will probably recur. This approach is similar to treating the symptoms of an illness but not actually curing the illness. The symptoms will continue to recur until the type of illness is identified, treated, and cured. Sometimes this effort will take a consistent effort over a period of time, but there is no greater reward for a teacher than to know that she or he has made a positive difference in the life of a student.

In all situations a teacher must determine whether it is desirable for a specific behavior to be increased or decreased. Behaviors that are to be increased should be reinforced and behaviors that are to be decreased should be punished. Types of positive reinforcers include verbal social reinforcers, nonverbal social reinforcers, consumable reinforcers, nonconsumable reinforcers, and privileges. Verbal social reinforcers are praise such as "terrific!" and "I'm proud of your effort." Nonverbal social reinforcers include a smile, nod, or a high five. Foods are examples of consumable reinforcers. These should be used sparingly, especially items that include sugar or that might cause allergic reactions. Instead nonconsumable reinforcers should be used such as certificates, stars by their name, or their pictures in the school newspaper. Privileges might include helping with equipment, selecting a class activity, or demonstrating a skill.[76]

Care must be taken in selecting appropriate punishments. What was selected as a punishment may actually be a reinforcer. For example "time out" can be quite effective for elementary students but not for a high school student. The high school student may actually want to sit out. The key is to take away something the student wants. For example, being with their own group is very important in middle school and high school. One main social opportunity is lunch time. A punishment might be that the student must eat lunch with the teacher rather than with peers.[77]

The best technique is to prevent misbehavior from occurring. This is best done by careful, thoughtful planning that results in lessons in which activities are developmentally appropriate and provide optimum challenges for each student; proper pacing is used; each student is engaged throughout the class; and the teacher is enthusiastic and respectful. The students are also held accountable for learning.

ACCEPTABLE DISCIPLINARY PRACTICES

Henkel studied teacher control strategies and classified them into three areas. First, teachers suspected or anticipated misconduct and took precautions to avoid problems. Second, when misconduct occurred, teachers tutored students to modify their conduct. Third, when serious misconduct occurred, teachers imposed unpleasant consequences, such as time-out or loss of privileges.[78]

When disciplining students, teachers typically make two types of errors.[79] The first error is to discipline the wrong student. From the world of sports, physical education teachers know that often the person who retaliates gets the penalty. The same is true for teaching. When disciplining students, teachers must make sure that action is taken with the instigator as well as the person who retaliates. The second error is to discipline the wrong behavior. Teachers must know which behaviors are likely to escalate into more serious behaviors and stop them quickly. Learning when to discipline students has been compared to driving a car—there are many things that must be coordinated simultaneously and the teacher must know when to push on the gas pedal and when to apply the brakes.[80]

Each student is an individual, so it may be necessary to vary actual discipline practices or consequences according to individual needs. When disciplining students, teachers must remember to let them know that it is the student's behavior that is the issue, not whether the teacher likes the student. Students may challenge teachers by saying "you don't like me." If teachers convey the attitude that they dislike certain students, they will never have a chance to establish a positive rapport with those students.

Teachers must decide what discipline practices work for them. Teachers striving to incorporate acceptable practices should remember the following guidelines: (1) solve your own problems whenever possible, (2) be available and visible, (3) admit mistakes, (4) take advantage of the teaching moment, and (5) look for causes of misconduct. The following are offered as suggestions when discipline strategies are needed.

Waiting Aggressively

Waiting aggressively is a teacher tactic that lets students know they must pay attention. Such waiting should be obvious. Waiting signals can include a frown, a shake of the head, a clearing of the throat, a disapproving look at an offender, a mild reproof, or movement toward the trouble spot. Often these techniques will resolve problems before they become difficult.

Rewards

Extrinsic and intrinsic rewards are based on reinforcement theory. Extrinsic rewards are external to the learner and are result-oriented—a good grade, peer recognition, or teacher approval. Intrinsic rewards are internally perceived and controlled by the learner. They include the pleasure derived from participation or competence in the activity itself, self-confidence, self-discovery, pride, or personal progress.

Studies have demonstrated that when intrinsic motivation is present, extrinsic rewards can actually decrease satisfaction in the activity.[81] Deci, however, isolated two kinds of rewards, only one of which results in a deterioration of intrinsic motivation. Rewards that intend to make students do what the teacher wants, when and where the teacher wants it done, are called *controlling* rewards. *Informative* rewards, such as "good work" written on a student's paper, provide feedback about their competence and self-determination. Deci's results showed that when teachers stressed the informative nature of rewards rather than the controlling nature, students were more intrinsically motivated, had more positive attitudes toward themselves, and were more self-directing.[82]

Harter described two general functions of rewards. *Motivational* rewards, used as incentives, increase the chances of a child's engaging in certain activities. The degree of pleasure or satisfaction experienced also influences the child's developing self-reward system. The *informative* function tells the child what goals are worthy and appropriate and provides feedback on the child's success in achieving those goals. When deciding how to behave in complex situations, younger children appear more responsive to adult feedback, whereas older children consider social (adult and/or peer) feedback and the objective consequences of their behavior as compared with their internalized standards of success and failure. As children develop, they need less extrinsic motivation. Intrinsically motivated students are capable of operating on a "relatively thin schedule of reinforcement."[83]

Harter also found that for older children, boys had significantly more intrinsic motivation, whereas girls relied more heavily on adult approval. However, tremendous variability existed within gender groups as well as considerable overlap between boys and girls. When girls are equally or more competent than boys on skills, no differences in intrinsic motivation have been found. Teachers can help students of both sexes acquire proficiency in activities and develop strong feelings of self-efficacy in movement patterns.[84]

Some teachers worry about the use of extrinsic rewards in the classroom. Remember that reinforcement is a part of life. Adults are rewarded with paychecks, recognition by society, praise from friends or bosses, and many other types of reinforcement. In fact, modifications in behavior are constantly being made by those who interact with others in the environment. It is the same in school. Teachers must take students as they are and assist them in trying out new kinds of behavior until they learn the satisfaction that comes from success in the activity itself. Students, like adults, choose whether they will respond to rewards. As La Mancusa stated, "The teacher does neither himself nor his students a favor by perpetuating the climate of failure."[85] Giving students attention for good behavior is far more desirable than giving them attention for misbehavior. Positive reinforcement occurs when a behavior is followed immediately by the presentation of a stimulus that will in the future increase the likelihood that the behavior will occur again. Students who are sitting in squad lines doing their stretches (behavior) and are praised by the teacher when he or she enters the gym (positive reinforcement) are likely to repeat that behavior. Negative reinforcement occurs when a behavior is followed immediately by the presentation of a stimulus that will decrease the likelihood that the behavior will occur again. Students who are made to run a mile (behavior) without previous conditioning are likely to experience pain (negative effect) and be unwilling to run in the future. When teachers try to decrease a previously reinforced undesirable behavior, they withdraw reinforcement. This is called extinction. When presenting information to a class, students will frequently call out answers rather than raising their hands to respond. Teachers who respond to those calling out are reinforcing that behavior. Instead, if the teacher will ignore those calling out answers and select other students to respond, the behavior (calling out) can be extinguished. Teachers should know that when attempting to extinguish a behavior, the behavior will likely escalate before it is extinguished.

When initially teaching a new behavior, teachers will want to reinforce the behavior each time it occurs. After students learn the behavior, teachers will want to "thin the schedule of reinforcement" by reinforcing the behavior less frequently (once every three times the behavior occurs and progressively less frequently). This will help prevent the reinforcement from losing effectiveness. As the behavior becomes part of the way students typically act, teachers must reinforce the behavior occasionally to ensure that it continues. If teachers see a previously learned behavior that is "slipping," they should begin reinforcing more often to ensure that it continues.

Rules can be taught using reinforcement. Rules should always be stated in a positive manner that explains how the student is to act (e.g., instead of saying "don't talk while others are speaking" the rule should state "listen while others are speaking"). Another strategy for using reinforcement is to reinforce a behavior that is an alternative to or incompatible with the undesired behavior (called DRA or DRI).[86] For example, if a teacher notices that students are moving around and interacting with their friends instead of listening when he or she gives directions, a policy could be implemented that requires students to sit in squad lines when directions are given.

Contingency Contracting

Most of us have practiced behavior modification on ourselves. You might be saying to yourself right now, "As soon as I finish reading this chapter, I'm going to eat a snack." That is an example of contingency contracting. *Contingency contracting* is reinforcement that is contingent on the performance of the desired behavior. An example of the technique is Grandma's law discussed in Chapter 12. A more sophisticated explanation was developed by Premack and is called the Premack principle.[87] It suggests that any behavior that occurs frequently can be used to reinforce a behavior that occurs less frequently. For example, "obtaining high performance scores" (a highly desired result) becomes a reinforcer for practicing one's skills (a less-desired result).

Contingency contracting can be used along with extinction to reduce undesirable behavior, to develop new behavior, or to strengthen and maintain existing behavior. Joyce and Weil described contingency contracting as "the heart of effective classroom management." According to Homme, contingency contracts should be

1. *Clear*—The directions should be stated in explicit terms that are easily understood by the student, such as
   If you do . . ., then you will get . . .
   If you do . . ., then I will do . . .
   If you do . . ., then you may do . . .
   (Note: *You* is a student or a group.)
2. *Fair*—The two sides of the contract must be of relatively equal importance.
3. *Honest*—The reward should be given immediately *after* the performance but *only* for the performance specified in the contract.
4. *Positive*—The contract *should not* say, "If you do . . ., then I will *not* do . . .
5. *Systematic*—The instructor should be consistent in reinforcing only the desired behavior.[88]

The following procedures will help when establishing a contract:

1. Clearly specify a few rules that tell exactly what is expected. Limit rules to five or fewer.[89] Establish the target behavior in terms of performance and criteria for achievement. Establish what the reward will be for correct performance. Stress academic achievement rather than obedience.[90] Academic achievement is usually incompatible with disruptive behavior. Maintain a fair contract.
2. Initiate a contract with students. The contract may be a short statement by the teacher that states the consequences to be gained by certain behaviors.
3. Ignore disruptive, nondestructive behavior.
4. Reward the student immediately after completion of the desired behavior. Initial rewards are given for behavior that approximates the goal (e.g., small, simple tasks). Later, behaviors should be increasingly close to the final objective.
5. Use a variety of reinforcers to reward appropriate behaviors. Work toward the use of higher-order reinforcers and an intermittent reinforcement schedule (random or unpredictable reinforcement) to increase resistance to extinction. This reduces teacher approval to only a few times a day. The needs of each individual will determine what things or events will serve as reinforcers. Teachers can plan in advance to see what is reinforcing and what is not for their particular students. To be worthwhile, rewards must be highly desirable and not obtainable outside the conditions of the contract.[91]
6. Be consistent in following the plan.
7. Progress from teacher-directed contracts to mutually directed contracts to student-initiated contracts.

Examples of contingency management programs include the Champions program, in which students earn points for good behavior and lose points for inappropriate behavior. By accumulating a certain number of points, students are awarded a Champions sweatband of the color earned. Colored chips have also been used as a behavior management tool. In one school, students earn soda cards that can be redeemed in the principal's office. Students should write their names on the cards so other students do not steal them.[92]

Several studies have been conducted in physical education settings. Vogler and French used smiley face and frowny face tokens, which students could exchange for free-time activities, to successfully increase on-task behavior. Paese rewarded students for appropriate dress with free gym time and choice of activities and increased the percentage of students dressed for activity from 71 percent to 92 percent.[93]

Different personalities of teacher and student, different student learning styles, and different environmental conditions can affect the success or failure of contingency contracting.

Contingent Activities

Contingent activities can be a reward for a goal fulfilled. Such activities should always be positive. Physical activity must never be negative, such as using running or push-ups as punishment for the losers of the game or for inappropriate behavior. Some possible activities include the following:

1. Reward class effort by letting students play novelty games or make up their own games.
2. Allow students who complete assigned tasks early to set up a game or match of their choice, practice on their own, or use specialized equipment (e.g., a ball machine).

Since preferred activities can serve as reinforcers, all instructors have to do is observe students to determine what activities they like to do best. Teachers can even ask students what activities are worth working for.

Social Reinforcement and Praise

How the teacher uses reinforcers frequently determines their success, because teachers themselves are one of the major sources of classroom motivation. Enthusiasm, facial expression, animation, and vocal intensity are some of the important qualities a teacher can exhibit.

Praise is used extensively in physical education even though research shows that it is often ineffective. Brophy found, however, that praise correlates positively with academic achievement for children of low socioeconomic status.

Introverts, low-skilled students, minority group students, and those with an external locus of control tend to respond to praise more than their counterparts. Students with the opposite traits are generally intrinsically motivated and may respond negatively to praise, resulting in decreased motivation. In fact, adults and high school students tend to perceive individuals who are praised for their successes, but given neutral feedback on their failures, as having lower ability levels, in contrast to those who receive criticism for their failures and neutral feedback for their successes. Praise, then, appears to convey information about teacher goals and desires and correct answers rather than serving as a reinforcer to student learning.[94]

The effects of praise vary with students' experience, personality, and previous successes and failures. Some students find praise embarrassing; others encourage and even elicit praise from teachers. Use praise only when it is sincere. However, either praise or criticism may be more motivating to many students than being ignored.

Praise correctly rather than often. Verbal praise can be effectively supplemented by giving written praise on student work and by teaching students to set realistic goals, evaluate their own performance, and provide self-reinforcement. Students also need to be taught to attribute success to their own abilities and effort rather than to external causes. As with the self-fulfilling prophecy, individual students react differently to praise. Catch students being good. Praise each student every day. Reinforce positive behaviors rather than focus on negative behaviors. Sander suggests written reports or letters to parents and positive verbal feedback.[95]

To be effective, praise must be contingent on correct performance, specific to the performance, and sincere. Privately given praise based on specified performance criteria (including effort) is effective.[96] General, nonspecific praise is not usually regarded by students as credible. Moreover, it can create anxiety and put students into a dependent mode. When students are praised for high achievement, they may feel insecure because they don't know whether they can maintain the high achievement. In addition, they are subject to criticism from their peers. The other students feel insecure because their efforts are not of value to the teacher unless they get high marks. Thus, self-worth and achievement are equated. Self-worth should not be based on performance. Students can also see praise as manipulative and react adversely. Expressing appreciation or positive feelings about the high quality of students' work can have a good effect.[97]

Brophy stated that boys get more praise and criticism simply because they are more active; they get more of all kinds of teacher interaction. Boys tend to be praised more for achievement and girls for such traits as neatness and following directions. On the other hand, girls are more often criticized for unacceptable achievement, whereas boys are criticized for speaking out of turn and sloppy work. These factors have serious implications for self-concept, especially for girls, who apparently internalize teacher criticism as a deficiency in their abilities, since they have been praised for their effort and obedience. Boys, on the other hand, generally blame their failures on external circumstances and their successes on their own abilities and, therefore, maintain positive self-concepts.[98]

Tokens or Points

Tokens or points can be collected to be exchanged at a later time for a specific reward. The object is not only to reward behavior but also to change it. Tousignant and Siedentop found that students who were rewarded for effort or performance reduced the quantity of their off-task behaviors.[99] Certificates, ribbons, stickers, special events, and other rewards might be used to motivate students. Siedentop specified a series of guidelines to implement this system:

1. Define the target in observable units.
2. Explain the target behaviors clearly to the participants.
3. Monitor the target behaviors consistently.
4. State the contingency (reward) clearly.
5. Use a simple reward system.
6. Think small. Make the system manageable.
7. Be consistent.[100]

The following examples illustrate the use of tokens or points:

1. Points are awarded during tournament play for game results. The following point system might be used:

   1 point = a loss
   2 points = a tie
   3 points = a win

   At the end of round robin competition, points are totaled to award first, second, third, or other place honors. Points might also be given for acts of courtesy and fair play.

2. Colored tickets are awarded for events in track and field throughout the unit.

   Blue = 1st place (Running events)
   Red = 2nd place (Running events)
   White = 3rd place (Running events)
   Orange = jogged a lap

   Blue, red, white, yellow, and green ribbons are also awarded for designated heights or distances in field events. Teachers might also designate criterion times for different running events and award ribbons based on achieving those times. Students are able to earn ribbons even though they might not place first, second, or third. At the conclusion of a unit, the point values of each ticket are calculated and students record their total score.

3. Extra credit points or tokens are awarded for participation outside of school hours in activities from archery to water skiing. Have students keep a log of dates and hours spent in each activity.
4. Points are awarded to units within a team for outstanding plays or goals achieved. For example, on

the basketball team the guards, forwards, and centers would compete as three separate units. An average unit free throw percentage would be kept and the unit with the highest average would get points or tokens.

5. Grades are based on a point system for completing learning tasks and policy requirements. When such a system is used, students know exactly what is required of them to earn a grade.

Punishment

Punishment is negative contingency contracting—"If you do x, you will get y," y being undesirable. Punishment involves external control over a student by the teacher. It usually implies mental or physical pain or discomfort. *Restitution* of things taken and *reparation* for things damaged or destroyed willfully are generally conceded to be fair forms of punishment. To be effective, this form of punishment must teach the student that when something is destroyed it affects the welfare of the entire group. This technique also teaches the student to make amends. The teacher's responsibility lies in explaining the reasons for the punishment and in following through to see that restoration is made. If the student is financially unable to pay expenses for reparation, the school should find a way for the student to work off the debt. When parents are too free with money, the school can solicit their cooperation in making the punishment effective by permitting the student to work out the debt to society.

Punishment has some undesirable side effects. Teachers must weigh the impact of these side effects before incorporating punishment into a system of discipline. Although a behavior may be temporarily suppressed when punishment or the threat of punishment follows behavior, it will often reappear later. One possible reason for this is that punishment tells the student what not to do but gives no direction as to the appropriate behavior, causing the student to experiment with a whole range of inappropriate behaviors while searching for the appropriate behavior. Reward, on the contrary, immediately tells the student what the appropriate behavior is. Other undesirable side effects of punishment, such as a negative self-concept or a dislike of school, the subject, or the teacher, can develop. These negative feelings may predispose the student to retaliate or withdraw. Further, punishment reduces the behavior only in the presence of the punishing agent. Students may learn how to avoid getting caught by more sophisticated cheating or lying. Finally, punishment teaches students to be aggressive through imitation of the aggressive behavior of adults.

Punishment should be used only in a planned, careful way to deal with problems that cannot be resolved by the alternative measures discussed, or when students know ahead of time that certain results come from their actions. Some school districts have a discipline code that categorizes student misbehavior and identifies administrative or teacher actions that may be taken. Becker suggested two circumstances in which punishment may be needed: (1) when direct reinforcement procedures are likely to fail because the negative behavior is so frequent that there is no positive behavior to reinforce and (2) when someone might get hurt.[101]

Punishment, when it is used, should be primarily a natural consequence of the choices made by students. Students should be counseled as to the consequences of alternatives when they make their choices. Negative reinforcement must never be used to punish one student in front of a group of students. The following procedures are suggested when using punishment:

1. Allow an undesirable act to continue (or insist that it continue) until the student is clearly bored with it. For example, a teacher could insist that a student throwing spit wads continue to make spit wads until the student has clearly learned how unattractive the behavior is and can make a decision to follow a desired behavior.
2. Always accompany punishment with a suggestion of something positive to do (e.g., the desired behavior).
3. End the punishment with the student's decision to perform the desired behavior.
4. Reward the positive behavior or the student will revert to the bad behavior to get recognition, even if it takes the form of punishment.

The Social Contract—Logical Consequences

Curwin and Mendler suggested the use of social contracts to achieve discipline with dignity. They noted the following components of a successful social contract:

1. Sound principles, which provide guidelines for classroom behavior, such as being respectful, courteous, prepared, practicing the Golden Rule, and doing one's best.
2. Effective rules, based on the principles, which define clearly what is and is not acceptable. Rules should be brief, stated in positive terms (if possible), and specific enough that students know what is meant by the rule. Students ought to be involved in this step. They might also create rules for the teacher. Make sure you can live with their rules before agreeing to them.
3. Consequences should be clear, specific, natural or logical, reasonable, and related to the rule, including a range of alternatives to meet the needs of various students. They are not punishments. Consequences should preserve student dignity. Since students are different, different types of consequences are necessary. Four kinds of consequences that generally meet the needs of a variety of students include these:
   a. Reminder of the rule. "Mary, we sit in our squads during roll call. This is your reminder."

b. A warning. "Chan, this is the second time you have forgotten your homework. This is your warning."
c. An action plan for improving behavior. "José, you are bothering Jackie again. I want you to write down how you intend to stop breaking this rule. List very clearly what you will do when you want to tell Jackie something." A conference with the student, parent, and teacher may be helpful in developing an action plan.
d. Practicing the behavior. When students lack the skills to follow the rules, the teacher may demonstrate how to follow the rule and have the student(s) practice. This may be done after class in private.

   Student involvement should be solicited in deriving appropriate consequences. The more students are involved, the better they feel about the plan.

4. A copy of the contract could be sent to parents, other teachers, and administrators with a letter explaining the contract and soliciting their suggestions. You might list some rules you are having difficulty with and ask for suggestions. This could be done with parents on Back-to-School night.
5. Test the students on the contract to make sure they understand the rules and consequences. Cite class privileges that they will earn by passing the test, such as being a student leader or earning free time.[102]

Be consistent in implementing the consequences. Simply approach the student, make eye contact, and softly but firmly state the rule and the consequence, without moralizing. Don't embarrass the student in front of his or her peers. This maintains student dignity. If students need help understanding the rule, teach them privately. Do not accept excuses or bargaining. Simply repeat the rule and the consequence. The student should understand that the teacher is enforcing a rule that the student chose not to follow. The teacher is merely following through with class procedures by implementing the consequences previously established.

Individual Conference

An individual conference with a student outside of class time is one of the most effective discipline techniques. A serious and frank talk is the logical first step in understanding behavior problems. Conferences help the teacher understand the causes of misbehavior and problems the student faces. They can also provide an opportunity for the teacher to explain school or class regulations to the student.

Group Discussion

When an entire class is disruptive, several possibilities exist:

1. Meet with the ringleaders. Tell them you are tired of yelling and threatening. Ask for suggestions on how to stop the disruption.
2. Abandon your lesson plan. Tell your students what you mean by disruptive behavior. Ask for verbal or written suggestions for changing their behavior and/or your teaching style.
3. Consider mutually creating a social contract, with students and teacher working together to set rules and consequences.
4. Have students make a list of rewarding activities and privileges. Tell them that they may earn these privileges by a daily or weekly record of improvement.[103]

Loss of Privileges

The loss of privileges, particularly those of a social nature, is generally a well-accepted method of discipline. When this method is applied, it should follow the offense as a natural, logical form of correction with no retributory attitude on the part of the teacher. After the student has had time to examine the misbehavior and agrees to follow class procedures, he or she can be restored to full privileges. Often students will plead to be allowed to work after being excluded.

Time-Out

Time-out consists of cutting off reinforcement for a period of time.[104] Usually the student is required to sit away from other students until he or she decides to engage in appropriate behavior. Some teachers use time-out to help students resolve interpersonal problems, such as fighting. Students are asked to leave the group until they have settled their differences, so that other students can continue to learn. The lack of an audience can be very effective in quieting emotions. Students may be asked to sit on a bench together and agree on what they are fighting about. This process helps children learn to resolve their own differences. Time-out is probably the most widely used technique to change behavior. When used correctly, time-out can be one of the most effective discipline tools an instructor can use for students of all ages. To make time-outs productive, Fronske recommends the following:

1. Students must enjoy the activity, the company of other students, or the teacher.
2. Use one warning before sending a student to a time-out box.
3. The student should inform the instructor when he or she is ready to return to activity and participate according to the rules. This will prevent a teacher from forgetting about a student who is in time-out.
4. On the third offense, the student loses the choice of when to return. It is now up to the teacher to make that choice.[105]

The use of time-out can be abused. The following cautions will help you implement time-out:

1. Use positive techniques before using time-out.
2. Never put a student in a time-out box for the remainder of the class.
3. Rarely put a student into a time-out box for a specified period of time on the first offense.
4. Avoid having students face the wall or stand behind a door where they cannot observe class activity. Remember, the instructor is legally liable for the activity of the student during time-out. Also, observing the fun other students are having increases the student's desire to return to activity.[106]

Use of Videorecorders

Videorecorders are becoming more and more common to prevent crimes and driving infractions. They are currently finding their way into school hallways and classrooms. Physical educators have used videorecorders to provide feedback to students on their physical performance. Kusky recommends their use in the classroom to encourage safe practices and to help students see their own behavior. He indicates his intentions to students and mentions that he might use the tapes in counseling sessions with their parents and with the school administration. When students ask whether it is an invasion of their privacy, he assures them that they are in a public building and what they do is a matter of public record. He is just making that record more permanent and transportable. Videotapes counter the tendency of students to play a different role in the office or at home and put the blame on the teacher. Confronted by the videotape, they are much easier to get started on the correction of the problem.[107]

Cooperation between Home and School

Genuine cooperation between home and school through conferences, home visits, and social contacts can achieve remarkable results, provided both parties are willing to understand the student's behavior and are sincere about wanting to help the student. Home-school cooperation can produce fruitful information and lead to correction of misbehavior. A positive, cooperative effort is usually most successful. Keep a record of student misbehavior.[108] Using three by five cards that can be filed in the teacher's office. Written and videotape records can help to identify patterns of behavior and to provide objective data for parents.[109]

Administrative Assistance

Administrative assistance should be secured only after the teacher has been unsuccessful in correcting a disturbing situation, or after repeated incidents of misbehavior. Sending a student to the office removes the offender from the class and facilitates instruction to the other students. However, it also bars the student from necessary instruction. Occasionally it creates a scene in which the offender may be humiliated or, on the contrary, become a hero to classmates. This method appears to be justified only in severe cases. However, a principal once told a teacher, "After you've done everything you can and the student doesn't improve, don't let it bother you out of proportion. Let it give the principal an ulcer." The administration has a duty to do everything possible to help the teacher deal with discipline problems for the sake of the student, the teacher, and the school as a whole. However, the teacher should refer a student to the administration only when all the resources at hand have been exhausted. Procedures for using administrative assistance include the following:

1. Before you are faced with a need to use administrative assistance, write down the rule violations you believe to be worthy of referral to an administrator. Then set up an appointment with your administrator to discuss your list.[110]
2. Know the student. A trip to the office may be just what the individual wants at that moment to get out of a difficult assignment.
3. When it becomes necessary to send a student to the office of the administrator, send along a note (with another student) that states the difficulty and the kind of treatment expected.
4. See the administrator as soon as possible to discuss the situation.
5. Do not send more than one student at a time to the office.
6. If the student is sent back to class, calmly readmit the student and ignore any face-saving behavior the student displays.

Mediation

Sometimes disciplinary problems cannot be solved by the teacher and the student involved. One method for alleviating such a problem is called mediation. Mediation uses an outside party to help settle a classroom dispute. The mediator is not a judge or jury. His or her sole purpose is to assist both sides in airing their grievances in a manner that will resolve the difficulty. By using a mediator in difficult situations, the teacher can reaffirm respect for student rights.[111]

Handling Explosive or Violent Situations

An explosive situation is one that requires immediate action to prevent personal injury or property damage. The most extreme situations are attack, robbery, rape, and hostage taking. Although students tend to be robbed by other students, teachers are more likely to be robbed by young intruders.[112]

It is best to prevent an explosive situation from occurring whenever possible by using the following suggestions:

1. Become a hard target. "Target hardening is a security concept that significantly decreases, deters, or prevents crime against specific individuals. . . . A soft target is an easy target; a hard target is a difficult one." Hard targets are much less likely to become crime victims.[113] Develop a healthy alertness about what is happening around you. Do not be distracted by reading or listening to a radio or cassette. Make eye contact with students as you pass through the halls. Walk with an erect bearing, emanating confidence. Walk down the center of empty hallways and on the street edge of the sidewalk away from buildings and shrubs where you have room to run. Better yet, don't walk alone anywhere. Do not wear expensive jewelry or carry much cash. Do not carry things in two hands; use an attaché case. Care about your students. They are not likely to injure someone they respect. "Target hardening can reduce your chances of being a crime victim by 70 percent or more."[114]
2. Do not let misbehavior go too far before attempting to handle the problem. Call for help if a situation may become explosive.
3. Do not lose your cool. Explosive situations become volcanic when the teacher and student are not in control of themselves. Maintaining a sense of humor will keep the student-teacher relationship on a personal level and can often defuse tense situations. Many discipline problems could be easily avoided if molehills remained molehills.[115]
4. Be decisive, act quickly, and disarm the situation. Insist calmly but firmly that the behavior be stopped immediately. Suggest an alternative behavior, an "out" by which the student can save face. Use a time-out or, if possible, remove the student or students from the classroom. Do not touch the student if this can be avoided. Seek help from others if possible.
5. Do not use too harsh a punishment as that can result in later aggressive behaviors.
6. Avoid confrontations with students. Do not accept a challenge as a personal matter.
7. Calm the class by restructuring the incident or using it as a topic for discussion. Introduce humor.

When an explosive situation does occur, the following procedures may be helpful:

1. In the case of a robbery or hostage attempt, do not resist. Do as you are told. Don't argue.
2. In case of a rape attempt, keep the intruder talking as long as possible. Negotiate without pleading. Negotiation and resistance will not work with a criminal rapist.
3. Mentally make a record of the attacker's description, especially any distinctive features.
4. Get help! If possible, send a student for another teacher, the principal, or a counselor. This may be after the robber has gone.
5. Do not touch anything the intruder has touched.[116]

Review Questions: What is an explosive situation?

What should be done when an explosive situation arises in the classroom?

Creative Techniques

Creative techniques can help you get your message across.[117]

1. Allow a student to play teacher. You take the student's place and act like he or she usually does. Then have a conference to discuss how you "as a student" could improve your behavior.
2. Use humor to defuse disruptive situations.
3. When students criticize, say, "There's a lot of truth to that. There are times when I . . . Thanks for pointing that out."
4. Make the behavior acceptable (throwing erasers—give the student a target) and ask the student to keep doing it, or tell a student he or she is not allowed to do homework. If the student stops, you win. If the student continues, he or she is doing what you said to do, so you win. If a student swears, ask him or her to define the term right now and you will write the definition on the chalkboard. The student has to behave more appropriately as a way of defying your authority. Have an eraser throwing contest to see who can throw the farthest or most accurately.
5. Throw a tantrum. Stand on the chair, knock things over, scream and yell. Save this for a few selected times a year.

Review Question: What discipline practices are compatible with your model?

UNACCEPTABLE PRACTICES

Some disciplinary practices used by teachers are generally considered unacceptable. Often they are initiated because the teacher is feeling the stress and tension of the situation. The use of such tactics normally generates resentment on the part of the student or causes the student to withdraw. Teachers must decide ahead of time that the following practices will not be employed no matter what the intensity of a circumstance might be. These practices include (1) coercion; (2) ridicule; (3) forced apologies; (4) detention without a specified purpose; (5) imposition of schoolwork or homework for punitive purposes; (6) punishment instigated on the spot, including grades; (7) group punishment for misbehavior by one or a few; and (8) corporal punishment. Using exercise for punishment can be considered a form of corporal punishment and may be prohibited by state law or result in a lawsuit. Other methods that generally result in a teacher's lack of control include appealing to the student's sympathy; the use of vague, unfulfilled threats; and exclusion of the student from the room without supervision. To avoid unpleasant situations caused by a disciplinary action the teacher must have in mind appropriate techniques that will be triggered automatically by the situation.

Review Questions: Why is it illegal to use physical activities as punishment?

What practices are never acceptable disciplinary technique?

Choosing Appropriate Techniques for the Situation

Teachers can be prepared to act instinctively when a disciplinary incident arises in class. Outcomes are often unpredictable. Predetermined rules and regulations might provide a solution to the problem, but the teacher still must react with a cool head and conclude the incident. Whatever problem might arise, proper action depends on (1) the teacher's philosophy and teaching style, (2) the students, and (3) the incident.

Understanding a variety of suitable techniques that match the model chosen or created by the teacher and success in carrying out different methods will allow you to select appropriate techniques for different conditions. Experiment to see what works best, because what works for one teacher may not work for another. Administrative policy may limit the choices a teacher is allowed to select. Often you must deal with the incident and at the same time direct students not involved in the action. No method of control is effective with all students. One must consider the age, sex, personality, and social values held by the student or group. Be alert to the individual needs of students. Occasionally, deafness, poor vision, or other disabling conditions create supposed discipline problems.

Try to determine the cause of the behavior and what actually happened without relying too heavily on statements made by students. Often the cause of the incident results from the classroom environment. Poor, haphazard, and unproductive instruction or a curriculum that is too easy, too hard, or not relevant to student needs may cause many discipline problems.

With these items in mind, first stop the ineffective behavior and then help the students overcome individual problems, thus preventing a recurrence of the problem. The action must be clear and definite, and be one in which you truly believe. By continually being alert to early signs of trouble and dealing with them firmly, calmly, and with consistency before they become serious, major discipline problems can be avoided.

An inexperienced teacher or one new to a school must still deal with discipline problems in a confident, controlled manner. Use preventive and positive discipline to prevent discipline problems. The following hints for new teachers are aimed at avoiding beginning pitfalls:

1. Learn school policies and procedures thoroughly.
2. Be an example the students can emulate.
3. Be a teacher, not a pal, to students.
4. Plan and organize.
5. Be flexible but consistent in carrying out plans.
6. Respect and appreciate students as individuals.
7. Let students know from the start what the payoff will be for working hard in class.[118]

Review Question: What factors affect the selection of a disciplinary technique?

Notes

1. W. Doyle, Classroom organization and management, in M. C. Wittrock, *Handbook of Research on Teaching,* 3rd ed. (New York: Macmillan, 1986), 392–431.
2. R. L. Curwin and A. N. Mendler, *Discipline with Dignity* (Alexandria, VA: Association for Supervision and Curriculum Development, 1988).
3. D. R. Hellison, *Goals and Strategies for Teaching Physical Education* (Champaign, IL: Human Kinetics, 1985).
4. Hellison, *Goals and Strategies.*
5. R. Wlodkowski, *How to Help Teachers Reach the Turned Off Student.* Unpublished paper. Cited in Curwin and Mendler, *Discipline with Dignity,* 16.
6. Curwin and Mendler, *Discipline with Dignity.*
7. H. Dunn, Listen to kids! *Today's Education 70* (1981, November–December): 37.
8. A. V. Carron, *Motivation Implications for Coaching and Teaching* (Kingswood, South Australia: Sports Dynamics, 1984); M. Hunter, *Motivation Theory for Teachers* (El Segundo, CA: Tip, 1971); M. C. Wittrock, Students' thought processes, in M. C. Wittrock, ed., *Handbook of Research on Teaching,* 3rd ed. (New York: Macmillan, 1986), 304.
9. Hunter, *Motivation Theory for Teachers.*
10. A. H. Maslow, A theory of human personality, *Psychological Review 50* (1943): 370–96.
11. R. M. Gagné, *The Conditions of Learning,* 2nd ed. (New York: Holt, Rinehart & Winston, 1970).
12. A. Bandura, Self-efficacy: Toward a unifying theory of behavioral change, *Psychological Review 84,* no. 2 (1977): 191–215.

13. Bandura, Self-efficacy.
14. S. Harter, Effectance motivation reconsidered: Toward a developmental model, *Human Development 21* (1978): 52.
15. M. Csikszentmihalyi, *Flow* (New York: Harper & Row, 1990).
16. A. Bandura, *Social Learning Theory* (Englewood Cliffs, NJ: Prentice-Hall, 1977).
17. D. L. Feltz and M. R. Weiss, Developing self-efficacy through sport, *Journal of Physical Education, Recreation, and Dance 53,* no. 3 (1982): 24–26, 36; E. McAuley, T. E. Duncan, and M. McElroy, Self-efficacy cognitions and causal attributions for children's motor performance: An exploratory investigation, *Journal of Genetic Psychology 150,* no. 1 (1989): 65–73; R. Weinberg, D. Gould, and A. Jackson, Expectations and performance: An empirical test of Bandura's self-efficacy theory, *Journal of Sport Psychology 1* (1979): 320–331.
18. Weinberg, Gould, and Jackson, Expectations and performance.
19. M. E. Rudisill, Influence of perceived competence and causal dimension orientation on expectations, persistence, and performance during perceived failure, *Research Quarterly for Exercise and Sport 60* (1989): 166–75; B. Weiner, *Human Motivation* (Chicago: Holt, Rinehart & Winston, 1980).
20. Bandura, Self-efficacy, 191–215.
21. Rudisill, Influence of perceived competence.
22. C. B. Corbin and C. Nix, Sex-typing of physical activities and success predictions of children before and after cross-sex competition, *Journal of Sport Psychology 1* (1979): 43–52; T. J. Martinek, Children's perceptions of teaching behaviors: An attributional model for explaining teacher expectancy effects, *Journal of Teaching in Physical Education 8* (1989): 327; Weinberg, Gould, and Jackson, Expectations and performance.
23. S. G. Maier and M. E. Seligman, Learned helplessness: Theory and evidence, *Journal of Experimental Psychology: General 105,* no. 1 (1976): 3–46.
24. C. B. Wortman and J. W. Brehm, Responses to uncontrollable outcomes: An integration of reactance theory and the learned helplessness model, in L. Berkowitz, ed., *Advances in Experimental Social Psychology,* vol. 8 (New York: Academic Press, 1975).
25. T. J. Martinek and J. B. Griffith III, Working with the learned helpless child, *Journal of Physical Education, Recreation, and Dance 64,* no. 6 (1993): 17–20.
26. C. S. Dweck, The role of expectations and attributions in the alleviation of learned helplessness, *Journal of Personality and Social Psychology 31* (1975): 674–85.
27. Martinek and Griffith, Working with the learned helpless child; Rudisill, Influence of perceived competence.
28. Martinek and Griffith, Working with the learned helpless child; M. K. Alderman, Motivation for at-risk students, *Educational Leadership 48* (1990): 27–30.
29. J. Brophy, Successful teaching strategies for the inner-city child, *Phi Delta Kappan 63* (1982): 527–30; J. E. Brophy and T. L. Good, *Teacher-Student Relationships: Causes and Consequences* (New York: Holt, Rinehart & Winston, 1974); R. Rosenthal and L. Jacobson, *Pygmalion in the Classroom: Teacher Expectation and Pupils' Intellectual Development* (San Francisco: Holt, Rinehart & Winston, 1968).
30. T. J. Martinek, Pygmalion in the gym: A model for the communication of teacher expectations in physical education, *Research Quarterly for Exercise and Sport 52* (1981): 58–67; T. J. Martinek, Creating golem and galatea effects during physical education instruction: A social psychological perspective, in T. J. Templin and J. K. Olson, eds., *Teaching in Physical Education* (Champaign, IL: Human Kinetics, 1983); T. J. Martinek and W. B. Karper, Canonical relationships among motor ability, expression of effort, teacher expectations and dyadic interactions in elementary age children, *Journal of Teaching in Physical Education 1* (1982): 26–39; T. J. Martinek, and W. B. Karper, A research model for determining causal effects of teacher expectations in physical education instruction, *Quest* 35 (1983): 155–68.
31. M. C. Wittrock, Students' thought processes, in M. C. Wittrock, ed., *Handbook of Research on Teaching,* 3rd ed., (New York: Macmillan, 1986), 304.
32. Martinek, Children's perceptions; T. J. Martinek and W. Karper, The effects of noncompetitive and competitive social climates on teacher expectancy effects in elementary physical education classes, *Journal of Sport Psychology 8* (1984): 408–21.
33. J. E. Rink, The teacher wants us to learn, *Journal of Physical Education and Recreation 52,* no. 2 (1981): 17–18; J. E. Rink, *Teaching Physical Education for Learning,* 5th ed. (New York: McGraw-Hill Higher Education, 2006).
34. S. Hutslar, The expectancy phenomenon, *Journal of Physical Education, Recreation, and Dance 52,* no. 7 (1981): 88–89.
35. J. S. Kounin, *Discipline and Group Management in Classrooms* (Huntington, NY: Klieger, 1997).
36. J. Lund, The Effects of Accountability on Response Rates in Physical Education (Unpublished doctoral dissertation, Ohio State University, Columbus, 1990).
37. K. Alexander, Behavior Analysis of Tasks and Accountability (Unpublished doctoral dissertation, Ohio State University, Columbus, 1982).
38. J. Shanklin, The Impact of Accountability on Student Response Rate in a Secondary Physical Education Badminton Unit (Unpublished master's thesis, Ball State University, Muncie, IN, 2004); Lund, *The Effects of Accountability.*
39. C. Tomlinson, Invitations to learn, *Educational Leadership 60,* no. 1 (2002): 7–10.
40. R. Sagor, Lessons from skateboarders, *Educational Leadership 60,* no. 1 (2002): 34–36, 38.
41. B. Coloroso, *Discipline: Winning at Teaching* (Littleton, CO: Kids Are Worth It, P. O. Box 621109, Littleton, CO 80162, 1983).
42. Coloroso, *Discipline.*

43. J. Raffini, *150 Ways to Increase Intrinsic Motivation in the Classroom* (Boston: Allyn & Bacon, 1996).
44. S. Faust, Effects of Ability-Labeling on Psychomotor and Academic Performances of Selected Sixth Grade Students (Unpublished doctoral dissertation, University of Miami, Coral Gables, 1974).
45. Raffini, *150 Ways.*
46. M. McKay and P. Fanning, *Self-Esteem* (Oakland, CA: New Harbinger, 1992).
47. W. Glasser, *Schools without Failure* (New York: Harper & Row, 1969).
48. K. H. Hoover, *The Professional Teacher's Handbook: A Guide for Improving Instruction in Today's Middle and Secondary Schools,* 3rd ed. (Boston: Allyn & Bacon, 1982).
49. V. Faust, *Self-Esteem in the Classroom* (San Diego: Thomas Paine, 1980).
50. Faust, *Effects of Ability-Labeling;* G. L. Chandler, Invitational physical education: Strategies in the junior high school, *Journal of Physical Education, Recreation, and Dance 59,* no. 4 (1988): 68–72.

    Purkey, W. W., *Inviting School Success* (Belmont, CA, 1978).
51. Cardinal, Motivation: Strategies for success, *Strategies 4,* no. 6 (1991): 27–28.
52. McKay and Fanning, *Self-Esteem.*
53. Curwin and Mendler, *Discipline with Dignity.*
54. S. K. Kovar, H. Ermler, and J. H. Mehrhof, Helping students to become self-disciplined, *Journal of Health, Physical Education, Recreation, and Dance 63,* no. 6 (1992): 26–28.
55. B. Bertel, Try what? *Journal of Health, Physical Education, Recreation 45,* no. 5 (1974): 24.
56. Faust, *Self-Esteem in the Classroom.*
57. D. L. Gallahue, Toward positive discipline in the gymnasium, *Physical Educator 42* (1985, late winter): 14–17.
58. Curwin and Mendler, *Discipline with Dignity.*
59. E. A. Locke, K. N. Shaw, L. M. Saari, and G. P. Latham, Goal setting and task performance: 1969–1980, *Psychological Bulletin 90* (1981): 125–52.
60. J. B. Oxendine, *Psychology of Motor Learning* (Englewood Cliffs, NJ: Prentice-Hall, 1984).
61. W. J. McKeachie, *Teaching Tips—A Guidebook for the Beginning College Teacher,* 7th ed. (Lexington, MA: Heath, 1978).
62. Curwin and Mendler, *Discipline with Dignity.*
63. McKay and Fanning, *Self-Esteem;* J. P. Sanford and C. M. Evertson, Classroom management in a low SES junior high: Three case studies, *Journal of Teacher Education 32,* (1981 January–February): 34–38.
64. E. Durkheim, *Moral Education: A Study in the Theory and Application of the Sociology of Education* (New York: Free Press, 1961); C. H. Madsen, Jr., and C. K. Madsen, *Teaching/Discipline* (Boston: Allyn & Bacon, 1970).
65. H. Wong and R. T. Wong, *The first days of school* (Sunnyva!e, CA: Harry K. Wong Publications, 1991).
66. Wong and Wong, *The first days of school.*
67. Wong and Wong, *The first days of school.*
68. M. Kniffin, Instructional skills for student teachers, *Strategies 1,* no. 6 (1988): 5–8.
69. Kniffin, Instructional skills; L. Canter, Assertive discipline—more than names on the board and marbles in a jar, *Phi Delta Kappan 71,* no. 1 (1989): 57–61.
70. T. Ratliffe, Overcoming obstacles beginning teachers encounter, *Journal of Physical Education, Recreation, and Dance 58,* no. 40 (1987): 18–23.
71. Canter, Assertive discipline.
72. Canter, Assertive discipline.
73. T. Gordon, with Noel Burch, *Teacher Effectiveness Training* (New York: Three Rivers Press, 2003).
74. Gordon, *Teacher Effectiveness Training.*
75. Curwin and Mendler, *Discipline with Dignity.*
76. R. W. French, H. L. Henderson, and M. Horvat, *Creative Approaches to Managing Student Behavior in Physical Education* (Park City, UT: Family Development Resources, 1992).
77. French, Henderson, and Horvat, *Creative Approaches.*
78. S. A. Henkel, STP—The teacher's edge to pupil control, *Journal of Physical Education, Recreation, and Dance 60,* no. 1 (1989): 60–64.
79. J. S. Kounin, *Discipline and Group Management in Classrooms* (Huntington, NY: Krieger, 1977).
80. K. LaMancusa, *We Do Not Throw Rocks at the Teacher* (Scranton, PA: International Textbook Company, 1966).
81. E. L. Deci, L. Sheinman, L. Wheeler, and T. Hart, Rewards, motivation and self-esteem, *The Educational Forum 44* (1980): 430.
82. Deci, Sheinman, Wheeler, and Hart. Rewards; E. L. Deci, L. Sheinman, L. Wheeler, and T. Hart, An instrument to assess adults' orientations toward control versus autonomy with children: Reflections on intrinsic motivation and perceived competence, *Journal of Educational Psychology 73* (1981 October): 642–650.
83. Harter, Effectance motivation reconsidered.
84. Harter, Effectance motivation reconsidered.
85. C. S. Kusky, Jr., Turning the cameras on them, *Phi Delta Kappan 74* (1992): 270.
86. J. Cooper, T. Heron, and W. Heward, *Applied Behavior Analysis* (Columbus, OH: Merrill, 1987).
87. D. Premack, Toward empirical behavior laws: 1. Positive reinforcement. *Psychological Review 66,* no. 4 (1959): 219–33.
88. L. Homme, A. P. Csanyi, M. A. Gonzales, and J. R. Rechs, *How to Use Contingency Contracting in the Classroom* (Champaign, IL: Research Press, 1969); B. Joyce and M. Weil, *Models of teaching,* 2nd ed. (Englewood Cliffs, NJ: Prentice-Hall, 1980).
89. W. C. Becker, S. Engelmann, and D. R. Thomas, *Teaching: A Course in Applied Psychology* (Palo Alto, CA: Science Research Associates, 1971).

90. J. P. Glavin, *Behavioral Strategies for Classroom Management* (Columbus, OH: Merrill, 1974).
91. Homme, Csanyi, Gonzales, Rechs, *How to Use Contingency Contracting.*
92. K. Major, *New Ideas, New Classes: Learning-Growing-Improving* (AAHPERD Convention session, New Orleans, LA, 1990); J. Carter, The "Champions" program—Behavior improvement in physical education, *Journal of Physical Education, Recreation, and Dance 60,* no. 5 (1989): 66–67; Coach Chipper, Box 27843, Santa Ana, CA 92799-7843.
93. P. Paese, Effects of interdependent group contingencies in a secondary physical education setting, *Journal of Teaching in Physical Education 2* (1982): 29–37; W. Vogler and R. French, The effects of a group contingency strategy on behaviorally disordered students in physical education, *Research Quarterly for Exercise and Sport 54* (1983): 273–77.
94. Wittrock, Students' thought processes.
95. Ratliffe, Overcoming obstacles; A. N. Sander, Class management skills, *Strategies 2,* no. 3 (1989): 14–18; Canter, Assertive discipline; J. Brophy, Teacher praise: A functional analysis, *Review of Educational Research 51* (1981): 5–32.
96. Brophy, Teacher praise.
97. C. H. Edwards, *Classroom Discipline and Management,* 2nd ed. (Upper Saddle River, NJ: 1997).
98. Edwards, *Classroom Discipline and Management.*
99. M. Tousignant and D. A. Siedentop, Qualitative analysis of task structures in required secondary physical education classes, *Journal of Teaching in Physical Education 3* (1983): 47–57.
100. D. Siedentop, The management of practice behavior, in W. F. Straub, ed., *Sport Psychology: An Analysis of Athlete Behavior* (Ithaca: Movement, 1978).
101. Becker, Engelmann, and Thomas, *Teaching: A Course in Applied Psychology.*
102. Curwin and Mendler, *Discipline with Dignity.*
103. Curwin and Mendler, *Discipline with Dignity.*
104. Becker, Engelmann, and Thomas, *Teaching: A Course in Applied Psychology.*
105. H. Fronske, personal communication, 1990.
106. H. Fronske, personal communication.
107. Kusky, Turning the cameras on them.
108. Sander, Class management skills.
109. S. D. Vestermark, Jr., and Blauvelt, P. D., *Controlling crime in the school: A complete security handbook for administrators* (West Nyack, NY: Parker 1978).
110. Curwin and Mendler, *Discipline with Dignity.*
111. T. Graham and P. C. Cline, Mediation: An alternative approach to school discipline, *The High School Journal 72,* no. 2 (1989): 73–76.
112. C. L. Quarles, *School Violence: A Survival Guide for School Staff* (Washington, DC: National Education Association, 1989), 17, 19.
113. Quarles, *School Violence.*
114. Quarles, *School Violence.*
115. R. G. Wegmann, Classroom discipline, *Today's Education 38,* no. 1 (1976): 18–19.
116. Quarles, *School Violence.*
117. Curwin and Mendler, *Discipline with Dignity.*
118. Becker, Engelmann, and Thomas, *Teaching: A Course in Applied Psychology.*

U N I T

IV

Evaluating Instruction and Programs

CHAPTER

14

ACCOUNTABILITY AND TEACHER EVALUATION

STUDY STIMULATORS

1. Who has the responsibility for worthwhile outcomes of physical education programs?
2. Why is teacher evaluation important?
3. List the steps in teacher evaluation.
4. What are the advantages and limitations of evaluation that is based on student achievement or improvement, informal analysis, informal analysis by students, descriptive analysis, and interaction analysis?

ACCOUNTABILITY

The 1980s and 1990s will be documented in history books as the years of educational reform. The barrage of reports in the early 1980s challenging the competency of our national education system sparked improvement by the schools. The "Education Report Card" released by the U.S. Department of Education showed four years of improvement by the schools that ended with a leveling off in 1985–86. Student test scores were up, as were teachers' salaries; the number of pupils per teacher was down; and expenditures per pupil were up.[1] Even with these positive gains the cry to do better was heard. Secretary of Education William J. Bennett emphasized, "We have to do better. Our children deserve better."[2] Legislators reinforced these words. In 2001, the federal government passed the No Child Left Behind Act (NCLB) in an attempt to close the achievement gap and make sure that all students, including those who are disadvantaged, achieve academic proficiency.[3] Under NCLB, teachers are to hold at least a bachelor's degree, be certified, and have proven knowledge in the subjects they teach. Operating under the assumption that no child should be trapped in an underperforming school, parents of children in Title 1 schools have the option of transferring their students to a higher-performing school within the district.[4] Most states have failed to include physical education in their tests for student competency.

The publication of the content standards by the National Association for Sport and Physical Education (NASPE) (see Chapter 1) makes it easier for parents and the public to know what physical education competencies they can expect from high school graduates. Teachers, schools, and districts would do well to further define these competencies with regard to their specific programs and to establish evaluation techniques to demonstrate that students are physically educated as defined. Failure to do so could make them vulnerable to educational malpractice suits. Failure to provide programs that result in skill proficiency in lifetime activities and increased health-related fitness and knowledge exposes teachers to public criticism.[5] Physical educators are responsible for the poor image they have created because of inadequate lesson preparation, poor personal appearance, failure to attend faculty and professional meetings, and inability to articulate objectives and their importance to the public, including students.[6]

Accountability, according to the law, tends to be limited to accountability of teachers and administrators for learning by students. However, accountability is more than that. Schools have a responsibility to educate students. Parents and taxpayers have a responsibility to provide the resources necessary for adequate learning experiences. Students must be accountable for their own behavior.

With the increased emphasis on accountability in core academic subjects, the pressure to increase time spent on those areas has, in many schools, led to a decrease in time allocated to physical education. Daily participation in high school physical education decreased from 42 percent in 1991 to 25 percent in 1995.[7] In 1996, the surgeon general published a report that outlined the benefits of participation in regular physical activity.[8] That report, coupled with a dramatic increase in obesity, points to the need for high-quality physical education programs. Additionally, research on the brain reveals the connection between cognitive learning and physical activity.[9] Physical educators must capitalize on public concern for these issues and emphasize the role that high-quality programs have on improving both the quality and quantity of life. Accountability is a key component of making that happen. Physical education programs must document their position as places where students learn rather than recreational venues associated with free play. At the same time that physical education programs are in jeopardy in the schools, the public has never been more active physically. People are spending millions of dollars to look and feel better. More than one hundred million people in the United States are actively engaged in fitness activities, an estimated 1,300 books on fitness are currently in print, and fifty thousand firms spend an estimated two billion dollars a year on fitness and recreation programs for their employees.[10] However, physical educators cannot claim a contribution to this increase in physical activity because their programs lag behind in teaching lifetime fitness concepts and activities. Griffey stated, "We have failed to provide an experience that our students perceive as meaningful. The sense of mastering something important is denied most students in secondary physical education programs."[11] Students should be expected to perform certain skills, know certain concepts, and behave in certain ways. This is what teaching is all about. Evaluation reflects success at doing these things.

Accountability requires, first, that students understand the worth of physical education activities so they become committed to improving their own performance and participating in vigorous activity throughout their lives. Class instruction must be more than "free play" and organized games. Students must be evaluated and results of achievement made available to parents, administrators, the general public, and the students themselves. Chapter 11 discussed ways to assess student achievement. Second, teachers must improve their effectiveness. Teacher evaluation will be presented in this chapter. Third, the public must be convinced of the worth of physical education programs so they will pledge their support to keeping them. Public relations was discussed as one of the roles of the teacher in Chapter 2.

Review Question: What is accountability? How can physical education teachers demonstrate accountability for educating students?

TEACHER EVALUATION

Teachers must be able to state performance objectives, assess student achievement of objectives, and use strategies that help students achieve objectives. Educators must also learn to evaluate and remediate weaknesses in their own teaching and in their programs. Administrators must be able to evaluate teachers' performances and help teachers improve their effectiveness.

Effective teachers have the ability to adapt their teaching behaviors to meet the needs of their students. Studies demonstrate that teacher evaluation increases teachers' awareness of these different instructional behaviors and helps them to improve both student achievement and teacher morale. This is true because teachers often perceive their teaching behavior as quite different from what actually occurs. Teacher evaluation enables the teacher to retain effective teaching behaviors and eliminate ineffective behaviors, thereby making actual behavior more congruent with desired behavior. Teacher evaluation involves the following steps:

Step 1. Determine what to evaluate.
Step 2. Choose or construct specific evaluation techniques: student achievement or improvement, teacher observation, student perceptions, systematic observation, and interaction analysis.
Step 3. Use the appropriate techniques to record information.
Step 4. Evaluate or interpret the data.
Step 5. Make changes and reevaluate.

Step 1—Determine What to Evaluate

The first step in any evaluation plan is to specify goals. This can be done by examining what you believe to be the most important goals of teaching and the behaviors necessary to achieve those goals.[12] Some examples of goals and related behaviors, based on some characteristics of effective teachers, are shown in Table 14.1.

TABLE 14.1 Goals, Behaviors, and Suggested Evaluation Techniques

Goals	Teacher Behavior	Suggested Evaluation Techniques
TEACHER WARMTH	Calls student by name. Provides more positive than negative feedback. Interacts with students.	Event recording Event recording Student evaluation of instructor Interaction analysis
TEACHER EXPECTANCY	Facilitates achievement of instructional objectives. Facilitates improvement in student learning. Selects tasks in terms of student abilities.	Student performance Student improvement Student evaluation of teacher Informal analysis
TASK-ORIENTED CLIMATE	Helps students spend a large amount of time in productive behavior. Monitors student progress. Provides feedback on behavior. Decreases time spent on class management.	Time analysis Spot checking Event recording Time sampling Event recording Time analysis Time sampling
EFFECTIVE INSTRUCTION	Provides appropriate model and explanation. Provides appropriate feedback for skills. Provides opportunity for student practice. Provides appropriate progression of content.	Informal analysis Event recording Event recording Time analysis Time sampling Number of practice trials/person Event recording

Step 2—Choose or Construct Specific Evaluation Techniques

Because teaching is so complex, a variety of formal and informal observation and recording techniques must be employed to describe the total teaching process. The techniques discussed in this chapter include (1) student achievement or improvement, (2) teacher observation instrument, (3) student perceptions, and (4) interaction analysis. These techniques generally assess either the performance of the students or the performance of the teacher.

Student Achievement or Improvement

The principal duty of teachers is to help students learn. Therefore, the key to evaluating teaching is to determine the extent to which learning has taken place. The use of performance objectives facilitates this process by providing an observable student behavior for each skill or content area to be learned. If students are learning and have positive feelings toward activity, then the teacher is effective, no matter how unorthodox the instruction appears to be. However, if students are not learning or do not have positive attitudes toward activity, then an analysis of the teacher's performance can help to pinpoint possible problem areas for remediation. Common techniques for evaluating student achievement include knowledge tests, skills tests, and various affective measurements. Each of these techniques is discussed in Chapter 11.

A second method for evaluating student learning is to record student performance each day and compare it with the objectives of the daily lesson plan. This can be as simple as having students check off skills as they accomplish them (as in gymnastics or swimming), count the number of successful attempts (as basketball free throws or tennis serves), or turn in a score (as in archery or bowling). See Chapter 11 for examples. If the lesson has been well planned, most of the students should be able to achieve lesson objectives. An accountability log can be kept each day showing not only students' achievement toward the objective for that day but also students' achievement of previous unit objectives. This log can be a tremendous eye-opener for how much review and practice students need to achieve course objectives. The log might include a list of objectives and the number of students who have completed each one.

Another method is to preassess students, teach, and then evaluate the improvement. Again, a knowledge or skills test or an affective measurement can be employed. Statistics from game play can also provide information about student improvement. Examples include

1. Sprint—Check for improvement in time.
2. Knowledge—Check the number of students improving their scores on a quiz, or check the class average on a quiz.
3. Attitude—Check the number of students changing from a negative to a positive attitude toward an

activity. Review Chapter 11 for specific suggestions on evaluating affective behavior.

4. Basketball strategy—Count the increases in successful passes per team.

There are limitations in evaluating teachers based on student performance. One of the major limitations is the difficulty of accurately evaluating student performance. Weather, time of day, illness, fatigue, and innumerable other factors can influence student performance scores. Subjective evaluation techniques and teacher-constructed tests may be unreliable. Measurements may not be sensitive enough to determine student improvement during short units of instruction. A second limitation is that it is difficult to establish a cause-and-effect relationship between a specific teaching behavior and learning. Students may have learned from a parent, from a friend, or from private lessons. Students may have begun with the skill level being evaluated. Students may learn because of or in spite of a teacher. When they do learn, it is difficult to prove which teaching behaviors may have caused the improvement. These limitations, however, should not keep teachers from making some educated guesses about their own teaching based on student achievement. Checking for achievement or improvement each day will provide a better idea of which teaching behaviors helped to create the changes in student behavior.

Teacher Observation Instruments

The most common method of teacher evaluation is informal analysis by oneself, a supervisor or administrator, another teacher, or by students. By videotaping the class, the teacher can record observations for self-evaluation and make changes to improve teaching performance. Since there are so many events occurring simultaneously in physical education classes, which make it difficult for an observer to see everything, teacher observation instruments that focus on specific components of a class are most useful.

A checklist can be used to direct the observer's attention to specific parts of the lesson. The observer simply checks each item that was included in the teacher's behavior during the lesson. The checklist provides the appearance of scientific accuracy, but vague, undefined statements or characteristics result in a very low level of reliability for most checklists. Such a checklist provides no information concerning the frequency with which a given behavior occurs. Requiring the observer to record anecdotal notes to support checking the presence of a behavior can increase the value of this type of observation. These notes will help define how the observer interpreted the behavior as well as provide examples of teacher behaviors that were used to indicate that the descriptor was demonstrated.

Rating scales can be valuable as a tool for self-evaluation and goal setting by teachers. They can also be completed by both teachers and supervisors and the results compared to encourage discussion of different points of view concerning the teacher's performance. Goals can then be set to evaluate and correct specific areas needing attention. Rating scales can be developed to evaluate specific items such as execution of teaching styles, demonstrations, or questioning skills.

An advantage of rating scales is that they take a minimum of time to complete and can provide information sufficient to get a teacher started on a personal improvement plan. However, as an evaluative device, the rating scale is generally less valid and reliable than many of the other techniques that will be presented in this chapter. This is especially the case when the ratings (i.e., "usually," "sometimes") are not clearly defined.

When constructing a rating scale, remember that providing fewer choice points increases reliability. However, enough points must be included to make the scale useful for its intended purpose. If numbers are used for choice points, they should be anchored with descriptive words at least at each end of the scale. Anchoring additional numbers with words will further help reliability. Any of the types of rating scales presented in Chapter 11 can be used to assess teaching performance. The choice depends on how an individual feels about a specific tool.

An analytic qualitative rubric could also be used for teacher observations. The example presented in Box 14.1 uses one of the Interstate New Teacher Assessment and Support Consortium (INTASC) Principles, develops four different descriptors or traits related to that standard, and then provides four levels for each of these descriptors to illustrate that level of teacher performance. If two observers complete the scale independently and then talk over discrepancies, items can be changed so that differences in understanding of the characteristics in question can be corrected. Then it is more probable that the differences are related to teacher performance rather than to raters' understanding of the scale.

Student Perceptions

Asking students how they feel about what they have learned and their perceptions about the learning situation can provide useful information. The most effective analysis by students is written, not oral, and is anonymous to allow for free and honest responses. Use caution when asking young students to analyze teacher behavior. Avoid using questionnaires with students who do not have the ability to understand the intent of the questions and to provide valid answers. Some examples of questions that might be asked on a student questionnaire include the following:

1. What are the two most important things you have learned in this class?
2. What factors helped you learn them? (Be specific. Who did what to help you?)
3. How could this class be improved to make it better?
4. List the strengths of your teacher.
5. Tell how your teacher could help you learn better.

To score the analyses, simply tally the number of times a similar response was given to each question. Then look

BOX 14.1

Sample Rubric

PRINCIPLE 5A:
The student teacher uses an understanding of individual and group motivation and behavior to create a learning environment that encourages positive social interaction in the classroom.

	Level of Performance			
Element	**Unsatisfactory**	**Basic**	**Proficient**	**Distinguished***
Management of Transitions	Much time is lost during transitions. May be unaware of lost time, does not plan for transitions.	Transitions are sporadically efficient, resulting in some loss of instructional time.	Transitions occur smoothly with little loss of instructional time. Specific procedures are taught and used effectively.	Transitions are seamless, with students assuming some responsibility for efficient operation.
Management of Time and Materials	Time and materials are inefficiently handled, resulting in loss of instructional time.	Time and materials are handled moderately well.	Time and materials are handled smoothly with little loss of instructional time or interest.	Time and materials are handled smoothly and efficiently with no loss of attention or interest. Students assume some responsibility for efficient operation of time and materials.
Directions and Procedures	Directions and procedures are confusing to the students.	Directions and procedures are clarified after initial student confusion or are excessively detailed.	Directions and procedures are clear to students and contain an appropriate level of detail. Frequently checks for understanding.	Directions and procedures are clear to students. Anticipates possible student misunderstanding; plans and monitors for it.
Pacing	The pacing is too slow or rushed.	Pacing is inconsistent.	Pacing is usually appropriate. Teacher adapts pace by monitoring students.	Pacing of the lesson is smooth, timely, and appropriate, allowing for reflection and closure.
Performance of Non-Instructional Duties: Attendance, Lunch Count, Distribution of Papers, Duties, Etc.	Performance of non-instructional duties is inefficient. May be inattentive to these duties.	Duties are handled fairly efficiently.	Duties are managed and completed in a clear, professional manner without loss of instructional time.	Systems for performing duties are well established, with students assuming appropriate responsibility for efficient classroom operation.

*Descriptions at the distinguished level may not be appropriate for some settings.
Source: *Evaluation of Student Teachers Guidebook,* Phi Delta Kappa International and Ball State University, 2000. Used with permission.

seriously at the ones listed most often. Also take note of responses that have never been given on previous questionnaires.

Checklists can also be used to obtain an overall estimate of student feelings toward specific aspects of teacher performance. Items might include some of the following:

1. Place a check beside *each* characteristic that describes your teacher:
   ___ Interesting ___ Organized ___ Strict
   ___ Smart ___ Pushover ___ Disorganized
   ___ Uninformed ___ Dull
2. Place a check beside the answer that best describes your feelings toward the teacher:
   a. The teacher helps me learn or improve my skills.
      Yes ___ No ___ I don't know ___
   b. The teacher has good discipline.
      Yes ___ No ___ I don't know ___

Several different types of rating scales can be used for student evaluation of teachers. Questions using a semantic differential scale to score student attitudes toward the teacher might appear as follows:

Friendly	::::::::	Unfriendly
Boring	::::::::	Interesting

Items are scored from one to seven, with seven being the most positive. An average of the scores for the entire class on each item would undoubtedly provide the most information.

A Likert-type scale can be used to determine student attitudes toward the teacher, or to compare how the students feel versus how the teacher feels about each characteristic. For example, in the following questions, *x* marks how the student feels, and *o* marks how the teacher feels on each item.

	Mostly True	**Usually True**	**Usually False**	**Mostly False**
1. The teacher is concerned about student learning.	o		x	
2. The teacher likes teaching.		x	o	

When a serious discrepancy exists between the teacher's and the students' feelings, as in item 1, the teacher becomes aware of the need to communicate feelings differently.

Students' perceptions about the instructional system can also be acquired via a rating scale. This scale could be a report card students use to grade the teacher at the end of a unit of instruction or grading period. The scale could be written at a lower level of reading ability for use by younger students.

Systematic Observation

One way to avoid the subjectivity inherent in informal analysis is to use systematic observation. Systematic observation is used to collect data that describe various components of the teaching performance. The data are then analyzed to determine the extent to which the intended teaching behavior actually occurred during teaching. The primary purpose of systematic observation is to collect objective data that accurately describe events occurring in the classroom. The data must be recorded in such a way that they can be used to analyze one or more components of the teaching/learning process.

Literally hundreds of analytic systems have been developed to encode student and teacher behaviors. Some are relatively easy to learn and use; others are so complex that only trained researchers use them. In this chapter, the simpler kinds of systematic observation that can be used for self-improvement are presented. These systems require only an observer, paper and pencil, and a stopwatch. A tape recorder or videorecorder can be valuable if teachers wish to analyze their own teaching behavior rather than have an outside observer evaluate them. The computer is another tool that aids the observer in teacher evaluation. The laptop models enable on-the-spot observation. Simple programs make it possible to keep track of time (e.g., minutes spent talking to the class) and behaviors (e.g., the number of times "okay" was said). Such programs usually convert tallies to percentages immediately and allow teachers to see results while everything is fresh in their minds.

Systematic observation is generally limited to a description of what the teacher and students were doing (i.e., how much time the teacher spends giving students practice or how much feedback students receive). It generally tells little about the quality of the performance (i.e., how well a teacher demonstrates a skill). Some studies have used time on task as a proxy for student learning. Byra is one of the few researchers to develop an instrument to accurately measure and describe qualitative aspects of the teaching process (quality of demonstration, clarity of presentation, and quality of feedback).[13] Other limitations are the limited sample size (sometimes only one student), the limited time sample, and the limited set of categories used for describing behavior. Systematic observation uses the techniques of duration recording, interval recording, group time sampling, and event recording. A discussion of each technique follows.

Duration Recording Duration recording analyzes time and is useful for determining the amount of time spent on the various functions that teachers perform.[14] Such functions include instructing students (demonstrating, explaining, or questioning); class management (roll call, organizing students, distributing equipment, discipline); active student practice with feedback from the instructor; and student practice with no feedback from the instructor. A stopwatch is used to record the amount of time spent in each category. Each time the teacher changes functions the stopwatch is restarted.

At the conclusion of the lesson, the time in each category is totaled and divided by the total class time to obtain the percentage of time spent in each category. Then the results are analyzed to see whether the time has been spent in the best way. Individual functions, such as roll call or demonstrations, can also be analyzed by duration recording to determine where the time is going, and changes can be made to eliminate the nonproductive use of time.

A variation of duration recording is to record the amount of time an individual student spends in actual practice. The teacher may discover that, although the class is engaged in what appears to be a large amount of practice time, individual students spend a large amount of time waiting for a turn or standing out in right field.

Duration recording can also be done for several brief periods of time spaced throughout a lesson. For example, three five-minute samples can provide a valid indication of the percentage of time spent in each type of behavior.[15] To obtain a percentage, merely divide by fifteen minutes instead of the total class time.

Interval Recording In interval recording, the observation session is divided into a number of equal intervals, and a specified behavior is observed and recorded at the conclusion of each interval. For example, in a thirty-five-minute period there are thirty-five one-minute intervals or seventy thirty-second intervals. The length of time selected for the interval will depend on the behavior to be sampled.

There are two types of interval recording. Whole interval recording requires that the behavior be present throughout the entire interval before it is recorded. Partial interval recording, which is more commonly used, requires the behavior to occur during the interval, after which its occurrence is recorded. Some time samples, such as checking on a student every five minutes to determine student involvement in activity, can even be done while teaching.

The easiest kind of interval recording involves only two categories, such as active or passive, productive or nonproductive. A student is selected, and at the end of each interval a check or tally indicates the behavior the student demonstrates. If a single behavior is targeted for the observation, several students can be observed by observing the first student during intervals 1, 4, 7, and so on; the second student during intervals 2, 5, 8, and so on; and the third student during intervals 3, 6, 9, and so on. To code a number of behaviors, the observer selects an average student and codes what the student is doing at the end of each interval. To make it easier, coding can be done for three minutes, followed by resting three minutes, and repeating the coding and resting throughout the period. While a watch or stopwatch can be used to time the length of the interval, it is difficult for the observer to watch the target student as well as the watch. A tape recording that cues the start and stop of the intervals can be prepared and played using an ear jack while the observer is doing the observation. Thus the observer can focus attention on the lesson and the cuing tape does not disturb others.

Box 14.2 shows an interval recording form designed by Anderson to determine how students are spending their time during a class session. It uses a five-second interval for coding. The categories are the following:

1. Performs motor activity—Plays game or sport, practices skill, does exercises or calisthenics, explores movement.
2. Receives information—Listens, watches demonstration, uses media, reads written material.
3. Gives information or assists—Talks to teacher or student, demonstrates, spots.
4. Waits—Waits for turn, waits for game or drill to begin.
5. Relocates—Moves from one place or activity area to another.
6. Other—Ties shoes, gets equipment, gets a drink.

At the end of each three-minute period, notes can be recorded to help the teacher recall information explaining the recorded behaviors. At the end of the period, each column is totaled and a percentage calculated. The behavior is then analyzed and goals set for improving teaching.

Group Time Sampling When you want to know what most of the students in a group or class are doing, an interval recording technique called group time sampling or placheck (planned activity check) is useful. This involves counting the number of students engaged in a particular behavior at the conclusion of a specified interval of time, such as every two or three minutes. Limit behaviors to be checked to two or three so the count takes only about ten seconds. The observer scans from left to right each time and records the number of students who are engaged in the less frequently occurring behavior. For example, in an actively involved class, the inactive students are counted and subtracted from the total number of students to get the number in the actively involved category. A group time sample spot-checking record is shown in Box 14.3.

Anderson suggested the use of the following categories for spot checking: active/inactive, on-task/off-task, safe/unsafe, attentive/unattentive, cooperative/disruptive, and interacting with others/isolated.[16] Most of the students should be engaged in appropriate and productive behavior for teaching to be effective.

At the conclusion of the class, the percentage of students in each category is calculated by dividing each column total by the sum of the two or three columns. The data are then analyzed, and changes are planned for improving teaching behavior.

Event Recording Event recording is merely tallying the frequency with which a given behavior occurs during a specified time period. It is done by identifying one person to observe (the teacher, an average student) and one or more behaviors to tally. The observer then proceeds to put down a mark each time the specified behavior occurs. If only a single behavior is being recorded a golf counter

BOX 14.2

An Interval Recording Form for Student Behavior

Sample Coding Form and Record

TIME SAMPLING OF A SINGLE STUDENT'S BEHAVIOR

RECORD A CHECK (✓) FOR EACH 5 SECONDS OF STUDENT ACTIVITY.

STUDENT'S NAME: Alice Smith

CLASS: Elementary Gymnastics

SEGMENT (3-MIN)	PERFORMS MOTOR ACTIVITY	RECEIVES INFORMATION	GIVES INFORMATION OR ASSISTS	WAITS	RELOCATES	OTHER	NOTATIONS
I 9:00–9:03	✓✓✓ (3)	✓✓✓✓✓ ✓✓✓✓✓ ✓✓✓✓✓ ✓✓✓✓✓ (20)		✓✓✓✓✓ ✓✓✓✓✓ (10)	✓✓ (2)	✓ (1)	Waited for teacher to begin Rec. info on class organization
II 9:06–9:09	✓✓✓✓✓ ✓✓✓ (8)	✓✓✓✓✓ ✓✓✓✓✓ ✓✓✓✓✓ ✓✓✓✓✓ ✓✓ (22)		✓✓ (2)	✓✓✓ (3)	✓ (1)	End instruction / began tumbling and head stand
III 9:12–9:15	✓✓✓✓✓ ✓✓✓✓✓ ✓✓✓✓✓ ✓✓ (17)	✓✓✓✓✓ (5)	✓✓✓✓✓ (5)	✓✓ (2)	✓ (1)	✓✓✓✓✓ ✓ (6)	Cont'd. tumbling "Other" = replaced mats
IV 9:18–9:21	✓✓✓✓✓ ✓✓✓✓✓ ✓✓✓✓✓ ✓✓✓✓✓ ✓✓ (22)	✓✓✓ (3)	✓✓✓ (3)	✓✓✓✓✓ (5)		✓✓✓ (3)	Performed on ropes
V 9:24–9:27	✓✓✓ (3)	✓✓✓✓✓ ✓✓✓✓✓ ✓✓✓✓✓ ✓✓✓✓✓ ✓✓✓✓✓ (25)		✓✓✓ (3)	✓✓✓ (3)	✓✓ (2)	Rec'd. instruction on bars
VI 9:30–9:33	✓✓✓ (3)	✓✓✓✓✓ ✓✓✓✓✓ (10)		✓✓✓✓✓ ✓✓✓✓✓ ✓✓✓✓✓ ✓✓✓✓✓ ✓ (21)		✓✓ (2)	Waits turn on bars and performs
TOTALS	f = 56 % = 56/216 = 26%	f = 85 % = 85/216 = 39%	f = 8 % = 8/216 = 3%	f = 43 % = 43/216 = 19%	f = 9 % = 9/216 = 4%	f = 15 % = 15/216 = 7%	

SUMMARY COMMENTS AND EVALUATION (made by Teacher of class)

Too much time spent waiting for teacher and getting organized.

Good activity levels on mats and ropes—too much waiting around on bars.

Overall, a greater proportion of time should be spent in performing activities.

Source: William G. Anderson, *Analysis of Teaching Physical Education* (St. Louis: The C. V. Mosby Co., 1980).

can be used to record frequency. Event recording can be used to record a behavior throughout the entire lesson or during specified time segments spaced at regular intervals (e.g., five three-minute segments).

Event recording can be used to collect meaningful data on a wide variety of teacher or student behaviors. It produces a numerical value that can be converted into rate per minute. The rate per minute on different occasions can then be compared to determine whether improvement in the behavior has occurred. Event recording can be used to record items involving instruction, student practice, and feedback.

Instruction The extent to which the intended concepts are conveyed to the students can be determined by listing each concept and recording a check beside the concept each time it is mentioned by the teacher. Asking questions during a lesson can make it more interactive and effective.

Box 14.3

A Sample Placheck Record

SPOT-CHECKING RECORD FORM

Class Track and Field Date May 10

	Time \ Categories	Off-task	On-task active	On-task waiting	Comments
High Jump	8:50	1	2	7	TIEING SHOES
	8:56	0	3	7	PRACTICED WHILE WAITING
	9:02	0	3	7	
	9:08	3	2	5	TALKING
	9:14	4	3	3	PLAYING AROUND
Long Jump	8:52	0	1	9	COMPLIMENTED OTHERS
	8:58	0	1	9	
	9:04	2	1	7	TALKING
	9:10	5	1	4	TALKING
	9:16	4	1	5	WANDERED OFF
Hurdles	8:54	0	4	6	
	8:00	0	4	6	PRACTICED WHILE WAITING
	9:06	0	4	6	
	9:12	1	3	6	GETTING A DRINK
	9:18	2	4	4	TALKING
	Column Totals	22	37	91	
	Total of All Columns	150			
	Percent of Total	14.7%	24.7%	60.7%	

Summary Comments and Evaluation:

on-task, active = performing or helping
on-task, waiting = watching performance
off-task = talking, wandering around, daydreaming

Students are spending a lot of time waiting and seem bored, especially at end of period.

BOX 14.4

Student Practice Record

STUDENT PRACTICE RECORD

Class Badminton Date March 17

Skills	Student #1 Period 2	Student #2 Period 2	Student #3 Period 2	Student #4 Period ___
Short serve	(/) / (/) /// (/) /	(/) (/) (/) // (/) (/)	(/) (/) (/) (/) (/) (/) (/) (/) (/) (/)	
Overhead clear	/ (/) // (/) / (/) (/)	(/) (/) (/) (/) (/)	(/) (/) (/) (/) (/) (/) (/) / (/) / (/) (/)	
Underhand clear	/// (/) /// (/)	(/) (/) (/) // (/) / (/) (/) / (/) /	(/) (/) // (/) / (/) / (/)	
Smash				
Drop				

Summary Comments and Evaluation:

I circled the successful attempts in a five-minute game. Student #1 needs to review basic skills. No student attempted drops or smashes. Perhaps I need to reteach the drop and smash.

Event recording can document the use of different types of questions (e.g., content related, procedural, multiple/run-on). Other teacher behaviors such as the use of meaningless words (e.g., okay, all right, like) and the use of student first names can be observed using event recording.

Student practice The number of practice trials a student attempts or the number of times a student touches the ball or uses a piece of equipment can be easily tallied, as shown in Box 14.4. This can be done during practice drills, in lead-up games, or during actual game play. A list of skills or tasks to be accomplished, with a check by each one attempted, provides an overall view of the distribution of practice over the entire range of tasks inherent in the activity. Box 14.4 shows how this can be done. A study of the record aids the teacher in determining the adequacy and distribution of practice trials.

Feedback Feedback has been defined as one of the key elements in the acquisition of psychomotor skills. Feedback also occurs in response to appropriate and inappropriate student behavior. Event recording can be used to record the extent to which both kinds of feedback occur. Both skill feedback and behavior feedback can be analyzed in the following ways:

1. Rate of feedback per minute.
2. Ratio of positive to negative feedback. Feedback should generally be in the ratio of four positive comments to each negative comment.
3. Percentage of specific feedback.

4. Percentage of value feedback.
5. Percentage of group-directed feedback.
6. Percentage of nonverbal feedback.
7. Ratio of reinforcement of appropriate behavior to punishment of off-task behavior.

Each column of the form can be used separately, or several columns can be recorded at once. Simple computer programs make such recording less tedious. Categories can be defined as follows:

1. Positive—A tone that conveys acceptance of a student's performance or behavior.
2. Negative—A tone that conveys rejection of a student's performance or behavior.
3. General—Feedback with no specific information given about the skill or behavior.
4. Specific—Feedback with specific information given about how to perform the behavior or skill.
5. Value—Feedback that tells why a specific behavior or skill should be done in a certain way.
6. Individual—Feedback to one student.
7. Group—Feedback to more than one student.
8. Verbal—Feedback that is only verbal.
9. Visual and verbal—Feedback that demonstrates how the skill or behavior should be performed.
10. Kinesthetic and verbal—Feedback that uses touch or manipulation of body parts to correct the movement (such as spotting in gymnastics).
11. Reinforces appropriate behavior—Feedback that rewards appropriate behavior.
12. Punishes off-task behavior—Feedback that is nonreinforcing or punishing for inappropriate behavior.

Academic Learning Time—Physical Education

Academic Learning Time—Physical Education (ALT-PE) is an example of a systematic observation system that uses both interval and event recording. Instead of coding actions of the teacher, a target student (average ability) is selected for observation. The assumption is made that the student reflects the impact of teacher behaviors, which is a good indicator of lesson effectiveness. For example, a teacher might be giving information, but if the student is not listening, the instructions are not effective. Noncontinuous interval recording is used, which means that the observer watches the student for a certain period of time (usually five seconds) and then records the dominant behavior observed during the following interval. This is a time-sampling technique, and in the calculation of how time was spent during the lesson, the first interval actually represents ten seconds of time rather than the five seconds that was spent observing the behavior. Although the behavior recorded during the five-second time interval is somewhat inflated, this system does provide a good representation of what occurred during the lesson. The five-second recording interval also gives the observer an opportunity to record other teacher behaviors (e.g., use of student names, feedback, overused phrases). ALT-PE has been used in several research studies and is simple enough for an observer to use while actually watching someone teach. After the lesson, the observer can provide immediate feedback by calculating the percentage of time spent in various categories (management, transition, wait, knowledge, activity, and off task) as well as the frequency of other teacher behaviors and relevant anecdotal notes. Box 14.5 is an example of a form that could be used to code a lesson with ALT-PE.

Computerized Observations

Laptop computers and handheld Palm Pilots are being used in systematic observations. Some computer observation programs are generic and require the user to customize the various features for the observation; others have been developed specifically for use in physical education. Changing the labels on the various timing and event recording categories allows the user to tailor the observation with relative ease. Computer timing programs are more accurate than the ALT-PE system described above as they use duration recording instead of noncontinuous interval recording. At the conclusion of a lesson, the data are calculated and can be used immediately during the post-teaching conference, as shown in Box 14.6. As computers become more powerful, other types of data will be possible. Box 14.7 is an example of a timeline

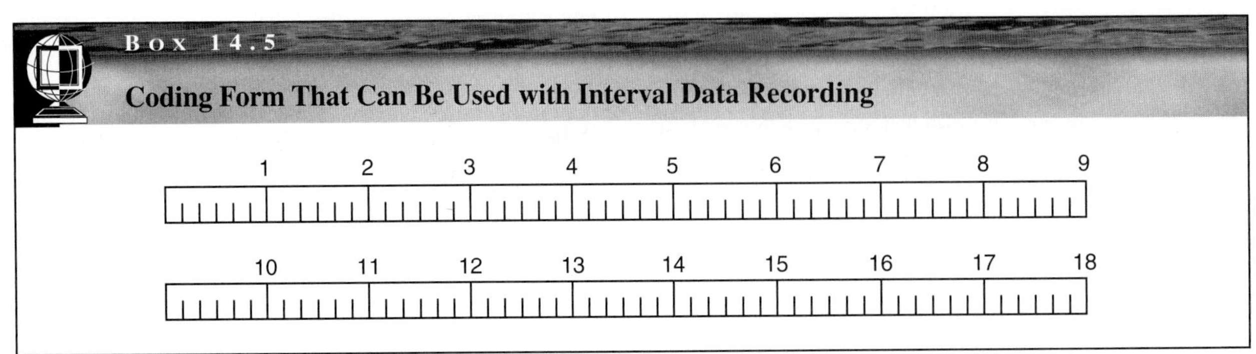
BOX 14.5

Coding Form That Can Be Used with Interval Data Recording

1 2 3 4 5 6 7 8 9

10 11 12 13 14 15 16 17 18

BOX 14.6

Example of an Observation Summary from a Computerized Observation System

OBSERVATION SUMMARY

ALT-PE Observation for Jane Newteach on 10/31/2004 10:11:46 AM

School Name:	Ballard High	**Class Type:**	Field/Court
Class Activity:	Volleyball	**Grade Level:**	8
Observer:	Dr Smith	**Number of Pupils:**	10
Subject:	Jane Newteach	**Total Time:**	00:10:04

Event	Event Type	Number of Incidents	Cumulative Duration	Cumulative Duration as % of Total Time	Threshold Level as % of Total Time	Average # of Counted Incidents /min	Average Length of of Incident	Length of Longest Incident	Length of Shortest Incident	Cumulative Duration between Incidents	Longest Length between Incidents	Shortest Length between Incidents
Management	Timed	1	00:00:30	05%	10%		00:00:30	00:00:30	00:00:30	00:09:33	00:09:33	00:09:33
Knowledge	Timed	3	00:02:31	25%	10%		00:00:50	00:01:30	00:00:30	00:05:01	00:02:00	00:01:30
Activity	Timed	4	00:06:31	65%	60%		00:01:38	00:02:00	00:01:00	00:03:01	00:01:30	00:00:31
Transition	Timed	1	00:00:30	05%	10%		00:00:30	00:00:30	00:00:30	00:03:02	00:03:02	00:03:02
Off Task	Timed	0	00:00:00	00%	5%		*	00:00:00	00:00:00	00:00:00	00:00:00	00:00:00
Waiting	Timed	0	00:00:00	00%	5%		*	00:00:00	00:00:00	00:00:00	00:00:00	00:00:00
Positive interactions	Counted	7				.70						
Negative interactions	Counted	1				.10						
Names called	Counted	8				.79						
Subject response	Counted	3				.30						

Comments

Source: From observa@www.bellsouth.net. Used with permission.

BOX 14.7

Example of an Observation Event Log Timeline from a Computerized Observation System

OBSERVATION EVENT LOG

ALT-PE Observation for Jane Newteach on 10/31/2004 10:11:46 AM

School Name:	Ballard High	**Class Type:**	Field/Court
Class Activity:	Volleyball	**Grade Level:**	8
Observer:	Dr Smith	**Number of Pupils:**	10
Subject:	Jane Newteach	**Total Time:**	00:10:04

Time	Management	Knowledge	Activity	Transition	Off Task	Waiting Interactions	Positive interactions	Negative Called	Names Response	Subject
00:00:01	Begin									
00:00:24										Occurred
00:00:31	End - 00:00:30									
00:00:32			Begin							
00:00:47									Occurred	
00:00:50									Occurred	
00:00:53							Occurred			
00:01:00							Occurred			
00:01:03										Occurred
00:01:08									Occurred	
00:01:25								Occurred		
00:01:44									Occurred	
00:01:52							Occurred			
00:02:13							Occurred			
00:02:18							Occurred			
00:02:32			End - 00:02:00							
00:02:32		Begin								
00:02:50										Occurred
00:03:13							Occurred			
00:03:25							Occurred			
00:03:33									Occurred	
00:03:38									Occurred	
00:04:02		End - 00:01:30								

Source: From *observa@www.bellsouth.net.* Used with permission.

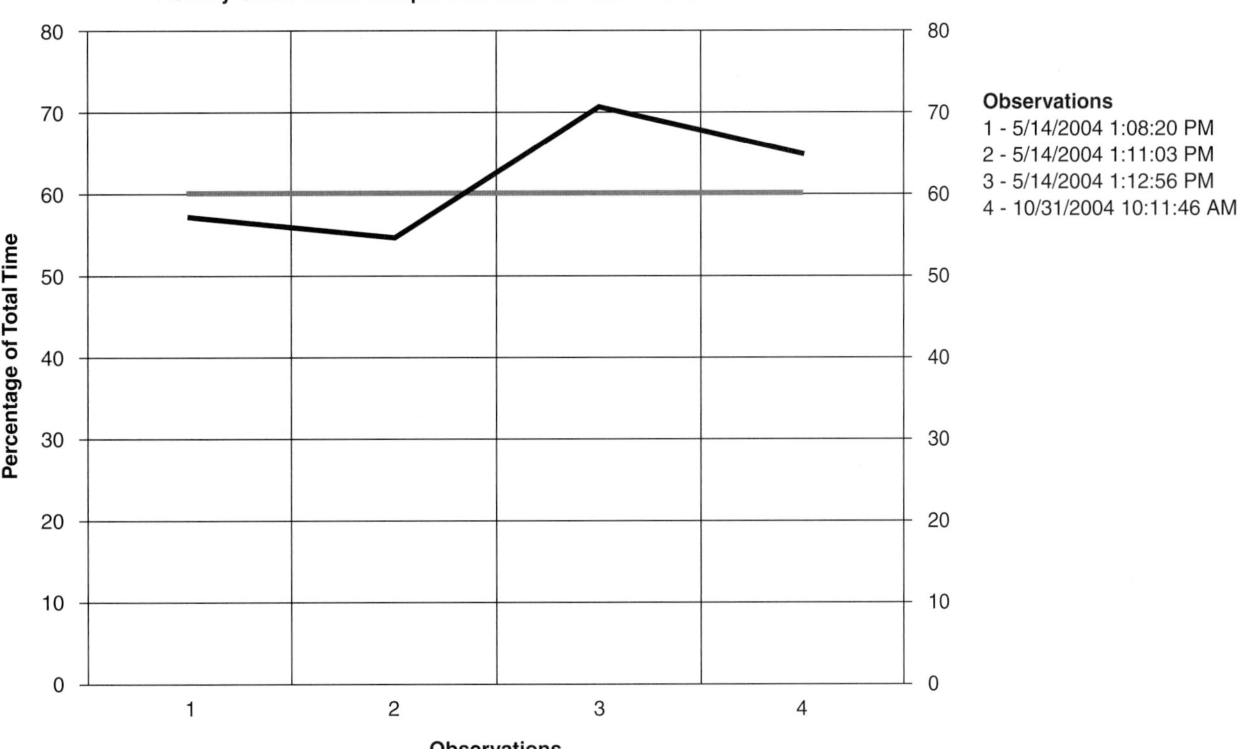

Figure 14-1

Example of a comparison chart from a computerized observation system.
From observa@www.bellsouth.net. Used with permission.

printout that shows when events occurred during the various timed segments. Such information is valuable when teachers wish to demonstrate that an event (such as feedback) occurred throughout a lesson rather than only during the beginning. A frequency count would only provide the total amount of feedback given and would not reveal when it occurred during the lesson. Computers can also generate charts that illustrate a teacher's progress over several different observations for a given teaching behavior (see Figure 14-1).

Creating a Personalized Descriptive System

Often evaluation instruments are not appropriate for specific situations. Those who know the situation best can create or adapt an appropriate tool for evaluation. Once an instrument has been formulated, try it out and check it for reliability. Make modifications until it brings the desired results. When preparing a descriptive system, incorporate the following components: (1) a single behavior focus, (2) a definition of categories, (3) an observation and coding system, and (4) reliability.

The Behavior Focus Select a single teaching component for analysis. Trying to analyze too much can defeat the system. Define the component to identify what is and what is not included in the behavior focus. An example for one teacher was to reduce the use of distracting words or phrases.

Definition of Categories Categories within the behavioral focus must be defined so that any observable behavior can be assigned to only one category. Provide examples of behaviors falling into each category. For example, "ok" or "all right" fit into the category of distracting words or phrases.

An Observation and Coding System Choose a technique such as duration recording, interval recording, group time sampling, or event recording; then develop a form for recording the data.

Reliability Reliability results when two observers obtain similar results after independently rating the same lesson or when one observer obtains the same results on two separate occasions from a videotaped recording. When this occurs, it reveals that the definitions of the behavior categories are sufficiently clear to ensure that behaviors are recorded accurately by the observer and reflect the actual behavior that occurred during the lesson.

Review Question: Define and give an example of each of the following teacher evaluation techniques: (a) student achievement and improvement, (b) informal analysis, (c) systematic observation, (d) duration recording, (e) interval recording, (f) group time sampling, and (g) event recording.

Step 3—Use the Appropriate Techniques to Record Information

The best evaluation technique is the one that provides precise feedback related to the specific teaching goal. Only a few events can be recorded during each lesson, so formulate a plan to utilize the most effective techniques for the objectives of the specific lesson. Keep the plan simple. Two or three evaluation techniques at a time are probably as many as can be checked accurately.

Step 4—Evaluate or Interpret the Data

Research on teaching has provided much useful information about things that good teachers do. For example, good teachers try to decrease management time and get students into activity as quickly as possible. Students who wait in line do not have time to practice; therefore, they are not learning and can cause problems when they become bored. Teachers should also try to use positive feedback and student names frequently. When teachers are presented with the results from a systematic observation, they have actual data about what is happening when they teach. The data become a starting point, and teachers can use them as goals for improvement. Beginning teachers can spend as much as 50 percent of their lesson in transition time, which means that much potential practice time is lost. Interpreting data to design an action plan is a critical part of the teacher evaluation process. Some questions to ask are as follows:

1. What teaching behaviors are satisfactory?
2. What changes in teaching behaviors might improve student learning?
3. Which changes are practical?
4. Which one or two changes in teacher behavior would result in the most important changes in student performance?
5. What will have to be done to implement these changes?
6. What target goal for the change would be indicative of a successful change effort (e.g., call ten students by name each period)?

Teachers should never try to change too many teaching behaviors at once. By targeting one or two behaviors and setting achievable goals, teachers can progress toward becoming more effective. Subsequent systematic observations will document this improvement and provide reinforcement and encouragement to teachers for their efforts. Teaching is very complex, and becoming a better teacher should be viewed as a journey that requires time and effort. Data obtained through systematic observations will document whether changes being made are having a positive effect in the person's teaching practices.

Step 5—Make Changes and Reevaluate

Try to incorporate the selected changes into the teaching repertoire. Make only one or two changes at a time. Teach the same or a similar lesson, concentrating on the intended changes, and reevaluate the lesson to determine whether the changes produced the desired results. If not, select a new procedure to try.

AN EXAMPLE OF TEACHER EVALUATION

Step 1—Determine What to Evaluate

For a softball unit, the teacher selected the following evaluation goals: (1) to increase student skill achievement and (2) to reduce class management time.

Step 2—Choose or Construct Specific Evaluation Techniques

The specific evaluation techniques selected were (1) student achievement, (2) duration recording and event recording of management time, (3) event recording of student practice, and (4) event recording of skill feedback.

Step 3—Use the Appropriate Techniques to Record Information

Student assistants were used to record student achievement and practice by tallying successful trials. Several lessons were videotaped for evaluation of management time and skill feedback. A sample evaluation plan for one of the lessons is shown in Box 14.8.

Step 4—Evaluate or Interpret the Data

The results of the data showed that students were spending too much time practicing without the help of teacher feedback and the feedback when given was primarily verbal. With regard to class management, the analysis showed that the teacher had to tell students several times before they proceeded to do what they had been told.

Step 5—Make Changes and Reevaluate

The teacher decided to use a golf counter to keep a tally of the number of feedback attempts he made during one period each day to increase the frequency of feedback. Later, an event recording of skill feedback also showed an increase in the number of nonverbal feedback attempts.

The second result of the evaluation occurred in class management. The teacher told the students what they were to do, asked several questions to determine whether they understood, and then refrained from repeating instructions. Students were timed to determine how long it took them to get into the next formation, drill, or game,

Box 14.8

A Sample Evaluation Plan

AN EVALUATION PLAN

Lesson Plan	Evaluation Plan	Data
Objectives		
1. Students will hit three out of five balls pitched to them during drill.	Students record number of successful hits during a specified time period.	
2. Students will hit 100 percent of the times at bat in one-swing game.	Tally number of students at bat and number of successful hits.	
Teaching and Learning Activities		
1. Demonstrate and explain batting.	Event recording of content of teacher's instruction.	
2. Pepper drill for maximum participation with teacher feedback.	Event recording of student trials during drill and skill feedback of teacher.	
3. One-swing softball game for application to game situation.	Event recording of student trials and successes during game.	
Specific Teacher Goals		
1. Reduce management time.	Time analysis of management time.	
Summary Comments and Evaluation		

and feedback was provided on the length of time it took. The result was a rapid decrease in management time.

A CHALLENGE TO TEACHERS

Evaluation challenges teachers to "put it all together" and, as a summarizing experience, gives teachers a sense of accomplishment by helping them realize how much they have achieved. As a learning activity it should also focus the teacher on how to improve the transmission of information and skills. By helping teachers check the effectiveness of the teaching process, evaluation tells the teacher whether students have achieved the course objectives and the progress they made in doing so. When evaluation materials show that students are not performing well, the teacher should examine unit and lesson plans to determine whether the achievement of performance objectives was pursued in a meaningful way. Next, the teacher must critically decide whether his or her teaching techniques were effective.

Because evaluation is so critical, it should be an ongoing process. Evaluation makes students accountable for their performance and teachers responsible for student achievement. Such accountability, which is often lacking, is vital to the credibility and effectiveness of the profession.

Review Question: How can teacher evaluation techniques help teachers improve their teaching?

NOTES

1. U.S. Department of Education, *Education Report Card* (Washington, DC: Author, 1987).
2. Staff, *The Daily Universe,* 11 February 1987.
3. http://www.ed.gov/print/nclb/accountability/index.html.
4. http://www.ed.gov/print/nclb/overview/intro/guide/guide.html.
5. G. W. Arbogast and L. Griffin, Accountability—Is it within reach of the profession? *Journal of Physical Education, Recreation, and Dance 60,* no. 6 (1989): 72–75.
6. N. J. Maggard, Upgrading our image, *Journal of Physical Education, Recreation, and Dance 55,* no. 1 (1984): 17, 82.

7. National Association for Sport and Physical Education, *SPEAK II: Sport and Physical Education Advocacy Kit II,* (Reston, VA: NASPE Publications, 1999).
8. U.S. Department of Health and Human Services, *Physical Activity and Health: A Report of the Surgeon General;* U.S. Department of Health and Human Services, Centers for Disease Control (CDC) Guidelines for School and Community Programs: Promoting Lifelong Physical Activity (Atlanta, GA: CDC, 1997).
9. Eric Jensen, Assessment and the Brain: Measuring What Matters. Recording# 503235, Association for Supervision and Curriculum Development 58th Annual Conference, San Francisco, CA, 8–10 March 2003. Read by author; Pat Wolfe, The Adolescent Brain: A Work in Progress. Recording # 503257, Association for Supervision and Curriculum Development 58th Annual Conference, San Francisco, CA, 8–10 March 2003. Read by author.
10. C. A. Bucher and C. R. Koenig, *Methods and Materials for Secondary School Physical Education,* 6th ed. (St. Louis: Mosby, 1983).
11. D. C. Griffey, Trouble for sure: A crisis—perhaps: Secondary school physical education today, *Journal of Physical Education, Recreation, and Dance 58,* no. 2 (1987): 21.
12. D. Siedentop and D. Tannehill, *Developing Teaching Skills in Physical Education,* 4th ed. (Mountain View, CA: Mayfield, 2000).
13. M. Byra, Measuring qualitative aspects of teaching in physical education, *Journal of Physical Education, Recreation, and Dance 63,* no. 3 (1992): 83–89.
14. Siedentop and Tannehill, *Developing Teaching Skills.*
15. W. G. Anderson, *Analysis of Teaching Physical Education* (St. Louis: Mosby, 1980).
16. Anderson, *Analysis of Teaching.*

CHAPTER

15

Evaluating and Revising the Instructional Program

Study Stimulators

1. Define formative and summative evaluation. What are the purposes of each?
2. Describe the process for evaluating a program in physical education.
3. Describe several kinds of data-gathering instruments and tell the advantages or disadvantages of each.

Physical education used to be a required subject at the secondary level, but the number of states with a physical education mandate has decreased dramatically over the past two decades. Programs of poor quality and increased attention to academic standards have both contributed to that decrease. Daily participation in high school physical education classes dropped from 42 percent in 1991 to 25 percent in 1995. Even good physical education programs are not immune to budget and time cuts. Rog proposed ten questions for measuring the vulnerability of physical education programs:

1. Does your building principal hold high expectation(s) of student achievement in physical education?
2. Do you hold high expectations of student achievement in your physical education classes?
3. Are your program and its goals clearly understood by others in the school and community?
4. Are the students in your physical education program evaluated primarily on their skill performance?
5. Does your program have frequent monitoring of student progress using criterion-referenced testing based on identified objectives of student achievement?
6. Do students in all of your schools have physical education programs available to them at least 150 minutes per week?
7. Does your state require that physical education programs be made available to all students in order for your school to receive state aid?
8. Are all of your physical education classes being taught by physical education specialists or specific skill specialists?
9. If your school system's athletic program were cut, would your physical education program survive?
10. Do you have evaluation data on the achievements of your students in physical education that would demonstrate to your school committee the value of keeping your program?[1]

Although Rog posed these questions over twenty years ago, they raise important issues today. If your program rates high on each of these questions, your program is exceptional. If not, you will become aware of some opportunities for improvement.

THE ROLE OF PROGRAM EVALUATION

Evaluation provides information to the public about the success of physical education programs. When physical educators can describe results, they are more likely to get the support needed for effective school physical education programs. Vogel and Seefeldt noted that erosion of physical education programs can be stopped only when physical educators identify the anticipated outcomes of their programs, select and implement appropriate instructional methods, evaluate the degree to which students achieve the desired outcomes, and alter programs or methodology so student achievement of objectives is realized.[2] It is critically important that physical educators share results of these evaluations with students, parents, and administrators to inform them of program quality.

Most school districts have a schedule for review of every curriculum area. These reviews are usually thorough and extensive, involving self-study as well as input from other stakeholders. Some programs use these reviews for accreditation by outside agencies, others use the results to guide curricular revision. Good programs do not wait for scheduled reviews to examine program policies and accomplishments. Curriculum review is seen as an ongoing process to optimize student learning. These interim reviews will look at a specific part of the program and evaluate its effectiveness. For example, if a school decided to implement an outdoor adventure or fitness program, an evaluation might examine certain aspects of the program to facilitate its implementation. When teachers add a new unit of study to their program, they might evaluate certain instructional aspects or sample student opinions for feedback on the process. Through constant appraisal and revision, the curriculum can be gradually improved to meet its purposes.

Program evaluation involves both measurement (quantitative) and judgment (qualitative) appraisals. For example, fitness tests are used to measure physical fitness. Knowledge tests measure concept acquisition. Questionnaires and inventories assess students' attitudes about physical fitness. The scores are then evaluated to determine whether the students achieved the objectives specified in the program.

With the increased concern for educational accountability, evaluation provides empirical data for reporting to students, parents, administrators, boards of education, state departments of education, public media, accrediting agencies, and sponsors of educational research regarding program successes or failures.

It is possible to develop an outstanding curriculum only to discover that students fail to achieve desired learning outcomes because the curriculum development has not been translated successfully into teaching methods. Evaluation can help determine whether the program works and how its effectiveness can be increased. The two major purposes of program evaluation are (1) to provide information for program improvement during the instructional process—formative evaluation—and (2) to assess the validity and effectiveness (or success) of the curriculum—summative evaluation. Both formative and summative evaluation provide feedback for improving physical education programs.

Formative Evaluation

Formative evaluation is done while the program or activity is in progress. By measuring students' achievement of specified goals and standards, evaluators can determine whether things are going as planned or change is necessary. When implementing a program, teachers should identify conditions of success and monitor whether they are being met. Formative evaluation components can be repeated throughout the unit and are usually done internally rather than using information from external sources. Information provided by the evaluation can signal the need for change before the conclusion of an activity. For example, if students are having difficulty learning badminton skills, it would be useless to wait until the posttest results reveal that the students did not learn. Self-testing activities conducted each day or week could expose students' specific learning problems. Perhaps the difficulty is a student's lack of hand-eye coordination or an instructional pace that is too fast. Once the cause is known, instruction can be redesigned to resolve the problems and increase student learning. Formative evaluation discloses whether the content is relevant or useless, practical or impractical. It reveals whether the instruction is too fast or too slow, too difficult or too easy. Student interest and motivation can also be checked.

Although formal evaluation techniques may be used, formative evaluation generally uses informal, criterion-referenced evaluation techniques, such as those reviewed in Chapter 11, to point out strengths and weaknesses of individual lessons or short units. Informal evaluation techniques vary in quality depending on the skills of the person constructing the instruments. However, when carefully constructed, these instruments can be valid for evaluating local programs. They provide data that can help to determine instructional effectiveness and feasibility in terms of cost, teacher time, and student and teacher attitudes toward instruction. When teaching strategies are discovered to be impractical or ineffective, changes can be made at once to revise, add, or subtract lesson content or to change methods to achieve the desired results.

Summative Evaluation

Summative evaluation, which is evaluation of the final product, is used to determine the overall merit or worth of a unit or program. It takes place at the end of a unit or program and provides feedback necessary for program improvement by revealing how well students have achieved specific objectives or whether a specific educational program is worth more than an alternative approach. Unexpected outcomes, such as negative attitudes or excessive costs, should also be analyzed. Although summative evaluation may utilize informal evaluation techniques, it tends to rely on formal evaluation methods, such as standardized tests and inventories that are norm-referenced. Often an external evaluator is called in to evaluate a program. Accreditation teams serve this function by evaluating the overall school program to determine whether the school curriculum meets the goals established by the accrediting association and the school. If the program is adequate, the school is accredited for five to ten years.

Two pitfalls that occur in summative evaluation are evaluating too soon and evaluating the results of a program that teachers never really adopted. Expecting complete results from a new program in less than three years is unreasonable as time is required to eliminate problems related to implementation. Some results might be more appropriately evaluated after five years. In a similar vein, evaluators must not automatically assume that teachers have adopted the program. An evaluation plan must include some way, such as classroom observation, to verify that the program has been implemented.[3]

Review Question: Define and give an example of

a. formative evaluation.
b. summative evaluation.

How to Evaluate Physical Education Programs

The following steps are suggested for evaluating the instructional program or a unit/component of that program:

Step 1. Describe the program to be evaluated.
Step 2. Identify the purposes of the evaluation.
Step 3. Establish criteria for judging quality and making decisions.
Step 4. Describe the information needed to make the decisions.
Step 5. Obtain, record, and analyze information.
Step 6. Interpret data in terms of standards.
Step 7. Make decisions and formulate recommendations.

Following a description of all of the steps, an example of the process will be presented.

Step 1—Describe the Program to Be Evaluated

The program description helps to avoid overlooking aspects that need to be evaluated. A description generally includes the following:

1. A statement of the program philosophy.
2. The people involved—students, their families, faculty, and administrators.
3. Standards to be met—this would include state and/or district standards for physical education. States and districts have established physical education content standards that, if met, should produce a physically educated individual. Content standards are defined as "what students should know and be able to do."[4] They identify the knowledge, skills, and dispositions important to the discipline of physical education. Content standards are somewhat broad and can be achieved using a variety of different activities and teaching techniques. When establishing the criteria for an evaluation, districts must look to the performance standards, which indicate "how good is good enough."[5] The performance standards must be defined by the district so that teachers will know the intended outcomes of their programs.
4. Subject matter content.
5. Instructional elements such as scheduling pattern, learning activities, student-student and student-teacher interactions, media use, motivation, and evaluation and grading techniques.
6. Resources—these include facilities, equipment, and time available for instruction.
7. Costs.
8. Administrative conditions.

Step 2—Identify the Purposes of the Evaluation

Identify areas of concern about the program and anticipate decisions that will have to be made by asking questions such as these: Are goals and objectives appropriate and worthwhile? Are students achieving the standards? What problems exist? What are the reactions of various audiences to the program? What unanticipated outcomes are there?

Vogel and Seefeldt asserted that positive responses to the following questions yield evidence of successful programs:

1. Does the program include the important potential contributions of activity to the quality of life?
2. Is the content of the program clearly defined? (What is being taught? When? Why?)
3. Do the content and the methods of instruction match the individual needs of the students?
4. Do the graduates attain the desired standards related to skilled performance, knowledge, fitness, and attitude?

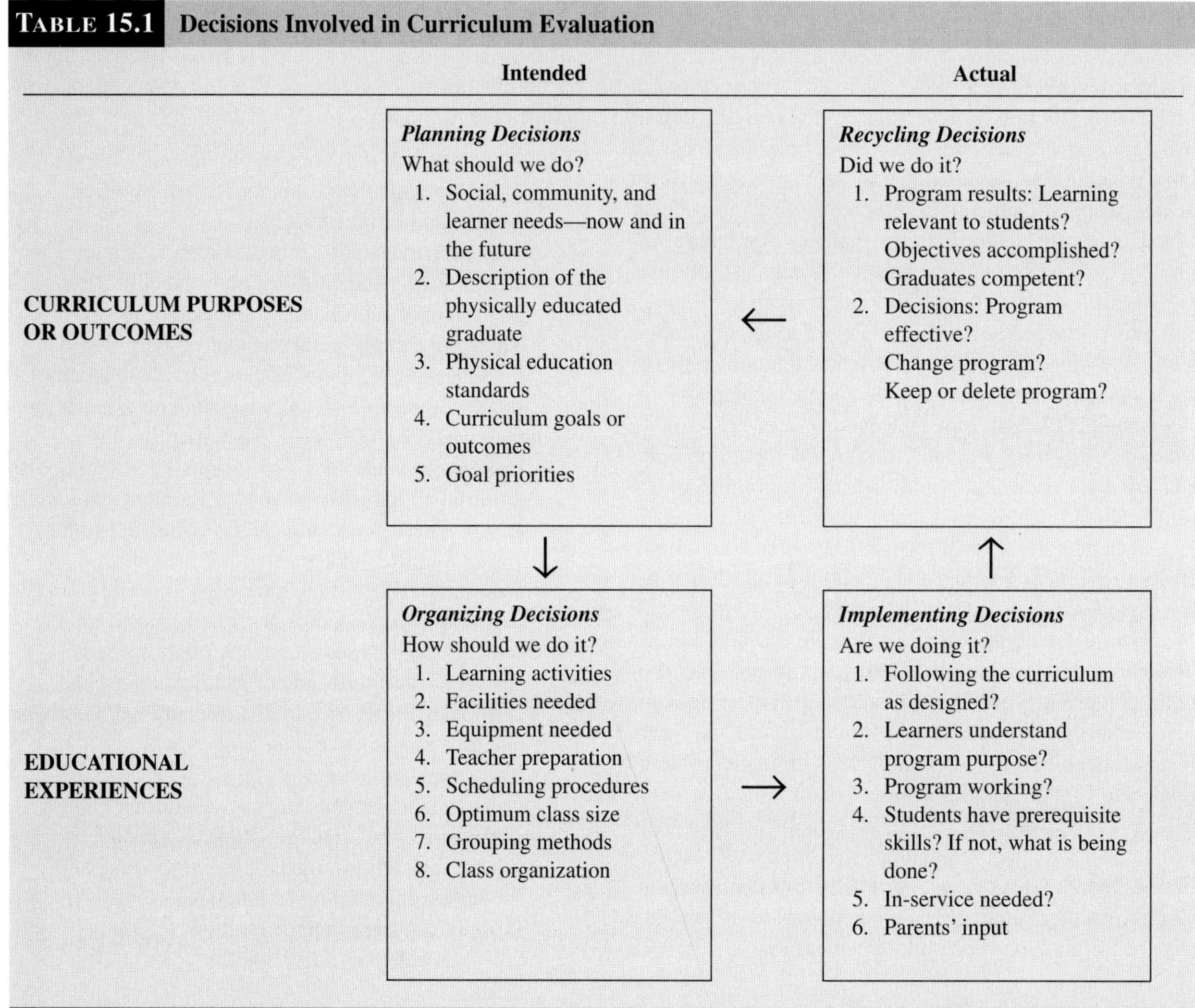

TABLE 15.1 Decisions Involved in Curriculum Evaluation

	Intended		Actual
CURRICULUM PURPOSES OR OUTCOMES	***Planning Decisions*** What should we do? 1. Social, community, and learner needs—now and in the future 2. Description of the physically educated graduate 3. Physical education standards 4. Curriculum goals or outcomes 5. Goal priorities	←	***Recycling Decisions*** Did we do it? 1. Program results: Learning relevant to students? Objectives accomplished? Graduates competent? 2. Decisions: Program effective? Change program? Keep or delete program?
	↓		↑
EDUCATIONAL EXPERIENCES	***Organizing Decisions*** How should we do it? 1. Learning activities 2. Facilities needed 3. Equipment needed 4. Teacher preparation 5. Scheduling procedures 6. Optimum class size 7. Grouping methods 8. Class organization	→	***Implementing Decisions*** Are we doing it? 1. Following the curriculum as designed? 2. Learners understand program purpose? 3. Program working? 4. Students have prerequisite skills? If not, what is being done? 5. In-service needed? 6. Parents' input

Source: Concepts from Daniel L. Stufflebeam et al., *Educational Evaluation and Decision Making* (Itasca, IL: F. E. Peacock, 1971); and Paul G. Vogel and Vern D. Seefeldt, "Redesign of Physical Education Programs: A Procedural Model That Leads to Defensible Programs," *Journal of Physical Education, Recreation, and Dance 58,* no. 7 (1987): 65–69.

5. Do the outcomes of the program justify the time, money, and energy expended to support the program?
6. Are there periodic evaluations and resultant program improvements?
7. Can the program continue if the current teacher(s) leave the district?[6]

Decisions to be made might include adopting a new program, discontinuing a program, changing student grouping patterns, increasing the budget, changing the staff, using community facilities, or implementing different instructional strategies. Possible alternatives should be identified in each instance. Four types of decisions included in program evaluation are (1) planning decisions, (2) organizing decisions, (3) implementing decisions, and (4) evaluating decisions.[7] Table 15.1 shows the questions that might be asked in each area, along with areas of concern.[8]

People responsible for making the decisions should be identified. These may include students, teachers, administrators, or the board of education. A date should be specified for making the decisions, along with policies within which the evaluation must occur.

Step 3—Establish Criteria for Judging Quality and Making Decisions

Two types of standards are used to judge program quality—absolute standards and relative standards. *Absolute standards* are those established by personal or professional judgment. Absolute standards are criterion-based and reflect a level of achievement independent of the performance of other programs. These criteria are established in the same way that performance objectives are created. The problem with using absolute standards lies in selecting the level that indicates program success. Because they are established by program evaluators, such standards often end up being "guesstimates" of performance. Absolute standards should be based on information obtained from outside resources and professionals. Preassessment scores of current students provide guidelines for developing standards. When students fail to achieve the standards, the program can be revised to produce the desired achievement, the objectives can be changed, or the program can be discarded and a new one created.

Relative standards are developed by comparing the program with other programs to determine which one has the best outcomes. National norms tell how students compare with other students nationally. Locally constructed norms can be used to evaluate how students compare with students who previously completed the program. Some difficulties are inherent in comparing two programs that look alike, since each may have some unique purposes the evaluation process may overlook. Thus, there may be no significant differences in the quantitative data when there are differences in the qualitative data. Both quantitative and qualitative data are necessary to overcome this deficiency.[9]

All evaluation studies should pay close attention to (1) validity—the extent to which the evaluation provides the information it is supposed to provide; (2) reliability—the degree to which the data collected are the same on different trials of the test; (3) objectivity—the extent to which the data are the same regardless of who administers the test; (4) cost-effectiveness in terms of the time, energy, and money invested; and (5) timeliness—the time required to make a decision.

Step 4—Describe the Information Needed to Make the Decisions

Prior to deciding which data sources will be used to obtain information about whether the standards are being met, evaluators should examine the performance standards developed when the content standards were unpacked. There should be a clear link with the physical education standards that govern the program (state or district). Standards should be clearly written so that teachers who will use them can understand the expectations associated with them. A logical progression or sequence with one activity building on and leading into the next will help teachers when they implement the standards. Students who successfully complete the program should be physically educated after achieving the standards that are identified. Additionally, students should have the skills, knowledge, and dispositions necessary to be physically active for a lifetime. The standards should also represent the program philosophy that will reflect the society in which students will live as adults. Last, the standards should be worth achieving; they must relate to the needs, interests, and abilities of the learners. Evaluators may want to compare their standards to those of other schools or districts as part of the process to determine whether they need revision.

After the program standards have been determined, it is necessary to decide which data sources will be used to obtain information about whether the objectives have been met. The nature of the evaluation (formative or summative) will help determine the types of data sources used. Information on achievement of the standards can be gained from the various stakeholders, including students, teachers, parents, and outside observers, using both formal and informal evaluation techniques. Some commonly used techniques include (1) controlled research, (2) structured external evaluation, (3) standardized tests, and (4) interviews with stakeholders.

Controlled research involves the use of randomization to assign control and experimental groups, and then the construction and testing of hypotheses. In this way the program results can be compared with a different or preceding program or the posttest results can be compared with the pretest results to see if they are statistically significant.

Structured external evaluation was one of the earliest methods used to evaluate the total physical education program. The first scorecard was developed by William Ralph LaPorte in the 1930s. Since that time a number of scorecards have been developed by various state departments of education. They are often used by evaluation teams from accrediting associations.

A program appraisal checklist has been created by the Middle and Secondary School Physical Education Council of the National Association for Sport and Physical Education.[10] Each checklist asks the evaluators to rate a number of statements relating to the curriculum; instruction; assessment; the student; facilities, equipment, and supplies; and the learning environment (see Box 15.1). A more comprehensive checklist for evaluating physical education programs prepared as part of the Michigan Exemplary Physical Education Programs Project is included in *Evaluation of K–12 Physical Education Programs: A Self-Study Approach.*[11] This checklist includes thirty-three categories divided into five parts dealing with the quality of the school-community environment; the program; instruction; personnel; and facilities, equipment, and safety.

Many teachers select AAHPERD's Fitnessgram, which is a *standardized test* designed to assess physical fitness.[12] *Performance-based assessments* have become increasingly more popular since the introduction of standards. Many of these assessment techniques are described in Chapter 11. New York and South Carolina have adopted statewide testing programs that require students to demonstrate knowledge, skills, and dispositions while engaged in a variety of activities (e.g., invasion, net, field games; dance and gymnastics performances; outdoor pursuits). Although performance-based assessments establish content validity very easily (they holistically represent what teachers want students to know and be able to do rather than representing part of the activity as a skill test does), care must be taken to develop rubrics or scoring guides that are both valid and reliable. In addition, teachers must be careful to establish appropriate norms for the levels of performance so that students are realistically able to achieve the standards. Programs that use performance-

BOX 15.1

Curriculum Established

CHECK YOUR PROGRAM IN THE FOLLOWING AREAS:

	Not	Established		Well
	1	2	3	4
1. A written curriculum based on NASPE's *National Standards for Physical Education* (2004) that is comprehensive, inclusive, progressive, and sequential is designed to guide appropriate physical education at all grade levels in the school. The curriculum for grades 9–12 includes a yearly plan, instructional units by grade level and activity, and lesson plans.				
2. Grade-level content standards are challenging, demonstrable, and relevant to learning essential concepts.				
3. The curriculum provides opportunities for students to recognize the benefits of regular physical activity.				
4. The curriculum allows students to integrate knowledge of kinesthetic experiences with concepts taught in the areas of health education, language arts, mathematics, social sciences, science, technology education, and vocational education.				
5. Lesson planning includes adequate time and opportunity for every student to have enough trials and adequate practice time to learn skills.				
6. Respect for diversity is taught and practiced.				
7. The curriculum provides opportunities for students to acquire the skills needed to develop a personal fitness plan.				
8. The curriculum offers opportunities for students to select activities in which they are interested and want to develop competency.				
9. The curriculum is based on the national and/or state content exit standards that are observable, measurable, and require evidence of students' ability to apply motor skills or to create new knowledge in new situations.				

Source: Reprinted from *Opportunity to Learn Standards for High School Physical Education* (2004) with permission from the National Association for Sport and Physical Education (NASPE), 1900 Association Drive, Reston, VA 20191-1599.

based activity usually require students to demonstrate the ability to participate capably in activities from more than one area (e.g., dance, invasion games, swimming, net games, outdoor pursuits) to meet the intent of NASPE Content Standard 1. Because student learning should be viewed from a variety of perspectives, programs should use several different types of assessments to document student skills, knowledge, and dispositions.

In addition to *teacher-constructed evaluation techniques,* other areas used to evaluate various components of a physical education program include student participation in extra-class or leisure-time activities, attendance, tardiness, discipline, dropouts, awards, assignments completed, and choices made in selective activities. Teachers and students can create graphs from class data demonstrating improvement in the psychomotor, cognitive, and affective domains.

Questionnaires, rating scales, and inventories can be constructed to determine student progress toward affective objectives. In general, assessment might include (1) whether student attitudes are positive or negative toward physical education or the specific activity engaged in, and how well students are applying the principles of appropriate social behavior such as good teamwork or fair play, (2) whether students appear willing to approach physical education or an activity as readily at the end of course instruction as when they began, and (3) what activities appeal to students.

For students to answer honestly on affective evaluation instruments, they must trust that results will not be used against them. To achieve this, use questions that require checking or circling the responses instead of writing, tell students not to put their names on the papers, and have students collect the papers and tabulate the responses, or ask for papers to be placed in a box in a nonthreatening place. Sample questionnaire items might include the following:

Student Goals and Interests

1. Indicate your interest in physical fitness *before* taking this class: highly interested/ interested/ neutral/ less interested/ highly uninterested.

2. How long do you plan to continue your present exercise program? throughout life/ throughout school years/ until school is out this year/this term only/ I don't plan to continue.
3. If you were asked to give a short talk about your favorite school subject, which subject would you talk about?
4. I took this class for the following reasons:

I was curious	_____
It was required	_____
I needed the challenge	_____
I've always liked it	_____
I wanted to learn something new	_____
I needed some easy credit or an easy A	_____
Nothing else was available and I needed an elective	_____
I don't know	_____

Student Perceptions of the Curriculum

1. I learned more this semester because I was able to take the activities I wanted. yes/no
2. I like being able to select the teacher I want. yes/no
3. There should be a limit on the number of times a student can take a given activity. yes/no
4. With regard to activities, I wish we had a class in _____.
5. In which of the following did you participate?
   intramurals _____
   extramurals _____
   varsity sports _____
   none of these _____
6. How do you prefer intramural teams be picked?
   by homerooms _____
   by physical education class _____
   by personal selection _____
7. If physical education were not required, would you still have taken it this year? yes/no

Rating scales usually include from three to nine choices. The number is based on the complexity of the information required. Fewer choices yield more reliable data. More choices provide more information. An even number of choices removes the option of letting students give a neutral answer, which tells those administering the survey little. Several types of scales exist. One form of scale is the continuum, on which the rater places a mark as shown in the following item:

Has positive attitudes toward self:

________/________/________/________

Very positive	Positive	Negative	Very negative

Another type has boxes to check:

☐	☐	☐	☐
Very positive	Positive	Negative	Very negative

Inventories are rating scales designed to yield two or more scores by grouping items in certain prespecified ways. Attitude inventories generally contain three types of questions. The first type is the following:

	Agree	Disagree
1. Physical education is a waste of time. (2.00)	_____	_____
2. Physical education is helpful in one's life. (8.00)	_____	_____
3. Physical activity is important to my mental, physical, and emotional fitness. (9.00)	_____	_____
4. Physical fitness is no longer essential in today's world. (3.00)	_____	_____

The student's score is an average of the scale factors (in parentheses) for all of the questions marked "agree."

The second type of question looks like this:

	Strongly Agree	Agree	Strongly Disagree	Disagree
1. I need a lot of exercise to stay in good physical condition.	( )	( )	( )	( )
2. Following game rules helps me be a better citizen in the community.	( )	( )	( )	( )
3. I prefer to engage in activities that require a minimum of physical activity.	( )	( )	( )	( )

When using this type of inventory, teachers should write questions so that the most desired answer is not always positive. Doing this will encourage students to read each question carefully and consider their answer before responding to the question.

The third type of question consists of bipolar adjectives. An example of this type of question is the following:

Physical education is

Pleasant	: : : : : : : :	Unpleasant
Good	: : : : : : : :	Bad
Active	: : : : : : : :	Passive

Another type of inventory is the interest or valued activities inventory (see Box 15.2). To score, simply tally the responses for each activity.

BOX 15.2

An Interest or Valued Activities Inventory

Instructions: Circle the symbol representing your interest in each of the following activities.

	Strong interest	*OK*	*Don't like*
Badminton	SI	OK	DL
Bicycling	SI	OK	DL
Bowling	SI	OK	DL
Dance	SI	OK	DL
Ultimate Frisbee	SI	OK	DL
Others (list)			
_________	SI	OK	DL
_________	SI	OK	DL

Adjective checklists differ slightly from inventories. Students select adjectives that apply to themselves or others from a list provided, such as the following:

Circle each of the words that tell how you feel about physical education:

interesting	dull	boring
fun	useful	very important
too hard	exciting	too easy
useless	tiring	

To score, compare the number of positive and negative words circled.

Ranking involves arranging items on a list in order of personal preference or some other specified quality. Usually the number of items to be ranked is limited to about ten. Two examples of ranking are shown here:

Example 1: List all the subjects you are now taking and then rank them in order from most interesting to least interesting. (1 is best)

Example 2: Rank order the following activities by placing a 1 by the activity you like to play best, 2 next, and so on down to number 6:

Badminton _____Inline skating _____
Basketball _____ Gymnastics _____
Folk dance _____Orientering _____

Do you dislike the activity you rated last? _____ Yes
_____ No

If yes, why?

To score, total the ranks from all students. The rank with the lowest score indicates the highest interest. One major disadvantage of ranking is that there is no way of knowing how much difference exists between items in adjacent ranks. Group scores, however, can provide valuable data.

Interviews with stakeholders such as teachers, administrators, parents, students, and community members can provide valuable information. Annual interviews or meetings to discuss goals and objectives, assess achievement of objectives, and predict needs and problems might deal with such questions as the following: Are goals and objectives appropriate? Should anything be added to or deleted from the program? Why or why not? What is not going well? How could it be improved?

All program evaluations should use a variety of evaluation instruments. Failure to do so can result in a biased interpretation of program effectiveness. Each technique is selected to correspond with the objective and the group to be evaluated.

A timeline or work plan is formulated to keep the evaluation proceeding on schedule. The plan describes who will do what, with what instruments, using what population sample, and by what date.

Step 5—Obtain, Record, and Analyze Information

Obtain and record the information specified in step 4, including such areas as student experiences, student gains and losses, unintended outcomes, and program costs in terms of time, money, and other resources. Determine a format for classifying and recording the information. Analyze the information by using appropriate statistical methods.

Step 6—Interpret Data in Terms of Standards

The purpose of program evaluation is to determine the worth or value of the program. Thus, after all the data have been collected, a judgment must be made as to whether the program has been successful. As in the other phases of curriculum design, many people should be involved in making these judgments, including students, parents, faculty, administrators, the board of education, and community and professional leaders. Conclusions should be drawn concerning program effectiveness and student progress.

Two questions must be answered when interpreting the information collected: (1) Were the standards and program goals achieved? (2) Was there a logical connection between entry behaviors, learning activities, and desired outcomes? Achievement of program goals is determined by comparing the data with the standards specified in step 3.

To interpret the relationship among entry behaviors, learning activities, and desired outcomes, pretest and posttest data must be analyzed. When students score high on the pretest, the instruction may be unnecessary. When students score low on the pretest and low on the posttest, the instruction was inadequate and needs revision or an alternative program should be adopted. Low pretest scores accompanied by high posttest scores demonstrate that sound instruction has occurred and students are learning as planned.

Step 7—Make Decisions and Formulate Recommendations

Once the data have been evaluated, decisions must be made concerning whether to retain the program as it currently exists or to make changes and adjustments. Data from the evaluation will identify both strengths and deficiencies; this information will indicate where and what types of changes should be made. The components of the program listed in step 1 will be considered during this step. The persons identified in step 2 as those responsible for the program must evaluate the data by the criteria listed in step 3. If the standards have all been met, the decision will be easy—to retain the program as is. If none of the standards have been met, the program will undoubtedly be replaced. However, when some of the criteria have been met and others have not been met, decisions will have to be made concerning whether the objectives are valid, whether the program can be changed in some way to achieve the objectives, or whether to adopt a new approach.

Recommendations provide a basis for administrative action in the form of further implementation, modification, or revision. The evaluation results, with accompanying recommendations, should be communicated to the faculty, administration, students, parents, and other interested community members.

Review Question: Define and give an example of the following formal and informal evaluation techniques: (a) absolute standards, (b) relative standards, (c) controlled research, (d) structured external evaluation, (e) standardized tests, (f) teacher-constructed evaluation techniques, and (g) interviews with stakeholders.

AN EXAMPLE OF PROGRAM EVALUATION

Step 1—Describe the Program to Be Evaluated

The Fitness for Life curriculum is designed to help students write and apply their own fitness plans during school and throughout their lives. Students contract with an instructor to do the following (see Box 15.3):

1. Pass five mastery tests on (a) how to write programs for cardiovascular endurance, weight control, and strength and flexibility; (b) how to measure cardiovascular endurance, strength, and flexibility; and (c) fitness concepts.
2. Complete a nine-week contract for cardiovascular endurance according to the specifications on the course handout.
3. Take a fitness appraisal before and after completion of the contract and show progress.

Students complete the contract on their own time and check with the instructor for assistance as needed or to take mastery checks. A fourth outcome desired in the program is that students will have positive feelings about fitness activities and about the unit.

Step 2—Identify the Purposes of the Evaluation

Some concerns about the Fitness for Life program included these:

1. Did students actually increase physical fitness during the nine-week contract?
2. Did students have positive feelings about physical fitness and about the unit?
3. Were the instructors satisfied with the program?
4. Was the new program better than the existing program?
5. What administrative problems existed?

Step 3—Establish Criteria for Judging Quality and Making Decisions

The following absolute standards in the form of objectives were selected at the beginning of the Fitness for Life program. Eighty percent of the students will do the following:

1. Achieve a good or excellent rating on the 1.5-mile run.
2. Achieve a percent body fat of 22 percent or below for girls and 15 percent or below for boys.
3. Obtain a score of 80 percent or better on all five tests of fitness concepts.
4. Complete a fitness contract for nine weeks at the contracted level of exercise.
5. Have positive attitudes toward participation in physical fitness activities.

With regard to relative standards, a comparison with the AAHPERD norms revealed that students in the Fitness for Life program were below the national average prior to participating in the program.

Step 4—Describe the Information Needed to Make the Decisions

The following measures were considered to provide the information needed to evaluate the program. The 1.5-mile run and percentage of fat measured by skinfold calipers were used to evaluate fitness. Students in Fitness for Life classes were tested and found to have improved significantly more

BOX 15.3

An Evaluation Work Plan for Fitness for Life

OBJECTIVE	ACTION BY	METHOD	POPULATION	DEADLINE
1. Pass five mastery tests.	Mr. Ames	Mastery tests.	All students in the school.	January and June
2. Complete contract.	Miss Jones	Count of completed contracts, analyze uncompleted contracts for problem areas.	All students in the school.	January and June
3. Take fitness appraisal.	Mr. Sims	Fitness appraisals recorded on class record sheets.	All students in the school.	January and June
4. Increase fitness.	Mrs. Garcia	Computer analysis of fitness appraisals.	All students in the school.	January and June
5. Positive feelings of students toward the unit; toward fitness.	Mr. Platt	Inventory of student feelings.	Random samples of 100 students.	January and June
6. Comparison with current program.	Mrs. Garcia	Computer analysis of fitness appraisals.	Test random sample of students in regular program and statistics from step 4.	January and June

in physical fitness than students who were enrolled in regular physical education classes at the same time. Therefore, it was concluded that the Fitness for Life program was better than the regular program for achieving fitness.

An attitude inventory was constructed to assess attitudes toward fitness. A questionnaire measured continued participation in fitness programs several years later. Another questionnaire requested feedback on preferred instructional methods.

An external evaluation team was invited to assess program effectiveness. They interviewed teachers, obtained questionnaire responses from students, and interviewed students who dropped the class.

Students in the fitness program were required to log in each time they requested individual help. Dates on which tests were taken were recorded. A contract was required on which students recorded their weekly participation in selected activities.

A continuous dialog between teachers and students in the program helped to provide feedback on what was or was not working. Teachers met weekly to discuss the progress of the program.

In the Fitness for Life program, teachers were frustrated by student procrastination in taking written tests. Students also complained about the need to log in each week.

Step 5—Obtain, Record, and Analyze Information

The faculty decided that a coordinator would be assigned to take responsibility for collecting each portion of the data. The final evaluation would be done by the entire faculty one month prior to the end of the school year. Note that only a sample of the total students participating in the program took the pretest on the mastery tests and completed the attitude inventory and instructional methods questionnaires. This was done by randomly assigning a few students in each class to each section of the inventory or questionnaire rather than by having all students complete all of the sections. This conserved student time and resulted in students being more attentive than they might have been to a long evaluation instrument. Since the fitness tests were used as a basis for the individual contracts, most of the students took them. The number of students achieving the 80 percent criterion on the mastery tests and the percentage achieving mastery are shown in Box 15.4.

Step 6—Interpret Data in Terms of Standards

Analysis of the data revealed that more than 80 percent of the students achieved the three unit objectives with one exception. In test 3, only 75 percent of the students achieved mastery. Data from the questionnaire revealed that some test questions were confusing to students. An analysis of the test showed that questions 6 and 10 were consistently missed. One solution was better instruction in the area of planning the weight control program. Another solution was to clarify the questions on the test.

The data showed that students in the Fitness for Life program achieved significant increases in all four fitness components. The differences in fitness between students in the regular program and the fitness program were also significant. Students appeared to be positive toward the instruction and toward physical fitness, with the exceptions noted. Some revisions in the program were made to resolve these problems.

Step 7—Make Decisions and Formulate Recommendations

In the Fitness for Life program, the following recommendations were made:

1. The program should be retained.
2. The grading system should be changed to an "A-pass-fail" system in which students can get an "A" grade or a "pass grade" (B or C equivalent) or a "fail" to provide more challenge to students to excel.
3. The test and the handout on weight control should be rewritten.
4. Students in the "good" or above categories must log in only every other week. This will provide more time for students needing help.
5. Test deadlines for each test will be posted to reduce procrastination.
6. A meeting should be held in December to evaluate the changes.

Cautions in Program Evaluation

Evaluators must be careful to use a variety of techniques to evaluate the instructional program or a component/unit of study within it. Exclusive reliance on quantitative assessment techniques may limit programs to outcomes that can be stated in precise terms and for which objective tests exist. Some of the most important goals for physical education will require other types of data sources to evaluate elements that are difficult to quantify. Even though these are sometimes perceived as "soft data," they are many times based on the perceptions of people who are professionals in the field (teachers and administrators) whose years of experience make their judgments and insights valuable data sources. Evaluators must be open to using all types of data sources in order to make the best decisions possible concerning physical education programs. Formative evaluations using a variety of assessment techniques can give us indicators of success or failure within the curriculum to help us adjust our course during the race.

The Curriculum Cycle

Evaluations are costly in terms of time and resources, so evaluators should ensure that they are used for program improvement rather than filed away in an administrator's drawer. These evaluations contain much valuable information that should be used to plan and implement effective and often necessary change. Following an evaluation, changes and improvements should be identified and a strategy for implementing them developed. The evaluation process should be viewed as an essential component of a continuous process to improve the instructional program.

Evaluation provides valuable information necessary to create an effective and dynamic program. Using data obtained from the evaluation, objectives must be reevaluated to see whether they are desirable within the constantly changing environment. Curriculum patterns and teaching and learning strategies must be revised so that student achievement more nearly approximates the objectives that have been established. Thus, the cycle of design, plan, implement, and evaluate begins again with redesign, plan, and so on.

BOX 15.4

A Recording Form for the Fitness for Life Program Data

OBJECTIVE	PRETEST DATA Number of Students	Number Achieving Criterion	%
1. Pass five mastery tests.			
Test 1	20	2	10%
Test 2	20	1	5%
Test 3	20	0	0%
Test 4	20	1	5%
Test 5	20	3	15%
Total			
2. Complete contract.	X	X	X
3. Take fitness appraisals.	200	200	100%

4. Increase fitness.	PRETEST MEAN Girls	PRETEST MEAN Boys
Percent fat.	19.43	15.10
1.5-mile run.	14:38	13:24

5. Positive feelings of students.	FAVORABLE	UNFAVORABLE
Orientation session.	卌 卌 |	||||
Mastery tests.	卌 卌 ||	|||
Contract.	卌 卌	||||
Fitness appraisals.	卌 卌 ||||	|
Grading system.	||||	卌 卌 |
Instructor assistance.	卌 |	||||
Toward fitness.	卌 卌 卌	

6. Comparison with current program.	CURRENT PROGRAM Number of Students	Number Achieving Criterion	%
Concept tests.	800	111	13.9
Percent fat.	800	500	62.5
1.5-mile run.	800	436	54.5

Continued

BOX 15.4 *Continued*

POSTTEST DATA

Number of Students	Number Achieving Criterion	%	CRITERION MET Yes	No
200	180	90.0%	X	
200	185	92.5%	X	
200	150	75.0%		X
200	190	95.0%	X	
200	195	97.5%	X	
200	165	82.5%	X	
200	192	96.0%	X	

POSTTEST MEAN Girls	POSTTEST MEAN Boys	SIGNIFICANT Yes	No
16.7	12.28	X	
13:27	12:11	X	

COMMENTS

Great!

Too easy, except Test 3, which had confusing questions.

Want ABC system.

Too busy to talk, too many log-ins.

FITNESS FOR LIFE PROGRAM

Number of Students	Number Achieving Criterion	%	CRITERION MET Yes	No
200	150	75	X	
200	152	76	X	
200	181	90.5	X	

NOTES

1. J. A. Rog, Will (should) your physical education program survive? *NASPE News* (1982, October): 6.
2. P. G. Vogel and V. D. Seefeldt, Redesign of physical education programs: A procedural model that leads to defensible programs, *Journal of Physical Education, Recreation, and Dance 58,* no. 7 (1987): 65–69.
3. J. Hill, Curriculum evaluation—Practical approach to dealing with the pitfalls, *NASSP Bulletin 69,* no. 478 (1985): 1–6.
4. National Association for Sport and Physical Education, *Moving into the Future: National Standards for Physical Education,* second edition (Reston, VA: Author, 2004).
5. National Association for Sport and Physical Education, *Moving into the Future: National Standards for Physical Education,* second edition (Reston, VA: Author, 1995).
6. Vogel and Seefeldt, Redesign of physical education programs.
7. D. L. Stufflebeam (Phi Delta Kappa National Study Committee on Evaluation), *Educational Evaluation and Decision Making* (Itasca, IL: Peacock, 1971).
8. J. C. Hill, *Curriculum Evaluation for School Improvement* (Springfield, IL: Thomas, 1986).
9. Hill, *Curriculum Evaluation.*
10. National Association for Sport and Physical Education, Middle and Secondary School Physical Education Council, *Opportunity to Learn Standards for Middle School Physical Education and Opportunity to Learn Standards for High School Physical Education* (Reston, VA: American Alliance for Health, Physical Education, Recreation, and Dance, 2004).
11. G. M. Dummer, P. L. Reuschlein, J. L. Haubenstricker, P. G. Vogel, and P. L. Cavanaugh, Evaluation of K–12 physical education programs: A self-study approach, in *Exemplary Phsycial Education Programs: Criteria for the Development and Evaluation of K–12 Programs* (Lansing, MI: Michigan Fitness Foundation, 1998).
12. Cooper Institute for Aerobics Research, *FITNESSGRAM Test Administration Manual* (Champaign, IL: Human Kinetics, 1999).

APPENDIX

Sample Unit Plan and Lesson Plan

UNIT PLAN

Unit Beginning Volleyball No. of Days 20 Name Angie Fluegetmann

Class Size 40 Grade Level 7th Skill Level Beginning

Special considerations: None

Skills/concepts to be taught: Forearm pass, set, underhand serve, spike, volleyball rules, pass-set-spike strategy

Facilities needed: Gym, 3 volleyball courts

Equipment needed: 40 VolleyLite volleyballs, 3 volleyball nets, net markers to divide nets into 2 half-courts per court

Media or other equipment: Videotape, VCR, and monitor

Preassessment: Ask students about previous experience in volleyball. After skill demonstrations, observe practice to determine how fast to move to the next skill.

Unit Objectives and Assessment	Objectives	Assessment	Content Standards
Skill Acquisition	1. Meet minimum standards for skills tests. 8 legal sets into the target area 8 forearm passes into the target area 8 legal underhand serves anywhere in the court 2. Complete 80% of all tasks on task sheets.	Skills tests Task sheets	1. Demonstrates competency in motor skills and movement patterns needed to perform a variety of physical activities.
Game Play	Execute the skills (pass, set, spike, serve) correctly in game play.	Subjective evaluation by teacher and student self-assessments	1. Demonstrates competency in motor skills and movement patterns needed to perform a variety of physical activities.
Knowledge	1. Pass a written test with 80 percent or better on minivolley rules. 2. Pass written quizzes with 75 percent or better listing the 3 cues for each skill—pass, set, serve, spike.	Written tests	1. Demonstrates competency in motor skills and movement patterns needed to perform a variety of physical activities. 2. Demonstrates understanding of movement concepts, principles, strategies, and tactics as they apply to learning and performance of physical activities.

Continued

Unit Objectives and Assessment	Objectives	Assessment	Content Standards
Physical Fitness	Complete physical fitness goals on contract.	Fitness log	3. Participates regularly in physical activity. 4. Achieves and maintains a health-enhancing level of physical fitness.
Personal/ Social Behavior	Exhibit a desire to become a more skilled volleyball player by participating in drills, attempting new skills in game play, and writing about feelings in personal journal.	Journal entries	5. Exhibits responsible personal and social behavior that respects self and others in physical activity settings. 6. Values physical activity for health, enjoyment, challenge, self-expression, and/or social interaction. 7. Understands that physical activity provides opportunities for enjoyment, challenge, self-expression, and social interaction.

Course Progression					
Week	**Monday**	**Tuesday**	**Wednesday**	**Thursday**	**Friday**
1	Model volleyball skills Preassessment	Forearm pass	Forearm pass	Set Review pass	Set Review pass Quiz on pass cues
2	Underhand serve Review pass and set Quiz on set cues	Spike Review other skills	Spike Review other skills Quiz on serve cues	Increase proficiency in all skills	Increase proficiency in all skills Quiz on spike cues
3	Increase proficiency in all skills	Increase proficiency in all skills	Quiz on minivolley rules Pass-set-spike strategy	Minivolley tournament Skills tests (repeatable each day)	Minivolley tournament Skills tests (repeatable each day)
4	Minivolley tournament Skills tests	Minivolley tournament Skills tests	Minivolley tournament Skills tests	Play official volley-ball games; introduce simple offensive and defensive strategies	Play official volleyball games; introduce simple offensive and defensive strategies

Note: Unit has been shortened for this example.

Day-by-Day Content			
Day (When)	**Content (What)**	**Learning Activities (How)**	**Assessment**
1	Model volleyball skills Preassessment	Videotape of youth volleyball championships.	Play minivolley
2–3	Forearm pass	Pass from partner toss. Pass from partner toss to side. Consecutive passes with partner. Consecutive passes with threesome. Toss over net, pass to hoop on floor. Play 3-pass game starting with toss.	10 times 10 times 15 10 5 into hoop Try to keep it going

Continued

Day-by-Day Content			
Day (When)	**Content (What)**	**Learning Activities (How)**	**Assessment**
4–5	Set Review pass Quiz on pass cues	Review pass drills. Catch ball in proper position from toss. Set ball from partner toss. Consecutive passes with partner. Consecutive passes with threesome. Consecutive alternating passes and sets with threesome. Pass and set to hoop. Play 3-hit game (pass-set-hit over).	See above. 1-min. quiz 5 times 15 times 15 10 15 5 into hoop Try to keep it going
6	Underhand serve Review pass and set Quiz on set cues	Review. Hit serves 15′ from net; work on force production, moving back with success to service line. Serve to partner who forearm passes to hoop on floor. Play serve game. Serve in court = 1 point Ace serve = 1 bonus point Receiver scores for pass-set-spike Play to 5 points and rotate. Play 3-hit game with serve; 1 point per 3 hits on side.	See above. 1-min. quiz Distance from net 5 into hoop Number of points Try to get as many points as possible
7–8	Spike Review other skills Quiz on serve cues	Review drills. Hit ball out of hand toward wall. Toss ball and hit toward wall. Jump forward, jump up, and scratch back of head. Practice approach footwork. Approach net, jump, and scratch back of head. Approach net, jump, and throw tennis ball over net. Approach and hit ball out of partner's hand (use chair). Approach and hit tossed ball. Approach and hit set ball. Toss ball over net, pass, set, spike.	See above. 1-min. quiz 10 times 10 times 10 times 5 times 10 times 5 times 10 times 25 times 15 times 10 times
9–12	Increase proficiency in all skills Quiz on spike cues	*Serve* in order to positions 1–5 on court. *Serve* at targets on floor. Partner keeps 1 foot in hoop and forearm passes back. *Set*—run to position and set ball. Set ball coming from different directions. *Pass*—retrieve ball from net. *Practice* setting a ball gone astray. *Spike*—Toss ball over net, pass, set, spike. *Game*—Play cooperative volleyball.	1-min. quiz. All 5 positions hit 5 reachable hits 10 times 10 times 10 times 10 times Points scored
13	Quiz on minivolley rules Pass-set-spike strategy	Play minivolley with bonus points for pass-set-spike sequences.	Quiz; score pass-set-spike sequences
14–18	Minivolley tournament Skills tests (repeatable each day)	Play games. Practice skills tests.	Pass-set-spike sequences Skills test scores
19–20	Play official volleyball game. Introduce simple offensive and defensive strategies.	Play games. Try W defense and 4-2 offense if ready.	Teacher observation of skills in game play. Student self-assessment based on incidence charts.

Grading Policies				
Category	**Category Weight**	**Assessments**	**Test Weight(%)**	**Possible Points**
Skills and Game Play	35	Skills tests—Pass	10	10
		Skills tests—Set	10	10
		Skills tests—Serve	10	10
		Teacher observation of game play	40	5
		Student self-assessment based on incidence charts of game play Bonus points—10 pts possible for most improved player	30	5
Knowledge	15	Minivolley quiz	50	10
		Cues quizzes	50	5
Physical Fitness	35	Setting and achieving own goals	100	35
Social Skills	15	Fair play—Teamwork rating scales Bonus points—25 pts for tournament Most Valuable Player, 25 pts for Most Inspirational Player (team player, tries hard, encouragement, leadership), 10 pts for each member of team whose members cooperate with each other the best	75	50
		Journal	25	5
Final Grade	100%			

LESSON PLAN

Ball State University Lesson Plan

Name: ____________________ **Date:** ____________________

Class/Grade level: ____________________ **Dates to be taught:** ____________________

Unit/Theme: ____________________ **Lesson #**____________________ of ________

I. Skills already developed by students ____________________

II. What happened last lesson? ____________________

III. Lesson objective(s):

Performance ____________________

Situation ____________________

Criteria ____________________

Performance ____________________

Situation ____________________

Criteria ____________________

IV. Indiana state standard targeted—indicate standard(s), number(s), and write out standard(s)

____

V. Assessment for measuring performance criteria ____________________

VI. My goal for improving my teaching ____________________

VII. Equipment and resources needed ____________________

VIII. Modifications needed for students with special needs ____________________

IX. Alternative activities for students with special needs (those unable to participate in regular activities with modifications) ____________________

X. Instructional / practice time / organization (see Sample Lesson Plan on the next page)

Time	Teaching & Learning Experiences	Student-Teacher Organization Formations	Description of Skills & Activities	Teaching Cues	Safety &Motivation
Closure					

SAMPLE LESSON PLAN

Ball State University Lesson Plan

Name: Jessie Weller **Date:** 9-4-2004

Class/Grade level: 1st–2nd **Dates to be taught:** 9/13–9/17

Unit/Theme: Soccer **Lesson** # 2 of 6

I. **Skills already developed by students:** Instep kick

II. **What happened last lesson?** Student learned the cues for the instep kick and practiced the skill in various situations. The beginning of class routine was also taught and practiced.

III. **Lesson objectives:**
-psychomotor: Students will be able to trap the ball with the sole of their foot on the poly spot at least 8 times.
-cognitive: Students will be able to verbally identify situations when dribbling is used effectively during a game situation.
-affective: Students are willing to try new activities and skills without receiving extrinsic motivation from the teacher.

IV. **Indiana state standards targeted**
#1: *Demonstrates competency in many movement forms and proficiency in a few.*
#7: *Understands that physical activity provides the opportunity for enjoyment, challenge, self-expression, and social interaction.*

V. **Assessment for measuring performance criteria:** teacher observation with checklist

VI. **My goal for improving my teaching:** I will keep my verbal explanations short and to the point.

VII. **Equipment and resources needed:** 30 soccer balls, 30 poly spots, 30 jerseys, 1 teacher checklist, 4 warm-up charts, 4 hula hoops.

VIII. **Modifications:** Use sponge ball, decrease distance, slow down movement, practice motion without a ball.

IX. **Alternative activities for students with special needs:** Practice focusing on one cue, student helper may assist, throw instead of kick.

Time	Activity/Task Development	Organization Management	Critical Elements/ Teaching Prompts	Reflection
	1. Daily warm-up routine a. Groups b. Class	1. Students are at their area practicing warm-ups. 1. Part 2 In rows.	1. a. Routine = —Come in, find your squad # on the wall. —Look at the warm-up chart on the wall next to your #. —Read the description of the task & perform as described. b. Pick one task. —When you hear the whistle go to your rows. c. Skills for the day = 1. Taps —Use bottom front of the foot to touch the top of the ball. Alternate feet & do in place. 2. Kicking against wall —Kick from different distances. —Kick toward targets.	

Time	Activity/Task Development	Organization Management	Critical Elements/ Teaching Prompts	Reflection
			***Feedback** *1. Great job keeping the ball between you and the wall.* *2. I like how you are trapping the ball when it comes back to you.* *3. You need to keep control of the ball. You are kicking a short distance, which means you shouldn't kick the ball hard.* *4. I like how your kicking leg is swinging in a straight line.*	
	2. Review kicking with instep cues	2. Same as above	2. Cues 1. Beside the ball 2. Behind the ball 3. Heel/ankle	
	3. Introduce trap a. Explain b. Cues—SAY AS A CLASS c. Demonstrate	3. a–c. Same as above	Have students explain each. 3. a. **? When do you think the trap is used in soccer?** b. Cues 1. *In front* = Body in front of ball with contact foot extended out in front of the body. Body weight is on other foot. 2. *Wedge* = Contact foot is on an angle with the toes flexed & higher than the heel. 3. *Sole* = Sole of contact foot contacts the back of the soccer ball at 12 o'clock.	
	Developmental Tasks: 1. Partners a. Explain b. Demonstrate c. Practice	1. a & b. Same as above. 1. c. Every student stands on a poly spot.	**? Where is the sole of the foot?** ***Feedback** *1. I like how your eyes and ears are on me.* *2. I like that you raised your hand to answer my question.* 1. a. —Students kick the ball to their partner. When ball comes their way they trap it and then kick it back. —Students aim for their partners' feet on the return.	

Time	Activity/Task Development	Organization Management	Critical Elements/ Teaching Prompts	Reflection
	2. Dribble straight **Introduce dribbling a. Explain/cues b. Demonstrate c. Practice	2. a & b. Students are in green circle. 2. c. Every student stands on a poly spot and goes from one black line to the other.	SIMPLIFICATIONS: 1. Decrease the distance EXTENSIONS: 1. Increase the distance 2. Pass with nondominant foot 3. Decrease # of steps taken before they kick *_**Feedback**_ *1. Great job following your kicking through to your partner.* *2. Your partner is not far away from you; you need to use less force.* **? When do you think dribbling is used during a game?** 2. a. Cues 1. *Face ball* = face ball, ball slightly in front of you. 2. *Inside* = Use inside of foot to contact the outside of the ball. 3. *Taps* = Many taps to move the ball. Ball moves ahead on an angle to the other foot. 2. c. Move into dribbling at different speeds	
	3. Poly spots a. Explain b. Demonstrate c. Practice **_Teacher Checklist_	3. a & b. Students are in green circle. 3. c. Students are scattered throughout the gym.	SIMPLIFICATIONS: 1. Move at own speed 2. Practice in place EXTENSIONS: 1. Move fast 2. Move in different pathways 3. # of times in 1 min. *_**Feedback**_ *1. Remember to look up with your eyes.* *2. Great job challenging yourself at different dribbling speeds.* *3. I like that you have control of the ball by keeping the ball between your feet.* 3 a. Dribble around the gym and when you approach a poly spot, trap the soccer ball on the spot and then move onto another spot. **? How can your eyes help you?**	
	Culminating Activity: 1. Hoops a. Explain b. Demonstrate c. Practice		SIMPLIFICATION: 1. Move at own speed 2. Practice with one spot	

Time	Activity/Task Development	Organization Management	Critical Elements/ Teaching Prompts	Reflection
		1. a & b Students are in green circle.	EXTENSIONS: 1. Move fast 2. # of fingers the teacher holds in the air 3. # of times in 1 min.	
		1. c. Students are in groups of 4 at hula hoops.	****Feedback*** *1. You need to keep control of your ball. Slow down your dribbling.* *2. Great job looking up from time to time.* *3. I like that you are giving little taps to the ball.*	
	Conclusion: 1. Review Trapping 2. Review Dribbling	1. & 2. In squads	1. a. Each team has a hula hoop with soccer balls for each teammate in the group. Goal is to move the soccer balls out of your team's hoop into another hoop. After two minutes the team with the fewest balls in their hoop wins. May only dribble the ball over to another team's hoop. ****Feedback*** *1. Great job moving safely.* *2. I like that you are not using your hands to stop or change directions with the ball.* *3. You need to keep control of the ball with the ball between your feet.* **? What are the trapping cues?** **? Why is it important that you trap the ball on back/top?** **? What are the dribbling cues?** **? What can you do to be successful at dribbling?**	

Index

A

B

C

D

H

I

J

K

L

Q

R

S

T

U

V

W

Y